T0325558

# Data Privacy and GDPR Handbook

Sanjay Sharma, PhD

with research associate
Pranav Menon

Cover design: Prudence Makhura
Cover image: © Starline / Freepik.com
Cover painting: Om Prakash (1932-2019)

Published by John Wiley & Sons, Inc., Hoboken, New Jersey.
Published simultaneously in Canada.

For general information on our other products and services or for technical support, please
contact our Customer Care Department within the United States at (800) 762-2974, outside the
United States at (317) 572-3993, or fax (317) 572-4002.

Wiley publishes in a variety of print and electronic formats and by print-on-demand. Some
material included with standard print versions of this book may not be included in e-books or
in print-on-demand. If this book refers to media such as a CD or DVD that is not included in the
version you purchased, you may download this material at http://booksupport.wiley.com. For
more information about Wiley products, visit www.wiley.com.

*Library of Congress Cataloging-in-Publication Data:*

ISBN 978-1-119-59424-6 (cloth)
ISBN 978-1-119-59425-3 (ePDF)
ISBN 978-1-119-59419-2 (ePub)
ISBN 978-1-119-59430-7 (obk)

Printed in the United States of America

V10015093_102519

*To my family and friends*

# Contents

# 1

# Origins and Concepts of Data Privacy

*Privacy is not something that I'm merely entitled to, it's an absolute prerequisite.*
— Marlon Brando

We generate enormous amounts of personal data and give it away without caring about our privacy.

Before the wake-up alarm rings on our smartphone, our heartbeats and sleeping patterns were being recorded through the night on the embedded app on our wrist watch. We turn on our customized morning playlist on Spotify, read the headlines tailored for our interests on Apple or Google news, retweet on Twitter, upvote on Quora, register likes on WhatsApp, post a snapshot of the snow outside our window, and look up on what our friends are up to on Facebook. We then check the weather forecast and ask Alexa to order cereal from Amazon. We are ready to go to work.

Unimaginable convenience for us commoners without a royal butler feels splendid. The invisible cost is that we are under constant surveillance whenever we use these services. All our choices, actions, and activities are being recorded and stored by the seemingly free technology-driven conveniences.

When we take an Uber or Lyft to work, our location and destination are known to them from previous trips. Today's journey is also recorded, including the name of the driver and how we behaved – spilling coffee may show up on our passenger rating if the driver notices it. A smile and thank-you wave to the driver are worth five rating stars. Our choice of coffee at Starbucks may already be programmed and ready based on our past preferences. Each swipe of our credit card is imprinted into our purchase habits.

As we exit the car, a scarcely visible street camera is recording our movements and storing those records for the local city police. The recording of our actions continue as we turn on our computer at work. We read and respond to e-mails, order lunch online, attend video conference calls, and check on family and friends again. Before noon, we have generated innumerable data on our laptops, tablets, phones, and wearables – with or without our conscious cognition or permission.

Everything that we touch through the make-believe cocoon of our computer, tablet, or smartphone leaves a digital trail. Records of our actions are used as revenue sources by data-gobbling observers in the guise of learning and constant improvement. In a different era, this level of voluntary access into our daily lives would have thrilled secret service organizations.

Numerous questions are raised in this fast-evolving paradigm of convenience at no cost: Whose data is it? Who has the rights to sell it? What is the value of the information that we are generating? Can it be shared by the Data Collectors, and, if so, under what circumstances? Could it be used for surveillance, revenue generation, hacking into our accounts, or merely for eavesdropping on our conversations? And, most importantly, can it be used to influence our thinking, decisions, and buying behavior?

Concerns regarding the privacy of our data are growing with advances in technology, social networking frameworks, and societal norms. This book provides a discourse on questions surrounding individual rights and privacy of personal data. It is intended to contribute to the debate on the importance of privacy and protection of individuals' information from commercialization, theft, public disclosure, and, most importantly, its subliminal and undue influence on our decisions.

This book is organized across three areas: we first introduce the concept of data privacy, situating its underlying assumptions and challenges within a historical context; we then describe the framework and a systematic guide for the General Data Protection Regulations (GDPR) for individual businesses and organizations, including a practical guide for practitioners and unresolved questions; the third area focuses on Facebook, its abuses of personal data, corrective actions, and compliance with GDPR.

## 1.1 Questions and Challenges of Data Privacy

We illustrate the questions and challenges surrounding individual rights and privacy of personal data by exploring online dating and relationship-seeking apps such as match.com, eHarmony, and OK Cupid. To search for compatible relationships through these apps, users create their profiles by voluntarily providing personal information, including their name, age, gender, and location, as well as other character traits such as religious beliefs, sexual orientation, etc. These apps deploy sophisticated algorithms to run individuals' profiles to search for suitable matches for dating and compatible relationships.

Online dating apps and platforms are now a global industry with over $2 billion in revenue and an estimated 8,000 sites worldwide. These include 25 apps for mainstream users, while others cater to unique profiles, special interests, and geographic locations. The general acceptance of dating sites is significant – approximately 40% of the applicable US population use dating sites, and it is estimated that half of British singles do not ask someone for a date in person.

The industry continues to evolve and grow, with around 1,000 apps and websites being launched every year in the US alone.

Most dating sites and apps do not charge a fee for creating user profiles, uploading photos, and searching for matches. The convenience of these apps to users is manifold. They can search through the universe of other relationship-seekers across numerous criteria without incurring the costs and time for the initial exchange of information through in-person meetings. More importantly, dating apps lower the probability of aspirational disappointment if there was disinterest from their dates.

### 1.1.1 But Cupid Turned Out to Be Not OK

In May 2016, several Danish researchers caused an outrage by publishing data on 70,000 users of the matchmaking/dating site OK Cupid. Clearly, the researchers had violated OK Cupid's terms of use. The researchers' perspective was that this information was not private to begin with. Their justification for not anonymizing the data was that users had provided it voluntarily by answering numerous questions about themselves. By registering on the dating service, the users' motivation was to be "discovered" as individuals through a selection process by application of the matching algorithm. The information was available to all other OK Cupid members. The researchers argued that it should have been apparent to the users that other relationship-seekers and thus the general public could access their information – with some effort, anyone could have guessed their identities from the OK Cupid database.

This case raises the following legal and ethical questions:

1. Were the researchers and OK Cupid within their rights to conduct research on data that would be considered as private by the users?
2. Did the researchers have the obligation to seek the consent of OK Cupid users for the use of their personal information?
3. Was it the obligation of OK Cupid to prevent the release of data for purposes other than dating?
4. If a legal judgment were to be made in favor of the users, how could the monetary damages be estimated?
5. What should a legal construct look like to prevent the use of personal data for purposes different from that which is provided by the users?
6. If users' information in the possession of and stored by OK Cupid was illegally obtained and sold or otherwise made public, who is liable?

## 1.2 The Conundrum of Voluntary Information

As humans, we have an innate desire to share information. At the same time, we also want to be left alone – or at least have the autonomy and control to choose when and with whom we want to share information. We may disrobe in front of medical professionals, but it would be unthinkable in any other professional situation. Similarly, we share our tax returns with our financial advisors but otherwise guard them with our lives. We share our private information personally and professionally in specific contexts and with a level of trust.

This phenomenon is not new but takes on a different dimension when our lives are inextricably intertwined with the internet, mobile phone connectivity, and social networks. With the ease of information dissemination through the internet, anyone with a computer or a mobile phone has become a virtual publisher – identifiable or anonymous. The internet provides near-complete autonomy of individual expression and effortless interactions with commercial services to bring tremendous convenience to our daily lives. At the same time, our expectations of control over our privacy have become increasingly overwhelmed by the power of commercial interests to collect our personal data, track our activities, and, most alarming, to subliminally influence our thoughts and actions. The growing power of commercial and other nefarious interests to impact our lives would have been considered dystopian not too long ago.

We generally understand that once we voluntarily share information with someone else, we lose control over how it can be used. However, two questions remain unanswered: Do we truly realize the extent to which our personal data is being monitored? What level of control and rights do we have over our personal information that is generated through our activities and involuntarily disclosed by us? As an example, mapping our driving routes to avoid traffic jams or ordering a taxicab to our location through an app on our mobile phones has become indispensable. This capability requires that our mobile phones act as monitoring devices and record our every movement with technological sophistication that would make conventional surveillance mechanisms look quaint. However, we would chafe at the notion of being asked to carry a monitoring device in the context of law enforcement, societal surveillance, or even as part of a research project.

The mechanisms for sharing information and their abuse are exponentially greater than in the days of print journalism and the school yearbook. Fast-evolving technology platforms are making our lives efficient and convenient, but these technologies require us to share personal information. Entities that receive and collect our data can use it to foster their commercial and sometimes nefarious interests. Our personal data can be abused through a multitude of ways that are becoming easier to execute – making it more profitable for commercial interests and more effective for law enforcement.

We need rigorous regulatory and legal mechanisms to govern how our information is used, regardless of whether it is provided voluntarily or otherwise. However, this is a very hard challenge because artificial intelligence and big data technology frameworks are constantly and rapidly evolving and can be easily mutated to circumvent regulations. Lawmakers are increasingly recognizing and adapting to these realities by laying the groundwork for legal frameworks to protect our privacy. Their challenge is that regulations for protecting individuals' data privacy should foster technology-driven personal convenience and not stifle ethical commercial activities and interests.

## 1.3   What Is Data Privacy?

### 1.3.1   Physical Privacy

Data privacy as a concept did not exist until the late twentieth century, with the birth of the internet and its exponential rate of adoption through computers and mobile phones. Until that time, privacy largely applied to physical existence and information as it related to an individual,[1] his home,[2] documents,[3] and personal life. The concept of privacy comes from a Western school of thought and had blossomed through common law, having its first roots in defenses against state action and *privacy torts*. Conflicts in this construct had mainly arisen in matters relating to journalism and state encroachment into the private life of citizens.

But how would the *right to be left alone* doctrine fare in a world where people willingly share private information in the public domain? How would the privacy of correspondence apply when documents are intangible, and conversations can be observed by hundreds of our friends? Is data an extension of ourselves and our private lives, or is it a commodity to be exchanged in a contract?

### 1.3.2   Social Privacy Norms

The traditional concept of privacy is centered around shielding ourselves and our activities from outsiders. It has the notion of secrecy. We associate personal privacy with "get off my yard" or "closing the blinds of our homes" to prevent outsiders from looking in. In business settings, privacy is associated with discussions and decisions "behind closed doors."

However, we readily disrobe behind a flimsy curtain in a clothing store without doubting if there is a secret camera. We hand over our suitcases for security inspection; we provide our Social Security numbers over the phone to our bank or insurance providers without asking for our rights to privacy. We may join a discussion group or a loyalty program and freely express our views. Concerns regarding our privacy hardly ever prevent us from providing our most intimate information to strangers.

In this construct, the roots and norms of privacy are based on social frameworks. The boundary of sharing information rests on who we have a relationship with (formal or informal) and who we trust. This implies a fiduciary responsibility from the individuals with whom we have shared the information; e.g. we trust that banks, security personnel, health insurers, etc., will not share our data with anyone without our explicit permission. Across all these situations, sharing is necessary and our trust in information receivers is inherent, but we provide it in specific contexts.

### 1.3.3   Privacy in a Technology-Driven Society

As technologies evolve, creating boundaries in the current societal environment is not an easy task by any means. We must think expansively to create a framework where the release, sharing, and use of our information is transparent, and discretion over it can be managed in our daily lives. It is relatively straightforward to create and enforce laws against premeditated and illegal use of our privacy or personal data, e.g. a hacker extracting confidential data through cyber intrusion – a clearly criminal activity akin to physical intrusion and theft.

This gets trickier when our private personal data may be used for public research (e.g. OK Cupid) or for targeted advertising. In addition, liability and assessment of damages is an uncharted territory for misuse when the underlying personal harm is nonmonetary and the question of liability attribution is unclear. This also applies to the transfer and sale of our personal data collected by apps and internet service providers. This becomes more complicated when it concerns the mining and collection of data that we have provided inconspicuously through our browsing – what we view when we buy, who we are likely to vote for, and who we may find to love. Abuses such as these have sparked the growth of the Doctrine of Information Privacy or "Data Privacy" in the modern age as an evolution to the traditional constructs of privacy in a "physical" or nondigital society.

## 1.4 Doctrine of Information Privacy

The use and mining of our personal data have existed from the time the first census was conducted. Researchers have used personal data for ages, but by and large without a commercial motive. With the advent of the internet and mobile technology, the pace and volume of personal data collection have grown exponentially. At the same time, it has become enormously valuable and is even traded in secondary markets like a commodity.

### 1.4.1 Information Sharing Empowers the Recipient

Through the disclosure and sharing of personal information, we intrinsically empower its recipients. This is most visible in doctor-patient (particularly for psychiatric conditions) and attorney-client information sharing. In journalism, it is a well-established and understood norm that "off the record" conversations are not attributed to the provider of information or commentary.

We understand this and exercise our contextual discretion by limiting the sharing of our professional compensation with our close family, supervisors, and human resources departments, and not always with our friends or work colleagues. We do not allow medical professionals to share our health information with our accountants or vice versa.

We have always cherished our rights and discretion privileges to limit the sharing of our personal information. Yet we continually provide information over the internet through mouse clicks and swipes and allow its unfettered usage.

### 1.4.2   Monetary Value of Individual Privacy

Across both our physical and digital existence, our right to our personal data and privacy is essential for our individuality and ownership of our thoughts and emotions. Historically, laws have considered health care, financial information, including tax filings, and other records to have enforceable rights to privacy. Ideally, these rights should extend to any form of data – even if it is seemingly innocuous. This includes data regarding our movements, events, and buying behavior.

The construct of intrusion of physical, property-based information has become the generally accepted construct of privacy. This is not entirely misplaced or ineffective. However, it can be argued that principles of privacy intrusion based on physical space can actually harm the right to privacy. This is because the decline of personal information as a property right raises the question: what is the monetary value of an individual's or a group's collective value of personal information? For instance, consider the case of US airline JetBlue Airways, wherein the company had shared some of its customers' information with a third party; a federal court rejected a breach of contract claim. The customers' case was that JetBlue had violated the obligations stated in its privacy policy. The court stated that even if it was assumed that a privacy policy could be interpreted as a contract, JetBlue's customers could not identify the damages and thus there was no support for the proposition that their personal information had any value. This can be significantly constraining in developing an effective legal framework to protect our data privacy.

### 1.4.3   "Digital Public Spaces"

The construct of intrusion of privacy in public spaces by traditional media – photographs and news stories citing individuals' specific traits, behavior, or life events – does not always extend to cyberspace. In the absence of monetizability of damages, judicial systems and policy makers tend to consider data privacy less worthy of legal protection than similar intrusions of physical space. In the case of cyber harassment, online intrusions of privacy, blatant theft, and even attacks are viewed as eminently preventable *ex ante* or stopped after the fact by shutting down a personal account or a webservice.

The most significant limitation of the construct of physical privacy is the implied definition of "digital public spaces." Individuals' rights to the privacy of their data should be applicable irrespective of the means of its acquisition or storage location. Privacy rights should not be conditioned by where individual data is stored. Privacy applies to the information and not where it resides or is derived from. This has direct implications for big data and machine learning techniques that isolate and predict our behavior based on collective data – that in the physical sense – is analogous to a public space.

Individuals provide data to retailers and other service providers as a necessity by virtue of their usage. This is unavoidable. The construct of privacy as seclusion from the public domain would imply two things – first, that the individual data provider has released the data into the public domain and has anonymized that data; second, that the distinction between public and private space in the digital domain cannot be well defined.

The perfect framework to regulate data privacy should enable us to control what, why, when, and with whom we share information, and how it will be used. This framework should allow us to revoke the continued usage of information through a collective choice or specifically for each entity. There should not be normative judgments regarding which data is important, or the context in which it is disclosed. The right to privacy is an individual choice including how, whether, and when anyone can use an individual's information that may be voluntarily provided or extracted.

### 1.4.4  A Model Data Economy

We have to create an environment where information willingly provided by us or extracted through our activities is not exploited for commercial or nefarious purposes without our thorough understanding and express time-bound permission determined by us. In addition, information that we consider truly private should not be released, re-created, or deconstructed. Researchers, governmental bodies, and businesses – be they social networks, search engines, or online advertisers – cannot use individual data under the legal representation that it is voluntarily provided or can be (inconsiderately) accessed through public sources.

A societal and legal framework for privacy should not encourage individual withdrawal from making connections and interacting with others. Rather, it should be designed to enable us to govern our private and public existence and contextual disclosure and usage of our private information. It should prevent any framework or mechanism from manipulating us into disclosing more information than we intend to, and once disclosed, to prevent its use in ways that may not have been represented to us *ex ante*. This framework must be legally enforceable with penalties for knowingly or otherwise violating the law or guidelines in any form.

Creating a legal framework for protecting the privacy of our personal information is a daunting task. While we must share our information for technologies, businesses, and societies to flourish and governments to function, we should also be aware of the collection of our data and its usage. As new information is being revealed about how Facebook provided access to user data, it is becoming shockingly apparent how providers can abuse data, and the extent to which they can manipulate our thinking and decision making.

For our social structures to persist and global commerce to thrive, we must trust collectively created frameworks in which there are legal standards to prevent prohibited or cavalier use of our information and with associated liabilities for its abuse. At the very least, this would encourage trusting relationships between providers and users of our personal data. This is indeed a momentous task that requires thoughtful and comprehensive laws through the participation of legal and social scholars, legislatures, and governmental and regulatory bodies.

With fast-evolving technology and the internet of things (wherein our physical beings and surroundings are wired and connected with transmitters) is around the corner, societies face a collective choice. We cannot let our rights to privacy be squandered away for the sake of convenience. A fine line has to be drawn between laws that are so onerous that they impede commerce and our own conveniences and those that guard against our privacy and exploitation of our likes, habits, and thoughts.

## 1.5 Notice-and-Choice versus Privacy-as-Trust

Notice-and-choice is based on the legal doctrine that as long as a data-collecting entity provides notice and discloses the specificity of the data they collect from a subscriber of the service, and how it will be used, we as data providers have sufficient information and discretion *ex ante* to make our choice/consent as to whether or not to interact and provide our information. This construct is inadequate because in our day-to-day lives, our information sharing is selective and contextual, and applies differentially. In addition, it is impractical for us to study a long disclaimer and terms of engagement with the entity that is collecting our information every time we click "*I agree.*" There are several other reasons why this construct is inadequate.

The bottom-line for our innate human trait to share information is that our actions to do so are contextual and based on trust. From a legal perspective, the paradigm of trust is based on a time-tested model of *fiduciary law* wherein the personal data-collecting entity is innately powerful once it has collected the data, making one vulnerable to the other; the entity with more power or control is legally required to act in the vulnerable party's best interest. Once again, the doctor-patient relationship is a classic example.

A construct of trust between providers and users of personal data could serve as a foundational component for design and enforcement of regulation. However, the concept of trust is hard to govern and enforce in practice. This is because our information has enormous economic value that would inevitably lead to its abuse by its collectors, intermediaries, and other agents in the process. The construct in which we have indelible trust in the data receiver and the aggregator will only be achieved when there is an "inform-and-consent" framework that is in place with strong deterrence for breach of trust.

## 1.6 Notice-and-Choice in the US

In the US, the notice-and-choice legal construct has a long history. The Fair Information Practices Principles (FIPPs), developed from a 1973 report by the US Department of Housing, Education and Welfare (HEW), are the foundation of notice-and-choice. Since such government agencies are privy to extensive personal data, HEW recommended that the agencies be required to make their data-use practices public, i.e. provide "notice." Thus, in theory, individuals may or may not consent to those agencies using or sharing that data.

The Federal Trade Commission (FTC) brought their recommendation of *notice* to the US Congress, emphasizing its importance as a component of FIPP. Since then, notice has been the framework for how legal obligations are placed upon companies, particularly online. There is no comprehensive federal law in place, however, that codifies the FTC's recommendations from the 1973 FIPPs report. Laws vary across states and industry sectors and are thus frequently modified. In contrast, the EU and Canada have more comprehensive laws in existence.

One of the most important and widely enforced example of sector-specific statutes is the Health Information Portability and Accountability Act (HIPAA), which protects users' medical and healthcare information. The Gramm-Leach-Bliley act is similar with respect to the financial sector. The statute that regulates activity specific to the internet is the Children's Online Privacy Protection Act (COPPA), which prohibits unauthorized use, collection, and dissemination of information of children 13 years old and younger, among other protections afforded to them. Most if not all of these acts deal with notice as their basis, but not necessarily protection of individual data privacy.

In the US, states' attorney generals have pressed for notice-and-choice along with the FTC. The California Online Privacy Protection Act (CalOPPA) was the first state law to require commercial websites to provide their users in the state with privacy disclosures. These disclosures include, generally, what information is collected, with whom it might be shared, and how users will be notified about the company's data-use practices. Similarly, in 2003, California enacted the "Shine the Light" law, which allows residents to obtain information from companies regarding their personal information that has been shared with third parties including agencies.

In New York, the Internet Security and Privacy Act also requires state agencies to provide the "what-when-how" of their own data-use policies. The provisions are essentially identical to California's trailblazing laws except that they are applied to New York's state agencies' websites. Connecticut and Michigan have similar frameworks but they apply to any person or entity that files a person's Social Security number. In Utah, the Government Internet Information Privacy Act requires notice of the what-when-how as well. Some examples of these what-when-hows (varying across states) of notice requirements on commercial and government websites are:

- Statement(s) of any information the entity will collect
- How the information is collected
- The circumstances under which such collected information will be disclosed to the user

- A description of the process by which the operator notifies of changes to the privacy policy to the user
- Whether and what information will be retained
- The procedures by which a user may gain access to the collected information

## 1.7    Enforcement of Notice-and-Choice Privacy Laws

The Federal Trade Commission has brought action against entities that it contends did not comply with applicable privacy laws. In the following cases, the company did not provide adequate notice of their data-use practices. Once again, the FTC and the corporate entities centered their complaints and settlements around the idea of notice. These can be referred to as "broken promises" actions.

### 1.7.1    Broken Trust and FTC Enforcement

In 2002 Eli Lilly and Company (Lilly) agreed, per the FTC website: "to settle FTC charges regarding the unauthorized disclosure of sensitive personal information collection from consumers through its Prozac.com website. As part of the settlement, Lilly will take appropriate security measures to protect consumers' privacy."[4]

Eli Lilly allowed users of Prozac.com to sign up for e-mail alerts reminding them to take and/or refill their prescriptions. The e-mails were personalized by data entered by each user. In 2001, a Lilly employee sent a memo to its users alerting them that the service would be discontinued. The "To:" line of that message included all 669 of the users' e-mail addresses, therefore making the users' medical information public. The FTC's complaint alleges that "Lilly's claim of privacy and confidentiality was deceptive because Lilly failed to maintain or implement internal measures appropriate ... to protect sensitive consumer information."[5] Lilly settled with orders to comply with notice of their data-use practices.

More examples include a case in which the FTC alleged that GeoCities – an internet web-based service expressly violated their own privacy policy by selling their customers' personal information. GeoCities settled and was required to comply with notice-and-choice guidelines. The FTC also took action against Frostwire, LLC, alleging that the company misled their customers into believing that certain files would not be accessible to the public, but they actually were, and that Frostwire failed to explain how the software worked. Lastly, in a case against Sony BMG Entertainment, Sony did not notify their customers that software installed on certain CDs could transmit users' music-listening data back to Sony. Once again, the company settled and was ordered to comply with notice-and-choice-style privacy practices in the future.

### 1.7.2 The Notice-and-Choice Model Falls Short

In theory, the notice-and-choice model assumes that if a data-collecting entity provides all the information required to inform users regarding the potential use of their personal data, they can freely make their own autonomous decisions regarding their privacy. It is based on the ideals of internet pioneers and *cyberlibertarians* (advocates for the use of technology as a means of promoting individual or decentralized initiatives, and less dependence on central governments).

However, notice-and-choice as a model for the law is inadequate because of several factors. First, the notion of autonomous decision making by an internet user has not turned out to be effective in practice. Second, the idea that users could remain fully anonymous has now been proven false. Most aspects of our lives are monitored; our activities are tracked and recorded. Our online experience is directed by artificial intelligence and complex algorithms in myriad ways.

Over the past two decades, notice-and-choice–based data privacy laws in the US have generally been pieced together as reactions to previous breaches of trust by companies and agencies over the "vulnerable" parties in the relationship. The laws themselves are based on somewhat arbitrary findings from the 1973 FIPPs report. This legal framework has led to administrative challenges with companies having to navigate a maze of rules, which vary across states, sectors, and at the federal level.

Differing laws mandate that company websites follow privacy policy guidelines that fall short of creating fairness on both sides of the company/user relationship. Usually the policies are confusing, lengthy, full of legal jargon, and as a result are read infrequently. Studies have found that the average internet user would spend 244 hours per year reading them. There is a growing body of literature addressing the monetary value of our time as well. According to one study, the average worker's time would cost more than $1,700 per year just to *skim* privacy policies.[6]

Notice-and-choice puts the bulk of the responsibility in the hands of the consumer of protecting their own privacy instead of powerful Data Collectors. Furthermore, once an individual agrees to a privacy policy and discloses their data, they have little or no control over how it is used. Tech companies that have access to their users' personal information should be legally required to handle that information with the highest level of trust. The current set of laws depends on the idea that if the company notifies its users of some of the what-when-how of their data-collection practices, users may then make educated decisions about whether or not to share that personal information. This model is flawed in myriad ways, from the very basis of the theory, all the way through to the logistical implementation of the resultant laws.

# 1.8    Privacy-as-Trust: An Alternative Model[7]

Online social networks are rooted in trust. This ranges from run-of-the-mill daily interactions with family, relatives, and friends to sharing information with strangers who may have or will reciprocate with us. Trust is the expectation that receivers of our information will not share it for their own interest and uses, commercialize it, or share it for other nefarious ends. If it is used for commercialization, information providers should expect consideration in the form of revenue-sharing fees.

The presumption of trust is at the core of our decisions to share our personal information with others. In the technologically driven online framework, the uses of our personal information include:

1. National security and law enforcement
2. Storing our data to provide convenience services
3. Commercialization of our information – selling information for commerce
4. Intrusion or theft of data
5. Influencing our thinking and decisions

The notion of Big Brother knowing everything about us with nonblinking eyes has persisted with time and has become more pronounced with the explosion in online connections and communication. It was originally enforced by law to monitor and ascertain allegiance to the ruling regime. This instrument was not sugarcoated under the guise of free services that foster trust.

The governmental Big Brother and his watching mechanisms are derived from public funds. And the means to the end is to ensure law enforcement and, in oppressive regimes, to observe allegiance and loyalty from the subjects of the regime. In contrast, Facebook, Amazon, Google, and other online Data Collectors do not have a Big Brother–like oppressive persona. In the guise of making life easier for their users, they provide seemingly cheap/free seamless services – be it finding a restaurant in our neighborhood at the very thought of hunger, selecting a movie to watch, or just finding our misplaced phone.

Privacy-as-trust is based on fiduciary (in Latin, *trust*) law. Most agree that Data Collectors have "asymmetrical power" over the average consumer. Thus, according to common law fiduciary principles, Data Collectors should be held to higher standards when entrusted with our personal data. They should act based on common principles of trust. As opposed to contract law (the body of law that relates to making and enforcing agreements) or tort law (the area of law that protects people from harm from others), fiduciary law centers around a few special relationships wherein the fiduciary – the individual who holds the more powerful role in the relationship – has an obligation to act in the best interest of the other party. Examples of fiduciaries include investment advisors, estate managers, lawyers, and doctors. If a patient goes into surgery their life is in the hands of the doctor.

Fiduciaries are entrusted with decisions about their clients' lives and livelihoods. When we share our personal information, we should expect it to be handled equally responsibly. The implication is that a fiduciary relationship between data brokers and users would help fight the power imbalance that exists in online interactions and commerce, and that is growing exponentially.

In this construct, companies like Google, Facebook, and Uber should be considered fiduciaries because of internet users' vulnerability to them. We depend on them, and they position themselves as experts in their fields and presumably trustworthy. Our contention is that corporate privacy strategy should be about maintaining user trust. Privacy leaders within corporations would often prefer to position the company in terms of trust and responsibility as opposed to creating policies that are designed to avoid lawsuits. They should go a step further and revisit their policies on a regular basis to keep up with the ever-changing and fair expectations of the clients depending on their understanding of the changing realities of internet privacy or lack thereof.

Many privacy policies on company websites are hard to read (generally in a light gray font), difficult to locate within their websites, confusing, and take too much time to review. Google continues to face criticism for its ability to track and record users' locations with their Maps application, even when the "Location History" feature is turned off. At a Google Marketing Live summit in July 2018, Google touted a new feature called "local campaigns," which helps retail stores track when Google ads drive foot traffic into their locations. They can also create targeted ads based on users' location data. Once Google knows where you spend your time, nearby store locations can buy ads that target you directly. Even when users have turned off location history, Google can use mechanisms in their software to store your information. For speed and ease, most users allow Google to store their location history without serious consideration.[8]

Fiduciary companies should have further obligations to the individual data providers/customers than being limited to clarifying their privacy policies. They should agree to a set of fair information practices as well as security and privacy guarantees, and timely disclosure of breaches. Most importantly, they should be required to represent and "*promise*" that they will not leverage personal data to abuse the trust of end users. In addition, the companies should not be allowed to sell or distribute consumer information except to those who agreed to similar rules.

## 1.9 Applying Privacy-as-Trust in Practice: The US Federal Trade Commission

In this construct, US companies should not be allowed by the Federal Trade Commission (FTC) to induce individual data providers' trust from the outset, market themselves as trustworthy, and then use that trust against us. As an illustration, Snapchat promoted their app as a way to send pictures to others that would only be available to the receiver for a preset time duration. However, there are ways for the viewer to save those pictures outside of Snapchat's parameters, such as taking a screenshot. While the image is "ephemeral" within the Snapchat app, the company failed to mention that the image does not necessarily disappear forever. Under privacy-as-trust law, Snapchat would be in breach of their legal obligations as a trustee.

In the US, the FTC has substantial experience with "deceptive business practice" cases under Section 5 of the FTC Act of 1914, which simply prohibits unfair methods of competition and unfair acts or practices that affect commerce. A good parallel to internet data collection could be drawn from the telemarketing industry. The Telemarketing Sales Rule states:

> ... requires telemarketers to make specific disclosures of material information; prohibits misrepresentations; ... prohibits calls to a consumer who has asked not to be called again; and sets payment restrictions for the sale of certain goods and services.
>
> – ftc.gov

In this rule, applying the clause "prohibiting misrepresentation" in general to digital data collection and commerce would be a profound change. Currently companies often use confusing language and navigation settings on their apps and websites to present their privacy policies. *It can be argued that this is misrepresentation of their goods and services.*

### 1.9.1   Facebook as an Example

The scope of Facebook's role within the complex issues surrounding data sharing and privacy cannot be overstated. Learning from the failures of MySpace and Friendster, Facebook has clearly triumphed in the social media domain. This is partly due to the public relations prowess of Mark Zuckerberg, its founder and CEO, "especially in light of the maniacal focus on an advertising-dependent business model based on mining users' data, content and actions."[9]

According to the Pew Research Center on February 1, 2019, approximately 68% of US adults use Facebook and three-quarters of those users visit the site at least once per day. However, 51% of those users state that they are uncomfortable with "the fact that the company maintains a list of the users' traits and interests." In addition, 59% of users said that the advertising on their NewsFeeds accurately reflected their interests (Pew). Ads on Facebook are seamlessly mixed with and appear in exactly the same format as our friends' posts, with the exception of the word "Sponsored" in a tiny, light gray font. If a friend "Likes" one of these sponsored posts, Facebook will alert us of that, and we are more likely to click on it, since we trust the friend. Once the algorithm has been proven to work, Facebook can charge more for their advertising real estate and continue to dominate the social media market. It is very likely that these types of strategies and constant honing of data analysis to target their users would violate privacy-as-trust.

There are no real alternatives for avoiding these formulas; other big social media sites like Instagram use similar tactics. As a counterpoint, a start-up company like Vero stores usage stats but only makes them available to the users themselves. However, Vero has only about a million users – it is unlikely that you will find your friends and family on it.

The FTC could intervene through several straightforward mechanisms. While eliminating third-party advertising altogether would be a heavy-handed and an unlikely action, the FTC could push for design changes to make it easy for users to spot advertising. Facebook could simply be prohibited from using personal data to create targeted ads. The FTC's deceptive practices actions have been broad and there are legal precedents for this. Any website exploiting this personal data against the interests of the users could fit under the FTC's existing authority and balance the power between users and data.

## 1.10   Additional Challenges in the Era of Big Data and Social Robots

The growing use of "social robots" adds a significant challenge to the data privacy debate. Social robots use artificial intelligence to interact and communicate with humans and possibly with their brethren. They require massive amounts of data to be effective. They learn from us through our choices and actions on their platforms, e.g. Facebook. By using their platforms, we feed them our data and train them. In turn, they increasingly evolve their abilities to influence our thoughts and decisions. This develops into a vicious cycle.

This phenomenon does not stop with our clicks and swipes. Social robots can also utilize data from our physical appearances. For example, robotic shopping assistants in the form of algorithms have been designed to keep track of our past purchases and recommend future buying. When sellers program robots to suggest weight-loss or wrinkle cream products based on appearance, the possibility of data-based discrimination with respect to sex, age, and race will be unavoidable.

### 1.10.1   What Is a Social Robot?

In order to address this challenge from a legal perspective, the term "social robot" should be defined. There are numerous examples in fiction and popular culture – Rosie from *The Jetsons*, C3PO, Wall-E, and even going all the way back to mythological legends of bronze statues coming to life. These myths have become a near virtual reality – Rosie, the Jetsons' memorable housekeeper is the closest to existing social robots.

The current generation of social robots utilize programmatic actions and have limited human-level autonomy, as opposed to C3PO, a more relatable human character, who while possessing "robotic" vocal and mechanical qualities, also comes with his own set of human emotions.

The legal definition of social robots should be characterized by the following traits/capabilities:

1. *Embodied* (they have a physical form – software)
2. *Emergent* (they learn and adapt to changing circumstances)
3. *Social valence* (they are thought of as more than an object and have the ability to elicit emotional social responses from their users)

### 1.10.2 Trust and Privacy

Because of our innate need for socialization, we are predisposed to anthropomorphize even inanimate objects. To feed this vulnerability, robots are designed to resemble humans in appearance, traits, and aura in their movements. Researchers have provided examples of humans bonding with robots and experiencing feelings of love, with some even preferring the company of robots over human beings.

Social robots are programmed to be more responsive and predictable than humans. They trigger our predisposition to relate to them on a human level to the point that they gain our trust. We are likely to develop *greater* trust in social robots than in humans. Trust leads to dependency, with susceptible consumers willing to spend unreasonably large amounts of money to keep them "alive" and functioning.

As our reliance on social robots to conduct our daily lives grows, we allow them to share our data – playing into the inherent mission of companies that create and deploy them.

Traditional constructs of privacy are based on individual separation, autonomy, and choice. As we choose to interact with technology that induces us to provide increasing amounts of data to feed social robots, how do we remain separate from it? Through our trust in social robots we are thus made increasingly vulnerable to the companies that create these artificial intelligence/social robot technologies.

### 1.10.3 Legal Framework for Governing Social Robots

It is extremely challenging for privacy policies to protect users from big data's algorithmic targeting and predictive analytics that drive social robots. This is because intellectual property laws protect the companies' algorithms, and thus consumers cannot be provided with sufficient information or notice to make informed choices to allow a company/website to access, store, or share that data. Social robots are not humans; they are virtual machines driven by software to collect our data by inspiring trust and inducing us to drop our privacy guards.

In a highly publicized case, the US retailer Target built customer profiles using data accessed from their recent purchases, their social media accounts, and data available from third-party data-sharing companies. Using all of this data, Target was able to determine the likely pregnancy statuses of its customers and send them mailers. They were not required to explain all of this on their website's privacy policy because the data was produced by mathematical equations, not from a direct source. Like the rankings of Google search results, these algorithms use our information to predict our choices.

According to the current model of notice-and-choice, it would be assumed that the very act of purchasing a social robot for home use provides our consent for unfettered data collection. Even if a consumer gives educated consent at the time of purchase based on knowledge of the robot's functionality, how can the consumer remain educated about the robot's functionality, as it is programmed to evolve and improve over time? In this framework the notice-and-choice model falls short in providing legal protection and relief.

Private citizens should be able to purchase and bring a machine connected to a social robot into their home, e.g. Alexa or other personal digital assistants, and enter into that relationship knowing that they are protected and would have legal relief when the implicit trust relationship is breached.

In public settings, social robots may also infringe on our basic human rights. Consider the fact that robots are equipped with facial recognition software. At a basic level, with robots in public places, we will not have a mechanism to exercise our notice-and-choice rights, as the data is written on our faces and is captured as we walk by unsuspectingly.

Could privacy-as-trust could be a more effective legal model compared to notice-and-choice? In this framework, companies that create the hardware and software that make up social robots should be considered information fiduciaries, like all professions and entities that access our data, e.g. healthcare professionals, accountants, and legal counsel. In the US, the Federal Trade Commission could take on an active role by exercising its authority to combat "unfair or deceptive trade practices," such as false advertising and misleading product demonstrations.

## 1.11 The General Data Protection Regulation (GDPR)

While efforts in the US and most other countries to ensure data privacy have not been robust (the US Constitution does not expressly provide for a right to data or informational privacy), the European Union has enacted the sweeping General Data Protection Regulation (GDPR). This regulation guarantees EU citizens and residents rights over the ownership of their own data and requires their permission (opt-in) for its commercial or other usage with substantial fines for intended or unintended use, release, or even theft/hacking by third parties. In addition to fines on Facebook and Google and continued investigations by the EU, the UK's

Information Commissioner's Office recently fined British Airways a record £183 million fine for the breach and theft of customer credit card data in 2018. It is the largest fine the office has ever handed out. It is inevitable that corporations – large and small – and other organizations will comply with GDPR in form, if not in spirit (in response to GDPR, Facebook moved 1.5 billion user profiles from Ireland – part of the EU – to the US to avoid it). It is inevitable that internet giants will attempt to create and use deception techniques to limit their users in EU who choose to opt-in for GDPR protection.

The challenges of ensuring data privacy are being made more difficult by the rapid evolution and incorporation of artificial intelligence (AI) that uses individuals' data to create behavior-prediction models ostensibly as a convenience, e.g. your online newsfeed preselects or highlights the news that is predicted to be of most value to you. *However, the boundary between individual behavior prediction and modification is blurred and is an enormous challenge for the creation and enforcement of rules.* This is because as AI-based techniques acquire new data from individuals' actions, the predictive power of the underlying algorithms becomes stronger. As AI algorithms become adept at anticipating individual thoughts, the line between the convenience provided by the internet and other data-collection platforms and their ability to modify behavior vanishes.

The concept of data privacy has been in the forefront for over two decades. However, before the finalization of GDPR, the legal and enforcement framework had not been structured across most countries. Episodic reports of intrusions into corporate and governmental databases and subsequent theft of individual identities and associated data have justifiably garnered outrage and hefty fines. However, the threat to individual privacy and manipulation of thoughts and decisions through the use of internet and social networks can lead our society into a dystopian future.

Beyond the pale of intrusion, driven by curiosity concerning individual information, the current framework and proliferation of technology and internet commerce through artificial intelligence techniques is increasingly being used to persuade and manipulate individuals. This stripping of individuality and associated agency is becoming prevalent. If Cambridge Analytica is a potential representation of the future where it was able to legally purchase – not by hacking and stealing – and harvest 87 million Facebook profiles to potentially influence the outcome of democratic elections, then we must take action to institute strong legislation and legal frameworks against such actions. This book is intended to address these developments within the context of GDPR.

## 1.12 Chapter Overview

In this book we outline the birth and growth of data privacy as a concept across the US and the EU. We also examine how data privacy has grown over time on a global platform, ushering in GDPR age and how it applies to Data Collectors like

Facebook. In Chapter 2 we provide an overview of the history of individual privacy and discuss how the construct is extended to information and data privacy. In Chapter 3 we discuss the primary actors under GDPR to whom this regulation applies. Additionally, we examine the legal scope of GDPR and its extraterritorial application to certain processing situations, making it a global undertaking.

GDPR requires organizations to make massive internal changes to their processing operations to enable legal handling of personal data. In Chapter 4 we discuss the top-down overhaul required by businesses to be compliant with the regulation. GDPR transforms personal data processing from an open to closed industry by creating strong mandates for "legally" processing data. In Chapter 5, we examine the legal and operational aspects of "legally" processing data in GDPR age. The regulation creates a "Magna Carta" of user rights in a digital age by reinforcing formerly existing rights in the previous EU DPD while also carving out new ones to protect user interests. In Chapter 6, we discuss how data subjects are protected in the digital age and how businesses will have to change to keep up.

As we have noted in this introductory chapter, regulation is ineffective unless there is enforcement. GDPR seeks to enforce compliance and change in the data culture by creating a powerful enforcement mechanism that delivers targeted strikes to offenders. In Chapter 7 we discuss the legal and administrative aspects of the regulation, which gives the law its teeth along with the venues for enforcement. Since a right is useless without enforcement, which in turn is ineffective without remedies, in Chapter 8, we discuss how GDPR provides for legal, curative, and punitive remedies.

As governments go paperless and try new initiatives that work harmoniously with data for effective governance, they will themselves incur personal data obligations. Chapter 9 first covers the relevant portions of GDPR which deal with the State, and then examines unique current topics regarding the use of citizen data for good governance. In Chapter 10 we provide a step-by-step guide to GDPR compliance and implementation of a successful system of personal data protection. Compliance is an ongoing investment, but necessary for the longevity of online retailers and providers of web-based services including social media.

In Chapter 11, we discuss the case of Facebook that has changed the dynamic of human interaction forever. It holds a unique place in our society as an omniscient community that lives in our pockets. We discuss the myriad legal issues surrounding the company and its management of billions of unique profiles and personal data. Continuing our previous discussion, in Chapter 12, we shift focus to Facebook's past, current, and future issues surrounding its personal data processing, specifically with regard to its GDPR compliance and ongoing investigations. Chapter 13 provides a glimpse into what the future may look like.

# Notes

1  *Union Pacific Railway Co. v. Botsford,* 141 US 250 (1891).
2  *Semaynes's Case,* 77 Eng. Rep. 194 [KB 1604].
3  *Boyd v. The United States,* 116 US 616 (1886).
4  Federal Trade Commission, "Eli Lilly Settles FTC Charges Concerning Security Breach," January 18, 2002, https://www.ftc.gov/news-events/press-releases/2002/01/eli-lilly-settles-ftc-charges-concerning-security-breach.
5  Federal Trade Commission, "Eli Lilly Settles FTC Charges Concerning Security Breach," January 18, 2002, https://www.ftc.gov/news-events/press-releases/2002/01/eli-lilly-settles-ftc-charges-concerning-security-breach.
6  Aleecia M. McDonald and Lorrie Faith Cranor, "The Cost of Reading Privacy Policies," *I/S: A Journal of Law and Policy for the Information Society* 4, no. 3 (2008): 543–568.
7  Ari Ezra Waldman, *Privacy as Trust: Information Privacy for an Information Age* (Cambridge University Press, 2018).
8  Ryan Nakashima, "Google Tracks Your Movements, Like It or Not," *AP News,* August 13, 2018, https://www.apnews.com/828aefab64d4411bac257a07c1af0ecb.
9  Gil Press, *Forbes,* April 8, 2018.

# 2

# A Brief History of Data Privacy

*What is history? An echo of the past in the future; a reflex from the future on the past.*

— Victor Hugo

The construct of individual privacy forms the basis of the current discussion and debates around data privacy. In this context, we present a brief historical overview of the concept of individual privacy to construct the paradigm for development of applicable laws.

## 2.1  Privacy as One's Castle

"A home is one's castle" was a simple, adequate, and robust framework for its time. It was one of the earliest cases on the Right to Privacy pronounced in 1604 by Sir Edward Coke in the King's Bench of England.[1] This elementary construct was fit for the times, as it addressed the private life of individuals within their homes and their rights to be left alone from public life. The doctrine was simple because the social life and modes of communication between people were eyes and speech.

The legal construct for protection of individual privacy has evolved since then. Over time it grew with the evolving technologies, but laws were rarely ahead of the curve in preventing abuse. Every development in the right to privacy follows the same story: a new technology is discovered: it starts being used commonly: the State finds a way to use the technology in law enforcement: and then the public starts to recognize the need for greater privacy.

This pattern has led to gradual growth of the individual right, either by law or judicial pronouncement, extending it from the privacy of man to his affairs, decisions, home, vehicle, documents, correspondence,[2] and communications. This extended the right to privacy from individuals' homes and personal lives more universally to protect us from excessive outside interference, be it public or private.

### 2.1.1 Individuals'"Castles" Were Not Enough

Individual rights to seclusion came under threat with the explosive growth in print media. From 1850 to 1900, the number of newspapers in circulation increased from 100 to 950 in the US alone with a 10-fold increase in readership to more than 8 million. The term "paparazzi" may not have been part of daily conversations, but the Kodak Brownie – a box camera spawned a multitude of photo-journalists who clicked on the private lives of the upper-class elite. The publishers' case to print the stories at that time is no different from now. They felt that they had an imperative to reveal the truth – the excesses of the rich and the elite – even if it conflicted with the individuals' rights to privacy. These stories fed the fast-growing readership interest in and frustration with the rich and famous.

## 2.2 Extending Beyond the "Castle"

As a response to the proliferation of print journalism into individual privacy, Samuel Warren and Louis Brandeis coined the phrase "the right to be left alone." Published in 1890 and adapted from an 1879 treatise on tort law, this is one of the most famous law articles on the right to privacy. They argued that modern technology had made "solitude" and "retreat from the world" more necessary than ever. The right to privacy was construed as separation from public observation and intrusion. They wrote that "our inviolate personality" – the dignity owed us as fully formed autonomous individuals – implies that we had the right to exclude others from our "thought, sentiments and emotions." Written 130 years ago, this construct is more relevant now than ever – even as the first-generation Kodak cameras are now museum pieces.

## 2.3 Formation of Privacy Tort Laws

In 1902, Abigail Roberson, then a teenager, sued the Flower Mills flour company in New York for "invasion of privacy." She asserted in her case that Flower Mills had used her likeness on advertising flyers without her consent, violating her privacy and causing her humiliation and injury. However, the New York Court of Appeals denied her claim because it could not find a precedent for bringing privacy action in Anglo-American common law. The public reaction to the decision was fierce. The *New York Times* published as many as five articles on the decision. As the criticism mounted, one of the judges in the case was compelled to justify the decision in an article in the *Columbia Law Journal*. This case was likely the catalyst for the first tort law that addressed individuals' rights to privacy: Section 51 of the New York Civil Rights law.

The Warren and Brandeis construct began to be followed by the courts. In the case of *Pavesich v. New England Life Insurance Company*, wherein the photograph of the plaintiff was used in advertising without his consent, the Georgia Supreme Court ruled against the insurance company. The court apparently followed Warren and Brandeis "edict" and stated that the claim was "derived from natural law." The court stated that subject to certain limitations, "the body of a person cannot be put on exhibition at any time or at any place without his consent." More importantly, the court went on to state that "a violation of the right of privacy is a direct invasion of a legal right of the individual." Over the next three decades, the US state common laws and court systems evolved to follow the *Pavesich* case – 14 states and the District of Columbia recognized at least one privacy tort.

### 2.3.1 A Privacy Tort Framework

In 1960, William Prosser,[3] a tort law scholar, delineated four distinct privacy torts – based on the cases mentioned in the Warren and Brandeis article. These torts are described below.

1. **Intrusion upon seclusion:** The intentional intrusion, physical or otherwise, into the solitude and seclusion of another or his private affairs or concerns in a manner which is highly offensive to a reasonable person.
2. **Public disclosure of private facts:** Publicizing matters related to the private life of an individual regarding information which is not of public concern is highly offensive to him.
3. **False light and publicity:** Publicizing matters concerning the private life of an individual in a "false light" (false impression) in a way that is highly offensive to a reasonable person and with reckless disregard to the falsity of the information shared.
4. **Appropriation:** Using the name or likeness of another for one's own personal gain or benefit.

These torts lay the foundation for determining violation of individual privacy rights and subsequent legal action.

## 2.4 The Roots of Privacy in Europe and the Commonwealth

During World War II the German army had seized the documents and effects of countless Jewish victims of the Holocaust. This was all made possible by a "punchcard" system, developed by none other than IBM, that was part of a German Social Security program.[4] This misuse of personal data with grave consequences provides a tragic historical context for the EU's cautious approach and has provided robust protection for the privacy of its citizens, their self-determination, documents, effects, personal, and family lives.

Conceptual privacy concepts raised across nations, with the Commonwealth members following a similar approach. But the most important aspect that sparked inspiration for GDPR is the security and privacy of citizens' personal informations from State seizure.

The initial roots of data privacy are found in the most basic Human Rights[5] enshrined under the *UN Declaration on Human Rights,* and subsequently echoed in the *EU Convention on Human Rights.* These rights include:

1. **The Right to a Private Life:** No person shall be subject to *arbitrary interference* with his privacy, family, home or correspondence, nor face any attacks on his honor or reputation.[6]
2. **Freedom of Speech and Expression:** The right to express one's views without interference and the ability to seek, impart and receive information and ideas through any media regardless of frontiers.[7]

These broader underlying freedoms helped shape the path for the growth of data-protection law with Germany leading the way in 1970 after the citizens of the State of Hessen became concerned over the dangers of automated processing. This started a trend that continued through to 1980s until more coordinated laws under the guidance of the Data Protection Doctrine (DPD) were enacted.

## 2.5  Privacy Encroachment in the Digital Age

As advances were made in the digital capture and transmission of print and visual media, the limits of personal privacy were beginning to be tested. The rapid acceptance of social media and personal networks created a dynamic that had never been experienced before in human history. The general population dropped their prior reservations regarding their privacy and voluntarily shared information among groups, which was subsequently circulated broadly and made available – with or without the knowledge of the providers of information. Family histories, personal information, images, and videos could be shared instantaneously in fast-growing social networks and other applications like Facebook, WhatsApp, and LinkedIn.

In less than a decade, the efficiency and convenience of instantaneous communication for a marginal cost or no cost at all has become an essential facet of our daily lives. We embraced and relished a more connected world. It is becoming increasingly evident that the price of this convenience – provided at little or no cost to us – was that our personal information became the asset that generated the revenue for Data Collectors. We became the product that was commoditized in the form of our persona, habits, and buying behaviors. Our personal data has become a new commodity that is traded and used by a multitude of businesses and applications.

## 2.5.1   Early Digital Privacy Laws Were Organic

Prior to the 1990s at the nascent stage of internet adoption, the US laws regarding privacy were limited in scope barring a few regarding wiretapping[8] and videography,[9] and did not provide robust protection to privacy rights. However, at an international level, particularly in several European States, important principles for data privacy were being formed as early as 1980. The Organisation of Economic Co-operation and Development (OECD) laid down Guidelines on protection of privacy and data collection based on eight principles:

1. **Collection Limitation** – Data should be collected lawfully and with the person's consent.
2. **Data Quality** – Data should be relevant to the purpose collected and be accurate.
3. **Specification of Purpose** – Data Collectors should specify the purpose at the time of data collection.
4. **Limitation of Use** – Collection and disclosure can only be done with the person's consent.
5. **Reasonable Security Safeguards** – Data security safeguards must be implemented.
6. **Openness Principle** – Users should be informed of the practices and policies of the entity collecting their data.
7. **Individual Participation** – People should be able to learn about the data processing and have a right to rectify any problems with their data.
8. **Accountability** – The entities responsible for the processing would be on the hook for any violation of these principles.

While the US system of online privacy operated on a presumption of trust between the data providers and collectors, the OECD had begun laying the foundation for a future of regulation in the digital age. At this point as data collection increased exponentially, legislatures slowly started to implement basic data-protection measures that were narrow, particularly in the US, where the protections were implemented on an as-needed basis.

## 2.5.2   Growth in Commercial Value of Individual Data

During the early 1990s, data-privacy concerns in the US were emerging with increasing adoption of online services like AOL and MySpace that required individuals' information. However, the collection of personal data was moderate, and the concept of commercializing it had not entered the mainstream. Providers of internet connectivity and other services increasingly started to realize the value of individuals' personal information. They voluntarily implemented privacy policies and disclaimers, but these were geared toward protecting corporate liability as several services had started using surreptitious mechanisms for data collection such as *cookies*[10] and *web-bugs*.[11] This can be considered as the beginning of the era of the mass commercialization of personal data.[12]

However, in the US the laws were only being actively legislating around specific problems and narrow areas.[13] Some examples are provided below:

- **Telephonic Consumer Protection:**[14] The US Congress passed laws regarding "do-not-call" lists that respected consumers' privacy from telemarketers.
- **Drivers Licenses:** The US Congress passed the Driver's Privacy Protection Act to regulate the sharing/sale of drivers' license-related information.
- **Health Insurance:** In 1996 the first law directly addressing privacy of individuals' medical/healthcare-related information was enacted in the US. It required patient authorization for any data shared with *anyone* other than the healthcare provider.[15]
- **Protection of Children:** The Children's Online Privacy Protection Act of 1988 provided for enhanced requirements on online consent and disclosure of information directed at children.

In addition to enacting legislation and laws, the US Federal Trade Commission (FTC) started bringing actions against companies that had violated their own data-collection standards and privacy policies. FTC and other legal actions were an effective mechanism to deter violations of data protection, particularly with the combination of class action suits, jury verdicts, punitive damages, and contingency fees for attorneys.[16] The FTC has continued this and can be considered as the enforcement wing with respect to privacy laws – it recently announced a fine of roughly $5 billion against Facebook for mishandling users' personal information, likely signaling a newly aggressive stance by regulators toward the country's most powerful technology companies. In contrast, Europe has adopted GDPR and is also enforcing it aggressively.

## 2.6 The Gramm-Leach-Bliley Act Tilted the Dynamic against Privacy

One of the catalysts for commercialization of data collection and sharing without providing individuals' consent was the Gramm-Leach-Bliley Act (GLB Act) of 1999. The implementation of this law led to a plethora of privacy policies being sent to customers of banks, informing them that their data might be shared with other companies. The GLB Act permitted financial institutions, including banks, to share "non-public personal information" with their affiliates and subsidiaries. The customers did have a right to be informed of such sharing but no right to object to it. The data held by these banks could also be shared with third parties, even though customers could object to such sharing, most did not. The GLB act opened the floodgates on data sharing in the banking industry. If a bank/financial institution wanted access to more data on customers to build their services, they only had to assume ownership interest in an entity that had access to individual data to become an "affiliate" and be entitled to access to the information without customer consent. Consumer data privacy rights began to be eroded, and the commercialization of individual information became more aggressive.

## 2.7 Emergence of Economic Value of Individual Data for Digital Businesses

As the early dot-com era was cooling off in 2000, an online toy store — Toysmart. com defaulted and went into bankruptcy protection. It offered to sell its customer lists containing contact informations, shopping, and financial information to the highest bidder to offset its debts. This news caught the public eye and brought into the mainstream the economic value of individuals' data. The blowback from this revelation was significant, with over a dozen bills proposed and pending in congress for federal data privacy legislation within the context of new technologies. However, before any bill related to privacy was passed into legislation, we endured the tragic events of 9/11 and their aftermath.

### 2.7.1 The Shock of the 9/11 Attacks Affected Privacy Protection Initiatives

The whiplash from the tragedy of the brazen and improbable 9/11 attacks caused US Congress to pass the Uniting & Strengthening America by Providing Appropriate Tools Required to Intercept and Obstruct Terrorism Act (USA PATRIOT Act), which gave legislative mandate for widespread surveillance of IP addresses, and interception of communications from internet and mobile service. Accompanying this were amendments to the Foreign International Surveillance Act (FISA), which allowed courts to provide warrants liberally to law enforcement bodies, sometimes for undisclosed suspects with less than sufficient probable cause. Subsequently, Congress passed the Intelligence Reform & Terrorism Prevention Act, 2004, which provided that information shared across federal agencies be provided in its most shareable form to promote a culture of information sharing. All forms of technologically enabled mechanisms were used to conduct mass surveillance of US citizens through tracking online activity and wiretapping telephonic conversations. This was a casual violation of due process and fundamental rights toward investigating terrorism. The Bush administration also gave the National Security Agency (NSA) unprecedented and wide-ranging surveillance powers. It could conduct surveillance without due process, which had been an artifact of the US Constitution from the Fourth and Fifth Amendments. The ethics and desirability of this is an ongoing debate and beyond the scope of this discourse.

### 2.7.2 Surveillance and Data Collection Was Rapidly Commercialized

It can be conjectured that the need for information to tackle terrorism created the *surveillance economy* in the private sector. Information on individuals readily available on their social media profiles, online banking services, delivery and shopping apps was accessed by a proliferation of vendors who provided these services. Technology advances on the internet led to rapid growth of social networks and media, online shopping and related services with numerous services such as Facebook, WhatsApp, Instagram, Snapchat, Amazon, and many others becoming ubiquitous. At the same time, data-mining practices were proliferating, enabled by the widespread practice of user-selected privacy policy and disclaimer settings.

We welcomed and embraced an atmosphere of sharing and connectivity, finding new ways to make friends and connections through platforms that facilitated these communications for little or no cost to users; their business model centered around the collection of data and selling to advertisers and governmental agencies. The PATRIOT Act created and encouraged an atmosphere of sharing between Data Controllers and governmental agencies. Commercial entities that collected data in the US complied with this practice as a legal process as most privacy policies had the common clause: "we may share your data to legal authorities in compliance with a law, legal order of the court, subpoena, warrant or in compliance with any legal process." The following list provides a representation of a typical data sharing cycle.

1. The user gives broad consent for the mining of his data.
2. The legal authorities require and seize data for their investigations and monitoring.
3. Legal authorities either create their own technology or approach a surveillance vendor for interception technologies to collect the data.
4. For certain types of data, volunteered by the public to Controllers, legal authorities directly access it from the Controller.
5. The Controllers, being *aware* of this need for data and its more sophisticated variations, increase their collection scope and capabilities with the services they provide. The data mined is sold for a profit.

The cycle can be endless with progressive severity with respect to individual privacy rights. As individual information became progressively more valuable, there was a proliferation of hackers, cyber terrorists, and surveillance vendors. Law enforcement in the US gradually caught up to handle the first two threats to privacy by creating cybercrime divisions in police forces and federal agencies.

### 2.7.3 Easing of Privacy Standards by the NSA Set the Tone at the Top

In 2009, Facebook changed its privacy policy without informing its users, and the mining of data and abuse set the stage for the Cambridge Analytica scandal that occurred in 2016. This came on the heels of Facebook changing all its users' default profile settings to "public" without their permission. A surfeit of data vendors including Axiom, Equifax, and TomTom cropped up around the world offering personal data for sale. In 2012, Google consolidated all its platforms: search engine, maps, Gmail, YouTube and others, presumably to optimize the collection and tracking of personal information. Data mining and analysis algorithms grew in complexity, with big data and artificial intelligence becoming overused buzzwords. The effect of this was palpable, e.g. Amex and other credit card companies lowered the credit rating of thousands of customers overnight using their shopping habits but not payment capacity to determine their creditworthiness.

It is remarkable that during this period very few protections were constructed and provided at a legislative level to encourage data privacy and discourage data commoditization and sales. Only a few state courts held companies liable for the way they disseminated personal data, requiring them to exercise reasonable care when disclosing information to a third party.[17]

## 2.8 Legislative Initiatives to Protect Individuals' Data Privacy

However, privacy was not dead in the US across all aspects because there were several legislations passed by Congress during 2000–2010:

- Credit reporting, identity theft, and handling credit card fraud.[18]
- Establishment of a national do-not-call registry, enforced by the FTC directly.
- The restriction on sending commercial spam disguised as legitimate websites or services to deceive or mislead recipients. Vendors had to provide for return addresses and allow users to opt out.[19]
- Other miscellaneous acts at the state level dealing with the basic necessary provisions of information technology law (such as data security, intermediary liability, revenge pornography, etc.).

These laws relate back to the conventional practice in the US of taking a market-based sectoral approach to data processing.

Despite the laws listed above, in 2005 several data brokers announced major data breaches of personal data belonging to 162,000 individuals by fraudulent companies set up by a ring of identity thieves.[20] This occurred soon after several courts ruled that general statements of privacy provided by a website were not contractual statements, giving rise to damages in the event of a breach by the service provider.[21] At this time the data protection debate had become mainstream in the public domain with attorneys arguing the basic principles before courts across the country. However, the lack of unified regulation contributed to it becoming a never-ending effort for privacy advocates because new industry entrants could easily create new websites and programs with emerging technologies.

Meanwhile, in 2005 the *New York Times* exposed the scale of NSA surveillance on the public,[22] and soon thereafter in 2006, Mark Kline of the Electronic Frontier Foundation discovered that AT&T had plans to work with the government on a communication-tapping program. This demonstrated that the US had indeed entered an age where "Big Brother is watching" through data that people themselves provide. This sparked national and international debate over the legality of then President George W. Bush's program as a violation of the Fourth Amendment privacy rights of the citizens. The main question was: Isn't one's personal data "a document" for which they may have a reasonable expectation of privacy?

As it stands today, that is not the case. This is owing to the Third Party Doctrine in Fourth Amendment jurisprudence, which mandates that law enforcement may collect information which has been willingly provided by the suspect to a third party,[23] in this case it being the data Controller. This logic has been applied in the past regarding bank records or any documents held by a conduit, with the reasonable expectation of privacy over the records lost once given to a third party. It is important to recall here the trespass theory of the Fourth Amendment, which equates a physical trespass by law as a violation of individual rights. This theory was employed by the US Supreme Court in 2012 in its ruling in *United States v. Jones*,[24] holding that a physical intrusion by the police in placing a GPS tracker on a car violates the Fourth Amendment, which was not the case here by the NSA. Without an operative US Supreme Court judgment on the matter, metadata collected by the NSA from Data Controllers is treated as equivalent to the government accessing individual bank accounts, resulting in the dismissal of numerous lawsuits filed against the Bush and Obama administrations.[25] Through this narrow loophole and the congressional power afforded to the government under the PATRIOT Act, the surveillance does not qualify as unconstitutional.

Despite the revelations of the NSA scandal and the abuse of the PATRIOT Act in 2005, the provisions remain in place today with no laws prohibiting the free sale and purchase of surveillance technologies and personal data in the US. Despite promises by Senator Obama to repeal the draconian legislations, President Obama chose to renew the controversial library provision of the PATRIOT Act, which was at the center of the NSA controversy. With the private sector collecting data indiscriminately and a healthy surveillance economy created with the government as a participant, the internet in the new millennium was truly the Wild West of business opportunities. With the mining of personal data, services became better, and the public reaped the benefits while the corporations increased their profit margins and governments analyzed the information. But of course, it came full circle at the turn of the decade as one scandal followed another leading to an end of the "good times."

## 2.9 The EU Path

While the US was the epicenter of the data market and surveillance economy, Europe had played it safer by taking the sure and steady route. While the drama of the new century unfolded in America, the EU Data Protection Directive (DPD) was in place guiding the Member States on how their data protection laws should be maintained.

Data privacy had initial sporadic growth in Europe with France implementing its first data protection regulation as early as 1970. A decade later in 1981 the Council of Europe, the predecessor of the EU, developed Convention 108, which protected data on an international level with provisions on transboundary data flows and basic principles of data processing. Simultaneously, many states in Europe were members abiding to the OECD guidelines for data transfers. Soon after, in 1983, a German Federal Constitutional Court had declared that people have a fundamental right of self-determination over personal data to remedy the wrongs of the past and ensure that something like the holocaust never happened again. This declaration became the cornerstone of the EU's views on data privacy today.[26]

The push for a single unified European market came as early as 1995, and the Member States of the EU knew the value of a secure data market for the consumers. This led to the promulgation of the predecessor to GDPR in 1996 by way of the Data Protection Directive (DPD). If the OECD guidelines were the initial blueprints for GDPR, the DPD would be the floor plan, crystallizing many rights of data subjects' rights and providing a broad overarching protection, rather than the sectoral approach of the US. Additionally, the directive provided specific requirements for international transfers of data, leading to the EU-US Safe Harbor Agreement, which mandated certain security safeguards for the transfer of personal data in accordance with the DPD.

The DPD helped unify Europe's laws on data privacy across the Union, keeping the basic rules of processing in place until the need for GDPR arose. The existence of these guiding rules helped the EU avoid many of the pitfalls of deregulation like the fiascos in the US. Here, one can observe a clear divergence across the approaches followed, which goes to the root of the philosophical differences in their governance. The general view is that the US has, in recent years, left the protection of privacy to markets rather than the law. In contrast, Europe treats privacy as a political imperative based on individuals' fundamental rights.[27]

This comparison of the "market" to a "fundamental right" approach essentially encapsulates the key difference between the two systems. At the close of the twentieth century, the US left data privacy largely to the markets until the market players abused their position as Data Collectors. After such an incident, a sector specific law came into place to prevent further data misuse. This goes in line with the commoditization of data as something a user can offer in exchange for a service, which can be subsequently bought or sold. On the opposite side of the coin, the EU takes a precautionary approach by treating data as an extension of the user's privacy and thus governed by fundamental rights. And in treating it as a fundamental right, broad directives are needed to control its protection.

### 2.9.1 The Internet Rights Revolution

The internet boom of the first half of the twenty-first century led to a period of loose regulation, near-anarchy, and a steady loss of online privacy felt by society. As phones and laptops became more advanced, so did the problems that followed with them with almost every app requesting permission for GPS use, proliferation in cloud computing services, introduction of wearable technologies, and new mediums such as virtual and augmented reality. It seemed that modernization was only entering its "first act" in mankind's history. The technology sector was on an exponential curve upward, and with it came unfathomable benefits and increased data collection by service providers. The rapid increase in data flow enabled entities conduct analytics in ways they could never do before, such as helping them prevent epidemics. But at the same time, data was sold and bought in larger quantities for those benefits, helping Controllers to maximize their bottom-line. This is the decade of Big Data, where our personal data is used for miracles, and profit.

### 2.9.2 Social Revolutions

On a social level, awareness of internet rights rose on a global scale, with the universe of users realizing that the internet is a public resource and not merely an alternative means of receiving services. Social media started to be used to protest authoritative regimes all over the world, such as in Egypt and Turkey. Developing countries such as India and China went from very little connectivity to becoming the largest markets for cell phones in the world within a span of a few years. And social media movements became a weapon for the public to challenge questionable state actions or international crises. But with these new tools available to the public, new rights were needed to empower them and keep up with the pace of development.

After some governments tried to silence opposition by controlling and cutting off internet connectivity, a global push was made to recognize a fundamental right to internet access for all people of the world, and not merely those who could afford it. Soon after protests broke out in Africa and the Middle East, a UN Special Rapporteur, Frank La Rue, released a report[28] stating that internet access should be considered a fundamental part of the freedom of speech and expression. He went on to state:

> Given that the Internet has become an indispensable tool for realizing a range of human rights, combating inequality, and accelerating development and human progress, ensuring universal access to the Internet should be a priority for all states.

As ambitious as the right may have been at the time, it was rooted in four basic human rights, which are enshrined under the UN *Universal Declaration of Human Rights*:

1. Freedom of speech
2. The right to information
3. Freedom of assembly
4. The right to development[29]

Despite the report and its recognition, in 2016, governments of Algeria and Turkey disrupted the internet connectivity of dissenters to quell possible revolutions. This led to the UN passing a nonbinding resolution in the summer of 2016 declaring that governments should not disrupt internet connectivity of their citizens to stifle free speech.[30] At present, there is no comprehensive declaration requiring that states provide internet access to their citizens, leaving the resolution largely aspirational. Globally, efforts can be seen by many countries to create a full blanket of internet protection for its citizens to increase their general quality of life, but the effort differs across nations. The flipside of a government's providing blanket internet access within its borders is that it controls the online world, leading to discretionary censorship and many other abuses of free speech.

Another key social change that took place is the movement of net neutrality, which many viewed as the ultimate battle between everyday users and internet service providers. Closely related to the right to internet access, net neutrality is a practice that emerged in the early part of the twenty-first century but gained momentum toward the turn of the decade. It is the practice of discriminating against different websites and services and the speeds provided to them by internet service providers (ISPs such as Verizon or AT&T) based on an amount paid for their services. Essentially, if a website paid an ISP a higher sum of money, it would receive a faster speed of connectivity while services that could not afford to pay could have their speeds lowered or throttled. This was yet another way to increase commercial profit in the private online sector and was the center of a heated debate all over the world for its discriminatory effect for the consumers.

Each country took the debate in its own way, leading to uneven stances on the issue throughout the world, depending on the government in charge. In the US net neutrality has a sordid history of constant change, with it initially being permitted, then outlawed, and subsequently challenged in court.[31] The FCC had issued an *Open Internet Order* in 2010, which stated that ISPs must provide internet service based on three principles:

1. Transparency
2. No blocking of websites
3. No discrimination

Soon after in 2014 Verizon challenged the order[32] on the grounds that it exceeded the authority of the US Telecommunications Act of 1996. This led to a partial upholding of the order and partial alteration of its scope for certain providers. As time passed and the public opinion submitted to the FCC greatly leaned toward neutrality, a fresh order was issued in 2015, which better complies with previous court orders. However, soon afterwards, the US Telecom Association filed a challenge against these new rules. While the case was pending, there was a period of online neutrality in the US where the debate slowed down and a system of preferential net pipelines for high-paying customers was permitted by the FCC. However, all of it was for naught as the administration changed in 2017, and the new FCC chairman, Ajit Pai, repealed all Obama-era net neutrality rules. As it stands today, there is no law for net neutrality in the US.

The EU on the other hand, had once again taken a precautionary approach and erred on the side of consumer empowerment. The first measure implemented in 2009 was in the form of a telecoms package that provided for a comprehensive framework for Member States consisting of regulations and directives on how ISPs should govern their broadband practices.[33] This package contained rules for transparency, pricing, discrimination, etc. Soon after, in 2015, the EU memorialized their policy of net neutrality by placing a binding mandate in a sweeping regulation that provided for equal internet access and speeds for connections within the EU.[34] The transition into a digital world of neutrality was relatively simple for the EU – unlike the US. And in true EU fashion, the Open Internet Regulation was carried out, keeping in mind the pillars of fundamental rights, transparency, and accountability which are also seen in GDPR to encourage the development of the single digital market in the EU.

If the first decade of the twenty-first century saw a learning curve, the second decade can be considered as the time for applying the lessons learned. The movement for digital rights and privacy started to gain real momentum leading to robust shifts in control of the internet. The full potential of social media was learned on all sides of the sector leading to tremendous feats of online activism such as the #MeToo movement in the past year to combat sexual harassment in Hollywood. The public has now accepted that the internet is not just a medium but a forum for discussion and exercise of one's fundamental rights, which makes the gradual shift into this new GDPR era seem long overdue.

## 2.10   End of the Wild West?

The first decade of the 2000s was one of unforeseeable and exorbitant profits for the companies that provided services to us. The volume of data casually bought and sold between vendors, online companies such as Facebook, Uber, and Amazon skyrocketed in value, with only a few the consumers asking the simple question, "How is this free?" Most of us happily availed ourselves of the services of these companies without paying a penny but did not ask the question, which would have made the protection of our rights paramount. It took numerous wake-up calls in the form of data-breaches and scandals such as Equifax and Cambridge Analytica for society to realize that there were fundamental issues with the entire industry of data collection and its effects on our daily lives.

The impeding threats to our privacy started to become widespread and were felt at personal levels. In 2012 Brian Leigh, an Irish student traveling to the US for vacation, tweeted "... free this week for a quick gossip/prep before I go destroy America? x" to a friend. He found himself detained and questioned by US Security Officers when entering the country.[35] In Britain this year, protestors of the royal wedding were arrested *before* their protest in anticipation of their creating an unlawful assembly. The British police based the investigation on the social media activity of members belonging to Facebook groups protesting the royal wedding on the days leading up to the event. Meanwhile, the apps and websites we rely upon are starting to eerily predict our needs, and data breaches of personal data have become more frequent in the news. This all culminated in the internet becoming an unsafe – albeit necessary – place, filled with Trojan attacks, fake news, spam bots, false advertising, and other invisible risks.

The 2016 US Election and the Cambridge Analytica scandal are the most notable incidents, that have once again sparked the debate for data privacy. It was the first time that the true dark side of the data trade market involved Facebook, a social connectivity service that the public holds so dear. This was punctuated by the fact that a foreign government potentially used this data and coordinated hacking efforts to rig the most prominent election on the world stage. If the positive side of Facebook was helping to stage peaceful revolutions for freedom, this was the darker side of how the service can be used for unimaginably nefarious purposes. To many, this may just seem like one isolated incident of a man and an organization gaming the system, but in retrospect, it was a sign of a broken system and a characteristic attribute of unregulated free enterprise.

## 2.11   Data as an Extension of Personal Privacy

As awareness of the erosion and abuse of our privacy entered the mainstream, it is becoming evident that the practice of releasing and selling of private information is compromising its safety with select recipients for viewing and with the

Controller for processing. Cyber security and data protection has become a prerequisite for a consumer to use a website, while personal data and electronic documents started to gain recognition under the law.

In 2012 the US Supreme Court had ruled that GPS tracking of vehicles requires a valid warrant since it qualifies as a physical trespass of one's reasonable expectation of privacy.[36] Soon after in 2014 the Court of Justice of the European Union (CJEU) passed the landmark *Right to be Forgotten* doctrine recognizing a people's right to delete certain content about themselves online and on search engines.[37] Governments all over the world started placing blanket and sector-specific data protection rules and laws for protecting privacy online. These included:

- Prohibition of child pornography and protection of minors' rights
- Protection from revenge pornography and other dissemination of private photos or videos
- Protection from online bullying
- Heavier enforcement of privacy policy terms
- Specific rules for contracting online and giving consent
- Data-protection rules for online transactions
- Intermediary liability
- Encryption, certification, public key infrastructures
- Oversight authorities
- Civil compensation for data breaches
- Criminal penalties for stealing or misappropriating data, hacking, impersonation, etc.

Clearly, this is not an exhaustive list, as the sophistication of the law would depend on the applicable jurisdiction (and in the US the list would be different across states). As the capabilities, scale, and generally well-intended creativity of technology platforms and providers continue unabated, lawmakers have to draw a fine line – protect individual privacy rights while not impeding commerce and the development of convenience. That is why many countries leave the task of making technical requirements and specifications to a delegated authority, such as the Supervisory Authority under GDPR. Regardless of the lack of uniformity in development, the critical infrastructure of cyber law was put into effect throughout the world.

China imposed tight state control over access to websites and data in their state, while others in Europe and North America provide nearly unlimited flexibility unless the content is objectionable, or in violation of national security or criminal laws. It is noteworthy that despite significant public discourse regarding privacy in general, a comprehensive data-protection law has not been passed in the US at the federal level. This leaves the enforcement of data privacy largely at the state level. There have been some initiatives at the state level, e.g. California recently enacted the California Consumer Privacy Act, which echoes the principles of GDPR[38] such as data minimization and opt-out consent. Unless broad legislation is enacted, the sporadic and inconsistent development of data privacy laws will lead to creative practices by Controllers to avoid their responsibilities.

Several countries are in the process of adopting new data-privacy laws with 109 countries having enacted data protection laws[39] and 35 countries with legislation in process.[40] In Europe, GDPR is viewed as a comprehensive, all-encompassing law that is likely to shift the culture of data privacy toward protecting the rights and interests of individuals. Over the next decade, we should expect increasing concerns and laws to enforce data privacy around the world.

## 2.12  Cambridge Analytica: A Step Too Far

An EU regulator recently compared Facebook and other data processing websites to the banking industry, where deregulation has only led to disarray and economic meltdown. This comparison was made this year when EU lawmakers questioned Facebook's Mark Zuckerburg regarding the Cambridge Analytica scandal. The future of data protection in the US and EU is best reflected in the inquisitions were conducted regarding the 2016 US election. The US had heavily pressed Mr. Zuckerburg with questions but left many unanswered for a later date. The congressional hearing resolved with the committee "warning" Mr. Zuckerburg and leaving Facebook to self-regulate its standards. Meanwhile, in the EU the tone was much less patient. Barraged with exasperated questions and a demand for answers, Mr. Zuckerburg left the hearing apologizing profusely, unequivocally assuring that Facebook will be GDPR-compliant. The tone of the EU lawmakers reflected that of the general public – full of frustration. Though Facebook's acts weren't illegal, they were certainly a clear violation of its users privacy.

## 2.13  The Context of Privacy in Law Enforcement

But this is just one side of the coin. The main struggle always lies with privacy in relation to state action, which is where the jurisprudence on Fourth and Fifth Amendment rights in the Constitution become relevant. The Fourth Amendment prohibits law enforcement from unreasonable searches and seizures absent a warrant issued for probable cause. It is a protection afforded to US citizens from overzealous law enforcement overstepping the bounds of privacy when conducting investigations or arrests. US legal culture places this right as the cornerstone of its democracy, because without it the thin line can be crossed between democratic and totalitarian governments by oppressive police forces. The passage of time has led to the well-known jurisprudence of the Fourth Amendment as it stands today, with elaborate rules for search and seizure of one's person, documents, possessions, and house for state actions. The most important rules are provided below:

- **Search warrant:** This is an order of a court issued by a competent magistrate to search one's property for the fruits, evidence, or instrumentalities of a crime based on facts supported by probable cause specifying the person to be searched and the specific area to be searched.
- **Wire-tap warrant:** Considered an offshoot of a search warrant, a wire-tap warrant is an order issued by a magistrate based on probable cause authorizing law enforcement to intercept and record communications relating to a crime. Such warrants require greater specificity from the police regarding the nature, duration, and content of the communications monitored.
- **Arrest warrant:** This is an order issued by a magistrate based on probable cause, specifying the name of the person and the crime charged. Police may reasonably enter a person's residence to arrest them even after they refuse; however, this may affect the validity of the evidence collected.
- **Probable cause:** Facts that point to it being more likely than not the defendant committed the crime.
- **Reasonable suspicion:** Articulable facts by a police officer that justify his suspicions (usually based on his experience). This is a lowered standard for actions such as physical stop and frisking in public.
- **Trespass theory of privacy:** Initial theories propounded by the US Supreme Court in *Olmstead v. The United States* in 1927 followed a *Trespass theory* of the Fourth Amendment, which extended a person's privacy to his property and its curtilage. As a result, the police violate the Fourth Amendment Rights of a citizen when they trespass on private property. This theory would later again be used regarding GPS tracking of a car by the police.[41]
- **Reasonable expectation of privacy:** This is the prevailing operating theory of privacy under the Fourth Amendment which overruled the trespass theory in *Olmstead*. This theory mandates that privacy follows the person and is not just restricted to his property. Thus, an individual has a Fourth Amendment interest wherever he has a reasonable expectation of privacy.[42] This includes a hotel room, a friend's house, a phone booth, a vehicle, etc.
- **Fruit of the poisonous tree doctrine:** This is the consequence for any illegal search or seizure conducted by the police. US case law mandates that the evidence that results from any invalid search will be suppressed at trial and be inadmissible. This doctrine is one of the truly unique factors of the US legal system because illegal collection of evidence can have potential downsides in what law enforcement sought to achieve in the first place, thus acting as a good deterrent for repeated violations.

The Fourth and Fifth Amendments for the US Constitution's Bill of Rights provide for an action in tort law for damages in all cases. This was an enormous shift in the then-existing culture, which had recognized bits and pieces of privacy, but not as a separate set of rights altogether. The Fourth Amendment is accompanied by the Fifth which protects citizens against self-incrimination by way of testimony or volunteering documents for their own criminal prosecution.[43]

These two amendments, though relating to criminal prosecutions, lay the bedrock for the concept of privacy in America. The belief is that there must be minimal governmental interference in the private lives of people in the US, truly keeping in line with Brandeis school of thought. But as the age of technology dawned on the country, it slowly eroded.

The US constitution is vocal about our rights to privacy. The Fourth Amendment of the US Constitution states: "The right of the people to be secure in their persons, houses, papers, and effects, against unreasonable searches and seizures, shall not be violated, and no Warrants shall issue, but upon probable cause, supported by Oath or affirmation, and particularly describing the place to be searched, and the persons or things to be seized."

Meanwhile the Fifth Amendment states:

> No person ... shall be compelled in any criminal case to be a witness against himself, nor be deprived of life, liberty, or property, without due process of law; nor shall private property be taken for public use, without just compensation.

The history surrounding these two amendments alone is sufficient to fill up an entire book. They are the source of power to challenge unreasonable government interference into the private affairs of US citizens. The law surrounding the Fourth Amendment is largely a result of precedent from the US Supreme Court.

## Summary

The key focus of data privacy law is to protect citizens from intrusions into their personal affairs and to prevent, if not regulate, the interception of personal communication. Essentially, the law seeks to protect the sanctity of individuals' privacy with themselves and their contact with society. In our view, the most important and sweeping rules that will likely be reference for what should be done in jurisdictions around the world is the General Data Privacy Regulation or GDPR – a modern-age privacy legislation with its origins in the darker parts of history. We describe this in depth in the following chapters.

## Notes

1 *Semaynes's Case,* 77 Eng. Rep. 194 [KB 1604].
2 *Ex parte Jackson,* 96 US 727 (1877).
3 William L. Prosser, "Privacy," 48 *Cal. L. Rev.* 383 (1960).
4 Olivia B. Waxman, "The GDPR Is Just the Latest Example of Europe's Caution on Privacy Rights: That Outlook Has a Disturbing History," May 24, 2018, http://time.com/5290043/nazi-history-eu-data-privacy-gdpr.

5 Sian Rudgard, "Origins and Historical Context of Data Protection Law," in *Europe and Privacy: Law and Practice for Data Protection Professionals*, ed. Eduardo Ustaran (Portsmouth, NH: International Association of Privacy Professionals, 2012), 3.

6 *UN DHR,* Article 12.

7 *UN DHR,* Article 19.

8 Electronics Communications Privacy Act, 1986. 18 U.S.C. §§ 2510-2523.

9 Video Privacy Protection Act, 1988 18 U.S.C. § 2710.

10 A text file that is imbedded on one's computer browser when visiting a website. When you return to the website, it identifies the text file and recalls your preferences.

11 A device which secretly uses *pixel tags* to gather data on the user.

12 *See* Daniel J Solove, "Privacy and Power: Computer Databases and Metaphors for Information Privacy," 53 *Stan. L. Rev.* 1393, 1407–1409 (2001).

13 Lothar Determann, *Determann's Field Guide to Data Privacy Law,* 3rd ed. (Edward Elgar Publishing, 2017), 21.

14 Telephone Consumer Protection Act, 1991.

15 Health Insurance Portability & Accountability Act, 1996.

16 Determann, *Determann's Field Guid ,* 22.

17 *Remsburg v. Docusearch Inc.,* 816 A. 2d. 1001 (N.H. 2003).

18 The Fair and Accurate Credit Transactions Act, 2003.

19 Controlling the Assault of Non-Solicited Pornography & Marketing Act (CAN-SPAM), 2003.

20 Joseph Menn, "Did the ChoicePoint End Backfire?" *LA Times*, March 13, 2005.

21 *Dyer v. NW Airlines Corp,* 334 F. Supp. 2d 1196 (DND 2004); *In re NW Airlines Privacy Litigation,* 2004 WL 1278459 (D. Minn. 2004); *In re Jet Blue Airways Privacy Litigation,* 379 F. Supp. 2d 299 (EDNY 2005).

22 James Risen and Eric Lichtblau, "Bush Secretly Lifted Some Limits on Spying in US after 9/11, Officials Say," *New York Times*, December 15, 2005.

23 *Smith v. Maryland,* 442 US 735 (1979); *US v. Miller,* 425 U.S. 435 (1976).

24 *United States v. Jones*, 565 U.S. 400 (2012).

25 John Villasenor, "What You Need to Know about the Third-Party Doctrine," *The Atlantic*, December 30, 2013, https://www.theatlantic.com/technology/archive/2013/12/what-you-need-to-know-about-the-third-party-doctrine/282721.

26 Waxman, "The GDPR Is Just the Latest Example."

27 Joel R. Reidenberg, "E-Commerce & Trans-Atlantic Privacy," 38 *Hous. L. Rev.* 717, 730 (2001).

28 Report of the Special Rapporteur on the promotion and protection of the right to freedom of opinion and expression, UN HRC, 16 May 2011.

29 The Right to Development is a third-generation right recognized by way of UN General Assembly Resolution 41/128. It mandates that every person has a right to social, economic, and personal development *equally; this includes an access to public resources that help development, such as the internet.*

30 *UN Human Rights Council Resolution,* A/HRC/32/L.20.

31 *Verizon v. The FCC,* 740 F.3d 623 (D.C. Cir. 2014).
32 *Verizon v. The FCC,* 740 F.3d 623 (D.C. Cir. 2014).
33 See Directive 2009/140/EC (Framework, Authorisation and Access directives); Directive 2009/136/EC (Universal services and E-privacy directives); Regulation No 1211/2009 establishing the Body of European Regulators for Electronic Communications (BEREC).
34 Regulation (EU) 2015/2120, 25 November 2015, laying down measures concerning open internet access and amending Directive 2002/22/EC on universal service and users' rights relating to electronic communications networks and services and Regulation (EU) No 531/2012 on roaming on public mobile communications networks within the Union.
35 Richard H. Parkinson, "'I'm Going to Destroy America and Dig Up Marilyn Monroe': British Pair Arrested in U.S. on Terror Charges over Twitter Jokes," January 31, 2012, www.dailymail .co.uk/news/article-2093796/Emily-Bunting-Leigh-Van-Bryan-UK-tourists-arrested-destroy-America-Twitter-jokes.html.
36 *United States v. Jones,* 565 U.S. 400 (2012)
37 *Google Spain v. Costejas,* CJEU, 2014, Case C-131/12 (ECLI:EU:C:2014:317); later discussed in detail in Chapter 6.
38 Heather Kelly, California Passes Strictest Online Privacy Law in the Country, *CNN Business,* June 29, 2018, http://money.cnn.com/2018/06/28/technology/california-consumer-privacy-act/index.html.
39 G. Greenleaf, "Global Data Privacy Laws 2015: 109 Countries, with European Laws Now in a Minority," (2015) 133 *Privacy Laws & Business International Report,* 14–17; European Commission, Communication from the Commission to the European Parliament, Exchanging and Protecting Personal Data in a Globalized World, Brussels, October 1, 2017, p. 7.
40 "Data Protection Regulations and International Data Flows: Implications for Trade and Development," UNCTAD (2016): http://unctad.org/en/PublicationsLibrary/dtlstict2016d1_en.pdf, pp. 8 and 42 (*note*: this is based on 2015 figures).
41 *United States v. Jones,* 565 U.S. 400 (2012).
42 *Katz v. The United States* 389 U.S. 347 (1967).
43 The core principles of these amendments have been made applicable to the individual states by way of the Fourteenth Amendment.

# 3

## GDPR's Scope of Application

*Virtue is more to be feared than vice, because its excesses are not subject to the regulation of conscience.*

— Adam Smith

Businesses and other organizations process data as a central component of their workflow or otherwise store data of their employees, customers or affiliates, etc. GDPR has broad scope and can be generally assumed to apply to all aspects of businesses and other organizations that receive personal data. Large Data Collectors must adapt and adhere to GDPR to reduce their exposure to liability in the long run. However, smaller businesses and organizations, particularly those or which principal activity does not entail receiving individual data, would find it hard to sustain the cost of ongoing GDPR compliance and would be concerned regarding the extent to which the regulation applies to their business activities. They have to balance between minimal processing, storage, and usage restrictions for individual information that may entail regulatory and reputational risks with comprehensive frameworks that would be cost prohibitive. Toward this goal, an evaluation of the applicability of GDPR is a critical first step toward its compliance. In this chapter we provide a framework for the assessment of the applicability of GDPR for individual businesses and organizations.

## 3.1   When Does GDPR Apply?

GDPR applies to all processing of personal data regarding the EU and its citizens.[1] This deliberately broad definition establishes a universal change in the perception of the importance of the privacy of EU citizens' individual data, its processing, usage, and sharing.

### 3.1.1 "Processing" of Data

Under GDPR, processing comprises any set of operations or treatments performed on personal data, regardless of whether it is carried out manually or with the help of automated mechanisms.[2] The "Material Scope"[3] of the regulation first and most importantly, applies to the processing of personal data. In this sense, any business that collects personal information of any type even if it is limited to its employees is subject to GDPR.

Specifically, to fall under the regulation, a business must:

1. Process personal data,
2. Wholly/partially by automated means, and
3. Process by other means
4. To form part of a filing system or intended to be part of one.

This includes the processing of data that can be used to identify a user either directly or indirectly.[4] Processing is an all-encompassing concept under the regulation, which consists of any one step from its collection to its destruction.[5] In brief, processing would include the use of personal data for:

1. Collection
2. Recording
3. Organization
4. Storage
5. Adaptation
6. Alteration
7. Retrieval
8. Consultation
9. Use
10. Disclosure by transmission
11. Dissemination
12. Aggregation
13. Blocking
14. Erasure
15. Destruction
16. Or otherwise making it available to a third party.

Under GDPR, the activities listed above are covered regardless of whether they are performed with or without human intervention. This prohibits the Data Processors' passing the responsibility to any technology framework(s) that may entail artificial intelligence (AI) that they may choose to employ; for example, Google cannot escape liability for unlawful data collection if one of its AI software technologies mines the data without the knowledge of an individual or a related website.

**3.1.1.1 Manual Processing**   The data collected under GDPR must be maintained in a repository, namely, a *filing system*. Additionally, GDPR includes certain types of manual processing within its scope. Manual processing is done without machine or AI involvement, carried out entirely by humans. Generally, such processing is not covered by GDPR unless the following criteria are met:

1. **Filing system:** If the personal data is placed in a "filing system" that is used to organize and manage the data.[6]
2. **Structured:** The files must be organized in a way that is based on a specific criterion[7] such as alphabetical or number-based structuring.

**Example:** A chartered accountant (CPA), Bo Dice, runs a small firm with a limited clientele of celebrities. As a cautious professional, he maintains all his clients' paper files in a filing cabinet in his office. All client files are organized in separate cabinets alphabetically, with each cabinet encompassing the prior one year of business information. As this is a "filing system" of personal information organized based on a specific criterion, Bo's business is subject to GDPR.

### 3.1.2 "Personal Data"

A business seeking to be compliant or a person seeking to enforce her rights must understand the scope of GDPR.[8] The regulation only affords protection to the personal data of **natural persons**,[9] which implies that legal persons such as companies are not provided protection. The regulation defines "personal data" as information relating to an identified or identifiable natural person.[10] Identifiability can be derived from a single set of information (example: a Social Security number or address) or from an amalgamation of information (e.g.: political or cultural views expressed on social media, or cookies and IP addresses).

**3.1.2.1 Relative Criteria for Identifiability** The term personally identifiable information does not require that the data set must have the person's name and intimate details available on its face; rather the test is whether the data as a whole could be used to establish a reasonable likeliness of identifiability.[11] If the data without further "supplemental" information (such as a *decryption key*) will lead to identification of the user, then it is "personal data." Controllers must consider the risk of data-subject identification in the long run under the regulation. The "risk" is insignificant if it involves a disproportionate effort of time, cost, and manpower[12] to protect the data against any potential identification. Controllers must also bear in mind the means likely to be used when trying to access such personal data including any potential technological developments.[13] Thus, "personal data" is not a "name-tag," but a piece of a jigsaw puzzle of information. GDPR covers a broad range of data such as IP addresses, cookies, and aggregated redacted information.

The broad definition of personal data is intended to cover any information that can help the recipient identify the data subject. For example, the Allentown, PA municipal corporation has a list of domestic properties subject to property tax. The individual tax payer data is held in a database separate from the "property file" maintained by the corporation. In the property file itself, the owners are not directly identified by name but have a unique account number, with the database holding the personal information. The account number in the property file qualifies as personal data as the payers can be identified "from other information in the possession of the data Controller."

**3.1.2.2 Individual Circumstances**   GDPR mandates that Controllers must also consider the individual circumstances of each case when carrying out processing.[14] This includes warrants paying attention to:

1. Technological availability and developments
2. Cost and time required for identification
3. The purpose of processing

The three factors above imply that "identifiability" is a general term and has no fixed prescription for its application. It requires Controllers to think a step ahead of any unscrupulous Data Collectors who may seek to breach the integrity of their processing operations.

**3.1.2.3 Special Cases**

*Special Case 1: Corporations*   Excluding company data seems logical as the objective of GDPR is to secure the rights of the users as enshrined and bolstered under EU law.[15] However, this exclusion leaves a vacuum in the rights of corporations and their data. Corporations who do business with a Data Processor/Collector will be unable to exercise the rights of access, rectification, erasure, restriction, and explanation, despite any harm caused.

**Illustration:** J-Mart is a large global retailer, known for doing business in a "socially responsible manner." They have accounts in place with all popular social networking websites, often communicating with their consumers through those platforms. All was well until unknown hackers found a way to breach all of J-Mart's social networking accounts, and they started putting up "confession" posts where they apologized to the public for violating numerous environmental codes globally, accompanied with false news articles and press releases. This leads to massive outrage online, making the news go viral, and causing a severe drop in J-Mart's stock price. J-Mart promptly regains access to the pages, removes the posts, and tries to set the record straight, by which time the PR damage is far too great. Under GDPR, J-Mart would have no rights to erase or rectify their profile, nor would they have remedies to retrieve compensation or damages under the regulation. They must retrieve their damages through alternate venues such as breach of contract or local data protection laws.

A critical question to be determined is whether a natural person acting for a legal entity by way of creating and operating a page on its behalf would be able to exercise their rights under GDPR. This would raise interesting issues of *standing* under GDPR and the scope of its protection. German personal data protection law, which has been the pioneer for most data protection law in Europe, extends applicability of their legislations to legal persons in two narrow scenarios:

1. Data regarding the individuals associated with the entity[16]
2. Data held by a one-man company, which is essentially treated as a natural person[17]

Whether these exceptions would translate to an EU-wide level for data protection has not been clarified.

*Special Case 2: Deceased Individuals*   The law governing the personal data of deceased individuals (such as a Facebook profile "remembering" a deceased loved one) would be left to the individual Member States to legislate.[18]

*Special Case 3: Gaming Profiles and Virtual Identities*   The impacts of GDPR must be considered in the context of online gaming websites. Considering that many current-day gamers have multiple profiles and accounts to their names, managing personal data obligations becomes difficult. At the same time, certain games allow users to customize their profile and create completely "unique" online personas that hide their true identity. Whether the information supplied to these websites can be considered as "personal data" – which leads to the identification of the individuals, and whether it falls under the scope of GDPR is not clear at this time.

*Special Case 4: "Bots" and "Fake Profiles"*   GDPR is silent as to whether Data Controllers/Processors would have to watch for "fake profiles," which are often made by natural persons or by AI technology such as "twitter-bots." Profiles such as these present themselves as actual people, without being "backed" by personal data or human involvement. GDPR broadly defines what data falls under its ambit but fails to mention whether the Controller has a duty toward any "fake" content on their websites. The "fake" content may have zero involvement of personal data, and merely exist to confuse users and dilute the customer base. GDPR imposes no positive duty on Controllers to ensure that websites rooted in personal data must only be used by natural persons. This oversight is likely to impede combating "fake" news in the future.

*Analysis with "Objectives"*   The above situations should be considered within the context of the true objectives of the Regulation, which are:[19]

1. Laying down the rules of protection of natural persons for processing of personal data
2. Protection of fundamental rights and freedoms of natural persons
3. The free movement of personal data within the EU

The objectives of GDPR, along with the limited protection to natural persons, demonstrate that the regulation is not concerned with commercial dealings of legal entities. However, these "carve-outs" do not drastically narrow the scope of what constitutes processing, as it is already quite broad, including short-term use of small amounts of data,[20] and data collected through unconventional inanimate objects such as cars and wearables.

**3.1.2.4 Anonymization**    Anonymization is the process of altering data to remove any connection between the information and the individual. In cases of effective anonymization of data, GDPR does not apply[21] as the information is either rendered unidentifiable or does not relate to one's personal data. Anonymization is carried out through two common methods:

1. **Generalization:** When data is grouped together by characteristics (example: age) and the attributes of data subjects are diluted thereby preventing identification.[22]
2. **Randomization:** As the name suggests, the data's accuracy is reduced by removing any strong link that exists with the underlying information, thereby rendering it uncertain and incapable of being identified.[23]

These methods are often applied in research and statistical use and can be beneficial if a business does not rely on personal data for commercial purposes but requires it for research. By effectively anonymizing the data, a Controller can avoid application of GDPR by minimizing data collection and deleting excess data that is not required (in line with the regulation). Note that the EU does not provide standards for anonymization,[24] and Controllers must conduct *risk-based analysis* of their data-processing activities before determining if their anonymization methods are suitable.

A good example of poor anonymization concerned the New York Taxi Company in 2014, where information regarding cab rides and addresses were released in an anonymized form in response to a Freedom of Information Law request. The data was released online, and many "hacktivists" promptly decoded the anonymization, causing an avoidable breach.[25] We discuss how measures such as these are an ongoing effort for corporations, and methods of application in the next chapter.[26]

**Illustration:** Data Bank LLP is a big data analytics company that has been contracted by a Member State government to help collect and analyze data for their 2019 census. The government, through mail, e-mail, and personal visits, collects the relevant demographic data for the census and provides the material to Data Bank, who transposes it into electronic format and runs it through their algorithms for analysis. Names, addresses, and contact and social ID numbers are not entered into the database; rather, the information is grouped by region and is subdivided by district. In March 2019, hackers broke into the census database and stole all the information. As Data Bank did not include any personal data in the demographics provided, they are not subject to GDPR penalties.

**3.1.2.5 Pseudonymization** Similar to anonymization, pseudonymization is the process of removing identification of personal data such that additional information would be required to attribute the data to the subject.[27] This is conducted by replacing the identifying characteristics with other indicators or encoding the information.[28] Unlike anonymization, this process does not take a business outside the purview of GDPR; rather, it is the recommended form of data protection listed in the regulation for processing.[29] Pseudonymization is a "technical measure" that can be implemented to ensure data privacy.

**Illustration:** An exclusive, high-end retailer that caters only to the wealthiest segment of the population maintains a common database where their clients' personal information, such as name, delivery and payment address, and phone number, has been allocated a *code name* corresponding to their data. For example, the business would refer to Mr. Bobby John as Mr. Orange to maintain secrecy in their internal orders and purchase slips. The main purpose for the secrecy is the company's goal to control their fashion trends by only selling to certain mainstream celebrities. No person outside the organization would be able to discern who Mr. Orange is, thereby making this an effective measure or pseudonymization under GDPR.

## 3.1.3 Exempted Activities under GDPR

Certain categories of personal data processing are exempted from the regulation.[30] These include:

1. Activities that fall outside of EU law.
2. Processing for furtherance of the Foreign Security policy of the EU.[31]
3. Processing by a natural person for a purely personal or household activity (for example, processing for leisure, household, entertainment, and social media platform collection of addresses, birthdays, and other important dates).[32]
4. Processing by competent authorities for crime:
   a. Prevention
   b. Detection
   c. Investigation
   d. Prosecution
   e. Penalty execution
   f. Safeguarding and prevention of threats to public security
7. GDPR is also inapplicable to the rules relating to intermediary liability.[33]

The EU and its legal instrumentalities and organizations must also adapt their own methods of processing data in accordance with GDPR,[34] by way of amending Union acts and enacting new laws.[35] The categories above follow a common "theme" of allowing certain larger state/Union activities that work for the "public good" to operate outside the scope of GDPR.

**Illustration 1:** An EU member country seeks to collect and process personal data of its citizens for creating a comprehensive no fly list to prevent the possibility of terrorism acts in the future. They may do so, as it falls under the category of "protecting public security" and "crime prevention and detection."

**Illustration 2:** Victor believes that some of the neighborhood boys are stealing his lawn ornaments during night hours. To catch them red-handed, he sets up a "home surveillance system," which covers his backyard, driveway, lawn, and entrances to the house. This can be considered as personal data processing for "purely household" reasons.

**Illustration 3:** Identical facts as Illustration 2, but Victor also watches the road outside his house and the adjoining driveways of his neighbors. This is not household processing, and Victor must be GDPR compliant in his surveillance.[36]

## 3.2 The Key Players under GDPR

Before proceeding further, it is important to define certain important stakeholders[37] under GDPR. Understanding who is affected by the regulation is valuable information to determine applicability. For a detailed explanation of the appointment, roles, and responsibilities of these parties, please refer to Chapter 4.

1. **The Controller** is the entity responsible for deciding the "purposes and means of processing personal data." The Controller can be a:
   a. Natural person
   b. Legal entity[38]
   c. Public authority
   d. Public agency
   e. "Other body"
   The Controller may act alone or jointly (in the case of larger enterprises) in its processing of personal data. The criteria for nominating a Controller may be specified by the EU or Member State law.[39] The legal status of the Controller is irrelevant, as the decisions may be made by the Board of Directors or CTO on behalf of the organization. The Controller spearheads the direction and purposes of processing, with their influence being determined by the following factors:[40]
   f. Freedom from instructions on processing.
   g. Merging data with their own databases.
   h. Use of data for the business's own purposes.
   i. The data was collected in line with a legal or contractual relationship with the data subject.
   j. Responsibility for processing falls on the entity.
   These factors help weigh the entity's decision-making power for processing purposes. When resolving this question, ask who began the processing and why is it being done.[41] This power comes from an explicit or implicit legal responsibility or from actual influence asserted over the processing.[42] The "decisions" must relate to important actions, while tangential decisions of less importance, such as the choice of software in the processing, may fall outside of the Controller's responsibilities.[43]

2. **The Processor** acts on behalf of the Controller in the processing of personal data. Like a Controller, the Processor can be a:[44]
   a. Natural person
   b. Legal entity
   c. Public authority
   d. Public agency
   e. "Other body"

   What can qualify as an "other body" for the purposes of being appointed as a Controller or Processor remains to be seen. The term "other body" is quite broad and could be subject to any number of interpretations in future litigation. Working on behalf of the Controller requires that the Processor be subject to the decision making mentioned above and must not exceed their contractual parameters.[45]

   The Controller and the Processor are often referred to jointly under GDPR as one activity usually includes another. The liabilities and duties between these entities differ in some areas, which we will discuss in Chapter 4.[46] Unless clearly indicated otherwise in this book, the Controller and Processor will hereinafter be referred to collectively as Data Collectors.

3. **The Data Protection Officer** (DPO) is designated by the Controller and Processor under certain circumstances where:[47]
   a. The processing is carried out by a public authority (except for courts in their official capacity).
   b. The activity carried out requires large-scale, regular, and systematic monitoring of the users.
   c. The activity involves large-scale processing of special categories of data or criminal convictions.

   The DPO is appointed to protect the data of the users when the processing requires regular supervision. A single DPO can be appointed to represent multiple entities so long as he remains easily accessible when needed. A DPO may also be a third-party contractor or employee hired by the Controller or Processor. The DPO is the primary line of defense for the protection of personal data under GDPR.

4. **Third parties** under GDPR are any natural or legal persons, public authorities, agencies, etc., who, under the direct authority of the Data Collectors, are authorized to process personal data. Simply put, they are any person or entity other than the user that is given the power to process personal data.[48]

5. **The recipient** can be any person (whether natural or legal or third party or public authority) to whom the personal data is disclosed. This does *not* include public authorities receiving personal data for a specific purpose under Union or Member law.[49]

6. A **data subject** (or "user," for our purposes) is the everyday "natural person" who is afforded the protections of GDPR. This could be a user or a customer of the website which collects personal data. Data subjects are the parties from whom the data is collected, at which point they gain rights under the regulation.

**Illustration:** Genepool.com is a new booming business that takes DNA samples from its users, analyzes them, and provides a diagnosis of any irregularities, vitamin deficiencies, etc., using a variety of tests. After the tests are complete, the users receive a "diagnostic prognosis" on their app-based platform. Subsequently, the corporation that owns the website, GeneMap LLC, diversifies and creates several websites for several different gene-based data analytics, with a range of cost for the specific types of diagnosis, with a separate holding company backing it. The CTO of GeneMap LLC, Mr. Ben Kim, decides to contract out the data-processing activities to Transpose Inc., located in Israel. Transpose and Mr. Kim agreed that they would hire CyberSec LLP as their cyber security firm for all of their operations. Transpose hosts its processing activity with the help of a large scale internet service provider, Chinese Wall LLC, who also provides ongoing security and access to the building for the employees of Transpose. The data-collection activities have a substantial footprint across several countries with close to 100 employees assisting in the collection, processing, and security of the personal data collected. Under GDPR:

- The **Controller** is Genepool.com, which is owned by GeneMap LLC and *represented* by Mr. Ben Kim, who acts on behalf GeneMap LLC's overall operations.
- The **Processor** is Transpose Inc.
- The **DPO** is CyberSec LLP.
- The **third parties** are the 100 employees involved in the operation.
- The **data subjects** are the users of the Genepool app.
- The **recipients** are *any* of the above individuals who receive personal data of users.
- The **conduit** or **data handler** would be Chinese Wall LLC, whose sole responsibility is to act as service provider but can in *no way* access the personal data hosted in the operation.

## 3.3   Territorial Scope of GDPR

The "territorial" provisions of GDPR represents the "long arm" of the law, extending the effect of this regulation beyond the borders of the EU. Article 3 determines whether a business is required to comply with GDPR by creating a broad territorial scope of application.[50] This brings cases within the EU's reach and prevents *forum shopping* by data-collection entities. Territoriality under GDPR can be broken into three independent categories as described in the following sections.

### 3.3.1   Physical Presence in the EU

A data-collection entity with an establishment within the EU is subject to GDPR regardless of whether the act of processing takes place within the borders of the

Union.[51] This concept in international law is known as the Establishment Principle, which mandates that a choice of law over a company's acts is determined by where it has its physical presence, not necessarily where the processing is conducted. However, the nature of the arrangement is immaterial as long as the company has effective and real exercise of activity through stable arrangements.[52] This means the regulation does not discriminate between a head-office and a subsidiary as the nature of the economic activity and the services offered are more reliable indicators.[53] Applying such a test would be determined by the specific facts on a case-to-case basis. It is important to remember that stability in the services offered is the dispositive point, with registration **not** being dispositive of "presence," though it remains an important factor in the analysis.[54] This leaves a range of possibility from holding a foreign bank account all the way to renting empty office space.

**Illustration:** Twitter sets up a branch in Germany to facilitate and serve its German and other European users. The key purpose of the new branch is to determine what changes must be made to tailor their services to this market. The specific act of data processing is done in their office in California and other locations outside of Europe. Twitter would have to be GDPR compliant, as the mere act of having a physical office within the EU, which determines the "purposes and means of processing,"[55] thus falling within the definition of a Controller. Twitter will not be able to escape liability merely because processing is done outside the borders of the EU.

### 3.3.2 Processing Done in the Context of the Activities

GDPR is triggered by minimal processing involvement by an entity, extending its reach even to cases where an organization simply economically supports processing. Though a connection must exist between the processing and commercial activity of a business[56] an entity can be subject to GDPR by carrying out processing on behalf of another entity.

**Illustration:** The data collected by a social networking website OhYo! based in Germany transfers and stores data through a *cloud-server* held by their subsidiary, Storagers LLP located in the Philippines. Storagers LLP, by maintaining data on behalf of OhYo!, has subjected itself to GDPR.

To summarize, a company operating inside or outside of the EU watch for GDPR applicability if their operations encompass any of the following scenarios:[57]

1. **EU entity processing personal data:** A good example would be the German-based company OhYo! described in our illustration above.
2. **EU Controllers and Processors across multiple Member States:** Consider an entity based in Germany with processing partners spread across France, Spain, and Belgium by use of cloud computing. Such a case would subject *all* parties, but primarily the Controller to GDPR.

3. **EU Entity carrying out processing with a non-EU entity:** Once again, consider our previous OhYo! illustration, where the Philippine-based cloud server would economically support their parent company based in Germany.

### 3.3.3 Users Based in the EU

Companies that are physically based outside the EU but have European customers which use their services, will also have to comply with GDPR if:[58]

1. They offer goods and services within the EU, regardless of whether payment is needed.
2. They monitor behavior within the EU.

This provision integrates the legal principle of *lex loci solutionis* which mandates that the law of contractual performance governs a contract between two parties. GDPR, in adopting this principle, looks to whether the services are being targeted within the EU internal market and EU consumers.[59]

**Illustration:** Glocal News is a popular news website, based in Canada, that provides comprehensive journalism and in-depth editorials to the users who sign in and create an account with them, free of cost. At the time of payment, the website makes it clear on their terms of use: "The news you read regularly will be processed by our in-house algorithm which will study your reading habits and recommend more articles that you would like." The website also offers services without users having to sign up, but their access will be limited in the number of articles they can read in a day based on the cookies on their computer. Glocal will have to be GDPR compliant to operate within the EU as the company satisfies both conditions mentioned above.

This type of "effects" territoriality clause is not uncommon in technology-related statutes. Take the example of the Indian Information Technology Act, 2000,[60] which provides for applicability where contraventions take place outside of the India, which results in "effects" felt within the border. Other reliable indicators of "targeting" services within the EU can be observed from:[61]

- The language employed
- Currencies accepted
- Delivery services
- Domain name geographical tags
- Customer base and testimonials

Additionally, any form of web tracking subjects a business to GDPR. Web-tracking tools include cookies, plug-ins, browser history, and any other data-analytic or customization tool which may be implemented. Consider the above "Glocal" illustration where the reading preferences, user history, and geolocation data in their analytics and services would attract compliance with the regulation. The effect of an extra-territoriality provision in GDPR creates a "shield" over the EU and the companies that do business with its citizens online.

### 3.3.4 "Time of Stay" Standard

In the internet age, residence or place of nationality are not reliable indicators of the degree of data protection a person is afforded. A consumer located in Dubai can simultaneously purchase socks from a US vendor and stream music from a company based in Brazil. The dynamic nature of online activity requires a change in previous standards of determining when data protection laws should apply. It is for this purpose that GDPR legislators cite the location of the data subject in the EU at the time of collection as the dispositive factor in applying the regulations.[62] Thus, a person's "time of stay" within the EU will afford them protection under GDPR and not their citizenship in an EU country.

**Illustration:** Zeke, a traveling businessman from Australia, has a five-hour layover in Paris, where he connects to the airport Wi-Fi. He provides his name, e-mail ID, and phone number to the Wi-Fi login service and uses the internet freely. Three hours later, he discovers that he is locked out of his phone and that all of his texts, pictures, and other data has been deleted. Subsequent investigation showed that a hacker breached his phone's integrity by using the airport Wi-Fi. Though not a citizen of the EU, Zeke has a remedy under GDPR.

## 3.4 Operation of Public International Law

GDPR also applies where processing may take place outside the EU, but a Member State's law would apply to that jurisdiction by an instrument of *public international law*.[63] Instruments here include bilateral or multilateral treaties, conventions, international agreements, etc. GDPR may also apply under this category by a Member's diplomatic mission or post in a foreign country.[64]

**Illustration:** Assume that France has a small group of territories in a cluster of islands (X Nation) in the Pacific Ocean, which used to be French colonies but now form an independent nation by an *international agreement* instituted at the time when France decided to relinquish its colonies. X Nation still follows the French law to this date. X Nation will have to be GDPR compliant if they have a Controller/ Processor within their borders, even if they are not falling into the "physical presence" or "effects" categories mentioned earlier.

## Notes

1  GDPR, Article 2.
2  GDPR, Article 4.2.
3  GDPR, Article 2.
4  See GDPR, Article 4.1.
5  See GDPR, Article 4.2.
6  GDPR, Article 2.1.

7 GDPR, Recital 15.

8 GDPR, Chapter I.

9 GDPR, Article 1.1.

10 GDPR, Article 4.1.

11 Paul Voigt and Axel von dem Bussche, *The EU General Data Protection Regulation (GDPR): A Practical Guide* (Springer, 2017), 12.

12 ECJ ruling of 19 October 2016, Breyer/Federal Republic of Germany, C-582/14, rec. 46; Opinion of the Advocate General, 12 May 2016, C-582/14, rec. 68.

13 GDPR, Recital 26.

14 GDPR, Recital 26.

15 GDPR, Article 1, Article 12-22, Recital 1.

16 S. Ernst, Arts. 2, 4 DSGVO, In B.P. Paal and D.A. Pauly (eds.), *Beck'sche Kompaktkommentare Datenschultz- Grundverordnung* (Munich: C.H. Beck, 2017), rec. 5.

17 P. Blume, "The Data Subject," *EDPL* 4 (2015): 258–264, 258

18 GDPR, Recital 27.

19 GDPR, Article 1.

20 P. Laue, J. Nink, and S. Kremer (eds.), "Einführung," in *Das neue Datenschutzrecht in der betrieblichen Praxis* (Baden-Baden: Nomos, 2016).

21 GDPR, Recital 26.

22 Article 29 Working Party, WP 216 (2014), 16.

23 Article 29 Working Party, WP 216 (2014), 12.

24 Article 29 Working Party, WP 216 (2014).

25 Alex Hern, "New York Taxi Details Can Be Extracted from Anonymised Data, Researchers Say," *The Guardian*, June 27, 2014, https://www.theguardian.com/technology/2014/jun/27/new-york-taxi-details-anonymised-data-researchers-warn.

26 Page 84 onward (Sections 4.7 and 4.8).

27 GDPR, Recital 28.

28 GDPR, Article 4.5.

29 See page 88 for a description of the Pseudonymization process.

30 GDPR, Article 2.2.

31 In accordance with the Treaty of the EU, Title V, Chapter II.

32 GDPR, Recital 18.

33 See EU Directive 2000/31/EC, Articles 12–15; GDPR, Article 2.4.

34 GDPR, Article 2.3.

35 In accordance to GDPR, Article 98.

36 This distinction of *public-private spaces* has been laid down by ECJ Ruling of 11 December 2014, Frantisek Rynes. Urad pro ochranu osobnich udaju, C-212/13, rec. 35.

37 Full definitions of the terms can be found under GDPR, Article 4.

38 *Note:* Any "legal person" carrying out activities on behalf of the Controller or Processor under GDPR must assign a "Representative" who can be held accountable.

39 GDPR, Article 4.7

40 Voigt and von dem Bussche, *The EU General Data Protection* Regulation (GDPR), 19.

41  Article 29 Working Party, WP 169 (2010), 8.
42  Article 29 Working Party, WP 169 (2010), 10−12 and 14.
43  Article 29 Working Party, WP 169 (2010) 14.
44  GDPR, Article 4.8.
45  GDPR, Article 26.10, Article 29 Working Party, WP 169 (2010), 25.
46  See Chapter 4.
47  GDPR, Article 37.
48  GDPR, Article 4.10.
49  GDPR, Article 4.9.
50  *Google Spain v. Costeja,* ECJ, 13 May 2016, C-131/12, Recital 54.
51  GDPR, Art. 3.1.
52  GDPR, Recital 22.
53  ECJ Ruling of 1 October 2015, Weltimmo, C-230/14, rec. 29.
54  Ibid.
55  GDPR, Art. 4.7.
56  *Google Spain v. Costeja,* ECJ, 13 May 2016, C-131/12, Recital 52.
57  GDPR, Art. 3.1.
58  GDPR, Art. 3.2.
59  GDPR, Recital 23.
60  See Indian IT Act, Chapter I, §1.
61  GDPR, Recital 23; ECJ Ruling of 7 December 2010, Alpenhof, joined cases,
    C-585/08 and C-144/09, recs. 80–84; *summarized by* Voigt and von dem Bussche,
    *The EU General Data Protection Regulation,* 26.
62  GDPR, Article 3.2.
63  GDPR, Article 3.3.
64  GDPR, Recital 25.

# 4

# Technical and Organizational Requirements under GDPR

*To create something exceptional, your mindset must be relentlessly focused on the smallest detail.*

— Giorgio Armani

GDPR secures a system of accountability for the protection of personal data by creating rules, bodies, and responsibilities entrusted to certain specific actors in the market. Accountability requires compliance in implementing technical and organizational measures within a business. The Controller and Processor have been defined briefly in the previous chapter we now examine the responsibilities of these bodies and the technical and organizational measures that form part of a coherent framework under GDPR.

## 4.1   Accountability

In the early years of the internet, it was difficult to hold businesses accountable for misconduct in their data collection and protection practices. This was partly because the law was not sufficiently developed to hold Data Collectors responsible for duties that did not exist at the time. Gradually, legal trends changed, with courts recognizing the value of data and its connection with privacy. However, Data Controllers and Processors managed to evade, or at least dilute, responsibility by hiding behind the complications created by technology.

For example, a business could allocate blame on their decisions to AI or a Subprocessor they were unaware of. Controllers could justify not mentioning a breach by placing blame on the Processor's inaction. GDPR creates a *chain of accountability* that runs from Subprocessor to Processor to Controller, with very little leeway for adjustment. The accountability chain is reinforced with how *liability* is allocated at the time of paying fines to the Supervisory Authority (SA).

## 4.2 The Data Controller

The Controller is the body that shoulders the most responsibility under GDPR. As discussed earlier, the Controller is an entity responsible for deciding the "purposes and means of processing personal data." The Controller, from an operational perspective, determines the "what, why, and how" of the processing activities. It is important to note that the Controller can be a(n):

- Natural person
- Legal entity[1]
- Public authority
- Public agency
- Other body

The Controller may be a single entity or acting jointly in cases of larger data enterprises. For example, Facebook owns Instagram, Whatsapp, and other data-processing apps and will likely have multiple Controllers under the same enterprise.

In most cases, the Controller is a corporate entity rather than a single individual making the decisions. Corporate officers such as the CEO or CTO are extensions of the data Controller, and their actions will be those of the company. An example of this would be to say that Facebook is the Controller in charge of your personal data for social networking purposes. Facebook decides the means of how your data is processed and is the responsible legal entity data "Controller" of data under GDPR. Notwithstanding the legal status of the Controller, when communicating with the user[2] the entity may include details to a representative, placing an accountable human face to the organization for the data subjects. In cases where the processing is done outside the EU, the appointment of a representative is mandatory.[3]

Controllers are not appointed by a company or the government but are the entities who plan processing activities. The criteria for nominating a Controller may be specified by the EU or a Member State.[4] That law may relate to the purposes and means of processing or for the specific criteria for the nomination of a Controller.[5]

**Illustration:** A Member State law called the Internet Banking Legislation requires that processing of individuals' financial information will require consent and certification of ISO27k certification and additional security measures both for the data at rest and in transit. Additionally, the law requires that "nomination" of a Controller will require approval from the newly created Online Banking Board of the State. The Controller nominee must have a representative who possesses experience in data protection and banking. People for Currency Equality (PCE) is a nonprofit association based in a small village in the Member State that helps the impoverished with their local banking needs. The PCE is represented by its CTO, Archie Banque, who hopes to bring these villages into the twenty-first century. Archie has experience in data protection generally but has never done any banking activities in his life. PCE has implemented security measures necessary under the law. PCE applies to be a Controller, and:

- The legislation is valid, and in accordance with GDPR.
- Under the strict GDPR requirements, PCE is a Controller as they are an Other Body determining the purposes and means of processing.
- However, under the requirements of the Internet Banking Legislation, they are likely to be rejected for such processing activities. This is because the Member State chose to give specific requirements for who may be nominated as a Controller. One of those requirements is to appoint a representative who has experience both in data protection *and* banking.
- Thus, as the Internet Banking Legislation specifies the criteria, Archie will have to be replaced with someone with both requirements for PCE to be a Controller.

### 4.2.1 Responsibilities of the Controller

Under GDPR, the responsibilities of ensuring compliance have been placed on the Controller. This includes the lawful processing of data, providing "information" on rights and obligations, and maintaining data security among many others. Chapter IV of the Regulation gives the General Obligations of the Controller, which broadly provides what the main responsibilities are.

**4.2.1.1 Demonstration**   The Controller must comply with GDPR and demonstrate it. The regulation requires the Controller to implement appropriate technical and organizational measures to protect the rights and freedoms of its users during processing. These measures are made considering the:[6]

- Nature,
- Scope,
- Context, and
- Purposes of Processing; along with the
- Risks, and severity of a breach (should it happen).

The above measures are to be routinely reviewed and updated. This can be carried out through technical and organizational methods such as adopting internal policies and codes of conduct and conducting routine web audits. Implementing these protective measures must accompany the ability to prove that the Controller has complied. This can be done by effective documentation of processing, making the company available to the local supervisory authority

(SA), and maintaining certifications or internal codes of conduct. The proof-of-compliance responsibility must also be demonstrated when the SA requests them to do so.

**4.2.1.2 Data Protection Policies**    It is the duty of the Controller to ensure that suitable policies are in place in the organization to protect the personal data of the user. These policies shall be included in the measures and must be proportionate to the processing done.[7] The data protection policies are read with the accompanying duty of data protection by design and default, which ensures the safety of the data as the de facto setting when carrying out processing activities.[8] This will be discussed in greater detail later in this chapter.[9]

**4.2.1.3 Adherence**    The final general responsibility of the Controller is to adhere to the:

1. *Codes of Conduct*[10] of the Controllers, which may be provided by the "Member State law" Data Protection Board, supervisory authorities, or even by the Controller themselves.
2. *Approved certification mechanisms*[11] such as a seal or mark provided for under GDPR to show that the processing is secure.

The two devices may be used as an element to demonstrate the compliance to the regulation as seen in the first basic responsibility established. Merely having codes of conduct or certification does not prove compliance, but it acts as a supporting point to show it.

**Illustration:** *Universe of War* is an interactive online fantasy game based on futuristic warfare. At the time of registering, the users must provide their name, age, e-mail address, password, and zip code. The Controller in charge is Gameverse .com, represented by Mr. Daichi. The website has been certified ISO27k and has implemented a data in transit protection model. Additionally, each player can create a "game ID" that keeps their identity shrouded when playing the game and interacting with other users. Only Gameverse.com knows the true identity of the user and utilizes the services of CyberSec LLP, a data security firm. Additionally, the website is governed by Gameverse.com's codes of conduct, which have been approved by the SA of their jurisdiction.

- Considering the nature, scope, context, and risks of processing, it is likely that Gameverse.com is GDPR compliant, as the protection given to the data is proportionate to the nature of the data collected.
- The Partnership with CyberSec LLP can be considered as an "organizational measure."
- The ISO27k certification can be used as evidence of data protection by default.
- The codes of conduct of Gameverse.com can be used to demonstrate compliance with the responsibilities under GDPR.

## 4.2.2 Joint Controllers and Allocating Liability

A single entity can have multiple Controllers to carry out their activities, collectively referred to as Joint Controllers under the regulation.[12] In such cases, the Joint Controllers would both[13] be determining the purposes and means of processing. Each entity involved in the "joint" processing must qualify as a Controller under the requirements of GDPR.[14] Joint Controllers need to cooperate in their processing,[15] with their status determined by an objective criterion. Joint Controllership is common in larger entities, or when the processing requires multiple Controllers by its nature. A Joint Controller relationship may even arise in an informal business relationship such as partial processing carried out by a specialized Processor for certain data, rather than an "all-in" joint venture type model between the Controller and Processor.[16]

The respective responsibilities of Joint Controllers must be disclosed in a transparent manner, particularly with regard to the transparency and information obligations[17] toward the user disclosed at the outset of the processing. The arrangement between the Joint Controllers can be determined by them internally unless EU or Member law provides otherwise. The arrangement includes providing a contact point for the users[18] and determining which Controller will be responsible to enforce the rights of the data subject. The arrangement should also reflect the roles and responsibility of the Controllers in relation to their data subjects.[19]

**4.2.2.1 Additional Obligations Placed on Joint Controllers**  After determining that multiple Controllers qualify as Joint Controllers, there is no major change of their obligations under GDPR. Each Controller in the arrangement is subject to the same obligations under the regulation as if they were acting independently in their processing. This includes maintaining data security and respecting user rights in processing. However, Joint Controllers must also respect several additional responsibilities which include:

- Entering into a *Joint Controllership contract* that allocates responsibilities between the Controllers and their measures of GDPR compliance.
- Expressly disclosing such arrangements to the data subject, with clear point of contact for the user in a written and concise manner.

Even the commercial decision to merge two Data Controller entities into a larger Joint Controller business requires compliance with the regulation as a Data Protection Impact Assessment (DPIA) which requires weighing any risks posed to the personal data held by the companies. For a greater discussion on DPIAs please see page 73 (section 4.5) onward.

**4.2.2.2 Joint and Several Liabilities**  A Joint Controllership arrangement must be communicated to the user, in line with transparency and information obligations. However, irrespective of the arrangement made between the Controllers, the user can exercise his rights against any of the Controllers in the organization.[20] This power to exercise the rights against any Controller of the organization is a prelude to the concept of joint and several liabilities under GDPR,[21] where the compensation for a contravention can be imposed against either the Controller or the Processor or both.[22] In turn, the Controllers and Processors would have a right of compensation for the amount they paid against the other.[23] GDPR prevents the entities responsible for the processing of personal data from evading liability because the responsibilities are diverse. The first objective would be securing the user's compensation/rights, which is followed by the data-processing entities dividing the liabilities among themselves.

**Illustration:** Timbuck2 LLC is a large online conglomerate that provides shopping, social networking, business, and streaming services. All services are provided by subsidiaries of Timbuck2 LLC, each with its own Controller determining the purpose for a particular processing activity. At the time of signing up, the Terms of Use for the users clearly state (across all platform agreements):

1. **Controller:** Timbuck2 Streaming Services Ltd. "**THE CONTROLLER**" is an independent entity from our parent company Timbuck2 LLC, registered in Hamburg, Germany.

The Controller of Timbuck2 Streaming is independently in charge of processing your personal data in cooperation with the Controllers of our parent company.

2. **Arrangement of Controllers:** Your data is processed in accordance with Timbuck2 LLC's Codes of Conduct (LINK) which provide for an arrangement between our entities of:
   a. Timbuck2 Streaming – Represented by Mr. Lau (lau@mail.com)
   b. Timbuck2 Shopping – Represented by Mr. Stieglitz (Stieglitz@mail.com)
   c. Timbuck2 Network – Represented by Mr. Bau (bau@mail.com)
   d. Timbuck2 Biz – Represented by Mr. Ken (ken@mail.com)

Though these Controllers work together under the same parent corporation, their responsibilities and duties are **restricted** to the services that their websites provide for. There is no "sharing" of their legal responsibilities and they all act independent of one another.

3. **Exercising Rights:** If at any point you decide to exercise your Rights listed under Chapter X of this agreement (LINK), it is preferable to contact the Controller responsible for those rights, namely, Timbuck2 Streaming. This is because that Controller would be best equipped to assist with the request you submit. **However,** this does **not** prevent you from contacting the other Controllers listed above who work for Timbuck2 LLC.

The above terms of use are a valid communication of the Joint Controller arrangement under GDPR.

**4.2.2.3 Controllers Outside of the EU**   As discussed in Chapter 2,[24] GDPR applies even in scenarios where the processing of personal data takes place physically outside the EU, but handles the data of people within the Union. Controllers outside the EU are subject to GDPR if the processing includes:

- Offering of goods and services within the EU (with *or* without compensation), and
- Monitoring behavior of EU Citizens.

When data-collection activities based outside the EU offer one of the services mentioned above, it is mandatory for the Controller to designate a representative in writing.[25] Compare this to appointing a representative under ordinary circumstances, where it is only optional. The representative appointed by the Controller shall be based in the EU in one of the Member States where the subject matter of processing[26] takes place. This ensures that even if the Controller is beyond the reach of EU authorities, their representative is not.

Once appointed, the representative must be addressed in addition to or instead of the Controller in all activities and matters of compliance relating to Supervisory Authorities and the users.[27] However, this does not prejudice the user's right to bring a legal action against the Controller or Processor directly for their activities.[28]

**Illustration:** Raters.com is a credit-rating agency based in the United States, providing services globally for individuals. As a credit-rating agency, Raters.com collects a large amount of data, both personal and special. As GDPR comes into force, they appoint Mr. Jacques Robert as their representative in the EU, with his small "home office" located in Paris, France. He is listed in all communications between the website and the users, with his name appearing next to the Company's in the initial request for consent and terms of use. Soon after, a massive data breach takes place and it is revealed to the world that Raters.com has been illegally mining data well beyond what is proportionate for their activities.

- The SA (or victims) of France may initiate action against Raters.com (USA) directly.
- The SA may initiate action also against Mr. Robert.
- The same rights exist for any SA or Victim in the EU against either Raters.com or Mr. Robert (jointly or separately).
- If Raters.com refuses to appear for the actions filed against them, Mr. Robert can still be held responsible on their behalf.
- However, GDPR does not expressly give Mr. Robert the right to claim compensation from Raters.com as that matter must be handled internally in the Company by way of contract or corporate rules.

GDPR creates a system of accountability for data protection so that Data Collectors cannot escape their liability. Article 27 provides for someone to be responsible, even if the Controller is beyond the reach of the EU courts. This is similar to how liability is attached for Joint Controllers, where one Controller may not evade liability because the responsibility has been placed on another.[29]

**Exceptions:** The obligation to appoint a domestic representative may be avoided under two specific scenarios:[30]

1. **Occasional processing** of personal data if such activities:
    a. Do not involve the large-scale processing of special categories of data; or
    b. Do not involve the processing of data relating to criminal convictions; and
    c. Is unlikely to pose a risk to the rights and freedoms of other users, considering the nature, scope, context, and purposes of the processing.
2. Processing by a **public authority** or body.

The data may be processed without listing a representative in the EU if a business falls under the exceptions above. Some of the exceptions are logical (such as processing relating to criminal convictions and public bodies), as a separate system of accountability is likely to be put in place. For example, if a foreign public body Controller is held liable under GDPR, traditional modes of diplomacy would likely control its disposition. However, the first exception relating to "occasional processing" can be subject to abuse owing to the reduction in accountability.

**Illustration:** Bloggey.com is a Canadian blog-based social media website with public posts and private messaging, hinged on exclusivity with services in the EU. As a result, the only way to join the website as a member is if three users "invite" you to join as a member. Bloggey.com only has about 2,000 "members" in the EU and 5,000 worldwide who submit personal data to be processed, while the remainder of the public may "view" the posts, without their personal data being processed. Bloggey.com has posts on highly controversial matters, often expressing the members' point of view on politics, religion and other "sensitive matters." Bloggey.com undergoes a massive data breach, and the SA of Belgium seeks to bring action against them for compensation. Bloggey.com does not respond to EU authorities.

- Without a representative in the EU, the SA must rely on traditional court procedures to hold Bloggey.com accountable.
- Can this be considered as a large-scale processing of special data? How much data should be collected to qualify? This is unclear under GDPR.
- Can the exclusivity of the website qualify this as "occasional processing"?
- When determining these facts, one must weigh it with the nature, scope, context, and purposes of the processing. This is likely to lead to a subjective result.

### 4.2.3 The Duty to Cooperate with the SA

Both Controller and Processor[31] must cooperate with the Supervisory Authority in carrying out their tasks when requested. This demonstrates that GDPR accountability is not an adversarial system against the regulatory authorities. On the contrary, they are required to submit to the authority of the SA in any investigation or action brought against them.

The duty is not expressly mentioned but can be drawn from various stipulations under GDPR regarding compliance.[32] The SA's broad discretion to request information on processing can trigger the "cooperation duty" on request and not on the Controller's own initiative. However, full transparency with the overseeing SA is always a helpful practice to build an organization's credibility in the market. The cooperation duty is not enforceable under GDPR, as enforceability is not mandated under the regulation. The EU has made an administrative procedure for the SAs to handle noncompliance with their requests in line with Member State Law.[33] Therefore, the cooperation duty though not enforceable under GDPR may find authority in the local law that grants legal authority to the SA. This includes the power to impose fines or force compliance with subpoenas and show-cause notices.

## 4.3 Technical and Organizational Measures

In line with the title of this chapter, the technical and organizational measures implemented for data protection are one of the most fundamental aspects of GDPR. Failing to maintain these measures can result in a €10,000,000 fine or 2% of the company's annual turnover.[34] This duty falls on the Controller, Processor, and any individual acting under their orders to process data.[35] The key objective is ensuring data security under GDPR, which will be elaborated further below and in finer detail later on in this chapter.

### 4.3.1 Maintain a Data-Protection Level

Within an organization that actively handles personal data, it is important to maintain an appropriate level of "data health" in processing. This requires protecting the data throughout its life cycle: from planning new online operations to storing old data. The data protection "level" a company wishes to maintain can be carried out by measures such as encryption, anonymization, conducting DPIAs, and training employees on data security practices.

**Illustration:** A university implements a policy to increase their data protection level after a massive breach. They contract with Microsoft Outlook to help maintain a university e-mail server with 2-Factor Authentication, encoded e-mails, and training all university employees on data breach practices. These can be considered as technical and organizational measures to hold an appropriate data-protection level under GDPR.

### 4.3.2 Minimum Requirements for Holding a Data Protection Level

To maintain an appropriate data protection level, GDPR requires the organization to implement the following measures:[36]

- Pseudonymize, encrypt, or anonymize the data.
- Ensure the ongoing security of the processing.

- The ability to restore and produce data in a timely manner in the event of a data loss (such as maintaining back-up systems).
- Regularly test and maintain the security systems.

The requirements mentioned above are the reasonable demands of a twenty-first century consumer who "lives" online. The complexity of technology and the capabilities of cyber-criminals change daily, and Controllers cannot escape their duty to maintain data safety because such a problem was not foreseen in the past.

### 4.3.3 Weighing the Risks

GDPR mandates a *risk-based* approach to data processing, where the appropriateness of data security is often weighed against the risk posed to the information held by the Controller. Perfecting the balancing act could be the difference in whether an organization pays a €10,000,000 fine or avoids it. When deciding whether the level of data protection is appropriate, consider the following types of risk posed to your organization.

**4.3.3.1 Risk to the Business**   A Controller or Processor must always consider the financial risk of noncompliance with GDPR, which could result in burdensome penalties. Aside from the regulatory fines issued by an SA, it is also important to consider lawsuits that could arise because of a violation of the data subject's rights or owing to a loss of data. In the United States, class-action lawsuits are the preferred form of handling high-profile data breaches, and GDPR gives the consumers a similar right in the EU.

While fines and adverse judgments against the business are foreseeable, it is always important to remember that these costs do not happen in isolation, as attorney's fees and loss of good-will and consumer loyalty can always follow. The minimal cost of compliance always outweighs the massive fines for contravening GDPR.

**4.3.3.2 Risk to Consumers**   The regulation creates numerous enforceable rights against the Controller in the hands of the data subject. Upholding these rights should be a number one priority in a data business, besides maintaining data health. The data subjects hold a vested interest in their data against any form of loss, alteration, deletion, accidental disclosure, and so forth.[37] The risk to one's consumers is significant in situations where:[38]

- The processing affects a large amount of people and data.
- The business handles special data.
- Behavioral monitoring is conducted.
- Vulnerable consumers such as children are affected.
- Data subjects might be denied access and control over their personal data rights.
- Loss of data would cause significant social or economic disadvantage or identity theft.

Again, we can see a fluid formula for balancing the risks, with levels of risk being shown. It would be beneficial for a business to classify their data risk levels based on the *nature* of their processing and information handled.

**4.3.3.3 Risks Caused by Third Parties**   Once the stakeholders of the risk have been identified, consider who causes the risk to the business. Often this may be unscrupulous cyber-criminals who find value in the data, or it could be business competitors who wish to learn trade-secrets. But it is also important to keep in mind a nonadversarial third party, the government. In certain highly regulated data fields such as telecommunications or healthcare, Data Processors are likely to receive standard requests for information from state agencies. It is important to maintain an internal policy for handling such requests.

## 4.3.4   The Network and Information Systems Directive

The "NIS" directive[39] was adopted by the EU in July 2016 in recognition of the Union's mutually dependent welfare regarding technological "backbones" in our society such as communications, defense, and energy. Today, our daily supply of information, transportation, energy, and contact with one another is hinged on a constant ecosystem of data and internet access. The EU in recognizing this has taken a risk-based approach toward the network security and availability of certain service providers.[40] The applicability of the NIS Directive is limited to *two* categories of services:

1. **Operators of Essential Services:**[41] As mentioned above, the NIS mandates a high level of network security for certain critical societal and economic activities where any breach would have a significant disruptive effect on the population. This would include:
   a. Energy
   b. Transportation
   c. Banking
   d. Financial market infrastructures
   e. Health infrastructure
   f. Water
   g. Digital infrastructure
2. **Digital Service Providers:**[42] If essential services are the "resources" for society, digital service providers give the "channels" for those resources to reach us. This includes providers of digital marketplaces, search engines, and cloud computing services. The inclusion of digital service providers is understandable, as a single security breach with a service such as Amazon would result in endless loss for *both* society and the company itself.

The NIS can be considered as a cohesive counterpart to GDPR, placing similar yet heightened requirements on these services providers. With GDPR in place now, businesses subject to the directive will unlikely undergo many major changes regarding their more stringent data protection requirements.

## 4.4    Duty to Maintain Records of Processing Activities

Though not expressly mentioned under Article 24, the Controller *and* Processor have an additional duty to maintain records of processing activities under their control,[43] the first purpose being that valuable data and subsequent evidence would not be lost or destroyed over the course of business. Personal data production often results in terabytes of information collected by organizations, leading to a valuable need to keep records of such activities. The second purpose of documentation is to increase transparency of processing operations to data subjects and the authorities. The records must be maintained in writing, which includes in electronic form, but GDPR does not provide further guidance on the amount of detail needed in the records maintained.

### 4.4.1    Content of Controller's Records

The record will include the following information:

1. Name and contact details of:
    a. The Controller
    b. Any Joint Controllers
    c. The representative
    d. The Data Protection Office
2. The purposes of processing
3. Description of the categories of users and data collected
4. The categories of recipients, both actual and intended[44]
5. The transfers to third countries or international organizations with identification and documentation of safeguards
6. Envisaged[45] time limits of erasure of different categories of personal data
7. A general description[46] of technical and organizational measures to protect data

In this age of constant digital cataloguing of information, this mandate under GDPR appears to be a logical inclusion to prevent any evasion of liability and lack of details on part of the Controller. This could be a "combat" measure against data-mining companies such as Facebook, which have sold data to numerous recipients and claim that they cannot produce records to keep track of those transactions. For this reason, GDPR mandates that this record be in writing[47] and made available to the supervisory authority by the Controller's representative on request.[48]

### 4.4.2   Content of Processor's Records

Mirroring the Controller's duty, the Processor also has a duty to maintain records[49] of all categories of data that is processed on behalf of the Controller. The record will include the following information:

1. Name and contact details of:
   a. The Processor
   b. Any Additional Processors
   c. Each Controller under which they act
   d. The Representative of the Processor or Controller[50]
   e. The Data Protection Officer
2. The categories of processing carried out on behalf of each Controller
3. The transfers to third countries or international organizations with identification and documentation of safeguards
4. A general description[51] of technical and organizational measures to protect data

As mentioned earlier, GDPR mandates that this record be in writing[52] and made available to the supervisory authority by the Processor's representative on request.[53]

### 4.4.3   Exceptions to the Duty

The duties to maintain records are similar between the Controller and Processor, with the only difference being that there are fewer requirements placed on the Processor regarding documenting the strategic ends of the processing. However, in both cases the duty to maintain records is not required if the Controller organization employs fewer than 250 people, unless:

- The processing likely poses a risk to the rights and freedoms of others.
- The processing is not occasional.
- The processing deals with special data.
- The processing deals with criminal convictions.

The above "small organization" exception is very narrow, but clearly seeks to reduce compliance costs for those businesses who need not maintain any records for their small-scale processing.

## 4.5   Data Protection Impact Assessments

In the physical world, the industries that make goods are responsible for maintaining the environment we share collectively. To ensure that, most governments require an Environmental Impact Assessment (EIA) before any large project is carried out, to assess the short-term and long-term risks that are posed to the natural resources of earth. GDPR creates a similar responsibility for the digital world we all share. For many organizations who seek to enter the data-collection market this would be their first step before beginning processing. For those businesses already in the market, this is part of the new risk-based approach of GDPR.

The current digital environment is constantly growing with new technologies, forms of data collection, and uses of that data. At the same time, like pollution in the physical world, the pursuit of technological advancement makes it easy for businesses to lose track of the data subject's rights and cut corners to achieve their larger financial goals. A data impact protection assessment (DPIA) is a report from the Controller of data who seeks to try out a new processing strategy that bears a high risk to the rights and freedoms of natural persons. The report shall be made with the assistance of the DPO if applicable[54] and should give an assessment of the origin, nature, and severity of risk.[55]

For example, let us consider a social networking website that seeks to enter the field of gene mapping by way of a DNA ancestry platform. To carry out the effort they will have to process large amounts of biometric and genetic information, which are special category data. Before implementing this new service, the website must create a DPIA and undergo prior consultation with the SA to show they are GDPR compliant.

### 4.5.1 Types of Processing That Require DPIA

When processing operations are to be changed, particularly by using new technologies, the Controller would be required to conduct a DPIA considering the:

1. Nature
2. Scope
3. Context
4. Purposes of the new processing
5. High risk to the rights and freedoms of natural persons from the new processing

The most important factor is the existence of a "high risk" to the rights of natural persons. This is a judgment call, which the Controller must make, and the DPIA must reflect what the impact of the envisaged processing operation will be.[56] The report may address multiple planned processing operations that present similar high risks. In some cases, the subject of the DPIA may be broader than one project alone.[57] The existence of any certification or approved codes of conduct can be used as valuable evidence in assessing the impact/purpose caused by any processing operation run by the entity.[58]

In certain operations, a DPIA is absolutely necessary and cannot be subject to discretion. These activities include:[59]

1. **Profiling:** Any processing operation where there is a systematic and extensive evaluation of personal aspects relating to natural persons, which is based on

automated processing and profiling. The decisions made as the result of such processing will have legal or significant effects on people.

2. **Special Data:** Any large-scale processing of special categories of data[60] or data related to criminal convictions and offenses.[61]
3. **Surveillance:** Any systematic monitoring of public areas on a large scale.[62]
4. **Big data operations:** Any processing activity that aims to process a considerable amount of personal data at the regional, national, or supranational level that could affect the rights of many data subjects.[63]

The above operations are in a way "larger than life" as they involve the processing of data which can be easily abused. For example, if a car company wishes to create the next generation of self-driving cars, it would involve a massive effort of mapping the geography of a country by using sensors, GPS technology, video logging, and satellite imaging. This qualifies as a systematic monitoring of public areas, and it would be wise for an SA to have a clear picture of how these processing operations would impact the everyday user. Note that in cases of processing in public interest or under the authority of law a DPIA may not be required if a "General Impact Assessment" is carried out before the operation.[64]

**Exception:** The processing should not be considered large scale if the processing operation concerns personal data relating to doctor/patient or attorney/client relationships. In such cases, DPIAs are not mandatory.[65]

## 4.5.2 Scope of Assessment

**4.5.2.1 Determining the Risk**   As alluded to earlier in this chapter, to determine the risk posed to the rights and freedoms of natural persons, of varying likelihood and severity, the Controller must pay attention to any processing that could lead to physical, material, or nonmaterial damage, specifically:[66]

1. Prevention of exercising control over their personal data
2. Limitation of user rights
3. Discrimination
4. Identity theft or fraud
5. Financial loss
6. Unauthorized reversal of pseudonymization
7. Damage to reputation
8. Loss of confidentiality of personal data protected by *professional secrecy*
9. Any processing of special data
10. Any processing of data relating to criminal convictions
11. Any evaluation of personal aspects to create or use personal profiles, such as health, personality, performance at work, economic situation, interests, preferences, reliability, behavior, location, movements
12. Processing of personal data of vulnerable persons
13. Processing of personal data relating to children

14. Processing of a large amount of personal data relating to many people
15. Any other significant economic or social disadvantage to the natural person concerned

The risks mentioned are exhaustive, but not all-inclusive or restricted to the above. These are some red flags the Controller must bear in mind when embarking on a new technology project. However, to enhance compliance with GDPR, the Controller should evaluate the factors keeping in mind the origin, nature, particularity, and severity of the risk posed. If after the assessment, the Controller feels as though the measures will not sufficiently mitigate the risk, the SA will be consulted.[67]

**4.5.2.2 Contents of the DPIA**  It can be expected that most DPIAs will be long, detailed reports containing highly technical matters and inner workings on the Controller's strategies. The regulation requires that at the minimum, the DPIA must contain:[68]

1. A systematic description of the envisaged processing operation
2. The purposes for processing
3. Any legitimate interest pursued by the Controller
4. An assessment of the necessity and proportionality in relation to the purposes of the new processing activity
5. An assessment of the risks to the rights and freedoms of natural persons
6. Measures envisaged to combat these risks and remain GDPR compliant. These include safeguards, security measures, and protection of the user's rights
7. Measures to demonstrate compliance and prove their legitimate interests

In certain scenarios, GDPR requires the Controller shall seek the views of the data subject on the intended processing operations.[69] This consultation can be made without prejudice to the commercial or public interests or to the security of the processing. This "public consultation" procedure is problematic, as the Controller, a business entity, can be required to consult their users on any new strategies they wish to take. This seems logical for smaller businesses with a curated client base but would pose problems for larger websites with millions of users globally. Public opinion could hinder technological and business opportunities that may arise.

The DPIA responsibility of the Controller also includes a responsibility to carry out a review to assess whether the processing is performed in accordance with the DPIA, and if any additional risks are discovered.[70] Thus, the DPIA, like data security, is also an ongoing responsibility that continues long after the plans are implemented.

**4.5.2.3 Involvement of the DPO**  When conducting a DPIA, it is best to involve the company's DPO in the entire process, having him advise on the following matters:

• Whether a DPIA is necessary
• What methodology to follow

- Whether to conduct the DPIA in-house or whether to outsource the work
- Determining safeguards necessary
- Mitigation measures for risk
- Oversight of the DPIA while it is being conducted internally

It is sound commercial sense to use all resources at your disposal when complying with the regulation. As the officer in charge of data protection in an organization, the DPO would be invaluable in mitigating risks in carrying out a DPIA.

**4.5.2.4 Prior Consultation**  The DPIA also requires oversight from the Supervisory Authority to "green-light" the project after review. Like large environmentally sensitive undertakings, any new project that has been discussed above should be assessed and then approved by the SA by way of prior consultation mechanism.[71] The Controller shall consult the SA when it comes to any DPIA that points to a high risk in the processing operations if no mitigating measures are put in place.[72]

1. Details to be provided to the SA:
   When approaching the SA for a prior consultation, the Controller shall provide:[73]
   a. The respective responsibilities of the Controller, Processor, and any Joint Controller/Processors (especially when a group of companies is involved)
   b. The purposes and means of the intended processing
   c. The measures and safeguards to be put in place to protect the rights and freedoms of the data subjects
   d. Contact details of the DPO (where applicable)
   e. The DPIA
   f. Any other information requested by the SA
   In addition to the above, the Processor has the duty to assist the Controller on request or when necessary to ensure compliance with the provisions relating to DPIA and prior consultation under GDPR.[74]
2. Approval or rejection of the DPIA:
   If after prior consultation, the SA believes the envisaged processing would infringe GDPR and does not sufficiently identify or mitigate the risk,[75] the SA may provide written advice to the Controller and exercise any of their powers under the regulation.[76] As will be discussed in Chapter 7, these include investigative, corrective, and advisory powers. In examining the powers of the SA, it is clear that the following can be applicable regarding DPIAs:
   a. Advise the Controller.[77]
   b. Authorize the processing.[78]
   c. Warn the Controller that the envisaged processing would infringe GDPR.[79]
   d. Order the Data Collectors to bring processing operations into compliance, within a specified time and in a specified manner.[80]
   e. Investigate further into the processing operations and conduct web audits.[81]

Though Article 58 does not expressly states that the SA has the power to reject the DPIA submitted, a collective reading of their powers can lead to the conclusion that they may exercise this power by way of a corrective measure in the form of a warning or prohibition.[82] It is unclear from GDPR whether the advisory power of the SA gives them the authority to alter the DPIA. It is likely that a more specific delegated legislation by the SA or Member States would give greater clarity to this.

In any event, this power to advise, approve, or reject the DPIA submitted must be exercised within eight weeks, with an option of extending the period by six weeks depending on the complexity of the case. The SA has a duty to inform the Controller/Processor as to the reasons of delay within one month of receiving the request. If information needs to be submitted with the SA, the time periods may be extended.

3. Other related responsibilities of Supervisory Authorities:

Other than prior consultation,[83] which is their primary duty, the SA has the following responsibilities in relation to DPIAs:

a. Maintain a public list of operations that require a DPIA[84] (*Black and White Lists*).
b. Maintain a public list of operations that do not require a DPIA.[85]
c. Communicate these lists to the consistency mechanism board when they relate to processing operations that offer goods or services, monitor behavior, or influence the free movement of data within the EU.
d. Consult and advise in any legislative process in the Member States relating to processing and mitigating that risk.[86]

### 4.5.3 Business Plan Oversight

A unique issue that arises under GDPR is the role of the SA in approving or rejecting DPIAs. Consider the scenario from the perspective of a data Controller business. With the use of a new generation of technology and new modes of processing, many business entities would seek to be the first in the market and to cut their costs in doing so. At the end of the day, the Controllers and Processors are businesses who seek a way to effectively monetize and run their online platforms while remaining GDPR compliant.

A DPIA is essentially a new business model for the Controller's processing operations, which has its risks but also its rewards. The DPIA must reflect the legitimate interests of the Controller, which includes their commercial objectives. However, GDPR balances any risks against the overarching data rights that a user may have. This gives the SA a unique role in reviewing and rejecting business models that may be created by the Controller. But what should be done when an eventual conflict arises between the commercial interests/efficiency of the operation with the potential infringements of rights?

When interpreting the objectives of GDPR,[87] the data subject's rights would superseed commercial interests in most scenarios. But if "user rights" act as the default tie breaker, one might see either a stifling in technological advancement or an increase in the competition in the market as DPIAs become standard in the industry.

Consider the following illustration.

In the competitive industry of online shopping, Shoppey.com has a new strategy of increasing their processing capabilities across borders by implementing new software that effectively maps and predicts the user's needs with even more precision than exists in the present market. It is a large undertaking, across several countries and a new "in-house" underwater processing plant and a patent pending for their processing technology. The DPO of Shoppey.com submits a DPIA to the lead SA that they report to. The detailed assessment report is 400 pages long. The SA, in accordance with the law, extends the prior consultation period by six weeks in addition to the original eight-week deadline.

Unfortunately, Shoppey.com's new processing model does not provide for mechanisms to review and demonstrate compliance with GDPR, and the SA rejects their model, asking them to review, edit, and refile. Additionally, the SA did not approve of how the risks are mitigated, claiming that the business model is "flawed" and needs to be completely reworked to be GDPR compliant. To rework the model there will be considerable costs and logistics involved.

During this period, Shoppey's fierce competitor MallMart.com submits a similar DPIA but with adequate protections by learning of their competitor's pitfalls over the prior months (by using the public register maintained by the SA and patent application filed by them). Such a scenario raises many questions:

1. Can the SA play a dual role of monitoring compliance of the law and reviewing future business plans of the Controller?
2. Can the order of the SA be upheld, even if the changes suggested would involve considerable costs, and even a change in the patent application?
3. Should businesses plan their future processing activities based on what the probable results of their DPIA might be?
4. What should be done when commercial interests are harmed by the ordinary actions of the SA?
5. How should the SA balance business competition with an effective DPIA system?

Thus, from this short illustration, we see practical issues arise outside the law. Especially when it comes to strategy planning and development of technologies in a business, as it demands privacy by design, and not merely innovations that favor commercial interests. In a sense, the SA is acting as ombudsman akin to new technology and processing strategies in ensuring that the culture of data protection created by GDPR is upheld. The SA's oversight covers not just design of the data, or the processing operation itself, but all future plans involving a new generation of data processing.

## 4.6 The Data Protection Officer

One of the main contributions of German data protection law is the appointment of a Data Protection Officer (DPO), providing strict requirements for having a point-person for all privacy-related matters within an organization. Generally satisfying the German requirements for a DPO would typically satisfy the requirements of GDPR.[88] GDPR requires that in certain scenarios further measures be implemented to ensure the security and protection of the data held. This additional protection takes form of a DPO who is responsible for safeguarding the security of the operation. The DPO can be an individual, or an entity (such as a third-party contractor), or even an employee of the Controller/Processor.

### 4.6.1 Designation of DPO

Unlike a Controller or Processor, a DPO shall be appointed by the Data Collectors in cases where:

1. The processing is carried out by a public body (except courts in their official capacity).
2. The core processing activities, by their nature, scope, and purpose of data collection, require regular and systemic monitoring of the users.
3. The core activities involve processing of special data or data related to criminal convictions on a large scale.

The three limited scenarios given above are the only cases where the appointment of the DPO is mandatory, unless EU or Member law expands the scope.[89] In all other cases, the appointment of a DPO is optional and may be done by the Data Collectors. The term "core activities" implies that the processing of personal Data is central to the Controller's overall business strategy and not a mere ancillary part of it.[90] For example, maintaining databases of employees may be ancillary, while having an online delivery platform based on creating user profiles qualify as "core" activities.

A group of undertakings can appoint a single DPO, provided he is easily accessible to all the entities.[91] Similarly, one DPO can be appointed to handle the activities of multiple public bodies and agencies, based on the organizational structure and size of the entity.[92] Additionally, a DPO may be appointed by an association representing Controllers or Processors,[93] or a staff member under the Data Collectors working under a service contract.[94] All these details must be published and communicated to the supervisory authority by the Controller or Processor.[95]

## 4.6.2 Qualifications and Hiring a DPO

The DPO can only be designated based on his professional qualifications and must have expertise in:

1. Data protection law,
2. Data protection practice, and
3. An ability to fulfill the tasks under GDPR.

Thus, from the above we can see that the DPO is a role that is dynamic and requires a good handle on GDPR and related data practices. Under German norms, the DPO must demonstrate diverse knowledge of the technical, organizational, and legal aspects of data protection.[96]

**Illustration:** Consider that over the course of taping of a physical-reality show *Rail-Road*, the medical team that works for a specialized subprocessing company, Healthee Data Inc., under the instructions of SATTV, the TV network airing the show decides to consistently monitor the vital statistics of the competitors to prevent any emergencies. This is done by way of providing the contestants with wearables that collect their biometrics and monitor markers such as heartbeat, blood pressure, calories lost, etc. As this data collection involves both special data and systemic monitoring of the contestants, a DPO must be appointed. SATTV appoints Dr. Bolton, a prominent cyber-law attorney and former computer programmer to work for the entire *Rail-Road* project, supervising the processing activities for all four entities involved.[97] Dr. Bolton will be working under a service contract with SATTV, and his details will be shared with the local SA. We use Dr. Bolton as our illustration to elaborate the concepts below.

## 4.6.3 Position of the DPO

DPOs hold a unique position in an organization. Unlike the Controller or Processor, they are given specific rights and obligations when commissioned to carry out data-protection activities.[98] Article 38 lays down specific rights and obligations of the DPO in relation to the Controller and Processor:

1. **Involvement:** The DPO must be involved in all issues that relate to the protection of personal data. The Controller/Processor must ensure this involvement. For example, the DPO must be contacted any time there is an attempted data breach of the processing activity or when determining the amount of security for a new category of data being processed by the Controller.
2. **Support:** The Controller and Processor must support the DPO in performing his tasks[99] by providing:
   a. The necessary resources
   b. Access to personal data
   c. Access to processing operations
   d. Maintenance of the DPO's knowledge

**Illustration** (continued): Cyber Pro, the cyber-security firm hired by SAT-TV, wishes for all their employees to undergo "digital awareness training" in accordance with their processing contract for the *Rail-Road* project. The DPO, Mr. Bolton, will oversee organizing the training program. He must be given a reasonable budget and access to the processing operations to carry out his task.

3. **Independence:** The DPO will exercise his tasks independently and will receive no instructions on how to exercise those tasks from the Data Collectors. **Example:** The DPO conducts an annual web audit of the processing operation and cannot fabricate the results just to maintain his contract.

4. **Reporting:** The DPO shall not be penalized for performing his duties. He shall directly report to the highest management level of the Controller/Processor entity. **Example:** If the results of a web audit are negative, the DPO reports directly to the chief technology officer (CTO). If the DPO happens to be an employee of the company, he cannot be removed for giving honest results of the web audit.

5. **Relationship with data subject:** The users may contact the DPO for all issues relating to the processing of their personal data, and for exercising their rights. **Example:** A social media website designating their DPO's office as the main point of contact if their users are hacked.

6. **Confidentiality:** In accordance to EU or Member Law, the DPO shall be bound by the obligation of secrecy/confidentiality.

7. **Other tasks:** The DPO may fulfill other tasks and duties. It is the responsibility of the Data Collectors to ensure there is no conflict of interests in the exercise of those tasks.

The duty to report imposed on the DPO reflects what the nature of his role in the company is, an independent watch dog. The regulation creates a delicate position in this legal ecosystem by giving the DPO *whistle-blower immunity* from any retaliatory action by the Controller.[100]

### 4.6.4 Tasks of the DPO

As mentioned above, the DPO has a prominent position in the organization when carrying out the tasks that are required under GDPR. The regulation requires that the DPO shall have at least the following tasks:[101]

1. To inform and advise the Data Collectors and their employees of their obligations under GDPR and related EU and Member laws
2. To monitor compliance with GDPR and related EU and Member laws, along with the internal policies of the Controller and Processor in relation to:
   a. The protection of personal data
   b. Assignment of responsibilities
   c. Awareness raising
   d. Staff training
   e. Related web audits

3. To provide advice and monitor performance of any data impact assessments
4. To cooperate with the Supervisory Authority
5. To act as the point of contact with the Supervisory Authorities in relation to any issues of processing and prior consultation[102]

Like other responsibilities under this regulation, the DPO must carry out his activities keeping in mind the risk of the processing operations, and the nature, scope, context, and purposes of processing.[103] Thus, we can see that the DPO's role is key in the overall processing operation as a human firewall regarding all things related to data security in an organization. This helps the regulation ensure overall accountability by having an accountable officer within an organization who oversees the operation and ensures compliance while processing personal data.

### 4.6.5 An Inherent Conflict of Interest?

An interesting issue to consider is the DPO's larger role in the system from the implementation of GDPR. To be a DPO one must be part legal counsel by advising the Data Collectors in their activities, but at the same time be an impartial body that monitors the organization from a technical perspective as well. Here, a crucial conflict arises. An attorney's role is to represent their client to the best of their interests, while as a DPO he is required to be as harsh and critical as he can be. Can the role be truly carried out without a conflict of interest?

Let us consider the qualifications required of a DPO under GDPR, where it states that he must be an expert in data protection law. It is then logical to assume that many qualified DPOs must be educated in the field of law, if not a qualified lawyer. It would be important for an organization to specify that the DPO in no way acts in the capacity of an attorney for the entity they report to. Even though much of the DPO's role would involve advisory and legal responsibilities, the primary role must be that of a data security expert. In such a case, the "practice of law" in the profession would be tangential, and none of the rights and liabilities of the attorney-client relationship would arise.

At the same time, the DPO cannot carry out tasks regarding data processing, as the DPO may not be in charge of determining his own compliance with GDPR.[104] The Article 29 Working Party itself recognized this to be an inherent conflict of interest in the DPO's duties and has mandated that the following employees are not permitted to take on the following roles:[105]

- Senior management
- Head of IT
- Head of marketing
- Head of HR
- Any other role in the organization if the candidate will lead to the determination of the means and purposes of processing

Perhaps the solution would be to treat the profession of DPOs like that of certi-fied or chartered accountants, where the skills involved would require knowledge of law, but keeping in mind a larger impartial role in overseeing the organization's activities and compliance with the regulation. Another option on a micro level would be to implement organizational measures to ensure that the DPO does not have any conflicts of interest and is legally bound to act in such a manner. Ad-ditionally, Controller organizations should categorize the positions mentioned above and others like it as ineligible categories of candidates.

### 4.6.6 DPO Liability

GDPR does not provide for any penalty to be imposed on the DPO for dereliction of duties. The liability for any of his shortcomings runs upward toward the Con-troller/Processor they report to. However, this does not prevent any claim against the DPO to be filed under Member State labor or contractual law by their employ-ers or harmed data subjects.

**Illustration:** Ingram, the DPO of an online e-commerce platform, OhYo!, left the office one day with his work desktop unlocked. An unknown party accessed the system and stole thousands of files, causing a €1 million fine being imposed on the company. The company brings a suit against Ingram for breach of his contractual duties and impleads Ingram in their defense in Civil Court filed by their users for the loss of data. These are both valid actions by OhYo! under GDPR.

## 4.7 Data Protection by Design and Default

Consumers are generally accustomed to using websites that they personally find trustworthy over those that seem risky. Many websites that contain malware and other viruses that steal personal data are rampant around the world, and GDPR seeks to curb this issue of introducing the principle of data protection by design and by default,[106] or privacy by design. This principle has long been known in tech-nological circles, and it has now made its way into data protection law. The con-cept primarily relates to the amount of data collected, the extent of processing, the period of storage, and its accessibility.[107]

### 4.7.1 Data Protection at the Outset

The regulation mandates that data must be secured by the Controller, at the out-set, placing it as one of the Controller's primary responsibilities. The principle of data protection by design requires that the personal data be protected by technical and organizational measures both:

1. At the time of determining the means of processing, and
2. At the time of processing.[108]

This dual layer of protection ensures that data protection is not just implemented but planned for. The measures must be effective enough to provide necessary safeguards to processing to meet the requirements of GDPR and to protect users. Certification from an authorized body can be relevant evidence to prove that data protection by design has been implemented.[109]

**Illustration:** An ad agency seeks to make an aggressive social media campaign to promote its client's new voice translation technology. The campaign strategy involves making the video go viral by way of using various social media platforms, using the client and the agency employees' social media accounts and buying generous ad space in these websites. These posts will then run through a complex algorithm and piggy-back onto the users' foreign friends' videos with an option to translate it live. The strategy cannot go through as both the ad agency and the website Controllers do not incorporate privacy by design into their initial plans.

It is important to note the slight nuance between data protection by design and privacy by design, both of which are used interchangeably, but often bear different meanings. Data protection by design entails any hardware or software "technical" measures implemented by the business for minimally invasive data processing. Meanwhile privacy by design speaks more to the principles of data minimization and the overall amount of data collected by a business. Thus, the two concepts collectively serve the purpose of protecting the data that is collected in a way that is not excessive. For example, a social networking site maintaining "privacy-by-default" settings on all profiles unless the user changes it.

### 4.7.2 Balancing the Amount of Protection

When implementing the technical and organizational measures, the Controller must consider the following:

1. The state of the art in technology
2. The cost of implementation
3. Nature of processing
4. Scope of processing
5. Context of processing
6. Purpose of processing
7. The varying likelihood and severity of risks in the rights and freedoms of data subjects

These seven considerations assist the Controller in weighing the amount of protection against the practical feasibility and nature of the processing. For example, the amount of protection given to merely collecting one's name would not be the same as data relating to one's health. To that end, GDPR suggests two measures to be implemented expressly: data minimization and pseudonymizing (or its broader practice of data encryption).

Data breaches can occur due to a lack of appropriate organizational measures to protect data. The value of the data determines the level of risk it faces from a leak. For example, confidential blueprints of India's new Scorpene submarines were hit by a breach in which approximately 24,000 pages of classified technical information were leaked by a disgruntled employee.[110] This leak had multinational consequences across India (who owned the submarine), Paris (where it was made), and Australia (which shares the information). The scandal had come to light when the employee decided to store the data on a disk and share it with an Australian journalist.

### 4.7.3  Applying Data Protection by Design

Encryption is a common capability in today's technology frameworks world to reassure the protection of one's personal data. It is embedded into our phones, direct messaging, e-mails, and all the data we hold dear. GDPR makes encryption a requirement for compliance by highlighting it as a suitable measure for data protection.[111] The concept of privacy by default can be technically implemented at any given moment during the processing, which makes it practical and relatively easy.[112]

*Step 1: Decide the Level of Protection Needed*   Depending on the type of data that is handled by the organization, the level of protection must be proportionate to avoid larger costs and burdensome maintenance of data security. It is here that the earlier measures of data mapping and minimization come into play, as GDPR mandates that the Controllers and Processors maintain a "lean data" practice of only collecting what is needed to achieve the larger purposes. Here, it is important to pay attention to the type of data handled by the organization:

- **Personal data:** Identifying information such as a person's name, age, address, postal code, Social Security number, family details, etc.
- **Special data:** Information that points towards a person's political, religious, philosophical or personal beliefs, or any genetic/biometric data.

*Step 2: Data Mapping*   Special data must be given a higher level of protection, but that does not entail that the regular personal data can be maintained with a low level of protection. The objective of data protection by design would require that any data that would lead to the identification of the user should have a minimum amount of encryption.

An effective mechanism to map data would be by conducting a web audit of the platform provided and categorizing the data as you proceed. Many providers such as Microsoft and IBM have programs that can map and minimize data to become GDPR compliant.

*Step 3: Data Minimization*   Once the type of data has been effectively mapped, it is important to start minimizing any superfluous data that may remain after the web audit is conducted. The technical and organizational measures must be implemented in such a way that, by default, only personal data that is necessary for each specific purpose is processed.[113] This obligation applies to the Controller with respect to:

1. The amount of personal data collected.
2. The extent of their processing.
3. The period of storage.
4. Its accessibility. Specifically, the personal data must not be accessible without the data subject's intervention to an indefinite number of natural persons[114]

The larger an operation is, and the more it depends on personal data for its functioning, the more difficult this weighing of factors will be. Certain organizations rely on a variety of data for research and development purposes, and for new features. Note that it is the Controller who has the burden of showing the proportionality of the processing operation[115] and to show that the level of data protection is sufficient.[116] Thus, the main task would be to use all data collected functionally and give a sufficient level of encryption to ensure that liability is kept to a minimum.

*Step 4: Deciding the Type of Measure*   Once a fair picture of the data handled by the processing operation is created, the next step forward would be determining the level of protection afforded to it. As mentioned earlier, there are levels to encryption with varying cost and technical expertise required. The prominent methods indicated by GDPR are pseudonymization, and data anonymization. Both achieve similar results but vary in the level of protection and accessibility given to it (see Figure 4.1). Let us examine them below, along with other viable options.

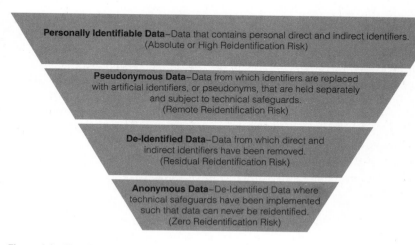

**Figure 4.1**   The Hierarchy of Data Protection

*Source:* Image retrieved from https://www.bryancave.com/en/thought-leadership/at-a-glance-de-identification-anonymization-and-pseudonymization-1.html.

**Option 1: Pseudonymizing:** It is clear from GDPR that this is the preferred method of protecting personal data, as it is used as a repeated example of technical and organizational methods. Specifically, the regulation defines pseudonymization in Article 3, as *"the processing of personal data in such a way that the data can no longer be attributed to a specific data subject without the use of additional information."* To pseudonymize data, the "additional information" must be *"kept separately and subject to technical and organizational measures to ensure nonattribution to an identified or identifiable person."*

Simply put, pseudonymization is a method to substitute identifiable data with a reversible, consistent value.[117] **Example:** User *Bill Putam, Palo Alto, CA* is processed and stored as *Libb Munpat, Lapo Apo, 03* with the Controller/Processor. In the event of a data breach, hackers would be unable to identify Bill's names and details without the identifying information held by the user/Controller to crack the code. This is known as pseudonymization by use of *"hash functions."*

Note that pseudonymization is not encryption. Encryption relies on a cryptographic key between the two parties, while pseudonymization only requires some sort of additional information. In practice, pseudonymization is not as effective as encryption itself as it allows reidentification of the data by either direct or indirect methods. A commonly known method of breaking pseudonymization is that of inference attacks that occurred at AOL in 2006. This can be done when certain personally identifiable information is pseudonymized, but surrounding information such as zip codes and online behavior is not, leading to abuse of the data by inference.

**Option 2: Tokenization:** Closely related to pseudonymization, is the practice of tokenizing personal data. Following similar principles of distorting the value fields of the data, tokenizing provides a consistent "token" for each unique name and requires additional information (a decryption key *or* static lookup tables/code books) to reidentify the data. **Example:** *Bill Putnam, Palo Alto, CA* will become *Xk1s Msjp9, Zbi Qou, T8.*

The small distinction that exists between the two above options is that pseudonymized data does not drastically change the value of the characters as tokenization does. Pseudonymization only blocks the identifying data to the extent that it can lead to the user, but still leaves a few important data fields unchanged to help easier identification. Meanwhile, tokenization replaces the data with "tokens" of similar value, using nonsensitive values, and without altering the length of the value. Having software (such as *Protegrity*) that can randomly generate pseudonyms and tokens of different types and formats are particularly useful in implementing such measures.

Tokenization as a nonmathematical approach involves less computational resources and costs to implement. This causes it to differ from classical encryption, where the length of the values can be changed for the data and render it completely unreadable when the data is at rest in a database/processing storage center. On the other hand, the "tokens" remain the same at rest and can also be easily subject to inference attacks. The main reason for this is that the "tokens" are the same for information for the same value. For example:

- Bill Putnam, Palo Alto, CA = Xk1s Msjp9, Zbi Qou, T8
- Bill Putty, Palo Alto, CA = Xk1s gfbf6, Zbi Qou, T8
- Paul Putnam, Palo Alto, CA = Dk7p Msjp9, Zbi Qou, T8

In this illustration the token values for certain terms remain the same across the board, which means that the code can be cracked if enough data is hacked. Tokenization and pseudonymization are two methods that are useful to protect the data at rest or in transit from being interrupted and abused. It can be compared to redacting and assigning code names to the personal data transferred into the Controller's possession, so that the default setting of the management of the data would avoid abuse. But the biggest factor leaning toward these forms of encryption under GDPR, despite its fallibility, is the retrievability of the data provided.

**Option 3: Anonymization:** Anonymization is one of the most effective forms of protecting personal data, by completely concealing the identity and identifiers of any nature. Broadly speaking, anonymization can be carried out by two categories of techniques:[118]

1. **Randomization:** Where the data's accuracy is altered by removing the strong link between the data and the user, making identification uncertain
2. **Generalization:** Where the attributes are diluted by altering the scale or order of the data

The methods mentioned above should be considered as data masking rather than complete data encryption, as they merely involve a rearrangement of the values in the data to give a desensitized result, which is protected. Anonymization on the other hand, does not "mask" the values but completely obliterates them to irreversibly prevent identification.[119] The lack of retrievability is perhaps why it may not be the preferred form of encryption from an operational standpoint. **Example:** *Bill Putnam, CA* will become *xxxx xxxxx, CA.*

All identifying information is removed and stored but does not give the Controller or the User the option of reidentifying the data. This is particularly useful in the field of data analytics or statistics, but not necessarily in the interactive use of personal data such as social networking.

**Option 4: Encryption:** Encryption is a technique of data security that encodes messages and information into an unintelligible format so that only authorized users may see the content. This is performed by way of *cryptographic keys.* Each cryptographic key is a string of characters such as letters or numbers that converts *plain text* into *cipher text.* The cipher text cannot be read until it is *decrypted* with the corresponding key. A good example of this would be the messenger service of Whatsapp that uses *end-to-end* encryption, which entails that no third party can read the messages in transit, as they are encrypted to all except the two (or multiple) users who may have the corresponding key.

**Illustration:** User 1: "Howdy!" -> **Encrypting key** <-"*7cjL2jcd85n@*"-> **Deciphering key** <- "Howdy!": User 2

Encryption offers the highest level of data protection by completely changing the value and format of the data so that it becomes incredibly difficult to access in transit. While the other measures mentioned above (other than anonymization) require a master database or "code" to crack the pseudonyms/tokens, encryption requires a specific *key,* which is held by the data subject, the recipient, or the creator of the key infrastructure.

The difficulty level of breaking encryption was recently seen when the US Department of Justice required Apple's assistance to break into a terrorist's iPhone. The only two key holders were Apple and the deceased terrorist himself. It took considerable effort on the part of the Department of Justice to eventually break into the phone. This issue of the state breaking into private encrypted data for official purposes will be discussed in Chapter 9.[120]

*Step 5: Implement Protection*   The Article 29 Working Party (*WP 29*) specifies that data may be encrypted/pseudonymized by the following methods:

1. **Noise addition:** The imprecise expression of any personal identifiers.
   **Example:** Bill Putnam, 38 years old, Caucasian = Libb Numpat, 42 years old, Dravidian
2. **Substitution/permutation:** Personal identifiers are shuffled and replaced with random values.
   **Example:** Wichita Kansas = Lone Mango
3. **Differential privacy:** The personal identifiers of one data set are compared against an anonymized data set held by a third party with instructions of the noise function and acceptable amount of "leakage."
   **Example:** The client who authorizes the processing of the data by the Processor insists on implementing code words to designate certain information. Location = Fruit, Name = Vegetable, Age= Meat, etc.
4. **Aggregation:** The identifiers categorized into a general range/group.
   **Example:** All clients who are over 50 years old are referred to collectively as "Dingo" and all females over 50 are referred to as "Gazelle."
5. **L-diversity:** The data is first "generalized," and then each attribute within a class is made to occur with a specific data set/value.
   **Example:** All residents of Kansas will bear a specific code of M6 (with a space on each side of the word), and names and addresses will be tokenized to create a long data set.
   a. Bill from Wichita, Kansas = Wu8 *M6* 795
   b. Grace from Kansas City, Kansas = Ngy *M6* 907
   c. Rich from Park City, Kansas= H4b *M6* 342
6. **Hash function pseudonymizing:** Replacing identifiers with artificial codes, like what has been discussed above. (Kansas = M6)
7. **Tokenization:** As discussed above.

While the WP29 has recognized the above methods, certain other acceptable methods have been suggested to be GDPR compliant:

8. **Directory replacement:** Modifying the names of the individuals but keeping consistency in certain values.

    **Example:** Bill Putnam, Kansas = Will Suttanam, *Kansas*

9. **Scrambling:** The mixing of letters and numbers.

    **Example:** Bill Putnam = Li66 N0mp2t

10. **Masking:** A part of the data is hidden with random characters.

    **Example:** Bill Putnam = whfwhif**b**dgdidjfkw**ll** p**h**387fgeh**u**f4hftif4if**n**738afgeu**M**

11. **Personalized anonymization:** Allowing the user to carry out their own anonymization techniques using a script or an application.

    **Example:** *Referrer* is a program that is used to anonymize links easily.[121]

12. **Blurring:** Utilizing an approximation in data values to render their meaning obsolete/impossible. This is similar to many of the methods discussed above.

*Step 6: Get Certified*    Once your data has been mapped, minimized, and given the appropriate amount of protection by use of one of the methods given above, it is helpful to certify the processing operation by receiving certification such as ISO27K or other services to demonstrate the compliance with GDPR. This helps to act as valuable evidence of GDPR compliance with the SA who oversees the processing operation.

### 4.7.4   Special Case: Blockchain Technology and GDPR

Before proceeding to the next topic of data security, we briefly discuss the impact of blockchain technology in the new GDPR ecosystem. For many, blockchain is a familiar term, which is associated with cryptocurrencies, specifically Bitcoin. However, its application goes far beyond cryptocurrency with applications in medicine, food safety, insurance, and any other field where information accountability is key. In fact, the Decentralized Identity Foundation states that blockchain is one of the key pillars of an open-source identity system.[122]

Blockchain is a shared, immutable ledger for recording the history of transactions.[123] The applications go well beyond the trading of currencies, as the blockchain platform creates a secure, transparent, and accountable record of transactions, which contains the data in a decentralized repository that is held by each user. As a result, breaking the integrity of a blockchain system is incredibly difficult, as the end-to-end chain of ledgers will have to fall apart in order to compromise the processing operation.

Blockchain has data protection by design and built-in security features. For this reason, blockchain can be considered as a suitable technology for the requirements of GDPR regarding the security of processing and its accountability. Blockchain uses complex cryptography and access controls to ensure confidentiality, integrity, and availability (CIA). The data remains secure through use of triple blind identity attribute provider and gives more power to the users to create a self-sovereign identity online, which can be altered or deleted through their control.

Aside from assuring CIA, blockchain also helps to build accountability under GDPR, with the ability to maintain meticulous records and keep track of its erasure and alteration. Every record in a blockchain platform provides independent proof that the records are maintained in their original state, and the history of any alteration or change can be tracked with cyber-forensics. The technology also assists in overseeing and maintaining compliance with any law by programming the records to reflect industry standards. For example, the US Food and Drug Administration (FDA) has been working with IBM to create a blockchain-supported database to keep track of global food safety and drug standards and their compliance in an immutable, decentralized ledger for all concerned to access and benefit from.[124]

While blockchain technology is secure and immutable, it is not infallible as it can also be subject to cyber-attacks and data breaches. Some of them include:

- Use of a vulnerable application connected to the blockchain database to gain unauthorized access to the disk/network
- Tampering, theft, and loss of an encryption key, leading to prevention of access
- Unverified participants impersonating valid users to gain access to the system

Thus, the mere fact that blockchain technology is used does not entail that the processing operation is GDPR compliant. Additional data security measures such as regular monitoring, restriction of access, user verification and encryption should be implemented to ensure that no risk is posed to the user's data.

## 4.8    Data Security during Processing

The principle of data protection by design is built into the foundation of the Controller's responsibilities both during processing and at the time of determining the means of processing. Data security, on the other hand, is an ongoing defensive mechanism that must be put in place to prevent the worst from happening.

Like most responsibilities under GDPR, the Controller is responsible for ensuring the ongoing security of processing.[125] The Controller must implement appropriate data security measures bearing in mind the following:

1. State of the art in technology
2. Cost of implementation
3. Nature of processing
4. Scope of processing
5. Context of processing
6. Purpose of processing
7. Varying likelihood and severity of risks in the rights and freedoms of data subjects

The measures implemented must be appropriate to the risk posed to the data. The above factors are a verbatim adoption of data protection by design, once again highlighting GDPR's pervasive approach to secure processing. Article 32 merely creates an ongoing duty on the Controller while carrying out the processing operations.

### 4.8.1 Data Security Measures

The technical and organizational measures that the Controller must implement include:

1. Encryption/pseudonymization of data
2. The ability to ensure the ongoing confidentiality, integrity, availability, and resilience of processing systems and services
3. The ability to restore the availability and access to personal data in the event of a physical or technical breach
4. A process for regular testing, assessment, and evaluation of the effectiveness of the measures to ensure the security of processing

These responsibilities of the Controller can be viewed as a broader, continuous duty, rather than the initial threshold duty of data protection by design. They run harmoniously, but the duty of data security further meshes out how protection is pervasive in GDPR. Consider the following.

| S. No | The duty | Type of measure |
|---|---|---|
| 1. | *Encryption*/pseudonymization of data. | A part of the principle of data protection by design, at the *initial stage* itself. |
| 2. | The ability to *ensure* the ongoing confidentiality, integrity, availability, and resilience of processing systems and services. | During the *stage of processing* where the operation is run in a reliable manner. |
| 3. | The ability to *restore* the availability and access to personal data in the event of a physical or technical breach. | A precautionary measure, *for the Plan B stage.* |
| 4. | A process for *regular testing, assessment,* and *evaluation* of the effectiveness of the measures to ensure the security of processing. | A preventive measure, to ensure the Plan B stage is never required. |

In addition to the continuous nature of data security, GDPR also provides for reactive measures in the event of a data breach[126] and proactive measures in the form of data impact assessments and prior consultations.[127] As mentioned earlier, relevant certifications or codes of conduct act as effective evidence to demonstrate compliance to the regulation.[128]

### 4.8.2 Determining the Risk Posed

While maintaining data security, the Controller must take a risk-based approach. In assessing this risk, a Controller must consider:[129]

1. Accidental damage or destruction
2. Unlawful destruction
3. Alteration
4. Unauthorized access
5. Unauthorized disclosure

The above considerations are a codification of how data security must be weighed under GDPR. Both the Controller and Processor have a duty to ensure that their employees do not access or process personal data except on their instructions, unless the employee is required to do so by law.[130] For example, an online banking corporation would have all the above risks inherent the sensitive financial data they process while an online chatroom has less to worry about.

### 4.8.3  Data Protection Management Systems: A "Technical and Organizational Measure"

Keeping track of numerous requirements and standards under a complex regulation such as GDPR can be an overwhelming task for most Controller organizations. That is why many data collection entities consider implementing Data protection management systems (DPMS) to manage their potential liability in a streamlined fashion. A DPMS is a system that oversees internal compliance within an organization in relation to their data protection standards and safety.[131] As the regulation primarily deals with human interaction with our technological counterparts, it seems logical that technology should help in complying with the technical and organizational conduct within a data-collection entity. Additionally, the DPMS documents the monitored activities to assist in compliance.[132]

Considering the efficiency that the DPMS can offer, it is a valuable recordkeeping and compliance monitoring technical measure under GDPR. It is advisable to keep the DPO or the respective officer in charge of oversight the task of ensuring that the DPMS itself is operating at full efficiency. The combination of the two will make it easier for a business to keep track of their GDPR compliance.

## 4.9   Personal Data Breaches

It is ironic that hackers and other threats to personal data are the driving force of data protection and cyber-security growth. As cyber-security mechanisms become tougher, hacking practices become more intensive. This creates a continuous cycle, where companies are unaware of how vulnerable their data is until the worst scenario occurs.

In earlier sections, we discussed how data must be protected under the regulation in the initial plans and ongoing processing operations. GDPR lays down responsibilities on Data Processors and Controllers if the worst-case scenario of a data breach were to occur. The regulation builds this practice by requiring data protection at every step. And, if the companies still face an attack, GDPR continues its system of accountability on the Controller.

### 4.9.1   Overview of Data Breaches

GDPR defines a "personal data breach" as[133] "*a breach of security leading to the accidental or unlawful destruction, loss, alteration, unauthorized disclosure of, or access to, personal data transmitted, stored or otherwise processed.*" The WP29 has issued guidelines to further clarify these terms:[134]

- **Destruction** of personal data should be clear: This is where the data no longer exists in a form that has any use for the Controller.
- **Damage** is where personal data has been altered, corrupted, or is no longer complete.
- **Loss** of personal data should be interpreted as implying that the data may still exist, but the Controller has lost control or access to it, or no longer has it in its possession.[135]
- **Unauthorized** or **unlawful processing** may include disclosure of personal data to (or access by) recipients who are not authorized to receive (or access) the data, or any other form of processing that violates GDPR.

When comparing this provision with that of determining the "risks posed" to the data processed, one can see a direct correlation between the duty and the result to be achieved. The obligation on the Controller to secure the data is performed with the aim of preventing data breaches from ever happening.

**4.9.1.1 Types of Data Breaches**   Though not expressly dealt with by GDPR, it is important to know the dangers faced by processing entities in their operations. Data breaches have long existed in many shapes, forms, and sizes, so let us first examine the types of data breaches. The WP29 in its Opinion 03/2014 on Breach Notifications, stated the types of breaches can be broadly divided into three categories:

1. **Confidentiality breach:** An unauthorized or accidental disclosure of, or access to, personal data. **Example:** A mid-level employee using his superior's code to access the main processing operations. The Cambridge Analytica scandal can be considered as this type of breach, as unauthorized access was given to the user's personal data.
2. **Availability breach:** An accidental or unauthorized loss of access to, or destruction of, personal data. **Example:** A DoS attack on an organization, or the Controller losing access to a decryption key.

3. **Integrity breach:** An unauthorized or accidental alteration of personal data. **Example:** Someone hacks into the Controller's main server to gain access to another individual's profile.

The WP29 goes on to state that these types of breaches are not mutually exclusive, and all three can happen in one attack. The classification given by the working party is broad and does not shed light on the finer activities of how such attacks happen. Another alternative would be to categorize the data breach based on the mode of execution:

1. **Physical breaches** entail "physical" theft or destruction of the electronic systems such as the laptops, external hard drives, physical systems, storage processors, etc. **Example:** To wipe out his record of debt with a credit agency, Robert breaks into their main processing center to set fire to the whole operation. This would be a physical breach.
2. **Electronic breaches** are the types of breaches that the common person is more accustomed to, where "hackers" gain unauthorized access to, or otherwise disturb, personal data processing. These include
   a. **Malware:** Viruses such as Trojan horses and worms are prominent in the internet, introduced into electronic systems by way of fake links or files.
   b. **Phishing:** Personal information is extracted by way of fake website requests, or concealed attacks that seem legitimate. Another form of this is a *cross-site request forgery* which is done by using "fake consent" to use cookies on one's laptops.
   c. **Password attacks:** If passwords to a service are not regularly attended to, criminals try to use *brute force attacks, remote code attacks,* and *combination attacks* to crack any unsecure passwords.
   d. **Ransomware:** This type of attack mainly targets businesses that deal with sensitive data, by collecting sensitive data or denying the Controller access to the website, in exchange for a *ransom* to access the data.
   e. **Denial of service attacks:** This method requires a website that is embedded with requests or data until the targeted system crashes. Once this happens, the system is hijacked, and neither the users nor the Controller can access the site.
   f. **Coordinated attacks:** This type of attack is newer, and most recently seen in the Cambridge Analytica scandal. This is a unique type of data breach, as it was not done by traditional methods of hacking (which Facebook was prepared for) but involved purchased data (which was arguably legally purchased by Cambridge Analytica) and the use of "fake" profiles which were created in accordance with Facebook's policies. This scenario does not entail just one type of attack, but a combination of several forms.

**4.9.1.2 Damage Caused by Data Breaches** A personal data breach may, if not addressed in an appropriate and timely manner, result in physical, material, or nonmaterial damage to natural persons, which includes:[23]

1. Loss of control over their personal data
2. Limitation of user rights

3. Discrimination
4. Identity theft or fraud
5. Financial loss
6. Unauthorized reversal of pseudonymization
7. Damage to reputation
8. Loss of confidentiality of personal data protected by professional secrecy
9. Any other significant economic or social disadvantage to the natural person concerned

**4.9.1.3 Degrees of Data Breaches** The Breach Level Index (BLI) is a project that was initiated by the foundation IT-Harvest and tries to measure the degree of severity of a data breach like how seismic waves are used to calculate the magnitude of earthquakes. BLI reporting is required in 46 US states and is presently pending in several legislations across the world, including the EU,[136] and would be relevant to briefly discuss to understand the amount of damage an organization could face.

*Step 1: Understand the Calculating Values* The BLI is based on a simple algorithm, which reads as Log10(NxtxsxA), with each letter value representing a factor that must be weighed.

**N =** The total number of records breached, or a dollar-value loss (in case of IP-based data).
  t = The type of data in the records with values which include:[137]
    1. Nuisance: E-mail adresses, affiliation, etc.
    2. Account access: Username/passwords
    3. Financial access: Bank account and card credentials
    4. Identity theft: Information that can be used to impersonate someone
    5. Existential data: Information of national security value or threatens a business
  **s =** Source of the breach with values that include:[138]
    1. Lost device
    2. Stolen device
    3. Malicious insider
    4. Malicious outsider
    5. State espionage

**A =** Action that has been used by the hacker to cause harm to the data:
    1. No action (value of 1)
    2. Publication of harmful/embarrassing information (value of 5)
    3. Impersonation to obtain funds or a loan by stolen financial credentials (value of 10)

*Step 2: Apply the Values* The algorithm is employed in a chart with the necessary data to give the BLI Score to show how secure a business may be. An illustrative example is provided below:

| Organization | Number of records breached (N) | Type of data (t) | Breach source (s) | Action (A) | BLI score |
|---|---|---|---|---|---|
| DJS Processing | 1,8000,000 | 4: SSN, Account info, DOB info. | 4: A malicious outsider | 1 | 7.5 |
| Cyber Sec LLP | 1,600,000 | 3: Financial information and access information | 4: A "hacktivist" | 10 | 8.5 |
| Gene Map LLC | 800,000 | 4: SSN, medical records and account info. | 1: A nonmalicious insider | 1 | 6.5 |

Thus, by merely applying the simple factors described above can present a fair assessment of how reliable a business may be in terms of their data protection history.

*Step 3: Categorize the Breach* Once a BLI score has been assigned by the methodology described above, Stiennon suggests that the scores be *categorized* like the Richter Scale for the broader understanding by society. The suggested format for this categorization and its meanings is shown below.

| Category | BLI Score | Characterization | Size |
|---|---|---|---|
| 5 | 9–10 | <ul><li>*Breach with an immense long-term impact.*</li><li>*Many victims and customers harmed.*</li><li>*Large amounts of sensitive data lost.*</li><li>*Huge financial costs to remedy the problem.*</li><li>*Breach notification is necessary.*</li></ul> | 10 to 100 million records lost |
| 4 | 7–8.9 | <ul><li>*Breach with significant exposure to the business.*</li><li>*Legal and regulatory impact.*</li><li>*Large amount of sensitive information lost.*</li><li>*Significant costs to remedy the issue.*</li><li>*Breach notification a must.*</li></ul> | 100,000 to 1 million records lost |

| Category | BLI Score | Characterization | Size |
|----------|-----------|------------------|------|
| 3 | 5–6.9 | • *Breach with short- to mid-term exposure with legal and regulatory impact.*<br>• *There will be some degree of financial loss.*<br>• *Some form of breach notification is necessary.* | 10,000 records or more lost |
| 2 | 3–4.9 | • *The breach has a low long-term impact.*<br>• *There is a limited breach notification and financial exposure.* | Several thousand records lost |
| 1 | 1–2.9 | • *Breach has no material effect.*<br>• *Notification required.*<br>• *Little damage done financially or legally.* | Less than 1,000 records lost |

The categorizations help businesses and lawmakers manage and supervise data breaches on a larger scale.[139] Each category requires notification and communication, which is reflected in GDPR. Despite general belief that data breaches are rare, many industry participants would argue otherwise, considering that the technologies available to hackers keep improving, leading to an increase in the frequency of data breaches. Some organizations have valuable data and face frequent attempts to breach their data security and can successfully defend the organization from damage. This should be reflected in the law and in other regulations as well; a "one size fits all" approach to data breaches is not advisable. It remains to be seen how the EU seeks to harmonize the BLI with GDPR, but it could be an effective combination.

**4.9.1.4 Types of Cyber-Threats**   Cyber-security is designed to prevent:

1. **Cyber-terrorism:** The disruption of essential services, by using technology to advance the political or ideological agendas. For example, hacking into a computer-operated dam system to flood a town.
2. **Cyber-warfare:** Where two governments use technology to propagate their agenda or stifle the independent activities of other countries. A topical example would be the allegation that Russian hackers accessed information from the Democratic National Committee's server.
3. **Cyber-espionage:** The use of information technology to obtain unauthorized access to confidential information to gain a commercial, strategic, political, economic, or military advantage over another. For example, hacking into another company's e-mails to access a trade secret.

4. **Cybercrime:** The use of technology to conduct a crime. Cybercrime is a term we have become more accustomed to over the past decade of cautionary tales. In some cases, it involves the use of technology to carry out ordinary crimes (example: A ransom-attack can be charged as a form of extortion under ordinary criminal law). Otherwise, cybercrime is a separate category of crimes that have been described by statute (example: online bullying, child pornography, and phishing).

While the first two varieties of security threats are larger and dealt with on a state-to-state level, beyond the scope of GDPR, the third and fourth are the most commonly referred to when it comes to personal data. Cyber-terrorism and warfare rarely relate to personal data as they are aimed toward more strategic targets. It is here that identifying the type of data processed and applying proportional security measures is key,[140] as the amount of protection cascades down in the operations mentioned above, using the nature of the personal data as the barometer for protection.

**4.9.1.5 Practically Implementing Cyber-Security**  Cyber-security has been more broadly discussed under the regulation as "security of processing" and as one of the key duties of the DPO. In terms of GDPR, it can be defined as the technical and organizational measures implemented by the Controller to combat any risk posed to the processing of personal data. GDPR mandates cyber-security in any processing operation subject to the regulation. There are several ways of addressing cyber-security in practical terms:

1. Implementing cyber-security measures and making the Controller/Processor responsible for its integrity[141]
2. Appointing a DPO and providing him resources (such as a cyber-security wing) in-house
3. Hiring a third-party contractor as the DPO (such as contracting a cyber-security firm for operations)
4. Conducting regular cyber-security educational seminars for the entire operation, led by the DPO

Though a DPO is not required in every circumstance,[142] it is advisable to hire/designate someone qualified to act as the organization's DPO. This assists in streamlining compliance, especially if the cyber-security is done in-house.

**4.9.1.6 Combating Cyber-Security Threats**  While there are diverse methodologies for combating cyber-attacks, the most common modes of executing the security of processing are:

1. **Software and programs** for cyber-security, such as those provided by IBM and Microsoft. Implementing such programs is more suitable for those processing operations that deal with less-sensitive data.

2. **Application security** is the protection provided to apps for cyber-attacks. These require a secure coding (data protection by design) and subsequent testing in the form of *fuzzing* and *penetration testing*.[143]

3. For larger businesses that operate across several platforms, a **network security** system that protects data across the entire organization would be recommended. This requires regular oversight.

4. Like network security, **cloud security** systems protect the data stored across several media and platforms. Strong cloud security requires robust network integrity, as a result these two types of protection require comprehensive due diligence. Furthermore, cloud security systems require greater understanding of individual access habits[144] for effective use.

The methods vary in their degree of protection, oversight, and efficiency and can be implemented in a variety of ways. These fall under the older "point product" approach of cyber-security, where each individual business oversees maintaining the security of processing by any mode they deem fit.[145] This tends to be inefficient as different types of protection are needed across various types of data and processing, leading to an accumulation of cyber-security mechanisms. An alternative to this would be implementing a security operating platform that provides prevention-based detection across the end-point, the data centers, the networks, clouds, and SaaS[146] environments.[147] This is undertaken by use of AI, which creates a system architecture that reduces the attack surfaces, increases visibility of activity across platforms, and provides a quick response mechanism to any threats.[148] This would be an ideal mechanism for larger, cross-border processing operations.

### 4.9.1.7 Breach Response Plan

In cases of a "digital" emergency, organizations should consider the following *breach response* measures:[149]

1. Identify the area affected.
2. Prevent further unauthorized use or disclosure of the data.
3. Preserve relevant evidence.
4. Clarify which data categories have been attacked.
5. Confirm who knows about the incident inside and outside the organization.
6. Investigate indications of future threat or harm.

Apart from these, there are several other practices a data collection organization can follow to prevent threats to cyber-security including:

- Restricting employee access to certain categories of data
- Segmentation of critical data
- Implementing a system of "user permissions" to give greater power to the users
- Implementing a policy and system of "notification" to the users in the event of a breach
- Ensuring that a system is in place to preserve any vulnerable data in the event of an attack

**4.9.1.8 Manual versus Automated Cyber-Security**   In the past, cyber-security practices required manual intervention to combat any potential attacks. This was done
by way of employing an effective cyber-security firm, or a CTO to take over the
situation if the attack was excessive and required immediate attention. However,
as automated processing and AI continuously evolve and grow, they will be the
future of cyber-security. This is because:[150]

1. AI can effectively correlate data and identify the sensitivities and vulnerabilities by assigning values while providing the algorithm. This helps to prevent
   attacks and identify weak spots effectively.
2. Automation can be used to generate and implement protections faster than a
   cyber-attack. As the machine keeps learning and operating, it will be able to
   locate vulnerabilities and build protections for it before or during an attack.
   As no manual intervention would be needed, the protections can be built and
   applied rapidly to stave off any attacks.

The growth of automated cyber-security technology is promising, but in no way
imply that the "human" aspect of cyber-security can be removed under GDPR.
The regulation mandates that AI cannot be used to make legal or significant
decisions regarding the data subject. Furthermore, the responsibility of secure
processing is on the DPO and Controller/Processor, and they cannot detach
themselves from that responsibility by using AI. It can be safely concluded that
even if a processing operation implements state of the art automation in their
cyber-security efforts, it will still require manual oversight and intervention for
full compliance.

**4.9.1.9 Cyber-Security Insurance**   In addition to certifications and approved codes
of conduct,[151] a smart business practice for any data-processing activity would be
to procure insurance against potential attacks. This is done by way of securing a
cyber-insurance policy that covers the envisaged damages in the case of a breach.

Traditionally, cyber-insurance was limited to covering specific types of breaches
in limited circumstances. Over the past decade policies have become comprehensive, covering the costs of litigation, money damages, reputation damages, compensation to users, etc. Cyber-insurance is a growing industry with a wide variety
of coverage models and legal issues of its own. Most policies cover costs/damages
relating to:

- Hacking
- Loss or damage of computer data
- Identity theft, fraud, theft of data
- Ransom attacks
- Digital forensic investigations
- Business interruptions
- Litigation costs in cyber-security operations

Conditions of coverage would depend on negotiated insurance coverage between the business and the insurance provider. Though GDPR does not address cyber-insurance, businesses would be wise to purchase to cover their liability.

This raises an intriguing issue about the future of the insurance industry. With the fines of GDPR well known, we can anticipate a shift in the terms of insurance policies, specifically the coverage of these policies to fit the amounts mandated by Article 83 of the regulation. The fines are well known for being deterrents to breaches of GDPR, and may lead to a shift in the circumstances, requirements, premiums, and coverage amount given to businesses in the EU.

Another interrelated issue would be impleading the insurance carriers into a GDPR lawsuit. The regulation does not provide for mechanisms to attach the insurance provider into any complaints or lawsuits filed against them, which would lead to the conclusion that domestic Member State law regarding impleading parties would be operative. But if the fines and punishments listed under GDPR are meant to be a deterrent, the court could decide to make the Controller/Processor himself pay it. Otherwise, a data-collection entity is less likely to be GDPR compliant as it would know that likely fines would be covered by insurance. and is less affected by the punishment imposed.

While the finer points of cyber-insurance and GDPR remain to be resolved, it is evident that carriers will have a prominent role in the future of the data-processing industry. Cyber-insurance generally has a "GDPR Endorsement clause," suggesting that their policies fit into this new legal regime.

### 4.9.2   The Controller's Duty to Notify

GDPR does not provide for how data breaches must be tackled but elaborates on how the Controller and Processor must proceed forward. The preceding duties of data protection by design and data security effectively hold the Controller accountable for the ongoing integrity of the data-processing operations, while Article 33 elaborates what must be done in the worst case scenarios. GDPR provides a two-prong duty to notify the SA and communicate the breach to the user within set time frame.

When a data breach has taken place, the Controller shall, without undue delay, and where feasible *no later than 72 hours* of becoming aware of the incident, must notify the competent SA[152] of the incident. The WP29 considers that a Controller should be regarded as having become "aware" when he has a reasonable degree of certainty that a security incident has occurred that has led to personal data being compromised. This will depend on the circumstances of the specific breach.[153] If the Controller cannot meet this deadline of 72 hours, he must report reasons for their delay.[154] Similarly, if such a breach occurs to the Processor, they must notify the Controller without undue delay.

The fact that the notification was made without undue delay should be considered with the nature and gravity of the personal data breach and its consequences or adverse effects to the data subject.[155]

**4.9.2.1 Excusable Delays**   A single data attack can qualify as a breach and must be notified within 72 hours. However, the WP29 Opinion on Data Breach Notification stipulates that the Controller may be excused from this deadline under extraordinary circumstances where damage control precludes timely notification to the SA. **Example:** multiple, repeated attacks within a short span of time. GDPR in such cases permits the Controller to submit a *bundled notification*, which details all the attacks made in one consolidated report, provided in phases[156] accompanied by reasons for the delay.

   **Illustration:** WebBank.com is an online banking platform with all the measures in place to be GDPR compliant. On Christmas day, their Data Processor Digi-Sphere encountered multiple, coordinated DoS attacks on their firewall and security systems. Immediately the DPO was contacted and their in-house cyber-security team were defending the data against the attacks. After 24 hours, the attacks were staved off, and the operations were put to repair. As the DPO and CEO of Digi-Sphere were writing their joint e-mail to WebBank.com, the attacks resumed in much greater force. These attacks persisted on and off for three more days. The cyber-security team could not protect the loss of some data but had effectively saved the operation from a complete shut-down. The Processor "bundles" the 87 attacks experienced into one report, and forwards it to the Controller, who then sends the report to the SA, along with the reasons for the delay. The Controller and Processor have acted in accordance with GDPR.

**4.9.2.2 Contents of Notification**   When dispatching the notification of data breach to the SA, the Controller must:[157]

1. Describe the nature of the breach.
2. Describe the categories and approximate number of data subjects and personal data records concerned.
3. Communicate the name and contact details of the DPO or other applicable contact point to receive the relevant information.
4. Describe the likely consequences of the breach.
5. Describe the remedial and mitigating measures proposed to be taken to address the breach and its adverse effects.

   Thus, continuing our earlier WebBank.com illustration, a simplified notice to the SA would read as follows:

1. On December 25, 2018, WebBank.com's data processing partner Digi-Sphere underwent a massive DoS attack, starting at 11:28 p.m. until 3:25 p.m. on the 29th of December. (There have been 87 such attacks, all listed in Appendix 1.)
2. The personal data lost in the defense of this attack are names, e-mail addresses, and passwords of 1,000 users across Germany.

3. For more information, documents, or answers to any questions you may have, please contact our DPO, Mr. Lau (e-mail, phone number, address).
4. The consequence of this breach is the likely abuse of these 1,000 user for fraudulently conducting banking services on their behalf.
5. The 1,000 affected accounts have been red-flagged; the users have been informed and requested to create a new password and account. If those accounts are used in the future, our cyber-security team will be notified. Also, we are acting to locate these remote hackers, with the help of the German Technological Police Division and our Cyber Security wing.

The report submitted by the Controller must also document any personal data breaches, with the relevant facts relating to the breach and the measures taken.[158] The examples given above are simplified, where in real life it would provide as many details to the SA as possible to reduce further investigation of compliance. It is expected that the EU or Member States will make their own guidelines for the format of the notification, and GDPR mandates that "due consideration" must be given to:

- Circumstances of the breach.
- Whether or not personal data had been protected by appropriate technical protection measures.
- Do those measures effectively limit the likelihood of identity fraud or other forms of misuse?
- Do the measures consider the legitimate interests of law-enforcement authorities where early disclosure could unnecessarily hamper the investigation of the circumstances of a personal data breach?[159]

**4.9.2.3 Exception** The notification duty is exempted if the personal data breach is unlikely to result in risk to the rights and freedoms of natural persons.[160] The use of the term "natural persons" rather than "data subjects" expands the scope of harm felt to any person who may be affected by the breach, instead of merely the users who provide their data. At the same time, it remains true to the objectives of GDPR, as any damage caused to the Controller/Processor/any other Business entity is irrelevant for the purposes of this regulation.

**Illustration 1:** WebBank.com undergoes a "phishing" attack and valuable personal and financial data is stolen from them. The data is encrypted, secured, and cannot be read without the confidential security key, which was not stolen by the hackers. Without the key, the data is unintelligible and useless. Though this was a data breach, the Controller does not have a duty to inform the SA as no risk is posed to the rights and freedoms of any natural persons.[161]

**Illustration 2:** The commercial banking wing of WebBank.com faces a large data breach resulting in the loss of important financial details of their corporate clients. Though this is a data breach, the Controller does not have a duty to notify the SA under GDPR. It does not apply to this breach as no "personal data" is involved, only the data of companies. As a result, the Controller would have to be liable under another law to act.

### 4.9.3 Controller's Duty to Communicate the Breach to Data Subjects

**4.9.3.1 A Timely Communication**   Under GDPR, the Controller is answerable to two main bodies: the SA and their data subjects. Therefore, in an event of a data breach, the Controller must continue this tradition by communicating the details of that breach to the users without undue delay. This must be done when there is high risk to their rights and freedoms. No specific time period is provided under GDPR to qualify what a "reasonable period" is to inform users. However, it is explained that the determination must be made by the Controller as soon as *reasonably feasible* and with close cooperation with the SA, respecting the guidance given.[162]

For example, a Processor who has undergone continuous, persistent attacks would not be expected to report immediately, while a Processor who has undergone one attack three weeks ago would be liable to communicate the breach to the users sooner. Regardless, the SA must be brought into the loop before the users. As a result, the Processor, Controller, and SA must work in tandem to handle the communication of the breach to the user.

**4.9.3.2 Contents of the Communication**   This section resembles the earlier notice requirements to the Controller, excluding only the first few details regarding the nature of the breach and the categories of data hacked. Therefore, the Controller must at least communicate:

1. The name and contact details of the DPO or other applicable contact point to receive the relevant information
2. The likely consequences of the breach
3. The remedial and mitigating measures proposed to be taken to address the breach and its adverse effects

These contents are the bare minimum standard that a Controller may communicate to the users. This communication must be provided in plain terms and clearly state what the adverse effects on the data subject will be[163] provided specific information on how the user can protect himself.[164]

A question arises: Why is the Controller not obliged to inform the users of the nature of the attack and the data lost? Is it because it would be impractical, or because it may hurt the long-term commercial interests of these Data Processors? On the one hand, an isolated data breach shouldn't have to be accompanied by all the details, but it would be advisable to have a well-informed base of data subjects (or on their right to information)? This exception provides a certain amount of leeway for Controller entities to manage their PR and tailer certain crucial facts when presenting the breach to the public.

**4.9.3.3 Exceptions** Communication to users is not necessary if the following conditions are met: [165]

1. Technical and organizational methods were implemented to ensure that the stolen data is unintelligible or protected from those who stole it, e.g. encryption.
2. Subsequent measures have been implemented by the Controller to ensure that any risk posed is unlikely to materialize.
3. Communicating with data subjects would be a disproportionate effort. GDPR permits public announcements in such situations. **Example:** A social media website with millions of users who are victim of data breaches (such as Facebook in the Cambridge Analytica scandal) are likely to undergo a disproportionate effort to send personalized notices to each affected user.

The exceptions given above are broader than the singular "no harm caused" exception to notifying the SA. This builds into the commercial objectives of the regulation as there would be no need for public outrage if the relevant authorities are informed and no harm is likely to be caused. If the Controller has not informed the users, it is up to the SA to determine whether the data subjects need to be informed and whether an exception can be claimed.[166]

The notification and communication duties under GDPR are based on history. In the past, companies have taken unduly long time periods to report breaches. For example, the widely known data breaches faced by large companies such as Yahoo!, Ebay, and Equifax were all a result of insufficient data protection, coupled with very late communication to the public. Equifax in 2017 took over two months[36] to report its momentous data breach to the public. GDPR seeks to curb the culture of secrecy by first holding the Controllers accountable for the safety of the data, second, having them react quickly to such attacks, and lastly requiring the Controller to be transparent if it does occur, in order to increase accountability.

## 4.10 Codes of Conduct and Certifications

### 4.10.1 Purpose and Relationship under GDPR

Once a business is compliant under the regulation, the next step would be to *advertise* that fact to the public through codes of conduct and certifications. These are monitored by independent bodies who essentially "vouch" for compliance by marking their approval over a company's processing activities. This serves several purposes:

- Signifies to the public that the business is GDPR compliant
- Informs the SA that an independent body has regularly checked on the company's processing operations
- Is a valuable factor in deciding proof of compliance in the event of a lawsuit or complaint filed against the company

### 4.10.2 Codes of Conduct

In addition to numerous bodies established under GDPR to regulate the processing of personal data, there are a series of devices used to control the entities responsible for those activities. We see its application in the requirement of mandatory contractual clauses between the Controller and Processor[167] and devices like certification, described below. Similarly, considering the needs of small and medium enterprises and the sectors of processing, additional codes of conduct may be drawn up by:

1. Member States
2. The board
3. The commission
4. The supervisory authorities
5. Associations of Controllers and Processors[168]

These delegated legislations providing for codes of conduct (codes) contribute to the overall application of GDPR by regulating the extent of processing that can be carried out. Like the certification mechanisms discussed in detail below, these codes of conduct may be used by processing, which falls outside of the scope of GDPR,[169] or for transfers of data to third countries or international organizations by way of legally binding instruments.[170] However, while certification acts as evidence of compliance from an independent entity, codes are specifications for compliance given by an organization or authority.[171]

**4.10.2.1 Codes of Conduct by Associations**  Just as larger corporations can create codes of conduct, associations and other bodies representing Controllers or Processors may prepare/amend/extend codes of conduct to comply with GDPR regarding:[172]

1. Fair and transparent processing
2. Legitimate interests pursued in the specific processing conducted by associated entities
3. The collection of personal data
4. The pseudonymization of data
5. The information provided to the public and the users
6. The exercise of data subject rights
7. The information provided to children, the protection of their data, and the manner of receiving parental consent
8. Responsibility of the Controller
9. Data protection and security measures
10. The notification of data breaches to SA and the users
11. Transfer of data to any third Country or international organizations
12. Out-of-court and dispute resolution procedures implemented to resolve any conflict between users and the Controller[173]
13. Mechanisms for monitoring compliance with GDPR[174]

It is likely that the development of sector- or technology-based codes of conduct between groups of Controllers will be adopted as association codes of conduct grow.[175] In situations where such associations create codes of conduct, the draft/extension/amendment must be submitted to the relevant SA, who then provides an opinion or approves of the codes if it finds that they provide appropriate safeguards.[176] Where the codes of conduct fall under the ambit of one SA, he shall register and publish the code after approval.[177] However, if multiple authorities are concerned with the codes, they shall approve the codes or provide opinions in accordance with their consistency mechanism.[178] Subsequently, the SA will approve the codes, publish them, and create a register of codes provided, which shall be made public.[179] An important point to note is that once these codes have been approved by the SA consistency mechanism board, it will have a general validity throughout the EU.[180]

### 4.10.2.2 Monitoring Approved Codes of Conduct

Once approved, compliance with the codes is monitored either by the SA or an independent party who has an appropriate level of expertise in relation to the subject matter of the code and is *accredited* for that purpose by the competent SA.[181] Public authorities are *not* subject to this requirement of monitoring,[182] and the scope is restricted to private parties who may decide to take such monitoring measures. Like accrediting certifying bodies under GDPR, a body may be accredited to monitor the compliance with the codes of conduct if:

1. They have demonstrated independence and expertise in relation to the subject matter of the code to the satisfaction of the SA.
2. Established procedures to assess eligibility of Data Collectors to apply the codes.
3. Established procedures for monitoring compliance and periodic review of the operation.
4. Established procedures for dealing with infringements of the code, and to enforce user Rights in accordance with GDPR.
5. They have demonstrated that the tasks and duties do not create a conflict of interest.

All the above must be shown to the satisfaction of the SA to receive accreditation.[183] The SA in the exercise of its powers and subject to its consistency mechanism may create a draft criterion for accreditation.[184] The SA has the power to revoke this accreditation for any subsequent infringement of the required criteria above.[185]

The Monitoring Body also has the power to take appropriate action when there has been an infringement of the codes,[186] including suspension or exclusion of the culpable Controller or Processor who breaches the code. They also have the power to report the responsible Controller/Processor to the SA in the event of a breach. It should be noted that codes do not have binding legal effect and merely act as a sign of "self-monitoring" compliance with the regulation. Thus, the efficacy of such codes is purely dependent on the implementation of the specifications within the entity/association itself.

### 4.10.3 Certification

GDPR creates instruments through which compliance can be proven. As mentioned earlier, certification can be an element to demonstrate compliance[187] or provide sufficient guarantees.[188] Like a certification mark that is placed on a good or service, the regulation places similar mechanisms for the practice of data protection. This is given by a "Certification Body" under GDPR.

**4.10.3.1 Certification Bodies**  A Supervisory Authority is the sole entity that regulates any potential certification body[189] and has the power to issue, renew, and revoke the accreditation of these bodies. A certification body with an appropriate level of expertise[190] relating to data protection may petition an SA to exercise its powers of issuance or renewal. This may only be allowed by Member States if they have been accredited by one or both of the following:

1. A competent SA[191]
2. A national accreditation body in accordance with:
   a. Regulation (EC) No 756/2008 of the EU Parliament[192]
   b. EN-ISO/IEC 17065/2012 of the EU Council
   c. Any additional requirements given by the local SA[193]

Thus, we can see that such independent bodies operate under the validation of law through a regulatory agency under GDPR, subjecting them to scrutiny.

**4.10.3.2 Factors for Granting Accreditation to Certification Bodies**  The above seals of approval by the SA and EU bodies are given only when the certification bodies have:

1. Demonstrated their independence and expertise to the satisfaction of the SA with regard to the subject matter of certification
2. Undertaken the criteria to receive a European Data Protection Seal, which is a common certification issued by the SA and EU Data Protection Board[194]
3. Established procedures for issuance, periodic review, and revocation of data protection certification/marks/seals given
4. Established procedures to handle complaints regarding the infringement and implementation of the seals given to the Controller and Processor, and transparency of those procedures and structures to the data subjects and public
5. Demonstrated to the SA that their tasks and duties do not cause any conflicts of interest

The final criteria will be determined by the SA or by the EU data protection board depending on the nature of the accreditation given.[195] The accreditation of these bodies shall be valid for a period of five years with an option to renew, provided that the certifying bodies comply with the regulation.[196] On infringement of the provisions of GDPR, the SA has authority to revoke any accreditation given.[197]

The SAs are responsible for making the criteria for accreditation public in an easily accessible form and transmitting those requirements to the EU Data Protection Board. It is then the responsibility of the Data Protection Board to create a comprehensive, public register of these requirements and the marks/seals/certifications in existence.[198]

**Illustration:** Cyber Sec LLP has been certified by a Blue Star, Triple Protection seal, which has been certified by Tech Cert. Tech Cert has been approved by the SA of several jurisdictions, with their established procedures approved by the consistency mechanism, and registered. They have also been certified in accordance to Regulation (EC) No 756/2008. The seal given to Cyber Sec certifies that they follow the highest level of data-security practices and submit themselves to an annual web audit by Tech Cert.

### 4.10.3.3 Responsibilities of Certification Bodies

The certification bodies are responsible for ensuring that a proper assessment is given before granting, renewing, or revoking certification,[199] but this is done without prejudice to the Controller/Processor's responsibilities under GDPR. When carrying out any certification or decertification, the certifying body must provide the SA with reasons for such grant or rejection.[200]

### 4.10.3.4 The Certification Mechanisms

GDPR stipulates that the SA and other EU/ Member bodies shall encourage the establishment of certification mechanisms, data protection seals, and marks so that Controllers and Processors may demonstrate their compliance with the regulation.[201] These certification mechanisms can also be used for data collection bodies that are not subject to GDPR,[202] or for transfers of personal data to third countries or international organizations.[203] This can be done by way of enforceable instruments such as contractual clauses or other legally binding methods. Further criteria and requirements may be provided by the EU commission by way of delegated acts.[204] Additionally, the EU Commission may specify technical standards for certification, marks, seals, and further promote the recognition of such devices.[205]

It is important to remember that certification is not mandatory but voluntary.[206] That is because certification is not proof of compliance but is only helpful evidence of the fact.[207] Thus, Controllers and Processors cannot avoid their responsibilities under GDPR by simply receiving a certification; rather it is used as a mechanism to reduce the burden of proving compliance to the SA should an investigation ever be initiated.

**Illustration:** A complaint is filed against Cyber Sec LLP before the local SA stating that inadequate oversight is given to the processing operations they conduct. The Triple Protection Seal will help rebut the initial presumption that the security measures are inadequate, but an SA may find otherwise after investigation and the seal would not in itself prevent such a conclusion.

When applying for certification, the Controller/Processor is required to provide full transparency to the certifying body, which is necessary to carry out their functions.[208] This would include providing all the information and access needed to their processing activities to conduct the certification procedure. Once granted, the certification will be valid for a period of three years and may be renewed if the necessary requirements are met. Similarly, certification may be withdrawn by either the certification body or the SA if the Data Collectors fail to meet the requirements.[209] To simplify:

- Certification is evidence of compliance with GDPR.
- Certification may be given by bodies who are accredited by either the SA or the EU Data Protection Board.
- Certification is granted after a full, transparent investigation by the certifying body of the processing operation conducted.
- This investigation is conducted in line with their established procedures (of the certifying body) submitted to the SA.
- Once granted, certification is valid for a period of three years with an option of renewal.
- The reasons for grant/rejection must be submitted to the SA.

Certifications are not new to the Data Protection industry as well-known marks such as ISO27k and Stampery have existed to show proof of credibility. Certification is not an instrument of accountability, but one of simplification. This voluntary mechanism is a way to help demonstrate compliance to this complicated data protection regulation by having the stamp of approval of an independent, disinterested third party.

## 4.11   The Data Processor

The collection and processing of personal data are often a concerted effort between entities governed by contract and business relationships. Unlike a Controller, however, the Processor's handling of the personal data of many is not borne through consent or legal justification; rather, it is based on its involvement with the Controller's operations.[210]

### 4.11.1   Relationship between Processor and Controller

As discussed earlier in this chapter, the Processor acts on behalf of the Controller in the processing of personal data. Like a Controller, the Processor can be a:

- Natural person
- Legal entity
- Public authority
- Public agency
- Other Body

Therefore, the Controller is the one determining the purposes and means of processing, and the Processor is the one who carries out the objectives. The Processor carries out activities under the instructions of the Controller, and GDPR specifies detailed criteria on how those instructions should be delivered. However, if the Processor infringes GDPR by determining the purposes and means of processing, he shall be treated as a Controller for the purposes of the regulation.[211] The distinction between the two types of actors under GDPR can be drawn by looking at the following criteria:[212]

1. Freedom from instructions as to the objectives of the data processing
2. Merging of data received upon delegation with the entity's own database
3. Use of the data for the entity's own purpose that may not have been agreed upon with the contracting party
4. Creation of legal relationship between the Data Collectors and the data subjects permitting the processing
5. Responsibility of the entity for the accuracy and lawfulness of processing

**Illustration:** A reality TV show, *Rail-Road*, has its competitors compete in intense physical and mental challenges over a period of two months, starting the competition with 40 players until they are down to the final winner of £3 million. Keeping in mind the grueling nature of the competition, the show runners keep a detailed database of their contestants' medical, psychological, domestic, and social details to manage their liability and ensure the safety of the contestants. To collect this information and create a "RR Database," the network, SATTV, enlists the services of a data-processing company, Cyber Pros LLP. SATTV here would be the Controller as they determine the purposes and means of processing, while Cyber Pros LLP would be the Processor, carrying out the activities under their instructions.

### 4.11.2 Responsibilities of Controller in Selecting a Processor

**4.11.2.1 Sufficient Guarantees**  Carrying on the "theme" of accountability that GDPR seeks to achieve, a Processor may only carry out processing on behalf of the Controller if they provide sufficient guarantees that they will implement appropriate technical and organizational measures to ensure:[213]

- Compliance with the requirements of GDPR
- Protection of the user's rights

Thus, just as a Controller must demonstrate their compliance to the SA, the Processor must do so to the Controller. In turn, Controllers are responsible for only hiring Processors who give such guarantees.

**4.11.2.2 Maintaining Processing Contracts**  GDPR has taken a step to regulate the contracts entered into between the Controller and Processor by mandating that certain clauses should be incorporated into their agreement. This is either by the

EU or Member State stipulating to the terms of the contract, or by the parties including the terms as part of their agreement. The regulation mandates that processing activities shall be governed by a law or a contract regarding the Controller which would broadly cover:

1. Subject matter of processing
2. Duration of processing
3. Nature and purpose of processing
4. The types of personal data
5. Categories of data subjects
6. The obligations and rights of the Controller

These requirements are supplemented by more specific clauses to ensure compliance with the regulation.

**4.11.2.3 Standard Contractual Clauses**  The legal measures above may also be implemented by way of using a "standard contractual clauses," which can provided by:

- A Supervisory Authority in accordance to a "consistency mechanism" measure[214]
- The EU Commission, by way of a delegated act[215]
- A certification granted[216]

These Standard Contractual clauses are an alternative way of imposing these mandatory terms upon the data-collection bodies. As a result, GDPR ensures implementation of the important terms between Processor and Controller by use of legal authority through contract or standard contractual terms to ensure that no party may evade accountability under the regulation.

### 4.11.3   Duties of the Processor

1. **Documented instructions:** The Processor may only carry out activities under the documented instructions of the Controller, which is essentially a restatement of the requirement of "general" or "specific" written authorization.[217] The Processor must follow these instructions to the letter, and this would include rules relating to third-country transfers and transfers to international organizations.

   Processor must also inform the Controller of any legal requirements placed on their processing, unless the law prohibits them from doing so. Even urgent oral instructions must be later documented without delay to avoid liability.[218]
2. **Confidentiality:** The Processor and anyone else authorized to process must be bound by a confidentiality clause during their activities. Otherwise, they must commit themselves to any statutory duty of confidentiality.

3. The Processor must take all security measures imposed under the Regulation.[219]
4. Follow the rules of subprocessing or subcontracting their responsibilities in line with GDPR.
5. Implementation of appropriate technical and organizational measures to assist the Controller in enforcing the user's rights. This must be done considering the nature of the processing and to the extent that such measures would be possible.[220]
6. **Ensuring compliance:** Considering the nature of the processing and information collected, the Processor must assist the Controller in ensuring compliance with the security of the personal data in accordance with GDPR.
7. **Termination of processing:** At the discretion of the Controller, the Processor must return or delete all personal data at the end of the provision of processing services. The Processor must also delete any copies that he may have of the data unless EU or Member law requires its storage.
8. **Assisting with demonstration:** The Processor must also assist the Controller in demonstrating compliance regarding his obligations under GDPR. This includes contributing to web audits and inspections initiated by the Controller or any other auditor authorized by him. This can be viewed as a complimentary duty to that of the Controller's duty to demonstrate.[221]
9. **Evidence of demonstration:** Once again, GDPR draws a parallel between the responsibilities of the Controller and Processor by stipulating that approved codes of conduct and certification can be used as an element to prove that sufficient guarantees were given by the Processor.[222]
10. **Authorized processing:** Individuals who are responsible for processing (such as the employees) under the authority of the Controller or Processor shall not process data unless:
    a. They have received instructions from the Controller; or
    b. Are required to do so under EU or Member law.[223]

**Illustration:** Continuing our earlier case of the *Rail-Road* show, let us consider that Cyber Pros LLP works with a series of different Subprocessors owing to the diversity of data collected. Cyber Pros generally contracts out its processing work to its sister company Cyber Sec LLP, which is also a cyber-security firm. However, medical data is collected directly from the patients and is processed by Healthee Data Inc., a company that specializes in processing and analyzing biometric and genetic information. Healthee Data Inc. has over 100 employees carrying out the processing for SATTV and Cyber Pros. One of the supervisory employees is persuaded by a contestant to change his records from "smoker" to "nonsmoker" to increase his chances of participation. The employee succumbs to the pressure and alters the data. This is illegal processing under GDPR, as it was not authorized by either the Controller or Processor.

### 4.11.4 Subprocessors

Under GDPR, there is a de facto prohibition against the Processor "subcontracting" or "subprocessing" the work assigned to him by the Controller. [224] This is only permitted when the Controller gives specific or general written authorization of the engagement. If the authorization is general, the Controller must be informed of any intended changes or replacement of Subprocessors, and be given the opportunity to object to any such changes.

Additionally, Subprocessors that carry out specific processing activities are subject to the same mandatory contractual terms/legal requirements that the Processors are. This would include providing sufficient guarantees that the Subprocessor will implement appropriate technical and organizational measures to ensure compliance with GDPR. If the Subprocessor fails to carry out his responsibilities, the Processor himself will remain directly liable to the Controller for the failure. [225]

Continuing our previous illustration: Cyber Pro's arrangements with Cyber Sec LLP and Healthee Data Inc. are put into writing and given to SATTV along with detailed reports of protection and compliance measures in place. SATTV agrees to the guarantees, and they conclude a firm contract with Cyber Pros LLP.

- Cyber Pros LLP remains the Processor.
- Cyber Sec LLP has a general written authorization to process by the Controller, SATTV.
- Healthee Data Inc. has a specific written authorization to process the biometric and genetic data of the participants.
- If there is any change in this arrangement, SATTV must be informed and given a chance to object.
- If Healthee Data or Cyber Sec fail to comply with GDPR, Cyber Pros LLP will remain liable to SATTV.

## Notes

1 *Note:* Any "legal person" carrying out activities on behalf of the Controller or Processor under GDPR must *assign a "Representative" who* can be held accountable.
2 GDPR, Articles 13 and 14.
3 GDPR, Article 27.
4 GDPR, Article 4.7.
5 GDPR, Article 4.7.
6 GDPR, Article 24.1.
7 GDPR, Article 24.2.
8 GDPR, Article 25.
9 See Sections 4.7 and 4.8.

10  GDPR, Article 40.

11  GDPR, Article 42.

12  GDPR, Article 26.

13  *Note:* "Both" does not mandate that Joint Controllers are restricted to only two per organization.

14  GDPR, Article 2.2.1

15  Article 29 Working Party, WP 169 (2010), p. 19.

16  Ibid.

17  GDPR, Article 13, 14.

18  GDPR, Article 13.1.a, 14.1.a.

19  GDPR, Article 26.2.

20  GDPR, Article 26.3.

21  GDPR, Article 82.

22  GDPR, Article 82.

23  GDPR, Article 82.5.

24  Section 2.3.

25  GDPR, Article 27.

26  This is the jurisdiction where the goods and services are offered *or* where the behavior is being monitored.

27  GDPR, Article 27.4.

28  GDPR, Article 27.5.

29  GDPR, Article 26.3.

30  GDPR, Article 27.2.

31  GDPR, Article 31: "… and, where applicable their **representatives** …"

32  For example, GDPR, Article 30.4.

33  GDPR, Article 31.

34  GDPR, Article 83.4.

35  Glenn Fleishman, "Equifax Data Breach, One Year Later: Obvious Errors and No Real Changes, New Report Says", Fortune, September 7th 2018, https://fortune.com/2018/09/07/equifax-data-breach-one-year-anniversary/

36  GDPR, Article 32.1.

37  GDPR, Article 32.2.

38  GDPR, Recital 75.

39  Network Information and Security Directive, (EU) 2016/1148.

40  Network Information and Security Directive, (EU) 2016/1148, Recital 49, 57.

41  Network Information and Security Directive, (EU) 2016/1148, Article 5 and Annex II.

42  Network Information and Security Directive, (EU) 2016/1148, Article 4 and Annex III.

43  GDPR, Article 30, 30.2.

44  GDPR, Article 30.1.d: "including recipients of third countries or international organizations."

45  GDPR, Article 30.1.f; "*where possible,* the envisaged."

46  GDPR, Article 30.1.g; "*where possible,* a general description."

47  GDPR, Article 30.3.

48  GDPR, Article 30.4.
49  GDPR, Article 30.2.
50  GDPR, Article 30.2.a: *"**where applicable**, of the Controller or Processor's representative."*
51  GDPR, Article 30.2.d: *"**where possible**, a general description."*
52  GDPR, Article 30.3.
53  GDPR, Article 30.4.
54  GDPR, Article 35.2.
55  GDPR, Recital 84.
56  GDPR, Article 35.1.
57  GDPR, Recital 92; "For example where public authorities or bodies intend to *establish a common application or processing platform* or where several Controllers plan to introduce a *common application or processing environment across an industry sector or segment or for a widely used horizontal activity.*"
58  GDPR, Article 35.8.
59  GDPR, Article 35.3.
60  GDPR, Article 9.1.
61  GDPR, Article 10.
62  GDPR, Article 35, Recital 91: "A data protection impact assessment is equally required for monitoring publicly accessible areas on a large scale, especially when using optic-electronic devices or for any other operations where the competent supervisory authority considers that the processing is likely to result in a high risk to the rights and freedoms of data subjects, *in particular because they prevent data subjects from exercising a right or using a service or a contract*, or because they are carried out systematically on a large scale."
63  GDPR, Recital 91: "This should in particular apply to large-scale processing operations which aim to process a considerable amount of personal data at regional, national or supranational level and which could affect a large number of data subjects and which are likely to result in a high risk, *for example, on account of their sensitivity, where in accordance with the achieved state of technological knowledge a new technology* is used on a large scale as well as to other processing operations which result in a high risk to the rights and freedoms of data subjects, *in particular where those operations render it more difficult for data subjects to exercise their rights.*"
64  GDPR, Article 35.10: Member State law may require that a DPIA be conducted in addition to the GIA as per Article 36.5.
65  GDPR, Recital 91.
66  GDPR, Recital 75.
67  GDPR, Article 84.
68  GDPR, Article 35.7.
69  GDPR, Article 35.9.
70  GDPR, Article 35.11.
71  GDPR, Article 36.
72  GDPR, Article 36.1.
73  GDPR, Article 36.3.

74  GDPR, Recital 95.

75  GDPR, Article 36.2.

76  GDPR, Article 58.

77  GDPR, Article 58.3.

78  GDPR, Article 58.3.

79  GDPR, Article 58.2.

80  GDPR, Article 58.2.

81  GDPR, Article 58.1.

82  GDPR, Article 58.2.

83  GDPR, Article 36.

84  GDPR, Article 35.4.

85  GDPR, Article 35.5; this responsibility is **optional**, as the term "may" has been used.

86  GDPR, Article 36.4, Recital 96.

87  GDPR, Article 1.

88  Lothar Determann, *Determann's Field Guide to Data Privacy Law,* 3rd ed. (Edward Elgar Publishing), 9.

89  GDPR, Article 37.4.

90  GDPR, Recital 97.

91  GDPR, Article 37.2.

92  GDPR, Article 37.3.

93  GDPR, Article 37.4.

94  GDPR, Article 37.6.

95  GDPR, Article 37.7.

96  Paul Voigt and Axel von dem Bussche, *The EU GDPR; A Practical Guide* (Springer, 2017), 57.

97  The Controller (SATTV), Processor (Cyber Pros LLP) and the two Subprocessors (Cyber Sec LLP and Healthee Data Inc).

98  GDPR, Article 38.

99  Pursuant to GDPR, Article 39.

100  GDPR, Article 38.

101  GDPR, Article 39.

102  GDPR, Article 36; see Chapter 6 .

103  GDPR, Article 39.2.

104  Article 29 Working Party, WP 243 (2016), 15.

105  Article 29 Working Party, WP 243 (2016), 15.

106  GDPR, Article 25.

107  S. Gierschmann, "Was 'bringt' deutschen Unternehmen die DS-GVO? Mehr Pflichten, aber die Rechtsunsicherheit bleibt," ZD (2016), 51, 53.

108  GDPR, Article 25.1.

109  GDPR, Article 25.3.

110  Defense News, "Submarine Data Leak Roils Three Governments," October 26, 2016, https://www.defensenews.com/naval/2016/08/26/submarine-data-leak-roils-three-governments.

111  GDPR, Recital 83.

112  Voigt and von dem Bussche, *The EU GDPR*. 64.

113  GDPR, Article 25.2.

114  GDPR, Article 25.2; It is unclear what GDPR means by "In particular, such measures shall ensure that *by default* personal data are not made accessible without the *individual's intervention* to an *indefinite number of natural persons.*" The wording creates confusion as it is not clear what qualifies as "an indefinite number," which leaves leeway for vexatious procedure. Perhaps the drafters intended that it meant "definite number" as that would leave less space for abuse.

115  GDPR, Article 6.

116  GDPR, Article 25, 32, 34.

117  Clyde Williamson, *Pseudonymization vs. Anonymization and how they help with GDPR*, January 5, 2017, https://www.protegrity.com/pseudonymization-vs-anonymization-help-gdpr.

118  Article 29 Working Party, *WP 216* (2014), 12 and 16.

119  Article 29 Working Party, *Opinion 05/2014 on Anonymization Techniques*, WP216.

120  Chapter 9, Section 9.10.

121  "Anonymizing Links: Advantages and Disadvantages of Dereferrer," Digital Guide, https://www.1and1.com/digitalguide/hosting/technical-matters/dereferrer-anonymizing-links-made-easy.

122  "Together We're Building a New Identity Ecosystem," DIF, http://identity.foundation.

123  IBM, *Blockchain and GDPR White Paper.*

124  Ibid.

125  GDPR, Article 32.

126  GDPR, Article 33, 34.

127  GDPR, Article 35, 36.

128  GDPR, Article 32.3.

129  GDPR, Article 32.2.

130  GDPR, Article 32.4.

131  P. Sholz, § 3a BDSG. In BDSG, 2nd ed., edited by J. Taeger and D. Gabel (Frankfurt am Main: Fachmedien Rech und Wirtschaft, 2014), Rec. 44; Voigt and von dem Bussche, *The EU GDPR: A Practical Guide,* 33.

132  Voigt and von dem Bussche, *The EU GDPR: A Practical Guide,* 33.

133  GDPR, Article 4.12.

134  WP29, *Guidelines on Data Breach Notification,* under Regulation 2016/679.

135  WP29, *Guidelines on Data Breach Notification*, under Regulation 2016/679.

136  Richard Steiennon, "Categorizing Data Breach Severity with Data Breach Index," IT-Harvest, https://breachlevelindex.com/pdf/Breach-Level-Index-WP.pdf.

137  The values correspond to the numbering given.

138  The values correspond to the numbering given.

139  For example, see Breach Level Index, "Data Breach Statistics," https://breachlevelindex.com.

140  See Chapter 5.

141  This option may be more suitable for small to medium-sized firms who are not required to have a DPO *and* do not handle sensitive personal data.

142   GDPR, Article 37.1.

143   J.M. Porup, "What Is Cyber Security? How to Build a Cyber Security Strategy," CSO, December 27, 2017, https://www.csoonline.com/article/3242690/data-protection/what-is-cyber-security-how-to-build-a-cyber-security-strategy.html.

144   Oror Liwer, "3 Little Known Secrets about Cloud Security," CSO, December 4, 2017, https://www.csoonline.com/article/3239747/cloud-security/3-little-known-secrets-about-cloud-security.html.

145   Cyberpedia, "What Is Cyber Security?," https://www.paloaltonetworks.com/cyberpedia/what-is-cyber-security.

146   That is, Software as a Service.

147   Cyberpedia, "What Is Cyber Security?," https://www.paloaltonetworks.com/cyberpedia/what-is-cyber-security.

148   Cyberpedia, "What Is a Security Operating Platform?" https://www.paloaltonetworks.com/cyberpedia/what-is-security-operating-platform.html.

149   Determann, *Determann's Field Guide to Data Privacy Law,* 155.

150   Cyberpedia, "4 Ways Cyber Automation Should Be Used," https://www.paloaltonetworks.com/cyberpedia/4-ways-cybersecurity-automation-should-be-used.

151   GDPR, Articles 42 and 40, respectively.

152   GDPR, Article 33.1.

153   WP29, *Guidelines on Data Breach Notification*, under Regulation 2016/679.

154   GDPR, Article 33.1, Recital 85.

155   WP29, *Guidelines on Data Breach Notification*, under Regulation 2016/67679; GDPR Recital 87.

156   WP29, *Guidelines on Data Breach Notification*, under Regulation 2016/679.

157   GDPR, Article 33.3.

158   GDPR, Article 33.5.

159   GDPR, Recital 88.

160   GDPR, Article 33.1.

161   GDPR, Article 33.1.

162   GDPR, Recital 86.

163   GDPR, Article 34.2; Recital 86.

164   WP29, *Guidelines on Data Breach Notification*, under Regulation 2016/67679; GDPR Recital 86.

165   GDPR, Article 34.3.

166   GDPR, Article 34.4.

167   GDPR, Article 28.3.

168   GDPR, Article 40.

169   GDPR, Article 3.

170   GDPR, Article 40.3.

171   Voigt and von dem Bussche, *The EU GDPR: A Practical Guide,* 71.

172   GDPR, Article 40.2.

173   This is to be done without prejudice to the data subject's rights under Articles 77 and 79.

174   GDPR, Article 40.4; *without prejudice* to the tasks and powers of Supervisory Authorities competent pursuant to Article 55 or 56.

175  GDPR, Article 40.2.

176  GDPR, Article 40.5.

177  GDPR, Article 40.6.

178  GDPR, Article 63.

179  GDPR, Articles 40.7 to 40.11.

180  GDPR, Article 40.9.

181  GDPR, Article 41.

182  GDPR, Article 41.6.

183  GDPR, Article 41.2, 41.3.

184  GDPR, Article 41.3.

185  GDPR, Article 41.5.

186  GDPR, Article 41.4. This is done *without prejudice* to the SA's power to take action against the Data Collectors.

187  GDPR, Article 24.3.

188  GDPR, Article 28.5.

189  GDPR, Article 57, 58.

190  GDPR, Article 43.1.

191  Pursuant to GDPR, Article 55, 56.

192  This Regulation provided by the EU parliament and council on July 9, 2008, sets out the requirements for accreditation and market surveillance relating to marketing products.

193  Pursuant to GDPR, Article 55 and 56.

194  GDPR, Articles 43.2.b *read with* Article 42.5, 58.3, and 63.

195  GDPR, Article 43.3.

196  GDPR, Article 43.4.

197  GDPR, Article 43.7.

198  GDPR, Article 43.6.

199  GDPR, Article 43.4.

200  GDPR, Article 43.5.

201  GDPR, Article 42.1; "The Specific needs of *micro, small and medium sized* enterprises shall be taken into account."

202  GDPR, Article 3.

203  GDPR, Article 42.2 *read with* Article 46(2).

204  GDPR, Article 43.8; 92.

205  GDPR, Article 43.9, 93.2.

206  GDPR, Article 42.3.

207  GDPR, Article 42.4.

208  GDPR, Article 42.6.

209  GDPR, Article 42.7.

210  G. Schmid and T. Khal, "Verarbeitung 'sensibler' Daten durch Cloud – Anbieter in Drittstaaten," ZD (2017), 54, 56–57.

211  GDPR, Article 28.10.

212  Voigt and von dem Bussche, *The EU GDPR*, 19.

213  GDPR, Article 28.1.

214  GDPR, Article 63; 28.8.

215  GDPR, Article 93.2; 28.7.

216  GDPR, Article 42, 43; 28.6.

217  GDPR, Article 28.2.

218  Laue, Nink, and Kremer S (eds.) *Selbstregulierung,* Rec. 18.

219  GDPR, Article 32; Article 28.3.c.

220  GDPR, Article 28.3.e: "taking into account the nature of processing, assists the Controller by appropriate technical and organizational measures, *insofar as this is possible...*"

221  GDPR, Article 24.1.

222  GDPR, Article 28.5.

223  GDPR, Article 29.

224  GDPR, Article 28.2.

225  GDPR, Article 28.4.

# 5

# Material Requisites for Processing under GDPR

*Success depends upon previous preparation, and without such preparation there is sure to be failure.*

— Confucius

Once the technical and organizational measures are put in place within the business to protect data, it is important to focus on the activity of "processing" itself. GDPR places numerous restrictions and rules on daily processing of data and the external interactions with consumers and foreign nations. Unlike previous laws surrounding data processing, which allowed for an expansive collection of information, GDPR is centralized around reducing data harvesting by sanctioning specific types of international data transfers along with ensuring compliance within the EU.

## 5.1   The Central Principles of Processing

Article 5 of GDPR lays down the essential matters that must be considered when personal data is being processed. Failing to follow these principles could result in a €20 million fine or 4% of the global annual turnover, requiring careful compliance. The term legitimacy in processing requires compliance with all existing law, which includes written common law, legislation, judgments, municipal decrees, constitutional principles, fundamental rights, and even other legal principles.[1] Essentially, the test is whether a court determining the case would consider the source as a law. Legitimacy is a fluid concept, which can change depending on the technology or societal/cultural attitudes.[2] The provisions lay the groundwork to establish how data may be collected and in what manner it may be continually processed and managed.

### 5.1.1 Lawful, Fair, and Transparent Processing of Data

The first principle of processing personal data mandates that the processing be lawful.[3] Prior to GDPR, the "lawfulness" of data processing as a concept was loose and open to interpretation. Article 5 requires legal permission along with user understanding of the basis. Translating these terms into their respective duties, it can be simplified as follows:

- **Lawful:** Processing operations must be in full compliance with the regulation.
- **Fair:** Data collection must be minimized and limited to its stated purpose.
- **Transparent:** All aspects of processing and data collection must be initiated to the data subjects and the relevant authorities.

Figure 5.1 presents the five pillars represent requirements that must be satisfied when processing under GDPR. Additionally, a sixth pillar, in the form of a duty placed on the Controller[7] — a duty of accountability, states the Controller shall be responsible for and must be able to demonstrate compliance to the lawfulness. Thus, we can see that Article 5 (1) gives the principles, and Article 5 (2) places the responsibility of obeying these principles on the Controller.

Under GDPR, personal data must be:[4]

| I | II | III | IV | V | VI |
|---|---|---|---|---|---|
| Processed in a manner that is | Collected for a purpose that is | Minimized to what is | Accurate in a manner that is | Stored in a way that it is | Secure from |
| Lawful | Specified | Adequate | Up to date | Identifiable | Unlawful/ unauthorized processing |
| Fair | Explicit | Relevant | Easily rectifiable or erasable | Limited to achieving its purpose[5] | Accidental loss or destruction or damage |
| Transparent | Legitimate | Limited to what is necessary for its purposes | | | |
| | Within the scope and for no further processing beyond what was consented to[6] | | | | |

**Figure 5.1** Principles of Processing, Breakdown

### 5.1.2    Processing Limited to a "Purpose"

GDPR mandates that Controllers communicate their purpose of processing to their users at the time of collection or soon thereafter,[8] which raises questions as to the form and content of the purpose communicated. As processing is rarely a uniform practice across the board, the level of detail will vary and can be determined on a case-by-case basis, bearing in mind the overall processing context along with the reasonable expectations of the user and the common understanding between the two parties.[9] Important barometers of this determination are as follows:[10]

1. **Big processing:** Larger processing operations handling high numbers of data subjects have a greater responsibility to provide detailed notices of purpose, categorizing subjects and the data collected, including factors such as cultural backgrounds and geographical locations.
2. **Superfluous data collection for a purpose:** If the processing needs more data than is customarily required for such operations, greater detail in the statement of purpose is required. For example, if an app deliberately collects dormant data from former users to study how to improve their service in the future, they must inform users that they have that option.
3. **Subpurposes:** It is unrealistic to expect that a Controller has only a singular purpose in data collection. For online conglomerates such as Google or Amazon, the data is often collected for a breadth of purposes. Breaking down the primary purpose into any "subpurposes" will assist in helping users understand data collection better.
4. **Layered privacy notices:** The Article 29 Working Party opines that "layering" privacy notices are an ideal way to help educate the data subjects. This has been adopted by larger companies (such as Gmail's privacy policy) where the critical information is presented to users in a concise manner, while full detail is provided to interested users by way of a hyperlink or new tab.

**Illustration:** An automobile GPS company, AGPS, wishes to expand its operations to the self-driving car industry. Since June 2018, AGPS has been selling its state-of-the-art GPS systems at a discount to consumers in exchange for their informed consent in allowing the company to study their driving habits for their new operations. The AGPS system will study the driver's habits, always including when the system is not in use. This is because the system requires constant data to improve its algorithms so that the company will be able to meet its targets for entering the market. In the layered privacy notices at the time of sale:

- Users were informed of the purposes and subpurposes of the constant data collection: namely, safety practices study, driving preferences, algorithm building, and ultimately the company's commercial purpose of the data.
- The company states in a large font, "THE AGPS SYSTEM COLLECTS DATA AT ALL TIMES AND WILL CEASE DOING SO ON JANUARY 12, 2019.

AFTER JANUARY 12, 2019, WE WILL REQUEST YOUR PERMISSION ONCE AGAIN, AND YOU HAVE THE OPTION OF DISCONTINUING THE PROGRAM AT NO LOSS TO YOUR SERVICES."

- The company lists its "R&D Partners" with whom they will share the data for their self-driving plans.

This layered privacy notice with clear "purpose limitation" is GDPR compliant.

**5.1.2.1 Restriction on Processing and Exceeding the Purpose**  GDPR permits the processing of personal data for a purpose other than that for which it has been collected which is not based on the user's consent or on the law.[11] This leeway is granted if such processing is a necessary measure in a "democratic society" to safeguard the objectives of the restrictions placed on processing under Article 23 of the Regulation.

Article 23 of GDPR permits the EU or Member States to make further law restricting the scope of Obligations and user Rights[12] in relation to the Principles of Processing discussed earlier in this chapter.[13] This can be exercised for a breadth of reasons to safeguard the democratic society, such as national security or judicial proceedings.[14] With that in mind, processing for purposes which is neither based on Consent nor based on EU or Member Law is allowed if such action is:

- Necessary
- Proportionate
- A measure in a "democratic society" to safeguard the objectives of the restrictions

**5.1.2.2 The "Compatibility" Test**  If the above requirements are fulfilled, processing for undisclosed purposes is permitted by the Controller. However, when making that judgment as to further processing, the Controller must ascertain whether the new purpose of processing is compatible with the purpose for which it was collected.[15] This is done by considering the following factors:

1. **The Link** between the purpose of collection and further processing
2. **The context** of collection, specifically the relationship between the Controller and the users
3. **The nature** of personal data collected, specifically special categories of data or criminal conviction data
4. **The possible consequences** of further processing
5. **The existence of security** in the processing, such as pseudonymization or encryption

The five-prong test above needs to be considered by the Controller when deciding on further processing of personal data. Let us consider an **Illustration:** Genepool.com is a new booming business that requests small DNA samples from its users, analyzes them, and provides a diagnosis of any irregularities, vitamin deficiencies, and a breadth of other tests. After the tests are complete, the users receive a "diagnostic prognosis" on their app-based platform. In the creation of the Unified Database in concert with the government, Genepool.com also additionally processed the personal data of its users to help the government detect and prevent outbreaks of common epidemics by providing the information received from the earlier samples of its customers that used their service within the borders of this state. The citizens identified would have to undergo mandatory vaccination. Before processing the data for such purpose, their CTO/DPO must apply the five-prong test, which we can analyze as follows:

1. **The link:** Here, it can be argued that a link exists between the purpose of collection, which was a diagnosis of any diseases or deficiencies. The purpose of further processing has a link of giving a diagnosis or pre-diagnosis to prevent the person from falling ill.
2. **The context:** Here, Mr. Kim might find some trouble justifying the context for the citizens whose data was collected at the time that Genepool.com was a private undertaking. This new processing could give the user a claim for a breach of the original purpose, as giving one's DNA info to a private corporation is a completely different context from giving it to the government.
3. **The nature:** Here, there is no denying that this falls under a special category of data as it has both genetic and biometric information involved.
4. **The possible consequences:** The result of such further processing in this situation leans in favor of Genepool.com, as it is done to prevent citizens from getting sick with deadly diseases, in furtherance of the public interest.
5. **Security:** Let us assume for the purposes of this illustration that Genepool.com has a very strong practice of cyber-security in partnership with CyberSec LLP.

Only point numbers 2 and 3 above might arguably cause trouble to Mr. Kim, as it is a special category of data being processed in a completely different context. However, Mr. Kim in this scenario has the "official authority" to carry out these operations in the public interest in accordance with Article 23, which permits him to restrict the user's rights as long as further processing is necessary and proportionate. This balancing should be done in a way that protects the fundamental rights and interests of other users.

**5.1.2.3 Processing That Does Not Require Identification**  Before proceeding with other aspects of compliance, it is important to mention that GDPR does not require any action if the processing is done in such a manner that:

- It does not require identification of the user, or
- "No longer requires" identification of the user.

In such cases, the Controller of the website is not required to maintain, acquire, or process any additional information for the mere purpose of complying with the regulation.[16] Article 11 also provides that if the Controller can demonstrate his inability to identify the user, he must accordingly inform the user of such a fact, if possible.[17] GDPR provides protection to the Controller by providing that an unidentified user cannot make a claim for any of the rights under the regulation until such time that they provide the Controller with such identifying information. Let us try to understand this through the following illustrations:

**Illustration 1:** EarWorm is an app that provides high-quality, high-speed music streaming services. To use the app, registration is not required, but the Terms of Use with the users permit the app to study the music taste, location, frequency, and other data accumulated while using the app to improve their services. As GDPR comes into force, EarWorm would not be required to start creating and maintaining profiles for the users, as they do not use the data to identify the user. Thus, they are not required to take any further action under the Regulation.

**Illustration 2:** Let us consider the same app above, EarWorm, and assume that they require registration of one's e-mail ID, username, and a password with a payment of a fee at the time of agreeing to the "Terms of Use" to avail their Premium Services. At the same they provide "Freemium Services" to those users who wish to remain unregistered. EarWorm would be required to comply with GDPR insofar as they handle the personal data of the "premium" users. The "freemium" users, on the other hand, are not protected or afforded rights under GDPR until and unless they provide the information that identifies them (username, e-mail ID, and password) to EarWorm.

### 5.1.3    Data Minimization and Accuracy

Data minimization is a practice that GDPR seeks to nurture. Older practices in the data-processing industries permitted broad and expansive harvesting of data under the umbrella of complex Terms of Service. When bringing one's processing into GDPR compliance, the technical and organizational measures must be implemented in such a way that, by default, only personal data that is necessary for each specific purpose is processed.[18] This obligation applies to the Controller with respect to:

1. The amount of personal data collected;
2. The extent of their processing;
3. The period of storage; and
4. Its accessibility. Specifically, the personal data must not be accessible without the data subject's intervention to an indefinite number of natural persons.[19]

The personal data held by Controllers must also be accurate and up-to-date and must constantly reflect reality. The business should take all reasonable steps to ensure that the data held is correct, giving their users the options of rectification or erasure without undue delay.[20] This is important for those Controllers who use personal data to produce legal or significant effects on the rights of their consumers.

**Illustration:** A tax-filing software collects consumer data based on their income, family details, and other expenses and uses the data provided to calculate tax returns and deductions. Naim uses the software and accidently puts in the wrong Social Security number, giving him a lower deduction than he was entitled to. After submitting his tax returns online (well before March 31), Naim learns of the error. He contacts the Controller to fix the problem, who tells him they can fix the issue for a €500 rectification fee paid to them. The Controller's demand for this fee violates GDPR because they do not allow Naim to rectify his own data to his financial detriment.

Working in closely with the purpose of limiting of data collection discussed above, data minimization is the technical mandate from GDPR to keep one's online operations lean and respectful of privacy.

### 5.1.4    Storage of Data

After a user deletes his "profile" and leaves the Controller's service, it is a misconception to say that the personal data is completely wiped off, as companies and countries have *document retention periods,* which require them to maintain the data for a period of time. Initially these periods were applicable largely to "official" corporate documents for law enforcement and litigation purposes. However, over the past decade a practice has been for Controllers to continue using the personal data of users even after they have left the service, citing "document retention" as the reason for doing so.

GDPR seeks to change this past practice by requiring that personal data permitting identification of the user only be retained for a period no longer than necessary to achieve the purposes of processing.[21] Here, it is important to draw a distinction between a storage period mandated by law and a company's document retention policy. Often, the two rules work harmoniously with one another, with the company's policies following the legally mandated period (depending on their interest in maintaining the document). As GDPR is a cross-jurisdiction regulation, it is logical that the regulation places this burden on the Controller entity itself, as the period of storage would be supplemented by Member State legislation.

The retention of personal data by the Controller will be limited to a strict minimum[22] with the organization required to set up suitable measures in place to periodically review those periods and the erasure needed. Thus, GDPR not only covers personal data processing from its inception or ongoing operations, but also its subsequent decommissioning and erasure from the storage "afterlife."

### 5.1.5    Integrity and Confidentiality of the Operation

While data minimization pertains to the technical measures that must be implemented in data processing, "confidentiality" and "integrity" relate to the organizational or "human" side of the business. Many of the historical data breaches have been caused by employee misconduct or human error, and this remains the hardest threat to track and contain. These past experiences have led the drafters of the GDPR to place a system of confidentiality within the data-processing eco-system by way of imposing a duty of confidentiality on:

- The Controller and their employees
- The Processor and their employees
- The DPO
- The employees of the SA (who are subject to a Professional Obligation of Secrecy)[23]

By maintaining this "wall-of-secrecy," confidentiality is maintained in all aspects of data processing under the force of law. Compare this with the Data Collector's duty of transparency to their users regarding their activities. From this dual relationship between confidentiality and transparency, we can see that the regulation pushes for internal secrecy in handling data and open communication of how the privacy is maintained.

## 5.2 Legal Grounds for Data Processing

As discussed earlier, processing under GDPR requires a legal basis under the regulation. An entity that wishes to process personal data for their day-to-day operations will have to claim one or more of the justifications listed below to avoid liability.

### 5.2.1 Processing Based on Consent

Under the earlier Data Protection Directive regime, the standard for "valid" consent was flexible. This reflected the tone of the industry where data minimization was not a priority, and verbose terms of service shielded Controllers from liability. GDPR provides stricter standards for consent, and receiving consent from minors, along with requiring explicit consent for collecting special data.

Consent is currently the most hotly debated topic in GDPR as it is at the center of the first complaints filed under the regulation.[24] The recent cases are not merely a case of GDPR violations but will have policy ramifications for privacy, consent, and online businesses. This section will first examine what GDPR considers consent to be and will then proceed to conduct a case study on the NYOB litigation and the effect it will have on the future of online contracts.

**5.2.1.1 What Constitutes Consent?**　　Article 4(11) of GDPR stipulates that consent comprises of any statement, clear affirmative action signifying agreement to processing that is:

1. Freely given,
2. Specific,
3. Informed, and
4. An unambiguous indication of the data subject's wishes (statement, written, clear affirmative action).

Article 7 of the Regulation provides the conditions for consent in the form of four requirements:

1. **Demonstration:** If the processing of personal data is rooted in consent, the Controller must be able to demonstrate that consent.[25] This provision essentially places the burden of proof of the consent provided on the Controller, mandating that he must be able to show compliance with Article 7 of GDPR when required. "Opt-out" consent is generally not permissible under the regulation (such as silence, *preticked boxes*, or *inactivity*) as they do not qualify as a *clear act* of demonstrable consent.[26] A sound practice would be to implement a *two-step consent* mechanism such as *confirmation mails* containing an *activation link* for enabling a profile.

2. **Distinguishability and transparency:** The terms of service must be unambiguous in its content and can be oral, written, or electronic[27] but must be demonstrable as discussed above. The multiple purposes of processing (such as registration combined with direct marketing or behavioral monitoring) must be clearly communicated as well. GDPR provides no specifications as to the formal requirements of consent. If the user gives their consent in a written medium that also encompasses other matters, the "Request for Consent" must be provided:
   a. In a clearly distinguishable form from other matters
   b. In an intelligible and easily accessible form
   c. Using clear and plain language

   For example, it would not be permitted to attain consent to process personal data if the request for consent is buried in 200 pages of confusing legal jargon. If a part of a written contract found to be in contravention of GDPR it will not be binding, creating a kind of severability provision.[28] The request for consent should be graphically demarcated and separate from the rest of the agreement.

3. **Withdrawal of consent:** Under the regulation, the data subject has a right to withdraw his consent at any time and must be informed of this right prior to giving consent. The regulation makes it clear that this withdrawal will not affect the lawfulness of processing that was done with the prior consent supplied by the data subject. GDPR goes on to say "It shall be as easy to withdraw as to give consent."[29] This last line might be the final nail in the coffin that causes a fracture between operating online businesses and the consensual processing of data. This will be discussed in greater depth in the next section in the case study of the recent cases filed.

4. **"Freely given" and conditional consent:** Consent requires a *clear affirmative act* to be valid. To that end, acceptable practices include:[30]
   a. Ticking an unticked box
   b. Selecting technical settings on the internet browser or cookies (example: automatic log-ins or preloaded passwords)
   c. Typing initials into a box next to "I agree"

A pivotal issue in the recent cases filed against Google and Facebook is determining what would constitute "freely given" consent. Article 7(4) states clearly that "utmost account" shall be given to whether the consent is conditional to attain the service applied for. A crucial factor is whether the consent to process data that is not necessary for performance of the contract is made as the condition for receiving the service of the platform. This issue and its ramifications on online contracts will be discussed in our subsequent case study.

**5.2.1.2 Consent of a Child**  GDPR provides special attention regarding consent given by children in relation to information society services.[31] An Information Society Service is an EU effort to unify their e-commerce market by creating a procedure for the provision for information in the field of technical standards by using long-distance technology.[32] The information service is generally provided in exchange for remuneration through:[33]

- A distance,
- Using electronic means,
- At the request of the data subject.

The services provided must be targeted directly to a child, using young consumers as their primary audience. Indicators of this fact (if not directly evident) can be inferred from the graphics, interface, content, language used, etc. Article 8 mandates that in relation to providing information services to a child based on consent, the processing will only be lawful under GDPR if the child is at least 16 years old. If the child is under 16, the processing will only be lawful if the consent of the parent/legal guardian is provided.[34] The Member States may lower this age requirement; however, it cannot be lower than 13 years for valid consent. Furthermore, the Controller shall make reasonable efforts to verify parental consent considering the available technology.[35] The Controller must also be able to document this consent as part of their demonstration duty. As the scope of this provision is limited to Information Society Services, it is limited to the EU by default.

**Illustration:** "Smarty Ted" is a new toy in the European Market that implements AI to communicate and educate consumers by acting as a responsive "plush-doll" for emotional well-being. Though the toy is not exclusively for children, several add-on "modifications" or "mods" assist the soft-toy in communicating with the consumer on certain subjects. Additionally, if a consumer gives the toys details regarding themselves, the toy will recall and use that information in their future conversations. Smarty Ted only speaks in simple language and is not designed to handle complex topics outside of basic education. The simple, appealing, and educational nature of the toy likely subjects Smarty Ted to the provisions of GDPR. As a result, Smarty Ted must first ask the parents to set the programming and provide consent before collecting the data. This is carried out by an e-mail verification link sent directly to the parent's e-mail at the time of registration. Smarty Ted is GDPR compliant.

The 16-year-old age of consent is not dependent on the child's individual personal development (such as mental deficiencies or greater intelligence). Additionally, this age limit is separate from any rules regarding minors provided under Member State general contract law. Additionally, GDPR does not prevent the Member States from legislating their own rules regarding contracts with children.[36] Placing measures to request "Parental Consent" is simple, but verifying success is difficult. Organizations must update existing consent policies to ensure that there is parental involvement in receiving consent (example: a confirmation code sent to a registered phone number). Businesses will also find value in developing multiple legal bases for their processing so that a "fallback" justification can be claimed if the standard for consent is not met.

Practically implementing an effective system for getting valid or parental consent of a minor is something companies presently struggle with. Children online primarily use social networks and streaming facilities. Age verification in social media companies is based on a trust system, which has cost companies millions. For example, in the US, the social media company TikTok paid a $5.7 million settlement to the FTC and agreed to implement measures to verify users under 13. TikTok's Musical.ly app knowingly hosted content published by underage users with no age-verification process in place until July 2017.[37] Since July 2017 the company inquired the date of birth for new users but did not verify existing users. This led to a "large percentage" of the 65 million accounts in the US being held by children on the app.[38] The FTC took notice when over 300 concerned parents complained to the company over a two-week period in September 2016. While the company deleted profiles of the children involved, the content the child had posted was not deleted. Additionally, TikTok retained the personal data of the children longer than was required. A delayed response by the company triggered an investigation under the Children's Online Privacy Protection Act.

In addition to the hefty fine, the FTC ordered the company to delete the children's data retained along with a mandate to verify age for existing and future users. While TikTok would be implementing age verification in the US, it would not be doing so in other countries it operates in.[39] But this raises the issue of how effective can verification be? The "trust-system" of consent only requires a user (existing or future) to enter their date of birth, which can be easily fabricated. Is there a practically feasible method for obtaining a child's consent? The first step is transparency in the collection and use of child data. Second is to find a mode to contact the child's parents to obtain consent. Lastly, *content moderation* and oversight of any "posts" that suggest the child is a minor. Content moderation requires the use of AI in "flagging" and young content, otherwise privacy concerns may arise from only-human moderation. TikTok's settlement highlights the difficulty of implementing child consent online, but it is evident that many issues were caused by the company's own actions of data misuse.

**5.2.1.3 NYOB.eu versus Google, Facebook, Whatsapp, and Instagram: A Case Study on Consent**  On the day that GDPR came into force, a prominent privacy rights activist Max Schrems and his not-for-profit organization, nyob.eu, filed complaints in four Supervisory Authorities (SAs) to act against the "Controllers" of the following companies:

1. Google's Android in the SA of France;
2. Facebook's Instagram in the SA of Belgium;
3. Facebook's Whatsapp Messenger in the SA of Hamburg; and
4. Facebook itself in the SA of Austria.

The complaints filed were all rooted in a lack of "free consent" in agreeing to use the service, but the issues run deeper than that. Most of us at one point have used the services of the platforms discussed above, and that is a key part of the debate. Their services of connecting us across our daily life, or Google for simply existing and making our lives easier, are starting to become indispensable. This is where contracting with a company becomes problematic; specifically, in this new GDPR era. When a company provides essential online services to average users, providing the service on their "non-negotiable" terms, is there ever any practical way to meaningfully consent? Is there any other way to give consent on bargained terms?

This section will examine the key issues and the nature of the claims in the four suits, while at the same time evaluating the broader policy implications that may arise. The issues discussed will not strictly adhere to format raised in the complaints filed;[40] rather, we will break it down into simpler practical portions.

*a. Vague and Complicated Information*   The Terms of Service of these four websites allegedly fail to provide proper notice under GDPR in relation to what data will be used for a specific purpose. Under the regulation, as discussed earlier, data processing must be necessary and proportionate in the provision of the service.[41] The consent is given by the user of the service for limited and specific purposes, and NYOB, the nonprofit organization headed by privacy activist Max Schrems, argues that the companies fail to clearly delineate:

1. What specific data will be used for what specific purpose
2. What sensitive data is being collected and for what specific purpose

NYOB argues that Google is engaging in "bundling" the data collection of all their services spanning from Chrome to the operating system of a phone (which is the subject of the complaint filed). This has led to a lack of specificity and broad data collection capabilities over multiple platforms, accumulating massive amounts of personal and special data essentially violating the Controller's duty to provide information.[42]

*b. Necessity of Processing*   The above argument regarding lack of "information" is hinged on the next question of whether the companies have changed their "data minimization" practices, collecting only the data that is necessary to provide the service. Here is where the debate expands, and we must look at the core services that these companies specifically provide:

**Google** is a conglomerate, with a dominant search engine, phones, operating systems, websites, browsers, apps, plug-ins, wearables, and Wi-Fi services.

**The scope** of processing by Google is almost all-encompassing, as buying a phone with it's OS or using the Chrome browser results in the collection of both personal and special data of an individual. Consider the user of the phone at the center of this litigation. The device was functioning on a Google-based OS with preloaded Google-based apps. The data collected in a phone is enormous as it is a virtual shadow of an individual and their lives. Thus, what is "necessary" for Google to process would largely depend on the service used.

**Instagram** is a photo/video sharing social networking platform with long-term posts, live videos, 24-hour long posts, and direct messaging services. It is also a strong business, PR, and public platform.

**The scope** of Instagram's processing is more limited as their website is "camera-centric." However, in putting up a post, an individual can share a written "caption," share their location, and tag their friends. Posts can be made public, or they can be made private, but the data being processed by the Controller will remain the same; the visibility to the public would not. As a result, the processing of Instagram should be limited to what is discussed above, or tangential activities.

**Whatsapp** is an online direct messaging service, with real-time responses, group chats, 24-hour long posts, and broadcasting systems.

**The scope** of Whatsapp's data collection should be relatively limited as a private direct messaging service should process only as much data as needed to facilitate the conversation. Here, however, the complaints raise an interesting point that Whatsapp's terms of use state that the data created will be shared for advertising purposes, which seems excessive.

The difference here would be that Whatsapp is a private messaging service between contacts, akin to texting a friend. The data collected would be a result of using private personal data that is not shared publicly. Thus, this can be a form of excessive processing.

**Facebook** is a jack of all trades social media platform with various modes of communication available.

**The scope** of Facebook's processing can be compared to that of Google, only not as pervasive across different mediums. But the size of the two companies prevents them from processing data with precision, as they provide numerous services on their platforms that collect different types of data. Thus, what data processing is "necessary" for Facebook to conduct remains largely unanswered.

According to a Working Party Opinion 06/2014, the term "necessary for the performance of a contract" needs to be interpreted strictly. The processing must be necessary to fulfill the contract with each individual data subject.

**GDPR versus the privacy policies:** An eventual conflict will arise between GDPR and the Privacy Policy/Terms of Use these companies adopt. GDPR Articles 13 and 14 provide that the Controller must supply "information" to the user regarding the legal basis of processing, the purposes, the storage, and recipients among many other things. However, the degree of specificity remains unanswered, as Controllers are only required to communicate it in a form that is clear, concise and in plain English, in a manner that is transparent and easily accessible.[43] Other than those simple instructions, the regulation fails to provide any "drafting tips," so to speak, for these Controllers.

If the Privacy Policy needs to be in plain English and concise, where is the room for specificity? NYOB's complaints allege that the Controllers fail to state precisely what data is being collected and for what specific purpose. But how would this be practically applied for a multilevel tech company like Google who collects data from its users and uses it in a variety of ways? If multipurpose tech companies had to list how every bit of data would be used in the larger scheme of their services, the "concise" requirement of GDPR would be defeated. Furthermore, one must ask if there is an effective way of communicating technical information on data processing with precision and simplicity.

The same can be said about Facebook and their allied companies in the case at hand. They had, in a way which is "simple" to understand, their advertising and data-sharing policies. But in simplifying their policies, they had sacrificed their precision and specificity of data processing.

*c. Granularity and Bundling Agreements*   Another interesting issue arises regarding the "bundling" of privacy policies, such as Google having one common policy for all its platforms. This amalgamation of the agreements creates a gray area when pinpointing the purpose of data collection to the data collected. Additionally, such action has the user agreeing to the terms of other services, which they may not have used or may never use.[44] This is also referred to as *granularity* or an "all or nothing" approach to services provided. Facebook and its companies are also "bundling" agreements by having users agree to the sharing of data between Facebook and their allied partner websites. GDPR considers such action as invalid consent,[45] as different processing activities require different consent. The concept of "bundling" agreements to process data that is not essential to the service is considered highly undesirable, and it is presumed that the consent given by the user is not valid.[46] However, this presumption cannot be considered in absolute terms, and there is limited leeway for such agreements to be enforced.[47] Guidelines issued by an Article 29 EU Data Protection Working Party (WP29) state clearly that "consent and contract cannot be merged and blurred."

Thus, it does not seem that "bundling" is the best practice for technology conglomerates as it is considered an undesired, risky practice. But what is the alternative? Should the user have to provide separate consent for every service they may use from Google, or Facebook, or even Apple for that matter? In certain cases, the services are so intermingled it might be practical and logical to have an all-encompassing Terms of Use.

**Illustration:** Like the data subject in the case at hand, let us consider a user who buys a Google Phone. The OS, browsers, services, and apps are all integrated and pre-set. Instead of bundling the agreements, Google requires the user to supply separate consent for each service they decide to use. This would begin from the moment the user switches on the phone for the first time, followed by a pop-up on the phone for each new intertwined service he wishes to use. Is this practical?

The WP29 seems to think not,[48] stating that excessive requests for consent will have a diminishing effect on its value, resulting in the requests not being read by users. However, WP29 provides no clue as to how this issue should be tackled, stating "GDPR places upon Controllers the obligation to develop ways to tackle this issue," leaving broad scope for error.

*d. Hidden Consent*   The issue of "bundling" leads to the next claim of "hidden" consent, where NYOB claims that the agreements hide the consent for processing in the bulk or the pages. They argue that this runs contrary to GDPR's require-ment of *distinguishability*[49] by preventing the user from being fully informed. For example, Whatsapp's Terms of Use takes up 89 screen pages of a mobile, which as a result is not in accordance to the conditions of plain language and accessibility.

Furthermore, Facebook, Whatsapp, and Instagram *all* have "tie-in" agreements with one another where they share data between platforms since they all exist un-der the same group of companies. This data shared would be used in direct mar-keting, advertising, and improvement of services. The claim is that such sharing of data between platforms contravenes GDPR as the user's data will be processed and shared across platforms in which they may not even be members. Further-more, it is alleged that these companies disguise the processing of the data as a "contractual obligation":

> Affiliated Companies – We are part of the Facebook Companies. As part of the Facebook Companies, WhatsApp receives information from, and shares information with, the Facebook Companies as described in WhatsApp's Pri-vacy Policy. We use the information we receive from them to help operate, provide, and improve our Services.

This scope of processing is problematic, because as stated earlier, Whatsapp is a private messaging company, and sharing of such data between other entities is not necessary for their processing. However, if Facebook, Instagram, and Whatsapp are all part of the same group of Facebook Companies, is the transfer between entity and entity under the same legal control truly considered as excessive pro-cessing? Though these entities are legally separate, they all belong to the same amalgamation and might even have the same Controller to handle their matters. At the end of the day, the data will remain under the "same roof."

The "slippery slope" arises when there are multiple data sharing "tie-ins" with other companies of the same conglomerate as there is greater risk of the data traveling to unauthorized recipients. It is important to note that when agreeing to the Terms of Service, a consumer not only agrees to share information with the affiliate companies, but also with their marketing partners. If each company has different marketing partners, an unmanageable chain of data sharing is created.

*e. "Freely Given" Consent*   **A "Realistic" Choice:** GDPR states that consent must be freely given to process personal data. This "freedom" entails that the user has a genuine right to accept or decline the terms with a realistic choice.[50] This sense of agency cannot be illusory or a result caused by a lack of bargaining power. If the user feels that he has no practical choice in accepting or declining the terms, the consent will not be valid.[51] GDPR scheme mandates that data subjects have two unequivocal rights regarding Consent:

1. A right to accept/decline the terms
2. A right to withdraw that consent[52]

The concept of "freely given" consent requires that the user, should he not agree to the data collection, would have a right to decline those terms without facing detriment.[53] Detriment implies negative consequences, or a "clear disadvantage," which may follow from declining the terms of use, such as additional costs, downgraded service, discontinuation of service, refusal of service, etc.

**"Illusory" Consent:** When determining whether consent was freely given, GDPR considers all the circumstances of that consent.[54] The WP29 clearly stipulates:

> If consent is bundled up as a non-negotiable part of terms and conditions it is presumed not to have been freely given.

This essentially states that "bundling" the consent with standard online terms and conditions of using a website would result in invalid consent, should the user not be offered a chance to decline. Under GDPR, certain factors indicate clearly that the user has no meaningful right of consent:[55]

- **Imbalance of power:** Where one party has a superior bargaining ability over the user, with an ability to dictate terms at the time of consent.
- **Conditionality:** GDPR mandates the service provided cannot be conditional on the user providing consent for the data collection. This is the centerpiece for the pending case, as all four companies refused to let the complainant use their platforms until consent was given.
- **Granularity:** This is the "all or nothing" approach in bundled online contracts, as discussed earlier.
- **Detriment:** The user must face a detriment in some form or other resulting from declining his consent, such as a denial of service.

**The Practicalities of Online Consent:** Looking at the above, we can surmise that these four factors, while idealistic in their approach, will be difficult to execute in practice. This is because it will require a change in the culture of online contracts and the overall data collection business. Let us consider the following counterarguments:

- **Imbalance of Power:** In most situations, an absence of imbalance in bargaining power between the Controller and the data subjects is rare. At one end, there is a business that requires personal data so consumers may avail their services. The websites are not reaching out to the consumers in most situations; it is the consumer requesting the service from the Controller. As a result, the Controller will always be in a superior bargaining position.
- **Conditionality:** Many data-collecting websites cannot function fully without the collection of data from the user. In many scenarios, the data the user creates on the websites is built up over time, and the Controller then uses that data to research and improve the service. It is for this reason Google and Facebook keep broad, sweeping provisions on the collection of data, both for monetization and development.

To that end, it is important to consider the "consent" for data collection as the signature on a contract for service with the website. At the time of entering a website or any platform and deciding to use their services (such as Instagram), the user enters into an ongoing agreement with the Controller for their services. But these services cannot go unregulated, and they require the processing of data for continuation of service. In such a case, would declining consent even be viable?

- **Granularity:** What if a website were interdependent on the data across their multiple platforms for optimum performance and development? What if corporations such as Google (which has a bundled Terms of Use) wish to let their users freely move between apps and join new apps on their servers without constantly pestering the users with a fresh consent request? If the requests were to pile up, users would be less likely to care, or they may choose not to use the app at all, bringing down the usage.
- **Detriment:** Would the denial of use of a privately owned, social media platform be considered a "detriment" to the user? At the end of the day, these are private companies providing a unique, exclusive service to the users based on their terms to ensure that the website functions fully. Would it be right to force such service providers to process the data even when the user declines their terms?

The questions raised above have no perfect answer. There is a thin line between consent for "necessary" processing and data abuse, and the Supervisory Authorities dealing with these matters must be very delicate in deciding this line.

**Implementing a "Bargaining Mechanism":** Online contracts over the past decade have made conditional consent their standard practice. Any user of a phone, laptop, or tablet would attest that the "terms and conditions" are simply a box to tick "yes," as saying "no" is not a practical option. The requirements of GDPR are considered as excessive in the tech industry,[56] considered to stifle the business aspect of data collection.

There is some truth to the criticism of the regulation. Declining terms of use can be interpreted as declining to contract with the website altogether by denying the terms provided. In such a case, what should a company do? A reduced service to the users who decline is not permitted as it is considered a detriment;[57] thus, companies could be arguably forced to provide full services to users without them accepting the terms presented or permitting the collection of their data. How can web companies effectively provide service if there is no meaningful way to communicate with the user and negotiate terms?

Some suggestions are:

- Different processing plans for different categories of users (that are not hinged on reducing their service to their detriment).
- Mechanisms to communicate with someone in the organization who has the authority and the option to bargain and alter terms of use with the users. This option would require a larger investment.
- Have clearly drafted privacy policies on the nature of data collected and its purpose.
- If further data is collected, it must be made clear how such data is necessary.
- Make it clear in the privacy policy how the company monetizes its activities and why data sharing is essential to those operations.

**Consent as Consideration?** An argument that may be made by the companies in the upcoming cases is that the consent to provide personal data acts as the consideration for availing the services of the website. As discussed earlier, these are private companies providing a service to the users on their terms, in many cases free of cost. This arrangement is a contract between the two parties, but a contract is only valid if there is consideration (i.e. an exchange of something of value for the service).

The Controllers of these websites could argue that these free services are provided to the world at large in exchange for one simple thing: data. And the consent to collect that data is necessary for the exchange of service to be a valid binding agreement. Furthermore, for a business to flourish, profit must be made. The advertising and sharing of data are instrumental for continued service to consumers. Monetization of resources available to the companies is critical to ensure its longevity.

This argument, though theoretically viable, faces a direct conflict with the terms of GDPR which mandates only necessary processing and an express prohibition against conditional consent. However, the key downfall in this argument is that the EU data subjects do not have a property right over their personal data, which makes use of the same as consideration highly questionable.[58] But this draws larger questions as to what the legal status of personal data is in the internet. Is it a property which can be sold or bought? Is it an extension of an individual's personality? Untangling this legal issue would involve a delicate balancing act of the commercial interests of the companies with that of the user's rights. The dual treatment of data under the law both as an extension of oneself and as a property that is bought and sold is bound to cause tensions in applying GDPR.

*f. Dominance in the Market*   There is no denying that the services provided by Google and Facebook dominate the market. The names of these services are known the world over, and their market share pales all competitors in comparison.[59] That is where the issue of "detriment" becomes a stronger one for NYOB. The position of these companies in the market creates the following issues:

1. Unique services with no comparable substitute
2. Indispensability of that service in our day-to-day lives
3. Highly superior bargaining position on their own terms
4. Detriment from loss of service is guaranteed

To understand the above, let us consider the user being represented by NYOB; he had purchased an android phone and did not consent. As a result he could not use his phone at all. That is because the phone is based on a Google OS, and without agreeing to their terms he cannot use any of the platforms he wanted as they are all linked to Google itself. If Google or Facebook decides to shut down their company and stop service, the world will suffer as GPS, basic communication, and information are provided by those companies. As a result, the scope of this suit expands to include antitrust issues as these companies hold a virtual monopoly providing an essential service. The freedom of choice would be made dependent on what other market players do, and whether an individual data subject would find the other Controller's services genuinely equivalent.[60]

This will lead the case to larger questions to consider. Is the denial of service by Google a detriment, or a mere exclusion from its platforms? How about the denial of the services of Instagram? How about Whatsapp? Can we force these companies to provide service to those who don't agree to their terms? Can we stifle the rights of users who wish to use their platforms, but don't want their data processed? Are there reasonable substitutes in the market? Would forcing these companies set a precedent of these websites acting as public resources? If so, how would such a system be implemented?

*g. The Burden of Proof*   After the filing of the Complaint, the Burden of Proof now shifts to the Data Controller[61] to demonstrate:

1. Consent of the users
2. The lawfulness of processing personal data
3. The legal grounds for processing special data

All four companies face a monumental task of demonstrating that inspite of poorly drafted privacy policy, no excessive processing of personal data has taken place. Additionally, they have a huge burden of proving consent was not conditional, which will be a tough task.

*h. Learning Curve versus Enforcement*   The crucial decision before the Supervisory Authorities now would be to determine whether they should hold a hard stance on GDPR enforcement or permit a "learning curve" to the Controllers. Considering this suit was filed on the day of GDPR coming into force, some degree of leniency should be expected as the Companies could argue that they have yet to learn how to "fully" comply with the letter of the regulation.

As several ambiguities exist as to how GDPR should be executed, in practical terms (such as privacy policies) those mandates have not been fully laid down by the regulation. As a result, if at the end of the SA's investigation it is discovered that violations occurred in the poor drafting of the Terms of Use in failing to state specific purposes of processing, a large fine may be imposed as an unjust result. However, any fines imposed owing to violation of the principles of consent mandate the highest penalty under the regulation, so it will be interesting to see how these four cases end up shaping the future of data processing and online contract law.

### 5.2.2 Processing Based on Legal Sanction

GDPR Article 6 acts as a revolutionary piece of law, which now restricts the circumstances under which personal data may be processed, limiting the scope of abuse. The bases listed are relatively "open-ended" and abstract because Member States are considering the discretion to add further specifics. For example, while GDPR lists "Vital Interests" of the data subject as a legal ground for processing Member States can specify what qualifies as a "vital" interest.

These "Opening Clauses" left in GDPR leave businesses to keep track of multiple standards for determining their legal bases, even though they may exclusively provide services within the EU. For example, different states may describe what forms of "advertising" are acceptable to qualify as a "legitimate basis" for processing personal data. State X may require explicit consent for native (subliminal) advertising while State Y may allow it based on normal consent. A business should ideally maintain a *master-list* of their legal bases and its parameters. Processing will be lawful only if it falls into one of the legally authorized situations which have been enumerated below.

**5.2.2.1 Formation or Performance of a Contract**   Processing of personal data is lawful when it is necessary for entering into a contract or for its performance. To fall under this category, the data subject must be a party to the agreement for processing. Otherwise, the data subject must be a *third-party beneficiary* to a contract initiated for processing of their data.[62]

Contractual necessity is a broad exception and shall apply regardless of which phase in the contract is concerned, so long as it occurs in the context of a contract.[63] Processing is necessary if the contract cannot be concluded or fulfilled without the personal data requested. This is a case-by-case determination and depends on the specific facts.

For example, social networking sites will require a certain amount of essential personal data, such as your e-mail ID to help you create your profile, to enter into a contract. Another example would be Amazon or an E-commerce website requiring delivery and payment details so that a contract may be performed fully.

**5.2.2.2 Compliance with a Legal Obligation** Processing is permitted where the Controller will be required to do so under a law to which he is subject. This law must be codified and adopted by parliament[64] and can cover multiple processing activities at once.[65] Member States have the authority to maintain and introduce new laws that provide more detail to these "legal obligations."[66] These obligations will likely relate to maintaining data in certain sectors such as healthcare, law, and finance.

**Illustration:** A recent executive order in one of the countries where the website operates has requested that all companies that work with DNA data analytics and with medical samples will be required to assist the government in its recent scheme of registering all citizens into a unified database. The companies will be required to actively assist the government in cataloguing and recording any information on citizens who do not feel like taking time out to register themselves. The website would also help the government in developing its own software of DNA data analytics by way of a partnership caused by radical nationalization. The Association of DNAnalytics, an industry association of all companies in the biometric data sector, would be subject to this law and would be legally obligated to process personal data of the users on its website in accordance with the law.

**5.2.2.3 Protection of Vital Interests** Processing for "vital interests" of the data subject is subordinate to other legal permissions under GDPR Article 6. This is because processing under this provision should only take place where no other legal basis can be claimed.[67] Personal data may be processed when there is a necessity to protect the "vital interests" of:

1. The data subject, or
2. Any other natural person.

Again, from the above we can see that the everyday user, namely, a "natural person," is afforded exclusive protection in line with GDPR objectives.[68] The term "vital interests" has not been defined anywhere in the regulation; however, Recital 46 clarifies that it relates to matters that are essential for the life of the data subject, essentially, creating an *Emergency/Health and Safety clause* for the processing of data, such as preventing epidemics, or logging blood types in the ER.

An example of this is a hospital processing personal data of a car accident victim based on their samples to ascertain blood type, treatment, and to track down their next of kin. If hypothetically, the victim at one point has raised strong religious objections to any form of treatment and the next of kin communicates this fact, the presumed will of the data subject will prevail over his/her presumed vital interests.[69]

**5.2.2.4 Public Interest and Exercise of Official Authority** Processing is allowed when it is necessary to carry out a task in the public interest. A good example of this would be the illustration provided above, where the Association of DNAnalytics subject to the data collection scheme can be deemed to be working in the public interest by helping the government create a unified database of citizens.

The Controller may also process personal data when it is necessary while exercising official duty. It is important to state that this official authority should have a basis in EU or Member law.[70] A large portion of this provision and the provision relating to "public interest tasks" can be determined by subsequent law which may lay down:

- The purpose of processing
- The type of data that may be processed and disclosed
- The data subjects concerned
- The limitations to such activities
- The storage periods
- Any other rules in the application of GDPR[71]

Using the illustration above once more, Mr. Ben Kim (DPO) by working in the newly nationalized Genepool.com (a member of the Association) as their Controller, acts in the public interest and is permitted to process data by exercising this newfound official authority. However, Mr. Kim's authority is limited to the parameters of the Executive Order alone and may not exceed its scope.

**Illustration 2:** A Regional Transportation Authority maintains a system that grants licenses to individuals and maintains a public register of licenses on that same website. At the time of applying online for a license, the RTO's page clearly lists a notice of:

- Name of the agency and establishing legislation
- Purpose of data collection
- Legal grant of data collection
- Information provided that will appear on the public register

Public agencies should clearly communicate the sources of its authority for the Controller to qualify as one acting in the "public interest" or under the official authority of law under GDPR Article 6.1.e.

**5.2.2.5 Exercising Legitimate Interests**   The Controller or third-party employee under the Controller may process data when it is necessary fulfill the purpose of their legitimate interests. This general clause adopted from the Data Protection Directive (the "DPD") states data may be processed when it is needed to fulfill the purpose for which the Collectors are permitted to conduct under law. Under DPD, legitimate interest was intended to be a narrow commercial exception; however, over time businesses have adopted interpretive liberties of the provision to their benefit, leading to lax enforcement.[72]

The ambit of "legitimate purposes" has once again been left undefined by the regulation, leaving space for the Member States to legislate on what qualifies for "legitimate purposes."[73] However, GDPR Recital 47 states that this may include matters such as preventing fraud or even processing for the purposes of direct marketing.

**Illustration:** Genepool.com and its employees routinely conduct a web audit of the database of its clients to prevent predictable cyber-attacks and fraudulent profiles.

This broad exception essentially permits the Controller to pursue its business interests and process for purposes which may be legal, economic, idealistic, or other nature.[74] This would include:[75]

1. Intragroup transfers
   **Example:** Employee monitoring, CCTV maintenance, HR databases.
2. Direct marketing
   **Example:** Behavioral tracking and targeted advertising to boost revenue.
3. Network integrity
   **Example:** Requesting additional "information" from consumers to prevent fraud or conducting web audits.
4. Strategic analysis
   **Example:** Using data analytics to improve new website interface.
5. Record keeping
   **Example:** Storing data past the company's document retention policy pursuant to a "litigation hold" to preserve evidence for trial.
6. Consumer assessments
   **Example:** Credit scores and eligibility tests for scholarships.
7. Data sharing with third parties and Joint Controllers
   **Example:** An accountant processing personal data for tax returns on behalf of clients or data transfers between merging companies.

**Balancing test:** When processing is necessary for "the purposes of legitimate interests pursued by the Controller" the decision must be balanced with the interests and freedoms of the users and cannot be carried out if overridden.[76]

The balancing test must be applied in evaluating the reasonable expectations of the data subject's privacy based on its specific situation with the Controller.[77] Evaluating these privacy interests could be based on social, economic, professional, and personal considerations, as the test depends on the relationship with the Controller or third party.[78] The rights of the data subject "override" the legitimate interests of the business if the consequences of the processing result in its impairment. The Data Controller must find an economically viable and minimally invasive way to exercise their legitimate interests without harming the interests of their consumer base.

To summarize, a business must balance:

- **Purpose:** Legitimate interests of Controller or third party
- **Necessity:** Processing that must be done to meet that interest
- **Rights:** The protection given to the data subjects' privacy rights under GDPR

Thus, if we were to extend our illustration of Genepool.com, consider that they participate in direct marketing to its users for pharmaceuticals and treatments based on the data they collect. If a user requests them to cease such direct marketing to them, Genepool.com is obliged to comply under GDPR, as their legitimate purposes cannot override the user's rights under the regulation.

**Exception:** The above circumstance will not apply to public authorities carrying out processing for their tasks.

This small exception leaves space for abuse, as public authorities would not be required to process exclusively for the furtherance of their legitimate interests. Under any other circumstance, the Controller would be required to process data only when he is doing so to do his job (or under other circumstances listed in Article 6), but public authorities, particularly their Controllers, are not subject to such a limitation or to the balancing test. This leaves a dangerous ambiguity, which can be abused.

From the above list we can conclude that lawful processing exists when there is either consent or necessity. Items 2 through 7 must be carried out only when there is a necessity to do so. This drastically limits the access to data and the amount of processing that can be processed. Instead of websites indiscriminately mining personal data from a user, they should only do so when needed. A sound rule of thumb to exercise is seeing whether there is a nexus or connection between the economic activity and the data processing conducted by the entity,[79] be it legal, financial, functional, administrative, etc. If the processing helps in boosting economic position of the Controller entity, then they cannot evade GDPR by reducing the activities.[80]

### 5.2.3  Changing the Processing "Purpose"

Business models operating online are fluid and tend to change their purposes of data collection. A business may have been processing under the authority of an expiring legislative act and would have to receive consent to continue working. GDPR allows for a change in the processing purpose only if certain conditions are met:[81]

1. The data subject consents to the new change.
2. The change is based on EU or Member State law and constitutes a necessary and proportionate measure in a democratic society to safeguard important public interest objectives.[82]
3. The new purpose is compatible with the purpose the data was initially collected for.

**The compatibility test:** While consent and public interest discussed above are self-explanatory in justifying a change in processing purposes, "compatibility" has a more nuanced application. GDPR specifies the following non-exhaustive factors to consider:[83]

- **Linkage:** The modified purpose should have a logical link with the original purpose for collection.[84]
- **Context and relationship:** The context for data collection and the data subject's relationship with the Controller are important factors to consider. What would a reasonable person in the data subject's position expect their data to be used for, based on the context they originally provided it for?[85]

- **Nature of data:** The type and sensitivity of data can also determine whether the change of purpose is appropriate.
- **Consequences:** Both positive and negative results of the change can affect compatibility.[86] If the change will be to the data subject's detriment, it is less likely to be considered as a "compatible" use.[87]
- **Data protection:** Applying appropriate safeguards and protections on the new processing operation (such as encryption) can help vouch for compatibility.[88] If a company has planned for the adverse effects of the change, it helps to offset any concerns the users may have.

If a company can successfully prove compatibility, they will require no separate legal basis from the original one claimed, which allowed them to collect the data initially. Let us apply the test in an example.

**Illustration:** A social networking site, exclusive for aspirational and amateur models named "Runways.com" operates as a platform for males and females to break into the industry by posting their photos on their profile. The boutique website originally operated as a "fusion" of LinkedIn and Instagram for individuals in the fashion business. The users of the site used it mainly for professional "social" networking.

In December 2018 Runways.com decided to use their resources to start the world's largest Online Talent Agency for fashion. The change occurred overnight after months of planning. Soon afterward, they started helping their users by providing them numerous openings and offers based on their geographical location. While some offers were great opportunities for the users, others were subpar or in some cases fraudulent.

The change here is not compatible because the link between social networking and being a client in a talent agency is minimal. Further, Runways.com went from being a "platform" for the users to a "professional manager," which changes the context and relationship in collection. Though the consequences were mixed, the adverse effects were not planned for properly or foreseen by the users.

## 5.2.4   Special Categories of Data

All data are not equal, with some being more valuable than others. Information that individuals would ordinarily keep private is afforded augmented protection under GDPR. Article 9 provides what constitutes a special category of data (special data), along with a long list of exceptions to the rule.

**Illustration:** The Health Ministry in conjunction with a civic hospital conducts a survey of its patients' lifestyles and overall health. The data collection for the survey is for "research" purposes, processing sensitive data under Article 9.2.a, GDPR which requires patients to provide explicit written/electronic consent. Civic hospitals must find a way to ensure patient confidentiality when releasing individually identifiable information to its collaborators, who compile data for the survey. Individual doctors obtaining consent must explain to patients the intended purposes of the survey for data sharing to be lawful.

**5.2.4.1 What Is "Special" Data?** In the broader scheme of the provision, processing Special Categories of data is generally prohibited outright, unless the activities fall into one of the exceptions subsequently elaborated.[89] Under the regulation, personal data cannot be processed to reveal:

1. Racial and ethnic origin
2. Political opinions
3. Religious beliefs
4. Philosophical beliefs
5. Trade union membership[90]

Additionally, there is a prohibition against processing of genetic and biometric data for identifying:

1. A person (specifically, uniquely identifying a person)
2. Data concerning health
3. Data concerning a person's sex life
4. Data concerning sexual orientation

The above categories are broad in the implications, and almost specifically targeted to the data mining and analytics entities such as Cambridge Analytica and Equifax. The first category of "profiling based" information specifically mandates that the data be processed in such a way that it reveals the information listed. This is a wise choice of words as the users do not always explicitly make such inclinations known on all the websites where they have submitted personal data. However, the data can be analyzed in a way as to profile the users, thereby tailoring the information they receive back to them. The second category of biometric and genetic data is a more straightforward privacy-based issue of personal matters.

GDPR Article 9 is a measure to combat the misuse of certain private information that can be valuable if used in a certain way (see Figure 5.2).

**5.2.4.2 Location and Behavioral Data** It is important to note that location data has not been included under this list as per GDPR. Perhaps the drafters knew that location data is becoming instrumental in most services provided; thus augmented requirements would prove to be burdensome for the businesses. However, as likely experienced by everyone at one point, Controllers generally request specific consent when accessing location data. In some places, such as California, Radio Frequency Identification tags ("RFID tags") in cars and other tracking services are permissible only subject to the consent of the user.

Even though GDPR does not bundle location data with the other special data, it would be worthwhile to look into your organization's cookies, which help to track both actively submitted data and passively tracked data.[93] Cookies can be used for:

- Website analytics
- Direct advertising
- Site functionality[94]

**Prohibition of Processing**

| S. No. | Profiling based data revealing: | Genetic and Biometric data revealing: |
|---|---|---|
| 1. | Race (includes names, languages spoken, lineage, parents name, place of birth, etc.) | Identification (includes any form of data that is unique to the person and has been handed down by genetics pointing to the physiology and characteristics of him/her)[91] |
| 2. | Ethnicity (same as above in race) | Health (includes data on the person's physical and mental health status, and whether they are receiving any healthcare)[92] |
| 3. | Political opinions (includes data relating to party affiliation, causes supported, opinions voiced, etc.) | Sexual activities (includes data relating to person's sexual life like websites visited, photos/videos received, dating app activity, etc.) |
| 4. | Religion (includes spiritual affiliations, opinions voiced, even lack of religious convictions, rejection of ideas, etc.) | Sexual orientation (includes the names of a person's partners, any indication of gender preferences, etc.) |
| 5. | Philosophical beliefs (includes the data discussed under religion and more abstract outlooks such as world view) | |
| 6. | Trade union membership (includes any data that points to affiliation or membership that may harm the user's collective bargaining position) | |

**Figure 5.2**  Special Categories of Data

Unlike location data, cookies track a user's behavior and preferences, which implies that the nature of use determines whether special data is collected. To ensure that the AI employed does not run outside of GDPR, determine whether the data collected is shared, whether the user has been adequately notified, and whether the user has an option of rejecting the use of such cookies.

**5.2.4.3 Processing Data Relating to Criminal Convictions** The processing of personal data of an individual relating to criminal convictions, offenses, and related security measures will be conducted exclusively under "Official Authority" that has been awarded to the Controller under EU or Member Law. Furthermore, any comprehensive register of criminal convictions shall be kept only under Official Authority.[95] The control maintained by EU Member States is necessary, as criminal data can cause great harm to a data subject if leaked. Member State legislations are likely to clarify how this data is handled internally in an employment context or for court procedures. Article 11 here ensures that the sensitive information relating to one's criminal past is not shared to any unscrupulous private party, and even if so, such data remains under the "Official Authority" of the Controller in public interest (example: The Controller of a "Private Prison service").

**5.2.4.4 The Exceptions to the Rule** GDPR heavily restricts the processing of special data by expressly stating that there is a "prohibition"; however, there are numerous exceptions to the baseline rule, which are listed below.

*a. Explicit Consent* The user has the authority to provide explicit consent to processing of special data for one or more of the above purposes. "Explicit" consent should be compared to regular consent,[96] which has its own requirements in the regulation. However, it is relevant to note that GDPR fails to state what exactly constitutes "explicit" consent and how it differentiates from regular consent.

**Illustration:** At the time of collecting biometric data from its customers, Genpool.com must ask for explicit consent to process the data, as it falls under the Biometric and Genetic category for the purposes of evaluating health. Which one of the following would be suitable in their terms of use?

1. **EXPLICIT CONSENT FOR COLLECTION OF SENSITIVE DATA:** We at Genepool.com will require that you give us your full, clear and knowing consent before proceeding forward with our services. The "Sample" you provide us will be converted into "Biometric and Genetic Data" for the limited purposes listed in Clause ____ of this Agreement. Genepool.com protects your data with our state of the art cyber security; more information here- __LINK__. The law requires that you give us your knowing consent when providing us with such data; if you agree please type "I consent" followed by your initials and date in the boxes provided below. [____]

2. **BIOMETRIC and GENETIC DATA COLLECTION CONSENT:** In order to fully service you and give a full and proper "Diagnosis" we require a sample of your Biometric and Genetic data which will be used in the analysis of your health, deficiencies, and any illnesses, which will be part of your diagnosis. Your sample must be sent as per our "Sample delivery system," which you can access here __LINK__. We require your consent, so please click the box below to indicate your consent to such analysis □.; OR

3. **CONSENT FOR COLLECTION OF SENSITIVE DATA:** We require your consent to conduct our testing of your samples as it is a "Special Category of Data" under the law. If you choose not to consent, we cannot fully service you. Please click "I agree" to indicate your consent □.

4. **CONSENT:** Genepool.com requires your consent to test the samples and the Biometric and Genetic information that is sent to us so that we may fully provide our service. Please type out "I Consent" or "I Agree" into the box below and click "Continue." [_____].

The four above examples are all examples of "consent" with varying degrees of specificity. From a plain reading of the above, we can see that option 1 is the best example of what constitutes "explicit" consent as it provides a full picture of the weight of the information provided, along with assurances as to its safety and purpose. The remaining options proceed in a descending order of the information and reasons provided to attain the consent. Option 4 is perhaps the weakest and may not constitute "explicit" consent as it doesn't fully educate the users as to the special nature of this data, even though the user will be required to type out his consent.

It is unclear as to what constitutes "explicit" consent and whether the same rules for regular consent can be applied to analyze this rule. However, some sound practices can be provided by looking at the above:

- Ask for explicit consent on a separate page rather than burying it in the main Terms and Conditions.
- Similar to the concept of explicit consent in medical and legal ethics, the consent should be given after a full, frank, and clear exposure as to the type of data collected, the purpose of collection, its security, and why the consent is important.
- Provide links to any provisions relating to other tangential matters such as the purpose of collection and its protection.
- Require the user to type out their consent, rather than simply clicking a box.

It is important to note that the user's right to provide explicit consent may be prohibited by EU or Member law.[97] An EU Working Party on "Consent" has indicated that there may be a breadth of methods that explicit consent may be implemented (full statements, two-step verifications, etc.) but leaves the decision of execution largely dependent on the situation,[98] stating that even electronic signatures may qualify as well.

*b. Employment or Social Protection*   In the field of Employment, Social Security, or Social Protection Law, necessary processing of special data is permitted for exercising the specific rights and obligations of the Controller or user. This can be done if:

- Authorization exists in either EU or Member law.
- Appropriate safeguards exist to protect the rights and freedoms of the user.

This exception recognizes that employers and governmental systems need to maintain sensitive data to carry out their functions. The best example would be to consider a corporate employer who collects employee health data to provide life and health insurance policies. At the same time, Member State legislations must provide a corresponding high level of protection to this data for ensuring its safety.

*c. Data Subjects with Incapacity*   Special data may be processed if it is necessary to protect the vital interests of the data subject or of any other Natural person who is either physically or legally incapable of giving consent. This is a limited exception to the concept of consent under GDPR, essentially being an "incapacity" defense. For example, if a patient brought into the emergency room requires treatment or maintaining a database of patients in a mental institution.

Processing special data under these circumstances should be based on the existential needs and interests of the data subject's physical integrity and life. The presumed will of the data subject should guide the Controller in deciding whether to process the data (such as a *Do Not Resuscitate DNR* provided in their living will). Going against the person's presumed will by collecting the data makes the processing illegal under GDPR.

*d. Associations and "Not-for-Profit" Bodies*   Here, the regulation creates a sort of "Membership" exception to processing special data in the following types of organizations:

- Foundations
- Associations
- Not-for-profits

Having a:

- Political,
- Philosophical,
- Religious, or
- Trade union aim.

The data collected must be limited to the members, former members, or individuals who have "regular contact" with the organization. The data can only be processed in furtherance of legitimate activities with appropriate safeguards to the information. To fall under this exception the entity's purpose is the deciding factor rather than its formal legal structure. It is important to examine how the special data was collected and why it was provided.

An example of this would be a Barge Workers Union keeping a detailed roaster on its members and their health data for their worker's compensation, or a political party keeping a list of the religions, ideologies, and race of its members.

*e. Public Data*   Special data that has been manifestly made public by the data subject himself can be processed. The data must be made public by a voluntary decision by the data subject. This exception is broad in its wording as it opens publicly available data for Controllers to use freely. Where is the line drawn before the information is considered "personal data" warranting protection under the regulation?

**Illustration:** Rich Putnam is a consistent blogger on left-wing politics, on a common blogging platform website named Bloggey.com. He is well known for not giving details of himself in his articles but keeping to the arguments on the issues and the facts. His voice in his articles is well known to represent the disenfranchised minorities, political and economic theories, and a critical voice to religious issues. However, no one has ever seen a photo of Rich, nor do they know his religion or ethnicity. The only thing that is known is that he lives in Sicily and is very sensitive toward racist comments on his blog page, removing such comments, saying that they "pollute the real discussion."

PolitiCAN is a political data analytics company that does a breadth of creative data analytics to help their client political parties to win elections based on public resources. Their most recent project for Dr. Buscemi, a candidate in the upcoming Italian elections, is to accumulate all political-based blogs and break down the potential "bases" where he may be lacking. The software mines the public data online; the AI analyzes the content of prominent bloggers and classifies them and their views on different categories from political stance to religion and so on. With this information, the candidate can tailor his speeches and campaign issues to reach dissenting voices. The software, while mining data, finds, reads, and analyzes Rich's posts and concludes that he is of Spanish origin, supports the far left, is a practicing Lutheran, and believes in a socialist democracy government.

Were all the details manifestly made public? Is it required that the user expressly and clearly makes these details known? Or is it enough that peripheral matters were public? This remains unclear from GDPR.

*f. Legal Purposes*    Processing of special data is permissible for:

- Establishment of legal claims
- Exercise of legal claims
- Defense against legal claims; or
- Courts acting in their judicial capacity.

This exception can be claimed in court or in out-of-court procedures[99] such as arbitration or administrative hearings. Note that this exception is likely subjected to more specific Member State legislation on personal data in court proceedings and litigations.

*g. Public Interest*    Like the earlier exception in "processing for further purposes," special data may be processed if it is necessary to achieve a substantial public interest involved. However, the following criteria must exist:

1. Basis in EU or Member law.
2. Processing must be proportionate to the aim pursued.
3. A respect for the essence of data protection.
4. Provision of suitable and specific measures to protect the rights of the user.

Processing special data under this exception requires respect for fundamental rights and must be based on preserving the interests of the state, or the lives, health, and freedom of its citizens.[100] Thus, in going back to our Genepool.com illustration for the creation of a unified state database, the above four factors must exist before the data is processed in the name of public interest.

*h. Prevention and Occupational Medicine*   Special data may be processed in the field of prevention and occupational medicine in

- Assessing the working capacity of employees
- Diagnosis
- Providing health and social care
- Providing treatment
- The management of health and social care systems

One can consider this as the "Hospital Exception," as it is only logical that processing sensitive data such as biometric and genetic information is needed in the field. Bear in mind, processing data under this exception must be pursuant to

1. EU or Member Law
2. A contract between healthcare professional and subject[101]

The "Hospital Exception" must be read along with other provisions of the regulation, as is the case when the exception is claimed by way of a contract between the healthcare provider and patient. Here if a contract designates the healthcare provider permission to collect the special data of the patient it should be read along with Article 9(2)(a), which relates to explicit consent, as the relationship between the parties is still rooted in contract, with an objective to collect special data.

Furthermore, when processing this data, the healthcare professional is bound by his *Obligation of Professional Secrecy* that the EU or Member State he is registered in adheres to.[102] In other words, the "Doctor," so to speak, must treat this special data as if it were privileged information provided to him from the client.

*i. Public Health*   Closely related to public interest, special data may be processed for the purposes of public safety and health for the greater good. Based on EU or Member law, keeping in mind the rights of the user and the obligations of professional secrecy,[103] such data can be processed to

- Prevent "cross-border" threats to health and safety (such as epidemics)
- Ensure a high standard and quality of healthcare
- Ensure the safety of medical products and devices

A common example of this is the processing of medical data to prevent the breakout of epidemics or using the data accumulated in a hospital to predict and improve treatment of diseases in premature babies. Another example is processing personal data to test new medical devices or pharmaceuticals entering the market.

*j. Archival Purpose*   Pursuant to EU or Member law, special data may be processed if it is necessary for archiving information. The legislative scope of EU or Member law can be used to derogate and limit the rights of the user,[104] but only insofar as the rights impair the objectives of the activity. The purpose of archiving can be for reasons relating to

- Public interest,
- Historical,
- Statistical, or
- Scientific research.

However, archiving can only be performed in a manner which is necessary and proportionate with safeguards in place to protect the rights and freedoms of the users. These safeguards include measures such as:[105]

1. Data minimization
2. Pseudonymization/encryption
3. Or any measure that prevents identification of the data subject.

The archiving exception is one that is observed throughout the regulation, as it is a common exception to data processing, provided that such activities are not excessive and only process to the extent that is needed for the operation.

**5.2.4.5 New Technologies Involving Special Data**   Developments in technology has led to physical devices becoming smaller, while data-processing capabilities become larger. In this section we will briefly identify GDPR issues for three developing technologies that implicate sensitive information in personal data processing. Additionally, we will discuss how to comply with GDPR requirements when engaging in such processing activities.

*Special Case 1: Big Data*   The big data approach to processing involves technologies that use large data sets to extract value. The "value" extracted can be monetary, commercial, scientific, statistical, educational, etc. Companies such as Google that possess an immeasurable amount of personal data study the general trends in human behavior and consumer attitudes. Big data analytics involve the use of factual data (example: studying weather trends) or personal data (example: studying pop-culture growth). The massive volume of data collected is used to understand, predict, and shape human behavior.[106]

Personal data involving tracking data and other behavioral information like direct advertising, predictive analytics, social media posts, geolocation data, etc., are valuable assets to businesses.[107] The information gained from the data is valuable for AI programs that profile data subjects in processing. Big data is used on a macro level to study trends in human behavior and at a micro level to study individual behavior. Big data firms face the following GDPR issues:

- **GDPR applicability:** With such a volume of data involved in analytics, even the smallest amount of personal data in processing will trigger GDPR compliance by a big data–processing firm. Minimal personal data will implicate the whole data set to compliance, so businesses must be mindful to accurately keep track of the data's nature.
- **Data protection:** If identification is not needed by the firm, implement measures to anonymize or pseudonymize the data for safe processing. Note, data

can be identifiable if a pattern is created with other surrounding information. Therefore, removing identifying characteristics is important.

- **Purpose limitation:** Big data firms need to revamp earlier broad data-processing policies as excessive data collection is a part of the overall business model. Considering the legal bases listed under GDPR for processing, the business must limit its data collection to what is needed for the analytics.[108] The "purpose" of the business must be clear and limited when conducting DPIAs or interacting with data subjects. Whether a big Data Controller has fully complied with its information obligations is determined on a case-to-case basis.[109]

- **Accountability:** Controllers are big data firms that provide the service of analytics to customers, while Processors execute the client's requests. In big data processing, these lines can be blurred owing to the nature of data collection. GDPR requires that businesses are accountable for their data flows starting at the source of data collection. Big data firms should keep track of their different sources of personal data and ensure those partners are also GDPR compliant.

*Special Case 2: Cloud Computing*   Cloud computing (Clouds) is an innovation that helped solve storage issues as the volume of data produced by individuals grew. Cloud computing uses internet-based technology and service models for the delivery of IT applications. This is commonly employed in office settings in virtual processing systems, IT infrastructure, software solutions, e-mails, etc.[110] Clouds help provide a *scalable* IT model to businesses at a reasonable price so that processing can be carried out without physical or financial hurdles,[111] for example, using Microsoft Office Suite services. Under GDPR, cloud computing Controllers face the following complications:

- **Client is a Controller:** The cloud computing service providers are Controllers, but at the same time their clients can qualify as Controllers themselves.[112] This is because they use the cloud service to process personal data based on purposes decided by them. This is not a blanket rule, as determining whether a business (relying on clouds) qualifies as a Controller is a case-by-case determination as in big data.[113] In most cases, the service provider will likely only be the Processor.

- **Joint Controllership:** There may be circumstances where both service provider and client are Controllers for their own purposes under GDPR. Under such cases, GDPR rules on Joint Controllership are applicable along with liability issues. Despite the fact that clients are rarely able to negotiate service contracts with providers, they are free to select from different providers based on allocating data protection responsibilities.[114]

- **Processors:** Cloud companies and their clients often contract-out processing to an appropriate entity who can handle the work. Controller businesses may lose exclusive control of the personal data they process and must ensure that

GDPR compliance carries to their business partners.[115] Controllers should take efforts to compare references, data protection standards, certifications, etc., before choosing a Processor to secure the confidentiality and integrity of the personal data.

- **Subprocessors:** Cloud companies should also ensure that any Subprocessors in the data-processing chain are also GDPR compliant by reviewing contractual stipulations with the cloud service company.[116]
- **International cloud companies:** Cloud services provided by companies based internationally should be authorized to carry out the processing by having a legal basis under GDPR.

*Special Case 3: The Internet of Things (IoT)*   Considered an instrumental channel for communication in the fourth Industrial Revolution,[117] the internet of things (IoT) refers to an infrastructure where billions of sensors are embedded into everyday objects to turn them into "smart" things.[118] The miniature sensors are designed to continuously record, process, and transfer data with one another for object maintenance, replacement, quality, and analytics. IoT is unique in that more data increases efficiency of processing and analytics. Considering the proximity IoT has with human environment, behavior, and privacy[119] it invariably implicates personal data, subjecting it to GDPR.

**Example:** Wearables and "fitness" trackers that study habits, behavior, daily preferences and schedules, etc. Juxtapose this with other IoT applications like sensors in clothes, lamps, heating units, etc. While some are deeply linked with personal data, others exist only tangentially around human activity.

The key issues facing IoT in GDPR compliance are:

- **Purpose limitation:** Establishing a lawful basis for data processing is the largest hurdle for IoT Processors under GDPR. As IoT technology relies on excessive processing for efficacy, defining the "purpose" of processing and a legal basis to do so is difficult under GDPR. Data minimization should be carried out internally, and collection must be tailored to a clear purpose that is communicated to customers.
- **"Legitimate" interests:** A basis that can be claimed by IoT Controllers is the exercise of legitimate interests in processing the personal data. However, this basis is risky because the omniscient nature of IoT will be overruled by the data subjects' rights[120] under GDPR. IoT relates to objects placed in human environments, and the data gained will likely shed intimate details of the data subject (like health, intimacy, location, etc.), raising serious privacy concerns.[121] Justifying economic interests as the sole basis in such situations is unlikely to pass GDPR's muster.
- **Consent:** User consent is always a strong basis for justifying IoT processing. Note that IoT involves processing special data which requires explicit consent from the data subject. Businesses must fully educate the user on IoT in

order to get a valid informed consent for processor. This can be carried out by implementing the terms into the device itself by obtaining permission at the time of data collection.[122]

- **Contractual "necessity":** Necessity for concluding or performing a contract is not always a viable basis, as it requires a direct link with the purposes of processing. This may be difficult for IoT Processors to prove, as data collection is required to be excessive. But contractual necessity can prove useful in limited circumstances: for example, using IoT services in car devices and housing devices to track maintenance needs.
- **Data protection:** Similar to big data (in some cases by using big data), IoT relies on large data sets for analytics. The personally identifiable information is usually supplemental to the main purpose of maintenance, study, and analytics of the thing itself. But IoT often maintains personal data for helping the seller keep a record of sales and units to maintain. For this reason, Data Protection and Privacy by Design should be implemented in IoT technologies moving forward. Data security in ongoing processing is also important, but GDPR places value on preventive data protection policies to avoid re-identification.[123] Practices like anonymization will be important to mask data subject movement patterns and behavioral preferences when the information is not needed for the IoT Controller.[124] The privacy-friendly design should implement user controls and transparency settings[125] to ensure that data subjects retain control of their rights under GDPR.

The three new technologies analyzed above will become the backbones of data processing in the future as IoT collects new data, big data analyzes it, and cloud computing stores it. Collectively these technologies will increase their processing capabilities, requiring more personal data for its efficacy. Planning for GDPR compliance fixes many foreseeable issues down the road and acts as a barrier to abuse by businesses.

**5.2.4.6 Developing the Law Further**   As stated earlier, the EU and its Member States are given leeway to further legislate on how to comply specifically with matters relating to:[126]

- Processing for performance of legal obligations, and
- Public interest tasks and the "official authority vested in the Controller."

The law on these matters can lay down a variety of requirements from what can be considered as "lawful processing" all the way to what the "storage requirements" can be, so businesses must be ready for sudden developments in the law as they come along. Once again looking at our Genepool.com illustrations, it would be left to the Member State that created the Executive Order to give the specific requirements for what processing can be done regarding the public database project and the parameters of processing.

## 5.3   International Data Transfers

GDPR is not a regulation that is confined to the borders of the EU alone. The subject matter of regulation, data privacy and protection, often involve issues that transcend normal geographic limitations of other activities. Most domestic cyber laws incorporate a form of extraterritoriality within their scope of application, because the technology and speed of communication on the internet require a state to exercise some degree of control over the data flows of their countries. This once again becomes a matter of national policy, with different states exercising different degrees of control; for example, China controls almost all data flow in and out of the country to effectively censor content; meanwhile, in a nation like Serbia the control is minimal.

So far in this book we parsed GDPR and how it is a "state-to-state" effort to implement the provisions of the regulations effectively to ensure data health within the EU. However, data processing is not a local activity, as it is now becoming necessary for the expansion of international trade and cooperation.[127] Considering the all-encompassing nature of this comprehensive regulation, it is no surprise that there are also rules on the transfer or processing of personal data by a foreign country or international organization.[128] Generally, a company has three hurdles to comply with foreign data transfers:[129]

1. **Comply** with requirements for collection and processing within the EU.
2. **Justify** the disclosure of the personal data to an international entity/ individual.
3. **Ensure** that the destination of the data is also in compliance with GDPR.

GDPR mandates that any transfers of personal data that are undergoing processing or are intended for processing after transfer to a foreign country or international organization can only occur if the Controller and Processor comply with the rules provided by the regulation.[130] The rules related to international data transfers also apply to onward transfers of personal data from or to another foreign country.[131] The key aim of these rules relating to foreign transfers is to ensure that the level of protection afforded to data subjects under GDPR is not undermined.[132]

International transfers can only be carried out if they are in full compliance with GDPR and are followed by the Controller and Processor handling the data.[133] However, the application of the regulation is without prejudice to any international agreement between the EU and other foreign governments and should include appropriate safeguards for the transfer of data outside the Union.[134] A prominent example of this would be the EU–US Privacy Shield, which provides rules for transfers of personal data between the countries. Member States are also entitled to enter into such international agreements; however, they must ensure that such agreements do not affect the application of GDPR or any other Union law,[135] thus, giving less freedom of the States to stray from the regulation. Additionally, when entering into such agreements, Member States must also provide for appropriate level of protection for the data.

### 5.3.1 Adequacy Decisions and "Safe" Countries

A transfer of personal data across the world can be permitted subject to several mechanisms provided under GDPR, one of which is an Adequacy Decision by the European Commission.[136] Such a decision certifies that the foreign nation provides a level of legal certainty and uniformity for adequate protections under the regulation.[137] Adequacy decisions are no new phenomenon in EU data-protection law. In fact, as early as 1995 the EU required this practice in their Data Protection Directive (DPD) with similar requirements to GDPR.[138] GDPR merely characterizes these decisions in greater detail to fit modern times. The Commission must determine whether the foreign country provides an adequate level of protection for data transfers and can relate to:

- A third country
- A territory of a country
- A specified sector(s)
- An international organization

Once the decision has been made that an adequate level of protection exists, a subsequent foreign transfer in line with it shall not require any specific authorization.[139] The Commission may give such a decision by way of an implementing act that provides for periodic review (at least every four years) based on all recent developments in the third country.[140] The implementing act must specify:

- The scope of application (territorial, sectoral, etc.)
- Appropriate SA who oversees such data transfers in the third country

Additionally, the Commission has a duty to monitor developments in these third Countries that could affect the functioning of any such adequacy decision.[141] A comprehensive list of foreign countries which provide or no longer provide an adequate level of protection shall be published by the Commission in the Official Journal of the EU and on its respective website.[142] Furthermore, any decision that was made under the Data Protection Directive of 1995 are "grandfathered" in and remain in force unless amended, replaced, or repealed subsequently.[143]

**5.3.1.1 Determining Adequacy** When determining if a foreign country gives an adequate level of protection to the processing operation, the Commission must consider the following elements:[144]

1. **The laws:** A foreign data transfer can be carried out only if the transferee country has a legal system[145] in place to essentially ensure that the country is not "lawless" when it comes to such transfers. This includes the foreign nation's:
   a. Rule of law
   b. Respect for human rights and fundamental freedoms

c. Relevant legislation, both general and sectoral
d. Implementation of legislations
e. Public security and defense
f. National security
g. Criminal law
h. Case law
i. Power of public authorities to access personal data
j. Existence of data protection rules
k. Existence of professional rules
l. Existence of security measures
m. The third-country transfer rules of that nation
n. Effectiveness and enforceability of data subject's rights
o. Effective administrative and judicial redress mechanisms for those data subjects

2. **Redressability:** Another factor considered by the commission is the existence and effective functioning of one or more independent Supervisory Authorities in the foreign country with a responsibility to ensure compliance with the data-protection rules and to help data subjects enforce their rights for any such transboundary exchange of data.[146] Such SAs must also be equipped with proper enforcement powers and must cooperate with SAs established within EU Member States.

3. **International agreements:** The Commission must also consider the international commitments of the foreign nation that arise from legally binding conventions or instruments,[147] particularly for those relating to protecting personal data. Such instruments also include participation in any multilateral or regional system such as the EU or South Asian Association for Regional Cooperation (SAARC).[148]

**5.3.1.2 Application of the Factors** The elements discussed above should be offered by the foreign country in the form of guarantees to the EU Commission.[149] The application of these elements may face problems in the future as the factors are subjective to the commission's views on the nation since not many countries follow the augmented requirements for protection and processing as laid down under GDPR. Furthermore, most countries outside the EU do not formally recognize the rights of the data subject enshrined under the regulation which might cause conflict.

When determining adequacy, the level of protection afforded by the foreign country only needs to be comparable or essentially equivalent to EU data protection standards.[150] The EU Court of Justice (CJEU) in 2015 when discussing the Police Directive in the Schrems case has clarified in the judgment that adequacy does not require a point-by-point replication of EU law.[151] Rather, equivalency requires a holistic look at the level of protection provided in the country with respect to:

- The substance of privacy rights afforded
- Implementation

- Enforceability
- Supervision

Essentially, protection of the data subjects is the name of the game, as the foreign legal system must provide the resources necessary for keeping the personal data and privacy of the individuals safe. Furthermore, there are certain countries with whom the EU will be actively pursuing dialogue to determine adequacy for increasing digital trade capabilities. In pursuing those countries, the EU Commission will consider the following criteria:[152]

1. The extent of the EU's (actual or potential) commercial relations with a given third country, including the existence of a free trade agreement or ongoing negotiations;
2. The extent of personal data flows from the EU, reflecting geographical and cultural ties;
3. The pioneering role the third country plays in the field of privacy and data protection that could serve as a model for other countries in its region;
4. The overall political relationship with the third country in question, with respect to the promotion of common values and shared objectives at international level.

The test laid down by the CJEU and the commission's criteria has led to diverse privacy systems throughout the world being recognized as "adequate" for international transfers of personal data. Though GDPR and its augmented requirements are now in force, any prior adequacy decisions made by the EU Commission under the auspices of the 1995 DPD remain valid[153] and have not been changed. Below, a brief **Global Status Quo** on the Commission's adequacy determinations has been provided.[154]

| S. No. | Country | Status | Transfer Scope |
|--------|---------|--------|----------------|
| 1. | Norway | Treated as part of the EU. | Transfers can be freely carried out as if it were an EU Country. |
| 2. | Lichtenstein | Treated as part of the EU. | Transfers can be freely carried out as if it were an EU Country. |
| 3. | Iceland | Treated as part of the EU. | Transfers can be freely carried out as if it were an EU Country. |
| 4. | Andorra | Determined adequate. | Free flow of data with no further safeguards necessary. |
| 5. | Argentina | Determined adequate. | Free flow of data with no further safeguards necessary. |
| 6. | Faroe Islands | Determined adequate. | Free flow of data with no further safeguards necessary. |
| 7. | Guernsey | Determined adequate. | Free flow of data with no further safeguards necessary. |

| S. No. | Country | Status | Transfer Scope |
|---|---|---|---|
| 8. | Israel | Determined adequate. | Free flow of data with no further safeguards necessary. |
| 9. | Isle of Man | Determined adequate. | Free flow of data with no further safeguards necessary. |
| 10. | Jersey | Determined adequate. | Free flow of data with no further safeguards necessary. |
| 11. | New Zealand | Determined adequate. | Free flow of data with no further safeguards necessary. |
| 12. | Switzerland | Determined adequate. | Free flow of data with no further safeguards necessary. |
| 13. | Uruguay | Determined adequate. | Free flow of data with no further safeguards necessary. |
| 14. | Canada | Partially adequate. | Commercial organizations who comply with the adequacy determination terms may transfer data freely. |
| 15. | US | Partially adequate. | Free transfer of data subject to compliance with the privacy shield. |
| 16. | Japan | Currently in negotiation. | To be determined. |
| 17. | South Korea | Currently in negotiation. | To be determined. |

### 5.3.1.3 Revocation of the Adequacy Decision
When conducting a regular review and monitoring developments in the foreign countries,[155] if the commission finds that an adequate level of protection is not provided to the processing of personal data by the nation/territory/sector/organization, they may:

- Repeal,
- Amend, or
- Suspend their decision.[156]

Such an act by the commission must be exercised to the extent necessary and will have no retroactive effect on any processing done thus far.[157] Any revocation must be accompanied with a full statement as to why the action is being taken.[158] Furthermore, the commission must, in a timely manner, consult with the foreign country for remedying the situation that led to the revocation of the decision.[159] The reassessment of an adequacy decision is generally subject to the examination procedure of the commission[160] and may be immediately applicable in cases of duly justified imperative grounds of urgency.

Adequacy decisions are only one part of international data transfer mechanisms and are separate from the other grounds listed under Chapter V of GDPR.[161] The revocation of an adequacy decision is without prejudice to the other grounds for foreign transfers that we shall discuss in this chapter.

### 5.3.2 Explicit Consent

As discussed above, explicit consent remains a valid justification for an international transfer of data, subject to the normal requirements of giving such approval under GDPR. The consent provided must relate explicitly to the proposed foreign transfers, with implied consent transfers generally considered insufficient. It is advisable to inform the data subject of:

- The risks of the foreign transfer
- The international recipient of the data
- The location of the recipient

Receiving explicit consent for foreign data transfers has proven difficult in practice. Many companies merely affix a hyperlink to a list of their international partners involved in the data exchange, with very few companies receiving approval for each transfer. These lists are constantly updated as business partners keep changing. Explicit consent is a sound mechanism if a business requires minimal foreign data exchanges, as repeated requests from data subjects for their permission may be burdensome. Customers may get annoyed with constant requests for explicit consent and can revoke their prior consent at any moment. For this reason, explicit consent is best suited for Controllers with a limited client base and international business.

### 5.3.3 Standard Contractual Clauses

Binding corporate rules or adequacy decisions may not be the ideal mechanism for most businesses that carry out international processing owing to the practical difficulties and administrative responsibilities that accompany it. An alternative that has existed in EU data protection law in the DPD are standard contractual clauses (SCCs), which have been adopted by the EU Commission. Similar to the mandatory provisions included in Processing Contracts,[162] SCCs are approved provisions by the commission that must be incorporated into any commercial agreement for the international processing of personal data.[163] Controllers can adopt these SCCs to compensate protection when the foreign country is not marked as "safe" for transfers by the EU Commission.

#### 5.3.3.1 Overview of Commission Decisions

The EU commission approves the wording and content of these clauses by way of commission decisions such as the ones laid down in 2001[164] or its alternative format issued in 2004.[165] In these decisions the clauses and the data-processing principles have been provided in the form of annexures and merely need to be incorporated into the commercial agreement between the parties. Broadly, the commission decisions can be categorized as follows:[166]

- **Controller-to-Controller SCC:** Under a category of transfers between two Controllers (for example, a transfer between Amazon and an online banking service) the commission presents two alternative clauses that could be implemented for such transfers. It is important to note that the two sets of clauses presented by the Commission are independent and cannot be combined.
  - Decision 2001/497/EC "Set I" follows a GDPR model of joint and several liabilities between the two Controllers.
  - Decision 2004/915/EC "Set II" allows parties to separate their individual obligations and allocates liability to parties for breach of their own duties.
- **Controller-to-Processor SCC:** EU Commission Decision 2010/87/EU permits foreign data transfers if the Processors can produce proof of compliance with GDPR.

At present the above-mentioned SCC decisions stand and remain valid; however, as GDPR comes into full effect legally and practically, one can expect more updates to the existing models. This is particularly evident after the ECJ's monumental decision in the *Safe Harbor* case.[167] Many SAs have raised concerns over the legality of transfers under the SCCs as they stand today, such as the Irish Data Protection Commissioner, who has taken up action in the courts of Ireland and intends to take referral to the ECJ on the matter. Though the Commission has acted and amended Set I of the SCCs to give more authority to the SAs,[168] it is more likely they will undergo further change to conform to GDPR.

**5.3.3.2 Content of SCCs**  SCCs must be adopted completely and unaltered, with parties accepting the baseline terms as they are. The protections afforded under SCCs cannot be made to contradict or reduce liability, but they can be expanded by contractual negotiations.[169] Controllers and Processors are encouraged to add protections to the basic SCC terms to protect their users.[170] If two parties wish to implement the SCC decisions into their foreign data transfer agreement, the following mandatory clauses must be incorporated into the agreement to cover the following matters:

1. **Obligations of data exporter:** The clauses require the exporting Controller to abide by core processing principles discussed in this chapter regarding data minimization, user rights, privacy by design, security, etc.
2. **Obligations of the data importer:** The data importer in the foreign country is also bound by the guiding principles of data protection and is additionally required to provide guarantees of compliance, communicate and facilitate with the exporter and EU authorities, and inform European authorities of any request to disclose personal data to the foreign government.

3. **Joint and several liabilities:** Both exporter and importer are left on the hook for any contravention and can later bring an action for compensation against one another.

4. **Data subject as a third-party beneficiary:** SCCs require that the parties recognize their data subjects as beneficiaries of the contract, thus giving the user the freedom to enforce any violation of the clauses with the relevant authorities.

5. **Choice of law:** Here, the EU requires that the law of the data exporter shall govern the agreement, making all regulations such as GDPR directly applicable to them.

6. **Dispute resolution:** The SCCs mandate that the enforcement of data subjects' rights be provided for by the parties through mechanisms such as negotiation, mediation, and arbitration. Additionally, parties must be provided the right to approach the court of the data exporter's country (located within the EU) as the final recourse for the user.

7. **Termination:** The parties must recognize that any violation of the SCCs will result in a termination or suspension of data flows to their organization for processing.

The above-mentioned clauses are only the beginning of the detail elaborated by the EU Commission, as the contract must also have an annexure of Data-processing Principles and a Description of the Transfer attached to the contract.

**5.3.3.3 Consequences of Breaching the Conditions of SCCs**  Breaching SCCs require two parties, the data exporter (based in the EU) and the importer (based abroad). Previous practice has implied that EU authorities lean toward acting against the data exporter for any breach of the SCCs.[171] This seems logical since it is easier to enforce any order against the local party itself, rather than executing a foreign judgment. The 2001 Commission Decision empowers the Member States to prohibit or suspend data flows to the third country in cases where:[172]

- It is established that the foreign nation's law imposes conditions that would require the data importer to derogate from the EU data protection laws in a manner that goes beyond the restrictions necessary for a democratic society and is likely to have a substantially adverse effect on the guarantees provided under the SCCs.
- The data importer has not respected the terms of the SCCs.
- There is a substantial likelihood that the SCCs are not being, or will not be, complied with and the continuation of the transfer would create an imminent risk of grave harm to the data subjects.

One of the key impediments from using SCCs freely is that the Processor would require all its Subprocessors to be subject to GDPR. For businesses heavily reliant on subprocessing (such as ISPs and payment service providers), this may not be the most ideal option.[173] If an SCC has been successfully adopted and implemented by the parties, no specific authorization would be required from the SA for any international transfer to that data importer.[174] Furthermore, GDPR permits parties to modify their contract to the extent that it will not directly or indirectly contradict the terms of the SCC.[175] Previously, SCCs were exclusively within the domain of the EU Commission, but GDPR now shifts that function of authorization onto the SA of the Member State,[176] which changes matters regarding oversight but not regarding the terms to be incorporated.

After the CJEU judgment that quashed the EU–US Safe Harbor Agreement, many Subprocessors voluntarily adopted SCCs as their mode of conducting transfers.[177] However, most entities prefer to not use SCCs when it is not mandated, as the clauses attach additional liabilities and obligations to exporter and importer, which is generally not required or rewarded outside the EU.[178] At present it is considered as the "international standard";[179] however, we are likely to see a change in these SCCs in the near future considering the terms must be adjusted to account for the newer GDPR principles.

**Pros and Cons of SCCs**

| Advantages | Disadvantages |
| --- | --- |
| Faster implementation | Lack of flexibility and individuality in terms |
| Subject to less negotiation over terms | Replaces the "risk-shifting" process of contractual negotiations |
| Certainty of legal compliance | Compliance is placed with rigorous terms, creating administrative burdens |
| Creates a contractual basis for foreign transfers between Controllers, Processors, and intra-group exchanges where one would not exist earlier | Binding corporate rules tend to be more suitable for repeated exchanges between entities |
| Can be used where multiple entities and parties are involved in processing | Liability and risk are often greater on the EU-based party under GDPR |

### 5.3.4 The EU–US Privacy Shield

A prime example of an international agreement related to the safe transfer of data between two countries is the Privacy Shield. This international agreement was put into place prior to GDPR under the auspices of the DPD that preceded it. As the world modernized and digital trade grew, both economic powers set up this agreement for the safe transfer of personal data across their borders. However, this does not qualify the US as a country that provides a fully adequate level of protection where a blanket protection exists for any transfer. As it stands today, the US only provides partially adequate protection limited to the transfers covered by the shield, and any business that is registered under program requires annual recertification.

The Privacy Shield contains seven Privacy Principles that must be followed by businesses as part of their *self-certification* under the regime:[180]

1. **Notice:** Users must be informed of the processing and its purpose, size, nature, etc.
2. **Purpose limitation:** Like GDPR, the Privacy Shield requires that data be collected only to the extent *necessary* under the original or compatible purpose cited.
3. **Choice:** The Controller must give the user an opportunity to *opt-out* of processing where there is a change in processing purpose. If special data needs to be collected the user must *opt-in* to the processing with explicit consent.
4. **Onward transfer accountability:** Controllers must be accountable for any transfers of data to third parties by ensuring they respect the Privacy Shield principles as well.
5. **Data security:** Controller must provide adequate data security in relation to the processing to prevent misuse by others.
6. **Right of access:** Data subjects are entitled to the right of access, rectification, and erasure when the principles under the Privacy Shield have been violated. This must be allowed unless granting such a request would be a disproportionate effort to the business.
7. **Enforcement:** Data subjects are entitled to suitable recourse of their rights under the Privacy Shield. Controllers are obliged to submit themselves to a voluntarily chosen dispute resolution mechanism.[181]

The scope of this agreement covers any companies involved in the transfer of personal data with the EU that have been registered with the US Department of Commerce (DOC), which is subject to an annual renewal of that license.[182] Like all other instruments listed under GDPR and DPD, the Privacy Shield is another way for the EU to ensure safe data transfers and accountability for data transfers that may go beyond the protective scope of their regulations. An American company that seeks to do business with the EU must:

1. Register themselves with the US DOC.
2. Abide by the Privacy Shield Principles (which are essentially the guiding factors of GDPR such as purpose limitation, data minimization, privacy by design, security, transparency, user rights, etc.).
3. Implement privacy policies that replicate and enshrine the principles.
4. Remain compliant and provide redress to the users under the oversight of the US DOC, the FTC and the EU DPA, and the Ombudsman.

Most third-country instruments recognized and implemented by the EU act as their *long arm* of the law, often reflecting the key practices that are central to their ideals of data protection. Even if the US does not have a federal data protection regulation in place, the Controllers who seek to work with the EU must abide by the shield principles to fill that vacuum in the law. This is Europe's way of ensuring that their consumers are not left out on a limb in the scenario where the company goes astray from the law. Redress is a key part of the shield, giving users a breadth of ways to enforce their rights, including:

1. **The Privacy Shield Company:** Akin to Articles 13, 14, and 15 of GDPR, all companies subject to the shield must provide "in-house" modalities for users to exercise rights such as erasure or rectification.
2. **ADR:** As discussed in Chapter 8, companies may implement ADR mechanisms such as mediation or arbitration to resolve their disputes with the users. Such services must be provided to the data subjects free of cost.
3. **The EU DPA:** Some companies are also free to opt for the EU Data Protection Authority to be the recourse for any complaints a user may have. In some cases, such as human resources–related data processing, the involvement of the DPA is mandatory.[183]
4. **US DOC:** Under the shield the US DOC also has oversight authority over companies through a dedicated contact point and 90-day response time.
5. **The FTC:** Overlapping with the DOC's authority, the Federal Trade Commission also accepts complaints for violation of the shield by way of their same system for other complaints on their website (www.ftc.gov/complaint). The US authorities have a close liaison with the EU DPA for any complaints.
6. **Privacy Shield Arbitral Panel:** If the other redress mechanisms above leave a complaint wholly or partially unresolved, it can be forwarded to an established "consumer friendly" arbitration tribunal for resolution of the complaint. This panel can be invoked after all other remedies have been exhausted by the complainant, and is funded by a specialized budget set up by the US DOC.
7. **The Ombudsman:** The users also have a right to complain of violation of the shield by US governmental authorities for activities such as surveillance and unauthorized access. The ombudsman is a senior official within the US Department of State who is independent from other intelligence agencies. This mechanism is intended for complaints relating to national security and involves close contact with the SA of the Member State as well.

The Privacy Shield seeks to improve on the inadequate protections of the now struck-down Safe Harbor Agreement[184] but has been criticized for its complex, inconsistent and difficult recourse mechanisms.[185] This difficulty in applying the Privacy Shield has resulted in it being challenged by Digital Rights Ireland Ltd. in the ECJ on September 16, 2016.[186] The complaint challenged the overall validity of the Privacy Shield but was dismissed by the ECJ due to Digital Rights Ireland's lack of standing.[187] This leaves numerous Privacy Shield concerns unanswered as GDPR comes into force.

The comprehensive nature of this international agreement helps GDPR's effect go to countries that do not otherwise have a suitable data protection law to regulate its Controllers. However, this raises the question as to why no recent action has been taken against companies that have clearly violated the shield, such as Facebook. The issue with international agreements of this scale is that they involve both countries to effectively enforce its provision. Consider the NSA-Prism scandal in the previous decade where the US government was itself culpable for data mining and surveillance which resulted in very few consequences over the course of time. Regardless, as it stands today the EU–US privacy shield is the standard and legal umbrella for transferring data across borders. However, considering that GDPR is now in force and its extraterritorial application in full swing, the US companies who seek to work with EU data have a new standard to meet, leading to likely changes in this international agreement.

### 5.3.5  Binding Corporate Rules

Of all the mechanisms discussed above, binding corporate rules (The Rules) are exhaustively provided for under GDPR. A larger tech conglomerate such as Google or Facebook who operate in numerous locations throughout the world with different subsidiaries giving different services are considered as a "Group of Undertakings" who may operate under a common set of processing rules for cross-border processing.[188] For example, Google's search engine, Chrome, Gmail, maps, and all other services can operate under a single policy for all their processing of personal data as this qualifies as a Joint Economic Activity. In application binding corporate rules cannot be used by entities outside the group[189] and do not serve as an independent legal basis for processing. The rules only act as proof of adequate protection for transfers within the corporate group. It proves useful in two main scenarios:

1. Controller transferring data to its non-EU Members.[190]
2. Controller transferring data to a Processor under service agreement with the Processor's binding corporate rules attached to the contract.[191] In such cases, Processors and Subprocessors in the group are authorized to transfer data to one another without specific authorization for individual transactions. But this does not include transfers to external parties like Subprocessors outside the group.[192]

It is important to note that binding corporate rules are self-imposed and not mandatory, and a Controller can choose to use other mechanisms[193] for transferring data internationally. It is merely a matter of corporate convenience as larger undertakings would find it difficult to manage foreign transfers of such a scale. The rules are subject to approval by the Competent SA in accordance with the consistency mechanism they operate under.[194] These rules operate as a sort of global privacy policy for a large business, with consistency of data protection between its undertakings.

**5.3.5.1 Legally Mandated Clauses**  Though the corporations are free to draft their own internal rules with the help of their attorneys, GDPR specifies essential clauses that must be incorporated into the rules. The content of these clauses largely resembles the requirements laid down by the Article 29 Working Party in their working papers.[195] The breakdowns of the specifications are exhaustive and have been elaborated in categories as follows:[196]

| I. Corporate Structure Information | 1. The structure and contact details of the group of undertakings or entities engaged in a joint economic activity (hereafter Conglomerate) and each of its members.<br>2. The legally binding nature of the rules both within the company and outside of it.<br>3. The complaint procedures.<br>4. The appropriate data protection training the employees who have regular access to personal data undergo. |
|---|---|
| II. GDPR Compliance | 5. The data transfers or set of data transfers, which include:<br>  a. The categories of data collected<br>  b. Type of processing activity<br>  c. The purpose of processing<br>  d. The type of data subjects affected<br>  e. The foreign countries involved in the operation<br>6. The application of GDPR principles, including matters concerning:<br>  a. Purpose limitation<br>  b. Data minimization<br>  c. Limited storage periods<br>  d. Data quality<br>  e. Data protection by design<br>  f. Legal basis for processing<br>  g. Special categories of data processed (if any)<br>  h. Data security measures<br>  i. Requirements for any onward transfers of data to bodies not bound by the corporate rules |
| III. The Data Subject's Rights and Its Enforcement | 7. The rights of the data subject regarding processing and the manner of enforcing those rights. Specifically, addressing:<br>  a. Right to explanation and protection against profiling and sole automated decisions<br>  b. Right to lodge a complaint with the competent SA and courts of the Member State<br>  c. Right to redress and compensation<br>8. The acceptance of liability by a Controller/Processor established within the EU for any contravention of the rules from its abroad affiliates. Those subsidiaries will be exempt from liability if they can prove that they are not responsible for the event causing damage.<br>9. How the information will be communicated to the data subjects in accordance to the Controller's duty of transparency.[197] |

| IV. Mechanisms and Procedures | 10. Tasks of the DPO or any other officer designated to monitor compliance, train employees, and handle complaints. |
| --- | --- |
| | 11. Mechanisms within the conglomerate which ensure compliance with these rules. This can include measures such as data protection audits or corrective actions to protect the rights of the data subject. Any resulting verification must be communicated to the DPO/responsible officer and must be available on demand to the SA. |
| | 12. Mechanisms of reporting and recording changes to the rules and reporting the same to the SA. |
| | 13. The cooperation mechanisms in place in the conglomerate to assist the SA in ensuring compliance and in making the results of verification available. |
| | 14. Mechanisms for reporting any legal requirements a foreign affiliate is subject to that are likely to have a substantial adverse effect on the guarantees provided under these rules. |

Additionally, the EU Commission may specify the format and procedures for exchanging information between Controllers, Processors, and SAs for the rules.[198] The 14 points listed above might seem like various other instruments that have been established by GDPR and discussed in this book, such as the conditions for adequacy, the privacy shield, mandatory Controller-Processor contract clauses, binding corporate rules, etc. That is because the drafters of the regulation are clearly trying to inculcate the principles of processing and rights of the data subject into all levels of data control, be it contractual, regulatory, or international.

This "soft-power" of the Union is key in sparking an overall change to data processing on a global scale by requiring compliance with GDPR both within its borders and beyond. At present, the effect may seem sporadic and discretionary, but in the larger scheme of time it will help bring most countries to incorporate their legal ideals when debating future legislation within their own countries. Furthermore, companies who are made to comply with these long-arm instruments of GDPR would find it more practical to apply the data-protection standards across the board for simplicity's sake, as demonstrated by companies who are following global GDPR compliance since the regulation was enacted.

**5.3.5.2 Conditions for Approval**  The competent SA shall approve binding corporate rules in accordance with its consistency mechanism, provided they:[199]

1. Are legally binding and enforced by all affiliates in the conglomerate, including their employees
2. Expressly confer enforceable rights to the data subject
3. Fulfill the requirements described above

Once approved, the conglomerate can freely transfer data within their organizations throughout the world for their joint economic activity without specific authorization of the SA for each individual transfer of personal data. However, the rules do not legitimize any data transfer to unaffiliated entities such as advertisers or service providers.

**Pros and Cons of Binding Corporate Rules**

| Advantages | Disadvantages |
|---|---|
| Rules can be customized to the entity's needs | Use is limited to intragroup transfers under GDPR. |
| They offer more flexible solutions for international transfers as opposed to SCCs and adequacy decisions. | Rules are subject to more scrutiny and approval from the SA, which may slow down business. |
| Formulating the rules helps businesses to better track their data flows and consumer needs. | Formulating the rules requires an exhaustive investigation into data-protection requirements across multiple countries, which can be time consuming for the business. |
| Once approved, international data transfers can be carried out freely between corporate groups. | Monitoring the rules and its compliance is an ongoing and expensive effort. |

## 5.3.6 Transfers Made with or without Authorization

### 5.3.6.1 International Data Transfers without the SA's Authorization 
Like most provisions in GDPR, international transfers are subject to the supervision of the SA with competence over that jurisdiction. However, there are circumstances where the appropriate safeguards implemented by the Controller do not require specific authorization of the SA. These measures include:[200]

1. A legally binding and enforceable instrument between public authorities or bodies. **Example:** A bilateral treaty between neighboring governmental investigative bodies to share criminal records with one another for extradition purposes
2. Binding corporate rules[201]
3. Standard Data Protection Clauses that have been adopted by the EU Commission[202]
4. Standard Data Protection Clauses adopted by the SA and approved by the Commission[203]
5. Abiding by approved Codes of Conduct[204] along with enforceable commitments by the Controller/Processor in the foreign country[205]
6. Certification mechanisms[206] followed by the Controller along with enforceable commitments from their foreign counterparts

To say that there is no authorization of a higher oversight body would be a misnomer. Most mechanisms discussed above are instruments of GDPR that require compliance and approval by the SA or the Commission. Rather, the instruments are in place as a sort of one-time investment, which a business must rigidly comply to so that they do not require specific authorization for every single international data transfer they do.

Here, we can see that GDPR is trying to create a dichotomy where on the one hand compliance must be respected by foreign businesses if they wish to do business with the EU, but on the other hand, businesses are given the flexibility of choosing an instrument that would best suit their commercial purposes. For example, a larger technology conglomerate would ideally implement binding corporate rules, while smaller and medium-sized businesses could use standard clauses for their purposes.

**5.3.6.2 International Data Transfers with SA's Authorization**   Certain transfers to third countries are subject to the authorization of the SA[207] by way of GDPR's consistency mechanism.[208] In such a case, international transfers of data may be carried out by using:

1. **Contractual clauses** between the Controller/Processor and the foreign Controller/Processor/Recipient of the personal data based in the third country.
2. **Inserting provisions** into administrative agreements between public bodies, which includes enforceable and effective data subjects' rights. This may also be implemented for international organizations with corresponding duties or functions who engage in such activities.[209] An "administrative agreement" includes any nonbinding arrangement such as an MoU between the parties.[210]

This narrow provision of the regulation provides for two kinds of authorizations that may be provided by the SA. The first mechanism of "contractual clauses" is quite individualized, as the SA would effectively approve a clause for data transfers between two contracting parties. Compare this with standard contractual clauses, which are adopted by the EU Commission directly and can be implemented in a boilerplate fashion and require no prior authorization. The first provision discussed above gives parties greater freedom to curate their clauses for their specific deal.

The second mechanism, on the other hand, has broader ramifications as it is an insertion of a clause into an arrangement between state entities involved in cross-border processing. The impact of such insertion would affect a larger category of individuals as opposed to authorizing contractual clauses between two parties. The reason for the SA's involvement is likely because public authorities who require international transfers of data to further their purposes may not be able to fulfill GDPR terms to its truest letter. As a result, if the rights of a data subject are haphazardly placed into administrative arrangements without an effective way to enforce them, it would run afoul of the regulation. Thus, this fluidity in GDPR keeps the SA involved in arrangements that require a more customized touch, be it public or private.

**5.3.6.3 Implementing Appropriate Safeguards**  Adequacy decisions from the European Commission are not the avenue for Controllers to legally transfer data to international countries or organizations. International transfers of data can be carried out in the absence of an adequacy decision if the Controller and Processor have provided appropriate safeguards for the processing.[211] In doing so, the Data Collectors must:

- Ensure that the data subject's rights are enforceable.
- Ensure that effective legal remedies are available for the data subject.[212]
- Comply with the general principles of personal data processing.
- Comply with principles of data protection by design and default.[213]

These safeguards echo the central part of GDPR, which is empowering the user of the service. The manner of implementing these minimal safeguards can be done with or without the prior authorization of the SA depending on its nature. The regulation creates a framework where there are several avenues open for foreign transfers of data, which is helpful in the larger scheme of keeping Europe connected with the rest of the world and giving its citizens a freedom of choice in the websites they wish to visit and who they give their data to. There are billions of websites that offer services within the EU but are based outside of the Union. If only one mechanism for international transfers is available under GDPR, such as an adequacy decision, it would stifle free trade online and end up isolating the EU from the global market.

## 5.3.7  Derogations

Like many aspects of the regulation, GDPR provides exceptions to its hardline rules on international transfers of data. The derogations discussed below are exhaustive, and businesses must be able to claim one of the bases to avoid liability. For an in-depth analysis of the provisions relating to public interest and state action, please refer to Chapter 9, where we briefly discuss derogations available to governmental authorities.

**5.3.7.1 Permitted Derogations**  In the absence of an adequacy decision, appropriate safeguards, and binding corporate rules, a transfer or a set of transfers internationally will be permitted only if carried out on one of the below conditions:[214]

1. The data subject has explicitly consented with full knowledge of the risks and the absence of any measures discussed above.
2. The transfer is necessary for performing a contract between the data subject and Controller and the implementation of pre-contractual measures implemented at the request of the data subject.

   There must be a direct and objective link between the contract and the transfer[215] and a substantial connection between the data subject and the purpose of contracting.[216] For example, a company booking hotel rooms and flights for its officers as part of arrangements for a corporate retreat.

3. The transfer is necessary for concluding or performing a contract executed for the interest of the data subject between the Controller and another person or entity.
4. The transfer is necessary for any important reason of public interest[217] (discussed in detail in Chapter 9).
5. The transfer is necessary for the establishment, exercise, or defense of legal claims.
6. The transfer is necessary to protect the vital interests of the data subject or other persons where the data subject is physically or legally incapable of giving consent.
7. The transfer is made from a register that is maintained under EU or Member law to provide information to the public and is open for consultation either with the public or with any person who can demonstrate legitimate interest (such as the recipient) who requests to be involved in the consultation.[218] A transfer made pursuant to this register shall not involve a bulk transfer of personal data or categories of data.[219]

When carrying out a foreign transfer of personal data on one of the conditions discussed above, the Controller/Processor has a duty to document[220] the assessment as well as any safeguards implemented for the transfer. If one looks at the entirety of this provision, barring consent and a transfer based on a register, any other foreign transfers of data must be necessary for achieving a purpose, be it the vital interests of the data subject or contractual reasons.

**5.3.7.2 Unauthorized Derogations**  Notwithstanding everything that has been discussed so far in this chapter, GDPR has a residual clause for international transfers of personal data that are not based on any of the above-mentioned mechanisms, including the specific derogations discussed in the preceding section. Such transfers must be of such a nature that they do not fall under any of the categories for transfer discussed above.[221] This new exception to EU data protection law allows for minute transfers to foreign countries and is accompanied by a series of conditions for being permitted:[222]

1. The transfer is not repetitive.
2. Concerns only a limited number of data subjects.
3. Is necessary for the purposes of compelling legitimate interests of the Controller.
4. Those interests are not overridden by the rights and freedoms of the data subject.
5. The Controller has assessed all circumstances surrounding the transfer of the data.
6. The Controller has implemented suitable safeguards based on that assessment.

7. The Controller informs the SA of the transfer.
8. The Controller informs the data subject of the transfer and the legitimate interests pursued in doing so in furtherance of the entity's transparency obligations.

The terms laid down in this provision are yet to be clarified under GDPR and remain ambiguous. What constitutes a "nonrepetitive" transfer has not been defined, leaving space for interpretation. The requirements above are mutually inclusive, and all must be present for the international transfer to be valid under GDPR. When assessing the circumstances surrounding the transfer and the suitable safeguards to be implemented, the Controller should give attention to:[223]

- Nature of the personal data
- Purpose of processing
- Duration of the proposed processing operation
- Situation in the foreign country of origin or destination of the data

It is evident that the provision is meant for a one-off transfer to another country for specific commercial purposes that do not fall under the categories above, and even then, must be subject to the bare necessity provisions of the regulation, namely, the data subject's rights and data security. An example of this would be scientific or historical research purposes where the legitimate interests of society for a general increase in knowledge can be considered.[224]

**5.3.7.3 Transfers Not Authorized by EU**   While GDPR has elaborate rules on the transfer of data to third countries and required disclosures by the EU itself, what if the foreign government seeks to place an order on the Controller? GDPR hinges this on reciprocity by stating that any judgment of a Court/Tribunal/Administrative authority of a foreign nation requiring the Controller or Processor to disclose personal data may only be recognized or enforced if it is rooted in an international agreement such as a *mutual assistance treaty* between the countries.[225] The reason for this is that any *extraterritorial application* of foreign laws on the data subject or Controller may impede the attainment of the protection assured to natural persons under GDPR.[226] A good example of a mutual assistance treaty is the EU–US Data Protection Umbrella Agreement of 2016, which encourages law enforcement to work together while respecting the principles of strong data protection.

This provision demonstrates a sort of "home-rule" bias in cases of conflicting values between the two countries. Earlier in this chapter we discussed how the elements for adequacy are subjective and may lead to some foreign nations being unable to deal with the EU when it comes to data processing. This hardline stance of the regulation demonstrates the EU's objective of having GDPR applied as the standard for data processing, ensuring the protection of their data subjects. For this reason, they mandate that an international legal document is necessary for the mutual respect for judicial orders to flow between the EU and the foreign nation. It can be argued as bias in some ways, but the underlying motives of the EU are necessary for creating a global practice of data protection for its citizens.

## 5.3.8    Controllers Outside of the EU

As we discussed in Chapter 3, GDPR applies even in scenarios where the processing of personal data takes place physically outside the EU, but dealing with the data of individuals within the Union if the activities include:

- Offering of goods and services (with or without compensation), and
- Monitoring behavior of EU Citizens.

In such a case Controllers (or Processors) engaging in such activities must establish a contact point within the EU to facilitate compliance.[227] When data collection activities are based outside the EU, it is mandatory to designate a natural or legal representative[228] in writing. This should be compared to appointing a representative in other scenarios, where it is considered a sound practice, but is not a must. The representative appointed by the Controller shall be based in the EU in the Member States where the subject matter of processing[229] takes place. This ensures that even if the Controller is beyond the reach of EU authorities, their representative would not be.

Once appointed, the representative will be inculcated into the activities, and must be addressed in addition to or instead of the Controller in all activities and matters of compliance regarding Supervisory Authorities and the users. This individual has a legal authority of representation,[230] but does not prejudice the right to bring a legal action against the Controller or Processor directly for their activities.[231]

**Illustration:** Raters.com is a credit-rating agency based in the US, providing services for individuals globally. As a credit-rating agency, Raters.com collects a large amount of personal data, both personal and special. As GDPR comes into force, they appoint Mr. Jacques Robert as their representative in the EU, with his small home office located in Paris, France. He is listed in all communications between the website and the users, with his name appearing next to the company's in the initial request for consent and terms of use. Soon after, a massive data breach occurs, and it is revealed to the world that Raters.com has been illegally mining data well beyond what is proportionate for their activities.

- The SA (or victims) of France may initiate action against Raters.com (USA) directly.
- The SA may initiate action also against Mr. Robert.
- The same rights exist for any SA or victim in the EU against either Raters.com or Mr. Robert (jointly or separately).
- If Raters.com refuses to appear for the actions filed against them, Mr. Robert can still be held responsible on their behalf.
- However, GDPR does not expressly give Mr. Robert the right to claim compensation from Raters.com as that matter must be handled internally in the company by way of contract or corporate rules.

The representative does not need to possess any specific qualification or affiliation to be appointed under GDPR. A single representative can be appointed to represent the interests of multiple Controller/Processor entities based outside the EU.[232] The obligations of the representative include:

1. Being a contact point for the company in the EU
2. Cooperating with the SA
3. Being subject to GDPR enforcement proceedings against the Controller/ Processor they report to
4. Maintaining records of processing activities on behalf of the Controller/ Processor

What GDPR seeks to create is a system of accountability for data protection in such a way that the Data Collectors cannot escape their liability. Article 27 provides for someone to be responsible, even if the Controller is beyond the reach of the EU Courts. We can see similarities in how liability is attached for Joint Controllers as well, where one Controller may not evade liability by the mere fact that the responsibility has been placed on another Controller.

**Exceptions:** The obligation to appoint a domestic representative may be done away with in two specific scenarios:[233]

1. **Occasional Processing** of personal data if such activities:
   a. Do not involve the large-scale processing of special categories of data; or
   b. Do not involve the processing of data relating to criminal convictions; and
   c. Is unlikely to pose a risk to the rights and freedoms of other users, considering the nature, scope, context, and purposes of the processing.
2. Processing by a Public Authority or body

In the above situations, the data may be processed without listing a representative in the EU who can be held directly accountable. Several of the exceptions seem logical (such as processing relating to criminal convictions and public bodies), as in such cases a separate system of accountability is likely to be put in place. For example, if a foreign public body Controller is to be held liable under GDPR, traditional modes of diplomacy would likely control its disposition.

However, the first exception relating to "occasional processing" can be subject to abuse owing to the reduction in accountability. "Occasional" suggests that the processing plays a subordinate role in the economic activity, or is for a limited period, but until the EU clarifies these terms, the definition remains ambiguous. This ambiguity can create issues when applying these exceptions in practice.

**Illustration:** Bloggey.com is a Canadian blog-based social media website with public posts and private messaging, hinged on exclusivity with services in the EU. As a result, the only way to join the website as a member is if three users "invite" you to join as a member. Bloggey.com only has 2,000 "members" in the EU and 5,000 worldwide who submit personal data to be processed, while the remainder of the public may "view" the posts, without their personal data being processed. Bloggey.com has posts on highly controversial matters often expressing the member's point of view on politics, religion, and other "sensitive matters." Bloggey.com one day undergoes a massive data breach, and the SA of Belgium seeks to bring action against them for compensation. Bloggey.com refuses to come to Europe.

- Without a representative in the EU, the SA must rely on traditional court procedures to hold Bloggey.com accountable.
- Can this be considered a "large-scale" processing of special data? What amount of data should be collected to qualify? This is unclear from GDPR.
- Can the exclusivity of the website qualify this as "occasional processing"?
- When determining these facts, one must weigh it against the nature, scope, context, and purposes of the processing. This is likely to lead to a subjective result.

## 5.4   Intragroup Processing Privileges

Larger conglomerates spread globally do not receive any sort of exemption for their data processing and transfers under GDPR. GDPR facilitates data exchanges in intragroup processing to a limited extent, requiring entities to be more diligent in their compliance efforts. It is important that these conglomerates work as one unit in their data-protection efforts, facilitating compliance with the regulation consistently. To that end, the following measures should be considered:

1. **Individual compliance:** Each entity in the group is responsible for maintaining GDPR compliance individually, with no inconsistency between group members. This implies a "Controller" in the group will be assessed separately from the rest, and will be responsible for the data protection, legal basis, and user rights relating to the data under their control. The overlap in large companies can make this task complex and time consuming.

   Data subjects should not be placed at a disadvantage because they are serviced by one subsidiary rather than another. Controllers must make detailed arrangements and allocations of liability for compliance. Regardless, GDPR imposes Joint and Several Liability on the whole group, when one Controller company contravenes its duties. Therefore, a data conglomerate is only as strong as its weakest link under GDPR.

   **Illustration:** TransferBro is a large conglomerate that specializes in assisting individuals in transferring money both within Country X (located in the EU, where it is based) and internationally. TransferBro's services are provided by three subsidiaries: TPay (an online "paypal" app), TBank (an e-banking app), and TGlobal (an international money transfer website). All subsidiaries and TransferBro rely on each other's resources for processing. While the first two subsidiaries maintain impeccable GDPR compliance, TGlobal's board of directors chose not to pursue it and implemented the older DPD-based compliance program instead. Even though TransferBro, TBank, and TPay have all complied with GDPR, TGlobal has not and cannot rely on the compliance of its sister companies to meet EU data protection standards. Thus, the local SA can bring action against all the entities in the group for noncompliance.

2. **Facilitation:** GDPR is cognizant of the fact that corporate groups work closely and allows facilitation of processing between these entities in certain scenarios. Binding corporate rules are an example of how GDPR creates instruments for easing compliance where normal mechanisms would prove burdensome. Additionally, the regulation recognizes that data sharing in corporate groups is a "legitimate" purpose for processing personal data.[234] Controller corporations should make full use of these methods to facilitate compliance with the regulation across the board.

Facilitation should follow individual compliance by sharing resources and information, like hiring a single DPO to handle all processing within the corporate group.[235] Companies can also consider sharing common templates, data-breach response plans, data protection and privacy policies, etc. Centralized processing and record-keeping can also assist in maintaining compliance with GDPR and helps economically manage the data.

## 5.5 Cooperation Obligation on EU Bodies

The transfer and free flow of personal data to a foreign country or international organization is not a singular effort that can be carried out with the EU alone. It involves coordination and cooperation with different nations to ensure the global safety of its citizens' personal information. When personal data moves across borders, an increased risk is put on the rights of the data subject when it comes to the disclosure of that information, and an SA's authority is usually territorial and cannot effectively use its authority to rectify the issues.[236]

GDPR mandates that the commission and SAs take appropriate steps to:[237]

1. Develop international cooperation mechanisms to facilitate effective enforcement of the laws relating to personal data.
2. Provide international mutual assistance in the enforcement of personal data laws which includes:
   a. Notification
   b. Complaint referral
   c. Investigative assistance
   d. Information exchanges[238]
3. Engage relevant stockholders in discussions and activities that aim to further international cooperation for the enforcement of the law and data subjects' rights.
4. Promote the exchange and documentation of personal data protection legislation and practice, including jurisdictional conflicts with other countries.

The purpose of such measures would be to reduce the administrative difficulties that come with any cross-border dispute, such as jurisdiction and resource constraints.[239] GDPR attempts to create a system where oversight authorities work together to prevent long, drawn-out disputes that may arise in international processing. Here, a conflict arises.

On the one hand GDPR mandates cooperation between nations, but on the other they restrict the applicability of foreign law and judicial orders if it does not fit the scheme of the regulation. The reason for this is clear, as the primary GDPR objectives must be met and cannot be effectively enforced if other countries hamper those goals. But the EU here essentially cuts off any recognition and applicability of a sovereign foreign law if it is not deemed "good enough" to meet GDPR standards. However noble the EU's intentions may be, disregarding another country's laws might cause long-term damage on an international scale with possible negative effects on trade within the Union.

**Illustration:** An E-commerce company, Dingo Bingo, based in a foreign nation processes the data of several EU citizens based on a standard contractual clause adopted by the European Commission. No other treaty or arrangement exists between the foreign nation and the EU or its Member States as the diplomatic history between the countries are strained. The Department of Financial Crime of that nation receives a court order for all the personal data of Zeke (a citizen of Belgium) hosted by Dingo Bingo, who they suspect has been indulging in credit card fraud. Dingo Bingo is at liberty to refuse the request stated as complying with such an order absent an international agreement contravenes GDPR.

Chapter V of GDPR is a continuation of the building blocks placed by the 1995 DPD and the OECD guidelines as a more comprehensive framework for adjusting the earlier practices into the new regulatory framework. The regulation permits variations for compliance and derogations to the rule because the legislators understand that controlling a free flow of data and services is instrumental for the long-term benefit of the union. Furthermore, the internet is unmanageable under a single approval mechanism as the digital economy grows at a faster pace than the law. It is for this reason, understandably, that the regulation creates instruments that can be implemented by small, medium, and large-sized businesses who wish to do business with the EU based on cross-border processing. The long-arm instruments of GDPR are subtle ways of ensuring that Europe's new policy on data health will help shape the world, by forcing foreign governments, international organizations, and data-importing businesses to make changes in the way that they handle the personal data in international transfers moving forward.

## 5.6   Foreign Law in Conflict with GDPR

Its foreseeable that a piece of legislation or regulation in another country will run counter to the user-centric objectives of GDPR, such as a law that directly regulates the processing activities of persons and legal entities who fall under the control of a Member State.[240] This may include a judicial order or legal act that requires the Controller/Processor to transfer or disclose personal data absent any overarching international agreement or mutual-assistance treaty between the EU or Member State and the foreign nation.

GDPR cautions that the extraterritorial application of that law might be contrary to international law or the attainment of the protection of personal data that is sought by this regulation. As a result, international transfers of personal data should only be allowed subject to the conditions laid down by GDPR explicated in this chapter.[241] Thus, the regulation closes off any kind of conflict or loophole in the law by restricting any foreign influence on the regulation which may arise.

## Notes

1. Article 29 Working Party, WP 203 (2013), 20.
2. Article 29 Working Party, WP 203 (2013), 20.
3. GDPR, Article 5.1.a.
4. GDPR, Article 5.1.
5. Data that is used for scientific, historical, and statistical purposes in the public interest is subject to "Storage Limitation" under GDPR, Article 89(1); Article 5.1.e.
6. Data that is used for scientific, historical, and statistical purposes in the public interest is subject to the "Storage Limitation" under GDPR, Article 89(1); Article 5.1.b.
7. GDPR, Article 5.2.
8. GDPR, Article 13 and 14.
9. Article 29 Working Party, WP 203 (2013), 51.
10. Article 29 Working Party, WP 203 (2013), 51 onwards.
11. GDPR, Article 6.4.
12. See: GDPR, Articles 12–22, page 194 onward in Chapter 6.
13. GDPR Article, page 125 (section 5.1) in Chapter 5.
14. GDPR Article 23, page 226 (section 6.9) in Chapter 6.
15. GDPR, Article 6.4.
16. GDPR, Article 11.
17. GDPR, Article 11.2.
18. GDPR, Article 25.2.
19. GDPR, Article 25.2; it is unclear what GDPR means by "In particular, such measures shall ensure that *by default* personal data are not made accessible without the *individual's intervention* to an *indefinite number of natural persons.*" The wording creates confusion as it's not clear what qualifies as "an indefinite number," which leaves leeway for vexatious procedure. Perhaps the drafters intended that it meant "definite number," as that would leave less space for abuse.
20. GDPR, Article 5.1.
21. GDPR, Article 5.1.

22  GDPR, Recital 39.

23  GDPR, Article 54.2.

24  Natasha Lomas, "Google and Facebook Face First GDPR Complaints over 'Forced Consent,'" *TechCrunch*, May 25, 2018, https://techcrunch-com.cdn .ampproject.org/c/s/techcrunch.com/2018/05/25/facebook-google-face-first-gdpr-complaints-over-forced-consent/amp/; Maya Kosoff, "The Next Big Anti-Tech Backlash Is Just Beginning," *Vanity Fair*, May 29, 2018, https://www .vanityfair.com/news/2018/05/the-next-big-anti-tech-backlash-is-just-beginning.

25  GDPR, Article 7.1 *read with* Controller's duty of accountability Article 5.2.

26  GDPR, Recital 32.

27  GDPR, Recital 32.

28  GDPR, Article 7.2.

29  GDPR, Article 7.3.

30  GDPR, Recital 32.

31  GDPR, Article 8; Article 4.25.

32  See *EU Directive* 98/48/EC.

33  GDPR, Article 4.25 read with EU Directive 2015/1535, Article 1.1.

34  GDPR, Article 8.1.

35  GDPR, Article 8.2.

36  GDPR, Article 8.3.

37  Dave Lee, "TikTok: Record Fine for Video Sharing App over Children's Data," BBC, February 27, 2019, https://www.bbc.com/news/technology-47396767.

38  Lee, "TikTok."

39  Lee, "TikTok."

40  To access the four complaints and its summary, see NYOB, GDPR, "noyb. eu Filed Four Complaints over 'Forced Consent' against Google, Instagram, WhatsApp and Facebook," May 25, 2018, https://noyb.eu/wp-content/ uploads/2018/05/pa_forcedconsent_en.pdf.

41  GDPR, Article 5.

42  GDPR, Article 13.

43  GDPR, Article 12, 13, 14.

44  *NYOB v. Google* Complaint, 2.2.3.

45  GDPR, Recital 32, 43; EU Data Protection Working Party, *Guidelines on Consent,* April 10, 2018, 10.

46  GDPR, Recital 43; EU Data Protection Working Party, *Guidelines on Consent,* April 10, 2018, 9.

47  EU Data Protection Working Party, *Guidelines on Consent,* April 10, 2018, p. 9.

48  EU Data Protection Working Party, *Guidelines on Consent,* April 10, 2018, 17.

49  GDPR, Article 7.2.

50  *NYOB Complaints;* EU Data Protection Working Party, *Guidelines on Consent,* April 10, 2018, 5.

51  See *Opinion 15/2011* on the definition of consent (WP187), 12.

52  GDPR, Article 7.3.

53  GDPR, Recitals 42, 43; WP29 Opinion 15/2011 on the definition of consent, adopted on July 13, 2011 (WP 187), 12.

54  EU Data Protection Working Party, *Guidelines on Consent,* April 10, 2018, 11.

55  EU Data Protection Working Party, *Guidelines on Consent,* April 10, 2018, 6–10; GDPR, Recital 42, 43.

56  Kosoff, "The Next Big Anti-Tech Backlash."

57  EU Data Protection Working Party, *Guidelines on Consent,* April 10, 2018, 10, 11.

58  Lothar Determann, *Determann's Field Guide to Data Privacy Law,* 3rd ed. (Edward Elgar Publishing, 2917), 158; rather, it is considered as an extension of *free speech and expression* rights. *If* property rights exist, they belong to the *Controller*, who generates the data and owns the database.

59  See: *NYOB Complaints,* under the heading "Dominant Market Position" (in each complaint).

60  EU Data Protection Working Party, *Guidelines on Consent,* April 10, 2018, 10.

61  GDPR, Article 6(1), 7(1), 13.

62  GDPR, Article 6.1.

63  GDPR, Recital 44.

64  GDPR, Recital 41, 45.

65  GDPR, Recital 45.

66  GDPR, Recital 45 *read with* Article 6.3.

67  GDPR, Recital 46.

68  GDPR, Article 1.

69  D.A. Pauly, "Vorbem. Zu Art. 44 ff. DSGVO; Arts. 46, 47, 49 DSGVO." In *Beck'sche Kompaktkommentare Datenshutz-Grundverordnung,* edited by B.P. Paal and DA Pauly. (Munich: C.H. Beck, 2017).

70  GDPR, Recital 45, Article 6.3.

71  GDPR, Article 6.3.

72  Determann, *Determann's Field Guide to Data Privacy Law,* 20.

73  GDPR, Recital 47.

74  Paul Voigt, Axel von dem Bussche, *The EU GDPR; A Practical Guide* (Springer, 2017), 103.

75  This list is not exhaustive.

76  GDPR, Article 6.1.f.

77  GDPR, Recital 47.

78  GDPR, Recital 47.

79  *ECJ Ruling of 13 May 2014,* Google Spain, C-131/12, rec. 52.

80  *ECJ Ruling of 13 May 2014,* Google Spain, C-131/12, rec. 52.

81  GDPR, Article 6.4.

82  Such as National Security, Defense, Public Security and others provided under GDPR Article 23.

83  GDPR, Article 6.4.

84  Article 29 Working Party, WP 203 (2013) 24.

85  Article 29 Working Party, WP 203 (2013) 24.

86  Article 29 Working Party, WP 203 (2013) 25.

87  Article 29 Working Party, WP 203 (2013) 26.

88  Article 29 Working Party, WP 203 (2013) 27.

89  GDPR, Article 9.1, 9.2.

90 Under Article 28 of the *EU Charter for the Fundamental Rights,* trade union membership requires specific protection to safeguard the individual worker's Freedom of Collective Bargaining and Action and to prevent discrimination of individuals in the marketplace based on the activities of their trade union.

91 GDPR, Article 4.13.

92 GDPR, Article 4.15.

93 Determann, *Determann's Field Guide to Data Privacy Law,* 168.

94 Determann, *Determann's Field Guide to Data Privacy Law,* 169.

95 GDPR, Article 10.

96 GDPR, Article 7.

97 GDPR, Article 9.2.a

98 EU Data Protection Working Party, *Guidelines on Consent,* April 10, 2018, 18.

99 GDPR, Recital 52.

100 GDPR, Recital 52.

101 GDPR, Article 9.2.h.

102 GDPR, Article 9.3, Article 90.

103 GDPR, Article 9.2.7.

104 GDPR, Article 89.2, 89.3.

105 GDPR, Article 89.1.

106 European Data Protection Supervisor, *Opinion 8/2016* (2016), 6.

107 European Data Protection Supervisor, *Opinion 8/2016* (2016), 6, 7.

108 Article 29 Working Party, WP 221 (2014), 2.

109 Article 29 Working Party, WP 203 (2013), 51.

110 Article 29 Working Party, WP 196 (2012), 4.

111 Article 29 Working Party, WP 196 (2012), 4.

112 Article 29 Working Party, WP 196 (2012), 7, 8.

113 Article 29 Working Party, WP 196 (2012), 8.

114 Article 29 Working Party, WP 196 (2012), 8.

115 Article 29 Working Party, WP 196 (2012), 5.

116 Article 29 Working Party, WP 196 (2012), 9.

117 Bernard Marr, "The 4th Industrial Revolution Is Here, Are You Ready?" *Forbes,* August 13, 2018, https://www.forbes.com/sites/bernardmarr/2018/08/13/the-4th-industrial-revolution-is-here-are-you-ready/#4ff2856b628b.

118 Article 29 Working Party, WP 223 (2014), 4.

119 Article 29 Working Party, WP 223 (2014), 4.

120 Article 29 Working Party, WP 223 (2014), 15.

121 Article 29 Working Party, WP 223 (2014), 15.

122 Article 29 Working Party, WP 223 (2014), 7.

123 Article 29 Working Party, WP 223 (2014), 8.

124 Article 29 Working Party, WP 223 (2014), 8.

125 Article 29 Working Party, WP 223 (2014), 22.

126 GDPR, Article 6.2, 6.3.

127 GDPR, Recital 101.

128 GDPR, Chapter V.

129 Determann, *Determann's Field Guide to Data Privacy Law,* 30.

130 GDPR, Article 44; Controllers and Processors *shall* comply with the rules laid down in Chapter V relating to *International Data Transfers.*

131 For the sake of convenience "***Foreign Country***" refers collectively to a Third Country **and** International Organizations who process personal data outside of the EU.

132 GDPR, Article 44.

133 GDPR, Recital 101.

134 GDPR, Recital 102.

135 GDPR, Recital 102.

136 GDPR, Article 45.

137 GDPR, Recital 103.

138 *EU Data Protection Directive,* Article 25.

139 GDPR, Article 45.1.

140 GDPR, Article 45.3.

141 GDPR, Article 45.4.

142 GDPR, Article 45.8.

143 GDPR, Article 45.9.

144 GDPR, Article 45.2.

145 GDPR, Article 45.2.a.

146 GDPR, Article 45.2.b

147 GDPR, Article 45.2.c

148 GDPR, Article 45 *read with* Recital 105: "In particular, the third country's *accession to the Council of Europe Convention of 28 January 1981* for the *Protection of Individuals with regard to the Automatic Processing of Personal Data and its Additional Protocol* should be taken into account."

149 GDPR, Recital 104

150 "Data Protection Regulations and International Data Flows: Implications for Trade and Development," UNCTAD (2016), http://unctad.org/en/PublicationsLibrary/dtlstict2016d1_en.pdf.

151 Judgment of the Court of Justice of the EU of 6 October 2015 in Case C-362/14, *Maximillian Schrems v. Data Protection Commissioner,* points 73, 74, and 96. *See also* GDPR, Recital 104.

152 European Commission, Communication from the Commission to the European Parliament, *Exchanging and Protecting Personal Data in a Globalized World,* Brussels, 10.1.2017, 8.

153 GDPR, Article 45.9.

154 *Source:* The EU Commission webpage on Adequacy Decisions, https://ec.europa.eu/info/law/law-topic/data-protection/data-transfers-outside-eu/adequacy-protection-personal-data-non-eu-countries_en.

155 GDPR, Article 45.3.

156 GDPR, Article 45.5.

157 GDPR, Article 45.5.

158 GDPR, Recital 103.

159 GDPR, Article 45.6.

160 GDPR, Article 93.2.

161 GDPR, Article 45.7.

162 GDPR, Article 28.3.

163 GDPR, Article 46.2.

164 EU Commission Decision, 15 June 2001, *On Standard Contractual Clauses for the Transfer of Personal Data to Third Countries*, under Directive 95/46/EC (2001/497/EC).

165 EU Commission Decision, 27 December 2004, *Amending Decision 2001/497/EC as Regards the Introduction of an Alternative Set of Standard Contractual Clauses for the Transfer of Personal Data to Third Countries* (2004/915/EC).

166 Voigt and von dem Bussche, *The EU GDPR: A Practical Guide,* 121.

167 ECJ Ruling of 6 October 2015, *Maximilian Schrems v. Data Protection Commissioner,* C-362/14.

168 European Commission *Implementing Decision (EU) 2016/2297* of 16 December 2016.

169 GDPR, Recital 109.

170 GDPR, Recital 109.

171 Determann, *Determann's Field Guide to Data Privacy Law,* 46.

172 EU Commission Decision, 15 June 2001, *On Standard Contractual Clauses for the Transfer of Personal Data to Third Countries*, under Directive 95/46/EC (2001/497/EC), Article 4.

173 Determann, *Determann's Field Guide to Data Privacy Law,* 37.

174 GDPR, Article 46.3.

175 GDPR, Recital 109.

176 GDPR, Article 57.1.r.

177 Determann, *Determann's Field Guide to Data Privacy Law*, 37.

178 Determann, *Determann's Field Guide to Data Privacy Law*, 57.

179 Determann, *Determann's Field Guide to Data Privacy Law*, 37.

180 EU–US Privacy Shield, Annexure II.

181 EU–US Privacy Shield, Annexure I and II.

182 European Commission, *Guide to the EU–US Privacy Shield,* 2016, 7.

183 European Commission, *Guide to the EU–US Privacy Shield,* 2016, 15.

184 ECJ Ruling, *Maximilian Schrems v. Data Protection Commissioner* C-362/14, October 6, 2015.

185 Article 29 Working Party, WP 238 (2016), 2–4.

186 ECJ, *Digital Rights Ireland v. Commission*, case T-670/16.

187 William Fry, "Challenge to Privacy Shield by Digital Rights Ireland Dismissed by EU General Court," December 5, 2017, https://williamfry.com/newsandinsights/news-article/2017/12/05/challenge-to-privacy-shield-by-digital-rights-ireland-dismissed-by-eu-general-court.

188 GDPR, Recital 110.

189 GDPR, Recital 110.

190 Article 29 Working Party, WP 204 (2013), 4 and 5.

191 Article 29 Working Party, WP 204 (2013), 6.

192 Article 29 Working Party, WP 204 (2013), 7.

193 GDPR, Article 46.

194  GDPR, Article 47.1, 63.

195  Article 29 Working Party, Working Papers WP 153 and 154.

196  GDPR, Article 47.2.

197  GDPR, Article 13, 14 *read with* Article 47.2.g. Specifically, the Controller must communicate the three abovementioned points to the data subjects (6, 7, 8).

198  GDPR, Article 47.3.

199 GDPR, Article 47.1.

200  GDPR, Article 46.2.

201  GDPR, Article 47; discussed in detail in the next section.

202  GDPR, Article 93.2.

203  GDPR, Article 93.2.

204  GDPR, Article 40.

205  GDPR, Article 46.2.e: "An approved code of conduct pursuant to Article 40 together with binding and enforceable commitments of the controller or processor in the third country to *apply the appropriate safeguards, including as regards data subjects' rights.*"

206  GDPR, Article 42.

207  GDPR, Article 46.3.

208  GDPR, Article 46.4, 63.

209  GDPR, Recital 108.

210  GDPR, Recital 108.

211  GDPR, Article 46.

212  GDPR, Article 46.1.

213  Though the requirement of complying with the general principles of processing and data protection by design *have not* been mandated by GDPR, Article 46, they have been mentioned *expressly* in Recital 108.

214  GDPR, Article 49.

215  Article 29 Working Party, WP 114 (2005), 13.

216  Article 29 Working Party, WP 114 (2005), 13.

217  GDPR, Recital 112- talking of data sharing between customs, tax, competition and financial authorities internationally.

218  GDPR, Article 47.2.

219  GDPR, Article 49.2, Recital 111.

220  GDPR, Article 49.6 *read with* Article 30.

221  GDPR, Recital 113.

222  GDPR, Article 49.1 paragraph 2 (the provision).

223  GDPR, Recital 113.

224  GDPR, Recital 113.

225  GDPR, Article 48.

226  GDPR, Recital 115.

227  GDPR, Article 27.

228  GDPR, Article 4.17.

229  GDPR, Article 27 *read with* Article 4.17.

230  GDPR, Recital 80.

231  GDPR, Recital 80.

232  GDPR, Article 27.2.b.
233  GDPR, Article 27.2.a.
234  GDPR, Recital 48.
235  GDPR, Article 37.2.
236  GDPR, Recital 116.
237  GDPR, Article 50.
238  GDPR, Article 50.1.b. The mutual assistance measures shall only be carried out "subject to appropriate safeguards."
239  GDPR, Recital 116.
240  GDPR, Recital 115.
241  GDPR, Recital 115.

# 6

# Data Subjects' Rights

*The rights of every man are diminished when the rights of one man are threatened.*

— John F. Kennedy

GDPR Recital 1 states: "The protection of natural persons in relation to processing of personal data is a fundamental right." This statement is the regulation's anchor and is the main objective to be achieved. With respect to digital rights, GDPR formalizes several preexisting rights and creates new ones for data subjects (or "users"). At the same time, the provisions under Chapter III are not only substantive by laying down rights and liabilities, but are also procedural. It creates a framework for answering the following questions:

1. What rights do the data subjects have?
2. How must it be explained to the users?
3. How can the rights be enforced?
4. What must be considered when enforcing it?
5. Under what circumstances may the Controllers derogate or refuse to enforce this right?

With the proliferation of technology, securing these rights is the primary responsibility of the Controller. GDPR is responsive to recent scandals like Cambridge Analytica and British Airways, combined with EU jurisprudence being formalized. Regardless, ensuring strong compliance will prevent paying fines up to €20 million or 4% of the business's annual turnover.[1] This chapter seeks to answer these questions and provides a framework for protecting these rights.

## 6.1 The Controller's Duty of Transparency

The first aspect of the scheme of rights under Chapter III is the manner of informing everyday data subjects that they have rights. Only informed users can exercise their rights over personal data creating an *information obligation* on the Controller. As opposed to the preceding Data Protection Directive (DPD) the information obligations of the Controller have been expanded under GDPR.[2] This must be performed by creating modalities rooted in transparency to communicate information to the data subjects.[3]

### 6.1.1 Creating the Modalities

GDPR mandates a procedural framework, placing the responsibility of the Controller to adopt measures to put into writing or electronic form, the information relating to the data subject's rights in a manner that is:

1. Concise
2. Transparent
3. Intelligible
4. Easily accessible
5. In clear and plain language[4]

The provision clarifies that this duty must be especially noted when communicating with a child. Conciseness requires that information be correct and comprehensive in its content but at the same time avoiding unnecessary information.[5] The shift to a "consumer education" model requires the Controller to break down the data use into its plainest terms without using jargon or legalese. This manner of communication must be adhered to in all correspondence with the data subject and not exclusively in the initial notices.

GDPR has the aspiration[6] that transparency can be achieved in combination of standardized icons that are:

1. Easily visible
2. Intelligible
3. Clearly legible
4. Machine readable[7]

At present, standardized icons have been left open to the EU Commission to create delegated acts clarifying its application.[8] The Controller's information obligation is the subject matter of a case filed against Google and Facebook recently by the digital rights group NYOB.eu. Though Google has made "modalities" necessary for users to access the information, the complaint alleges the information supplied is insufficient to justify their processing activities.[9] Thus, merely maintaining "icons" does not compensate for the level of information that must be provided and will be unlawful.

Clarifying how the modalities need to be made should be considered by the EU legislators. Controllers must balance a conflict between the principles of conciseness and plain language. Providing "concise" information on complex data processing can be difficult for businesses, especially when this information needs to be explained in simple terms. For social networking sites that work with numerous advertisers, Processors, Subprocessors, and businesses, it is important to be cautious when communicating the purpose of collection and recipients of the data.

### 6.1.2 Facilitating Information Requests

The Controller shall facilitate the exercise of their information obligation and cannot refuse when requested unless the company can show that it is not in a position to identify the data subject.[10] This complements the Controllers' liability for processing where personal data is not collected or the user is unidentifiable.[11] Essentially a Controller must facilitate any exercise of the rights, electronically in writing, within one month of the receiving the request.[12] The time limit may be extended to two months if the Controller can justify the delay.[13] Delays can be justified in complex cases with multiple data subjects or processing operations, and when the request itself is difficult to answer.

The Controller also has a right to request additional information to confirm the natural identity of the data subject where reasonable doubts exist.[14] For example, asking for a confirmation code or a user ID number. Maintaining a confirmation system is helpful on websites like Twitter where usernames are creative. If the Controller does not act or intends to pursue a judicial remedy, he must inform the data subject within one month of receiving the request.[15]

The form of responding to information requests must mimic the request itself. If a user makes the request electronically, then the Controller should respond in the same manner electronically when feasible. Oral requests can be made under GDPR[16] in exigent circumstances after the identity of the data subject is confirmed. As the burden of proving the information obligation is on the Controller, it is advisable to always respond to the request in writing, even if the data subject insists on an oral response. The oral response to the data subject must be accurately documented immediately, if not soon after the communication.

### 6.1.3 Providing Information to Data Subjects

Generally, the Controller must provide the information discussed above free of cost to the data subject.[17] But the Controller also holds certain rights that can be used to prevent abuse by the data subjects who seek to disrupt business. If the requests are:

1. Manifestly unfounded or
2. Excessive, in particular because of their repetitive character.

The Controller has the option of:

1. Charging a reasonable administrative fee, or
2. Refusing to act on the request.[18]

This gives the Controller a reasonable right of refusal, for requests could argu-ably be made by "internet trolls" who seek to only annoy, or even from hypersen-sitive users who actively try to critique the modalities available to them. However, what the terms manifestly unfounded or excessive mean are left open to interpre-tation, and the burden of proof is on the Controller.[19] "Manifestly" unfounded would require the request to be exceptionally baseless and should be evident from first glance itself. The lack of definition in these terms would likely result in inter-pretive confusion in the future.

**Illustration:** Devon submits an erasure request with the search engine Con-troller "Searchy," which has collected substantial data on him based on his minor fame on several reality shows in which he competed in and fared horribly over 10 years ago. Searchy reviews his request and finds that answering it would re-quire a massive effort of automated and human effort, which would cost the com-pany at least $5,000. Responding within a month, Searchy informs Devon that his request is "excessive" and he will have to pay $4,000 in order for the website to fulfill the request. In this simple scenario itself, there are numerous legal ques-tions that arise. What can be considered as an excessive request? What would be a reasonable "administrative fee"? If Devon were to refuse, can the Company go on to ignore his request? What would the liability be if the Controller's determination turned out to be misguided? The evident point is that the Controller would have a heavy burden of proving to a court that the rights of refusal or charging a fee are exercised diligently.

### 6.1.4 The Notification Obligation

Though not included as part of the Controller's transparency duties under Article 13 or 14, another important responsibility is notifying users when they have re-quested him for:[20]

  i. Rectification,
 ii. Erasure, or
iii. Restriction of processing.

In such cases, the Controller has a duty to communicate this information to each recipient of the personal data, unless this proves to be impossible or requires a *disproportionate effort*. The Controller also has a duty to inform the user of who those recipients are if so requested.

**Example 1:** David requests Facebook to erase his profile. Facebook is not re-quired to inform each of his friends (to whom the data has been disclosed) that he has erased his profile, as such an undertaking would be a disproportionate effort.

**Example 2:** David erases his account on Amazon.com. Amazon must inform all third-party advertisers who have his personal data that David has erased his profile. The Controller must also ensure that all copies, links, and replications of David's profile are erased.[21]

**Illustration:** A government department that maintains a large "client" database uses an external IP addresses file to validate postal locations of its constituents. The department regularly receives new data that confirms addresses and uses it to update the information on the database. The department does not need to provide an explanation to individual data subjects each time a new version of the address file is processed. This is because doing so would involve disproportionate effort.

## 6.2 The *Digital Miranda* Rights

With the framework in place for the manner of communication of the rights, the next step would be to determine what information must be provided to the users at the outset, whether data is provided to the Controller directly or indirectly.[22] Similar to the US's "Miranda Rights" this information must be provided to data subjects, and they may demand its protection at any time. The information obligation consists of two categories of information that must always be provided to the data subject: accountability information and transparency information.

### 6.2.1 Accountability Information

Regardless of whether a website holds personal data related to the data subject that is collected from them directly[23] or whether the data has not been personally provided by the Subject,[24] the Controller shall provide the following information:

1. The Controller (or their representative's) identity or contact details.
    **Example:** GeneMap LLC, Represented by Mr. Ben Kim
2. Contact details of the Data Protection Officer, where applicable.
    **Example:** Please mail BKim@GeneMap.com
3. Purposes of Processing.
    **Example:** We collect your personal data in order provide our services and to develop better ways to increase our efficiency by incorporating that data into our algorithms, which study the data to maximize performance.
4. Legal Basis of Processing.
    **Example:** The data you provide is processed legally by us in accordance with the law based on:
    a. Your consent, and
    b. So that we may perform our end of the service.
5. If the processing is based on legitimate interests of the Controller or third party, it must be explained.[25]

**Example:** We share your data with third-party advertisers so that they may suggest goods and services you may be interested in. You may turn off or manage this feature by following this __LINK__.

6. Intended recipients or categories of recipients of the data

**Example:** Your personal data will be shared with the following recipients:
   a. Your friends
   b. Third-party advertiser X
   c. Third-party advertising agency Y
   d. Our employees who help to run our website

7. Whether the Controller intends to transfer the data to a third country or international organization; the existence or absence of adequacy decision or suitable safeguards.[26]

**Example:** We have a processing center in Japan, DaichiPro Ltd., which helps us manage, protect, and handle the data you provide us. The transfer of your data to our Processors has been approved by the EU by way of Adequacy Commission Ruling 123/2018, available here __LINK__.

It is clear from the information above that the details lay down the basis for accountability in the website. A data subject can read this information and understand who is entrusted with their data, who will receive their data, and for what purpose. Recall that this information must be presented in a very simple, clear, concise, and plain manner,[27] and legalese cannot be used to confuse the purpose and recipients in any way. Users must also be informed of the existence of any affiliates who subsequently become recipients of the personal data and who they are. Merely stating that the data will be shared with the Controller's "trusted business partners" or "advertisers" would fall below the new GDPR standard and would require some degree of identification or specificity.[28] A sound option would be to hyperlink the list of affiliates for the consumers to read at their discretion.

### 6.2.2 Transparency Information

The second set of disclosures necessary under GDPR involves educating the data subject on their rights and the modalities to exercise them. Here, there are additional requirements placed on Controllers who possess personal data, but not collected from the subject directly.[29] The information listed below is required in both the direct and indirect collection of data under Articles 13 and 14:

1. Period of data storage or criteria used for calculating that period.

**Example:** We store your data actively in our servers for as long as you decide to use our services. If you choose to erase or deactivate your account, we hold your data for a period of five years in accordance with X Data Retention Law.

2. Existence of the right to request erasure, rectification, restriction, or data portability of one's data from the Controller.

**Example:**

a. If at any point during the use of our services you wish to erase or rectify your account please click on this ICON.

b. Please note, while we are erasing or rectifying your account, you may request our Controller to restrict us from processing your data further.

c. If you wish for us to give a collection of all the data you have created in a "machine readable format" please click this ICON on your home page.

3. The right to withdraw explicit consent.[30]

**Example:** If you decide that you no longer agree to the collection and processing of your personal data by our website, you may withdraw your consent by following this __LINK__.

4. The right to lodge a complaint with the Supervisory Authority.

**Example:** If you feel we have violated the terms or the law in any way, you have a right to lodge a complaint against our website in the Supervisory Authority of Hamburg, who oversees our authority.

Note that Controllers are only obliged to mention the general existence of remedies, and are not required to identify the appropriate competent authority.[31]

5. Whether the processing of the data is required by contract or statute or a prerequisite to enter into a contract.

**Example:** We require your personal data so that we may fully perform our activities for your benefit. To understand what data is used and how we use it, please read our section on PROCESSING __Link__.

6. Whether the data subject is obligated to provide it and the consequences of not doing so.

**Example:** By law we require your personal data in order to carry out our purposes. EU regulation on X requires you to provide this data to us; failure to do so means we cannot provide our services to you as it would be against the law.

7. The existence of AI and automated decision making and a description of the logic, significance, and consequences of such processing.

**Example:** Our website uses cutting-edge AI to help manage our website and improve our functions. The AI uses the data you provide us and runs it through an X algorithm that weighs the information you give us with Y and Z factors to constantly improve our website's performance. This helps us to redesign our pages and increase our processing capabilities.

8. Where the data is intended to be collected for further processing for a purpose that it was not originally intended for, such information must be provided prior to further processing.[32] A sound practice would be to describe predictable future uses of the data in the notice to prevent expenses of future notices. These purposes must be in line with the rules on changing processing purposes under GDPR.[33]

**Example:** If we change the use of your data and process it for different purposes than what is mentioned in this agreement, you will receive a notification pop-up on your laptop or mobile device and can decide whether to consent to such processing.

The above-mentioned details must be provided regardless of whether the personal data was collected directly by the data subject or from an indirect source.[34] However, when personal data is possessed by the latter method, additional information as to the point of origin or the source of the personal data must be provided as well.[35]

**Illustration:** The collection of unpaid fines is transferred from court A to court B. Court B writes immediately to the payment defaulters concerned, identifying its authority/designation and explaining that the file has been transferred for collecting unpaid fines. The notice further states that disclosures may be made to agents of court B. Here, the obligation to provide information to the data subject under GDPR coincides with the need to contact him to collect the fine regardless.

### 6.2.3 Timing

Note a slight difference in the timing of when both categories of this information must be disclosed to the user. Controllers who directly collect personal data from the subjects must logically provide the information at the time of collection.[36] If the data was collected and possessed indirectly, Controllers must notify the data subject:

1. Within a reasonable period after obtaining the data, keeping in mind the circumstances (within one month at the latest),
2. At the time of the first communication with the data subject, if the data was used for that purpose,
3. If the data is envisaged to be shared to another recipient, disclosure must be made at the time of disclosure at the latest.

### 6.2.4 Defenses for Not Providing Information

Under both direct and indirect possession of personal data, information does not need to be provided if the data subject already has the information.[37] When comparing Articles 13 and 14 one can see that this is the only exception available to those who directly collect data from the subjects; at the same time, more leeway is given for Controllers who indirectly possess the data. The broader exceptions include:[38]

1. Impossibility
2. Disproportionate effort
3. Superseding Union or Member law that provides appropriate safeguards
4. Confidentiality or privilege based on Union or Member law.

Invoking the defenses of impossibility or disproportionate effort for archiving in public interest, scientific, historical or statistical analysis[39] has been specifically noted by GDPR drafters. The disclosure of the information is not required insofar as it would likely render impossible or seriously impair the objectives of such processing for archiving purposes.[40] Furthermore, if this exception were to apply, the Controller must adopt appropriate measures to protect the rights of the data subjects. It is unclear whether Article 14(5)(d) restricts its defense of impossibility and disproportionate effort to processing for archival purposes. The provision uses the wording "in particular," which does not expressly exclude the use of the defenses in other circumstances. However, the wording is sufficiently vague and can be interpreted to be a restricted exception rather than a broad one. This will require either court intervention or delegated legislation to clarify whether other forms of processing can avail this defense.

Thus from the above we can see that Controllers are the administrators of this new species of rights by way of a *full, frank, and plain* disclosure of the data subject's rights, a sort of digital *Miranda*. The regulation makes this a mandatory requirement, placing the burden on the Controller, based the most serious penalty for contravention.[41] The information obligation should be considered as a part of the data subject's rights rather than the Controller's duty.

## 6.3 The Right of Access

GDPR Article 15 provides the first "substantive" right of the data subject. The right permits the data subject to verify the lawfulness of the processing by giving them a right to demand for information and access from the Controller.

### 6.3.1 Accessing Personal Data

Unlike the information obligation which is general, the right of access requires Controllers to go beyond normal detail in response provided. The right mandates the data subject shall have the right to approach the Controller:

1. For confirmation as to whether personal data of his is being processed; and if so
2. For access to the personal data and the information relating to:
   a. The purpose of processing
   b. Categories of data processed
   c. Recipients or categories of recipients of the data
   d. Period of data storage or method of calculation of said period
   e. Existence of the right of erasure, rectification, restriction, and data portability
   f. The right to lodge a complaint against the Supervisory Authority
   g. Source of the data, if the data has not been provided directly
   h. The existence of AI and its logic, significance, and consequence of such automated decision making
   i. Existence of appropriate safeguards in cases of transfers to third countries.[42]

The right of access corresponds to the transparency disclosures made by the Controller at the time of processing. Article 15 lays down the affirmative right to exercise those disclosures, making it a matter of law and not merely one of contract. The appropriate response of a business faced with a rectification request depends on the individual situation. Immediate action is always needed, and Controllers must provide detail in responding. Establishing a two-step process for responding to information requests is not recommended because GDPR Article 15 requires detailed information to begin with, and responses should not be provided in phases. Overall, businesses should maintain a system that the data subject can access easily in reasonable intervals, so they can best exercise their rights.[43] Access must be in a commonly used electronic form and can include measures like remote access through another's computer.

Data subject access is not always an easy right to provide for. In some cases, competing interests may require restricting the breadth of access. For example, consider an HR department handling a complaint regarding an alleged incident involving the company's officers. The complainant requests all personal information held regarding her by the department. Practically, the officer dealing with the complaint must also handle the subject access request to maintain a single channel of communication with the complainant. At the same time, the HR officer must work with the DPO to ensure that the statutory requirements for subject access are met without intruding into other employees' privacy.

### 6.3.2 Charging a "Reasonable Fee"

As with Article 12 (5),[44] the Controller has a duty to provide a copy of all personal data undergoing processing, and the right to charge a reasonable administrative fee for any further copies requested by the data subject.[45] Both provisions possibly conflict with one another as the parameters for charging a reasonable "fee" are different, stating it may be charged for "further copies" in place of being "excessive" or "manifestly unfounded." This creates confusion as to whether a reasonable fee can be charged as a matter of convenience or a matter of deterring excessive/unfounded requests. The discussion becomes more complex when considering Article 15 (4), which says that copies "shall not adversely affect the rights and freedoms of others." This statement is not subsequently explained in the regulation. The vagueness of Article 15 (4) if liberally interpreted by a Controller can result in multiple requests for copies not being granted because of the adverse effect on others' interests.

**Illustration:** Max requests a copy of all his data processed by Facespace. com, a social networking website. Max is very active on the website, posting on his friend's wall, commenting on photos, sharing links and memes along with creating several events over the years. Max has 3,000 friends, of whom 2,000 have a high degree of privacy settings. Without Max noticing, many of his past friends (with whom he actively communicated in the past, publicly) have removed him from their friend lists. Facespace.com could reject Max's request for a full copy of his processing history, as that would involve going into others' profiles, which include those who removed him and those with a high privacy setting. The website could cite the protection of "the rights and freedoms of others" and specifically, their right to privacy. Whether such a denial would be valid under GDPR remains to be seen and would require court intervention or delegated legislation.

When collectively reading Articles 12 to 15, data subjects have rights not only to access personal data, but also to be informed with a mechanism for exercising those rights. GDPR compliance can be achieved by thoughtful drafting of a website's terms of use, and initial disclaimers and disclosures. Despite gaps in the regulation, many of the issues can be resolved by a uniform internal policy of granting requests for access, the facilitation of rights, and the circumstances under which a reasonable fee will be imposed by the Controller for such an exercise. Assuring accountability and transparency is the cornerstone of the substantive rights under GDPR. Absent a court or the EU Commission clarifying the ambiguities, Controllers must "self-clarify" these points in their terms of use, erring on the side of data protection in order to prevent subsequent claims and fines.

## 6.4   Right of Rectification

GDPR provides for the user a right of rectification of any inaccurate or incomplete data.[46] This right corresponds to the principle of accuracy in processing under GDPR.[47] Users may erroneously give incorrect information to a website and find no way of correcting the errors. Article 16 mandates that the users be provided a choice and mechanism[48] to correct inaccurately maintained personal data. Rectification encompasses two aspects:

1. The correction of incorrect data
2. The completion of incomplete data

Though users do not have to provide reasons for their request, the burden of providing inaccurate or incomplete personal data lies on the data subject. This right of rectification must be asserted by the data subject itself and not by any third party. While this may appear to be a logical requirement, the hardline stance under the regulation is likely to raise issues to those data subjects who become incapable of exercising their rights.

For example, consider medical records or any online service that keeps track of death records for the public. Or consider a social media profile that hosts inaccurate data to the friend list of an incarcerated or deceased data subject. The close family/friend who wishes to rectify the data to "honor" the person's memory would not be entitled to exercise the right on behalf of the user.

### 6.4.1 Inaccurate Personal Data

Inaccuracy occurs when the data provided is not in accord with reality such that the information submitted would be untrue or misrepresentative.[49] GDPR does not specify what constitutes "fact" or "reality," which creates problems in the "fake-news" era of information. In a business setting, the value judgments on facts by Controllers or data subjects is necessary, as the company cannot conduct detailed investigations into the truth of all requests it receives. Controllers should undertake a reasonable inquiry into the request's veracity and make value judgments into whether it is genuine. It is important to balance the data subject's right to restriction and the business's freedom of opinion and information.

**Example:** Requesting Instagram to remove a "fake" profile that represents itself as a user. The Controller would need some time to verify the request by looking into whether the profile predates the claimed one and other factors like personalization, friends, location, content posted, etc.

### 6.4.2 Incomplete Personal Data

Incomplete data is missing information that renders personal data incomplete. The missing personal data must be necessary for reaching the purposes of processing. The personal data provided earlier may be accurate, but the missing "incomplete" data prevents the information from accurately reflecting reality. The Controller should consider the following factors:

- Does the missing information serve the purpose of processing?
- Is completing the data a proportionate effort for the business based on the specific processing needs?
- What risks do the data subjects face if the information is not rectified?

When making such a request, the Controller should allow the user to submit a *supplementary statement* to explain the situation in detail. Considering the burden of proof is on the data subject, its sensible to give them adequate means to justify their request.

### 6.4.3 Handling Requests

As discussed earlier, the right of rectification must be informed to the user at the outset,[50] by way of an easily accessible mechanism. Once the request is made, it must be handled without undue delay on the part of the Controller.[51] When a request is made for adding to incomplete data, GDPR considers the purposes of processing, a judgment call made by the Controller. The degree of user freedom and value of "correct" data depend largely on the specific processing situation.

**Illustration 1:** Ram discovers that his date of birth is entered incorrectly on the online shopping website Nowshop.com. He requests the Controller listed to rectify his profile. The Controller takes five months to respond to the request. Nowshop.com has violated GDPR.

**Illustration 2:** Ram discovers that his address is incomplete on Nowshop.com. He clicks their "PROFILE SETTINGS" icon and fills it up himself. The website is GDPR compliant.

**Illustration 3:** Ram joins a survey link shared by a friend on the educational service Surveyjunkie.com. When entering the website, he is prompted with a page asking for details such as his name, age, city of residence, and occupation (which is optional to fill in). Ram only fills in his name and answers the survey. Later, Ram feels regret for leaving out the personal details as it may have bearing to the final survey results and requests the Controller of the website to allow him to fill in those incomplete details. The Controller mails back, stating that filling up those details is not possible as the survey is immediately sent in to an algorithm, which compiles the result, and no mechanism is in place to change those results. The Controller is GDPR compliant, as the purpose of the processing does not require those incomplete details to be completed, and it is reasonable not to fulfill the requests as the integrity of the survey would be hampered.

**Illustration 4:** Based on incorrect information Ram accidently gave, TaxMan .com's algorithm reported that his tax return for the year was only €200 when it was €700. Ram realizes his mistake before the documents were sent to the tax authorities and tried to rectify the form (weeks before "Tax Day"). The service does not permit him to change his information once the data has been "finalized" as the algorithm would require a fresh application from another e-mail ID. As TaxMan.com does not allow Ram to rectify the data, resulting in a loss of €500, it is likely that a court or Supervisory Authority is likely to find this as a "legal or significant effect" on Ram as a data subject; therefore, he likely is entitled to object to the algorithm's assessment under Article 21. For this reason, it is advisable for the Controller to place a "form" in the "rectification system" for cases where special requests are made by the consumer.

## 6.5  Right of Erasure

In 2014 the court of Justice of the European Union (CJEU) delivered a historic and controversial judgment of *Google Spain v. Costeja*. The judgment established that all EU citizens have a fundamental right to be forgotten when potential damaging or private details regarding them have been placed online. In the EU it is now considered a human right[52] as evidenced from its inclusion into GDPR.

### 6.5.1  Development of the Right

Contrary to public belief, the "right to be forgotten" (hereinafter referred to as erasure) was not born in the *Costeja* judgment but existed in the legal systems of several countries prior to 2014. As early as the 1978, France had recognized that its citizens had a *right to oblivion*, that was an erasure of personal data which is no longer relevant.[53] This right remained in French data protection law, and then traveled to the neighboring countries of Spain, Italy, and Germany. By 1995 the EU Data Protection Directive[54] formally recognized erasure as part of the "subject access" rights.

Subsequent litigation in countries such as Argentina,[55] India,[56] and other countries all have raised Google as the focus of the exercise of this developing right. That is perhaps because unlike other websites where personal data is uploaded by the user itself (or their friends/connections), Google presents public search results without the user's consent.

The case that received the most attention and relevance was in the Spanish Apex Court and subsequently the CJEU judgment in *Google Spain v. Costeja.* In 1998, Mr. Costeja-Gonzalez, a citizen of Spain, was unable to pay his social security debts, resulting in the foreclosure of his house. As per Spanish law, such auctions must be advertised through a local newspaper. One such daily, *La Vanguardia,* had published this notice of auction with his name listed, and as a result the article appeared on any Google search with Mr. Costeja's name. On requesting Google to remove the content, Google opposed as it is an article lawfully published by a newspaper. This led to a long drawn-out legal battle, which began at the Spanish data protection agency (the AEPD) and ultimately went to the CJEU to dispose of a series of issues, which have now been dealt with under GDPR.

The order by the Court of Justice formally recognized the right to be forgotten and held that intermediary search engines such as Google shall be responsible for the content that arises from their search result. An interesting fact to note is that the court does not directly reference the right, but draws on its existence by examining EU data protection[57] and privacy rights.[58] The ruling required "Data Controllers" to remove content from their search engines if it is *inadequate, irrelevant, excessive, out of date, or unnecessary* in relation to the purposes of processing. An interesting point to note is that the information does not have to be false to qualify for erasure. Controversial as this decision may be, it gave the blueprint for the right of erasure in GDPR as it stands.

## 6.5.2 The Philosophical Debate

As with any other legal issue, there are two sides to the debate. The supporters of erasure recognize that it protects privacy, while critics oppose the *chilling effect* on the right to information and the freedom of speech. This is especially so in a country like the United States, where the scope of freedom of speech is broad and has far-reaching implications. Reconciling these differences is a very difficult task, and GDPR itself does not leave a robust framework for resolving such disputes.

A perfect example of this would be the *Costeja* case, which sparked critical and scholarly debate over the existence of the right, perhaps more so because it was a newspaper article that was removed from the public's dominant search engine. Legal arguments can be narrowly drawn to determine where the line in the sand lies, or broadly presented, asking whether individuals are entitled to rewrite their history. Below we examine the primary legal arguments and conflicts to erasure in light of the facts of the *Costeja* case and illustrations.

1. **The right to privacy:** Most nations recognize that citizens have a fundamental right to privacy in their affairs, property, and things.[59] The champions of privacy rights consider the right of erasure as a positive step forward in this internet age, as it gives users a degree of power to determine what information about them exists on the internet. It is important to note that erasure serves mainly as a response to "revenge pornography" or other highly sensitive content being shared to the internet at large. This is preferable to a system where inappropriate, false, and dated information is uploaded online with no remedy left to the user.

2. **Freedom of speech:** The right of erasure will always conflict with ideals of free speech. It is discussed repeatedly under GDPR as a factor the Controller must consider when deciding erasure requests.[60] This is because erasure will involve stifling someone else's speech on some level. It is simple to execute when the user has access to the profile and control over their contents, but complexities arise when the content is posted by a third party. Furthermore, the fact that the information need not necessarily be false creates a way for individuals to suppress the truth about themselves.

   Consider the *Costeja* case, where the search results of a news article were removed, despite the fact that the information had to be printed by law. A newspaper in its routine practice will publish articles that mention some person or other in a negative light, and this is linked to the people's right to know the information. This becomes even more subjective as one applies the "freedom of speech" requirements of different countries. For example, the US gives the press wide latitude to report on matters, even if the reporting may not be 100% accurate. Could Mr. Costeja succeed in his action in US courts? It is likely the same view would not be adopted.

3. **The right to information:** Modern democratic societies recognize that a well informed electorate is essential to the fair and effective governance of the state. With that in mind, most countries recognize that individuals have a fundamental right to information, save for several exceptions in public interest.[61] Unsurprisingly, erasure and information do not mix. Once again a delicate balance must be struck between the privacy of one and the information of many, which will be difficult to implement.

   Note that erasure does not necessarily result in complete and permanent deletion of the information, but merely a removal of the content that the Controller is in charge of. For example, Mr. Costeja's request would lead to the search engine removing the article from the search results, but not in the article being removed. Thus, when dealing with search engines, it is not the information being erased; it is the access to said information. Hypothetically, someone who would like to find out more about Mr. Costeja's case could go straight to La Vanguardia and find the article themselves, which will not be displayed through Google.

**Illustration:** In 1975, Butch went hunting in the African savanna with some local poachers and took a picture with a lion that he had shot. At the time, a picture was printed with a small article by several local and national newspapers, which caused strife in Butch's life at the time. After that, the news died down, and Butch moved away and never looked back. Recently, Butch noticed that an "internet shaming" hashtag has gone viral online to protest poaching in light of similar events coming to light[62] with other poachers. In response, Butch wants to silently have his old newspaper articles removed from search engines which may report it. Which is more important: Butch's right to privacy or the freedom of speech of the newspaper and the public's accompanying right to that information? Whichever answer one may arrive at, the solution will be subjective.

4. **Censorship:** Free speech advocates are concerned that allowing a system of erasure will result in excessive censorship and misuse of information flows.[63] This is because a private corporation such as Google or Facebook is responsible for balancing the fundamental rights of its users and must make a judgment as to what must be removed and what can be kept. It is clear that GDPR seeks to solve this issue by bringing in regulatory backing to the concept.

   Prior to GDPR, thousands of erasure requests submitted to Google were made behind closed doors, with a panel of "experts" determining whether to allow or grant the requests. Many of the details and parameters were not shared with the public. As a result a group of internet scholars and legal academics wrote an open letter[64] to Google requesting them to give insight into the inner workings of their system. Google had not complied with the request, stating that they publish a yearly report with the relevant details.

   Regardless, the line is always drawn somewhere in the sand. For example a court in The Netherlands has held that erasure does not apply to a convicted killer seeking to remove information on his past from Google's search results.[65] GDPR lists a series of guiding factors and mechanisms for streamlining this right further.

5. **The "Streisand effect":** Though not a legal argument, the "Streisand effect" is an internet phenomenon where an attempt to enforce privacy rights will inevitably attract more media attention to what is hidden from the public eye. This irony is not restricted to what occurred in the actress Barbra Streisand's 2003 privacy case in which the term arose, but it has been consistently seen in the past with entertainers such as Hulk Hogan in an attempt to suppress his "sex tape," and with businesses like Trafigura attempting to hide a waste dump in the Ivory Coast.

The argument states that enforcing a right of erasure in the internet age will result in greater attention to the subject that is being hidden, as the internet acts as a sort of "quicksand," producing content faster than the speed it can be erased at. With erasure requests becoming more commonplace under GDPR, perhaps this effect will lose its potency.

While there are numerous hurdles in place to enforce erasure under GDPR, the EU drafters had pushed forward, taking the "user friendly" privacy-driven approach. Strategically, the drafting committee had decided not to refer to it as the "right to be forgotten" under GDPR. Perhaps because being "forgotten" is unachievable in the internet age but erasing one's data is.

### 6.5.3 Circumstances for Erasure under GDPR

Let us now analyze GDPR Article 17, where the right of erasure has been elaborated. The provision gives users the right to request erasure requiring that the Controller "shall" carry out the request. The Controller in fulfilling the request must act without undue delay if one of the following grounds exists:

1. The personal data is no longer necessary for the purpose of processing. Erasure is also allowed where the purposes of processing no longer exist under law. But if the business finds another purpose that overlaps completely or partially with the original, or a purpose that is compatible, erasure is not available.
   **Example:** David decides to delete his Twitter account after years of nonuse, which would render the purpose of collection no longer necessary.
2. The consent or explicit consent is withdrawn and there exists no other legal ground for processing.
3. The user exercises his right to object to the processing[66] or profiling activities. Erasure is often the remedy to an objection made by a user to automated processing. The data subject should demonstrate his/her modified interests based on the specific processing situation.
   **Example:** David objects to the way that LinkedIn uses his personal data to profile him for certain types of products he does not want. He requests the Controller to restrict processing and investigate his objection. If his objection is granted after an investigation, we can request erasure of the personal data.
4. The data was unlawfully processed.
   **Example:** Data processed in contravention of GDPR or EU-NIS directive.
5. The data must be erased in compliance with a legal obligation under EU or Member law. These obligations relate to the national peculiarities in data-protection law within the EU as per the various opening clauses under GDPR.
6. The data was collected in relation to an Information Society Service (ISS).[67] This provision gives additional benefit to children who have consented to data processing with an ISS. Because children are the most vulnerable members of society, EU legislators provide a broader erasure right to children. A child

may not be fully appraised of the risks of data processing and should not be harmed by their data on the internet.[68] Note, this right can be exercised even after reaching maturity,[69] provided the data was collected during minority.

The circumstances for granting erasure interlinks other provisions of GDPR, as the request is tied with other portions of the regulation, such as consent, necessity, lawfulness, etc. Furthermore, there is a close relation between the right and obligation, as the user's right to request is hinged on the Controller's duty to grant the request.[70] The irony here is that GDPR does not use the same wording of the *Costeja* judgment, which held that personal data which is "inadequate, irrelevant, or excessive in relation to the purposes of processing, that they are not kept up to date, or they are kept for longer than is necessary."[71] In a way, the regulation does cover all of the grounds when one collectively looks at the processing obligations of the Controller[72] in relation to user rights.

**Illustration:** Calibri Ltd is hiring new sales managers for its new venture in western India. During the recruitment, several applicants are eliminated from the hiring pool for reasons like salary, notice period, and experience. The rejected applicants receive letters of rejection through e-mail from the HR department. Calibri Ltd processes personal data legally for recruiting new employees. However, Calibri Ltd does not need the data of rejected applicants; hence those candidates have the right to demand the erasure of their personal data from the database of Calibri Ltd.

**Public figures:** GDPR does not differentiate between personal data collected from normal individuals and that of public figures. Public figures are individuals in the public eye, such as celebrities and politicians. This is a curious decision as the CJEU had ruled that the right to be forgotten may be trumped by the public's right to information keeping in mind the "role played by the data subject in public life."[73] Public figures often have a reduced right to privacy in many jurisdictions because of their prominent position and giving an equal right of erasure may lead to abuse by parties who wish to hide certain important details of their life that the public has a right to know.

**False news and posts:** While many may assume that erasure will be a mechanism for removing "fake news" from the internet, this is far from the case. That is primarily due to the fact that inaccuracy or falsity is not a ground for erasure, but a ground for rectification,[74] and even then data subjects can only raise requests related to his own personal data. Thus, a remedy for removing "fake news" posted by third parties is left to the website that is providing the service, leaving an interesting vacuum in the regulation.

**Illustration:** Clint is a citizen running for parliament in his country, which is a member of the EU. Most citizens of the country use a common social networking website called Facespace.com. Several days before everyone votes, a story breaks out on Facespace.com that Clint has an illegitimate son with his former maid. The story is not true but was made using certain true facts received from his personal data (which was public) and was shared by a "spam-bot." The news went viral and was subsequently shared by both uninformed swing voters and opposition members, fueled by continuous sharing by these bots. Clint requests erasure of the false news from both Facespace's and Google's Controller. Clint does not have a remedy against either.

- His suit against Facespace.com will fail, as the news was posted by a third party and not in relation to the data he gave to the website. He can only erase the news posted if Facespace.com has a "take-down" policy or mechanism.
- His suit against Google would fail as he did not give the personal data to them himself.
- In both cases, he has no grounds, as the irrelevance or falsity of the news article is not a ground for erasure.
- The fact that Clint is running for public office would not be considered under GDPR.

From looking at the above, it becomes clear why GDPR has a right to erasure and not a right to be forgotten. A right to be forgotten carries with it a broader weight and ambit, giving a data subject the right to approach a Controller and have a wider array of objectionable material removed in the interest of his privacy. Erasure on the other hand, is the right to control personal data provided directly or indirectly to the Controller for their processing activities in connection to GDPR itself. Thus, the scope of erasure is restricted to the rights and obligations provided for under the regulation, but not beyond that scope.

### 6.5.4 Erasure of Personal Data Which Has Been Made Public

Under GDPR, if the Controller makes the personal data of the user public and subsequently receives a request for erasure, reasonable steps must be adopted, including technical measures to coordinate with the other Controllers that are processing that personal data to ensure that the request is carried out. The coordination between the Controllers processing the data must be made considering the:

1. Available technology; and
2. The cost of implementation.

After informing the other Controllers processing the data of the erasure, reasonable steps must be made to erase the:

1. Data
2. Links
3. Copies and
4. Replications.

This provision gives user protection in situations where the data provided is shared between different websites/apps/platforms, etc. Using our earlier Illustration of Clint, let us consider now that the false news was made using the true personal data that was part of his Facespace.com profile, that was shared with his consent across their sister companies. When receiving his request to delete all data which was processed by Facespace and their subsidiaries, the Controller of Facespace.com should take reasonable steps and technical measures to ensure that all of Clint's data made public by the company (including their subsidiaries) is subsequently erased.

**Illustration:** In a conference held by a state power company to discuss poor electricity facilities in a town, transcripts and key notes were written by the staff, which included information regarding individual residents, their families, corporations, and social workers impacted. The information on file is not segmented, so that personal data can be separated from the main notes. If a surveyor requests a copy of the key notes, it can be released in full without severing any of the third-party information contained in it. Third-party consent is not required as they voluntarily attended the conference and shared the information.

### 6.5.5 What Is "Erasure" of Personal Data?

For lay consumers not versed in technology, erasure likely suggests permanent deletion of the data off the "face of the earth," or rather, the internet. This is a common misconception as Controllers and Processors are subject to other considerations like corporate and legal data retention policies, service efficiency, record-keeping purposes, etc. Erasure requires that data be rendered unusable by physical destruction or technical deletion in a way that no other person or entity may use it for their purposes.[75] For example, placing data into the computer's recycle bin is not erasure, but clearing the recycle bin may qualify.

The value of the data decides the level of erasure necessary. GDPR gives no bright-line rule as to what constitutes an "erasure," but what may be a reasonable action by the Controller involves an individual analysis, weighing the value of the data and the comprehensive nature of the protection required, depending on the organizational effort required.[76] The fact that data could be restored again by using "specialized" software does not necessarily lead to the conclusion that that the Controller had failed in "erasing" the data.

### 6.5.6 Exceptions to Erasure

Erasure shall not apply to the extent that the processing is necessary for the following purposes:

1. For exercising the freedom of speech and the right to Information.
   **Example:** A citizen journalism website with "crowd-sourced" news where everyone contributes to the website.

This exception is subject to the parameters of the Member State opening clause and carries value for the press industry. The exception can be claimed by both natural persons and entities. But this exception is problematic, as websites like Google, Facebook, and Twitter can claim that they process data for these purposes to fall within the exception. Drawing the line requires more guidance from the EU. Furthermore, the exception can be invoked by anybody and not merely press entities. GDPR fails to state how Controllers must deal with removal content surrounding personal data like opinions, exaggerations, puffery, satire, irony, etc., all of which are nuanced and interlinked with the right to erasure.

2. For compliance with a legal obligation under EU or Member law. This depends on GDPR opening clauses and national peculiarities like tax and commercial codes.

    **Example:** An EU regulation specifies that a Controller may not carry out erasure requests in websites that host "journalistic content."

3. For reasons of public interest and health.

    **Example:** A convicted criminal requests erasure of all information on Google reporting that fact. This request is unlikely to be granted as processing here would be in the public interest.

4. **Archiving**, insofar that it seriously impairs the objective of the processing.[77]

    **Example:** David asks that his Snapchat profile be erased, and all the data completely deleted by the Controller. The Controller refuses, stating that while they will erase his profile for public access, his personal data will be tokenized and used for their statistical reports. This is permissible under GDPR.

    Archiving under GDPR will likely face scrutiny at a domestic, Member State level, as the scope of the exception is left open. Erasure requests in statistical and historic archiving likely occur after the research has been completed, which may interrupt the results of the study itself. This will not be an issue if the data has been anonymized properly for the study.

5. For establishing, exercising, or defending legal claims.

    **Example:** David is the defendant in a defamation suit for his offensive tweets against his business rival. The personal data may not be erased even though David requests the Controller to do so. This is because his tweets will be used as the subject matter of the case.

The five exceptions are broadly worded to give discretion to the Controller in conducting their business while balancing the competing rights of others. But do the exceptions fully do justice to handling such a controversial right? It does not necessarily sort out the threat of a Controller making such important decisions that affect the rights of many individuals, as evidenced by scholarly objection to Google's erasure practices.[78] For erasure to become a streamlined practice in data processing, GDPR drafters must clarify:

- The standard for assessing erasure. At present Controllers use *subjective judgments* to decide whether erasure should be permitted, leading to numerous disagreements with consumers and the public. GDPR needs to specify an *objective criterion* for handling erasure requests.

- The geographic scope of erasure orders. As discussed above "freedom of speech" standards differ between countries, and erasure orders in one jurisdiction may not be suitable in another.

    **Illustration:** Country X has a law which states that erasure of "journalistic articles" based on personal data requires the Controller to implement the measures with every Controller who hosts the article (either directly or indirectly). This is because the public policy of X favors privacy over all other rights. Country Y's law states that the Controller must erase only the article on their website, and other Controllers are free to keep sharing the article until they receive an individual request. Country Y's jurisprudence favors a strong freedom of information policy for its citizens. Country Z's law states that only search engines are required to delete journalistic articles under erasure because their public policy favors free speech over all other interests. All three countries are within the EU.

    If a request is granted in Country X but implicates Controllers subject to GDPR in Countries Y and Z, which obligation must be fulfilled? What is the appropriate geographical extent for erasing data in such situations? GDPR has left this unanswered.

The CJEU in *Costeja* stated the right to privacy and data protection should overcome other competing rights such as the economic interests or public access to that piece of information.[79] If a Controller, acting under GDPR were to follow the interpretive principles provided by the CJEU, the data subject's rights will trump the public's in most circumstances unless he/she holds a larger role in public life,[80] which GDPR does not cover. There is a lack of harmony in the CJEU right to be forgotten and GDPR erasure. This may be restricted to wording alone, but will likely have larger effects in interpreting erasure as GDPR complaints increase. Going by GDPR objectives moving forward, a "pro-privacy" approach needs to be adopted by Controllers when receiving requests for erasure.

## 6.6    Right to Restriction

Closely related to rectification and erasure is the accompanying right to restrict processing of personal data.[81] Restriction reconciles conflicting interests between the data subject's erasure right and the Controller's interest in continuing processing. It is a temporary or permanent solution to verify processing integrity. The "verification" must be carried out as soon as possible and involves the following steps:

1. Confirming user identity (if needed)
2. Examining the veracity of the request

3. Determining whether the request for erasure/rectification should be granted
4. Acting to grant or deny the request

## 6.6.1  Granting Restriction

Restriction requires marking stored personal data with the aim of limiting its processing in the future.[82] The data subject shall have the right to restriction when:

1. The accuracy of the data is contested, and the Controller is given a period of time to verify the request.

    **Example:** David contests that his match.com dating site profile incorrectly lists his age and height. He gives a rectification request to the Controller, who suspends his profile while the request is being carried out.
2. The processing is unlawful and rather than erasure, the user requests restriction. Here, the data subject is interested in preventing erasure.

    **Example:** David discovers that another dating site cupid.com has the same details from his match.com profile and Facebook page and keeps suggesting "dates" to him based on this unlawfully collected data. David requests the Controller to stop collecting more data on him. He requests them to rectify incorrect information and erase some personal details posted. However, he decides to keep the profile up on cupid.com based on this restriction.
3. The Controller no longer needs the data, but the user requires it for establishing/exercising/defending a legal claim.

    **Example:** After many years of nonuse of his match.com profile, the Controller mails David stating they will be deleting his profile unless he states otherwise as part of their new "data minimization policy." David asks that they keep his profile, but on an "inactive" status as he requires his old "direct chats" to prove an alibi in a criminal trial.
4. The user exercises his right to object to the AI or logic involved, and the Controller is verifying whether overriding legitimate grounds exist to continue processing.

    **Example:** David objects to the profiling practices of the algorithm that cupid.com uses, insisting that they keep suggesting matches to him based on his ethnicity. His processing will be restricted while the Controller investigates the matter.

The legal effect of restricting processing is the nonuse of the personal data by the Controller in processing. Methods for carrying this out include:

- Moving the personal data to another processing system temporarily
- Making the data unavailable to other users
- Temporary removal of published materials[83]

On granting the request the Controller must inform other recipients of the personal data if requested by the user.[84] Other Controllers are not automatically obliged to enforce erasure/restriction/rectification rights, but must do so when another Controller informs them that the rights are being exercised.

### 6.6.2 Exceptions to Restriction

After the restriction has been implemented, further processing of the data may not occur place unless:

1. The user consents,
2. The data is needed for the establishment/exercise/defense of legal claims,
3. The protection of another natural or legal person's rights, or
4. In accordance to EU or Member public interest.

The practical scope of "consent" remains unclear and likely applies in circumstances where personal data is being disclosed to third-party recipients notwithstanding the restriction. **Illustration:** A discharged employee in a law firm asks for them to stop processing his personal data and erase the contents from their servers immediately. The firm agrees to stop processing his data for active purposes but requires a week to speak to his company insurance carriers and retrieve his data from them. The employee consents to this limited processing. This is a partial processing restriction.

An important exception to further processing in cases of restriction is the storage of the data. If the Controller has concluded his investigation and intends on lifting the restriction of processing he must inform the data subject prior to doing so.[85] GDPR Article 18 acts as a buffer between the time of requesting rectification or erasure, and the disposition of the request. In the time it takes the Controller to verify a request under the regulation, the data remains protected in favor of the user like an interim measure to prevent further harm from occurring to his interests.

## 6.7 Right to Data Portability

Data Portability is a new right created by GDPR, requiring that the personal data provided to the Controller will be available on demand to the user to transfer to another Controller. The right is a specification of an individual's right to privacy and self-determination guaranteed by EU law.[86] The right allows users to move, copy, and transmit data from one IT environment to another[87] and to change services with more ease. Portability of data is another indicator that the EU is shifting its digital market toward a "consumer-friendly" approach, as implementing portability to comply with GDPR will likely impose considerable efforts on Controllers.[88]

**Illustration:** Raviraj purchases a car financed by a leasing agreement with the Controller, a car distributor. In the leasing agreement, Raviraj, the data subject, consented to transfer data on his driving behavior to the Controller to help resolve any potential question of liability in case of a car accident. This data is held by an insurance company to maintain a file on his driving behavior. Raviraj requests the transfer of said data to another financer with whom he wishes to negotiate a potentially more beneficial leasing agreement. The Controller must contact the insurance company and provide the data in an interoperable format. The transfer can be made for Raviraj's own personal reasons but may not be done for furthering the Controller's commercial interests like marketing.

### 6.7.1   The Format of Data and Requirements for Portability

The provision is aimed at online service providers, encouraging a market where users can transfer their data with "one-click." GDPR Article 20 mandates that on request, users shall have the right to receive the personal data provided to the Controller in a format which is:

1. Structured
2. Commonly used
3. Machine readable; and
4. Transmittable to another Controller.

In terms of technical requirements, Controllers are encouraged by GDPR to develop *interoperable formats* that enable data portability.[89] "Interoperability" entails data be in a format that would support *reuse* by another Controller.[90] GDPR encourages adopting such formats and does not create an obligation on Controllers to maintain processing systems that are "technically compatible."[91] "Commonly" used would require an examination of the technology's state of the art in the industry. For example, PDF, Word, HTML links are acceptable, while a floppy disk would not be. "Reuse" requires that the user be able to access the data at any time, such as having a downloadable copy on demand.

Such an undertaking between Controllers will require consistent cooperation and harmonized technology. Carrying out such a task will soon become necessary as all Controllers processing on the bases provided below are required to have a data portability right. This may be an easier task for the Controllers of larger and fully-monetized companies but would be difficult for SMEs[92] in the market. The processing capabilities must be agreed on between these enterprises to carry out their GDPR obligations.

The user has a right to receive the data in the above format and has the right to transmit the data to another Controller without hindrance from the Controller who has the data. In cases where the Controller handles large quantities of data on behalf of the data subject, the entity may request specification of the data required by the user before acting on the request.[93] It is also important to keep in mind that data portability applies not only to the actively provided information by the user, but also passive data created over the course of the service such as one's browser history, metadata, preferences, cookies, etc.[94] The portable data may contain the personal data of other third parties (which may be the case in social networking sites) and as a result the Controller may be obliged to turn over some data that relates to other individuals.[95]

The Controller must not take an overly restrictive approach in portability requests and can only deny a request when it would have an adverse effect on the rights of another. When providing the portable data, the Controller must also cite the justification for processing the data on behalf of a third party[96] (like legitimate or vital interests).

Where technically feasible, the user shall have the right to have his data transferred directly from one Controller to another. The right to data portability exists in scenarios where:

1. The processing is based on consent[97]/explicit consent[98] or based on contract;[99] and
2. The processing is carried on by automated means.

Any activities that do fall under the above categories are not required to comply with data portability. This seems logical when reading the activities listed under Articles 6 and 9, whose nature usually does not require data portability. **Example:** processing for medical purposes or compliance with a legal obligation. The use of automated means is also a logical choice, as a person manually processing the data would have a hard time implementing the right.

### 6.7.2 Business Competition Issues

The objective of data portability is to create fair competition and protect consumers from a "lock-in" online market. However, GDPR is silent as to whether providing personal data in a portable format for transfer between Controllers is mandatory. It merely says that it must be performed when technically feasible leaving question as to whether it is a "duty" of the Controller. This requirement of Controllers to develop an "interoperable format" discounts market competition that exists between entities. Entities consistently use personal data in an altered or modified format that is classified to fit the business purposes (like tracking data). Consider the following scenario.

**Illustration:** Silver Spoon is a large restaurant-food-delivery service that provides menu and food delivery by way of their app. When joining (by giving consent), one would be required to give in personal data regarding their name, address, credit card details, phone number, etc. Flint is a long-time member of the app. He now wishes to join another food service app called FooNow. He submits a request to Silver Spoon's Controller to give him his data. Under GDPR, Silver Spoon will be required to give the data to Flint in a machine-readable, commonly used and structured format; but will he be required to directly transfer it to FooNow even though they are competitors? Whose interests will prevail?

This is one of the situations where GDPR may cause hurdles in healthy market competition by assuming cooperation between businesses. The Article 29 Working Party has opined that data generated by the Controller as part of the processing by user categorization or AI profiling is not covered by this portability right. Rather, only the raw data provided by the user himself/herself will be covered.[100]

Thus, in the illustration discussed above, the data provided by Flint is to be portable, but the personalization and recommendations by the app are not.

Another issue in data portability is whether the right should be provided to third parties (like employers, hospitals, and banks) who process personal data based on consent. GDPR does not clarify what "provided" implies under Article 20.1, and whether entities can claim portability rights on behalf of the consumer. Employers are not excluded from this responsibility and process personal data based on national law requirements. This allows a broader range of processing that may not be related to their main purpose. In the illustration above, if Flint requests his employer to transfer his data in a portable format for him to register in Silver Spoon, will they be obliged to comply?

### 6.7.3   Intellectual Property Issues

The internet is filled with content that is both protected and unprotected from claims of legal ownership. Intellectual property (IP) is often the appropriate vehicle for a person/entity to stake their interest in online content or programs. Briefly listed, the predominant types of IP in the online world are as follows:

- **Copyright:** For literary, artistic, and other forms of expression that are originally created by the owner and fixed on a tangible medium such as a blog post. Often the underlying algorithm of a software or service is protected by this law. **Example:** A format for arranging data in a system, like Google Maps using public geo-data to create a unique navigator.
- **Trademark:** To protect one's brand and trade names/symbols used to represent a product or service and distinguish it from others in the market. **Example:** The firm brand represented in the website's logo and domain name.
- **Patents:** A temporary monopoly granted by the state to use and exploit an invention that was made by the creator for gain. This form of IP often relates to the more technical aspects of a company's processes in creating their product or service. **Example:** An e-commerce website providing a unique "one-click" checkout technology.
- **Right of publicity:** The common law or statutory right held by a person to protect the unauthorized use of their image for financial gain. **Example:** An attire company using someone's social Instagram photos to advertise the clothes they are wearing.
- **Trade secrets:** Closely-held information by an entity that is highly valuable to competitors and that is not well known to the public. Often this trade secret is closely linked to one of the key factors in a product/service's success. **Example:** The "secret recipe" of Coca-Cola.

Though there are other forms of IP, the forms discussed above are the most relevant to the present discussion on personal data protection. Data portability stands as a threat to potential interests in IP, especially if a company's underlying copyright and patent interests in the data software are used by the Controller.[101] If an overwhelming threat to the Controller's business interests exists, the data need not be made portable or transferred. However, rejection of the request is not assumed[102] as the Controller should attempt other measures such as redaction or anonymization of the data.[103]

### 6.7.4   Restrictions on Data Portability

The data portability cannot be exercised:

1. To prejudice the right of erasure of that user[104]
2. Where the processing is necessary in the public interest or under the official authority of the Controller[105]
3. When it will adversely affect the rights and freedoms of others

Data portability and erasure do not have linked consequences. Simply requesting portable data does not equate to requesting erasure, and the Controller may not terminate the contractual relationship that exists. The Controller also holds the right to continue processing data despite the transmission of the data set. Erasure only occurs after data subjects make specific requests to the Controller.

It is unclear from GDPR whether Controllers can contractually exclude data portability with consumers. Its unique position in the regulation as a subordinate right (unlike rectification which is mandatory) creates difficulties in practice. If processing is based on consent, Controllers may exercise the option of removing portability altogether as there is no clear mandate from GDPR. Considering that portability is a subset of the fundamental right to privacy,[106] it would be risky to exclude its application when it can be feasibly carried out in processing.

**Illustration:** Let us consider that Silver Spoon (discussed previously) allows its users to link up their profiles, giving them the ability to "chip in" for meals, and even pay for their friends' meals as a gift. On Flint's profile, he has his friend Maggie's card registered along with his own. When the Controller of Silver Spoon is creating the "personal data file" of Flint for portability, he should not include Maggie's or any of the details of Flint's friends as that would adversely affect their rights.

Data portability under GDPR is an ambitious step forward to a more user-friendly internet. For years individuals utilized the "cookies" and memory features of browsers to make life easier, but the regulation now makes it a legal right. The conflict arises when applying portability practically in the digital environment where technical capabilities and competition in the market are not all harmonized. If Controllers can agree on a common method to carry out data portability in the future, the right will become streamlined for the everyday user, opening fair competition in the market. As Controllers are unlikely to enforce GDPR to their own detriment, clarification from EU legislators on the right is the need of the market.

## 6.8   Rights Relating to Automated Decision Making

With the increase of sophisticated Artificial Intelligence (AI) carrying out more processing activities, Controllers have often found ways to avoid processing liability in the past. This is because many processing decisions made in modern platforms handling personal data are carried out using "automated individual decision making" and AI.

For example, in the recent Cambridge Analytica scandal, the profiling activities of Facebook for the 2016 US elections were allegedly based on "racial" profiling by using AI. While profiling was not carried out specifically using "race" as a factor in the algorithm, it is alleged that Facebook and Cambridge Analytica used "surrounding" personal data that helped the AI identify racial background. The key issue in the above situation is allocating liability. If the technology becomes intelligent enough to make its own automated decisions based on logic and algorithm, the Controller can avoid liability insofar that the decision was not made by it, the Processor, or any of their employees. Rather, the decision was not even made by a human. GDPR seeks to solve this problem by empowering the users and holding the Controller responsible with relation to AI and its use. The regulation gives users a right to object to certain types of processing, following a specific right of explanation of AI activities.

### 6.8.1   The Right to Object

GDPR Article 21 is directed against lawful processing activities that do not correspond to the expectations of the data subject. When processing personal data is necessary for either public interest or prevailing legitimate interests of the Controller,[107] the user shall have a right to object on grounds that are relating to his particular situation.[108] This right to object can be raised at any time and includes profiling activities relating to the processing discussed above. This right also exists in relation to the use of Information Society Services[109] implemented by way of "technical specifications." If this right is successfully exercised, the Controller can no longer process the personal data of the user if processing would have a future effect on the user.[110]

Nowhere in GDPR is "particular situation" elaborated, only specifying that the processing is done in the course of public or legitimate interest-based activities. Interpreting the provision above leads to the conclusion that exercising objections is situational and would depend on the specific facts of the case. It is important to reiterate that this right can be exercised both for the processing done in a situation by the Controller and for profiling activities. This right cannot be interpreted extensively, as it would interrupt the legal bases for processing. Specific situations could relate to one's family circumstances or professional interest in confidentiality.[111]

**The balancing test:** When receiving an objection to processing, the Controller shall no longer process the personal data, unless he shows compelling legitimate

The Controller's                                                                                                    The User's

Interests, Rights, and Freedoms

**OR**

Compelling Legitimate Grounds                    versus                    Establishment/Exercise/Defense
of Legal Claims

**Figure 6.1**   Balancing the Right to Object

grounds to override an individual's rights and interests **or** the establishment of legal claims of the user. The burden of proof in proving "compelling legitimate grounds" rests on the Controller.[112] Let us apply the test presented in Figure 6.1.

**Illustration:** The city of Townsville has started a recent initiative with the home security app "Castle Guard" to link the processing of the data related to home invasions with the police department's statistics and crime reports to increase public safety after a recent spree of break-ins. The app collects the "break-in alerts" of Castle Guard and consolidates the information with housing and police records while keeping the data well protected. David objects to this processing as he is afraid that the data will be misused by the police against him, as he is a prominent criminal defense attorney who is despised by the department for his success.

- David has a right to object to the processing based on his particular situation.
- The processing is carried out in furtherance of public interest of maintaining safety.
- The Controller's compelling legitimate grounds may override David's objection as the protection of the data is secured, and it is unlikely that David's paranoia will negate the project.
- David will likely have a right to erasure or restriction if he wishes to pursue other remedies.

**Direct marketing:** The right to object also extends to situations where the processing of personal data is carried out for "direct marketing" purposes, which includes profiling the data subject.[113] If the user chooses to object, GDPR mandates that the personal data cannot be used for those purposes any longer.[114] This right can be invoked at any time free of charge.[115] Here, there is no "balancing test" provided by the regulation, showing the user's right to prevent excessive direct advertising online. For example, Facebook after the implementation of GDPR has introduced a panel to regulate and control the advertisements presented on one's newsfeed. This can be considered as implementing the right to object to direct marketing.

Regarding advertisers at large, ensure that the three following steps have been covered to avoid GDPR liability:[116]

1. The data has been obtained legally, i.e. not from a data brokerage firm or from an "ad-exchange" company that obtained it illegally to begin with.
2. The entity is permitted to conduct direct marketing or behaviorally targeted advertising by receiving appropriate consent or any other legal basis.
3. Employ a method that is not prohibited under SPAM-prevention laws.[117]

**Notice:** In accordance with the user's "digital Miranda" right that accompanies the Controller's information obligation,[118] this right to object must be brought to the attention of the user at the time of the first communication. The right must be communicated:

1. Explicitly
2. Clearly; and
3. Separately from other information.[119]

Controllers should develop ways to demarcate automated-processing provisions to users such as pop-up windows or highlighted forms.

**Archiving:** The right to object exists in relation to archiving activities for historical/statistical/scientific purposes that are done in accordance with the regulation.[120] The grounds for such an objection are relating to his or her particular situation, and the user shall have a right to object unless the performance of the task is performed in public interest. Note that "statistical" archiving here is not restricted to scientific or public interest purposes but can also relate to consumer or business studies that implement AI in analysis. But if that statistical use of data is subsequently used to affect the data subject, they will maintain their right to object and explanation.

If the data subject successfully enforces this right, the Controller must cease processing of personal data.[121] The right to objection has a future-effect on the Controllers' processing activities. If the objection is based on profiling, the Controller cannot claim a possible counter-exception to continue processing the data.

## 6.8.2 Right to Explanation

Though many believe this right is a creation of GDPR, the prohibition against sole machine decision making has existed for more than 15 years in Europe,[122] specifically by way of German law. The purpose of this restriction was to prevent everyday consumers from having legally significant decisions made by machines alone. A common example are the scandals of arbitrary credit ratings assigned to consumers in America from algorithms implemented by agencies. Under GDPR, the user shall have the right not to be subject to a decision that is solely made by automated processing (AI) that either legally or significantly affects him. To simplify it, let us use a formula:

$$\text{Sole decision making by AI} + \text{Legal or Significant effects}$$
$$= \text{The right of Explanation}$$

A "decision" based on automated processing includes profiling. GDPR Article 22 appears to be a response to Controllers who avoid liability stemming from decisions made by the AI they employ, by specifically preventing them from using technology to dispose of important functions. Even if human intervention is used to verify final decisions made by the machine logic, a Controller remains liable if a human cannot influence the final decision-making determination by the algorithm.[123]

"Legal effects" under this provision include any decision that would change the data subject's legal position either to his detriment or benefit. For example, denying a housing application based on an AI's determination of creditworthiness or denying a job application using e-recruiting AI software to categorize resumes. Meanwhile "significant" effects go beyond the law and consider other factors like economic or personal consequences. **Example:** denying one's bid for fan-based memorabilia on an online auction website based on an analysis of their previous purchase history.

If the right is successfully enforced, the adverse decision against the data subject will be "cut-off," and a human would have to make a separate determination on the contentious portion. Thus, the implementation of GDPR requires Controller entities to make organizational changes to ensure a "human face" handles an "appellate function" to the decisions made by algorithms.

**Illustration:** Anil wants to insure his car, and the insurance company XY carries out "driver scoring." In scoring, XY's computer system analyzes Anil's previous driving behavior data such as car accidents or other traffic offences. The system then rates his behavior based on a predetermined criterion. Based on the result of the scoring, XY will decide whether it wants to conclude an insurance policy with Anil and at what rate. Here the contractual objective of Anil and XY's agreement is to insure Anil's car, and the company requires automated decision making to provide their rate to the customer. Though the AI is necessary for XY's calculations, this can be considered as legal/significant decision making affecting Anil, giving him rights under GDPR.

### 6.8.3 Profiling

Processing that measures and evaluates personal aspects relating to a user based solely on automated decision making is considered profiling.[124] This includes the automated data processing "evaluating the personal aspects relating to a natural person, in particular to analyze or predict aspects concerning a data subject's performance at work, economic situation, health, personal preferences or interests, reliability or behavior, location or movements, where it produces legal effects concerning him or her or similarly significantly affects him or her." Many have been subjected to profiling by AI at one point or another in their digital lives. The responsibility has been left to the EU Data Protection Board to make further guidelines on how profiling must be executed.[125]

**Illustration 1:** Nowshop.com is an online marketplace that employs AI to recommend new products and services to users based on their GPS, previous shopping habits relating to preferences for goods, cost of purchase, and frequency of use. This is legal profiling under GDPR.

**Illustration 2** Nowshop.com uses indicators based on ethnicity and race to help suggest goods and services to its users (in addition to the factors discussed earlier). This is impermissible profiling under GDPR.

### 6.8.4  Exceptions

The rights related to automated decision making do not apply when the decisions are:

1. Necessary for creating/performing a contract between the Controller and user
2. Authorized by EU or Member law with suitable safeguards for the users
3. Based on explicit consent of the user

When the "decisions" are made based on contract or explicit consent, the Controller shall implement suitable safeguards to protect the rights, and legitimate interests of the user.[126] The regulation does not discuss the scope of these safeguards but specifies that the user at least has the right to obtain human intervention on part of the Controller to contest the decision. The requirement of "human intervention" is a creative invention of the regulation, which ensures that the decisions made by the AI are not absolute and cannot leave the user without remedy.

**Illustration 3:** Nowshop.com also has a section in their website called "Concierge Shopping" where exclusive, limited-edition items are sold to the highest bidder in silent online bids. The website determines who gets the good by employing AI that examines the factors discussed in the prior illustration and on the basis of the user's employment and salary earned (with the user's explicit consent). David wishes to buy a limited edition suit of armor from his favorite mythical TV show. The algorithm determines David does not have the funds to purchase the good as the bid he made exceeds his monthly salary and previous shopping history. David has a right of explanation by the Controller as to the logic employed and the basis of denial.

### 6.8.5  Special Categories of Data

GDPR expressly prohibits using automated decision making insofar as the personal data provided is "sensitive,"[127] such as biometric or genetic data. However, if the Controller implements "suitable measures" to safeguard the data, processing can be carried out if:

1. Explicit consent is obtained.
2. The processing is necessary to achieve a substantial public interest.

The "suitable measures" above include "appropriate mathematical or statistical procedures for the profiling, implement technical and organizational measures appropriate to ensure, in particular, that factors which result in inaccuracies in personal data are corrected and the risk of errors is minimized, secure personal data in a manner that considers the potential risks involved for the interests and rights of the data subject, and prevent, inter alia, discriminatory effects."[128]

When dealing with data relating to a person's ethnicity, religious, political, and philosophical views, GDPR places stringent data-protection requirements to prevent scandals such as Cambridge Analytica from taking place. Thus, the regulation first restricts the scope of using AI for such information and secondly ensures protection by the Controller.

## 6.9 Restrictions on Data Subject Rights

No right is absolute, and GDPR follows that rule by providing for numerous exceptions under Article 23, which permit EU or Member law to restrict the rights discussed in this chapter, along with the principles of processing[129] and notification of data breaches[130] insofar as it relates to the rights of the data subject. This requires keeping track of national peculiarities in the Member State law based on where the business operates.

### 6.9.1 Nature of Restrictions Placed

Though rights may be restricted under GDPR, the EU places minimum guarantees that must be followed by Member States when legislating over this topic. The restriction must be made to:

1. Respect the essence of fundamental rights and freedoms.
2. Be necessary and proportionate measure in a democratic society.

The restrictions to user rights are a delicate matter, which can often result in challenges to the law itself if poorly executed. GDPR tries to remove this hurdle by requiring specific provisions be incorporated into the legislative measures. The law must provide for:[131]

1. Purposes or categories of processing
   **Example:** This law relates to all manual and automated processing of personal data by Controllers of e-commerce platforms and websites.

2. Categories of personal data

   **Example:** The restriction shall apply to any personal data that is collected in the course of e-commerce, specifically to data submitted relating to the payment for goods and services.

3. Scope of the restrictions

   **Example:** The restrictions will apply insofar as it is necessary for ensuring smooth and streamlined payment of goods and services.

4. Safeguards to prevent abuse or unlawful access/transfer

   **Example:** The Controller shall adopt measures to protect the data such as pseudonymization or anonymization of the data along with two-step verifications for payment.

5. Specification of the Controller or category of Controllers

   **Example:** This law shall be applicable to all Controllers who engage, facilitate, or host the sale and purchase of goods on the internet.

6. Storage periods and applicable safeguards[132]

   **Example:** The data shall be stored for a period of five years in an encrypted manner, with protection both the data in transit and the data at rest.

7. Risk to the rights and freedoms of data subjects

   **Example:** The Controller shall ensure that the actions taken do not adversely affect the rights and freedoms of other data subjects on their websites.

8. The right of the user to be informed of such restriction unless it would be prejudicial to the purpose of the restriction

   **Example:** On enacting this law, Controllers are required to inform the users of the restrictions placed on their rights in a clear and plain manner, explaining the reasoning for such an act.

GDPR not only lays down the restrictions to processing but ensures that Member State legislatures will not go too far in curtailing these rights. The restrictions under Member State law must be carefully drafted to prevent overreach.

### 6.9.2  The Basis of Restrictions

The legislative restrictions can be made as a necessary and proportionate measure in a "democratic society." This includes safeguarding the following interests of the State:

1. National Security

   **Example:** A law preventing suspected terrorists from erasing their social media profiles.

2. Defense

3. Public Security

   Consider our Nowshop.com illustration discussed above as an example.

4. The prevention, investigation, detection, or prosecution of criminal offenses

> **Example:** A law that prevents criminal defendants accused of fraud from erasing their trading profiles online.

5. The execution of criminal penalties, including safeguarding and preventing threats to public security
6. Other important objectives of public interest of the EU/Member State. This includes economic and financial interests, with matters relating to:
   a. Monetary interests
   b. Budgetary interests
   c. Taxation
   d. Public Health
   e. Social Security
7. The prevention, investigation, detection, and prosecution of breaches relating to professions regulated by ethics

   > **Example:** The use of AI to track prescription pharmaceutical sales to determine which doctors are overmedicating their patients. In such a case, using AI "solely" for that purpose would be permissible.

8. The monitoring, inspection, or regulatory function connected, **even occasionally,** to the exercise of authority for the restrictions discussed above

   > **Example:** A prosecutor investigating the breach of legal ethics by an attorney may be able to monitor his social network profile to prove conforming conduct of the attorney.

9. The protection of judicial independence and proceedings
10. The protection of the user and the rights of others
11. The enforcement of civil law claims

The restrictions act as a ceiling to the rights that form the foundation for GDPR. While rights such as erasure and portability are necessary to transfer the authority to the users, leaving them absolute would cause inefficiencies under the new "single digital economy" that GDPR seeks to achieve. The restrictions serve this purpose to ensure the new rights created do not hamper the larger interests of the State or the EU, while keeping the essence of these rights intact for the beneficiaries of the new regime.

## Notes

1  GDPR, Article 83.5.
2  Data Protection Directive, Articles 10, 11.
3  GDPR, Article 12.1.
4  GDPR, Article 12.1.
5  Paul Voigt and Axel von dem Bussche, *The EU GDPR: A Practical Guide* (Springer, 2017), 142.
6  GDPR, Article 12.7: It is important to note that the drafters used the term *"may be provided"* rather than a compulsory *"shall."*

7  GDPR, Article 12.7.
8  GDPR, Article 12.8.
9  Complaint against Google LLC, filed with the French DPA (CNIL), May 25, 2018 (https://noyb.eu/wp-content/uploads/2018/05/complaint-android.pdf).
10  GDPR, Article 12.2.
11  GDPR, Article 11.
12  GDPR, Article 12.3.
13  GDPR, Article 12.3.
14  GDPR, Article 12.6.
15  GDPR, Article 12.4.
16  GDPR, Article 12.1.
17  GDPR, Article 12.5.
18  GDPR, Article 12.5.
19  GDPR, Article 12.5.b.
20  GDPR, Article 19 *read with* Article 16, 17, 18.
21  In accordance with GDPR, Article 17.2.
22  GDPR, §2, Article 13, 14.
23  GDPR, Article 13.
24  GDPR, Article 14.
25  GDPR, Article 13.1.d *read with* Article 6.1.f.
26  GDPR, Article 12.1.f: Elaborating on the "adequacy decision" by the commission and appropriate safeguards has been discussed in Chapter 4 (Section 4.3.1).
27  GDPR, Article 12.1.
28  Lothar Determann, *Determann's Field Guide to Data Privacy Law*, 3rd ed. (Edward Elgar Publishing, 2017), 72.
29  GDPR, Article 14.
30  "Explicit Consent" is with relation to the consent given under Article 6.1.a or 9.1.a of GDPR.
31  GDPR, Article 12.2 ¶2.
32  GDPR, Article 13.3 and 14.4.
33  Chapter 5 (Section 5.1.2).
34  GDPR, Article 14.
35  GDPR, Article 14.2.f.
36  GDPR, Article 13.1.
37  GDPR, Article 13.4 and 14.5.a.
38  GDPR, Article 14.5 (b) to (d).
39  The archiving exceptions are subject to the safeguards provided under GDPR, Article 89 (1).
40  GDPR, Article 14.5.c.
41  GDPR, Article 83.5.b.
42  Pursuant to GDPR, Article 46.
43  GDPR, Recital 63.
44  Relating to the provision of information by the Controller, "Free of Cost."
45  GDPR, Article 15.3.
46  GDPR, Article 16.

47  GDPR, Article 5.1.d.

48  GDPR, Articles 13, 14.

49  C. Worms, Arts. 16, DSGVO. In *Beck'scher Online-Kommentar Datenschutzrecht,* 18th ed., edited by H.A. Wolff and S. Brink (C.H. Beck, 2017). Rec. 49 and 53; Voigt and von dem Bussche, *The EU GDPR: A Practical Guide,* 154 and 155.

50  GDPR, Article 13.

51  GDPR, Article 16.

52  Lilian Mitrou and Maria Karyda, "EU's Data Protection Reform and the Right to Be Forgotten: A Legal Response to a Technological Challenge?" pp. 29—30. Fifth International Conference of Information Law and Ethics, Corfu, Greece, June 2012.

53  Droit d'oubli, French Law 78-17/1978, Article 40.

54  EU Directive 95/46/EC, Article 12.

55  Edward Carter, "Argentina's Right to be Forgotten," *Emory International Law Review* 27, no. 1, http://law.emory.edu/eilr/content/volume-27/issue-1/recent-developments/argentinas-right-to-be-forgotten.html.

56  Abhinav Garg, "Delhi Banker Seeks 'Right to Be Forgotten' Online," *Times of India,* May 1, 2016, https://timesofindia.indiatimes.com/india/Delhi-banker-seeks-right-to-be-forgotten-online/articleshow/52060003.cms.

57  EUCFR, Article 8.

58  EUCFR, Article 7.

59  EUCFR, Article 7; *US Constitution,* 4th Amendment; *Constitution of India,* Article 21.

60  GDPR, Article 17.3.a.

61  See for example The Freedom of Information Act, 1967 5 U.S.C. § 552, Section 8(A); and more broadly the Espionage Act, 1917, 18 U.S.C. § 792; The Official Secrets Act (India), 1923, Section 3; GDPR, Article 23.

62  See Don Melvin, "Zimbabwean Officials: American Man Wanted in Killing of Cecil the Lion," CNN, https://www.cnn.com/2015/07/28/africa/zimbabwe-lion-killed/index.html.

63  Index on Censorship, May 13, 2014, http://www.indexoncensorship. org/2014/05/index-blasts-eu-court-ruling-right-forgotten.

64  Natasha Lomas, "Call for Google to Show Its Right to Be Forgotten Workings," *TechCrunch*, May 14, 2015, https://techcrunch.com/2015/05/14/call-for-google-to-show-its-right-to-be-forgotten-workings/.

65  Emiel Jurjens, "Third Dutch Google Spain Ruling: Convicted Murderer Does Not Have 'Right to Be Forgotten,'" Inforrm Blog, https://inforrm. org/2015/06/10/third-dutch-google-spain-ruling-convicted-murderer-does-not-have-right-to-be-forgotten-emiel-jurjens.

66  GDPR, Article 17.1.b; *read with* Article 21.1 and 21.2, specifically, "profiling" based processing balanced against the *legitimate overriding interests of the Controller.*

67  GDPR, Article 8.1.

68  GDPR, Recital 65.

69  GDPR, Recital 65.

70  C. Worms, (2016) Art. 17, rec. 23, DSGVO. In Wolff and Brink (eds.), *Beck'scher Online-Kommentar Datenschutzrecht.*

71  *Google Spain v. Costeja,* CJEU [2013] C-131/12, ¶92.

72  GDPR, Articles 5 and 6.

73  *Google Spain v. Costeja,* CJEU [2013] C-131/12, ¶99.

74  GDPR, Article 16.

75  C. Worms (2016) Art. 17, rec. 55, DSGVO. In H. A. Wolff and S. Brink S (eds.), *Beck'scher Online-Kommentar Datenschutzrecht,* 18th ed. (Munich: CH Beck).

76  Worms, Art. 17, rec. 56, DSGVO.

77  GDPR, Article 89.1.

78  Lomas, "Call for Google to Show Its Right to Be Forgotten Workings."

79  *Google Spain v. Costeja,* CJEU [2013] C-131/12.

80  *Google Spain v. Costeja,* CJEU [2013] C-131/12, ¶99.

81  GDPR, Article 18.

82  GDPR, Article 4(3).

83  GDPR, Recital 67.

84  GDPR, Article 19.2.

85  GDPR, Article 18.3.

86  EU-Charter of Fundamental Rights, Article 8 and TFEU, Article 16.

87  Article 29 Working Party, WP 242 (2016), 3–4.

88  Voigt and von dem Bussche, *The EU GDPR,* 169.

89  GDPR, Recital 68.

90  Article 29 Working Party, WP 242 (2016), 13.

91  GDPR, Recital 68.

92  That is, small and medium enterprises.

93  GDPR, Recital 63.

94  Article 29 Working Party, WP 242 2016, 8.

95  Article 29 Working Party, WP 242 2016, 7–9.

96  Article 29 Working Party, WP 242 2016, 8.

97  GDPR, Article 6.1.a.

98  GDPR, Article 9.2.a.

99  GDPR, Article 6.1.b.

100  Article 29 Working Party, WP 242 2016, 7–9.

101  GDPR, Recital 63.

102  GDPR, Recital 63.

103  Article 29 Working Party, WP 242 2016, 10.

104  Here, GDPR is ambiguous in its 68th recital as to the reach of this exception: "Furthermore, that right should not prejudice the right of the data subject to obtain the erasure of personal data and the limitations of that right as set out in this Regulation and should, *in particular,* not imply the erasure of personal data concerning the data subject which have been provided by him or her for the performance of a contract *to the extent that and for as long as the personal data are necessary for the performance of that contract.*"

105  GDPR, Recital 68, "By its very nature, that right should not be exercised against Controllers processing personal data in the exercise of their public duties. It should therefore not apply where the processing of the personal data is

necessary for compliance with a legal obligation to which the Controller is subject or for the performance of a task carried out in the public interest or in the exercise of an official authority vested in the Controller."

106 EU-Charter of Fundamental Rights, Article 8 and TFEU, Article 16.

107 GDPR, Article 6.1. e and f.

108 GDPR, Article 21.1.

109 GDPR, Article 21.5; *EU Directive* 2002/58/EC.

110 Voigt and von dem Bussche, *The EU GDPR,*179.

111 Voigt and von dem Bussche, *The EU GDPR*, 177.

112 GDPR, Recital 69.

113 GDPR, Article 21.2.

114 GDPR, Article 21.3.

115 GDPR, Recital 70.

116 Determann, *Determann's Field Guide to Data Privacy Law,* 107.

117 For example, see the US CAN- SPAM Act.

118 See GDPR, Article 13, 14, 15; Chapter 6 (Section 6.2) of this book.

119 GDPR, Article 21.4.

120 GDPR, Recital 162.

121 GDPR, Article 21.1.

122 Specifically, German Law *BDSG,* §6a.

123 Voigt and von dem Bussche, *The EU GDPR*, 181.

124 GDPR, Recital 71.

125 GDPR, Recital 72.

126 GDPR, Article 22.3.

127 GDPR, Article 9.

128 GDPR, Recital 71.

129 GDPR, Article 5.

130 GDPR, Article 34.

131 GDPR, Article 23.2.

132 GDPR, Article 23.2.f: "... taking into account the *nature, scope, and purpose* of the processing or categories of processing."

# 7

## GDPR Enforcement

*Vigilant and effective antitrust enforcement today is preferable to the heavy hand of government regulation of the Internet tomorrow.*

— Orrin Hatch

In our previous chapters, we discussed the duties and responsibilities of the Controllers and Processors under GDPR. Securing a legal basis for processing data subject rights and protecting the data are the central concerns of a Controller. Now, let us examine how those rights and responsibilities can be enforced under the scheme of the regulation. There are four ways to enforce GDPR compliance:

1. Through "in-house" modalities and mechanisms,
2. By approaching the appropriate SA,
3. By going to court, and
4. By having an ADR mechanism in place.

In this chapter, we shall examine all of the above.

## 7.1   In-House Mechanisms

GDPR encourages Controllers to assist data subjects in exercising their rights in processing personal data.[1] This is a form of self-regulation as a part of GDPR compliance. Some of the measures discussed below are mandatory while others are advisable business practices to avoid liability. Mechanisms must be set up by modalities or easily accessible icons to help the users easily access and control their personal data.

### 7.1.1 A Quick Review

Earlier, in Chapter 6, we discussed the Controller's information and transparency obligations requiring them to provide details to users regarding their rights and the duty to create modalities to exercise those rights.[2] Let us review what GDPR requires before proceeding. The Controller has the responsibility of adopting measures in writing, providing information relating to the data subject's rights. The information must be provided in a manner that is:

1. Concise
2. Transparent
3. Intelligible
4. Easily accessible
5. Using clear and plain language[3]

The information must be provided free of cost by the Controller to the data subject.[4] This transparency can be achieved in a combination of *standardized icons* that are:

1. Easily visible
2. Intelligible
3. Clearly legible
4. Machine readable

However, standardized icons have been left open to the EU Commission to create delegated acts for clarifying its application.[5] Complimenting the Controller's information and transparency obligations, there is concurrent data subject right to approach the Controller:[6]

1. For confirmation as to whether his personal data is being processed; and if so,
2. For access to the personal data and the information relating to:
   a. The purpose of processing
   b. Categories of data processed
   c. Recipients or categories of recipients of the data
   d. Period of data storage or method of calculation of said period
   e. Existence of the right of erasure, rectification, restriction, and data portability
   f. The right to lodge a complaint against the Supervisory Authority
   g. Source of the data, if the data has not been provided directly
   h. The existence of AI and its logic, significance, and consequence of such automated decision making
   i. Existence of appropriate safeguards in cases of transfers to third countries.[7]

The Controller shall facilitate the rights exercise and cannot refuse to do so when requested unless an inability to identify the data subject is shown. If the Controller does not act or intends on pursuing judicial remedies, he must inform the data subject within one month of receiving the request.[8] Additionally, the Controller also has a right to request additional information to confirm the natural identity of the data subject where reasonable doubts exist,[9] such as asking for an ID number.

Thus, GDPR mandates that users have right of access and compliments it with an information and transparency obligation on the Controller. This requires that mechanisms be easily available for the two to coexist. A "platform" provided by the Controller is the first step for users trying to enforce GDPR. It is important to note that this does not prevent the user from exercising rights before the SA or court, as the regulation permits that option. Commercially, it is sensible to implement such a "self-enforcement" option for users to exercise their rights. Beneficially, both parties stay out of court/SA's Office and try to resolve the issue internally.

## 7.1.2 Implementing an Internal Rights Enforcement Mechanism

In GDPR compliance, a Controller must provide a suitable system of providing information, educating the user, and modalities for exercising rights.

**7.1.2.1 Step 1: Getting the Information Across** At the time of collecting user data or a reasonable period after attaining it,[10] the business must provide the information listed above to the user. The effective mechanisms used widely in practice are disclosures or terms of use when commencing service. GDPR requires a change in the way that the terms of use can be presented to the user; the major adjustments would be:

1. Plain English must be used.
2. The information that must be provided must be clearly demarcated.
3. Excessively long and complex legal contracts are not permitted.
4. Information cannot be deliberately technical to mislead the user.
5. When the user consents, it must be freely given, with full knowledge of the terms and clearly separated from the rest of the information.

GDPR permits a level of creativity in how businesses put information across, allowing videos and visualizations to educate users. If a Controller cannot find a way to concisely provide the information for the user (for example, multipurpose platforms that provide a breadth of services), it is advisable to clearly describe and demarcate the headings and titles of the agreements. Consider the headings in the model contract illustrated below:

*What we use your data for. (Collapsible LINK.)*
*How long we store your data for. (Collapsible LINK.)*
*What are your rights under the law? (Collapsible LINK.)*
*How do you exercise your rights? (Collapsible LINK.)*
*For any complaints, help, objections, or assistance regarding these Terms of Use, your rights, and our service may be mailed to Mr. CONTROLLER @e-mail and Address.*

**7.1.2.2 Step 2: The Privacy Policy** Though many businesses may choose to "bundle" the privacy policy with the terms of use, it is wise to separate the two. Though GDPR does not expressly require it, having a separate policy simplifies legal documents for a comprehensive and understandable account of the business for the user. At the same time, users must know that their privacy is implicated and protected by the service provided by the Controller.

A safe way to divide the two would be to include the commercial terms, general information (regarding advertising), and the purposes and means of processing in the terms of use. Separately, all privacy and rights related matters are provided in the privacy policy. A broad division that can be followed has been provided below:

| S. No | Terms of use | Privacy policy |
| --- | --- | --- |
| 1. | The purposes of processing | Relationship between data provided and purposes of processing |
| 2. | Where the processing is based | Types and categories of data processed |
| 3. | Existence of any further processing | Consent and explicit consent procedures for further processing and special data |
| 4. | The legitimate interests of the Controller | Existence of the data subject's rights |
| 5. | Existence of advertising and its relation to the processing | The data subject's right to control advertising, direct marketing, and profiling |
| 6. | Third-country transfers and permissions | The recipients of the data |
| 7. | The right to lodge a complaint before the SA for infringement of GDPR | The right to lodge a complaint before the SA for violation of these rights |
| 8. | Whether the processing of data is required by contract or law | Whether the processing of data is required by contract or law |
| 9. | The existence of AI and meaningful information regarding the logic involved | The relation between the AI and the user's rights/privacy |
| 10. | The identity of the Controller and representative (where applicable) | Period of data storage |
| 11. | Legal basis of the processing under GDPR | The right to withdraw consent |
| 12. | The Controller's data breach policies | Users' rights in the event of a data breach |
| 13. | Contact details of the DPO | Contact details of the DPO |

The content of the two documents are similar and interlinked. The terms of use provide a broader palate of information, while the privacy policy is a digital *Miranda* of the user's rights in processing. Thus, larger organizations that have voluminous information to provide the user are advised to separate the privacy policy and initial disclosures.

The two documents listed above are in no way the only forms of documentation that may exist within a data processing organization. For sound measure, let us consider the categories which have been provided below:[11]

1. Notices (example: Notice for collection of special category data)
2. Consent forms (example: Requesting explicit consent for collection of special data)
3. Contractual agreements (example: Agreements with advertisers)
4. Protocols (example: Employee confidentiality protocols)
5. Data-submission forms (example: surveys or registration forms)
6. Descriptions (example: Hyperlinks to explain how AI is employed in the process with technical detail)
7. Government notifications (example: A subpoena)

The label assigned is nearly irrelevant so long as the consent is well demarcated and separated. In the broader practice of online contracts, a "privacy policy" is nothing but a combination of notice, protocols, and statements regarding one's personal data security.[12]

**7.1.2.3 Step 3: Create the "Technical" Measures**   Once users are fully informed and processing has legally begun, the next step is to ensure that a mechanism exists for enforcing the agreement and the rights[13] maintained internally. This technical and organizational effort involves both digital resources and manpower. There are several ways to implement this:

1. **Full control model:** Give data subjects complete power over the data processed on the website and the exercise of their rights. This would include:
   a. Necessary modalities to access their rights
      **Example:** A tool bar, icons, user-profile settings, or other methods of easily accessing the data collection settings.
   b. Necessary modalities to enforce their rights
      **Example 1:** A section in the settings tab where the users can personally rectify/erase data.
      **Example 2:** An icon to receive personal data in a portable form.
      **Example 3:** An "Advertisement Control Panel" to switch off and regulate the ads presented.
   c. A section to contact the Controller or DPO in an efficient manner
      **Example:** A "complaint and inquiry" box that is accessible from the user's profile with a 48-hour response time. The Controller/DPO should take care to ensure that any request filed should be answered as soon as possible to avoid liability.
   d. An alternative to contact the Controller or DPO to access and enforce their rights
      **Example:** An "Emergency Contact" page on the website with the DPO's details in cases of any data breach. The DPO or Controller must ensure that

a second avenue of communication (such as e-mail or text message) is easily accessible to the user with a high speed of response.

The "full control" model is ideal for GDPR compliance but demands significant costs and technical expertise. Furthermore, in certain types of activities that level of control with data subjects might interrupt the efficiency and purposes of processing. Thus, this model may not be ideal for small and medium-sized businesses who cannot afford the costs or the effect.

2. **Partial control model:** This model mixes users' control with Controller involvement, where the organization's intervention is needed for certain requests. This model requires:

   a. Necessary modalities for accessing their rights

      **Example:** A tool bar or a user settings profile

   b. Necessary modalities to request the exercise of rights

      **Example 1:** A "Request" tab where the user can efficiently inform the Controller for restriction and erasure of his data with a 48-hour response time.

      **Example 2:** A "portability-request" button, with user-friendly "settings" to adjust the period, nature, and contents of the data needed. After the user submits the request, the Controller must give the data in a machine-readable form within 24 hours.

   c. A mechanism to contact the Controller or DPO

      **Example:** An AI Management section in the website that enables users to request meaningful explanations of the logic, specific information of profiling, logic and processing operations, and an "Objection to Automated Processing" form that can be submitted to the Controller/DPO directly.

   d. An alternative to contact the Controller or DPO to access and enforce their rights, as discussed above

      While rights like rectification are easier to place in the users' hands, erasure, data portability, objection, etc., may interrupt the processing activities or require extra processing itself. GDPR only requires that users be provided an option to request the Controller for exercise of these rights,[14] giving space for businesses who cannot afford to give that level of control.

3. **"Request-based" model:** If an organization cannot implement new modalities owing to costs, lack of expertise, or the nature of the processing operation, they can create the minimum mechanism of having the users "Request" exercise of their rights. This model is based on establishing a low-cost mode of communication with the user, which must be regularly monitored. In this model, manpower is more valuable as requests need to be answered immediately to avoid GDPR liability.

   **Illustration:** A medium-sized healthcare data analytics firm, Health Pro, relies heavily on the specifics of data in their records provided by their customers. As a result, only the doctors and designated employees of Health Pro's "Processing Wing" are permitted to change the information on their records. If a customer wishes to rectify, delete, or port their data, they will have to go to their profile and fill out a singular REQUEST FORM which has categories of

SUBJECT FIELDS, which help them specify which action they can take. The request form has all the sections necessary to request Health Pro to act on the right in question. Health Pro requires a period of 48 to 72 hours to verify the information from the doctor and respond. So long as all requests are answered in a timely fashion, Health Pro is GDPR compliant.

Note, there is no model based on No-Control as GDPR mandates data subjects hold some degree of control over personal data. The exercise of GDPR rights must be easily done and not difficult for the user. Therefore, organizations should be careful not to be rigid and to give users free access to their data to the maximum practical degree.

**7.1.2.4 Step 4: Implement the "Organizational" Measures**  Behind the modalities and mechanisms, it is important to keep a human face, or a team of employees dedicated to the cause. This is, of course, dependent on available resources and human capital of the business. However, GDPR requires that technical mechanisms available to users have the regular involvement of the Controller. Thus, any processing operation will require some level of oversight, even if it is a "full-control" model.

Assuming the resources exist, it would be ideal for an organization to:[15]

1. Hire a dedicated department to handle data subject requests.
2. The department should be qualified to carry out the functions and answer directly to the Controller or DPO.
3. Categorize the requests according to which require the most employee-intervention to execute.
4. Give a fixed period to users for response.
5. Follow approved codes of conduct for processing in order to regulate how specific requests and objections may be dealt with.
6. Have the same codes of conduct dictate clearly the criteria for rejection of user requests.
7. Follow fixed data breach protocols for the processing activity and inform the user.
8. Any extraordinary requests should be reported to the Controller/DPO directly.
9. Any contentious requests should be referred to the legal department and Controller/DPO.
10. If the modalities provided are largely automated, regular oversight and maintenance are needed.

**7.1.2.5 Step 5: Create a Dispute Resolution Policy**  The first priority of a Controller organization would be successfully enforcing users' rights under GDPR and operate with no complaint or objection. If all fails, its best to be prepared for a dispute with a plan of action. This includes:

1. Planning settlements with users and *settlement policies* internally for alleged GDPR violations
2. Providing a *Choice of Forum* or *ADR clause* in initial privacy policies and disclosures[16]

3. Having a legal team ready to work with Processors and other bodies involved for any potential problematic complaints
4. Maintain a Compliance department that oversees GDPR matters and assists the SA with their investigations (under the direct orders of the Controller)
5. Being transparent with the SA for any documents or information they may request

The measures above require having resources ready for the worst-case scenario where normal in-house mechanisms in place do not satisfy the request/complaint filed. Planning for eventual disputes is always a better option than being caught off guard.

Creating a fluid and efficient system of enforcing data subjects' rights involves a solid base of information by educating the user. After that, users only require the tools necessary to enforce those rights when the occasion arises. Beyond that, the steps discussed merely help the business to streamline the mechanisms to prevent legal action from being commenced. An effective implementation of an in-house rights enforcement mechanism will reduce GDPR liability, making it an investment worth the cost and effort.

## 7.2  Data Subject Representation

Before proceeding to enforce GDPR, let us briefly discuss issues of standing to bring complaints and suits. It is evident that any GDPR complaint or suit can be filed by the data subject directly or through a legal representative/attorney to represent their rights before the SA/court. Another option available to the data subjects is enlisting the services of a not-for-profit body/organization/association (hereinafter referred to as NPO) to represent their rights.[17]

### 7.2.1  Standing of NPOs to Represent Data Subjects

NPOs representing data subjects must be legally established, with statutory objectives in public interest and encouraging rights and freedoms of data subjects in processing. A qualified NPO is entitled to represent the interests of the user in any GDPR forums to:

1. Assist the data subject in exercising the infringed-upon **rights.**
2. Assist the data subject in receiving **compensation.**

This GDPR crafts a system that encourages digital rights activism by allowing use rights represented by entities that are focused on ensuring the growth of those rights. **Example** NYOB is presently representing undisclosed, confidential data subjects against Google and Facebook.

### 7.2.2 Digital Rights Activism

This GDPR's encouragement of digital rights activism has been made clear by allowing NPOs to act independently of the data subject's mandate to lodge a complaint in the SA or court, allowing them to report infringements freely.[18] This opening clause is subject to a specific Member State law giving it more detail. The provision allows NPOs to report a violation without being instructed to do so if it considers that the processing violates the rights of any users. However, this liberty of NPOs is limited to that of reporting infringements and enforcing rights, not for claiming compensation.[19]

This provision again demonstrates that GDPR places primary importance on average data subject rights by ensuring compliance and accountability. Compliance is secured if Controllers and Processors are aware they are being watched not only by users who may not be well educated, but also by NPOs that lobby and encourage the rights. This helps keep any processing business alert, but also can lead to abuse. If a Controller is not careful, it could be barraged with complaints from NPOs simply for pushing an agenda forward in the public eye.

Consider the recent NYOB v. Google and Facebook complaints, for example, where the central issue is "conditional consent." Such consent was common industry practice prior to GDPR, but if enough complaints are filed, the public and legal conversation can eventually be manufactured based on pending complaints. In the same vein, business practices can be changed, for better or worse by using permissive activism under GDPR.

## 7.3 The Supervisory Authorities

GDPR pushes a framework of accountability from entities processing personal data. The Supervisory Authorities (SA or SAs) are enforcement arms of the regulation. GDPR text is centered on formalizing this regulatory agency, spread across the Member States of the EU, with a unified purpose, powers, and rules for their functioning. Almost every aspect of GDPR is overseen by the SA of the Member State, holding the authority to investigate compliance to keep Data Collectors alert. In this chapter we will discuss the salient points on SAs in relation to its position and enforcement powers under GDPR.

### 7.3.1 Role of Supervisory Authority

The SA is an independent public authority whose main responsibility is:

- Monitoring the application of GDPR
- The protecting of fundamental rights and freedoms in relation to processing

- Facilitating the free flow of information throughout the EU[20]
- Contributing to the consistent application of GDPR throughout the EU[21] by cooperating with other SAs and the Commission

Similar to a market regulator such as the US Securities and Exchange Commission, the purpose of the SA is to be the enforcement wing of the law. GDPR text implies that rather than being a central agency, SAs are decentralized with each Member State having authority to establish an SA's office. It is not necessary that each Member State have only one SA, as several may coexist so long as they are created by law[22] and a single SA is designated to represent them in the consistency mechanism.[23]

### 7.3.2   The Members of the Supervisory Authority

Like other public agencies, the SA is run by natural persons qualified to carry out its functions. GDPR provides for the general conditions for the appointment of these members.[24] Each Member State of the EU shall be responsible to provide for a transparent method of appointment, by way of:

1. Their parliament
2. Their government
3. Their heads of state
4. Any independent body entrusted with appointing under their law

The members of the SA must have the qualifications, experience, and skill necessary to protect personal data and carry out the necessary functions of the job. Their responsibilities continue until:

- Expiration of their term,
- Resignation, or
- Compulsory retirement.[25]
- Dismissal only in cases of serious misconduct or an inability to fulfill the conditions required to perform the duties of the office.[26]

In the appointment of members to the SA's Office, there is considerable leeway afforded to Member States to fill in the finer details of the requirements. Specifically, Member States by way of law must provide for:[27]

1. Establishing an SA
2. Qualification and eligibility of members
3. Rules and procedures for appointment of members.
4. Duration of the members' terms, which may be no less than four years
5. Existence of reappointment and eligibility
6. Conditions and obligations of the members, which includes prohibitions on benefits, incompatible occupations, and cessation of employment

The regulation only provides conditions that must be met by the individual states, giving space for inconsistent standards in human resources within these

SAs. However, this result would be unlikely as these authorities must work together constantly in the consistent application of GDPR, which includes standards for hiring officers.

### 7.3.3 An Independent Body

A Supervisory Authority is required to carry out its functions with complete independence in performing its tasks in accordance with GDPR.[28] This would entail:

1. They operate free from external influence, whether direct or indirect.
   **Illustration 1:** The SA of a state seeks to make rules on certification. Many industry players large and small in private data protection try to lobby the SA to draft the rules with simple requirements. On the other hand, there are digital rights activist groups who lobby for stricter requirements. Both forms of lobbying would qualify as "external influence" and violate GDPR.
2. They neither take nor seek instructions from anybody.
   **Illustration 2:** The law of a Member State that establishes an SA empowers the Minister for Technology to "set directives, objectives and goals" for the SA. This provision would violate GDPR.
3. They do not take any actions that are incompatible with their duties.
   **Illustration 3:** Due to a backlog of complaints, the SA's office decides to prioritize certain larger, "high-profile" cases, rather than the complaints filed against smaller companies. This would be incompatible to their duties and violate GDPR.
4. They shall not during their term in office engage in any incompatible occupation, gainful or not.
   **Illustration 4:** A member of the SA is also the chairman emeritus of a digital rights activism foundation. This violates GDPR.

**Budget and resource independence:** The foundational rules above are accompanied by a requirement that each Member State provide human, technical, financial, and infrastructural resources to carry out their tasks.[29] The SA members also have the independence to choose their own staff, who operate at their exclusive direction.[30] Additionally, the SA must not be subject to financial control and must have a separate allocated public annual budget, which is part of the overall state or national budget.[31]

The SA is a *quasi-judicial* body, with the broad authority to shape, enforce, investigate, and punish the infringers of GDPR. Therefore, independence from external influences and consistency in enforcement is critical. A key requirement for SAs throughout the EU is "cooperation" and "consistent application" of GDPR.

### 7.3.4 Professional Secrecy

The SA's members and staff are bound to obligations of professional secrecy in accordance to EU or Member Law.[32] Through this opening clause, GDPR allows for delegated legislation on how employees of these agencies should maintain secrecy. This obligation requires that SA employees must maintain confidentiality for information that comes to their knowledge while conducting tasks and exercising their authority. Specifically, this relates to natural persons reporting GDPR infringements. This confidentiality duty is ongoing and must be followed both during and after the course of employment.

GDPR creates a new species of privilege or professional secrecy where the SA's duties in relation to their work with Controllers and Processors. Like privilege, the secrecy covers the information from the personal data received or obtained in exercising their duties.[33] It is left to Member States to legislate the extent of this new professional secrecy, but it must be exercised in a manner that is necessary and proportionate to reconcile the right to protect personal data with professional secrecy.[34] It remains to be seen how this test can be applied in cases of criminal investigations, public interest, and even private need for information.

### 7.3.5 Competence of the Supervisory Authority

The SA's "competence" is a way of defining the regulatory body's reach. The competence of the SA is largely territorial,[35] empowered to perform their tasks assigned within the borders of its establishing Member State. This competence extends to public authorities and private entities carrying out public functions,[36] but does not include courts acting in their judicial capacity.[37] GDPR does not provide a criterion to allocate competence but refers to the SA's authority and tasks as the criteria.

The basis for allocating competence is the data-processing location of Controllers, Processors, data subjects, and other industry players. SA competence can result from:[38]

1. The complaint is lodged with the SA.
2. The Controller/Processor is established within the EU Member State where the SA operates.
3. Data subjects who are substantially affected or likely to be substantially affected within the Member State they reside in.

In the past, parallel competencies led to data subjects being forced to interact with multiple SAs, which proved to be complicated and time consuming. GDPR tries to fix this problem by creating a one-stop shop mechanism to consolidate any conflict between authorities. The change allows processing entities to interact and report to a single SA. The one-stop shop mechanism exists for the benefit of businesses to ease GDPR compliance. Keep note that this will not exclude an investigation initiated in another jurisdiction. For example, a company registered in Germany would report to the German SA for Data Protection Impact Assessments ("DPIA") and certification monitoring. But if their customer files a complaint in France, the company and the German SA must work together to resolve the issue.

**7.3.5.1 The Lead Supervisory Authority**  In cases of cross-border processing, the SA, which operates wherever the main establishment of the Controller/Processor is, will operate as the lead supervisory authority (LSA) for those operations.[39] The LSA is the interlocutor between the Controller and Processor for the cross-border activities pursued.[40] The term "establishment" requires the effective and real exercise of activity through *stable arrangements* within the EU.[41]

In larger multinational entities, it becomes crucial to determine the *main* establishment within the EU to determine the LSA. The main establishment for a Controller is located where its *central administration*, which determines the purposes and means of processing, sits. The test boils down to locating where the objectives of the processing are adopted or implemented.[42] For multinational Processors, similar rules apply with the central administration or whichever establishment is hosted within the EU, for its activities will act as the geographical indicator for determining its LSA.[43]

The test relating to groups-of-undertakings above are complex in practice, as each entity within the corporate structure individually determines the purposes and means of their processing. For example, Facebook's conglomerate (comprised of Instagram, Whatsapp, etc.) are each Controllers and would have an individual SA to report to for GDPR compliance. Resultantly, the entities within the groups would be responsible for local compliance and the one-stop shop mechanism would not apply. Main establishment rules are difficult to apply and have shortcomings in resolving overlapping competencies. GDPR requires that SAs internally resolve any conflict and decide which authority should lead an overlapping investigation.

**Illustration 1:** Entity BVC has its central administration in Germany (where it is registered) and has two additional branches. The first branch is in France and administers the industrial property rights of BVC. This is carried out by two employees who use a remote access to BVC's German-based IT system. The second branch is in Ireland and is responsible for BVC's entire marketing. The Irish branch develops marketing concepts for all BVC branches and determines where customer data goes for marketing purposes. The marketing and customer data are processed solely through BVC's German-based IT system. Marketing is the main activity of BVC. Here, even though BVC Germany processes the data and acts as the registered corporate headquarters, BVC Ireland is the main establishment as it determines the purposes and means of processing. Both the Ireland and Germany branches are independent Data Controllers, but the Irish Supervisory Authority is the competent LSA.

**Illustration 2:** A Danish entity, targeting consumers in Denmark and Germany, uses video surveillance for its premises in Denmark. As the entity's processing activities concern individuals located in Denmark and Germany, ordinarily an LSA would usually have to be determined. However, as the surveillance only relates to the Danish office and primarily affects data subjects there, the Danish Supervisory Authority can handle the case. This is because GDPR allows

Member States to handle processing concerns of domestic employees' personal data processing in specific employment context of the Member State. Since the surveillance only concerns those employees in the Denmark office, Denmark can act as LSA.

**7.3.5.2 Local Competence** At a domestic level, SAs have competence for simple and efficient handling of local cases. The "local" SA will be the most proximate authority for a business entity in their day-to-day operations. Notwithstanding any determination of a LSA, other SAs are still competent to handle any infringements in their jurisdiction if:[44]

1. It relates to an establishment in their borders, or
2. Substantially affects their data subjects.

In such scenarios, the SA must inform the LSA of its decision to pursue the complaint within three weeks.[45] In conflicts, or if the LSA decides to take the case up themselves, the consistency mechanism elaborated under Article 60 must be followed.[46] GDPR establishes an elaborate network of SAs to ensure the safe processing of data within the EU, without delayed jurisdictional conflicts over activities as fluid and pervasive as data processing. Fulfilling GDPR compliance requires prior interaction with the competent SA, making it commercially sensible to identify the SA ahead of time.

Under the Data Protection Directive (DPD), authorities had interpreted data protection obligations differently, creating multiple standards for data protection. Having an empowered oversight body is necessary to simplify the data market by giving Controllers an authoritative regulator to facilitate compliance. This reduces inconsistencies in national peculiarities between Member States by harmonizing procedures between Controllers, Processors, and the SAs themselves. Formalizing the need for a locally competent SA or LSA as a sole contact point for Controllers helps resolve the issues that existed under the DPD framework. But this GDPR framework may also face problems relating to differing national standards and parallel competencies when entities undertake compliance. These provisions of GDPR remain incomplete and are linked with future cooperation between SAs for its efficacy.

### 7.3.6 Tasks of the Supervisory Authority

The powers of the SA accompany its numerous duties under GDPR. Let us examine the major tasks that an SA accomplishes within its competent territory.[47]

#### 7.3.6.1 Advisory Duties

1. Give advice on processing operations.
2. Advise the other governmental bodies and lawmakers on legislative and administrative measures relating to processing.

### 7.3.6.2 Promoting Knowledge and Compliance

3. Promote awareness of the duties and obligations of Controllers and Processors.
4. Provide appropriate information to data subjects regarding their rights and cooperate with other SAs to help them.
5. Promote public awareness on the risks, rules, safeguards, and rights in relation to processing, with activities specifically addressed to children.
6. Monitor recent developments and their impact on the regulation, specifically the development of information and communication technologies, and commercial practices.

### 7.3.6.3 Investigative Duties[48]

7. Monitor and enforce GDPR.
8. Facilitate the submission of complaints filed by introducing measures such as electronic submission of complaints (without closing other avenues of communication).[49]
9. Handle complaints lodged by data subjects, bodies, organizations, and associations.[50]
10. Investigate the subject matter of the complaint to the extent necessary. This includes conducting web audits, on-premises investigations, requests for information, and seizing access to IT systems of the entity under investigation.
11. Inform the complainant on the status of the complaint.
12. Conduct further investigation and coordination with other SAs if needed.
13. Conduct investigations into the application of GDPR, based on information received from another SA, or public authority.

### 7.3.6.4 Cooperation

14. Cooperate with other SAs and provide mutual assistance towards the uniform application of GDPR.
15. Contribute to activities of the board.

### 7.3.6.5 Regulating Compliance

16. Adopt standard contractual clauses between Controllers and Processors,[51] and for transfers to third countries.[52]
17. Establish and maintain a list of requirements for data impact assessments.
18. Encourage drawing up codes of conduct and approve those that provide "sufficient safeguards."
19. Encourage data certification mechanisms, and for data protection seals and marks, and approve the criteria for certification.
20. Conduct periodic reviews of those certifications granted.
21. Draft and publish the criteria for accreditation of certification bodies.

22. Conduct accreditation of bodies monitoring the enforcement of codes of conduct.
23. Authorize contractual clauses for third-country transfers.[53]
24. Approve binding corporate rules.[54]

#### 7.3.6.6 Internal Responsibilities

25. Keep internal records of infringements of the regulation and measures adopted.
26. Draw up an annual activity report of their activities, which shall be made public.[55]
27. Fulfill any other tasks relating to the processing of personal data.
28. The performance of the tasks of the SA shall be done free of charge for the data subjects and, where applicable, for the Data Protection Officer. However, manifestly unfounded, excessive, or repetitious requests may be charged a reasonable fee based on administrative costs, or even a refusal to act on a case. It will be the burden of the SA to prove the above when charging a fee.[56]

The SA's duties include shaping the law, enforcing the regulation, and maintaining standards of compliance. GDPR creates a sort of quasi-judicial agency as a one-stop shop mechanism for all actors in the industry.

### 7.3.7   Powers of the SA

The previous Data Protection Directive framework gave broad discretion to Member States to lay down the SA's authority.[57] This led to inconsistent enforcement powers and diverse national peculiarities in data protection within the EU. GDPR solves this problem by exhaustively providing consistent authority to SAs. To carry out the tasks discussed above, the SA has an assortment of powers to enforce GDPR. The structure of the authority held by the SA complements the tasks they are assigned.[58]

#### 7.3.7.1 Investigative Powers

1. To order the Controller, Processor, or their representative to provide any information
2. To carry out investigations and perform data audits
3. To carry out a review of certifications issued
4. To notify the Controller/Processor of any alleged infringements under GDPR
5. To obtain access to personal data necessary for the performance of their tasks from the Controller/Processor
6. To obtain access to any premises of the Controller/Processor, including any data processing equipment and means in accordance with the law

Investigations require factual indications that data processing activities are being carried out by the Controller/Processor entity. Inquiries are not limited to GDPR compliance and can include general information regarding the entity's organization and the measures implemented internally that form the basis of their data processing. The responsibility to comply with investigations includes not only the processing entities but their organs and representatives as well. Responses to SA inquiries are not in a prescribed form and may be carried out orally or in written and digital formats.

The SA's authority is executed in accordance with national procedural laws, with GDPR providing the legal basis for their actions. Investigative measures must be a necessary, appropriate, and proportionate measure to ensure GDPR compliance.[59] GDPR empowers SA officers to conduct unannounced on-site inspections of the processing activity and web audits. Such measures do not require an instigating event from the Controller/Processor to take place. Parameters of these physical or digital inspections must be clarified by Member State law (though data protection audits are not often legally prescribed). For an investigative measure to be binding it must be:[60]

- Reduced into writing
- Clear and unambiguous
- Indicate the Supervisory Authority issuing it
- Bear the date of issue
- Bear the signature of a Member or Head of that SA
- Give reasons for issuance
- Refer to the right to an effective remedy against the order

The content of an investigative order listed by GDPR is standard practice in the EU, which has now been formalized. Keep in mind that Member States can place additional formal requirements for procedural matters.

**7.3.7.2 Corrective Powers**  Under the SA's corrective powers, the least severe measures are:

1. To issue warnings to the Data Collectors that their intended data-processing operations would infringe GDPR
2. To issue reprimands to those Data Collectors who infringe GDPR

The first two corrective measures are a "slap on the wrist" to Controllers or Processors for minor GDPR violations. The remaining measures demonstrate the quasi-judicial authority of the SA to force compliance and punishments:

3. To order the data-collecting entities to comply with a user's request to enforce their rights
4. To order the Data Collectors to bring their processing operations into compliance with GDPR, with the authority to specify a manner and time to do so
5. To order the Controller to communicate a personal data breach to the users
6. To impose a temporary or definitive limitation including an overall ban on processing
7. To order the rectification, erasure, or restriction of processing of a user's data that has been disclosed to other parties

8. To withdraw or order the withdrawal of certification given
9. To order a certifying body not to certify any further
10. To impose an administrative fine,[61] in addition to or as an alternative to the measures discussed above
11. To order the suspension of data flow to a third country

### 7.3.7.3 Authorization and Advisory Powers

12. To advise the Controller in accordance with the prior consultation procedures[62]
13. To authorize processing after the prior consultation procedure (if Member State law requires such authorization)
14. To issue on its own, or on request, opinions to the national government or other public bodies on issues related to the protection of personal data
15. To issue an opinion and approve draft codes of conduct
16. To accredit certification bodies
17. To issue certifications and approve the criteria for certification
18. To adopt standard data-protection clauses between Controller and Processor, or for transfers to third countries
19. To authorize such contractual clauses for third-country transfers of personal data
20. To authorize administrative arrangements for third-country transfers of personal data
21. To approve binding corporate rules

**7.3.7.4 Appropriate Safeguards** The fact that the SA has far-reaching authority does not make it an "all-powerful" agency acting as "judge, jury, and executioner." The SA acts as a market regulator, rather than a specialized court of justice. The SA can bring infringements to the attention of the judiciary, or even commence an action for infringement to ensure GDPR enforcement.[63] However, the exercise of the authority will be subject to effective judicial remedy and due process.[64] The true scope of the SA's authority, as discussed, can be expanded under Member State Law.

## 7.3.8 Cooperation and Consistency Mechanism

The tasks and duties of Supervisory Authorities are all subject to national peculiarities within the EU as discussed throughout this section. Implementing the one-stop shop mechanism internally for legal and administrative clarity requires consistency and cooperation between SAs. To encourage simplified access to the regulatory bodies, GDPR places mechanisms for resolving any issues between SAs with overlapping competencies. A secondary purpose of the consistency and cooperation mechanisms under GDPR is to prevent forum shopping by Controller/Processor entities.[65]

From a business perspective, this mechanism is of little relevance for GDPR compliance, as it handles issues between SAs. However, before examining how SAs enforce GDPR it is important to gain an overview of their inner workings.

**7.3.8.1 EU Data Protection Board**   Formerly known as the Article 29 Working Party, the EU DPB replaces the Working Party as the data protection oversight body at the Union level.[66] The DPB is comprised of the head of one Supervisory Authority of each EU Member State and of the European Data Protection Supervisor.[67] The DPB is represented by a Chair, elected by the members. The DPB is an *independent monitoring body* tasked with:[68]

- Issuing guidelines, recommendations, and best practices on data protection
- Making final decisions on conflicts in the cooperation and consistency mechanism

Like the Article 29 Working Party, which consistently issued clarifications and studies on legal issues surrounding data protection, the DPB will likely advise further on GDPR opening clauses by issuing recommendations. Keeping a close eye on DPB activities will be an active part of the DPO/IT department's role within an organization, as some mandates will affect GDPR compliance. The DPB's role as *final decision-making body* at the EU level will be discussed later.

**7.3.8.2 The Cooperation Mechanism**   Alluded to earlier in discussing the Lead Supervisory Authority (LSA) working in concert with other SAs,[69] a system of cooperation is required by GDPR. This cooperation requires an effective information exchange and mutual assistance to one another.[70] The objective of GDPR one-stop shop mechanism is for SAs with overlapping competencies to reach a consensus on how to proceed with a multi-jurisdictional processing case. Cooperation encompasses the following aspects:

1. Exchanging relevant information.[71]
2. Creating a cooperation mechanism with the LSA to handle the processing case.
3. Submitting draft decisions to the LSA expressing relevant and reasoned objections.
4. LSA shall consider the views of the other SAs and, if needed, change the draft mechanism.[72]
5. The cooperation mechanism shall lead to a final decision on how to proceed with the case adopted by the assigned LSA. The final decision shall reflect the views of other SAs involved.
6. The final decision can also allocate partial authority to other SAs over aspects of the processing case. This allows LSAs and SAs to adopt their own decisions regarding portions of the same case.[73]

In cases of conflict between the SAs that cannot be resolved by the cooperation mechanism, the matter is referred to the EU DPB pursuant to the consistency mechanism.[74]

**7.3.8.3 The Consistency Mechanism**   The DPB is responsible as the final decision-making body when the cooperation mechanism fails.[75] The consistency mechanism triggers only when SAs cannot reach a consensus over how to proceed with processing a case.[76] The DPB then considers the matter and issues binding decisions to resolve the disagreement.[77] This effective tool helps to close any debate that may exist between regulatory bodies on a Union level. SAs are often governmental bodies and can easily be entangled in bureaucratic delays. This would stall the overall case, harming interests of EU data subjects. GDPR encourages use of the consistency mechanism where a significant number of data subjects are harmed throughout several EU Member States.[78] The mechanism exists to contribute to the consistent application of GDPR throughout the EU[79] by eliminating possible hurdles at a State-to-State level.

### 7.3.9   GDPR Enforcement by Supervisory Authorities

If the in-house mechanisms for resolving disputes (discussed in Section 7.1) fail, the next option open to data subjects would be approaching the SA. We have discussed extensively the investigative, corrective, and advisory authority that the SA yields,[80] and this is where the powers come into use. As a new investigative agency entrusted with GDPR enforcement, the user has a right to lodge a complaint with the SA of his/her:[81]

1. Member state
2. Place of habitual residence
3. Place of work
4. Place of alleged infringement

It is important to note that complaints do not need to only be for a violation of the data subject's rights but can also be for general infringements of GDPR by the processing operation.[82] In other words, the data subject's right to approach the SA is triggered anytime a Controller's personal data processing infringes the regulation. Thus, data subjects do not have to face direct attacks on their rights to approach the SA, but can be a whistleblower for any GDPR contravention by the Controller.

**Illustration:** JT lives in Hamburg, Germany, and was born in Vienna, Austria. His work frequently takes him to Brussels, Belgium, four days a week, where the home office of his business is. One day, he discovers that a dating website he uses, Honey Trap (based in Paris, France) has been selling his data to adult website advertisers without his consent. The advertising activities were based in Spain. Below, as we examine how the case proceeds, we can see an amalgamation of different rights and duties working together in tandem:

- JT can file his complaint in the SA of Germany (place of habitual residence) or Austria (the Member State he belongs to) or Belgium (place of work) or Spain (where the alleged infringement took place). He has the freedom to choose under GDPR.

- If he by chance files in the wrong SA's office, the duty of cooperation requires them to forward it to the correct jurisdiction.[83]
- If the duty of cooperation is implicated, the SA must inform the user of the coordination.[84]
- The Controller/Processor has a duty to inform him of who the appropriate SA is and his right to lodge a complaint at the time of providing the initial information.[85]
- Once the Complaint has been filed, the SA may exercise its investigative and corrective powers.[86]
- The investigation following the complaint will be carried out subject to judicial review to the extent appropriate.[87]
- The data subject has a right to be informed on the progress and outcome of the Complaint[88] by the SA within a reasonable period.[89]
- The data subjects must also be informed of the possibility of a judicial remedy available to them by the SA.

## 7.4 Judicial Remedies

The above modes of GDPR enforcement are *without prejudice*[90] to the right to pursue other avenues, creating multiple ways to ensure compliance. Logically, one of the avenues open to the user involves approaching a court or other "judicial body" to report infringements, noncompliance, and violation of his/her rights.[91] A competent court has *full jurisdiction* over the legal and factual questions before it based on national procedural law.[92]

### 7.4.1 Judicial Action against the Controller or Processor

A complaint can be filed in court against the Controller or Processor for any potential GDPR noncompliance. This can be done when the user feels that GDPR rights have been infringed in processing his personal data. **Example:** Lack of sufficient notice for a data breach, refusal to let the user "erase" her profile, allegations of "conditional consent" to process data, etc.

When bringing action against a Controller or Processor, the choice of venue is narrow compared to the choices available to data subjects when picking an SA to lodge a complaint with.[93] The suit can be filed:

1. In the State where the data subject's rights have been infringed.
2. In the State where the Controller/Processor has an establishment. The use of the phrasing "has an establishment" would lean toward the interpretation that the jurisdiction extends to any place where a processing operation has been set up, and not merely the head office.
3. Where the data subject resides. **Exception:** Where the processing is carried out by a public authority of the Member State, in exercise of its official authority.

Let us apply these rules in our previous illustration: If JT wishes to sue Honey Trap in court, he can file his law suit in the courts of France (where the Controller is based), Spain (where the rights have been infringed), or Germany (where JT resides) in accordance with their procedural laws. If JT files in Germany, France, and Spain (in that order), the courts, rather than "cooperating," will be required to suspend their proceedings and allow the German court to proceed first.[94]

### 7.4.2 Courts versus SA; Which Is Better for GDPR Enforcement?

The judicial venues that the data subject can approach are restricted, as opposed to selecting a competent SA. This is perhaps because a court carries a distinct legal authority. Unlike SAs, a court is not created specifically for GDPR purposes. A judicial body is likely to deal with diverse matters and must divide its focus to each case, while the SA is dedicated to personal data-protection causes. Therefore, regardless of which SA is approached, a built-in "consistency mechanism" and "duty to cooperate" ensure that GDPR enforcement is streamlined and coordinated. Courts on the other hand, especially if in different countries, lack the same freedom. Furthermore, simultaneous lawsuits filed in different courts likely lead to conflicting authorities and jurisdictional issues.

Thus, while going to court is an option for data subjects, approaching the SA is far more advisable because:

1. The SA has specialized authority and the power to enforce GDPR.
2. The SA is more likely to be staffed with more technical personnel.
3. The SA is bound by specific duties under GDPR to carry out their functions in a specific manner, while a court is bound by a broader, less specialized statute such as the Constitution.
4. The SA has a wider range of powers spanning from investigative to advisory.
5. The SA is required to carry out their functions (as far as possible) free of cost, while court tends to be expensive.

### 7.4.3 Judicial Action against the Supervisory Authority

Similar to how judicial action can be taken against Controllers, under certain scenarios, the data subject has a right to sue the SA in court.[95] Data subjects can bring actions for demanded performances of SAs, but not discretionary acts (**Example:** approving codes of conduct or assessing DPIAs). This right is without prejudice to other remedies the user may have, and may be raised against:

1. A legally binding decision of the SA concerning him/her.[96] This is available to any natural or legal person who is concerned with the decision made.
2. A delay in acting on a complaint filed with a competent SA.[97] This also includes a delay in informing the data subject of the progress or outcome of their

complaint, which exceeds three months. This ground is only available to data subjects themselves, unlike the previous ground, which is broader.

The grounds are quite narrow and apply only to a specific set of circumstances, making this a limited data subject right. Simply, the only two scenarios for exercising judicial remedies against the SA are for appeal and delay. Beyond that, the SA remains an independent and competent regulatory agency subjected to the establishing law of the Member State that created it.[98] It logically follows that users can only sue an SA in the courts belonging to the Member State territory that establishes it,[99] in accordance with the domestic procedural law.[100] Note that mere inactivity by an SA does not give a claim to sue under GDPR as there is no legally binding decision to challenge.[101] An order must be passed or exceed GDPR deadlines to qualify for judicial challenge.

The right to approach a court for "appealing" SA decisions echoes an EU Citizen's right to *effective judicial remedy*, which is a basic facet of their human rights framework.[102] This provision is reasonable, as SAs cannot be given "unimpeachable" authority to carry out the functions of GDPR. Thus, right to appeal the order of a SA exists, if data subject rights are infringed by:[103]

1. Partially rejecting the complaint
2. Wholly rejecting the complaint
3. Dismissing the complaint
4. Acting in a manner that is inconsistent/not necessary to protect the rights of the data subject
5. Inaction

Any of the five grounds above trigger a user's right to bring a suit against the SA handling the complaint. The SA's "decision" can concern the exercise of investigative, corrective, and authorization powers in relation to the dismissal/rejection of the complaint.[104] It does not include nonbinding measures such as opinions and advice provided.[105] When adjudicating a GDPR case, a court is entitled to use its full jurisdiction to examine all relevant questions of fact and law before them.[106] However, the regulation is unclear whether a court in exercising its full jurisdiction can rule on the underlying complaint that was originally filed, or if the order is restricted to the decision made by the SA alone.

**Illustration:**[107] JT submits a complaint with the SA of Spain with regard to Honey Trap (a dating website's) selling his data to unauthorized adult entertainment advertisers located in Barcelona. The SA responds promptly, stating they have begun the investigation. Three months go by without any contact between JT and the Spain's SA. After three months, the SA sends him a detailed report, including a consistency mechanism decision. The main part of the report stated:

> Your complaint has been partially rejected as Honey Trap LLC has a legitimate commercial interest in the sale of your personal data. Your agreement with the Controller allows them to use AI to analyze your dating

preferences and suggest advertisers you may be interested in. However, we have issued a warning and a $1 million fine to the Controller for not maintaining settings which allow you to control profiling and direct advertising. The fine has been reduced because they have not engaged in "illegal processing" since the sale of your personal data was lawful.

JT can approach the courts of Spain to:

1. Challenge the partial rejection of his complaint stating that the processing was legal
2. Challenge the reduction in the fine, arguing that the SA is not acting in a manner that protects his rights
3. Challenge the lack of notice provided regarding the consistency mechanism deliberations and decisions
4. Challenge the lack of notice throughout the entire investigation
5. Challenge the delay in investigation, and why no reasons were provided

The illustration presents a range of options available to the data subjects and echoes the accountability theme of GDPR. Even the SA, an oversight body of the regulation, is not immune from violating its duties.

### 7.4.4   Controller Suing the Data Subject?

GDPR neither prohibits nor allows the Controller to sue the data subject. This raises an interesting lacuna in GDPR enforcement. While data subjects, digital activists, the SA, and the DPO have the authority to enforce the regulation, the Controller and Processor do not.

The Controller has the right to claim compensation from the Processor, and vice versa,[108] in relation to their joint and severable liability. However, this scenario is limited, and the Controller/Processor does not have any other rights under GDPR. For most, this seems a logical choice as the regulation's objectives are centered on data subject rights and accountability. Controllers are required to comply with GDPR and ensure its smooth functioning, while data subjects, the SA, DPO, and courts are entrusted with keeping a check on those entities. This leaves the Controller's hands "tied" in cases where the organization would be harmed by the actions of their data subjects.

It is important to note that the Controller has a limited right to compensation or refusal if the data subject's requests to exercise their rights are manifestly unfounded or excessive, in particular because of their repetitive character.[109] But the regulation is silent as to how the Controller can exercise this right. Could Controllers request the user directly, or does a request have to be made before the SA/court? This limited right overlooks other situations where Controllers might need to claim compensation from the data subjects, because it is safe to assume that certain users would be likely to cause problems for the Controller.

Consider the following illustration.

Gameverse LLC is an online gaming platform that provides a warcraft game called Sole Gunman. Gameverse carries out its own processing, giving users the freedom of creating their own usernames and profiles, and playing anonymously in real time. As users improve in the game, they receive more and more advantages and weapons. At the time of registering, the users are expressly told that they are bound to the terms of use and the privacy policy and cannot use the platform in a way in which it was not intended to be used. Over the next five years of their operation they faced a series of issues from certain users:

- Yoko99 had found a way to hack the platform and study the underlying code. From that he created a series of "cheat codes" and shared it with the public. Because of this, Gameverse had to completely rework its algorithm.
- Munk48 had sent a request for a "meaningful explanation" of the automated processing of his data. Gameverse responded with an explanation, but Munk48, a computer technician by profession, kept filing repeated requests for more specific explanations, with each new request costing the company extra cost to answer.
- Mala05 wanted to know the identity of several of the users she plays with. She used the cheat codes and information that Yoko99 put online and found a way to reverse engineer and decode the usernames of four other players.

In the above scenarios, Gameverse quite possibly only has a compensation claim against Munk48 if it is proven his request is excessive and repetitive. Meanwhile, under GDPR framework, Gameverse has no claim against Mala05 or Yoko99, even though they caused violation of other gamer's rights. At the same time, Gameverse has no claim under GDPR for any commercial loss face because of its users' actions (like reworking the original algorithm).

The aim of GDPR is to encourage, promote, and protect the rights of the user, and the SA is bound to act in a way that is consistent with those aims.[110] This leaves little room for claims based on financial losses that harm the user. The Controller Gameverse would likely find their claim's basis in other legal statutes, but not GDPR. However, bringing a claim against users is always a "double-edged sword," as any breaches caused by them, or any deficiency in the rights afforded to them, might cause a claim for contributory liability against the business for GDPR noncompliance.

## 7.4.5 Suspending the Proceedings

Simultaneous lawsuits of the same subject matter and parties require a suspension of related proceedings under GDPR.[111] "Related proceedings" are actions so closely related and intertwined with the original suit that it is expedient to hear and determine them together and avoid the risk of irreconcilable judgments on the same subject matter.[112] In collateral proceedings initiated in a court against the same Controller or Processor, regarding the same subject matter as a suit previously filed, the court shall follow the following procedure:

1. Contact the other Member State court to confirm the existence of the proceedings.
2. If yes, then any competent court other than the court first seized may suspend their proceedings.
3. The court engaged in subsequent proceedings also can decline jurisdiction if the original court has rightful legal jurisdiction over the matter and their law permits such consolidation.[113] Note that this authority to decline will have to be requested by one of the parties.[114]

To summarize, if two similar cases are pending before two different courts, the first court to take up the matter has priority and can proceed forward. Simultaneously, the second court has the option of either suspending or declining the case, creating a sort of "first-come-first-served" rule for dealing with jurisdictional conflicts. GDPR infers this by using the phrase "any competent court other than the court first seized," requiring that the first court not be required to suspend its proceedings and may push forward. Just as SAs have their own internal mechanisms to work through jurisdictional conflicts, GDPR tries to create finer rules to avoid multiplicity of proceedings in the development of data protection law.

**Illustration:** Tailored.com is a custom clothing online service based in Italy. When users register for their service, they collect data relating to name, age, address, measurements, fashion preferences (which is a detailed and nuanced questionnaire), accessory preferences, etc. They also continue collecting data by use of direct profiling software. Locke is one of their customers (in France), and seeks to join another custom fashion service Flyby.com. He makes a data portability request to find out that tailored.com does not offer such a service. On further inquiry with the Controller, they refuse his request again. He files a suit in court, first in France, then in Italy. The suit begins in French court, and three weeks later it begins in Italian court. Tailored.com informs the Italian judge of the other proceeding, and the judge confirms this fact and suspends the proceeding until that is resolved. After another two weeks, Tailored.com returns to Italy and requests the court to decline jurisdiction. The judge rejects the request because Italian law does not permit premature dismissal of proceedings. The case will not proceed but will remain suspended.

## 7.5  Alternate Dispute Resolution

The final option for enforcing data subject's rights and GDPR itself would be employing an Alternate Dispute Resolution (ADR) mechanism in contractual arrangements. This option is controversial as it is unclear if GDPR would permit these mechanisms to enforce its aims.

ADR is a nonjudicial, out-of-court mechanism for resolving disputes, which is rooted in consent between the two parties in a legal instrument, perhaps as a clause in a contract or a separate agreement altogether. ADR includes the following mechanisms:

1. **Negotiation:** The disputing parties discuss the terms of settlement and try to enter into a mutually beneficial arrangement to avoid proceeding forward with their case. Concessions and admissions made in a negotiation settlement are not admissible in any trial (in most jurisdictions). A validly executed settlement agreement is binding on the parties.
   **Example:** The data subject and the Controller discussing the amount of compensation the data subject would like in exchange for not filing a formal complaint for an isolated violation of GDPR.

2. **Mediation:** A neutral third-party "mediator" facilitates a discussion between the parties to help them arrive at a settlement. Mediation is an informal process, where the mediator's duty is to merely facilitate conversation and not give his judgments. The mediation proceedings are confidential, and any agreement reached because of a mediation is *nonbinding,* unless they execute a valid settlement agreement.
   **Example:** After a long-drawn-out dispute with heated arguments, Clint and Joe decide to refer the matter to Bob, a man who both companies know to be a neutral friend. Bob is the mediator and will help Clint and Joe resolve their differences by communication and negotiation.

3. **Conciliation:** Like mediation, conciliation uses a third-party neutral to facilitate conversations and steer the parties into repairing broken relationships and arriving at a settlement. It differs from mediation as the conciliator is entitled to be more liberal and direct the parties to "reconcile" their disputes. However, like a mediator, the conciliator's recommendation is *nonbinding* on the parties.
   **Example:** Clint and Joe (who represent data-processing companies A and B, respectively) are unsuccessful at mediation as Bob's methods of communication are not able to cut to the heart of what is wrong. They refer the matter to Richard, a known conciliator from the law firm XYZ LLP. Richard cuts through their surrounding issues and focuses their attention on the main issues by steering the arguments.

4. **Arbitration:** A well-known method of resolving disputes in the business world, arbitration is a binding out-of-court procedure where parties employ a neutral panel of legal/industrial experts to decide on the dispute. Arbitration and international arbitration have become the preferred way to handle "cross-border" disputes, as parties have the freedom to modify the procedures, hire experts to decide their case, and have it resolved efficiently and at a low cost. The award made by the arbitrator/arbitrators shall be binding pending enforcement by a court in accordance to domestic law or the New York Convention on the Validity and Enforcement of International Arbitral Awards.

**Example:** Clint and Joe decide to give their case to a three-member tribunal to give an award by way of a "submission agreement." Each party will appoint their own arbitrator and the two party-appointed arbitrators will appoint the chairman.

Of the above, negotiation is routine in legal disputes, while arbitration remains popular among commercial parties. Mediation and conciliation are niche to certain fields and business relationships. When discussing further on this topic, we shall primarily be referring to arbitration and mediation as these are the most likely methods to be used to enforce GDPR. Negotiation is a standard practice, while conciliation is less used and more specialized. Nonetheless, the key question for our purposes is whether it is a sound fit in the larger scheme of GDPR.

### 7.5.1 Is an ADR Arrangement Allowed under GDPR?

GDPR Articles 77, 78, and 79 when discussing the user's right to approach the SA and court (for suing the Controller and SA) all use curious wording "without prejudice to any available administrative. or non-judicial remedy each data subject has the right...." This wording gives the regulatory allowance needed to explore the idea of using arbitration and mediation to enforce GDPR, as it does not expressly exclude the possibility of parties making nonjudicial arrangements.

However, this is highly dependent on domestic and EU stances on what that wording implies. While some countries require express exclusion to prohibit the use of ADR, others require express inclusion for it to be a possibility. The wordings of these three articles suggest that at the least, there is an implied inclusion of ADR mechanisms being used to enforce user rights under GDPR. Regardless, this will be a greater issue as time passes.

### 7.5.2 ADR Arrangements

Dispute resolution mechanisms such as arbitration and mediation[115] are "creatures of contract." This suggests that the neutral third parties giving judgment are bound by the mandate of the parties who bestow that authority in their legal arrangement. The source and basis of the arbitrator's authority are rooted in the agreement and cannot be imposed upon them unilaterally.[116] Thus, let us consider the arrangements under GDPR that can be implemented:

1. The data subject consents by way of an "arbitration clause" when agreeing to the initial terms of use with the Controller.
2. The data subject enters into a subsequent "submission agreement" after the dispute arises with the Controller/SA.
3. The establishing law that sets up the SA requires disputes with the SA to be resolved by arbitration or mediation.
4. The data subject and Controller agree to go to mediation once the dispute arises to reach a beneficial settlement.

Aside from the above, the Controller, Processor, and DPO have greater liberty to choose the mode of executing their own internal disputes by ADR. The focus is primarily on entering into such agreements with data subjects or the SA itself in relation to the processing.

### 7.5.3    Key Hurdles of Applying ADR to GDPR

As discussed earlier, the regulatory mandate is unclear,[117] making the playing field complicated with possible issues. Specifically, when looking at binding processes such as arbitration,[118] legal challenges can exist at every step of the way. Several of them are listed below.

**Adhesion and Unconscionability:** When creating an arbitration clause, both parties must willingly consent into the process. Measuring the freedom to contract depends on the jurisdiction and its legal framework. While many allow ADR clauses to be included in a "standard contract" between a commercial party and online user, others may require a more knowing consent to the terms. If some unfairness in the formation or execution of the clause is shown, it may be invalidated by a court or tribunal.

This is known as an adhesion contract, where one party with the superior bargaining position (such as the Controller) can impose unjust terms on the weaker party (the data subject). This could include matters such as:

- Forcing the clause on the user
- Deliberately creating expensive procedures (such as choosing an expensive arbitral institution to administer the proceedings)
- Drafting the clause in a way that favors the stronger party (example: Only giving the Controller the right to choose who the Arbitrator may be)
- Creating inconvenient procedures (example: Requiring the arbitration to be conducted in a foreign country)

Considering the strict position of GDPR on "free consent" and the ability to withdraw that consent, this problem is augmented, giving a more favorable view to the user's weaker position.

**Limitation of other forums:** A binding arbitration clause requires mandatory language to bind the parties to the award given by the tribunal. To make an effective clause, the mandatory language would have to limit the user's ability to approach a court or the SA. This will create a clash of the jurisdiction of these bodies, as it is unclear whether the involvement of the SA can be ousted by way of an alternate arrangement. Can effective drafting techniques be used to limit the involvement of the SA? It is likely that it cannot as the SA's involvement is pervasive in GDPR.

**Choice of law:** Arbitration is well known for giving the parties the freedom to choose their own substantive and procedural law to govern their dispute. The question then becomes whether GDPR can be contracted around. For example, if a US-based Controller governing an agreement with EU users under US data-protection laws and procedures, rather than EU law. This is also unlikely to be allowed as GDPR can be classified as mandatory law whose application cannot be done away with.

**Arbitrability:** Certain fields of law are not capable of being settled by arbitration because of their nature. For example, in most jurisdictions matters relating to criminal law and family law are not arbitrable. The extent of this rule would depend on each individual country, but rests on the same principle that fields subject to mandatory law are not arbitrable as they implicate public interest. This has caused different norms of arbitration, which are unique to each country.

It remains to be seen if GDPR and personal data-processing cases are arbitrable under EU law. Would user rights under GDPR be enforceable using an arbitration award? Can the arbitrators give the same remedies such as compensation and administrative fines to the user as a court or SA would? This would have to be determined, as arbitrability is not something that relates to the entire body of law; rather, it can be analyzed depending upon the nature of the issues raised. For example, a contractual dispute between user and Controller is more likely to be arbitrable than a determination of the lawfulness of processing.

**Confidentiality:** While arbitration is binding between the two parties subject to it, the award of an arbitrator has no value as precedent. In fact, most arbitrations are conducted under complete secrecy and confidentiality. This presents several issues:

- Businesses can hide GDPR violations and processing shortfalls by using the confidentiality in arbitration.
- The confidentiality may conflict with the theme of transparency and accountability under GDPR.
- Important questions of law will be left "undeveloped," as the awards made have no future legal value in building it further.
- Inconsistencies may arise in awards applying GDPR.

While confidentiality makes sense from a strategic, commercial standpoint, it may cause long-term problems for the growth of GDPR jurisprudence.

**Enforcement:** All the above issues ultimately play into the enforceability of the arbitral award in domestic courts. An award is enforced against the losing party in jurisdictions where they have their assets. The New York Convention provides that award enforcement must be made easily, giving the domestic court the power to "rubber-stamp" the award in enforcing it. That is unless the award is challenged under the scenarios provided under the convention.[119] Like all issues in international arbitration, enforcement thresholds differ from country to country based on the challenge grounds raised. GDPR, being such a heavily regulated law, would create problems for the enforcement of awards and simultaneously give new grounds for challenging those verdicts.

**Costs:** Despite arbitration being hailed as a less costly alternative to litigation, it has become more and more expensive in the recent past, especially in international disputes. Normal everyday users might face problems in handling the cost of this "specialized" brand of justice.

**Consistency:** GDPR requires that the law be applied and interpreted consistently across the EU. Arbitration and new law regarding the relationship between GDPR and ADR will likely cause inconsistencies in the growth. As it stands today, the countries in the EU all follow different rules regarding arbitration, so GDPR creates another wrinkle for those differences to expand. Until the CJEU rules on what the position of ADR is in this new legal ecosystem, we are likely to see the strategic use of certain country's laws to improve the position of the Controller/Processor.

### 7.5.4 Suggestions for Implementing ADR Mechanisms

Despite the numerous issues listed earlier, ADR and arbitration specifically are ideal for resolving most business disputes because of their flexibility, efficiency, and transboundary use. In activities such as cross-country processing, predictability in dispute resolution is a strong asset. Therefore, it would be prudent to at least examine the best practices for implementing an ADR system to reduce the likelihood of it being invalidated.

1. Clearly incorporate it into the initial terms of use with the data subject. Ideally it should be differentiated or put on a separate page and communicated to the user.
2. Reduce the likelihood of an adhesion claim by drafting the terms favorably to the users. This may seem counterintuitive from a commercial standpoint, but it reduces hurdles in enforcement. Every part of the clause should give the data subject an equal amount of power in all parts of the process, spanning from appointment of the tribunal to the procedural evidentiary aspects.
3. Reduce costs by avoiding expensive institutional administrators or bearing the bulk of the cost yourself until the tribunal comes to a final determination. Any reduction in the overall expenditure for the user will reduce the likelihood of challenging the clause.
4. The conduct of the arbitration should be convenient. Avoid keeping the venue of the proceedings in faraway locations. Reduce the amount the data subject would have to travel and undergo to reduce adhesion claims. A relevant example of this would be Amazon's Online Arbitration Model, where the dispute is resolved virtually through document submissions and virtual webcam proceedings.
5. Draft the scope of the clause broadly to encompass all issues that may arise before the tribunal. **Example:** "Any and all issues arising out of and relating to this agreement, including the validity of this agreement shall be referred to

Arbitration with a panel of three arbitrators." This would prevent court intervention while proceedings are under way.

6. Account for GDPR expressly in the contract, recognizing and identifying the user's right to approach the SA. It is likely that the role of the SA cannot be contracted out; however, the arbitration clause could be used to circumvent any court remedy. Thus, clearly recognizing the applicability of GDPR and the scope of the arbitration will help uphold its validity. **Example:** "By agreeing to binding arbitration, you are excluding the involvement of any court regarding any dispute arising out of or in connection with this agreement. Nothing in this clause prevents you from exercising your right to approach the appropriate Supervising Authority to exercise your rights under GDPR. This Arbitration clause only precludes the involvement of a court of law in the dispute."

7. If GDPR applies to the dispute in hand, choose a seat of arbitration[120] that is a liberal, "arbitration-friendly" jurisdiction within the EU.

8. Tier your arbitration clause. Arbitration, mediation, and other ADR methods are not mutually exclusive of one and other. Some clauses can be specially crafted to include ADR in each step to help streamline the dispute and avoid any minor claims. **Example:** "In the event of a dispute, the parties shall first negotiate for a period of two weeks. If negotiation fails, the parties agree to submit their dispute to a 'good-faith' mediation administered by a mediator they both agree on. If mediation fails, the dispute shall be referred to Arbitration."

9. **Opt-out of confidentiality.** This is a strategic determination, which each party must make when drafting the clause. Complete transparency in the proceedings can help to demonstrate compliance and present that there is "nothing to hide," while at the same time may end up garnering negative publicity and unwanted attention.

ADR and GDPR might be a perfect match in enforcing the rights of the user, but the ambiguity in the law and the lack of clarity in its future make it a gamble. If arbitration is carried out and the court annuls the award, it ends up being a waste of time and effort. That is why a well-drafted, fair, and cautious ADR clause can help avoid the foreseeable issues that could arise in the future.

| | Supervisory authority | Court | Arbitration |
|---|---|---|---|
| **Type of authority:** | Regulatory oversight. | Judicial. | Nonjudicial. |
| **Functions:** | Ensuring GDPR compliance. | Dispute resolution. | Dispute resolution. |
| **Source of authority:** | GDPR and establishing statutes. | Act of State. | Contract. |

|  | Supervisory authority | Court | Arbitration |
|---|---|---|---|
| **Type of powers:** | Investigative, corrective, and advisory. | All judicial powers generally given to a court. (**Example:** Administering oaths and issuing subpoenas.) | Generally, the same powers of a court, but often limited by law or contract. |
| **Issues:** | Advisory opinions, orders, fines, rules, and standard communications. | Judgment of law. | Arbitral award. |
| **Binding power:** | Subject to court supervision and review. Certain orders are binding. | Binding on all parties. Depending on which court, the judgment can be binding on society at large. | Binding between the parties only. No precedential value. |
| **Independence:** | An independent body that is entrusted with supporting the enforcement of user rights. | A completely independent and impartial body. | Even though the parties appoint their tribunal members in most cases, it remains an independent body. |
| **Confidentiality:** | While the inner functions of the SA is bound by professional secrecy,[121] their overall orders are not confidential. | Most proceedings are not confidential as "open-court" is a facet of most democracies. | Awards and proceedings are confidential. |
| **Cost:** | Free of Cost in most circumstances. | Tends to be expensive. | Less expensive than litigation. |
| **Flexibility:** | Low flexibility. They are bound by their mandate in GDPR and Establishing Act. | Not flexible. | Flexible and can be changed by way of agreement. |
| **Subject-matter dealt with:** | GDPR. | Anything legally and rightfully brought before it. | Whatever issues mandated by the parties in their arbitration agreement. |
| **Adjudicators:** | Legal and data protection professionals with qualifications specified by their State. | Qualified judges trained in law. | Anyone the parties appoint or agree to. Usually legal, industry, and technical experts. |

## 7.6 Forum Selection Clauses

A close replacement to arbitration clauses is the more traditional *forum selection clauses,* allowing parties to agree upon a specific court in a specific country to resolve the dispute. Like arbitration, a forum selection clause is rooted in consent between the parties and can suffer from similar issues but provide similar benefits. **Example:** Any dispute arising out of this agreement shall be determined by the civil courts of Rome, Italy, which have jurisdiction over the matter.

Drafting and including such clauses for GDPR purposes relies on the same wordings discussed earlier, which permits users to exercise rights without prejudice to any other administrative and nonjudicial remedies.[122] Forum selection clauses differ by being less scrutinized opposed to ADR as GDPR already permits users to go to court. The ambiguity is in whether Controllers and users can contractually assign the jurisdiction to one court. Note that users' rights are without prejudice to any other administrative and nonjudicial remedies, which does not include courts.

GDPR nowhere prohibits or allows a forum selection clause, leaving a vacuum in answering the issues. For example, if such clauses were allowed in initial terms of use, is it fair for the Controller to limit the data subject's freedom to file wherever GDPR permits? Even if the terms of the forum clause are fairly drafted, it still limits user rights to enforce GDPR in the "most convenient" court to him. Until the CJEU or the EU DPB gives further determination, this question will be difficult to answer.

## 7.7 Challenging the Existing Law

To complete this chapter, let us briefly discuss how to challenge GDPR provisions or their delegated legislations in the EU. This legal challenge is not relating to facts or noncompliance; rather, it is a direct challenge to the law itself, on the basis that it violates one's rights. Any person has a right to bring action to annul the decisions of the EU DPB[123] before the CJEU. The "decisions" mentioned are any kind of delegated legislation made by the EU DPB under GDPR. A challenge can be raised in the CJEU within two months of its publication. The CJEU has the authority to determine the validity, legality, and interpretation of EU law.[124]

This right exists for any natural or legal person who is affected and concerned with the law, and even Supervisory Authorities can raise a challenge to the law within two months of publication.[125] If SAs while applying legislations of the EU DPB are challenged in a court by any person, the matter must be referred to the CJEU, so that it may be resolved by the lower court. This power of the CJEU also applies to situations where a lower court will require their interpretation on the meaning and validity of a provision of law so that the case may move forward.[126] It is the petitioners' prerogative to bring the claim within the two-month period. If the period expires, the lower court is not required to refer the matter to the CJEU.

Similar to the bodies that operate under GDPR, even the law itself is not infallible and can be subject to review. This is the mode open to those who critique and object to how the opening clauses of GDPR are being drafted by the DPB in the years to come. It is this system of constant challenge, defense, and growth that helps to create strong and efficient legal protections for all the players in the market.

# Notes

1   GDPR, Articles 12 to15.
2   Sections 6.1 and 6.2.
3   GDPR, Article 12.
4   GDPR, Article 12.5.
5   GDPR, Article 12.8.
6   GDPR, Article 15 *read with* Articles 13 and 14.
7   Pursuant to General Data Protection Regulation, Article 46.
8   GDPR, Article 12.4.
9   GDPR, Article 12.6.
10  GDPR, Article 14: In cases of where the Controller has the user's personal data, but has not collected it from the users directly.
11  Lothar Determann, *Determann's Field Guide to Data Privacy Law,* 3rd ed. (Edward Elgar Publishing, 2017), 64.
12  Determann, *Determann's Field Guide to Data Privacy Law,* 65.
13  When discussing "rights" in this chapter, we refer to *all,* including rectification, erasure, restriction, data portability, explanation, objection, etc.
14  GDPR, Article 15.
15  The above measures are suggested for the needs of large to medium-sized businesses. They can be scaled *down* or *up* in size depending on the processing operation.
16  It is not entirely clear from the text of the regulation whether Controllers have the liberty of resolving disputes with their users by using a "dispute resolution" clause in their terms of use. This ambiguity becomes amplified when we look at the *overlap* of enforcement mechanisms under GDPR. We shall examine this further as we proceed to our other sections on court and ADR.
17  GDPR, Article 80.
18  GDPR, Article 80.2.
19  GDPR, Recital 142.
20  GDPR, Article 51.1.
21  GDPR, Article 51.2.
22  GDPR, Article 51.4.
23  GDPR, Articles 51.3, 63.
24  GDPR, Article 53.
25  GDPR, Article 53.3: *In accordance with member law.*
26  GDPR, Article 53.4: Once again, Member State law provides for these specifics.
27  GDPR, Article 54.
28  GDPR, Article 52.
29  GDPR, Article 52.4.
30  GDPR, Article 52.4, 52.5.
31  GDPR, Article 52.6.
32  GDPR, Article 54.2.
33  GDPR, Article 80.
34  GDPR, Article 80.1.

35  GDPR, Article 55.1.
36  GDPR, Article 55.2.
37  GDPR, Article 55.3.
38  GDPR, Article 4.22.
39  GDPR, Article 56.1; Subject to the *consistency mechanism.*
40  GDPR, Article 56.6.
41  GDPR, Recital 22; for further discussion see Chapter 3, Section 3.3.1.
42  GDPR, Article 4.16.
43  GDPR, Article 4.16.
44  GDPR, Article 56.2.
45  GDPR, Article 56.3; *in accordance to* the procedure under Article 60 if conflicts exist.
46  Section 7.3.8.
47  GDPR, Article 57.
48  GDPR, Article 57.f.
49  GDPR, Article 57.2.
50  GDPR, *in accordance with* Article 80.
51  GDPR, Article 57.1.j; *read with* Articles 28.8.
52  GDPR, Article 46.2.
53  GDPR, Article 46.3.
54  GDPR, Article 47.
55  GDPR, Article 59.
56  GDPR, Article 57.4.
57  *DPD,* Article 28.3.
58  GDPR, Article 58.
59  GDPR, Recital 129.
60  GDPR, Recital 129.
61  GDPR, *in accordance with* Article 83; 58.2.i.
62  GDPR, Article 36; see Chapter 4, Section 4.3.2.4.
63  GDPR, Article 58.5; the scope of the enforcement power is subject to Member State law.
64  GDPR, Article 58.4.
65  *"Form shopping"* is the act of choosing the *most favorable jurisdiction* out of other options to gain advantage in a legal dispute. This advantage may be commercial, legal, economic, etc. Forum shopping is considered undesirable in most jurisdictions as it's often used by parties to pick legal regimes that protect their interests. However, forum shopping is not *illegal.*
66  GDPR, Recital 139.
67  GDPR, Article 68.3.
68  GDPR, Articles 68–76.
69  Section 7.3.5.
70  GDPR, Articles 60–62.
71  GDPR, Article 60.1.
72  GDPR, Article 60.4.
73  GDPR, Article 60.9.

74  GDPR, Article 60.4.
75  GDPR, Articles 63–67.
76  GDPR, Recital 138.
77  GDPR, Articles 64 and 65.
78  GDPR, Recital 135.
79  GDPR, Article 63.
80  §7.3.1 onwards of this book.
81  GDPR, Article 77.
82  GDPR, Article 77.1.
83  GDPR, Article 57.1.e.
84  GDPR, Recital 141.
85  GDPR, Article 13.2.d; Recital 141, which states, "In order to facilitate the submission of complaints, each supervisory authority should take measures such as *providing a complaint submission form which can also be completed electronically,* without excluding other means of communication."
86  GDPR, Article 58.
87  GDPR, Recital 141.
88  GDPR, Article 77.2.
89  GDPR, Recital 141.
90  GDPR, Articles 77, 78, and 79; all these provisions provide that the exercise of one venue is done *"without prejudice* to any available administrative or non-judicial remedy," which opens the door for Forum Selection and ADR clauses, discussed later in this chapter.
Article 79, relating to Judicial Remedies states: "Without prejudice to any available administrative or nonjudicial remedy, *including the right to lodge a complaint with a supervisory authority* pursuant to Article 77, each data subject shall have the right to an effective judicial remedy."
91  GDPR, Article 79.
92  GDPR, Recital 143.
93  GDPR, Article 79.2.
94  GDPR, Article 81.
95  GDPR, Article 78.
96  GDPR, Article 78.1 *read with* Article 78.4, which states; "Where proceedings are brought against a decision of a supervisory authority which was *preceded by an opinion* or a decision of the Board in the *consistency mechanism,* the supervisory authority *shall forward that opinion or decision to the court."*
97  GDPR, Article 78.2: "... each data subject shall have the right to an effective judicial remedy where the supervisory authority which is competent pursuant to Articles 55 and 56 *does not handle a complaint* or *does not inform* the data subject within three months on the *progress or outcome* of the complaint lodged pursuant to Article 77."
98  GDPR, Article 51.
99  GDPR, Article 78.3.
100  GDPR, Recital 143.
101  GDPR, Article 78.1.

102  The EU Charter of Fundamental Rights, Article 47.

103  GDPR, Recital 141.

104  GDPR, Recital 143.

105  GDPR, Recital 143.

106  GDPR, Recital 143.

107  Continued from the previous illustrations.

108  GDPR, Article 82.5.

109  GDPR, Article 12.5: The Controller bears the burden of proving these facts.

110  GDPR, Article 79.

111  GDPR, Article 81.

112  GDPR, Recital 144.

113  GDPR, Article 81.3: "Where those proceedings are pending at first instance, any court other than the court first seized may also, on the application of one of the parties, decline jurisdiction if *the court first seized has jurisdiction over the actions* in question and its *law permits the consolidation* thereof."

114  GDPR, Recital 144.

115  The discussion in this section would be limited to these two forms, mainly *arbitration.*

116  This is excluding any Statute mandated ADR that a country may have.

117  GDPR, Articles 77–79.

118  In this section we do not focus on mediation and other ADR techniques. As a "nonbinding" resolution method, inclusion of mediation is *less likely to raise any issues* in the scheme of GDPR. Mediation, conciliation, and negotiation are all processes that can be backed out of *at any time* after a *good faith attempt.* Thus, this section is focused on the issues that face *binding arbitration.*

119  New York Convention on the Validity and Enforcement of International Arbitral Awards, Article V.

120  The seat of arbitration is a way of denoting which Country's procedural law will govern the proceedings.

121  GDPR, Article 90.

122  GDPR, Article 77–79.

123  GDPR, Recital 143.

124  This is done in accordance to the Treaty on the Functioning of the EU (TFEU), Article 263.

125  GDPR, Recital 143.

126  GDPR, Recital 143; *TFEU,* Article 267.

# 8

# Remedies

*Extreme remedies are very appropriate for extreme diseases.*

— Hippocrates

In Chapter 7 we discussed the enforcement mechanisms open to data subjects under GDPR; now let us examine the remedies available in those actions. This chapter will discuss the "teeth" of the regulation, focusing on how noncompliance is punished. Throughout this book, we discussed how GDPR creates a market of stern compliance by incorporating Controller/Processor accountability at all stages of processing. Remedies are how the law penalizes those who break it.

GDPR has two species of remedies available to carry out enforcement, compensation, and administrative fines. *Criminal penalties* such as *imprisonment* or *deprivation of profits*[1] are left to the Member States to legislate on further, subject to the rules of double jeopardy.[2] Compensation is a civil remedy for damages by the user, while administrative fines are handed down by the SA in exercise of their corrective authority.

## 8.1 Allocating Liability

The Controller and Processor are the two players under GDPR who will be held responsible in the event of a contravention. Despite sharing this liability, the burden can be shifted between the two based on the following rules.[3]

### 8.1.1 Controller Alone Liable

The Controller bears liability for any damage caused in processing that infringes GDPR.[4] The entity bears this burden as a default unless it can prove that it (the Controller) is in no way liable for the event that caused the damage.[5] This requires proof of full compliance with GDPR.

**Illustration:** Discover Tech is a prominent "litigation discovery services" management company based in Austria that helps law firms process data relating to litigations based on documents and transcripts to help them efficiently manage their disputes. They work with the processing company Lit Pro LLC located in Ireland. A compensation suit has been filed by Fabio, after his patent case suffered a data breach at their hands. At trial, it was discovered that Discover Tech's employee was bribed by an unknown party to leak the documents online. Discover Tech will remain solely responsible.

### 8.1.2  Processor Alone Liable

The Processor will solely be held liable if damage caused by processing was a result of noncompliance of "processor-specific" responsibilities under GDPR.[6] This is a change from the preceding DPD framework where only the Controller can be held liable.[7] The Processor can also be held liable for not following the lawful instructions of the Controller.[8] Like the Controller, liability can be avoided if it has been proven that they were not liable for the event leading to the damage caused.

**Illustration:** Consider the facts above, and now consider that the data breach was caused because Lit Pro had engaged another processing company, Sub Pros, to carry out their work for Discover Tech. Sub Pros did not implement the security instructions provided by Discover Tech, which was unaware of any such subprocessing arrangement. Lit Pro will be solely responsible for the Compensation.

### 8.1.3  Joint and Several Liabilities

GDPR provided a *graduated liability system* based on cascading roles played by the Controllers or Processors. This topic had been discussed in Chapter 3, when speaking about the combined liability shared by entities involved in a processing operation. To succeed in a claim for damages, the claimant must prove a *plausible submission of facts* to establish the liability of the Controller/Processor.[9] A comprehensive knowledge of the other party's processing operations is not needed. Joint and several liability applies where the infringement has been caused by:

- Multiple Controllers
- Multiple Processors
- The Controller and Processor together
- Multiple Controllers and Processors together

In cases of damage caused by a "joint" processing operation like the combinations discussed above, each Controller and Processor shall be held liable for the entire damage to ensure effective compensation of the data subject.[10] This is the legal concept of "joint and several" liability. Liability can be avoided if it is proved that the entity was in no way responsible for the event giving rise to the damage and subsequent claim.[11] As opposed to the preceding DPD, the scope for exemption has shrunk as even the smallest involvement on the part of the Controller/Processor will subject them to GDPR liability.[12]

If one of the Controllers/Processors paid full compensation for the damage suffered by the data subject, they have a separate right of compensation or *recourse proceedings*[13] against the other parties involved in the damage. This "compensation" from the other Controllers/ Processors in the suit filed will be proportional to the liability they bear based on the rules of allocation discussed above. GDPR allows flexibility for data subjects to recover from entities and permits co-defendants to handle their dues independently with one and other.

**Illustration:** Let us adopt the facts of the above illustration and assume that the data breach was caused due to both infringements discussed above by Discover Tech's employees and the arrangement with Sub Pros. Fabio can recover his compensation in full either from Discover Tech or Lit Pro. He recovers damages amounting to €1 million from Lit Pro. Lit Pro can then file a reclamation suit against Discover Tech to compensate the portion of the €1million that was caused owing to their fault.

## 8.2  Compensation

GDPR gives any person who has suffered material or nonmaterial damage because of an infringement caused by the Controller or Processor the right to claim compensation for the damage suffered.[14] Compensation is a private action initiated by a data subject for any person harmed by the processing operation. Compensation can be claimed for violating GDPR and delegated acts:[15]

- Which are made under GDPR for its implementation.
- Member State Law made pursuant to opening clauses.

The provision acts as a legal basis for claiming damages caused by processing businesses. Without this remedy under GDPR, claimants would have to find an analogous theory under common law like unjust enrichment, negligence, or breach of contract. GDPR removes the need for an independent basis and provides a formalized remedy for noncompliance.

### 8.2.1  Quantifying "Full Compensation"

Material and nonmaterial damage caused as a consequence of data breaches can be monetary or intangible. Intangible harms are diverse and can include issues like social discrimination, psychological stress, barriers to trade or free personality development, etc. For example, the victims of the Ashley Madison data breach did not face monetary loss but faced psychological harm in having their extramarital affairs made public.

A person suffering damages under GDPR is entitled to full compensation of their loss from the Controller/Processor. The concept of "damage" here is to be interpreted broadly in line with precedent established by the CJEU.[16] ECJ jurisprudence mandates that generous quantification of damages is likely to have a genuine deterrent effect on the liable party and subsequent infringers.[17] Furthermore, the regulation specifies that data subjects are entitled to full and effective compensation for the damage caused.

**Illustration:** Continuing our above Discover Tech illustration, let us assume that Fabio's patent case leak had caused him €500,000 in financial loss as the value of his patent has been reduced because of the leak, €200,000 lost in legal fees for filing the suit, and an additional €300,000 for the damages he would have gained if the litigation went on without the data breach. He is entitled to the full €1 million for effective compensation.

## 8.2.2 Conflict in the Scope of "Standing" in Court

The scope of litigants who can claim for compensation is broad, giving the right to anyone who has been harmed by the infringement. "Any" person can claim compensation under GDPR Article 82.1 but a causal link to their harm and the service provided must exist. A data subject always has standing for compensation as the personal data holder, but third parties should possess some connection with the processing to entitle them to compensation. For example, a deceased relative or a durable power of attorney holder objecting to processing data of a relative or client.

This is a broader scope than the right to an effective judicial remedy against the Controller/Processor,[18] which limits standing only to data subjects. It also conflicts with the right judicial remedies against an SA,[19] which allows for any natural or legal person and data subjects affected by an action of an SA to sue.

Consider the following breakdown and see the differences in the wording used:

| Forum and defendant | Cause of action | GDPR article | Wording used |
| --- | --- | --- | --- |
| Suing the Controller/ Processor in court | Infringement of rights and noncompliance | 79 | "Each data subject" |
| Suit against SA in court | Appeal of an order | 78.1 | "Each natural or legal person" |
| Suing SA in court | Delay in response or action on a complaint filed | 78.2 | "Each data subject" |
| Complaint filed in the SA against Controller/ Processor | Noncompliance or infringements of rights | 77 | "Every data subject" |
| Compensation suit against Controller/ Processor | Material/ nonmaterial damage caused because of infringement | 82 | "Any person" |

Essentially every cause of action against the Controller/Processor is based on an "infringement," but the venues and the individuals who may exercise those rights differ depending on the scenario provided by GDPR drafters. Note that data subjects can enlist the services of NPOs that specialize in digital rights, and those NPOs may work independently of their mandate when filing complaints. This creates a system where different rights can be exercised by different categories of claimants.

These conflicts may be minor but will create a great deal of confusion in future cases, as it will be unclear what the status or standing of the one claiming compensation needs to be. While only data subjects can file a "complaint" in court, anyone can claim "compensation" in court. This creates a wider ambit for monetary suits, only based on complaints filed. This confusion is increased when we consider that compensation suits are subject to the same rules of jurisdiction and venue as complaints listed under Article 79.2. Namely, this includes an analysis of the Controller's establishment and the place of habitual residence of the data subject. "Habitual" residence in this context does not equate to legal residency (as for tax purposes), but only requires a degree of permanence in the data subject's stay in the country.[20]

Thus, while data subjects are the only ones who can file a complaint in court, any person can file for compensation in court. It is unclear why GDPR drafters chose to make this distinction. Perhaps this was adopted as a deterrent measure since "damage" always requires redress. Regardless, the involvement of a wide breadth of natural and legal persons affected along with data subjects and NPOs makes a system of constant checks on Controllers and Processors to maintain compliance.

## 8.3  Administrative Fines

Unlike compensation suits, which can be filed in court, administrative fines are issued by the SA as part of their corrective powers.[21] These fines can be issued by the SA in addition to or instead of their other corrective powers and must be imposed in each individual case to be effective, proportionate, and dissuasive. This clear mandate from GDPR implies that the fines are intended to be deterrents imposed to prevent any future infringements.

### 8.3.1  Fines for Regulatory Infringements

GDPR divides its administrative fines into two main categories. The first category of fines can be up to €10 million or in cases of an undertaking up to 2% of their total worldwide annual turnover of their preceding financial year, whichever is higher.

The fines can be imposed on the Controller or Processor for the following infringements:

1. Violation of consent rules relating to children[22]
2. Maintaining personal data information and records where the processing no longer requires identification[23]
3. Failure to maintain data protection by design or default[24]
4. Failure of the DPO in relation to their tasks for the Controller/Processor[25]

Additionally, fines can be imposed on certification bodies[26] and monitoring bodies[27] of codes of conduct for infringements of their obligations under GDPR.[28] If we look at the nature of the violations described under this section, we can see it centered around regulatory infringements, which may not cause harm or damage but contravene GDPR nonetheless.

### 8.3.2  Fines for Grave Infringements

The second category of fines discussed is greater in quantification and is for violations that go to the overarching GDPR objectives. The administrative fines imposed under this category can be up to €20 million or in cases of undertakings, up to 4% of their annual turnover of the previous financial year, whichever is higher. They can be imposed for:

1. Violation of the basic principles of processing[29]
2. Unlawful processing of personal data[30]
3. Insufficient consent to processing[31]
4. Processing special data without a basis[32]
5. Infringing the rights of a data subject[33]
6. Unauthorized and unlawful third-country transfers[34]
7. Infringing any obligations under Member State law related to specific processing situations[35]
8. Noncompliance with any order from the SA imposing a temporary or definitive limitation on their processing[36]
9. Failure to provide access to the SA while they exercise their investigative powers[37]
10. Noncompliance with any corrective measure imposed by the SA[38]

In comparing the two categories of fines above, a clear shift in GDPR priorities is highlighted. This category of fines is higher than first-category penalties as they cut to the essential duties of the data collecting entities, rather than infringements of "black letter" requirements of the law.

### 8.3.3  Determining the Quantum of the Fine

While compensation may vary case to case based on the damage caused, administrative fines have more significance, with fixed amounts spanning to millions of euros, which have become the key selling point for GDPR compliance. When determining the amount imposed, the SA must consider:[39]

1. The nature, gravity, and duration of the infringement considering the nature, scope, and purpose of the processing
2. Number of data subjects affected
3. Level of damage caused
4. The intentional or negligent character of the infringement
5. Any mitigation action adopted by the Controller to reduce the damage
6. The degree of responsibility of the Controller/Processor based on the technical and organizational measures implemented
7. Any relevant previous infringements
8. Degree of cooperation with the SA to remedy or mitigate the damage
9. Categories of personal data affected
10. The manner in which the infringement was communicated, and whether it was informed or discovered by the SA
11. Any previous corrective measures imposed upon the Controller for the same subject matter, and subsequent compliance to those measures
12. Adherence to codes of conduct or any certification awarded
13. Any other aggravating or mitigating circumstances, which include financial benefits or losses avoided, because of the infringement, either directly or indirectly

The extensive formula provided helps the SA weigh important factors necessary to impose a fine. For example, an SA can issue a reprimand in the case of a minor infringement by a natural person,[40] whereas a larger conglomerate can be given the full fine.

**Sanctioning corporate groups of undertakings:** When administrative fines are imposed on natural persons and not undertakings, the SA should take account of the general level of income in the Member State as well as the economic situation of the person in considering the appropriate amount of the fine.[41] On the other hand, sanctions against a group of undertakings would entitle the SA to impose the fines across not only the legal entities in the undertaking, but every entity that is engaged in the economic activity regardless of its legal status or manner of financing.[42]

**Multiple infringements:** Complex processing situations may lead to intentional or negligent contravention of GDPR in the same or linked activities. If the Controller/Processor during processing infringes several GDPR provisions, the total fine imposed shall not exceed the amount specified for the gravest infringement.[43] Imposing administrative fines is subject to appropriate procedural safeguards such as effective judicial review and due process,[44] or provision of appeal.[45] The cap on fine recoverability exists for events of widespread GDPR infringements across several millions of hypothetical consumers. Such cases would require a separate analysis for each individual infringement, which would prove to be cumbersome and ineffective.

**Illustration:** Brigade Ltd. is a home security system that utilizes the internet-of-things platform with smartphone technology to give digital protection from intruders. Brigade has several subsidiaries in car, mobile, hotel, and payment security forming a large conglomerate with a total worldwide turnover of €1 billion. In January 2019, the Brigade group faced numerous brute-force attacks from hackers, which took place sporadically for three weeks. The group kept the breach private for several months until users started complaining the data provided has appeared on the dark-web marketplace. After an investigation, the LSA determines that the Brigade group breached obligations relating to data security, data breaches, information obligations, and user rights over the three-week period in January. The SA may only issue a single maximum fine based on the worldwide turnover of the whole Brigade group for the most severe GDPR violations. Resultantly, the Brigade Group must pay 4% of €1 billion, leading to a total penalty of €80,000,000.

Pursuant to GDPR opening clauses, Member States are given the liberty to lay down rules for local business established in their State and for public authorities (without prejudice to the SA's corrective powers).[46] The SAs may exercise the consistency mechanism to harmonize the amounts for fines for a consistent application and uniformity across the EU.[47] Additionally, if Member State law does not permit "administrative fines" such as in Denmark and Estonia,[48] they must create an alternate system of imposing effective, proportionate, and dissuasive punishments, such as using national courts.

**Responding to SA investigations:** Practically, when receiving a request for information or a corrective order from the SA, it is important to diligently prepare the response from the organization. If the entity has a DPO, involve him immediately in the process to assess the complaint. Broadly, follow the steps below:

1. **Assessment:** At the outset, determine what type of inquiry has been made. Is it in response to a complaint, or is it made *suo moto* by the SA? Is it investigative, advisory, or corrective?
2. **Fact gathering:** Collect all relevant facts and data involved in the request and see if any illegal oversight exists.
3. **Legal examination:** Depending on the seriousness of the complaint, refer the matter to the organization's attorney or DPO. Have the officer prepare a short legal examination and prepare a proposal for moving forward.
4. **Cooperate:** All inquiries and complaints should be dealt with in a nonadversarial manner if possible. Cooperating with the SA by an in-person meeting or by providing additional information will always help resolve any misunderstandings.

The steps facilitate compliance to serve the purpose of disposing of any inquiries at the earliest stage. This helps to avoid fines and reduce the quantum of the fine if issued. If there is a genuine legal conflict with GDPR itself or the compliance requirements, then it is best to follow legal strategies that involve less cooperation and an adversarial approach.

## 8.4 Processing Injunctions

Injunctions are court orders commanding that a person or entity stop an activity they are engaged in, either temporarily (pending a final judgment from the court) or permanently. Injunctions are well known judicial remedies that can prevent harm from occurring or from rights being violated, while damages can compensate the harm that already has been caused. Curiously, GDPR has not provided injunction remedies for data subjects in its text. This seems counterintuitive, as injunctions are powerful tools, which can be utilized well in processing since they can effectively prevent infringements of important rights. In common law countries, injunctions are *equitable remedies* that can only be issued by a court. This may justify why injunctions have not been included in GDPR expressly.

Consider the following **illustration**. Kent discovers one day that his trusted social media website Friendly.com has been continuously processing his data and keeping his profile "alive" and "online" even though he had "deactivated" his profile for the past three months while he studied for his exams. Notwithstanding the deactivation, the website continued to use his data in their operations stating that he "liked" and "suggested" certain posts, when he did not. Rather than approaching the SA to impose a fine, or requesting compensation for the breach by Friendly.com, Kent requests the court to issue a "permanent" injunction requiring that the website stop all processing activities until they address this problem. GDPR does not empower a court to issue an injunction in relation to processing activities. Does that suggest Kent has no remedy to stop Friendly.com? Not quite. There are several ways of achieving this remedy, which we shall discuss next.

### 8.4.1 Domestic Law

The simple fact that GDPR does not expressly empower a court to issue an injunction does not necessarily lead to the conclusion that no remedy exists. Courts are awarded authority by the sovereign state that establishes them. Therefore, each Member State of the EU has its own specific rules and laws regarding the court's power, in addition to what circumstances warrant an injunction.

Injunctions are usually treated as an equitable remedy that is left to judicial discretion. Speaking generally, most jurisdictions place the following requirements for granting "temporary" injunctions:

1. The plaintiff/movant's likelihood of success on the merits.
2. The plaintiff has experienced irreparable harm, or is likely to face such harm.
3. The harm faced by the plaintiff from the activity outweighs any harm faced by the defendant in allowing them to carry on the activity (the *balance of equities*).

Similarly, for granting "permanent" injunctions, the following requirements must be met:[49]

1. The plaintiff has suffered an irreparable injury.
2. Other remedies such as damages would be *inadequate* to address the injury.
3. The "balance of equities" favors the plaintiff.
4. Granting the injunction would not harm the public interest.

The above requirements for granting injunctions are the general requirements placed globally, as they require balancing interests between two conflicting parties. There is no reason why a domestic court would be prevented from applying these elements in the backdrop of processing personal data. This would be a beneficial remedy as damages can increase at a fast pace and the Controller may be unable to effectively fix or prevent the damage caused later on.

### 8.4.2   The EU Injunction Directive

Separate from GDPR but related to our purposes is the EU Injunction Directive,[50] which is an effort to harmonize the procedure of granting injunctions and provides a mode of "cross-border" injunctions across the Union. Unlike GDPR, this is a "directive" and not a "regulation," which implies that it has no binding force over the Member States and subjects. The central focus of this directive is on consumer interests with respect to previous directives issued on:

1. Consumer rights
2. Consumer credit
3. Package travel
4. Unfair commercial practices
5. Unfair consumer contract terms
6. Sale of consumer goods and associated guarantees[51]

Though the injunction directive has no binding force and requires a collective reading with other directives and national laws, it seeks to achieve a similar goal as GDPR: the collective interests of a consumer in an internal market. GDPR was made with intent to harmonize the digital marketplace and strengthen the user's rights. In fact, if we look at the six categories of consumer interests above, each is implicated and affected by GDPR in one way or another. Rather than reading the directive as a separate way to enforce injunctions, consider it as a supplement used to unify and strengthen the remedy across the EU.

However, this requires that the data subject be considered as a consumer for the purposes of the directive. Let us apply this to our earlier illustration and consider that Kent has approached a court in Germany (where he lives) for an injunction. The Court can place an injunction on further processing and have that order enforced throughout the EU by using the directive if Kent is proven to be a "consumer." Further, the injunction would have to be a specific limitation on the processing activities and not a general order on all processing as initially requested by Kent.

### 8.4.3 The SA's Power to Restrain Processing

While GDPR does not expressly for injunctions as a remedy, it implicitly gives the authority to the SA.[52] This is the SA's power and not a duty.[53] This implies restraining orders are discretionary and can be issued as the situation demands. However, GDPR evades using the term "injunction" because there are several key differences between the two remedies. The SA's corrective and advisory powers give them a wide range of authority to control the processing of data, which includes:

1. Imposing a temporary or definitive limitation on processing including a ban on processing
2. Ordering the suspension of data flows to a recipient third country or international organization
3. Ordering the Controller/Processor to bring processing into compliance of GDPR, in a specified time and manner
4. Ordering the Controller/Processor to enforce the rights of a data subject or to comply with any such request

While these powers are not characterized as injunctions, they have the same effect, which is to stop an infringing activity. However, the restriction powers are broader than traditional injunctions. The powers do not work as negative orders that restrain an entity from processing but can also specify how and when to comply.

GDPR Article 58 provides the authority but does not give a clear criterion for exercising them and what considerations the SA should use. Unlike injunctions, the requirements for restraining orders are not entirely certain and are left to SA discretion. This leads to the conclusion that the SA's authority to restrain processing is a regulatory measure that can be exercised to ensure the smooth functioning of GDPR, subjecting it to subsequent judicial review.[54]

Continuing our Friendly.com **illustration**, let us assume that Kent has filed his request with the SA of Hamburg, who initiates an investigation and comes to the initial conclusion that the processing violates Kent's rights. Pending the final conclusion of the investigation, the SA orders Friendly.com to stop all processing activities until the matter is resolved. Friendly.com strongly protested the order, and requested a hearing, citing that such a limitation would result in immense financial loss for the Company, and is a disproportionate order for a single "isolated" complaint, which will cause them irreparable harm. The SA imposes the restriction nonetheless stating that "User's Rights prevail over the website's commercial interests under GDPR." Friendly.com can appeal this order to a court[55] on the grounds that the SA made the detrimental order without following due process.

**Differences Between Injunctions and Restraint of Processing**

| Point of difference | Injunction | Restraint of Processing |
|---|---|---|
| Who can issue? | A lower court. | The SA |
| Authorization | A jurisdiction-specific statute, usually related to civil procedure and remedies. | GDPR, Article 58 |
| What must be considered? | Jurisdiction-specific factors based on harm and balance of equities. | Unspecified by GDPR |
| When is it issued? | To prevent irreparable harm. | Discretionary |
| Scope | Can be used to stop an activity that infringes the rights of others, either temporarily or permanently. | Can be used to stop, restrain, suspend, or authorize the flow and processing of data |
| Circumstances of use | Must be requested by a movant. | Can be issued by the SA *suo moto*, without an application made |
| Nature of the remedy | Equitable. | Regulatory |
| Possibility of review | Can be subject to subsequent appeal by a higher court. | Can be subject to judicial review by an authorized court |
| Uniformity | The EU Injunction Directive tries to harmonize the factors across the Union. Regardless, the requirements remain largely similar from country to country. | Uniformity might differ from SA to SA |
| Regarding | Anything that infringes/could infringe the rights of another. | Personal data processing activities |

The differences in the table above are academic but are important for understanding what remedy is suitable to enforce user rights. GDPR, rather than leaving this authority with the courts, consolidated the power entrusting it to the enforcement agency of GDPR. This increases the SA's discretion for issuing restraining orders, but concurrently can be used to enforce GDPR without dealing with vexatious court petitions and procedures.

As discussed earlier in this book, GDPR acts as a "digital environment" regulation that adopts precautionary and reactive measures to ensure compliance. Injunctions are often effective tools in preventing pollution and stopping physical harm before it occurs. Similarly, these judicial mechanisms can be used to prevent any pollution of our digital environment, cutting off any unsavory data-processing practices before they cause long-term, irreparable harm to our common shared mediums.

## 8.5 Specific Performance

Like injunctions, specific performance is an *equitable remedy* in law that is used to direct another to do a specific act. Specific performance usually exists in contract law, specifically in the sale of goods and services. The remedy is often issued when money damages or injunctions are unsuitable. Generally, the factors for specific performance are as follows:

1. Inadequacy of alternate legal remedies
2. Ability of the defendant to carry out the requested performance
3. Balancing of equities and hardships

Specific performance is often rooted in contractual relationships and involves providing a specific or unique good or service. This uniqueness in the good/service makes other remedies like damages or an injunction inadequate to prevent injustice for one party. Compared to an injunction, conditions for specific performance are narrow and less likely to be granted. In the context of GDPR, it may not be the best remedy. Even though the relationship between Controller and data subject is likely governed by contract, it's unlikely that the service would be unique and cause injustice. However, situations may arise under GDPR where the data subject requires the Controller to take specific action regarding the processing of his personal data.

Here once again, it is relevant to discuss the authority of the SA in restraining and controlling processing activities as those powers will likely be exercised. The SA has the authority to order the Controller to comply with GDPR in a time and manner that they specify. Additionally, the SA has the authority to order rectification, erasure of personal data, and restriction of processing from the Controller.[56] In a sense, this acts as a GDPR form of specific-performance remedy, where the SA can order the Controller to act in a certain way in processing. This is subject to the same judicial reviews as injunctions but has a smaller scope, as the remedy is not contractual, but regulatory limited to the field of processing.

The remedies of injunction and specific performance should not be confused as the SA's function is to essentially give orders to the Controller/Processor. This particular corrective power assists them in ensuring compliance on their terms alone, with "specific performance" required for GDPR compliance or enforcing data subject rights. The various devices of compensation, fines, restriction of processing, etc., available to the SA demonstrate the intent of GDPR drafters to make the agency a powerful and capable enforcer of the regulation. While many of these powers can be executed by a court by using traditional judicial process, empowering SAs reduces delays, costs, and other negatives that follow litigation.

In entrusting the SA with a wide array of authority, GDPR creates more efficiency at the cost of regulatory discretion. The agency holds powers usually entrusted to a judicial body, with the ability to issue orders without request as they deem fit, if the situation demands it. In normal situations, it would be dangerous for one regulatory agency to have such a power, but GDPR provides numerous "checks and balances" to their power by giving an option of judicial review for orders and mandating that the SA always operate in furtherance of the data subject's rights. GDPR fixes the imbalance by erring on the side of caution to prevent abuse.

## Notes

1 GDPR, Recital 149, Article 84: These penalties must be *separate* from the Administrative Fines and shall be effective, proportionate, and dissuasive.
2 GDPR, Recital 149; "However, the imposition of criminal penalties for infringements of such national rules and of administrative penalties should not lead to a breach of the principle of ne bis in idem, as interpreted by the Court of Justice." *Ne bis idem* translated from Latin means "not twice in the same thing" acting as the EU doctrine for double jeopardy, which holds that no legal action can be instituted twice for the same cause of action.
3 GDPR, Article 82.
4 GDPR, Article 82.2.
5 GDPR, Article 82.3.
6 GDPR, Article 28, 82.2.
7 *DPD,* Article 23.
8 GDPR, Article 29, 82.2.
9 P. Laue, J. Nink, and S. Kremer (eds.), Haftung, "Sanktionen und Rectsbehelfe. Zusammenarbeit mit Aufsichtsbehorden." In *Das Neue Datenschutzrecht in der betrieblichen Praxis* (Baden-Baden Nomos, 2016), Rec. 8.
10 GDPR, Article 82.4.
11 GDPR, Article 82.3.
12 Laue, Nink, and Kremer (eds.), Haftung, "Sanktionen und Rectsbehelfe," Rec. 15.
13 GDPR, Recital 146.
14 GDPR, Article 82.1.
15 GDPR, Recital 146.
16 GDPR, Recital 146.
17 ECJ Ruling of 17 December 2015, Ajorna Camacho, C-407/14, rec. 31.
18 GDPR, Article 79.
19 GDPR, Article 78.
20 Note that GDPR places more importance on the data subject's *location* and *time-of-stay* in the EU, rather than formal citizenship. See GDPR, Article 3.2.
21 GDPR, Article 83; 58.2.
22 GDPR, Article 8.
23 GDPR, Article 11.
24 GDPR, Article 25.

25  GDPR, Article 39.
26  GDPR, Articles 42 and 43.
27  GDPR, Article 41.4.
28  GDPR, Article 83.4.
29  GDPR, Article 5.
30  GDPR, Article 6.
31  GDPR, Article 7.
32  GDPR, Article 9.
33  GDPR, Articles 12 to 22.
34  GDPR, Articles 44 to 49.
35  GDPR, Chapter IX.
36  GDPR, Article 58.2.
37  GDPR, Article 58.1.
38  GDPR, Article 83.6.
39  GDPR, Article 83.2.
40  GDPR, Recital 148.
41  GDPR, Recital 150.
42  ECJ Ruling of 23 April 1991, *Hofner & Eler v.Macrotron*, C-41/90, rec. 21; *read with GDPR*, Recital 150 which gives the definition of *"Undertaking,"* placing it under the same definition given under EU competition law (which must be read with Articles 101, 102 of the Treaty on the Functioning of the EU).
43  GDPR, Article 83.3.
44  GDPR, Article 83.8.
45  GDPR, Article 78.1.
46  GDPR, Article 83.7.
47  GDPR, Recital 150.
48  GDPR, Article 83.9, Recital 151.
49  Once again, this is a generalized list of requirements. Each State would likely differ in their specifics in small ways.
50  EU Directive on Injunctions for the Protection of Consumer Interests, 2009/22/EC.
51  See "Injunctions Directive," European Commission, www.ec.europa.eu/info/law/law-topic/consumers/injunctions-directive_en.
52  GDPR, Article 58.
53  Compare GDPR, Articles 57 and 58.
54  GDPR, Article 58.4.
55  GDPR, Article 78.1.
56  GDPR, Article 58.2.g.

# 9

## Governmental Use of Data

*Always eyes watching you and the voice enveloping you. Asleep or awake, indoors or out of doors, in the bath or bed – no escape. Nothing was your own except the few cubic centimeters in your skull.*

— George Orwell, 1984

As the world modernizes and goes paperless, governments are also keeping pace. Over the past few decades, technology is integrated into most aspects of state activities, spanning from the ability to file online applications to internal functioning. At the same time, technology revolutions are crucial to develop and increase the efficiency of the state with ambitious projects under development all over the world. While some of these projects are bold (such as China's project, One China, which aims to give free internet to all its citizens), other undertakings have far more problematic implications (such as the UK's arrest of citizens protesting the royal wedding prior to the protest itself based on their social media posts).

In this chapter we examine how GDPR interplays with these projects and what exceptions can be claimed by state entities under the regulation. The impact of the exceptions provided to the state under GDPR helps to give the governmental bodies the leeway they require to effectively carry out any future projects. We will also examine the implications of "public-private" partnerships in these projects. Additionally, we shall examine how certain projects can be subject to abuse, considering the lessons in recent history.

## 9.1  Member State Legislations

GDPR, as a regulation passed by the EU, is directly applicable on the States, and unlike a directive, it does not require a transformative act to be binding. The regulation does permit Member States to further legislate on specific areas of data protection through "opening clauses." Before examining how the State operates under GDPR as a Controller, it is important to study what rules can be made. These delegated legislations are often practical measures, designed to suit the legal framework of a country. The degree of customization a State can exercise over that area is broad in some aspects and narrow in others, giving rise to *national peculiarities* in data-protection law within the EU.

National peculiarities are inevitable as the EU legislators cannot be expected to regulate all aspects of personal data protection. Specializing GDPR rules to fit every situation would be best left to the Member States who would have a keener awareness to the economic, societal, and public interest needs of their citizens. Opening clauses can cover general or specific processing obligations depending on GDPR mandate. General processing opening clauses are those areas within GDPR that Member States can legislate over relating to general processing obligations. General clauses are deliberate gaps left in the regulation, permitting further definition, expansion, restriction, derogation, and overall refinement of GDPR principles of processing by the Member States to suit their situations. In some cases, GDPR makes it mandatory to create delegated legislation.

Specific processing opening clauses relate to situations where Member States can more liberally and substantially regulate by legislation over a specific area of processing. Areas like journalism, employment, and professional secrecy have not been covered at all under GDPR and have been left to Member State competence. The existence of these opening clauses creates a risk of data protection inconsistencies throughout the EU, with Controller/Processor businesses subject to multiple regimes simultaneously. The assessment of these standards will have to be done on a case by case basis, keeping in mind:

- The jurisdictional omissions
- The jurisdictional derogations
- Any additional requirements for compliance
- Differences between GDPR obligations and Member State data-protection standards

Larger entities spread over multiple Member States and international Countries will likely face greater difficulty in compliance, as their processing obligations are likely to differ based on the location of the data.

GDPR's opening clauses can also provide flexibility to public bodies processing data for their employees as well. For example, consider a government department receiving a request to reveal the duties and payments made to employees incoming from the private sector. Under a national Right to Information statute, the department would have to release the information unless it is likely that it would breach any existing data protection obligations. At the same time, the department can decide that such requests are unfair processing, on the basis that the transferred employees were working in the public interest and were remunerated by public funds. The department also has the freedom to require transferred employees to release those details at the time of appointment by formal request. The fluidity gives States the freedom to manage the unique roles of public servants and their data.

**General Processing Opening Clauses**

| GDPR article and section | Opening clause content |
| --- | --- |
| 4.7 | Member States may define the purposes and means of certain processing activities along with the criteria for nominating a Controller in their country. |
| 6.2 | Specifying what "lawfulness" of processing is when based on legal obligation and public interest. |
| 8.1 | Member States can lower minimum age of child consent, provided it is not below 13. |
| 9.2 | States can deviate from normal special data rules by excluding certain categories of sensitive data based on consent, and create rules on employers handling sensitive data. |
| 9.4 | Conditions, limitations, and maintaining rules on genetic and biometric-sensitive data. |
| 10 | Maintaining processing rules for criminal conviction and arrest data. |
| 14.5.c, d | Exempting Controllers from their information obligation toward data subjects if the law requires the data be kept confidential. |
| 17.1.e and 17.3.b | Controller must erase all personal data if required by Member State law. Additionally, the Controller does not have to erase data if Member State law exempts them. |
| 22.2. b | Member State law can authorize automated decision making as an exemption to the general prohibition against its use. |
| 23 | Data subject rights can be restricted by Member State law for reasons of public interest. |
| 26 | Specific rules on allocating data protection obligations between Joint Controllers. |
| 28.3.a, g and 28.4 | • Permitting Processors to continue processing in certain situations without Controller authorization.<br>• Exempting Processors from deleting data held after terminating services with Controller.<br>• Specify rules for Subprocessors. |

*(continued)*

*(continued)*

**General Processing Opening Clauses**

| GDPR article and section | Opening clause content |
| --- | --- |
| 32.4 | Requiring certain individual employees to continue processing data despite being ordered to do otherwise by the Controller/Processor who employs them. |
| 35.10 | Controllers handling data in public interest are permitted to conduct a General Impact Assessment (GIA) in lieu of a DPIA under specific member law. |
| 36.5 | Requiring Controllers to regularly consult with, and receive authorization from, the SA when carrying out public interest processing. |
| 37.4 | Introducing further obligations for appointing a DPO. |
| 39.1.a, b | Introducing additional obligations and responsibilities on the DPO. |
| 49.1.d, g and 49.4 and 49.5 | Maintaining a register that provides information to the public regarding "recognized" international data transfers made in the public interest. Member States may also restrict international processing of special data for public interest reasons. |
| 58.1.f and 58.6 | On-site inspection procedures and granting additional powers to the SA in the jurisdiction. |
| 84.1 | Laying down additional rules on other penalties for infringement where it has not been specified under GDPR. |

**Specific processing opening clauses**

| GDPR article and section | Opening clause content |
| --- | --- |
| 85 | Reconciling freedom of expression and information with journalistic, academic, artistic, literary purposes. |
| 85.2 | Derogations to GDPR for key regulatory areas in the nation. |
| 88 | Employment law and personal data. |
| 89.2 and 89.3 | While the article itself lays down minimum standards for protecting personal data during processing for public interest, scientific historical, or statistical research purposes, Member States can provide for the derogations and limitations to user rights in those scenarios. |
| 90 | Allowing or exempting certain Controllers or Processors from the obligation of professional secrecy to protect them from disclosing information to the SA in investigations. |
| 95 | Special exemption of GDPR application to certain Controllers already subject to the E-Privacy Directive.[1] |

The opening clauses of GDPR serve an important purpose of harmonizing data protection across diverse legal traditions. The content of these opening clauses will be discussed in greater detail as this chapter proceeds.

## 9.2 Processing in the "Public Interest"

Throughout GDPR, a common exception to many of the rules provided are processing operations that are performed in "the public interest" or if the Controller is acting under "official authority" granted by the Member State. This is not a given exception for all requirements under GDPR but provides enough leeway for Member State entities to carry out functions without burdensome hurdles in their way.

### 9.2.1 What Is Public Interest?

Public interest is a term with an intensive legal background and varied definitions, often depending upon the context in which it is used. To understand the true meaning, nuances, and scope of the term, the ECJ has provided a series of rulings depending upon the right at stake and the law being challenged.[2] Let us examine several basic definitions of the concept.

Public policy is a narrow concept, invoked in the event of a genuine and sufficiently serious threat to the fundamental interests of society.[3] Public interest is loosely defined and is seen as the opposite to private or individual interests,[4] and deals with the collective public benefit even if it runs contrary to a combined group of individual interests.[5] Under EU law, public interest must be substantially and concretely defined[6] and involves any of the following:

1. Public security
2. Matters of defense and military affairs
3. International relations
4. The financial, currency, or economic policy of the community or of a member state

Throughout the regulation, one can notice varying levels of "public interest," requiring that it be "substantial,"[7] "important," or "necessary," all giving varying degrees of protection for the State. In fact, GDPR extends the four bases discussed above in Article 23, providing a broader ambit to create restrictions on the rights of the data subject.[8] In some portions of the regulation it is specified that the public interest claim be rooted in EU or Member State law. Defining this complex term is nearly impossible, as its meaning is contextual and subject to interpretive factors. For the purposes of this chapter, let us understand the term to be any activity that is done with the greater public benefit as the objective to be achieved.

For example, anticorruption initiatives in the public sector involve data sharing between authorities or require matching various data sets supplied by different agencies. The Indian National Governance Initiative conducted under the auspices of the Audit Commission is one such project. The initiative relies on statutory mandate to require bodies under audit to provide sets of data. The data requested can be broad and can cover information like personnel, benefits, and licensing, which are then analyzed to identify possible cases of fraud.

### 9.2.2 Public Interest as a "Legal Basis" for Processing

At the outset, note that processing which is necessary for the performance of a task in public interest or under the exercise of official authority, creates a legal basis for processing under GDPR.[9] Furthermore, a Controller's (or a third party's) legitimate interests when working in public interest can override the fundamental rights and freedoms of a data subject that require the protection of personal data.[10] This is the first critical exception under GDPR, which gives States a fair amount of autonomy in processing personal data for the purposes of their own projects.

**Illustration:** A governmental agency that provides healthcare seeks to initiate a new program that creates a unified database with all information on hospitals, doctors, clinics, patients, insurance providers, and pharmaceuticals. The program is called "Homeostasis" and is developed in partnership with a healthcare data analytics company, Healthee Data LLC, who will be the designated Controller and Processor for the operation by way of a legislative resolution. The Homeostasis project will require all healthcare providers and patients (discussed above) to submit their files maintained on patients and upload them to the database. Once the data has been fully uploaded, there is no option of rectification, erasure, or portability without the authorization of the patient's designated doctor.

- Though no consent or permission is received for the processing, Homeostasis is a lawful operation, and Healthee Data LLC has the authority to process the data.
- Despite the restriction on the rights of rectification, erasure, and portability, the legitimate interests will prevail since the processing is necessary for a task in public interest.

### 9.2.3 State Use of "Special" Data

As discussed in Chapter 5,[11] special categories of data are those which reveal sensitive information or involve biometric and genetic data.[12] GDPR places a *de facto* prohibition on processing such data unless the activity is based on one of the exceptions under Article 9.2. Governmental bodies can claim several of the exceptions carved out expressly for their use under GDPR.

Processing special data is permitted for reasons of substantial public interest based on Union or Member law, and must be done in a way that:[13]

- Is proportionate to the aims pursued
- Respects the essence of the right to data protection
- With specific safeguards to protect the fundamental rights and interests of the data subject

Like normal processing of personal data, processing for public interest creates its own legal basis for the activity. However, simply by comparing the two bases discussed above, one can see that there are augmented requirements for processing personal data. First, the public interest claimed must be substantial and must be rooted in law. Second, unlike normal processing of personal data, special data must be accompanied with safeguards, data protection, and proportionality. This is logical, as sensitive data needs to be protected suitably even by the State. If the processing of personal data is based on a statutory obligation, such a requirement must be conveyed to the data subject at the time of receiving the personal data.[14]

It remains unclear what respecting the "essence" of data protection entails. It is also unclear why that wording has been used. One could argue that it, in fact, reduces the responsibility of the Member State in setting up security measures for the data that is considered the most vulnerable. For example, if a state agency puts up the minimal amount of protection needed, which is not comprehensive, does it respect the essence of data protection? It can be argued that it does, as the provision only mandates a minimal protection.

Closely related to the substantial public interest exception is that of public health concerns, which includes preventing cross-border epidemics and ensuring "high standards" of quality and safety for healthcare, medical products, and devices. Like the preceding exception, the public health basis for processing must be rooted in EU or Member State law and must provide for suitable measures to safeguard the rights and freedoms of the users.[15] Thus, applying what has been discussed in our earlier illustration, we see that the legal basis claimed by Healthee Data to process the biometric data is strengthened by their authority to do so for the overarching public health concerns and prevention, in furtherance of a substantial public interest.

The last category of "public interest" processing of special data that is permitted by GDPR is that of archiving for scientific, historical, or statistical purposes. Archiving activities are usually performed in furtherance of public interest to build the population's knowledge and awareness on certain subjects. We shall be examining this exception in more detail later in this chapter.

### 9.2.4   Processing Relating to Criminal Record Data

GDPR provides for a state-sanctioned monopoly over the processing of personal data relating to the criminal history of the data subjects. Processing such information relating to convictions and offenses can only be performed under the control of an official authority, or by authorization provided by EU or Member law.[16]

This processing must be carried out with appropriate safeguards for the rights and freedoms of users. Additionally, this state monopoly over such "criminal record" data includes providing for related security measures based on the lawfulness of processing.[17] Any comprehensive register of such criminal record data must be kept only under the control of official authority.

Article 10 creates a state monopoly over criminal record data, and rightfully so, as this has long been a subject of government domain. Criminal law and process is often an area of exclusive state control, and the data produced from it should be no different, as such convictions are one of the most private things an individual may hold about themselves. With the advent and growth of private prison services the industry has recently observed more nonstate involvement in the process. However, GDPR requires that they also have the requisite legal authorization to process such data.

**Illustration:** Menlo Prison Solutions LLC is a private jail that operates in State X by way of a contract with the State's Department of Crime. Under the agreement, Menlo will be responsible for maintaining a comprehensive database of all convictions, offenses, behavior records, health, and all other data relating to the prisoners they hold. This database would be subject to a full web audit once every two years to ensure that it is done properly. Beyond that (or without a complaint filed in court) State X will leave Menlo to maintain its own database. The arrangement with Menlo violates GDPR because the authorization to process criminal record data was not provided by law, and because Menlo does not act under sufficient "control" by State X.

## 9.3   Public Interest and the Rights of a Data Subject

It is inevitable that the public interest will come into direct conflict with the digital rights that are provided to the data subject under GDPR.[18] Plainly, one can see that "public interest" will often trump the limited rights of the "individual." We shall examine the rights that have been restricted under the regulation in relation to public interest purposes.

### 9.3.1   Erasure and Restriction of Data Processing

This data subject has a right to have all personal data relating to him erased from the services of the Controller for a numerous reasons spanning from unlawfulness of processing to a lack of consent given.[19] As discussed in Chapter 6, there are several exceptions that a Controller may claim when refusing a request for erasure, and for our purposes there are four specific grounds that a state entity may claim:[20]

1. Compliance with a legal obligation under EU or Member law to which the Controller is subject
2. Performance of a task carried out in the public interest or in exercise of official authority
3. For reasons of public health, which we discussed earlier
4. For archiving purposes

These exceptions are a near-verbatim reproduction of the "legal basis" for processing, which has been discussed earlier.[21] This combined reading of the lawfulness with the limitation on erasure demonstrates GDPR's priorities when balancing public and private interests. Even a right of restriction on processing is subject to the public interest exception.[22] Consequently, we can surmise that these rights are in no way absolute unlike other human rights such as the right against slavery or the right to due process of the law before punishment.[23]

## 9.3.2 Data Portability

Public interest can also be used to restrict the user's right to data portability in a machine-readable format.[24] Data portability is a unique right that exists when processing is based on consent or is necessary for the performance of a contract. However, it should not apply where the processing is based on any other ground outside of the two discussed earlier.[25] In fact, the drafters specifically point out its inapplicability of data portability to public interest processing by stating:

> By its very nature, that right should not be exercised against Controllers processing personal data in the exercise of their public duties. It should therefore not apply where the processing of the personal data is necessary for compliance with a legal obligation to which the Controller is subject or for the performance of a task carried out in the public interest or in the exercise of an official authority vested in the Controller.[26]

This unambiguous wording in the regulation shows that, unlike erasure or restriction, data portability as a right does not exist for any processing done by the State in furtherance of public interest. In fact, GDPR specifies that in an event of a conflict between erasure and portability rights being exercised, erasure should prevail.[27]

### 9.3.3 Right to Object

Unlike the previous two categories of rights discussed, which provide for exceptions in the public interest, the right to object goes in the opposite direction and creates a direct inclusion for public interest projects. In situations where the processing of personal data is carried out under official authority or for public interest purposes, the data subject shall have a right to object to the processing of his personal data based on his situation.[28]

This shows that the right to object would still exist and can be claimed even when the processing is done for a public interest and not on consent alone. Contrast this with erasure, which provides for limitations on the right, or with portability, which outright excludes the right from being exercised altogether in cases of state processing. However, the mere fact that there is an inclusion of the right to object to public interest–based processing does not mandate that the objection be effectively exercised in each circumstance. This dichotomy is observed when the right to object extends to objecting to archiving activities for historical, scientific, or statistical purposes, unless such archiving is done in the public interest.[29] Thus, while a data subject can invoke the right to object, it is not absolute.

### 9.3.4 Right to Explanation

While objecting to the processing in the name of public interest is expressly allowed, the right of explanation of automated decision making shall not apply if the decision is authorized by EU or Member law that provides for suitable safeguards for the data subjects.[30] This plots a different course from its sister provision, "objection," and veers toward the side of express exclusion which data portability follows.

This creates an interesting loophole, in which the State, by way of legislation, can mandate that certain legal or significant decisions be made solely by AI. If the law requires such processing, the user will not be able to receive a meaningful explanation of the logic involved from the Controller unless the law permits such a right. GDPR drafters expect that any further law made on this topic shall provide for "suitable safeguards" but do not actually specify what those must be.

If the EU/Member law that authorizes the automated decision making does not include any leeway for explanation, the data subjects might be left with their hands tied behind their backs, thus rendering this right meaningless. As a result, the most likely alternative available to the data subject would be to challenge the law altogether in the CJEU[31] to ensure that the right remains in place even though it is a public interest project with a legally authorized AI making decisions. See Figure 9.1.

| The right | Applicability in public interest processing |
|---|---|
| Access | Data subject must be informed if processing is based on public interest, and if giving the data is mandatory. |
| Rectification | No change in applicability or scope. |
| Erasure | The enforcement of the right may be refused if it interferes with public interest. |
| Restriction | The enforcement of the right may be refused if it interferes with public interest. |
| Portability | Inapplicable when processing is based on public interest. |
| Objection | The right shall continue especially for public interest projects. |
| Explanation | EU or Member law may make this right inapplicable so long as suitable safeguards are provided. |

**Figure 9.1** Treatment of Data Subjects' Rights in Processing Carried Out under Official Authority

## 9.4 Organizational Exemptions and Responsibilities

In GDPR framework, the "public interest" rule runs far beyond the confines of processing and the accompanying rights. It also includes certain organizational exemptions and specific responsibilities imposed on the State when processing personal data for the greater good. For simplicity, we discuss them briefly below. For an in-depth examination of each of these individual concepts and responsibilities, please see the respective chapters in this book.

### 9.4.1 Representatives for Controllers Not within the EU

Foreign public authorities or bodies who process personal data within the EU are exempt from establishing a representative within the territory.[32] This separates processing activities by any foreign state with that of processing by foreign Controllers, who must do so. This is probably because any data dispute that arises will likely have to be resolved by diplomacy and international law.

### 9.4.2 General Impact Assessments in Lieu of a Data Protection Impact Assessment (DPIA)

Under GDPR, a DPIA is required when the processing would involve:[33]

- Systematic and intensive evaluation of subject's personal aspects derived using AI, including profiling that can produce a legal or significant effect on them

- Large-scale processing of special data or data relating to criminal convictions
- Systematic monitoring of a publicly accessible area on a large scale

The above-mentioned activities are almost always conducted by a State in one form or another. Some of these activities (such as processing criminal records) will solely be in their domain. GDPR is aware of this fact and provides that where the processing is legally based on EU or Member Law and involves one of the above activities, then the State may conduct a General Impact Assessment that includes a DPIA in lieu of a separate DPIA. This is, of course, subject to a more specific Member law requirement, as is the decision as to whether projects relating to public interest, health, and social protection must undergo the prior consultation procedure with the SA.[34]

### 9.4.3 Designation of a Data Protection Office (DPO)

Processing carried out by a public authority or body must designate a DPO to oversee their operations.[35] Additionally, whenever the processing involves a large-scale systematic monitoring of individuals[36] or involves large-scale processing of special data or criminal records,[37] it would also require a DPO. This requirement does not apply to courts acting within their judicial capacity.[38] A similarity exists here between the requirement to designate a DPO and the requirement to conduct a DPIA. The relationship seems logical as the activities discussed often would require a specific officer to oversee its safety.

This requirement cements in place the involvement of a DPO in any public interest project as it is a legal necessity. Essentially, the DPO can be treated as a new type of public officer with a fixed office in a "governmental" capacity. The question then arises as to whether a DPO can be treated as a "public official" holding an office in the government overseeing any data projects, or whether the same responsibilities and liabilities are beyond his scope.

**China's Social Credit System, an all-encompassing illustration:** One of the most ambitious personal data collection projects by a government would be China's nascent Social Credit System initiative where citizens are assigned a score between 1 and 100 based on a range of factors like creditworthiness, social media use, purchases, fulfillment of contractual obligations, etc. The project involves mass surveillance of online behavior tracking, facial recognition software, citations issued, and criminal records. The data is processed through a centralized database, created with a private-public data analytics partnership that is controlled by the government itself. China's centralized processing clearinghouse and data-sharing platform will end up housing the data of more than a billion citizens from resources provided by the Central Bank, Governmental Agencies, and over 44 financial concerns.[39] Profiling algorithms and AI then utilize the data and assign each citizen a credit score based on five subcategories:

1. Social connections
2. Consumption behavior
3. Security
4. Wealth
5. Compliance

The key objectives of this initiative are to ensure governmental, judicial, societal, and commercial integrity. Essentially this creates a *reputation system* in our modern era with a long-term aim of creating a "law-abiding" society where the number of points citizens earn directly correlates to the quality of life they live for things ranging from education to travel and governmental jobs. Every aspect of this system that China seeks to implement[40] encompasses all the above requirements to conduct a DPIA[41] and to designate a specialized DPO for the project.[42]

Any project of similar magnitude by a government subject to GDPR must consider the augmented requirements placed on them to insure special care of the personal data of their citizens. Furthermore, any centralized state processing operation will contain a massive amount of all kinds of data and must provide the strongest form of data security. Obviously, any big data project will have to consider the economic, financial, and social impacts when drawing up their plans in the context of their data protection measures and not merely be decompartmentalized. *Datafication projects* must join the citizen's data with their personal identity and not a merely link to it.

### 9.4.4  Monitoring of Approved Codes of Conduct

Processing carried out by public authorities and bodies is not required to maintain a monitoring body to oversee compliance with approved codes of conduct.[43] The practice of approved codes of conduct itself is not mandatory under GDPR unless mandated by a law or a delegated legislation.[44]

### 9.4.5  Third-Country Transfers

A transfer of personal data to a third country in the absence of an adequacy decision[45] or appropriate safeguards[46] is allowed if the transfer is necessary for important reasons of public interest.[47] This same authority exists to limit the transfer of specific categories of data to foreign countries,[48] by way of EU or Member law in absence of an adequacy decision by the European Data Protection Board. This is a large power, which is given to States to authorize and limit transfers to other countries who do not meet the standards of GDPR. For this reason, the regulation uses stringent language emphasizing the necessity and importance of the greater public interest, which must be recognized by EU or Member law.[49]

Furthermore, the EU or Member State law can maintain a register of authorized foreign data transfers that are maintained to provide information to the public. This list will be open to consultation, either with the public or with a person who has demonstrated a legitimate interest, but only to the extent that the specific law requires;[50] for example, a transfer of data between two tax authorities or even a transfer of health information for matters of public well-being.[51]

GDPR gives States considerable freedom in determining foreign transfers of data. In fact, many provisions relating to such transfers are inapplicable to public authorities exercising their official powers.[52] They are listed below briefly:

- In the absence of an adequacy decision or appropriate safeguards, the data subject's explicit consent is required for the transfer to be valid.[53]
- In absence of an adequacy decision or appropriate safeguards, the transfer will be valid if it is necessary for performance of a contract or to implement precontractual measures.[54]
- In absence of an adequacy decision or appropriate safeguards, the transfer will be valid if it is necessary to conclude a contract between Controller and another person or entity.[55]
- The balancing test helps the Controller and the authorities to determine whether a transfer made in absence of an adequacy decision or safeguards would be valid. This test gives a series of factors that must be borne in mind when the Controller decides to make a transfer of personal data to a foreign country and would help the authorities determine if the transfer is legal.[56]

All the above provisions are inapplicable to a public authority transferring personal data to a foreign country in exercise of their official powers. Some are understandable exceptions, although it is unclear why the State agencies would be exempt from the balancing test, which contains a reasonable number of factors that should be borne in mind that protect the interests of the data subject.[57] The exceptions and powers looked at cumulatively in this section alone shows the true extent of the States' authority to determine foreign-country transfers of its citizens' data. Essentially, the public authorities are afforded true freedom from being subject to cumbersome provisions relating to third-country transfers under GDPR. See Figure 9.2.

| 1. | Public interest |
| 2. | Data subjects' rights |
| 3. | Compliance |
| 4. | Commercial interests of Controller |

**Figure 9.2** Hierarchy of GDPR Objectives

## 9.5 Public Documents and Data

GDPR mandates that a public authority that carries out processing in the public interest may disclose those documents in accordance with EU or Member law.[58] This obligation may be extended to a private authority carrying out a public function as well. This objective of publishing official documents must be exercised in a way that reconciles the public's access to official documents and their right to data protection under GDPR.

This provision of GDPR is aspirational, but not mandatory. Perhaps it can be considered as a countermeasure to the governmental practice around the world that shrouds itself in secrecy. Scandals like Wikileaks have revealed how much can be concealed from the public with regard to the work their government does. On the opposite side of the coin, revelations like the NSA-Prism incident show us how much our government knows about our lives. Reconciliation of official secrecy laws and freedom of speech and information has been a timeless tug of war. For this objective of GDPR to be achieved, a strong responsible government at the Member State level is necessary.

### 9.5.1 The Network and Information Systems Directive

The "NIS" Directive[59] was adopted by the EU in July 2016 in recognition of the Union's mutually dependent welfare on technology backbones in our society such as communications and energy. In 2018, our daily supply of information, transportation, energy, and contact with one another is hinged on a constant ecosystem of data and internet access. The EU in recognizing this has adopted a *risk-based approach* toward the network security and availability of certain service providers.[60] The applicability of the NIS Directive is limited to *two* categories of services:

1. **Operators of essential services:**[61] As discussed above, the NIS mandates a high level of network security for certain critical societal and economic activities where any breach would have a significant disruptive effect on the population. This would include:
   a. Energy
   b. Transportation
   c. Banking
   d. Financial market infrastructures
   e. Health infrastructure
   f. Water
   g. Digital infrastructure
2. **Digital service providers:**[62] If "essential services" are the resources for society, digital service providers are the proverbial "roadways" for those resources to reach us. This would include the providers of digital marketplaces, search

engines, and cloud computing services. This is understandable, as a single security breach with a service such as Amazon would result in endless loss both for society and the company itself.

The NIS can be considered as a cohesive counterpart to GDPR placing similar yet heightened requirements on these services providers. With GDPR in place now, businesses will unlikely undergo major changes in relation to their more stringent requirements as they stand at present.

### 9.5.2 Telemedia Data Protection

The most common device used to produce, collect, and store personal data is a mobile phone tucked away in a person's pocket. Telecommunication (Telecom) providers operate the data channels by offering communication through airwaves and wireless connectivity on the internet. Through messaging, instant messaging, apps, network, and internet-based phone calls, these entities hold private conversations between individuals and operate in a highly regulated industry. Considering the diversified nature of data processing across several airwaves, it is appropriate to classify these companies as telecom-media (telemedia) companies.

Telemedia Controllers are required to maintain the confidentiality of communications between individuals[63] free from unwanted intrusion and monitoring. The EU the e-privacy Directive[64] controls the personal data obligations of telemedia Controllers, requiring them not to use or store personal communications without consent.[65] GDPR Article 96 requires that additional obligations not be imposed on telemedia Controllers subject to the e-privacy directive. This treats the e-privacy directive as the *lex specialis* over communication data and gives it precedence over GDPR. As an e-privacy "directive," the law has been implemented domestically by Member State transformative acts. This is likely because Member States prefer to maintain data sovereignty over the communications within their borders, with requirements suited to their criminal/civil subpoena procedures.

Implementing the e-privacy directive by national legislation has been incredibly difficult and has led to inconsistencies in its applications. For example, German law incorporates the e-privacy directive by two legislative acts, the TKG, which regulates personal data protection in telecom, and the TMG, which regulates telemedia and ISP services. The complexities of these two regulations surpass GDPR and likely supersede it.[66] But which law prevails in the event of a conflict? GDPR is silent on this issue.

The e-privacy directive applies to personal data processing in connection to providing publicly available electronic communication services in public networks.[67] From this, two terms are important to explore:

1. **Public networks:** To qualify as "public" the network must service an indefinite number of individuals. For example, landlines, IP networks, mobile networks, etc. Juxtapose a "public network" with a publicly accessible network,

which can be accessed to the public under limited circumstances (example: a hotel or café Wi-Fi). Publicly accessible networks are not governed by the e-privacy directive.

2. **Public electronic communication services:** Communication must be the primary purpose of the service to fall under the e-privacy directive. This is where a business is dependent on providing channels for communication like e-mail, telephone, and messaging services. The business must transmit the signals or airwaves needed for the communication to take place. If communication is secondary or tangential, it is outside the e-privacy directive.

   **Illustration 1:** A news company has a booming online journalism following among users. They provide chat rooms and comment boxes for their users to discuss articles and pressing issues facing the country. The communication services provided here are secondary because the primary purpose of the business is journalism

   **Illustration 2:** Sky Conf Inc. provides state-of-the-art webcam conference technology, along with "secure" networks for long-distance business between companies. As their primary purpose is providing a channel for transmitting communications, they are subject to the e-privacy directive.

The nuanced and complex nature of internet communications requires greater clarification on how the e-privacy directive can be reconciled with GDPR. The scope of terms discussed above should be greater defined so that telemedia Controllers know which obligation should have precedence. Already we are seeing practical examples of this ambiguity being used by Controllers such as Facebook, Google, and other social networking sites that provide communication services but claim that this is secondary to their purpose of providing a platform for advertisers, businesses, and individuals.

GDPR does not discriminate which Controllers are subject to it, as the regulation applies to any entity processing personal data regardless of the service they provide or the nature of data they hold.[68] This overlap and eventual conflict in the two frameworks (three if one considers transformative State legislations) has been recognized by EU legislators as well, who have called for the e-privacy directive to be reworked.[69] On January 10, 2017, a proposal was submitted to create an e-privacy regulation for the EU to remedy the fragmentation of telemedia data protection obligations. At present EU legislators are debating the terms of the incoming regulation and how it will fit into the new GDPR regime.[70] Creating a binding EU regulation for telemedia Controllers will help streamline and clarify what obligations they must follow to protect their consumer's personal data.

### 9.5.3 National Identification Numbers

The Member States also have the discretion to create "National Identification Number" schemes for their citizens or any other general identifiers[71] that they may deem fit for their general application. GDPR only requires that appropriate safeguards be implemented to protect the rights and freedoms of the data subject.

Whether governments can be trusted to implement appropriate safeguards remains to be seen, as a lack of care spells disaster for the project. Consider for example India's Unique Identification Aadhar Card system (UID System), which relies on a centralized database of biometric and personal data on its citizens. In 2017 they faced big data breaches, which resulted in a loss of sensitive data for millions of citizens, leading to many concerns on the project and the safety of the information itself. Like China's Social Credit System, the UID is one of the largest biometric data collection projects in history and links personal, financial, residential, biometric, and legal information into one identification number. However, unlike China, the UID system has already faced countless court challenges in its implementation leading to monumental Supreme Court judgments in India on the privacy rights of individuals.[72]

GDPR operates on the assumption that its Member States all operate competently on any similar projects. The logistical and administrative hassles that second and third world countries face are a considerable hurdle to a global implementation of the regulation. This is perhaps why the EU mandates that their Member State governments all act in line with the regulation with certain indispensable requirements such as data protection[73] or the scope of their derogating legislations passed.[74]

## 9.6 Archiving

In the larger scheme of mankind, recording history is a necessity to ensure forward momentum of future generations. In the digital age, an insurmountable amount of data is produced, adding to the endless volumes and records of data that already exist. The importance of consistent archiving is recognized by GDPR and afforded special protection throughout the regulation. Archiving encompasses the processing of personal data for purposes relating to:[75]

1. Public interest
2. Scientific or historical research
3. Statistical purposes

These activities are independent of one another, and therefore may not be subject to exclusive State control. Any archiving is subject to appropriate safeguards mandated by GDPR to protect the data subject's rights.[76] Those safeguards include:

- Technical and organizational methods such as data minimization.
- Encryption or pseudonymization measures. When further processing must be done of the data, but does not require identification of the data subject, use of anonymization would be preferred.

Discussed throughout this book and GDPR is the archiving exception that may be imposed by EU or Member law allowing derogation of the rights of the data subject where the rights would likely render impossible or seriously impair the achievement of the specific purpose.[77] This exception exists for all archiving activities, but the scope is broader for public interest processing, which permits derogation of more rights of the data subject.[78] However, any derogation to data subjects' rights must be provided the appropriate protection as provided for under GDPR.[79]

## 9.7 Handling Government Subpoenas

The first and foremost thing to do if your Controller/Processor entity receives a government order is to refer it to counsel before acting on it. In certain jurisdictions compliance with such requests is strict, while in others it can be objected to in a court. Notwithstanding, any communication with the State will bring in larger legal implications, so it is prudent to involve attorneys at the outset.

The complexities arise when a company is based in multiple countries and faces a conflict of laws when complying with such orders. Many companies have been caught in legal entanglements where complying with one subpoena would likely result in violating privacy obligations in another country. In such cases, it's important to weigh the consequences of breaching one or the other. A prominent example of this would be the case where US tax authorities "strong-armed" a Swiss bank to break its secrecy laws to answer their request for documents (in the form of data).

## 9.8 Public Interest Restrictions on GDPR

As discussed in detail in Chapter 6, states are afforded a wide discretion to restrict the rights of the data subjects and the principles of processing by way of law for a breadth of purposes.[80] These restrictions must be a necessary and proportionate measure in a democratic society that respects the essence of fundamental rights. The basis of these restrictions is briefly listed below:

1. National security
2. Defense
3. Public security
4. The prevention, investigation, detection, or prosecution of criminal offences
5. The execution of criminal penalties, including safeguarding and preventing threats to public security
6. Other important objectives of public interest of the EU/Member State. This includes economic and financial interests, with matters relating to:
   a. Monetary interests
   b. Budgetary interests
   c. Taxation

    d. Public health; and

    e. Social security.

7. The prevention, investigation, detection, and prosecution of breaches relating to professions regulated by ethics

8. The monitoring, inspection, or regulatory function connected, even occasionally to the exercise of authority for the restrictions discussed above

9. The protection of judicial independence and proceedings

10. The protection of the user and the rights of others

11. The enforcement of civil law claims

    The exhaustive list above is accompanied with drafting guidelines[81] and is the final safety blanket needed by States to carry out their activities. All the exceptions and responsibilities above are the benefits that are provided to public authorities under GDPR, while the restrictions can be considered as the tools. When reading the regulation, one can surmise that the Controller and Processor bear the main responsibility for ensuring compliance, followed by the SA, and finally the delegated legislations itself. However, not many measures are put in place for the accountability and responsibility of the public authorities. GDPR places a large amount of faith in its Member States to operate correctly within the bounds of the regulation and gives the public agency the freedom to push forward and develop the law and practice of data processing as they deem fit. This leaves in place a system where the strength of GDPR hangs on how well governments enforce it. But this may leave a large window for abuse to those less-than-honest governments that could easily use the many legal resources available to them to make a quick profit.

## 9.9 Processing and Freedom of Information and Expression

GDPR is primarily a law that protects personal data in a digital age by giving people rights attached to the data they provide. The rights enumerated by the regulation are all rooted in the larger concept of the right to privacy. This right to privacy is often in direct conflict with the freedom of speech and expression and the right to information. These three rights are all fundamental to a democratic society but cannot co-exist together in complete harmony, and balancing those interests has been a struggle in every country on earth throughout history.

### 9.9.1 Journalism and Expression under GDPR

Though GDPR is a privacy regulation, it mandates that Member States draft laws that reconcile the protection of personal data with the freedom of expression and information.[82] This includes processing for:

- Journalism
- Academic expression

- Artistic expression
- Literary expression[83]

When discussing the forms of expression discussed above, one can reasonably assume that it will include accommodations for content control, fact-checking,[84] IP, data sharing, etc. Keeping in mind the need for those measures, the Member States are permitted to provide exemptions or derogations from provisions of GDPR relating to:

- The principles of processing: Chapter II
- The Rights of the data subject: Chapter III
- Controller and Processors: Chapter IV
- Third-country transfers: Chapter V
- Supervisory authorities: Chapter VI
- Cooperation and consistency: Chapter VII
- Specific data-processing situations: Chapter IX

GDPR gives a broad ambit to the Member States to change the law regarding the processing of journalistic and expression-based data. The authority to make exemptions or derogations is far reaching, covering all aspects of GDPR except the provisions relating to:

- The general applicability and objectives: Chapter I
- Remedies, liabilities, and penalties: Chapter VIII
- Delegated acts and implementing acts: Chapter X

If one looks at the regulation, the accommodations made for journalistic and artistic expression are broader than those made for national security and other purposes.[85] To ensure the free flow and sharing of information, Member States can derogate from GDPR liberally and across the board. While national security and public health matters can only derogate the rights of the data subject, journalism and artistic expression can be fluidly adjusted into GDPR. This is understandable considering that incorporating rules regarding copyright and journalistic freedoms and ethics would involve a change in many aspects of the regulation and not the data subject's rights alone.

### 9.9.2 Combating "Fake News" in the Modern Age

One of the larger considerations of this provision of GDPR is the leeway Controllers will require to manage the content on their platforms. An unregulated amount of "free speech" has led to a proliferation of false news and effective mediums to carry the information across making it the "subjective truth" to the masses. Facebook's founder recently testified before EU regulators stating that their organizations would work closely with governments during elections to control disinformation. Facebook is also working with third-party fact checkers to verify and rate news content on their website.

Other states have adopted a more proactive approach, such as the government of India, which seeks to create a Social Media Hub that will regulate, oversee, and collect information on data produced in social networking sites in the country. The government cites this as a measure for a "free and open internet" and to take a pulse on national sentiment. Additionally, the project combats "fake news" from such websites. Though the objectives seem pure for the project, it has already raised several privacy concerns resulting in legal action already being initiated against the Ministry of Information and Broadcasting.[86]

Regardless of how false news is combated, it is apparent that it is a practical problem that goes beyond a small segment of the population. This has led to blurring of what qualifies as facts and what can be considered as the verifiable truth. A system needs to be put in place that can solve the following issues:

- What is a fact?
- How is a fact verified?
- Who can determine the credibility of the news story?
- What can be considered as dispositive proof of that credibility?
- Who gets the final say on whether something is an established fact?
- How should the individuals creating and knowingly sharing false news be punished?
- What is an effective way of communicating falsity to the public?
- Is a Controller legally a "publisher" or merely a "platform" for other publishers to share content?
- When should a Controller be held liable for the content on their website?

The above questions are simple in theory but have proven to be a problem in practice. Dispute over the answers of these basic questions is what prevents a democracy from being well informed and focused on the issues. If governmental bodies are left as the sole verifiers of what qualifies as a fact, only a thin line will separate a democratic and totalitarian flow of information. Whether it is by law or corporate codes of conduct, a system to maintain journalistic credibility must be established to fix the problems in the long term with mechanisms for verification and accountability.

## 9.10  State Use of Encrypted Data

In Chapter 4 on data security and breaches (Sections 4.7–4.9), we discussed how encryption and data anonymization practices are an absolute must in processing data under GDPR. Data encryption is something that is instrumental to our daily lives without our knowledge. Almost all the data we frequently create and share is encrypted for our privacy. Even essential services conducted by companies and public authorities rely on some form of encryption to protect the data from cyber criminals and terrorists. But with every boon, there is a bane.

Encryption is a tool to protect personal data and to conceal criminal activities. A well-known instance of this is the recent controversy where the US government wanted Apple to create a *master key* or a "backdoor" to the encryption placed on their iPhones so that law enforcement might access the files of a deceased terrorist. This led to widespread debate as to whether a master key should really exist and placed into the hands of the government. Regardless of Apple's protests and refusals to comply, the US Government had found a way to break the encryption mechanism.

The EU follows a different approach to master keys. An Article 29 Working Party (WP29) has recently noted that master keys are a larger threat to society than they would be a benefit.[87] This is primarily because the safety of a master key is not impenetrable. Even service providers and manufactures agree with this view,[88] with companies such as Apple unable to create such a key without keeping the vulnerabilities and abuse by authorities at bay. The WP29 takes the position that this danger of abuse and the potential downfalls on society at large will make the invention of such a master key redundant as it will cause the very harm that it seeks to prevent.

However, this would not necessarily entail that law enforcement would be powerless in such cases. The law enforcement agencies of Member States are entitled to use other legal mechanisms when authorized to access data that is otherwise encrypted, including:[89]

1. Access communications metadata and unencrypted data held by Controllers.
2. Social engineering to infiltrate criminal organizations.
3. Require alleged criminals and persons of interest to provide their encryption key.
4. Targeted interception tools such as IMSI catchers and electronic communications interception through network providers.
5. Specific and targeted tools to guess or intercept passwords, documents, and keystrokes before or after encryption on the suspect's device.
6. Obtain individual encryption keys held by Controllers or key escrow services.

GDPR therefore, by way of WP29, is of the stance that the Member State cannot create a master key for encryption and prefers the methods discussed above as far more secure and appropriate to tackle cybercrime and terrorism. This is in line with the more cautious approach to data security that is promoted in the EU throughout GDPR.

## 9.11 Employee Data Protection

As recognized earlier in this chapter, the opening clauses under GDPR permit Member States to exercise their legislative competence over some specific processing situations such as employment.[90] For many businesses, the only data processing conducted is relating to that of their employees, which is regulated by national law. Multinational companies often conclude their employment contracts domestically with employees, subjecting them to the overall employment law of the nation, which can include requirements on protecting their data.

This leaves several national peculiarities to employee data protection, requiring employers to keep track of data-protection standards by maintaining a central HR administration or regional/national HR databases. In some Member States, employee data protection is detailed and requires the involvement of mandatory co-determination bodies for representing employees. These co-determination bodies are mechanisms for employees to exercise control and interests over their personal data.

### 9.11.1  The Opening Clause

GDPR allows Member States to provide specific data protection rules in the field of employment under the framework of their domestic labor laws.[91] The delegated legislation may be adopted for the following purposes:

1. Recruitment
2. Performance of employment contract, law, or collective bargaining agreement
3. Management, organization, and planning work
4. Increasing diversity and equality within the business
5. Work health and safety
6. Protection of employer/consumer property
7. Exercise or enjoyment of employment rights and benefits by individual or collective employees
8. Termination and retirement of employment

The items listed above are nonexhaustive, with Member States given the discretion to make further rules on processing personal data based on employee consent.[92] In the employer-employee relationship, personal data is used to document and track workers and facilitate daily workflows. Negotiating these terms under most circumstances puts the employee at a disadvantage because the employer holds the stronger bargaining position.

**Illustration:** Paul receives a job offer to be a junior associate in a prestigious law firm Wayne Carlson. He is provided a generous offer from the firm's name partner and hiring commission consisting of two senior partners. At the time of discussing terms of employment, the partners inform him that all his key strokes and computer use while in the law firm will be tracked to ensure that hourly billing is proper. This is part of a firmwide policy that seeks to minimize excessive client billing. Paul realistically has no choice in denying these terms if he wishes to work with the firm.

Member State law on employment data must conform to certain minimum requirements under GDPR.[93] The law must provide for:

- Suitable and specific measures to safeguard the data subject's human dignity, legitimate interests, and fundamental rights
- Transparency in processing
- Intragroup data transfers
- Work surveillance and monitoring

### 9.11.2 Employment Agreements

From the above parameters, we can see that GDPR leaves reasonable space for domestic legislations. The minimum requirements of the regulation will be implemented through company policy (as part of compliance) and employment agreements. There are two main *bargaining mechanisms* that are used to impose data processing terms on employees:

1. **Employment contracts:** Individual agreements that cover the terms of employment concluded either through negotiation or as a standard offer based on the company's practice. Some provisions in these agreements may be mandatory under domestic law, such as minimum wage, paid leave, etc.

   **Illustration:** Law firm Wayne Carlson (discussed in the previous illustration) extends an offer to Paul to be a junior associate. Under national law, they must pay him minimum of €30,000 yearly along with two weeks' paid leave. The firm makes it clear that other aspects of the agreement are "industry-standard" for junior associates (hours, billing practices, drug-testing, medical insurance, etc.). This is a standard employment contract.

   Extend the illustration and consider an offer to an incoming partner to the firm, Dominic. Dominic brings a large client list, reputation, and money into the firm. Dominic will likely have the luxury of negotiating his contract with the firm. In both illustrations the junior associate and partner will be likely agreeing to Wayne Carlson's data protection policies as it only coincides with the job requirements.

2. **Collective bargaining agreements (CBAs):** For unionized workers, individual contract negotiation is rare. Trade Unions and Employers Associations negotiate terms collectively for the members they represent. The CBA covers all important aspects of the work such as remuneration, hours, vacation leave, work conditions, injury compensation, etc. The manner of negotiation and essential terms of the CBA are provided for in domestic labor law.

Data protection will legally flow downward in implementation, starting with GDPR opening clauses into Member State law acting through the SA who oversees compliance by companies in their policies and employment agreements. Employees assert their rights through *works councils* and *co-determination bodies* within the EU

Member States. Though data protection policies may not be expressly included in every contract, the law will require that businesses respect GDPR principles.

### 9.11.3  The German *Betriebsrat*

German data protection law is considered as the gold standard holding strict requirements for processing. The *Betriebsrat* or Works Council is an employee representative body, which must be established by organizations with a minimum of five employees. The Works Council plays an instrumental role in protecting employee data from misuse by employers and third parties under German law. The council ensures that employers have properly implemented laws, regulations, safety regulations, work agreements, and CBAs for the benefit of its representatives[94] including GDPR mandates.

The participation rights of the Council permit it to oversee GDPR compliance giving comprehensive information rights regarding:

- New IT systems or revised programs
- Involvement of a Processor in employee data management
- Introduction of a centralized HR processing for the corporate group[95]

The co-determination rights of the council allow them to voice their objections to forms of work-place surveillance of employees.[96] This includes the introduction of technology designed to monitor the conduct or performance of an employee. The objections can cover the IT systems and protection measures placed on collecting and storing the data. Additionally, the council must consent to any reworking of the existing IT systems used to monitor employees. Codetermination rights relate to the technical aspects of processing and not the legal basis itself. However, involvement is a must, and employers should consult with the council at the earliest stage to obtain consent. In cases where there is no agreement, the issue must be resolved using the Conciliation Board mechanism under German law.

German participation rights are limited to receiving information, with no decisional or enforcement authority over the objections made by the council. The employers are not bound to accept council recommendations, and plans can proceed forward, notwithstanding the objections if the employer decides to do so. On the other hand, participation rights require consent from the Works Council, and violating the right entitles the employees to an injunction. If granted, employers must reverse their previous actions and remove any measures taken as part of the monitoring program.

**Illustration:** Trucker Ltd. is a registered trucking company in Germany with over 500 employees. They have an established Works Council representing their 400 truckers who have unionized to collectively represent their interests. Up until 2018, the company monitored the truck deliveries by synching to their standard-issue GPS systems in the vehicle. The movements of "on-the-clock" truckers were logged and tracked "real-time" with the help of the company's technology wing. The Works Council had full access to these systems and information of how it works as part of their participation rights. The council also regularly informs the union of any changes in the system to get their timely objections.

In November 2018, Trucker Ltd. announced it would be implementing AI into its trucks' systems to ensure that drivers are rested and running on schedule. This involved installing webcams, which activate when drivers exceed their hours of work, and using self-stopping safety features that track retina and motor movements to prevent crashes. The system activates when a trucker logs in to start the vehicle. Trucker Ltd. allowed the council to review the new IT systems but ignored all their objections. The Works Council approaches a court for an injunction over the new monitoring systems. A court is likely to grant the injunction, requiring the company to halt all surveillance until a solution is arrived at by a Conciliation Board.

### 9.11.4   The French "Comité d'enterprise"

Like German law, France requires an entity of more than 50 employees to establish a Works Council or *Comité d'enterprise*, presided over by an employer representative, consisting of employee representatives.[97] Organizations of the same size must also establish a Health and Safety Committee (Comité d' hygiène, de sécurité et des conditions de travail) to oversee the physical and mental well-being of employees. Smaller organizations can create a Works Council if the CBA permits so. Businesses of 11 employees or more must organize elections for Employee Delegates (Délégués du personnel).

French law provides more authority to the council as opposed to its German counterpart to protect the social, economic, and professional interests of its members. French Works Councils are entitled to information and consultation rights regarding the introduction of any new technologies which will likely have consequences on the employees':

- Employment
- Working conditions
- Training
- Payment[98]

The aspects discussed above invariably implicate workplace surveillance technologies or other matters that affect the job itself. When changes in technology affect the overall working conditions of employees, the Health and Safety Committee must be consulted as well.[99] Like German law, the council can voice its objection, but the employer is not bound to follow their terms. However, once again, involving the council in the decision making is a must. Failure to do can result in injunctive relief and a reversal and removal of a previous "technological" decision made by a business. French law also criminally punishes employers for violating the Work Council's rights in the consultation process.[100] Violating the consultation obligation can also result in fines up to €10,000.00 being imposed on the business.[101] Therefore, the Work Council's decisions help to validate a processing decision made by an employer under French law.

## Notes

1 EU "e-privacy" Directive, 2002/58/EC.
2 See Alexander J. Belohlavek, *Public Policy and Pubic Interest in International Law and EU law,* Czech Yearbook of International Law paragraph 7.16 onwards.
3 ECJ Judgment of 14 March 2000, C-54/99, *Association Eglise de scientologie de Paris and Scientology International Reserves Trust v. The Prime Minister* [2000] ECR I-1335, Marg. (17).
4 ECJ decision of joined Cases T-109/05 and T-444/05 of 24 May 2011 (in matters of *Navigazione Libera del Golfo Srl. /formerly Navigazione Libera del Golfo SpA/ v. EU Commission*) (unpublished).
5 Vladimír Hyánek, *Problémy definování a prosazování veřejného zájmu (The Issues of Defining and Enforcing Public Interest)*, in SBORNÍK REFERÁTŮ Z TEORETICKÉHO SEMINÁŘE POŘÁDANÉHO KATEDROU VEŘEJNÉ EKONOMIE ESF MU V BRNĚ VE SPOLUPRÁCI S ASOCIACÍ VEŘEJNÉ EKONOMIE (Anthology of papers presented at the theory seminar organized by the Department of Public Economy of the Faculty of Economics and Administration at Masaryk University in Brno in cooperation with the Public Economy Association), Brno: Masaryk University 60 (I. Malý ed., 1999).
6 See, for instance, the following ECJ decisions: (·) ECJ Judgment of 1 July 2008, in joined cases C-39/05 and C-52/05, Sweden et *Maurizio Turco v. Council of the European Union* [2008] ECR I-4723, Marg. (49); (·) ECJ Judgment (General Court/First-instance court) of 11 March 2009, T-166/05, *Borax Europe Ltd. v. EC Commission.*
7 GDPR, Article 9.2.
8 Chapter 6, Section 6.9.
9 GDPR, Article 6.1.e.
10 GDPR, Article 6.1.f, *the provision.*
11 See Chapter 5, Section 5.2.4.
12 GDPR, Article 7.
13 GDPR, Article 9.2.g.
14 GDPR, Article 13.2.e.
15 GDPR, Article 9.2.i.
16 GDPR, Article 10.
17 GDPR, Article 10; *read with* Article 6.1.
18 GDPR, Chapter III.
19 GDPR, Article 17; Chapter 6, Section 6.5.3.
20 GDPR, Article 17.3.
21 Chapter 6, Section 6.5.6.
22 GDPR, Article 18.2: "Where processing has been restricted under paragraph 1, such personal data shall, with the exception of storage, only be processed with the data subject's consent or for the establishment, exercise or defence of legal claims or for the protection of the rights of another natural or legal person or for reasons of important public interest of the Union or of a Member State."

23 EU Convention on Human Rights, Articles 4.1 and 7 respectively: "The term 'absolute' mandates that the Rights are non-derogable and unqualified."

24 GDPR, Article 20.3.

25 GDPR, Recital 68.

26 GDPR, Recital 68.

27 GDPR, Article 20.3.

28 GDPR, Recital 69; Article 21.

29 GDPR, Article 21.6.

30 GDPR, Article 22.2.b.

31 GDPR, Recital 143; *TFEU,* Article 263.

32 GDPR, Article 27.2.b.

33 GDPR, Article 35.3.

34 GDPR, Article 36.5.

35 GDPR, Article 37.1.a.

36 GDPR, Article 37.1.b.

37 GDPR, Article 37.1.c.

38 GDPR, Article 37.1.a.

39 Alexander Mortensen, "The Chinese Social Credit System in the context of Datafication and Privacy," Medium.com, https://medium.com/@alexanderskyummortensen/the-chinese-social-credit-system-in-the-context-of-datafication-and-privacy-cafc9bb7923b.

40 Though implemented in phases in the Country as of now, China hopes to fully enact its Social Credit System by 2020.

41 GDPR, Article 35.

42 GDPR, Article 37.

43 GDPR, Article 41.6.

44 GDPR, Article 40.1.

45 GDPR, Article 45.3.

46 GDPR, Article 46.

47 GDPR, Article 49.1.d.

48 GDPR, Article 49.5.

49 GDPR, Article 49.4.

50 GDPR, Article 49.1.g.

51 GDPR, Recital 112.

52 GDPR, Article 49.3.

53 GDPR, Article 49.1.a.

54 GDPR, Article 49.1.b.

55 GDPR, Article 49.1.c.

56 GDPR, Article 49.1, second sub-paragraph provision.

57 GDPR, Article 49.1. second sub-paragraph provision.

58 GDPR, Article 86.

59 Network Information and Security Directive, (EU) 2016/1148.

60 Network Information and Security Directive, (EU) 2016/1148, Recitals 49, 57.

61 Network Information and Security Directive, (EU) 2016/1148, Article 5 and Annex II.

62  Network Information and Security Directive, (EU) 2016/1148, Article 4 and Annex III.

63  EU Charter of Fundamental Rights, Articles 7 and 8, read with EU "e-privacy" Directive, 2002/58/EC, Recital 3.

64  EU "e-privacy" Directive, 2002/58/EC.

65  EU "e-privacy" Directive, 2002/58/EC, Article 5.1.

66  GDPR, Article 95.

67  EU "e-privacy" Directive, 2002/58/EC, Article 3.1.

68  WP29, WP240 (2016), 4.

69  GDPR, Recital 173.

70  Natasha Lomas, "ePrivacy: An Overview of Europe's Other Big Privacy Rule Change," October 7, 2018, *TechCrunch*, https://techcrunch.com/2018/10/07/eprivacy-an-overview-of-europes-other-big-privacy-rule-change.

71  GDPR, Article 87.

72  *Justice KS Puttaswamy v. The Union of India,* Writ Petition (Civil) No 494 Of 2012; Reaffirming that Indians do have a Fundamental Right to Privacy under the Constitution, striking down other previous judgments of the court.

73  GDPR, Article 87.

74  GDPR, Article 23.

75  GDPR, Article 89.

76  Such as Data Protection by Design & Data Security.

77  GDPR, Article 89.2.

78  GDPR, Article 89.3 (which permits derogation for Articles 15, 16, 18, and 21) compared with 89.4 (which permits derogation for Articles 15, 16, 18, 19, 20, and 21).

79  GDPR, Article 89.1.

80  GDPR, Article 23.

81  GDPR, Article 23.2. For detailed information on these restrictions, see Chapter 6, Section 6.9.

82  GDPR, Article 85.

83  GDPR, Article 85.1.

84  Such as third-party fact checkers for "fake news."

85  GDPR, Article 23.

86  Akasha Sachdev, "Government's Social Media Analytics Tool Is Illegal & Unconstitutional," *IFF,* The Quint, https://www.thequint.com/news/india/iandb-ministry-social-media-analytics-tool-rathore-internet-freedom-foundation-illegal. Thus far a legal notice has been sent to the MIB based on the "Request for Bids" issued by the Ministry for the project.

87  WP29, Statement of the WP29 on encryption and their impact on the protection of individuals with regard to the processing of their personal data in the EU, Brussels, April 11 2, 2018, p. 2.

88  WP29, Statement of the WP29 on encryption, p. 2.

89  WP29, Statement of the WP29 on encryption, p. 3.

90  GDPR, Article 88.

91  GDPR, Article 88.1.

92 GDPR, Recital 155.
93 GDPR, Article 88.2.
94 *BetrVG,* Section 80.1.1.
95 *BetrVG,* Section 92.
96 *BetrVG,* Section 87.1.6.
97 Code du Travail, Article L2322-1 et seq.
98 Code du Travail, Article L2323-29.
99 Code du Travail, Article L4612-8-1.
100 Code du Travail, Article L2328-1.
101 Code du Travail, Article L4741-1.

# 10

# Creating a GDPR Compliance Department

*Well begun is half done.*

— Aristotle

The volume of GDPR requirements and the changes they bring within an organization make compliance a daunting task. Basic filing and organization of personal information can trigger GDPR compliance, with data protection becoming an absolute necessity in era of fast-evolving digitization technologies and connectivity. In this chapter we discuss the frameworks necessary for implementing the regulation by creating a *GDPR Compliance Department* (or a *GDPR Team* for smaller businesses).

GDPR brings new standards of data protection, which are likely to be different from those provided under the Data Protection Directive. A business should abandon the DPD standards in assessing data-protection standards and adopt GDPR standards so that there is no gap in privacy measures. The guide provided in this chapter follows a *Waterfall Model* where each step of the implementation process is divided into pre-established phases, which are executed according to their timelines and scope.

## 10.1  Step 1: Establish a "Point Person"

One of GDPR pillars is accountability in processing, particularly by allocating liability clearly to Controllers, Processors, Subprocessors, and their foreign counterparts. Within an organization, categories of processing activities involve appointing a Data Privacy Officer (DPO)[1] to oversee the operation. This is also a reasonable business practice as processing sensitive personal data attracts scrutiny from regulators. Keep in mind that the DPO is an independent role and has whistleblowing responsibilities regarding GDPR contraventions. The officer should be suitably qualified and knowledgeable in the technical, legal, and (ideally) business aspects of processing.

Another option for businesses not required to hire a DPO is to synthesize GDPR compliance into one of their existing departments such as:

1. **Legal:** This is a sound option for companies with in-house attorneys well versed in both legal and technical aspects of the organization. However, it is not the best choice as overlapping ethical obligations might hinder attorneys from fully carrying out either duty.

   **Illustration:** During a data breach, Richard, the in-house attorney (and DPO) for the e-commerce site "Bingo" discovers the damage to be well beyond GDPR parameters. After an initial assessment he finds that the breach went on for 12 months, with the company discovering it 4 months ago and only resolving the issue 2 months ago. The public and authorities are unaware of the breach, and if they were to know the company would go under with lawsuits, GDPR fines, and loss of goodwill. Both a DPO and an attorney would be responsible for giving a full report to the board of Bingo, but the DPO is legally required to report to the authorities. An attorney would be legally prohibited from reporting the breach as it is detrimental to Bingo's interests.

2. **IT:** Like synthesizing the responsibilities in the legal department, IT is more suited to responsibilities of GDPR compliance as they work closely with processing and are more versed with the technical aspects. On the other hand, the project manager or department head would have to be well acquainted with the legal aspects of compliance.

3. **Marketing or sales:** Unlike the previous options, departments that are profit centers including marketing and sales are not suited to oversee GDPR compliance, simply because the regulation's objectives and business motives are unlikely to align. An objective, independent department is necessary for strong GDPR compliance.

   **Example:** "Sales" departments that work on commission are unsuitable for overseeing GDPR compliance.

4. **HR:** Best suited for traditional businesses where commercial activities are "physically" carried out (not online), and data is processed internally for logistical or HR purposes. If personal data is used only for employment purposes, an officer in HR may be best suited to handle GDPR compliance.

   **Illustration:** "Tea-Time" is a medium-sized tea manufacturer based in France. Tea-time conducts all its sales physically by contracting with brick and mortar stores and their partners. The company does not provide any online services like ordering and delivering on e-commerce platforms, as they are "traditional." The company has 100 employees whose personal data is maintained by Tea Time's HR department located in Paris. The central server of employee information is maintained by HR with a specialized Technology Officer who handles GDPR compliance. The Technology Officer is contractually entitled to carry out all functions of a DPO for Tea Time and is responsible to report any misconduct by his superiors in HR overseeing processing. Note, Tea Time also has to comply with local requirements on processing personal data as GDPR leaves employee data processing to its Member States.[2]

It is important to note that *conflicts of interest* rule out any corporate officer who is motivated by collecting personal data. In general, this rules out the owners, business managers, board members, high-level officers, etc., as the DPO or the head of compliance department. Regardless of the route chosen, it is advisable to have a single person report directly to the CEO/CTO on GDPR compliance. Depending on your jurisdiction's legal regime, consider assigning personal liability for breach of his or the office's tasks, holding him directly responsible for illegal processing that occurs during his employment. However, such clauses must be carefully drafted as GDPR does not provide generous possibilities for Controllers to evade liability.

Without an officer in-charge the organization will face gaps in communication, a higher risk of confidential information leaking, and possible confusion over the "chain of command." For larger entities with data processing integrated into their business models, a possible option is have a GDPR oversight employee in any department handling personal data, having each employee report regularly to the DPO.[3] The DPO will then report directly to the CTO/CEO or board. There are several variations that can be tailored to suit a specific business, but these points should be used as reference.

## 10.2   Step 2: Internal Data Audit

The next step would be to identify, categorize, and prioritize the personal data your organization handles. Essentially this would be the step of data mapping as we discussed in Chapter 4 (Sections 4.3 and 4.6). Broadly, work with the DPO and chart out the:

1. Amount of data handled.
2. Amount of data needed.
3. Nature of data processed.
4. Why it is needed.
5. Was it obtained directly from the user or through another commercial party?
6. What would be your consumer's expectations regarding future processing?
7. What data is not necessary at this moment, but can be useful in the future (example: data for analytics)?
8. How sensitive is the data?
9. How many employees have access to the data?
10. What safeguards are in place (technical and organizational)?

Data mapping helps in analyzing the gap in data-protection policies existing between GDPR and DPD (or whichever legal regime the company is subject to). The analysis helps in identifying the degree of change in data protection obligations. It can be carried out by:[4]

1. Employee workshops
2. Self-assessments
3. Questionnaires
4. Specialized interviews
5. Department reports

Analyzing the gap in data protection policies will help assess the risk posed to personal data. GDPR follows a *risk-based approach* in data processing and links an entity's obligations to the risk of a breach. The risk is assessed based on the value of the data held by the business. Thus, after mapping the data from different departments, create a priority list of valuable data to categorize the risk posed to it. The data at the highest risk should be addressed first and given the highest level of protection. Likewise, an organization will find benefit in mapping data based on these cascading priorities.

This step will help in determining the scale of compliance needed for your business and for the next step itself. Data mapping is a necessary part of data minimization under GDPR and can be carried out manually or digitally using automated means. Many software vendors in the industry provide data mapping and minimization services to businesses depending on their size of processing. From the results of data mapping and minimization, create a strategic plan of action with deadlines to formalize the objectives and goals of GDPR compliance.

## 10.3 Step 3: Budgeting

Step 2 should provide a clear picture the business's processing size. Generally, GDPR applicability is not dependent on the size of the companies (small, medium, large), but it does derogate from some requirements for small and medium-sized enterprises. Larger businesses face augmented GDPR requirements bringing them under greater scrutiny. Regardless, GDPR applies to minimal personal data processing, so variations in the steps discussed are limited.

When creating a budget, be mindful of organizational resources and the cost of the present measures in place. GDPR mandates that technical and organizational measures be implemented to regulate compliance and requires ongoing processing and potential future business plans account for data security. Unsurprisingly, one of the staunchest criticisms of GDPR is the overall cost of compliance as it would involve a fair amount of resources. Several things to consider are:

1. The cost of implementing any *data protection management systems* or other AI-based compliance programs like the ones provided by businesses such as IBM and Microsoft.

2. The amount of human capital needed for oversight in relation to the size of processing. Accordingly, the cost of their salaries and benefits should be factored in.
3. The legal costs in formalities.
4. Expenses involved in changing processing operations into a privacy-by-design model.
5. Expenses involved in creating modalities and icons for the exercise of data subject rights.
6. The cost of receiving a certification or ascribing to a code of conduct.
7. Companies carrying out foreign data transfers (bringing data in and out of the EU) or based abroad should consider the cost of establishing a physical presence in the Union.
8. Any expenses required in changing website interface to provide more "rights-friendly" account settings for the user.
9. The payment scheme laid out for the human resources in the department, (hourly, weekly, salary, annual fixed fees, etc.). This would depend on whether the organization hires employees or external contractors for compliance.
10. The expense of *cyber-insurance* for data breaches.

When evaluating these expenses, also account for the predicted income generated by compliance, for example, goodwill gained by consumers for being GDPR compliant. It is helpful to create this budget with the DPO's assistance, as this budget would be utilized under his authority. GDPR mandates DPOs maintain organizational and monetary independence to conduct his activities with the Controller bound to provide it.

## 10.4 Step 4: Levels of Compliance Needed

Certain companies have numerous subsidiaries, employees, processing plants, assets, and customers spread over multiple jurisdictions. In such cases, it is important to isolate and identify the countries implicated in the processing and the degree of international, local, and regulatory compliance required. A sound practice is to categorize business interests by country or by the layers of regulations involved in the processing.

### 10.4.1 Local Legal Standards

Despite GDPR being a Unionwide regulation, several provisions are left open to Member States for further legislation on its practical application. Although the standards are harmonized by GDPR, each Member State is likely to vary in its thresholds for compliance based on where the business operates. This presents national peculiarities in data protection obligations, which tend to create difficulties in online commerce. At the outset, it is pivotal to identify the local Supervisory Authority and comply fully with domestic directives provided by the SA under GDPR.

### 10.4.2   Enhanced Legal Standards for International Data Transfers

If your company works across jurisdictions, consider the stricter compliance requirements for international data transfers. Based on the business's size, determine which compliance method would be best suited to your budget (SCC, binding corporate rules, etc.). Each method carries its distinct set of advantages and disadvantages based on the processing capabilities of a business. For more information, please see Chapter 5 (Section 5.3).

### 10.4.3   International Legal Standards

In addition to identifying the compliance method that is best for the business under GDPR, note that other foreign legal frameworks may have different requirements. These foreign requirements may be stricter or more lenient depending on the policy objectives of the international country. This can create two levels of data-protection compliance for a business in a single transfer of data between the nations.

If standards vary, the organization must alter compliance efforts in the other country to fit their standards. GDPR prioritizes its compliance over foreign standards that may conflict with its objectives. GDPR also requires that businesses ignore any foreign governmental requests that infringe on compliance.[5] If a business is faced with conflicting standards, it is best to consult the SA rather than taking an independent decision on the matter. This will shield the business from future penalties from non-compliance caused by a state-to-state dispute on data protection standards.

### 10.4.4   Regulatory Standards

If the business operates in a heavily regulated industry like aviation or health, there are likely to be additional regulatory standards and oversight that must be complied with. Compliance with GDPR does not excuse any failure to act on any additional standards that may be imposed. This is where a sector-based evaluation of legal frameworks should be conducted to identify and juxtapose the standards of data protection. **Example:** Telemedia Data Controllers are subject to both GDPR and *EU e-Privacy Directive* standards for personal data protection.

### 10.4.5   Contractual Obligations

Regardless of statutory obligations, also consider standards of data protection promised to customers through the entity's consent agreements. This is also commercially prudent, as the privacy sold by the company may be what makes clients use the service. Also consider that enhanced GDPR standards are permissible, but reduced requirements are not permissible even if the customer consents. Therefore, when drafting privacy policies and terms of service, use GDPR as a floor and not a ceiling.

### 10.4.6   Groups of Undertakings

Special mention should be made for larger conglomerates who process personal data across numerous entities and jurisdictions. Businesses should decide whether to implement a *blanket data policy* or phase GDPR compliance across smaller groups for a more coherent approach. Commercially, it is advisable to implement changes across the board, rather than on an entity-by-entity basis as the latter likely causes more confusion and inconsistency. The data protection obligations can be organized by:

- Sector
- Entity
- Country
- Specified "groups"

**Illustration:** An e-commerce platform, Bingo, runs services relating to online shopping, banking, social networking, and auctions. Bingo's main establishment is in Ireland, but has operations spread throughout the EU and globally, with subsidiaries and processing partners spread all over. Each subsidiary handles a unique service or a geographical market. Bingo begins its GDPR compliance by sectorally having its e-banking companies adopt their strongest and most expensive "compliance plan" drafted by their attorneys and DPO. For its foreign subsidiaries offering services within the EU, Bingo adopts a country-wise plan of compliance, bringing their largest service providers working in Ireland into compliance first, using an *Ireland-GDPR compliance plan* drafted by their legal department. All plans adopted by Bingo's legal department adopt the minimum GDPR standards.

Categorizing entity groups and arranging uniform policies will help capitalize on GDPR devices like binding corporate rules which help streamline international data transfers within a business group.[6] All entities in a group should also keep track of their partners who receive personal data, as identifying those parties becomes harder in larger organizations.

## 10.5   Step 5: Sizing Up the Compliance Department

Under GDPR, an organization must assist the DPO "by providing resources necessary to carry out those tasks and access to personal data and processing operations and to maintain his or her expert knowledge."[7] This provision requires that the

Controller give the DPO (and his department) the budgetary and resource independence necessary to execute GDPR functions. With that said, the proportionality of the expenses would have to be made keeping in mind what the entity seeks to achieve and the scale of processing as determined in Step 2.

In larger conglomerates, with departments established for each aspect of the business, one option would be to have a representative employee in each department in charge of oversight, who reports directly to the DPO. Other organizations may find it easier to set up one comprehensive GDPR Compliance Department with access to all processing operations within the company. The method chosen must provide these officers suitable oversight and access powers. Another alternative would be to absorb GDPR oversight into an already existing compliance department within the organization to streamline legal responsibilities.

## 10.6 Step 6: Curating the Department to Your Needs

Once the mode and resources for carrying out compliance are determined, the next logical step is to stock the department with the necessary talent required to carry out the task. Following are two sensible options for establishing the "human capital" of the department.

### 10.6.1 "In-House" Employees

The first option is to stock the department with payroll employees experienced in data protection and its legal aspects to conduct GDPR oversight. This is a smart route if the business heavily relies on processing for its daily functions. Payment and access are the benefits of this compliance method. Salaries and fixed hours with the DPO's office make GDPR oversight easier.

Having someone under the organization's direct supervision can help facilitate communication with DPO, the relevant parties in a dispute, and for handling emergencies (for example, data breaches). Additionally, confidentiality remains within the company and no third party will access company IT systems. Keep note of the ethical obligations the DPO is subject to, and plan for independent oversight of the company's obligations. The unique role and obligations of the DPO should be discussed at the time of recruitment itself to cement his/her independence.

### 10.6.2 External Industry Operators

The risk in hiring employees for GDPR department is that the efficacy of compliance would be contingent on the talent hired. This makes oversight dependent on hiring the right employees in the department. In such cases, the employees' knowledge might be isolated to fields such as IT exclusively, requiring them to further educate themselves on the legal aspects of GDPR compliance.

Companies lacking the resources to educate employees from scratch should consider hiring independent contractors in the market who specialize in data protection and GDPR compliance. External contractors are beneficial because:

- They bring in already-existing industry expertise.
- The job of compliance is effectively shouldered by the contractors themselves, freeing the company to focus on commercial activities.
- As outsiders, the contractors have more freedom to act independently and report on any wrongdoing.

The risk of hiring contractors is that the entity must open its systems, processes, and security measures, leaving its management to an unknown third party. The business should be cautious and hire a credible contractor, with a proven track record. Certifications, codes of conduct, market reputation, and data protection practices are sound indicators for assessing contractor qualifications. Reinforce legal responsibilities in the contract drafted between the entity and external operator. Be sure to have modes of regular and emergency contact with the external contractor to avoid gaps in communications. The payment mechanism can be altered depending on the business's needs and can be made monthly, quarterly, annually, etc.

In legal circles the term "independent contractors" often helps businesses to shift liability to the contractor itself as the doctrine of vicarious liability only applies to employees under a master-servant relationship. However, this doctrine exempting independent contractors does not apply under GDPR as Controller/Processor entities are held directly liable for noncompliance. As a result, hiring external contractors can be used for commercial reasons like those discussed above, but cannot be implemented to evade GDPR liability.

### 10.6.3   Combining the Resources

"Curating" the department does not necessarily require that businesses adopt only one mode of stocking their department. The two methods above can be mixed, considering the diverse responsibilities under GDPR. Therefore, an entity could hire a cyber-security firm to handle data protection but have other aspects like data subject rights, legality, and data minimization maintained "in-house" by employees.

## 10.7   Step 7: Bring Processor Partners into Compliance

Data processing is rarely a sole effort by a single entity. Processing often requires partnership with other entities such as Processors and their Subprocessors. GDPR mandates that all entities in a processing chain be in compliance with requirements applicable to them to operate. This duty flows from the Controller who determines the "purposes and means" of processing down to the entities who carry it out. A Controller organization must ensure that all processing contracts in the chain contain *mandatory clauses* that are provided under GDPR.[8] Commercially, this maintains the overall security of processing and avoids liability from a "weak link" in the compliance chain.

## 10.8   Step 8: Bring Affiliates into Compliance

Certain business partners are not directly subject to GDPR but are deeply intertwined with the processing, either financially or by otherwise using personal data collected by the organization. This can be any entity ranging from advertisers to data brokers and their recipients of the data. Controller entities remain liable for any breach of GDPR, requiring scrutiny in any entity that may use customers' personal data in their business. Maintaining clean "data health" in the company is relevant at all times. For example, erasure requests made by users require removing the data from both the entity's platform and any service the data has been disclosed to.[9]

## 10.9   Step 9: The Security of Processing

With all pieces in place to minimize personal data use by the business, the next step is to ensure its safety at all stages of the processing. The organization should impose measures to ensure that data produced is safe by design at its very inception. For businesses, this is a shift from previous processing models and practices where excessive data collection is the norm. This makes it worthwhile to invest in external assistance from players in the industry to revamp it. Broadly, this requires:

1. Technologically designing personal data to protect privacy by default (data protection by design).
2. Internal confidentiality within the business to ensure no personal data leaks take place (privacy by design).
3. Ongoing cyber-security over personal data being processed. This is carried out by implementing software or IT networks that monitor, report, and combat data breaches.
4. Regular maintenance of all the practices discussed above. Technology becomes outdated quickly, so the business must be ready to follow the changes.

If the organization is larger with an in-house IT department, increase security measures in the existing processing operations. Additionally, organizations should account for data security when establishing the compliance department and (if feasible) have a dedicated employee in charge of regular oversight. For a more in-depth discussion on implementing cyber-security, please refer to Chapter 4.[10]

## 10.10 Step 10: Revamping Confidentiality Procedures

"Security in processing" under GDPR does not exclusively speak to the technical side of processing, but also covers the interpersonal aspects in confidentiality within the organization. Employees in charge of maintaining data security, along with the DPO and others with access to users' personal data within a company are legally bound to confidentiality[11] in carrying out their functions.

With that in mind, update existing contracts with employees who are subject to official secrecy under GDPR Article 90.[12] If internal employment contracts do not contain a confidentiality clause, draft one according to the business's specific needs. It is important not to create a "wall of secrecy" within your company by having all matters sealed from the public eye. Carefully determine:

1. Who is subject to confidentiality
2. What they cannot discuss outside the company
3. The scope of when it is acceptable to break this confidentiality (**Example:** When the DPO requests so, or when presented with a request from a state agency under the law, etc.)

Additionally, ensure secrecy is maintained by including suitable *liquidated damages clauses* for breaches of confidentiality. Note, such clauses depend on the legal framework of the jurisdiction where the business operates. The quantum of damages is likely subject to negotiation, but should be proportional to the value of the data handled along with the position of the officer. Be very careful to liquidate an amount that is not punitive or excessive so as to overburden the employee. Clauses with unreasonably high liquidated damages are likely to be voided by a court if ruled to be "unfair."

Finally create *internal confidentiality protocols* for communications *between* officers handling personal data. Clarify rules on electronic communications between employees and reporting confidential information up the corporate command. The clearer the rules of secrecy are within the office, the lesser exposure to GDPR liability is faced for breaches caused by inadvertent or deliberate leaks.

## 10.11 Step 11: Record Keeping

GDPR requires businesses to maintain records of all processing activities. This must be done in line with Member State *document retention laws* and internal corporate *retention policies*. Businesses commonly align both of these time frames and maintain a single period for retaining and destroying records. In creating a document retention policy, consider the following:

1. Include data in the purview of those policies. Most legislations globally have expanded the definition of "documents" to electronic files and data.
2. Record an overview of processing activities across departments. The overview will include the department name, a short description and name of department contact.
3. Maintain data records as required by law.[13]
4. Maintain a *custodian of records,* either according to department or centrally. Central record custodians are advisable to keep consistent oversight over compliance.
5. Ensure that Processors and Subprocessors also maintain records. Processors can log, use, and systemize the data by virtue of their processing agreement with the Controller.
6. Keep track of *"litigation holds"* on documents maintained by the business. Litigation holds are court orders requiring a company to preserve documents for upcoming legal disputes.

Modern technology makes it easier to log and maintain accurate records of processing under GDPR. The business should give the DPO or compliance department access to the records so they can execute their duties. But access should be limited to those employees necessary for overseeing and maintaining the records.

## 10.12   Step 12: Educate Employees on New Protocols

GDPR encourages data protection knowledge within Controller/Processor organizations, and it is sound business practice to facilitate it. Retooling an entity to be GDPR compliant is likely to change the business technologically and logistically. It is worthwhile to:

1. Educate employees on any changes and security protocols within the entity.
2. Conduct periodic seminars on data protection protocols (either a large seminar once a year, or piecemeal presentations every month/few months).
3. Provide material or seminars for new incoming employees.
4. Circulate regular memos on security protocols for personnel to get accustomed to them.
5. Create "video-lectures" on GDPR compliance, which can be accessed by employees at their convenience as part of their training.

These formats are not legally mandated and are merely illustrative. Educating employees within the organization does fall under the purview of the DPO's responsibilities under GDPR. Thus, employee education should be carried out in collaboration with his/her department.

## 10.13   Step 13: Privacy Policies and User Consent

Whether you are a new business trying to enter the EU market, or an existing one becoming GDPR compliant, processing personal data generally requires user consent. Absent consent, the entity must establish a legal ground for processing personal data.[14] Privacy policies and consent requests are the tangible communications of the entity's GDPR compliance with the consumer base. Earlier, when data processing was largely unregulated, Controllers were free to draft policies to their commercial needs, following the minimum requirements of the law. Now the regulation mandates what information should be communicated and how it should be presented.[15]

The data subject has a right of access to this information, and businesses should take efforts to present GDPR rights and obligations transparently with appropriate modalities on website interfaces for exercising user rights. Follow the drafting tips for privacy policies provided in this commentary along with the requirements for valid consent under the regulation.[16] If the entity processes personal data not acquired directly from the user, then employ your IT team to track down these users and provide them notice that their personal data is being processed.[17] Bear in mind, these documents should be communicated in the form and manner prescribed by GDPR and cannot be traditionally drafted to be overly legalistic or technical. If the entity has the resources, hire a contract administrator who can help facilitate the entire process.

## 10.14   Step 14: Get Certified

This step is discretionary, but with all the mandatory requirements for GDPR compliance in place, it is advisable to have these efforts verified and given a "stamp of approval"[18] by an independent third party. Depending on the business's size, determine which verification method is best suited for the entity's processing (certifications or monitored codes of conduct).[19] Getting certified helps communicate to the public consumer-base that the business has changed its processing to fit GDPR standards. Communicating data practices to the public helps in increasing company goodwill in the market by assuring safety.

## 10.15   Step 15: Plan for the Worst Case Scenario

The final step in setting up a GDPR department is to always be prepared for the worst. The regulation punishes noncompliance and increases fines based on the level of recklessness in the breach.[20] Subject to the business's disposable resources, consider the following measures:

1. Have a Data Security Breach Protocol that clearly explains to your employees what must be done in the event of a data breach.
2. Purchase cyber-insurance that covers GDPR fines.

3. Conduct regular data protection impact assessments when planning future projects and consult with the local SA as to the legality of the intended processing.

4. Conduct periodic *web audits* and oversight of all processing activities run by all entities in the service provided.

5. As far as legally practical, receive all necessary and discretionary approvals of ongoing and future processing activities with the local SA. This helps build credibility with the public agencies and serves as evidence of GDPR compliance in future actions.

In the past, data breaches have been a "PR" issue for businesses, but GDPR now makes it a regulatory breach. To prevent breaches effectively, regularly update technology practices to stay ahead of any cyber-criminals. Have the compliance department or DPO regularly monitor developments in technology to keep track of when network system protections become outdated.

## 10.16    Conclusion

Always consider the ramifications of GDPR in all aspects of the business's processing activities. Future commercial plans created by the company should also keep in mind data protection measures to avoid unnecessary delays in its implementation. This checklist may be excessive for smaller businesses and may not be functionally suitable for its processing size. Customize the steps provided above and do what is best for your business by curating it to meet your commercial needs. Prioritize the business's needs when budgeting expenses, keeping in mind what requirements are mandatory and which are discretionary in GDPR compliance. Then begin pushing forward in phases, keeping the mandatory requirements at the front-end of the organizational checklist. Determine if the company will be proactive or reactive to data protection, and when in doubt, opt for the former. In GDPR compliance, prevention is the cure.

## Notes

1  GDPR, Article 37.
2  GDPR, Article 88.
3  For all intents and purposes, in this section "DPO" will include the DPO himself, *or* any officer employed in the organization responsible for GDPR compliance.
4  This list is *not* exhaustive or mandated by GDPR.
5  GDPR, Recital 115.
6  GDPR, Article 47.

7  GDPR, Article 38.2.
8  GDPR, Article 28.3.
9  GDPR, Article 17.2.
10  Chapter 4 (Sections 4.7 and 4.8).
11  GDPR, Article 90.
12  *Note:* This duty will *differ* depending on the Member State within the EU. This area has been left to the Members under their delegated legislation capabilities under Article 90 of *GDPR.*
13  GDPR, Article 30.
14  GDPR, Articles 5 and 6.
15  GDPR, Articles 13 and 14.
16  Chapter 5 (Section 5.2.1).
17  GDPR, Article 14.
18  GDPR, Article 42.
19  GDPR, Article 41.
20  GDPR, Article 83.

# 11

# Facebook: A Perennial Abuser of Data Privacy

*We don't sell any of your information to anyone, and we never will.*
— Facebook data policy

## 11.1 Social Networking as an Explosive Global Phenomenon

Facebook (FB) has revolutionized virtual social interactions in major parts of the world. Before its inception in 2004, other communication and networking platforms including AOL, Yahoo!, and Orkut laid the foundation for the concept of online social networking as a free service, or nearly so. FB made it mainstream with over 2 billion members worldwide. It has aptly been dubbed the most successful thing in human history.[1] Since its inception the company has expanded its operations rapidly into nearly all forms of human communication increasing its reach, and more importantly, its data collection capabilities.

## 11.2 Facebook Is Being Disparaged for Its Data Privacy Practices

At the time of writing this chapter, the latest controversy surrounding the company is regarding the *10-Year Challenge* meme shared by users on the FB/Instagram platforms. Some allege that the 10-Year Challenge meme was started by FB itself to develop its facial recognition algorithms by collecting a diverse range of aging features from its data subjects, perfectly set to a 10-year comparison.[2] None of these allegations have been confirmed, with FB denying any involvement in making the Challenge go viral. But the company's denial comes at a time when its data practices are under strict public scrutiny following the Cambridge Analytica scandal and their recent data breach in 2018.[3] After 15 years of providing and expanding social networking "services" on its platform, accompanied by numerous scandals, legislative bodies, regulators, and the public are now acutely aware that FB's business model and valuation are dependent on its data practices. This was evidenced during Mark Zuckerberg's US Congressional hearing in April 2018. where it became clear that lawmakers would leave the website to self-regulate its data practices. After the hearing, the valuation of the FB's stock rose on the NY Stock Exchange, as the market surmised that the company's profitability would not be affected by the Cambridge Analytica scandal.[4]

## 11.3  Facebook Has Consistently Been in Violation of GDPR Standards

With GDPR now in force throughout the EU, FB has made assurances that it is compliant with the regulation's requirements, stating that it would be implemented globally where practical. But many questions surround the company's implementation of the regulation and how its business model has changed following GDPR compliance. At the same time, it is important to remember the unique position FB holds in the online market as one of the Big Four technology companies.[5] The diverse range of services provided, along with the corporate structure of the FB Group, makes GDPR compliance extremely challenging for the platform.

## 11.4  The Charges against Facebook

FB is currently embroiled in a series of lawsuits and regulatory investigations outside of GDPR that illustrate a history of data abuse by the company. The legal actions are a result of poor data protection and privacy practices, which many allege have been deliberate inaction on part of the corporation.[6] As of September 2018, the Irish data protection commissioner has been investigating FB for a security breach affecting 50 million users. Similarly, the UK information commissioner issued a maximum penalty of £500,000 for FB's involvement in disinformation campaigns during the Cambridge Analytica scandal. In February 2019 the UK House of Commons followed suit by issuing a damaging report on the disinformation campaigns of 2016 and how the company violated the 2011 FTC Consent Decree leading to the Russian interference.[7] Additionally, the report reveals FB violated its own privacy policies and granted *preferential access* to advertisers by maintaining *whitelisting agreements*.[8] The whitelisting practices led to another recent litigation filed against FB by the app developer Six4Three, who claims the company wrongly revoked its preferential access and sold it to the highest bidder.

The series of investigations noted above are those that are outside of the Company's GDPR breaches and deal with the larger abuse of the platform and its data practices. With the multi-jurisdictional legal challenges being the opening act of

FB's problems pre-GDPR, the company must make radical changes to be fully compliant with this new regulation.

## 11.5   What Is Facebook?

As of December 2018, FB had 1.52 billion daily active users and 2.32 billion monthly active users. As Google+ shut down in April 2018, FB gained a greater market share of global social networking. By any measure this is a unique phenomenon in human history. "Facebook.com" is owned and operated by Facebook Inc. and Facebook Ireland Ltd.[9] and offers the company's original social networking platform. "Facebook Products" include services like FB messenger, Instagram, and boomerang,[10] which are owned by the two holding companies above. Additionally, FB is the parent corporation for the companies listed below.

- **Facebook Payments Inc.:** Handles FB Group's online payment systems and services to users.
- **Onavo:** FB's online mobile services company,[11] providing apps like Protect, and Free VPN+ Data Manager.
- **Oculus and Oculus Ireland Limited:** FB Group's virtual and augmented reality services.[12]
- **WhatsApp Inc. and WhatsApp Ireland Limited:**[13] Offers the popular WhatsApp messenger, a private, direct messaging service hosted online.
- **Masquerade:** Provides FB's "mask-technology" for "selfie" cameras in creating moving/stationary "filters."[14]
- **CrowdTangle:** An FB subsidiary that "controls the use of your information" on behalf of the group by using data for analytics, security, and marketing.[15]

## 11.6   A Network within the Social Network

Like most large corporations, FB shares personal data freely within its family of companies.[16] The formally stated purpose of data sharing is to facilitate, support, and integrate the conglomerate's activities and to improve services. However, data sharing within the group takes place in accordance with each company's respective terms of service and privacy policies. This implies the individual services provided by the companies in the group control the amount of data collected and shared. For example, Facebook Payments Inc. has the strictest data policy in the group and protects personal information from being shared even within the FB Group.[17] Meanwhile, data collected by Masquerade or WhatsApp messenger services are shared more freely between companies and advertisers. Note that many companies in the FB Group maintain separate terms of service for data subjects located within the EU, which can lead to jurisdictional differences in their compliance obligations.

Within FB's Terms of Use itself, the following supplementary agreements are listed as binding on the user:[18]

- **Community standards:** FB's content moderation rules.
- **Commercial terms:** Applicable to users availing themselves of FB's services and products for a commercial or business purpose. **Examples:** Advertising, operating an app on the platform, using FB measurement services, managing a group or page for business, or selling goods or services.
- **Advertising policies:** Specify what types of ad content are allowed by partners across the FB Products.
- **Self-serve ad terms:** These terms apply to users utilizing self-serve advertising interfaces to create, submit, or deliver advertising or other commercial or sponsored activity or content.
- **Pages, groups, and events policy:** Applicable to users who create or administer a FB page, group, or event, or who use FB to communicate or administer a promotion.
- **FB platform policy:** These guidelines outline the policies that apply to platform use. **Examples:** Developers or operators of a platform application or website or using social plug-ins.
- **Developer payment terms:** These terms apply to developers of applications that use Facebook Payments.
- **Community payment terms:** These terms apply to payments made on or through FB.
- **Commerce policies:** Outlining rules for offering products and services for sale.
- **FB brand resources:** These guidelines outline the policies that apply to use of FB trademarks, logos, and screenshots.
- **Music guidelines:** These guidelines outline the policies that apply to users posting or sharing musical content on FB.

## 11.7    No Shortage of "Code of Conduct" Policies

Internally, the FB Group is likely following a set of Binding Corporate Rules and monitored Codes of Compliance for intra-organization transfers of personal data,[19] but the divergent data collection practices will cause confusion in investigations. When transferring data internationally to its affiliates, FB is GDPR compliant by adopting the SCCs provided by the EU commission along with adequacy decisions.[20] Organizationally, the corporate group manages its data sharing by directing users to hyperlinks which lead them to a list of Processors, Subprocessors, and advertisers they share profile data with.[21] Users have the power to control data sharing with these affiliates through their privacy settings, but not if the data sharing is necessary for their FB services. For example, if users wish to donate money to a cause through FB, they must agree to the terms provided by Facebook Payments Inc., as payment data is necessary for processing the transaction. But after acceding to the terms of processing, the extent of shared data and the mechanisms have not been explained in detail in FB's Data Policy.

## 11.8 Indisputable Ownership of Online Human Interaction

After Google+ shut down in April 2018, FB gained a greater market share as the social networking site. As of December 2018, FB had 1.52 billion daily and 2.32 billion monthly active users. The order from Germany's Federal Cartel Office to collect and combine less data comes at a time where the FB Group plans on bringing data processing across all company platforms under one framework.[22] FB also planned to integrate the technology behind the chat services of Instagram, WhatsApp, and FB Messenger, which would lead to the company aggregating the data they have. FB justifies the practices by citing:

- More focused direct marketing for users.
- The single processing framework will assist advertisers in measuring the success of a campaign.
- The processing change will make it easier to identify fake accounts, combat terrorism, and protect users otherwise.[23]

## 11.9 Social Networking as a Mission

FB began as a social networking website, providing a platform for communication and "connecting" with friends, family, acquaintances, and one's personal community. FB revolutionized communication by helping individuals expand their definition of community by providing a simple, unified platform for increasing day-to-day interactions. Through using this platform, users stay in touch with friends with whom they would ordinarily lose contact by removing the hurdles of traditional communication and simplifying the manner of expressing oneself to the public. Previous mediums like text messaging, phone calls, letters, etc., did not have the ability to transmit communication publicly or the ease of assimilating information from multiple sources at once.

For example, "calling" someone (like an old college friend to catch up) requires investing time in the initial "formalities" of conversation, and unreliability in receiving an answer. Additionally, long-distance communication tends to be costly. By using FB, a person can simply view that friend's profile and immediately find out where they are, what they've been up to, and any "life events." With "web-based calling" becoming an easier alternative to telecommunications, FB also provides phone and video calling services. The degree of information shared with the public is left to the user itself. A profile can reveal all details of a person's life, their views, pictures, videos, "links" they like, family members, close friends, "public" posts between friends, etc. A profile can also be set to be a closed network with minimal details and essential information. Customization is a key part of FB's service.

Many argue that the "open" nature of FB's service causes an erosion of human privacy in communication. The argument is fair as the company has increased the ways individuals can express themselves by introducing "Feelings," "Stickers," "GIFs," "trending news," "24-hour story" features along with numerous plug-ins, apps, devices, and "tie-ins" with other services provided by the Facebook Companies. The unique power of FB is its ability to create and expand the definition of social networking. At the forefront of the industry and at a dominant position in the market, the company has the power to dictate the scope of the industry and the direction of its growth. This is evidenced as the company extends its reach to gaming, virtual reality, employment, trade, and advertising services, while also providing platforms for political, social, financial, and philanthropic causes.

This leaves the question of what is a "social networking service"? FB's Terms of Use lists the following "services" provided by the website:[24]

1. Provide a personalized experience for the user
2. Connect users with people and organizations they care about
3. Empower users to express themselves and communicate about what matters to them
4. Help discover content, products, and services that may interest the user
5. Combat harmful conduct and "protect and support our community"
6. Use and develop advanced technologies to provide safe and functional services
7. Research ways to make services better
8. Provide consistent and seamless experiences across the Facebook Company products
9. Enable global access to FB services.

The "services" listed by FB provide minimal guidance on how data collection relates to a specific function of their platform. Like many social media websites, FB finds it challenging to link collection with purpose, which lands the companies in legal scrutiny. If we look at the "services" above, we can see that they are generalized and broad. Providing a "consistent and seamless experience" across the FB group can justify any number of data-collection activities. Helping users with a "personalized experience" might justify why FB keeps expanding its modes of data production and collection.

## 11.10 Underlying Business Model

FB's business construct is straightforward: extend the existing modes of communication and connectivity, thereby enhancing "user experience" and more importantly, data collection. By increasing the number of services provided, the company keeps expanding what social media means and entails. While FB has been harshly criticized for pushing an "open" culture of sharing personal information, one might ask: Isn't that the *purpose* of the company? Every new feature, plug-in, and app has an audience with users employing these devices without serious objections. FB's new services help in "facilitating" communication and increasing human interactions by providing a platform for expression. "Expression" and "social networking" are ambiguous terms without structural definitions in law or society. This gives the company the leeway it needs to set its own purposes of processing personal data. New features increase personal data production but fall within the original mission of the company, social networking. With no rules in place to dictate what qualifies as appropriate "tools," any new data-collecting service can be deemed as a part of the social networking experience.

## 11.11    The Apex of Sharing and Customizability

Social media services are premised on the assumption of "sharing" personal details with a public or private group of people. Individuals join sites like FB primarily to "reach out" to their community and provide "updates" on their daily lives, while others do so to expand their network of friends. Users also exclusively use FB for commercial reasons to advertise their brand and products. When joining the service, users assume the "public eye" will be on what they share unless they say restrict it in their "settings."

In an environment like this, can privacy and data protection by design be practically implemented? Consumers of FB's services knowingly enter an "open" space premised on "sharing" details with a network. Can the company be faulted in facilitating this "sharing culture" toward their commercial benefit?

This is where customizability plays a key role. The sharing culture created by FB is not universally appreciated, and the company is strongly cognizant of that fact. FB remedies this problem by giving full user control over his profile's privacy. Commercially, the idea is sensible, as users decide how much to share and with whom, providing each consumer a "customized" service. At the same time, the decision legally helps FB in shifting privacy interests and responsibilities onto the user. Users are primarily responsible for controlling their data production by adjusting the public and corporate recipients of the information they share. As a result, data subjects have the discretion of making a public or private profile on the platform, giving each a unique, modified service. Whether the full user control model passes GDPR regulations and their interpretation remains to be seen.

## 11.12    Bundling of Privacy Policies

The FB Group follows a practice of bundled privacy policies, where in an exhaustive reading of several documents is necessary to fully understand the terms. Additionally, bundling requires a user to consent to all terms of an agreement with no meaningful option to reject the selectivity.[25] To its credit, the company elaborates its policies well, in plain English, by breaking down its data collection practices for the user.[26] By utilizing tabs and hyperlinks the accompanying policies are accessible for users to read at their convenience. The tabs also repeatedly direct users to their privacy settings to change default practices offered in the standard terms. Essentially, FB provides users its standard data policy and practices along with information on how data is collected, shared, and stored as a default. If the user disagrees with any of those terms, the website provides the option of blocking such practices. Since the Cambridge Analytica scandal, FB has updated its policies across all services[27] and offers a series of privacy features like "privacy check ups," instructive videos on their services, and providing "shortcuts" on users' home pages.

However, the practice of bundling privacy policies has already landed FB (and Google) in legal crosshairs of European regulators. In January 2019, the NYOB.eu complaints (discussed in Chapter 5) resulted in Google being fined $56.8 million for inadequate consent and information practices.[28] Bundling policies and hyperlinking important processing information across several documents were found to be an excessive dissemination, thereby failing GDPR's standard of free and voluntary consent.[29] FB has yet to face GDPR penalties for its consent and information practices, but its dominant market position and similar practices have created issues with the German antitrust authorities, as mentioned earlier. Considering the fact that the company similarly hyperlinks its multiple policies, we can expect similar actions to be taken by the Irish SA.

## 11.13   Covering All Privacy Policy Bases

In its Data Policy, FB states the reasons for personal data collection are as follows:[30]

1. **Provide, personalize and improve products:** FB as a website constantly updates its platforms, services, and overall "social networking experience" for users. This includes platform analytics, facial recognition, location-based services, direct marketing, and cross-platform[31] consistency.
2. **Provide measurement, analytics, and other business services:** This legal basis primarily services FB's advertising interests where data is used in products like Pixel, which help advertisers in targeted marketing and analytics.
3. **Promote safety, integrity, and security:** Data is used for purposes of combating cyber threats, security breaches, and data protection.
4. **Communicate with user:** Personal data may be used when the company itself wishes to contact users on any changes or updates to the services provided.

## 11.14   Claims of Philanthropy

FB also processes data for philanthropic purposes like studying migration patterns to aid authorities. Personal data is processed for causes such as general social welfare, technological advancement, public interest, health, and well-being.[32] This comes under the larger practice which enables the use of personal data for the larger social welfare, for example, the use of cell phone and location data and anonymized mails to study migration patterns of diseases. A similar example would be when the mathematician Stephen Wolfram worked with data donated by FB users to show how the data reveals signals about how a person and their life changes over time.[33]

**Data resources:** "Donation" is a key word in the examples given above as it is rarely that FB itself carries out the philanthropic analysis. FB often provides data needed for the study, but the analysis and research are likely to be carried out by external data analytics firms. The company holds a rich trove of valuable personal data that gives insight into the human condition and society. The user information can help data philanthropists to get the raw data they require for their analysis without the hassle of a questionnaire or survey. But privacy concerns always exist, even with utilitarian processing in public interest. Therefore data philanthropy firms require donations, consent, or anonymization of personal data for conducting a study that respects privacy. However, these factors can have negative impact by limiting the pool of available information or incorrect user data.

**Philanthropic modalities:** Other than giving the resources for philanthropic studies, FB also conducts its own public interest services by providing features like:

1. Marking users "safe" during natural disasters and emergencies.
2. Modalities to give and receive donations for charitable causes.
3. Modalities for creating "fundraisers."
4. Listing nonprofits who require or accept donations.
5. Modalities to organize and mobilize "community actions" over causes.
6. "Crisis response" that provides a live dashboard of emergencies globally, which can be tracked. Users can also use the feature to offer services like providing supplies.
7. "Town Hall," which links users to their local bodies of government and representatives.

Each of the features above provides users a specialized channel for carrying out their own personal philanthropy online, using the FB platform. With each service used, an independent legal basis is created under the processing purpose of "public interest" under GDPR. But note that the philanthropic purpose of data collection does not change the breadth of data sharing by FB and its partners, and this data is given the same treatment as ordinary data created for social networking.

**Technological advancement:** Products offered by the FB group rely on the data created and shared on the website to improve services for the users. "Technological advancement" in this context connotes that the entity will use personal data for the greater public good, which is a highly subjective matter. Arguably, any technological advancement is in "the public interest" as the public benefits from the increase in efficacy. Whether FB can use its own data for this purpose remains discretionary as this category easily overlaps with the company's data collection for R&D. It is likely that this provision points to projects like "Aquila," a bold effort undertaken by FB to bring drone-based solar-powered Wi-Fi to poorly connected areas across several countries. This project was discontinued in 2018 following organizational difficulties,[34] but it demonstrates the type of activities that the entity may classify as "technological advancement." Development comes with increased data processing, but historically the company has been on the frontlines of modifying the social media experience for "greater" user enjoyment of its service. A restriction on these types of processing may result in stifling technological growth in the larger scheme of commerce.

## 11.15    Mechanisms for Personal Data Collection

Over the past decade, FB has substantially increased its modes of collecting personal data from users. Relating back to our discussion on FB "defining" what social networking is, the company expands its data collection capabilities by offering new ways of expression. "Expression" is a broad concept, especially online, where users can utilize multiple aspects of the platform to put forward their views. If FB introduces features like geo-tagging or "feelings," it increases data production by users but also serves to enhance user expression. Before criticizing these practices, one should ask whether the new feature helps in connectivity, communication, and expression. If the answer is yes, the next question to ask is whether the new service is outside FB's original social networking mission. Any new feature introduced on FB's platform will inevitably increase data production by users. Does that imply that the website should abstain from bringing in new features?

When commencing its social-networking service in 2004, FB offered the following modes of communication:

- Profile with biographical, contact, "relationship status," and family information.
- Profile pictures.
- "Tagging" friends in photos.
- "Wall-posts" between users for public communication.
- "Comments" and the ability to "like" other users' posts.
- Notifications about responses to a user's personal activities.
- Private messaging on FB (though this was introduced soon after 2004).
- Seeing "friendships" between two users. This may be the interactions, pictures, videos, etc., between two users, which can be viewed by the users themselves or even by mutual friends.

- "Statuses" by users presenting public thoughts and opinions to their network.
- Viewing a user's friends and mutual friends.
- Friend suggestions (provided by FB).
- Pages, events, discussions which a person can "like," "share," or "join."
- Birthdays of friends.

FB currently offers the following modes of expression in addition to its core services listed above:[35]

- Cover photos on profiles
- Geo-tagging locations on photos uploaded
- Auto-recognition of friend's faces in pictures for "tagging"
- User activity logs
- "Following" prominent user activities
- Account verification for popular users
- Notifications on other user's activities (example: Bill uploaded a link on his profile)
- Notifications on birthdays
- Expressing feelings to statuses (example: Bill, feeling happy!, shared a post on his graduation)
- Emojis to comments, likes, messages, and posts (example: Bill, feeling sad ☹, shared a post on his father's death. James held the "like" button and expressed ☹ to the post rather than commenting)
- Geo-tagging and location check-ins on statuses
- Image and video sharing (here, the speed of file sharing has made this service much easier than the preexisting platform)
- Image and video filters that can be applied to user photos
- Linked sharing with Instagram and other FB companies
- FB "memories" where users can reminisce on past activity
- Friendship anniversaries where FB creates automated videos on activity between two friends
- Group chats and direct messaging
- GIF media keyboards
- Stickers in messaging
- Hashtags and trending news
- Direct advertising
- Commercial and business pages
- Gaming
- Job searches
- A "Marketplace" where users can sell their goods
- A listing of local public events
- A listing of "local" sights and restaurants
- City guides
- Movies
- Recent "offers" available
- Messenger kids service

- Job searches
- Fundraising
- Payment services for donations, repayment, and online purchases
- Beginning causes, discussions, and political "town-hall" meetings
- Marking a user's safety during a natural disaster
- Crisis response
- Live video streaming
- 24-hour stories
- FB TV
- Virtual and augmented reality

These services are provided on FB's core platform and become more diverse across its other products and companies FB Group offers countless products, plug-ins, apps, social media users, business partners, and advertisers, across interconnected platforms. This creates a self-sustaining data-collecting ecosystem from a broad sampling of the population. Each new service triggers a new basis for processing, new forms of expression, and, more importantly, new data. An emoji or a "feeling" can tell more about a user than words could, and multimedia sharing helps shed light on a person's humor, interests, and views. An analysis of the multimedia a user regularly sends or routinely uses provides the corporation a clearer *digital blueprint* of a data subject.

## 11.16   Advertising: The Big Revenue Kahuna

FB and other social media platforms have been a revolutionary force in the advertising industry. Consumer focus in the past decades has gradually shifted from the television screen to handheld mobile devices as social media became the primary source of entertainment and news. Both FB and advertisers capitalized on this shift by utilizing technology to target users directly rather than through broadcast. The popularity of practices like "nudging" and "native advertising" grew, since technology provided companies a subtle way of entering consumer's minds. Advertising influence online grew to such an extent that consumers *expect* to be barraged with pop-ups and sponsored links.

GDPR specifically addresses direct advertising to protect users from unwarranted targeted intrusion. FB allows users to manually object and suspend direct marketing on the website, but not advertising altogether. This again is part of the full user control model implemented by FB. Some users prefer targeted advertisements while others would prefer to restrict data sharing with external entities. By allowing users to customize ad preferences personally, the company remains GDPR compliant. This is because there is no outright prohibition against advertising, but direct marketing remains regulated.[36]

GDPR drafters recognize that behavioral targeting and direct marketing are powerful tools in the hands of corporations with deep implications for individual privacy interests. The regulation allows users to object to such targeting, exercise greater control over ad preferences, and demand that organizations take greater caution when processing (like requiring a DPIA and a DPO). In the past, FB has been referred to as an advertising company rather than a social media platform owing to the steady commercialization of their personal data services. We will later examine whether FB's advertising policies are GDPR compliant.

## 11.17   And Then There Is Direct Marketing

FB's advertising policy provided in users' Ad Preferences and the company's help page provide how advertisers collect and use data on the platform. At the outset, it is important to note that the data provided to advertisers are masked, with identification data removed. FB allows advertisers to specify a demographic to target but cannot specify the users. The following table demonstrates how advertiser specifications and direct marketing is linked on FB:[37]

| Advertiser specifications | User targeted and data presented |
| --- | --- |
| 1. Car enthusiasts | 1. "FB user" (name redacted) |
| 2. Between 18 and 35 years old | 2. 30 years old |
| 3. Female | 3. Female |
| 4. Within 20 miles of my store | 4. Menlo Park, CA |
| 5. Interested in mechanics, racing, F1 and professional driving | 5. Interested in car engineering, movies, cooking |
| 6. Mobile or Pad users | 6. iPad and iPhone user, car shopper, gamer |

## 11.18   Our Big (Advertiser) Brother

Advertisers collect personal data directly or indirectly by using FB information about users. Personal data is collected directly based on user "activity" across FB Group products and services. This includes:[38]

- Pages users and their friends "like" or post
- Information from FB and Instagram profiles
- Locations checked-in to

Similarly, indirect personal data collection takes place when information like phone numbers and e-mail addresses are shared with businesses who add the user to their customer list, which can be matched with a FB Profile. FB's advertising services help companies "match" the advertisement with the most relevant audience. Businesses collect data indirectly when users:

- Sign up for an e-mail newsletter.
- Make purchases at retail stores.
- Sign up for a coupon or discount, etc.

Indirect personal data collection is also carried out by utilizing FB's business tools (APIs, SDKs, plug-ins, and other platform integrations) to suggest ads based on products and services viewed by the user. These tools can be triggered by:

- Viewing webpage of a business
- Downloading a mobile app
- Adding products to shopping carts or making a purchase

The methods of data collection are also closely linked to the location data created by the user for FB group services, mobile apps, and IP addresses. The above methods of data collection are not exhaustive and are illustrative as per FB's legal policies.[39] Understandably, a large company like FB cannot practically list all sources of data collection but attempts to summarize them for its users. But the company carries the risk of contravening their information obligations under GDPR if data collection is outside the parameters provided to users.

For example, consider a user who has FB, Instagram, and WhatsApp accounts and uses all those services (i.e. utilizing all features of the platforms). Additionally, that user is a regular online shopper in many e-commerce websites that implement the FB business tools like a "log-in" and "share" social plug-ins. The single user alone creates enough data to provide advertisers a digital blueprint of their behavioral tendencies and shopping activities. The user provides all this data from multiple sources simultaneously feeding information into other FB business tools like "pixel," which helps advertiser analytics for targeted marketing. Additionally, users' activities open channels for data collection from their friends as well, thereby expanding the bases for analytics. This constant cycle of data production, collection, analytics, and use aptly creates an internal "ecosystem" of information for advertisers.

Advertisers run ads based on a contact list uploaded by their company or a partner entity, which includes data fields related to relationships, employment, education, etc. The data fields are used only to determine if an ad should be shown to a user.[40] Additionally, advertisers are not allowed to alter profile and data visibility. The data fields help categorize users for advertising demographics and help create an audience network elaborated below.

## 11.19   A Method to Snooping on Our Clicks

The "ad system" discussed above helps prioritize ads and match them to a desired audience based on the specifications provided by advertisers.[41] FB expressly claims that they do not sell individual data (like names) to advertisers, with users remaining completely anonymous. The purpose of this processing is to provide users "relevant and useful" ads for products and services that might interest the user. It is important to note that FB does not list this as their legitimate commercial interest, but rather includes it as part of their services. The direct marketing process is provided below based on FB data policies:

1. **Advertiser specifications:** A "business goal" is given by advertisers such as selling a product or increasing awareness of a brand.
2. **Audience identification:** A demographic or desired base of users is laid down by advertisers. This is done by using the FB Audience Network, which allows advertisers to display ads on websites and apps across devices such as computers, mobile devices, and connected TVs. When companies buy ads through FB, they can choose to have their ads distributed in the Audience Network.

   Audiences are identified by using personal data relating to users' interests as represented in their FB activity.[42] This includes users' interests related to:
   a. News
   b. Entertainment
   c. Business and industry
   d. People
   e. Hobbies and activities
   f. Shopping and fashion
   g. Education
   h. Travel
   i. Sports
   j. Technology
   k. Fitness
   l. Food
   m. Lifestyle
   n. Etc.[43]
3. **Ad creation:** Probably handled by the ad agency or business itself, social media campaigns are created for the desired platforms based on the business tools used.
4. **Direct marketing:** FB utilizes the advertisers' goals and matches them with the audience they target without direct identification.

Commercially, a hurdle that advertisers face is the veracity of information they receive from users' FB Profiles. A large section of users tends to dishonestly represent their "interests" and personal information on their profiles for any number of reasons (like social, professional, or "romantic" motivations). This variable corrupts the process of "audience identification" as users may be wrongly categorized and shown irrelevant advertisements.

## 11.20   What Do We Control (or Think We Do)?

FB provides great deal of flexibility to its users to control direct marketing but not the option of stopping exposure. Advertising is a part of FB's business model, and users cannot opt out of advertising altogether like other channels of marketing.

Users can modify the access to their personal data by advertisers, but not the overall activity itself.

User controls allow data subjects to:

- Limit the data provided to advertisers.
- Limit the data provided to third-party apps/services.
- Exclude or include advertisements from certain entities.
- Review advertisers viewed based on a website or app using FB technology.

The relationship between personal data "submission" and "use" by advertisers is controlled by the users' Ad Settings in their FB Profile. FB allows users to control advertisements based on the source of data collection, which we discuss below.

### 11.20.1   Ads Based on Data from FB Partners

The first source of data for advertisers is the users' activity off FB Company products and services. This data is collected from "partners" and includes online activity on third-party websites, apps, and certain offline interactions with those services (like purchases).[44] The data collected from these partners results in the advertising seen across the FB Group's products, services, and devices.

**Illustration:** Keith buys plane tickets to Hong Kong for his parents on Trip.com, a travel website. Trip.com uses FB's plug-in to help users register an account. Later that day, Keith sees advertisements for hotels and sightseeing packages on his FB newsfeed. He also sees sponsored articles titled "11 things to see in Hong Kong!" Keith becomes annoyed with these ads because he himself would not be traveling to Hong Kong. He goes to his Ad Settings in his profile to switch off all ads created from his activity on Trip.com and FB partners.

The effect of "switching off" ads from FB partners does not delete the data[45] but stops these entities from processing his data for direct marketing on FB. Keith will still see the same number of ads, but they will be based on activity on FB group services and products. Keith may also see advertisements from third parties with whom he specifically shared his contact information that have been matched with his profile by FB.

### 11.20.2   Ads Based on Activity on FB That Is Seen Elsewhere

Like direct advertising, the reverse is also allowed by default by FB. The company's advertising services complement the use of data generated from FB company products (like websites, apps, and devices) by showing users "relevant" advertisements on other services. Other services that work with FB advertising utilize the Audience Network (discussed above) to help create targeted markets for their products. Users have the option of switching off this form of direct marketing by choosing whether FB Ad Preferences are used to show ads on apps and services not normally provided by FB.

### 11.20.3   Ads That Include Your Social Actions

"Social actions" on FB represent the act of liking, sharing, or commenting on a page that runs an ad. As a default, FB shares this data with a chosen audience (public/only friends/friends of friends, etc.) as "People want to know what their friends like." The setting applies to the "likes, follows, comments, shares, app usage, check-ins, recommendations, and events" a user participates in that appear in ads their friends see. Advertisements based on these social actions are only visible to networks specified by the user in their profile.

Here, FB takes the role of "suggesting" products based on social relevance and mutual connections. Users would be more likely to take an advertisement seriously if they knew their friends are also interested. This is why FB's interface mentions, "X, Y, Z and 10 more liked this," so that a user can look at a post with greater credibility. The "social actions" shared and used by FB effectively brings word-of-mouth advertising to a digital domain, by having users suggest pages and products without even being aware of doing so. Ordinarily, suggesting pages, products and services for word-of-mouth advertising require conscious suggestion by a user. FB cut out this step by placing passive endorsements based on site usage.

Whether this is proper use of data and an effective implementation of privacy by design is highly debatable in a social networking context, as endorsements are part of the social experience, but not integral to it. The main issue with word-of-mouth advertising in the past was the inability to tangibly identify and utilize customer suggestions in attracting future business. FB has learned how to track, identify, and show "social actions" and more importantly, how to use those actions for advertising.

### 11.20.4   "Hiding" Advertisements

The ad controls provided by FB serve to help "see ads that are more interesting and relevant to you." But as we pointed out earlier, advertisements on the platform are inevitable, even if a user disables direct marketing by FB. Users may still see ads based on:

- Age, gender, or location
- The app or website content used
- Activity off FB company products

However, data mentioned above would not be as "relevant" to the user as direct marketing would be as information used by FB is more general. The ability to hide advertisements once again plays into the customizability of FB's services to consumers, even to the extent of hiding certain ad topics like those related to alcohol, parenting, and pets. The customizability plays into the other aspects of content control, which has recently been a high priority for the website.

Note: **We are in the process of restricting developers' data access even further to help prevent abuse**. For example, we will remove developers' access to your FB and Instagram data if you haven't used their app in **3 months**, and we are changing Login, so that in the next version, we will reduce the data that an app can request without app review to include only name, Instagram username and bio, profile photo and e-mail address. Requesting any other data will require our approval.[46]

The above notation in FB's data policy is reflective of the company's past advertising practices. After Cambridge Analytica and the Six4Three cases, the abuse of personal data for advertising and direct commercial and political marketing damaged FB's credibility in self-regulating their business. Presently the company is trying to rebuild its reputation by having "user-friendly" explanations of their advertising and data practices, insisting that personal data is not sold. While FB does not trade personally identifiable information with advertisers, its "lookalike audiences" feature in their advertising products cleverly uses a GDPR loophole by selling behavioral characteristics using inferred data. We will discuss this loophole later in this chapter when examining the UK House of Common's report on Fake News and Disinformation.[47]

## 11.21 Even Our Notifications Can Produce Revenue

"Notifications" are a central part of a social networking website's business model. It is an external tool outside of the interface that "reminds" users of activities affecting them while they go offline. Notifications help companies ensure that users regularly return to the service and keep their social networking activities at the forefront. GDPR does not legislate regarding notifications and the privacy implications in regularly informing users of activities, leaving considerable discretion to Controllers for determining the extent of sharing information through these mechanisms.

On FB (and many other websites), any activity involving the user will always remain "on."[48] This seems logical as users should ideally be informed if an activity related to them is taking place on the service. However, over the past decade FB has increased the amount of information shared by notifications in expanding this feature to activity by friends as well. The change was gradual and subtly invasive while staying in line with FB's theme of community and connectivity. FB's algorithms help identify which friends a user is close to, and what activity may interest them and make them return to the website.

From a "consumer" perspective, users enjoy being informed of their friends' activities, and certain users place high value on having many notifications in their inbox. Psychologically, more notifications lead a user to believe in increased popularity and social involvement. From a "business" end, more notifications help ensure users will return to the service either out of curiosity, social involvement, or even just to clear the "clutter" of older notifications. The commercial goal is to have returning users (rather "customers") instead of sporadic and inconsistent use of the service. FB notification practice has become expansive, going beyond "user-based" activity to:

- Activity from friends (example: "Bob just uploaded a new post!" Or "Bob and 3 other friends are interested in an event near you!").
- Birthdays, pages and events (example: "Bob and 4 others have their birthday today!" "Bob started a new page named GDPR enthusiasts!"). It is noteworthy that "page-based" notifications have been expanded from page invitations to general information on the formation, activity, and membership on these pages.
- Live videos (example: "Bob just started a live video! Stream it now").
- Location-based notifications (example: "Bob is close to your area!").
- Connecting with new friends on FB (example: "Bob accepted your friend request! Say hello to your new friend Bob!").
- Marking "safety" in natural disasters (example: "Bob has been marked safe in the Cambodian earthquake").
- Memories (example: "You have memories with Bob, Rich and 3 others!").

Notification frequency will likely increase as users avail more services from the website. For example, if a user conducts a transaction on the FB Marketplace, they will likely be included in further communications from the service.

## 11.22 Extent of Data Sharing

FB has been widely criticized for its data-sharing practices, as particularly reflected in the pre-set options of the website's processing. For example, facial recognition is allowed by default along with direct marketing from advertisers. Advertisers also gain access to profile information and personal data of friends of users in the direct marketing process. But this is not to say that all settings are made public by default, as many protections have been put in place after the past scandals facing the company. These include:

- Privacy tools to review and manage future, present, and past posts.
- Audience control features like blocking and "close" friends lists.
- Privacy "check-ups" where the website reviews privacy settings and suggests measures for increasing security.
- Two-step authentication (optional).
- The "your activity" and "how people find and contact you" sections are a default setting open to friends except for certain features like requests, which are available to friends of friends.
- Location and log-in history, which can be controlled, managed, and deleted by the user.
- Activity logs, which can be controlled by the user.

- Optional and limited public posts, which can be customized by the user. The default presumption by the website is that posts would like to be made "public" to increase their network, but users control the ultimate result.
- Popular users with large networks are given "follower-based" profiles, where the public can see their posts, but only limited friends can directly contact the user.
- Identity confirmation for users seeking to advertise politically or on issues of national importance.
- FB also maintains a separate Cookie Policy, which governs the use of their internet cookies. Read with the Data Policy, it lays out the modes, uses, and restrictions on FB's collection of cookies. Users can opt out of seeing online interest-based ads from FB and other participating companies by contacting the Digital Advertising Alliance (US), the Digital Advertising Alliance of Canada, the European Interactive Digital Advertising Alliance, or otherwise through mobile device settings.[49]

Balancing privacy with reasonable data collection in social networking is yet to become a precise science. Many object to the public defaults created by FB, but the premise of the website is to create a "network" for users. "Publicity" is what many users utilize the service for, and FB tries to balance user objectives with customizability, which has only created problems for the company in the past. The main reason is that publicity of personal data directly coincides with the company's commercial interests. The financial gain in "public" data by FB indicates a habit of prioritizing shareholder needs over data subject privacy.

## 11.23 Unlike Celebrities, We Endorse without Compensation

Sharing user activity with other users is inherent to FB's business model and interface to keep users "connected" with one another. Contractually, FB will disclose user activity on advertisements and sponsored content with other users.[50] Users, when signing up for the service, automatically give their consent to have their name, profile picture, and information disclosed in connection with their advertiser actions without compensation. Many regular FB users consider this a normal aspect of the website, but the practice raises the issue of unauthorized endorsement of products by users and indiscriminate use of their publicity rights.

The right to publicity, recognized in most nations, is the right of a person to prevent unauthorized use of their name, image, persona, signature, and likeness for commercial purposes.[51] Many jurisdictions like the US Lanham Act recognize that a person's image cannot be used to sponsor or endorse products and services without their prior permission. This mode of advertising by FB can arguably qualify as a *digital endorsement* of a product/service since a user's friend will see their interest in a product and likely consider buying it more seriously based on that fact. Image interests and publicity can be very valuable based on the popularity of the user.

**Illustration:** Bo has over 5,000 FB friends owing to his popularity in a national singing competition. Many of his friends see that he is "interested" and have" viewed" sponsored pages relating to recreational marijuana paraphernalia. Bo only clicked the page and purchased items for his cousin in Amsterdam, a regular recreational user. Bo himself does not use such products, but when his "friends" see that he has visited the page and purchased goods it causes two major events:

1. Many fans are outraged by Bo's failing to be a "good role model" for the children who idolize him after the TV appearance.
2. Increased traffic on the sponsored pages that sell the marijuana products by other users who idolize Bo and considered him a customer. This drove up the overall sales of the sponsored page.

Both the "outrage" and increased sales are indicative of the two major issues discussed above. Bo's valuable endorsement helped both FB and the seller financially, but at the same time it breached his privacy interests by making his shopping habits public. Conversely, "public" figures sacrifice privacy for commercial rights in their image interests. In normal "physical" trade, Bo's endorsement of the marijuana service would be lucrative and clear to the public. The public would know that Bo endorses the product (as controversial as it may be), and Bo would be compensated for his "fame" bringing in sales. But a simple provision in FB's Terms of Service represents a deeper conflict in the intersection of online privacy, advertising and publicity interests on social media sites.

## 11.24  Whatever Happened to Trust

Certain commentators have strongly suggested that personal data should be treated as a fiduciary obligation for Controllers.[52] Just as lawyers and doctors are required to hold personal information confidential based on trust, similar principles should be implemented in personal data processing. In practice, implementing such a regime on financially motivated entities would be difficult in the absence of strict legislative mandate from the state. Additionally, on social networking websites a user may not value the same degree of privacy unlike other fiduciary arrangements. Categorizing Controllers and the type of data processed would become instrumental if this theory were to be enforced by law.[53]

## 11.25  And to Security of How We Live

FB has a decade-long track record of poor data protection practices. From cyber-security breaches, to selling data to third parties and the most recent social engineering hack of Cambridge Analytica, it is clear that the FB group faces larger systemic problems in protecting data. The UK information commissioner, Elizabeth Denham, noted that a tension exists between social media companies' advertiser-based business model and human rights like data privacy.[54] This was noted in our earlier discussion on the purpose limitation on data collection in websites rooted in "connectivity" and "openness." But this conflict is also extended by the company's decision in mid-2012 to change FB's business from a games and apps-driven desktop model to an advertising business model, delivered via smartphones.[55] The decision led the company to consistently violate self-imposed privacy restraints, grant preferential access to high-paying advertisers, and increase data collection and analytic activities in processing.

## 11.26  Who Is Responsible for Security of Our Life Data?

A brief overview of major security breaches is given below:[56]

- **2005:** Researchers at MIT created a script that downloaded publicly posted information of more than 70,000 users from four schools.
- **2007:** FB paid $9.5 million as part of a class action settlement agreement for adding user activity from other websites to be automatically included in FB profiles as part of Beacon. This was one of the website's first attempts at monetization by direct marketing.
- **2009:** Information believed to be "private" profile data was being shared publicly by the website, leading to a consent decree with the FTC in 2011.
- **2013:** A "bug" accessed over 6 million accounts in the span of a year by creating shadow profiles that collected personal data of users and their friends.
- **2014:** Cambridge Analytica and related data-gathering activities began. This became public in March 2018.
- **April 2018:** Mark Zuckerberg and other senior corporate officials were allegedly given access to user profiles ordinarily not open to others. Using this access they remotely deleted personal messages sent by the officials to others on FB.
- **April 4, 2018:** FB announced that "malicious actors" abused the search function to gather public profile information of "most of its 2 billion users worldwide."
- **June 3, 2018:** The *New York Times* reported that FB maintained data-sharing partnerships with mobile device manufacturers like Apple, Amazon, Black-Berry, Microsoft, and Samsung. Under the terms of this personal information sharing, device manufacturers were able to gather information about users to deliver "the Facebook experience" allowing those parties to obtain data about a user's FB friends, even if those friends configured their privacy settings to deny data sharing with third parties.
- **July 3, 2018:** FB acknowledged a "bug" that unblocked people who users had blocked between May 29 and June 5, 2018.
- **June 5, 2018:** New reports allege that the Chinese device manufacturers Huawei, Lenovo, Oppo, and TCL were granted access to user data under this

program. Huawei, along with ZTE, are facing scrutiny from the US government for national security risks.

- **July 12, 2018:** CNBC reported that a privacy loophole was discovered and closed by FB. A Chrome plug-in intended for marketing research called Grouply.io allowed users to access the list of members for private FB groups.
- **August 22, 2018:** FB removed the FB-owned security app Onavo from the App Store for violating privacy rules. Data collected through the Onavo app was shared with FB.
- **September 28, 2018:** FB disclosed details of a security breach that affected 50 million users. Attackers devised a way to export access tokens to gain control of user accounts by exploiting a vulnerability in the sites "view as" feature. FB is currently under investigation from the Irish Data Protection Commissioner.
- **October 25, 2018:** FB was issued a £500,000 maximum penalty by UK's Information Commissioners Office for the Analytica scandal. The same day, Vice reported that FB's advertising procedures were easy for abuse by running "false" political advertisements for many political candidates. Vice conducted a second run at the exercise on October 30, 2018 only to discover no changes have been made to FB's advertising procedures.
- **February 14, 2019:** The UK House of Commons released a comprehensive report on the Cambridge Analytica scandal and FB's involvement in disinformation campaigns by Russia. The investigation concluded that FB violated the 2011 FTC Consent Decree, and were it not for that violation the events of Analytica would not have happened.[57] Additionally, FB violated its own privacy policies and granted preferential access to advertisers by maintaining whitelisting agreements. The final report concluded that the companies on the "white list" are permitted to access friend data even if platform controls were set to private. A November 2013 e-mail discussion revealed that FB was managing 5,200 whitelisted apps.[58] Microsoft, Spotify, and Amazon were among those companies.[59]
- **March 11, 2019:** FB sued Andrey Gorbachov and Gleb Sluchevsky, of Ukraine's Web Sun Group.[60] The suit alleges that the defendants exceeded their granted permissions in harvesting data from over 63,000 profiles by using "personality quizzes." The quizzes allegedly use FB log-ins and gave the developers access to full profiles, causing over $75,000 in damages to FB. The initial permissions given by FB extended only to limited public data, thereby violating the FB Terms of Service.[61]
- **Currently pending:** The determination of the Six4Three litigation filed against FB in California district court. Six4Three were one of the whitelisted developers granted access to otherwise inaccessible data using FB products in 2012. FB revoked this access allegedly when more lucrative offers came from other advertisers. FB claims it is a publisher of online content, which gives them editorial discretion over the data Six4Three wished to access.[62]

- **Currently pending:** Another decision that will be important to the company's data protection practices is the result of GDPR investigation over FB's user monitoring and consent policies by the Irish Data Protection Commissioner.

The developments outlined above are numerous and indicate a culture of poor data protection by FB. Whether the company implements enough data security in its daily processing remains to be seen. As a "treasure-trove" of information, FB is always going to be at the center of cyber-crime, which requires stronger security in ongoing processing. The UK House of Commons' investigation into the Cambridge Analytica scandal definitively concluded misconduct and widespread data trade by FB. The "user-controls" for customization and educational tone of FB's data policy are useless if the company simply disregards privacy for revenue maximization. The actions of FB in the past decade have been justified as "mistakes" from "learning on the job,"[63] but the white-listing agreements combined with preferential access and disregarding privacy policies and user controls made widespread data abuse easy for both political and financial gain.[64]

Despite all these scandals, FB still fails to prominently publish its data-protection measures and policies. It is generally known that the website employs AI in content moderation and oversight. The automated programs help track suspicious behavior, fake profiles, bots, and cyber-crimes on the website platform. Additionally, profiles are password protected, and activity is carefully tracked. Private messaging services like Messenger and WhatsApp are protected with end-to-end encryption and can only be accessed for legally authorized purposes (like preventing crimes). But technical details of FB's data protection policies are not provided in their main pages and are rather provided in hyperlinks and secondary sources. Considering the tumultuous history discussed earlier, and GDPR's importance on data protection, it is advisable for social networking Controllers to be transparent about such measures for interested data subjects.

Facebook's data practices have already landed them under scrutiny in the US with the FTC issuing a record-breaking $5 billion fine against the social media giant for their involvement in Cambridge Analytica. Part of the settlement – which is yet to be approved by a Federal Court – gives the FTC unprecedented oversight powers over the Company's privacy practices. Notwithstanding the fines and oversight, FB is still in the process of reversing the damage of 2016 by announcing that they're suspending around 10,000 third-party apps which were harvesting user data. The details are minimal, with the company not disclosing names of the app developers or the basis for the suspension, only citing that the apps are being targeted for a "variety of reasons."[65]

## 11.27   And Then There Were More

The diversification of FB's services increases as new projects are undertaken by the company in different fields. FB Group has recently shown interest in tele-media data processing by introducing its newest product, "Portal," a voice-activated calling and webcam service for communication. Competing with Amazon's Alexa or Google's Home Assistant, FB is attempting to enter the market with physical devices, which allows for traditional or augmented[66] online communications. The webcam in Portal follows the user's movements, unlike traditional laptop/mobile cameras, which are stationary.

Additionally, FB is entering the realm of original TV programming and virtual reality using services like FB TV and Onavo. All new projects undertaken by the tech conglomerate simply increase their data collection and analysis capabilities across new mediums. But aside from GDPR obligations, internet TV brings a new set of problems related to censorship, content moderation, and larger costs. For example, consider the recent situation where a Turkish 22-year-old committed suicide on FB Live Streaming, which gave the company no opportunity to be able to censor.[67] While the services are likely operated under different privacy policies and data collection standards, the ultimate flow of information will be through the FB Group itself and the increase in mediums will change their data-protection obligations.

## 11.28   Who Is Responsible for Content?

As the FB app and Messenger become the preferred form of private and public communication, it becomes the responsibility of the Controller to moderate platform content. Websites like FB, Twitter, and Google all share a common element of providing a third-party platform for hosting free expression. Powerful discussions and movements have flourished on FB as the website helps facilitate public communication in a revolutionary medium. Users on FB utilized the variety of multimedia services provided by it to express personal and public issues and share audiovisual information and materials.

On the other hand, mediums like FB and Twitter have been powerful instruments of hate and violence with many users abusing the anonymity of the internet. SPAM links, fake accounts, cyber-bullying, and online "hate-speech" on websites like FB helped create new species of criminal law and civil liability. Cybercrimes and lawsuits primarily targeted disputes between users with companies insulated from direct liability. For example, if User 1 wants to bring a criminal action for cyber-bullying by User 2 on FB, he would direct the suit against User 2 and not FB. Or consider a defamation and hate-speech suit filed against User 1, the administrator of an anti-LGBTQ group. User 1 would be liable rather than FB, since the website is only an intermediary to the speech.

Intermediaries or "platforms" are websites that do not directly create or publish content, but merely provide a service for facilitating content and communication on its servers.[68] Modern internet legislations do not hold intermediaries liable for the content published on their websites but rather require them to remove "offensive" content within a few days of receiving notice from a user or legal authority. This requires intermediary Controllers like FB to maintain Community Standards,[69] which regulate the content moderation on the website. "Posting Guidelines" such as this help serve the following purposes:

1. Inform the users what constitutes "acceptable speech."
2. Establish the website's take-down policy of user-generated content.
3. Give clarity and support to legislative mandates imposed on the company.
4. Provide an objective policy for "moderating" free speech on the platform.
5. Evidentiary value in eventual suppression of free speech claims by users.

The presence of standards for moderating user speech is insufficient, as there should be a body responsible for overseeing the application of company rules. The oversight can be conducted by human or artificial capital, though it is advisable to combine both resources. FB maintains a team of content moderators[70] considering the widespread use of their service and recent difficulties controlling "fake" news. FB has also faced issues with fake accounts, cyber-bullying, content suppression, content prioritization, and other scandals that demonstrate the company has a challenges in managing free speech and commercial interests.

Community standards combined with content moderation and a strong "take-down" policy help many online intermediaries avoid liability related to free speech issues. In this section we briefly examine the FB Community Standards, followed by the company's content-moderation process and finally investigate the website's role in controlling fake news in the backdrop of recent investigations by UK regulators.[71]

## 11.29   Why Should Content Be Moderated?

> The fundamental reason for content moderation—its root reason for existing—goes quite simply to the issue of brand protection and liability mitigation for the platform.
>
> —Sarah T. Roberts, assistant professor, UCLA[72]

"Content moderation" is not covered by GDPR, as it tends to go beyond the subject of personal data protection. Curiously, very few laws expressly mandate content moderation by networking platforms, many times the effort is taken by the companies themselves to avoid liability. Commercially, the objectives of content moderation are laid out perfectly by Professor Roberts:

1. **Brand protection:** What users post and upload on a platform greatly defines what the website is about. If a website poorly regulates its content, the user's

newsfeed will be filled with spam, advertisements, and objectionable content such as adult entertainment and aggressive speech. But what users see and can do with the service becomes part of the platform's brand image with the public.

Twitter struggled with this issue in the first decade of its existence, where in initially the platform encouraged free speech in all forms. The popularity of the service grew with users recognizing the platform for universal free speech, where views no matter how extreme would be accepted and discussed. The appealing premise was ultimately abused with proliferation of Twitter-bots,[73] hate speech, threats of violence, and cyber-bullying. Like FB, Twitter is a platform that hosts speech and expression that is always a hotly debated topic of constitutional importance. The parameters of free speech are usually determined by the highest courts of a country, but when private companies facilitate this speech on their platforms, self-regulated content moderation becomes a necessity. Government censorship of the internet is more objectionable to companies keeping a "check" on their own platforms.

The need for content moderation led Twitter to steadily increase the specificity of its Posting Guidelines along with the removal of objectionable posts.[74] This is because the company's overall brand value was being reduced from unmoderated content from users. Twitter gained popularity for "free" speech, but became known for fake accounts, cyber-crimes, dangerous activity, and hate speech. The Twitter Rules were introduced under heavy criticism by users, but ultimately serve the purpose of protecting the Twitter brand from the downside of unregulated speech.

2. **Liability mitigation:** Though content moderation is not legally mandated, protecting users from certain speech is required in several legal frameworks. Modern criminal and civil laws recognize the harm caused from a person's activity online. Matters like illegal trade,[75] cyber-bullying,[76] hate speech,[77] and intellectual property[78] are independently covered by legislations within a country where the website offers its services. Modern legislations would likely hold FB liable as an intermediary if "illegal" posts remain on their server. Therefore, social networking companies choose to remove content preemptively to reduce liability. In some cases, the company may be held directly liable for failing to control certain content; for example, if a user is encouraged by other users to commit suicide by using hashtags or other website services.

## 11.30 There Are Community Standards

As a host for billions of individual interactions each day with a global presence, FB must moderate content for commercial and legal purposes. The first step toward self-regulating content is to memorialize a set of rules for both the users and company to follow. Content-based rules should be drafted based on the following factors:

- The purpose of the platform. **Example:** E-commerce, social networking, business networking, dating services, etc. Each platform will likely regulate the extent of open communication of ideas in their services.
- Consumer expectations. **Example:** A user of a dating website will expect more privacy than a FB user. Similarly, FB also has a "young" consumer base requiring it to regulate content strictly, while Reddit allows users to post more freely.
- Legal boundaries and requirements for "free speech and expression." The definition of "free speech" depends on a specific country's jurisprudence. While the US and EU provide broad protections, censorship remains a nuanced issue in countries all over the world.
- **Other legal mandates:** Content moderation also requires compliance with other surrounding legislations around speech, like a hate speech prohibition and removal of official government secrets from a server.
- **Maximum financial value:** From a commercial perspective, a business should consider the content that best represents their brand image to the public. Monetizing the content on the platform is best done without disrupting the brand image.

FB's intricate business model and platform are governed by their Community Standards (FB Standards or standards) that, combine the factors above and distill them. Over time the standards have developed into an independent "body of law" providing what is acceptable speech on FB. The FB standards prohibit users posting content related to:[79]

I. **Violence and criminal behavior:** "Calling" or "inciting" violence on a digital platform to cause real-world harm is difficult to identify and enforce in practice. Users may use violent threats while being sarcastic, ironic, or in nonserious ways. It is the job of FB content moderators to identify "genuine" threats and separate it from other acceptable forms of expression.
   1. Violence and incitement: FB removes content, blocks accounts, and works with law enforcement relating to genuine credible threats made against other users, individuals, groups, or places (cities or smaller). This broad provision covers the real-world harms caused by activity on FB and includes instructing, misinformation, political suppression, etc.
   2. Dangerous individuals and organizations: FB maintains an inclusive and open digital society but holds the role of fighting crime on their website. The company removes posts that are involved in or that praise organizations engaged in terrorism, "organized" hate, mass murder, human trafficking, and organized crime. This provision prohibits using FB services for large-scale criminal activity that carries the most risk for the company in the countries they operate in.

      FB is notorious for poorly enforcing this provision with numerous reports of speech suppression by foreign governments working with the website against dissenting voices.[80] Defining a "terrorist group" or "organized hate" is dependent on the social, historical, and political context of a country, which makes FB vulnerable to state misuse of the service.

3. Promoting or publicizing crime: Supporting criminal activity by creating "content depicting, admitting, or promoting the following criminal acts committed by you or your associates" is prohibited by FB. Content moderators are responsible for separating rhetorical and satirical posts relating to criminal activities. Users are also allowed to debate or advocate for the legality of the crimes as well.

4. Coordinating harm: While §I.2 of the FB Standards prohibits the use of the service by certain organizations, §I.4 prohibits criminal acts by individual users and those groups. For example, drug dealers using FB wall-posts for coordinating with their customers. Or a political page misrepresenting voting details to suppress voter turn-out on election day.

5. Regulated goods: FB prohibits posts that promote, encourage, coordinate, or advertise the sale and purchase of regulated goods such as pharmaceuticals, marijuana, nonmedical drugs, firearms, organs, alcohol, etc. The policy is carried out consistently across its platforms regardless of their overall legality. If a product or services is regulated, retailers (example: firearms) are permitted to operate on FB if they comply with all applicable laws and regulations.

   A criticized prohibition under this Section is the bar against "Content that attempts to sell, gift, exchange, transfer, promote or otherwise provide access to instructions for 3D printing or computer-aided manufacturing of firearms or firearm parts." The company faced significant dissent from users and free-speech advocates for including this prohibition after blueprints uploaded by a user caused physical harm.[81]

   §I.5 lays a broad prohibition and must be read with the FB Commerce Policies for full compliance. It is important to note that FB only restricts visibility to adults over 21 for content posted by a brick-and-mortar store, legitimate website, or brand that "coordinates or promotes the sale or transfer of firearms, firearm parts, ammunition, or explosives." This provision gives FB discretion in presenting regulated goods to users based on where the users are located and creates an exception to the prohibition against regulated goods. By prohibiting users to post content related to such goods but allowing stores to advertise, FB manages to control the sale and purchase of regulated goods on their website.

**II. Safety threats:** The second category of prohibited content relates to targeted activity against other users that may place their safety in jeopardy. FB uses this provision to encourage safety on their platform and has the power to remove posts, work with law enforcement, and encourage awareness for these causes.

6. Suicide and self-injury: Encouraging, promoting, coordinating, or giving instructions for suicide, self-harm, and eating disorders is prohibited on FB. Users may only post content to promote awareness of self-harm or if the content shared is newsworthy. However, clear warnings and disclaimers[82] must be provided to protect sensitive users.

7. Child nudity and sexual exploitation of children: As one of the unanimously accepted cyber-crimes around the world, exploitation of children is often strongly enforced online. FB provides detailed guidelines on protecting children and reports any abuse to the National Center for Missing and Exploited Children (NCMEC), in compliance with applicable law.

8. Sexual exploitation of adults: Like §II.7, FB also protects adults from non-consensual sexual exploitation and violence. FB maintains a "Guide to Reporting and Removing Intimate Images Shared Without Your Consent,"[83] which helps simplify the posting rules. This provision is likely in response to the trend of "revenge-porn" posting that existed in the early years of social networking. Considering the recent Me Too movement and other instances of victims sharing their stories to bring attention to crimes against them, FB allows discussion of such events based on the context/caption given.

9. Bullying and harassment: As mentioned earlier, cyber-bullying is a newer crime, which grew as social media sites were used to belittle or torment individuals to inflict physical or emotional harm. Bullying polices apply to individual users but do not apply to public figures (insofar that the posts do not violate other policies like hate speech or credible threats). Like the sexual exploitation of minors, cyber-bullying is a crime that bears extra attention by FB since it directly affects their young users who are especially vulnerable to attack. For this reason, the company maintains a Bullying Prevention Hub to report abuse and protect users.

   Social media platforms gave rise to internet-trolls who try to "annoy" and "harass" other users for amusement. The FB harassment policy applies to both public and private individuals to prevent unwanted or malicious contact on the platform. This provision does not qualify as a "credible threat" but may cover posts that fall under the subjects mentioned above. This includes sending messages related to the prohibitions in the FB standards, repeatedly messaging a user despite their clear desire and action to prevent that contact, or repeatedly contacting large numbers of people with no prior solicitation.

10. Privacy violations and image privacy rights: FB standards prevent the theft and dissemination of users' personal data by other users through a variety of prohibitions. The prohibited content identifies a user in some form, collected or "stolen" by hacking,[84] phishing, or other methods.

    **Example:** User 1 posts the picture and address of User 2 along with the caption "User 2, whose details are below is a recently released SEX OFFENDER now allowed to stay in our neighborhood! Everyone, keep a vigilant eye out for this man and address. Someone...please get him to move far far away!!" Though the information of User 2 is obtained from his FB profile and public records, the post can still be removed for violating user privacy.

    This provision of the FB standards is deeply intertwined with the company's GDPR compliance as they need to maintain data integrity on their servers. Processing security cannot be achieved when user privacy is being eroded by other users on a Controller's servers. Though it may be ironic for users to make "privacy" requests on a platform rooted in "sharing," FB as an intermediary is responsible for removing any identifiable information to protect users under GDPR and other domestic legislations. Removing such posts will also coincide with the data subjects' right to erasure.

The second aspect to this rule relates to the Right to Publicity and Image Interests held by a user in his/her appearance and persona. Considered one of the three main privacy torts laid down by Warren and Brandeis,[85] publicity gives a person the right to protect their image from unauthorized use and commercial exploitation. FB removes photos/videos of minors (under 13, or between 13 and 18 years), a foreign national who can cite legal authority for removing the post, and incapacitated adults. Note that the claimants under FB standards are narrower than those under statute, which is open to any competent plaintiff. This is likely because "competent" users can utilize the other removal services available on their FB settings.

III. **Objectionable content:** While the previous categories dealt with objective threats to a user's safety, "objectionable" post removal is more subjective. Issues like nudity, "hate" speech, and violence can be considered as acceptable to a user based on their sensitivities.

**Example:** User 1 is a "city-grown" individual with a strong "stomach" for violence and nudity, while User 2 from a rural background would likely find a "nude" video to be pornographic. FB plays the role of censor in moderating this content and uses intricate posting guidelines under §III to specify what is unacceptable.

11. Hate speech: Legislators and Supreme Courts have struggled to define what hate speech is and what qualifies as "hate" speech. This is mainly because hate speech walks a fine line between free speech and suppressing dissent, with courts struggling to quantify what "hate" is. FB defines hate speech as a direct attack on people based on legally protected attributes like race, ethnicity, national origin, religious affiliation, sexual orientation, caste, sex, gender, gender identity, and serious disease or disability. The website also offers limited protection to a person's immigration status as well.

"Hate" is triggered in cases of violent or dehumanizing speech or posts that call for exclusion or segregation. Online hate speech may be defined by the Supreme Court of a country, but the enforcement of that definition falls on platforms like FB, Twitter, Tumblr, etc. To effectively enforce this subjective concept, FB follows a three-tier system based on the content and wording of the posts.

12. Violence and graphic content: "Graphic" violence or content are posts that glorify or celebrate violence and suffering of others. Social media platforms cannot outright ban violent content as many viewers may enjoy,

and a prohibition will reduce the website's use. As a result, FB creates three categories of posts with varying degrees of violence. Based on that classification, FB either prohibits posting or includes disclaimers, age filters, and warnings of the sensitive content.

13. Adult nudity and sexual activity: While FB strives to become the platform that digitally represents society and its communication, many sectors of society object to "adult" content. Like the provision on violence, FB censors its platform by restricting and removing posts that represent sexual imagery or displays of sexual activity. The "nuanced" provision of the FB standards considers the educational, humorous, satirical, medical, and artistic motivations behind nudity and its use.

14. Sexual solicitation: Posts by users are removed "when content facilitates, encourages or coordinates sexual encounters between adults." Note that the prohibition against sexual exploitation deals with serious crimes,[86] while standards relating to nudity and sexual activity (discussed above) control adult content posted by users. "Sexual solicitation" relates to the commercialization of "sex" on FB and is prohibited in all forms.

15. Cruel and insensitive: This "catch-all" provision of the FB standards is short but broadly prohibits content that targets victims of serious physical or emotional harm. This includes "content that depicts real people and mocks their implied or actual serious physical injuries, disease, or disability, nonconsensual sexual touching, or premature death."

    Posts that are "cruel and insensitive" cover matters not otherwise discussed in the preceding provisions that may hurt certain users. A relevant example of this would be the repeated attacks made against Christine Blasé Ford during the Brett Kavanaugh US Supreme Court senate confirmation hearings, where she admitted to being targeted by many users in cyber-bullying attacks. Her case falls under "non-consensual sexual touching" and should be read with §2.10 on harassment.

IV. **Integrity and authenticity:** Closely linked to GDPR compliance (as opposed to the categories discussed above), §IV of the FB standards handles matters related to data protection and security on the platform and the overall integrity of the website.

16. Spam: "Commercial spam" was one of the first issues that the website faced in its early years of operation as FB faced a proliferation of "fake" actors on its website. The standards prohibit users from using misleading or inaccurate information to collect likes, followers, or shares. This includes creating fake accounts, artificially increasing post likes or shares, restricting access to posts, using false pretenses to encourage post activity, using personal data or log-in credentials, and promising nonexistent FB features. The standards prohibit users from tampering with the website's natural functions to gain popularity or money.

17. Misrepresentation: Read with FB Naming Policies, users are required to create authentic accounts based on their everyday identities. After a decade

of "fake" news and profiles, the standards prohibit misrepresentation, account misuse, impersonation, and inauthentic behavior. Each activity under §IV.18 serves to prevent the creating, managing, and perpetuating of profiles on FB that mislead as to the identity of the account holder. This includes sharing accounts, maintaining multiple profiles, fake naming, and stealing other users' identities. Note that GDPR does not require Controllers to maintain "true" data expressly but may require inauthentic profiles to be removed in line with erasure, restriction, and data minimization/security.

18. False news: FB's procedures relating to false news will be examined in detail later on in this section along with the recent report issued by the UK House of Commons on February 14, 2019.[87]

19. Memorialization: GDPR only deals with the personal data of the living, and not the dead.[88] However, FB hosts the personal data of deceased users by memorializing the account. Once a user passes away, the website ads a tag "Remembering" a profile for those friends who wish to pay their respects. The tag makes it clear that the account is a memorial protected against attempted log-ins and fraudulent activity, with the profile's original state maintained.[89] Permanent account deletion takes place either by a pre-mortem expression of will by the user or by the legacy contact they provide to the website. Account deletion can also be raised by a next of kin, who can express the user's living wishes for erasure.

## V. Respecting Intellectual Property

20. Intellectual property: Trademarks and copyright are the most valuable intangible properties hosted on FB servers. IP rights are created, used ("fairly"[90] and commercially) and flow through FB daily. Many modern IP statutes consider the fluid nature of internet infringement and provide strong remedies to the rights holder for enforcing those interests. Social media platforms are considered as intermediaries in IP infringement cases and are legally required to remove infringing content within a designated time period (such as 72 hours). For this reason, FB and other websites take IP policies seriously and incorporate respecting those rights in their Terms of Service directly.

IP in social media websites is a complex subject considering the speed of file sharing and difficulties in tracking infringement. A useful practice is to categorize IP interests by type and ownership. On websites like FB, content is created and owned mainly by three parties: the user, the platform, and third-party affiliates. As a website for "expression," FB hosts user-generated creative content protected by IP statutes (like Trademark, Copyright, Software,[91] Publicity,[92] etc.). Though ownership of the content remains with the user, platforms like FB acquire a mandatory license for using that content. FB's Terms of Service lay the following condition:[93]

"Specifically, when you share, post, or upload content that is covered by intellectual property rights (like photos or videos) on or in connection with our Products, you grant us a non-exclusive, transferable, sub-licensable, royalty-free, and worldwide license to host, use, distribute, modify, run, copy, publicly perform or display, translate, and create derivative works of your content (consistent with your privacy and application settings)."

The broad license given to FB is the industry standard in social networking websites and other services that allow user-generated content. For example, food delivery apps that allow for user reviews do so on the condition that the Controller get a license to those posts. Essentially users receive means to express creativity and originality in exchange for the platform to broad and nonexclusive permission to use that content. Users can only opt out of the license by deleting their profiles, and it cannot be altered by their settings.[94]

For many users, this provision of the Terms of Service is inconsequential as they are unlikely to create content with monetary value. However, users who create something valuable are likely to see a dilution in their IP's value as one corporate entity already has authorized access to use it.

**Example:** A user who posts poetry and prose on her FB profile is approached by a publishing house to make a book compiling those posts. FB already has a legal right to distribute and display the works based on their Terms of Service.

Conversely, the FB platform protects its own IP very strictly[95] by retaining rights over its trademarks, source code, products, etc. Under the Terms of Service, users are prohibited from using FB's IP without prior written permission and it can only be done so in compliance with FB's Brand Usage Guidelines.[96] The Brand Usage Guidelines along with the licensing provision and Community Standards are the three instruments FB uses to regulate IP on its servers. The commercial nature of the platform clearly orients IP interests to align with FB's business goals, but this is the standard model of most social media platforms, indicating a need for a more systemic change in online IP rights.

VI. **Content-related requests:** Requests under this category coincide with GDPR requests related to erasure, restriction, and protecting minors.

21. User requests: Removal requests made by the user, their legacy contact, or an authorized representative will be respected by FB. Note that §VI.22 does not relate to a larger "policy" like the preceding categories of content, but only includes a directive.

22. Additional protection of minors: FB also removes content relating to underage accounts, child-abuse imagery, and posts that attack unintentionally famous minors.

The Community Standards create a secondary, independent body of law for FB content moderation. While the State may provide for the protections through law, FB's content rules help to enforce nuanced concepts of free speech by giving a codified source of application. Users automatically consent to the Community Standards when consenting to the FB Terms of Service making the standards binding on all users of FB. However, the community guidelines fail to state that FB takes the role of curating the content seen by users. The FB standards only provide what is or not allowed but do not highlight the content moderation process that removes and shows content to the users. What users see in their newsfeed is entirely determined by the company's algorithms, which is proprietary and often kept secret.

Tailoring newsfeed content is FB's discretion and is designed to attract maximum usage from consumers. This leaves FB with the power to control the information flows on its platform, which has been abused in the past by the website. Aside from the well-known facts of the Cambridge Analytica scandal, FB has been accused of trying to increase website usage by allowing "outrage porn" that incites strong emotions from users. For example, the website allegedly "neglected" to remove a post that depicted a child being beaten multiple times to increase discourse between users and attract new users.[97] Another example would be FB escalating illegal content in India and Pakistan regardless of humor or context to increase user involvement.[98]

The rules provide for the backbone for content moderation on the platform, but its application needs to be carried out genuinely by the Controller to be effective in practice.

## 11.31 Process for Content Moderation

With 2 billion users posting in over a hundred different languages, and generating over a billion posts daily, content moderation is a complex logistical problem for FB.[99] Setting Community Standards is only the first step towards content moderation and serves as a codification of user rules. Overseeing rule-application, tailoring, and moderating the platform content requires a combination of AI and human intervention. FB aims to review content with an error rate of less than 1% with a response within 24 hours.

### 11.31.1 Identifying and Determining Content Removal Requests

FB employs roughly 7,500 human moderators who follow the Community Standard written by a Policy Team consisting of lawyers, public relations professionals, ex-public policy wonks, and crisis management experts.[100] The first layer of protection in moderation is the artificial intelligence FB utilizes to identify posts that violate the rules and flag content for the human moderators. AI is effective in identifying objective violations of the standards like pornographic and violent images/videos, or spam and fake accounts. For subjective violations of the FB standards like hate speech, privacy violations, and "credible" threats, the second layer, namely, the human moderators intervene. Moderators review content flagged by the AI or on user request and decide whether to remove the post or abstain from acting. Human moderators employed by FB are divided into the following teams:[101]

- Content moderation crisis team
- Software writing and AI development

- Accuracy and consistency team overseeing global application of the standards
- Oversight and coordination team who ensure the other teams are working together

Decisions on removing content in FB are made through exchanged e-mails and meetings conducted across the company's headquarters based on the policy considerations of the FB standards.[102] Determinations outside of the rules must fit the spirit of the policy behind the rule. During "crisis" events FB launches lockdowns where policy teams focus on a single urgent content moderation issue for extended period of time.

## 11.32 Prospective Content Moderation "Supreme Court"

The determinations of the FB content moderation team are often subjective and widely criticized. Free speech advocates claim that the company polices stifle expression, while privacy advocates claim the policies are too lax. This is primarily because FB performs the task of censorship which leads to subjective determinations on free speech and expression. Other platforms like Twitter and Tumblr faced the same issues when they decided to tighten their content-moderation policies. In response to these difficulties FB announced in November 2018 that it plans on establishing a FB Content Moderation Appeals Court to review subjective complaints against posts.[103] Mark Zuckerberg wrote:

> First, it will **prevent the concentration** of too much decision-making within our teams. Second, it will **create accountability** and oversight. Third, it will provide assurance that these decisions are made in the **best interests of our community and not for commercial reasons**.

Despite the "user-oriented" purposes cited by the website's founder, this decision will likely concentrate the power to decide free speech disputes with the company itself. Speech is considered a constitutional issue in most nations, and the decision to create a private "supreme court" for content moderation will virtually give the website the power to unilaterally decide what is seen on their platform. FB expects to establish the appellate system by the end of 2019, and it will likely mark a change in the content moderation business with other companies following it. Whether this system will be implemented by binding arbitration awards or judicially appealable orders shall determine the overall legality of the proposed system.

## 11.33 Working with Governmental Regimes

As a key form of communication globally, FB is subject to a diverse set of legal requirements that affect the free speech and privacy expectations of its users. Government requests to reveal or stifle speech are routine, and FB has been used as a weapon of oppressive regimes on numerous occasions.[104] Interface with governmental content requests can trigger the following:

1. Privacy violations of users from state requests to reveal personal data and profile history
2. Free speech violations from requiring FB to remove content due to domestic restrictions and prohibitions on expression
3. The user's right to information on matters of public interest published on FB
4. Underlying public policy of the law governing the request
5. Commercial interests of FB in being allowed to operate in a country

Balancing the competing interests will likely create a result that harms at least one of the stakeholders mentioned above. The main concern occurs when political policies and requests are prioritized by the website to ensure the commercial goal of operating their service in the country. FB has in the past aligned its business motivations with political objectives resulting in free speech being stifled. At present, nine countries actively pursue issues around holocaust denial with FB policies.[105] To comply with local laws that mandate removal of any holocaust denial posts, FB blocked users with IP addresses from these nine countries. In doing so, FB prevents users from those countries from viewing such content. The solution complies with domestic requirements on free speech but does so by stifling the user's information flow. At the same time, FB ensures that the service does not get blocked in that country, thereby securing their commercial motivations.

## 11.34  "Live" Censorship

As FB steadily increases its platform's services, the complexity of content moderation also rises. For example, in October 2016 a 22-year-old Turkish man logged into FB livestreaming services and said:[106] "No one believed when I said I will kill myself ... So watch this." (The user proceeded to commit suicide on "live" camera.)

This incident along with cases of live hate speech, terrorism threats, and violence alerted FB to the new layer of complexity in platform censorship. While moderating texts, photos, and videos can be easily identified and banned quickly, it is difficult for content moderators to censor videos that happen "live" as the damage is harder to control. FB will have to come up with creative solutions to censor live videos as the service gains popularity on its sister platform Instagram. Merely removing the archive of the live video is not effective in preventing liability or harm to users. One option is for FB to create time delays between the recording and streaming of the live video to provide moderators a chance to review the content. However, the appeal of "live" recording is the ability to interact real-time with the user on the video, which implies that time-delays will hurt the quality of the live services.

As FB expands its operations into the IP TV sector with FB Watch, it can anticipate more issues in real-time censorship. The unpredictability of "live" streaming demands more human moderator involvement in reviewing videos. Additionally, removing "live" content requires immediate action to minimize any PR or legal issues. Any censorship of live videos will lead to users "gaming" the system by starting misleading videos only to introduce objectionable content later on in the performance. FB in expanding its services attracts more regulation of their business and more rigorous oversight of its content. Transitioning into the IP TV and telemedia will only augment these issues in the coming decade.

## 11.35    Disinformation and "Fake" News

FB's ability to control the flow of information was highlighted after the Cambridge Analytica scandal that surrounded the 2016 US presidential elections. Recently in February 2019 the UK House of Commons Digital, Culture, Media and Sport Committee issued a final report titled "Disinformation and 'Fake News'" ("final report"), which outlines the investigations of the committee into FB and Russian involvement in the Analytica Scandal. The comprehensive report outlines:

- FB's excessive personal data collection
- FB's advertising policies and practices
- FB's data sale to third parties and advertisers
- FB's data analytics services and creation of "psychological profiles"
- People and corporations involved in the Cambridge Analytica scandal
- How FB was used to spread disinformation during political elections
- How elections were influenced by the disinformation
- Which elections were affected

The final report links all the matters listed above and creates recommendations for fighting disinformation on social networking websites. The final report also includes how the investigation was conducted along with evidentiary support. With US Special Counsel Robert Mueller's final report finally released to the public, misconduct on FB's part and Russian involvement is evident. Mark Zuckerberg assured EU lawmakers that FB will make fundamental changes for fighting fake news like implementing AI and third-party fact-checkers. But this leaves the company with the problematic task of determining

- What is "truth" on the internet?
- Who decides if something is "true"?

### 11.35.1    "Disinformation"

"Fake" news is a term popularized by US President Donald Trump, but a more apt technical term is disinformation. This is not uncommon in history with many nations resorting to disinformation campaigns when trying to push military or political agendas. As information and mass communication shifted from print to phone, disinformation grew on a new medium. In this era, users know better than to believe everything read on the internet, but not all users have the time or drive to fact-check whether journalism is true.

While "digitally educated" users know to check the journalistic source, supporting materials, and secondary sources, "digitally illiterate" users tend to believe news that looks "official." It is important to remember that in many nations large sectors of the population (and more importantly, voters) are not "digitally literate" and only recently joined FB to stay connected. Foreign nations, companies, political parties are highly cognizant of this fact and manipulate "illiterate" users to push forward an agenda or ideology. In its final report, the UK House of Commons defined disinformation as:

> The deliberate creation and sharing of false and/or manipulated information that is intended to deceive and mislead audiences, either for the purposes of causing harm, or for political, personal or financial gain. "Misinformation" refers to the inadvertent sharing of false information.[107]

This strategy is employed in all forms of disinformation, but technology and personal data collection has helped to customize it. The investigation revealed that personal data, collected from users' FB profiles and other sources that utilized FB products (like apps, plug-ins, like and share buttons, pixel, etc.) were utilized with data analytics to create a *psychological profile* of the user. As discussed earlier in this chapter, FB hosts a variety of methods for data production and collection that give the company access to personal *and* special data. The information collected helps identify a user's interests, political and philosophical outlook, humor preferences, etc. Additionally, FB had access to data that helped point to what outraged users, what they "like" and "share," and most importantly, the captions tailored to show the user's views on the subject. The mined data along with the psychological profiles helped Russian hackers accurately target the disinformation to "swing"/ "undecided" voters in elections.

**Illustration:** David wanted to buy a property in Anglewood to open a second branch of his business. To lower the property price, David creates multiple fake IDs on FB using different e-mail addresses. All the fake FB profiles were created with proxy IP addresses to represent that the users live in Anglewood. The fake profiles then "friended" users and joined pages that relate to Anglewood. David then creates multiple "authentic-looking" websites and FB pages that spread stories of a "tainted water" and "lead pollution" in Anglewood, which caused mass paranoia with the public and local news stations. Additionally, David's fake profiles and pages shared the disinformation, which caused the price of the property to drop significantly. Brett, Bob, and Rich, David's FB friends, all shared the stories, believing them to be true.

In the illustration above, David is guilty of spreading disinformation for personal and financial gain as his actions were clearly deliberate. Brett, Bob, and Rich are guilty of misinformation since they inadvertently shared the disinformation. Note that the House of Commons definition of disinformation does not include targeting specific audiences, but is only conditional on actions to mislead them. Therefore, the fact that David did not customize and/or target users does not prevent him for being charged with spreading disinformation.

### 11.35.2  False News Policy

FB Community Standard §IV.19 elaborates the company's policy for moderating disinformation on their platform. This recent addition to the FB standards was crafted against the backdrop of the Cambridge Analytica scandal but lacks specificity, unlike the other provisions that deal with content moderation. While provisions dealing with misrepresentation, nudity, bullying, etc., all contain definitions, posting guidelines, and examples of acceptable activity, the False News provision does not.

Owing to the volume of information shared on FB, the platform takes the sensitive role of regulating the news flow for the public. But unlike traditional platforms of print and broadcast journalism, FB does not investigate, fact-check, certify, or publish the news stories. At the same time, FB controls what news stories are seen. The company is in a unique position to moderate journalism and information without being responsible for the authenticity of the story. This requires it to be more responsible.

At the outset, it is important to note that FB does not remove false news but only "significantly" reduces its distribution by showing it lower on the newsfeed.[108] This is likely because "removal" of a false post will attract claims of stifling free speech and censoring public information.[109] Removal will also require more involvement from the FB moderators, as each story will have to be fact-checked, interpreted, and verified for FB to confidently remove the post.

**Illustration:** Kenneth is a prominent left-wing conspiracy theorist who uses interlinked facts from broadcast and print journalism to "hypothesize" the larger picture. His FB profile and group consistently post his "theories" in the form of an FB Note. One of his theories alleges that the presidential candidate had an affair with the secretary of agriculture. Users and journalists on FB complained the news is baseless and false, with Kenneth responding "I laid out my theory. Please prove me wrong if you want to say I'm lying!"

In the illustration above, if FB were to remove the post, Kenneth's supporters can likely allege that the platform is stifling valid "commentary" on political events and determining what is and is not true. As a result, FB exercises its discretion in reducing visibility of his "news" stories. As the content moderator, FB can prevent Kenneth from having a voice in the public. Whether this compromise by FB is an appropriate "fix" to the fake news problem remains to be seen. Reducing visibility shields the company from liability in free speech claims and serves a smart commercial purpose. Removal attracts public attention to a matter that was seen recently with Alex Jones and other right-wing commentators being removed from services like Spotify and Pandora.

§IV.19 also sheds light on how FB is generally combating fake news. The provision does not provide specifics on how the measures are being carried out. FB's measures to "reduce the spread of false news" include:

1. Disrupting economic incentives for people, pages, and domains that propagate misinformation
2. Using various signals, like community feedback, to inform a machine learning model that predicts which stories may be false
3. Reducing the distribution of content rated as false by independent third-party fact-checkers
4. Empowering people to decide for themselves what to read, trust, and share by informing them with greater context and promoting news literacy
5. Collaborating with academics and other organizations to help solve this challenging issue

The measures above speak in general terms and do not cite how the mechanics of combating the issue will be undertaken. It would be difficult for regulators to oversee if FB is "disrupting" economic incentives or "reducing" distribution. Machine-learning models and "collaboration" are aspirational and yet to be implemented by the website. For FB to effectively combat fake news and the issues that surround it, the Community Standards need to be updated to:

- Better define "false news" and the concepts of disinformation and misinformation.
- Define the position, role, and appointment process of the third-party fact-checkers.
- State the threshold between true, false, and subjective "facts" that guide the fact-checkers.
- Elaborate on the company's *visibility policy* and how distribution of FB will be reduced.
- Elaborate on how "economic incentives" will be reduced.
- Exhaustively state what "signals" will be used in the prospective AI to reduce personal data misuse.

### 11.35.3 Fixing the "Fake News" Problem

The changes to the Community Standards on disinformation/false news should be read with the recent recommendations of the UK House of Commons final report. The 108-page report provides conclusions to the Analytica investigation, which points to the culpability of FB and other entities like SCL, AIQ, and Cambridge Analytica and proceeds to provide measures on how to fix disinformation on social networking platforms. The relevant recommendations have been summarized below:

1. **New category of entity:** A long debate that surrounds social networking websites is the legal categorization of the entities for determining liability. FB, Twitter, and other websites claim to be "platforms," which enable communication and distribute information rather than "publishers" with editorial discretion

over the content distributed. In its early years of operation FB claimed to be a "neutral" platform, which only facilitates communication and hosts user-generated content. However, as content moderation has grown into a central issue for social networking companies, websites like FB have been aggressively regulating and censoring written and visual content.[110]

In the US, the status of social networking sites is a longstanding debate under Section 230 of the Communications Decency Act with Controllers like FB claiming to be "platforms" for connecting entities like AT&T or Verizon. Platforms only provide the channels for communications with minimal power to moderate consumer activity on the service. For example, a company like Verizon cannot block or restrict calls and conversations made on their phone-lines by their consumers. Therefore, communication platforms are not liable for user activity on their services.

Publishers, on the other hand, hold editorial discretion, which is a free speech right protected constitutionally in many nations, giving them the power to decide what not to publish. Editorial discretion is accompanied by liability for content published by the website, even if it is user-generated. Social networking companies in the US (and many other countries) still claim platform status, thereby insulating them from liability notwithstanding the fact that the websites moderate user content. Mark Zuckerberg has admitted that the company is "responsible for the content" on its platform, that justified the removal of pages and groups which support certain political ideologies.[111] But this "responsibility" comes without a change in entity status to publisher.

The status of FB is further convoluted when examining recent claims in court proceedings by its claim that the website is a publisher entitled to First Amendment protections.[112] In response to a lawsuit filed by Six4Three alleging wrongful removal of developer access to "friends' data," FB claimed that data access decisions by the company are a "quintessential publisher function" thereby entitling them to constitutional protection. The conflicting positions of FB in court and in public once again raised questions as to the true legal status of the company under Section 230 of the Communications Decency Act. Meanwhile, a separate case pending in the US Supreme Court will soon determine if users can file First Amendment lawsuits against social media operators.[113]

The pending Six4Three court case and official related documents were crucial in the UK House of Commons' final report. This is because FB's dealings with Six4Three highlight the company's excessive data collection, preferential data access using "white-lists," and the denial of access previously given to developers (defrauding those entities). The personal data sharing by FB played into the events of Cambridge Analytica and the consequences that followed. The House of Commons recommended that social networking companies be reclassified into a new category of regulated entities separate from platform/publisher status.[114] The recommendation claims that social networking companies cannot evade publisher liability by claiming to be a platform. The new category of entities will be liable for content created by users on their websites.

2. **Imposing a levy:** The recategorization of social media companies into independently regulated entities requires consistent oversight of the overall information flows and content moderation practices by the UK ICO. The committee recommended that the government consider imposing a digital services tax on social media companies operating in the UK to fund the ICO's increased role in the system.[115]

3. **Digital campaigning:** The 2016 US presidential election and the alleged Russian influence on the process by weaponizing social media platforms opened a series of investigations into foreign disinformation campaigns to advance political causes. The final report concluded that disinformation campaigns are more common than initially anticipated with elections in EU member states, Iran, Venezuela, Ukraine, and the Brexit referendum suspected to be tampered by Russian influence.[116] While targeted commercial advertising erodes privacy for financial gain, digital campaigning on social media platforms can change history.

   The final report recognizes the power of targeted political campaigning and recommends that the UK Government create a law which would:[117]
   a. Define digital campaigning.
   b. Elaborate what constitutes valid political campaigning online.
   c. What disclaimers and statements should be made when ads are not sponsored by a specific political party.
   d. Acknowledge the "role and power" of unpaid political campaign FB groups that influence the outcome of elections/referendums.
   e. Mandate that paid-for political advertising be publicly accessible, clear, and easily recognizable. Recipients should be able to identify the source, who uploaded it, who sponsored it, and its country of origin.[118]
   f. Political advertising items should be publicly accessible in a searchable repository stating who is paying for the ads, which organizations are sponsoring the ad, who is being targeted by the ads. This way the public can understand the behavior of individual advertisers. The repository should run independently of the advertising industry and of political parties.[119]

4. **Shell companies and targeted advertising:** FB's digital advertising supply chain is complex by design. In terms of scale, FB has 2.2 billion users globally who produce and/or provide personal data. This data is shared with advertisers and their subsidiaries using FB products like plug-ins and pixel. Those same products help to gather data from external sources which feed into the trove of data available to advertisers. The Six4Three case and the committee investigation revealed that FB maintained "white lists" that gave certain wealthy advertisers preferential access to otherwise private data.[120] FB claims users have "control" over their data and content, which can be deleted at will. However, users cannot access, control, or delete the advertising profile that FB maintains on them.[121]

This is arguably a violation of GDPR Article 15 as it denies data subject access, but the advertising profile likely only contains inferred data based on personal characteristics.

The scale of users, and mass data production, sharing, and gathering between FB and its advertising partners is made complex by a network of corporations that share personal data with one another for financial and political gain. The information flowing internally and externally through FB requires greater scrutiny for effective regulation.

The final report recommends[122] that concerned entities must be transparent and disclose shell companies operating in their digital advertising supply chain. Companies cannot hide the identity of advertising purchases, especially regarding political causes. The UK government should explore methods of regulating external targeting and advertising transparency.

5. **Publicize disinformation campaigns:** The final report also recommends that social media companies share information on any foreign interference on their sites with the public.[123] This information includes who paid for political ads, who has seen the ads, and who has clicked on the ads. Companies will be held financially liable if disclosure is not done properly. To ensure that a "real" person is behind an account, FB should implement security certificates and authenticate profiles.

6. **Tracking and research on advertiser data use:** The final report recognized certain tools have been developed that help users oversee their data use like "Who Targets Me?,"[124] a browser extension that helped users understand how they were being targeted with ads during elections. FB users can view personalized statistics on their advertising exposure. The data is also collated into a master database, shared exclusively with researchers and journalists interested in exposing misinformation, election overspending, and microtargeting, and other issues. On January 9, 2014, Who Targets Me? and all other organizations operating in this space, like ProPublica and Mozilla, lost access to this data.[125] FB blocked researcher access to this data to conceal advertiser activity. Since then, research on FB-advertiser data sharing has been minimal.

The ICO along with the committee recommended a Code of Practice be created to publicize the use of personal information in political campaigning, which includes an age-appropriate design code and a data protection and journalism code.[126]

7. **Digital literacy:** The committee also recommended that digital literacy be included in the fourth pillar of education, alongside reading, writing, and math.[127] The programs should be based online, and a comprehensive educational framework should be created by charities, NGOs, or regulators.

8. **Code of ethics:** As mentioned at the beginning of this section, many countries do not have a "Content Moderation Law" that dictates what should or should not appear on FB newsfeeds. Rather, moderation is carried out based on an amalgamation of legal mandates from different sources of law. Social media companies were free to remove and tailor content as they saw fit with minimal interference.

The final report recommends that the new category of entity created should be regulated like the broadcast sector operating under an independent code of ethics. The code should be developed by technical experts and overseen by an independent regulator. The regulatory guidelines should codify what is or not acceptable on social media. This includes harmful and illegal content referred to the companies for removal by their users, or that should have been easy for tech companies themselves to identify.[128]

How this new code of ethics will interplay with GDPR remains to be seen. Any new legislation should be drafted to complement GDPR mandates and standards or provide for even stricter requirements.

I think this finds the right balance between ubiquity, reciprocity, and profit.
—Mark Zuckerberg[129]

The description of FB's advertising deals is best summed up by their founder in the quote above. Behavioral monitoring leads to inferred data that matches advertisers to lookalike audiences with terabytes of personal data flowing in and out of the company daily. FB is a corporation focused on revenue maximization and profitable contracts. As the size of the company grows to dominate the social media market, app developers pay large sums for advertising, while FB uses the money to target and acquire any direct or potential competitors who enter the market.[130]

Legislation on content moderation, but more importantly, on online disinformation and "false news" is the safest path forward. Foreign influence in social media is not limited to FB alone. In October 2018 Twitter released an archive of tweets that had been shared by accounts from the Internet Research Agency, with the goal of "encouraging open research and investigation of these behaviors from researchers and academics around the world."[131] The datasets consisted of 3,841 accounts affiliated with the Internet Research Agency originating from Russia, and 770 other accounts, potentially originating in Iran. The accounts included more than 10 million tweets and more than 2 million images.[132] The Twitter accounts were used to influence the 2016 US presidential election, as well as elections, referenda, and issues of national importance in several other countries, including the UK and Ukraine.[133]

FB, on January 17, 2019, removed 289 pages and 75 accounts from its site. The accounts removed had approximately 790,000 followers spending $135,000 on ads between October 2013 and January 2019. The sites were run by employees of Sputnik, a Russian state-owned news agency. Additionally, around 190 events were hosted by these pages beginning in August 2015; the most recent was scheduled for January 2019.[134] The numbers alone show the scope of the influence social networking websites hold over the masses, acting as a primary form of communication, internet, and news. Like broadcast journalism, consistent regulatory oversight is required to ensure truth and newsworthiness in the information presented to the voters of a nation.

## 11.36 Conclusion

FB's greatest value to society comes from its noncommercial services like those based on connectivity and philanthropy. Many of the contraventions by FB have been caused by pursuing its "legitimate" financial interests by exploiting loopholes in the commercial aspects of personal data. The scandals of the past decade have damaged the company's public image, daily usage, and market value, but have not stopped it from being an essential part of modern human communication. GDPR seeks to oversee a previously unregulated field to create a new culture of data minimization that comes in direct conflict with the preexisting culture, which allowed social networking to grow and flourish.

It is important to note that FB set the tone for social networking and has gained its dominant market position not by a stroke of luck. The platform's popularity is based on sharing and connectivity, which fit well with the unregulated data culture, but now finds itself at odds with the restrictive changes. While some practices (like poor data security) are objective violations of GDPR, others like the information obligation, purpose limitation, and privacy by design, are subjectively complied with. In the coming years, regulators need to specify:

- What constitutes a social networking purpose?
- How should the technological and legal aspects of online contracts be presented by all-encompassing services like FB?
- How can "voluntary" consent be given for complex processing operations?
- Which regulatory agencies can oversee and enforce GDPR compliance?
- What role can customizability play in GDPR compliance?
- How to reconcile "sharing-based" platforms with data privacy?
- How to effectively regulate content, disinformation, and commercial goals of the Controller?

The questions posed above are preliminary issues in a complex regulatory field for the twenty-first century. GDPR's consumer objectives indicate that the trend will be to protect data subjects over the companies that provide online services, but this trend may be limited to the EU alone. Other countries that remain unregulated will likely take different directions, which in turn will lead to companies changing the location of their main establishment to reduce compliance efforts. Consistency of data protection across the globe is necessary to force companies to self-comply with GDPR obligations, and to avoid forum or require shopping. The following table provides a comparison of privacy policies and GDPR standards of mainstream internet-based services.

Comparison of Privacy Policies and GDPR Standards in Big Tech

| GDPR requirement | FB policy as on April 19, 2018 | Twitter policy as on May 25, 2018 | Netflix policy as on May 11, 2018 | Amazon policy as on August 29, 2017 | Uber policy as on May 25, 2018 | Spotify policy as on May 25, 2018 | YouTube policy as on January 22, 2019 |
|---|---|---|---|---|---|---|---|
| Information and Transparency | Data collection practices are explained across the Terms of Use, Data Policy, Cookies Policy, Commercial terms. FB also has a series of other policies and rules like its Community Standards, Platform Policy, Advertising Policies, Self-serve Ad terms, IP and Music Guidelines, etc. Many aspects of FB's policies are explained through hyperlinks including FAQs and explanations to terms. The purposes for collecting data is explained using examples. | Data collection practices are outlined in the Privacy Policy. Additionally, users are bound by the Terms of Service and Twitter Rules. Twitter maintains a separate set of these three policies for EU residents. Terms and concepts are explained through pop-up windows on the policies. Cookies and API policies are hyperlinked separately. Data collected is linked with the purposes of sharing with third parties. | GDPR compliance is governed through Netflix's Privacy Statement, which also explains the Cookies and Web-Beacon policies of the website. | Amazon's Privacy Notice regulates its services provided under the Conditions of Use. As an online marketplace, there are several other legal notices users must comply with. The Privacy Notice is short and hyperlinks examples, information, and explanation to terms and concepts in the document. Additionally, the Privacy Notice should be read with the Interest-Based Advertising Notice. Examples of data collection and subsequent use are hyperlinked, but the Privacy Notice also discloses the circumstances for data-sharing externally. The two have not been linked. | The Uber Privacy Policy and Terms of Use are the operative documents for data protection. The Privacy Policy contains hyperlinks to other policies and sections within the policy itself. The Privacy Policy has a specialized GDPR section, which gives additional protection to users within the EU. | Spotify's Privacy Policy along with its Terms and Conditions of Use govern the company's GDPR obligations. Uniquely, the Privacy Policy categorizes, separates, and links the data collection with the purpose of use. This is done in a table format in the Privacy Policy. Spotify does not externally hyperlink additional sources that effect privacy; the agreement encompasses all aspects. | YouTube is covered by Google's Privacy Policy and Terms of Service. The Privacy Policy uses hyperlinks to explain certain terms, concepts, and additional policies of interest. The data collected and purposes are listed in the Privacy Policy but are not linked with one another. In a large online conglomerate like Google, failing to accurately list the purpose limitation can create legal troubles. The excessive hyperlinking along with the inability to effectively educate users has led the French SA to conclude that users gave "forced consent" and issued a €50 million fine against Google under GDPR.[135] |

*(continued)*

| GDPR requirement | FB policy as on April 19, 2018 | Twitter policy as on May 25, 2018 | Netflix policy as on May 11, 2018 | Amazon policy as on August 29, 2017 | Uber policy as on May 25, 2018 | Spotify policy as on May 25, 2018 | YouTube policy as on January 22, 2019 |
|---|---|---|---|---|---|---|---|
| **Data subject access and interface** | User control model that customizes privacy interests of the user and publicity of information.<br><br>User settings, Privacy shortcuts, Privacy "check-ups," and Activity logs are the modalities data subjects use to control privacy.<br><br>Users have full access to data created by them but not to their advertiser profile, which is maintained by the company. | Users can access their data from the Your Twitter Data section of their profile settings.<br><br>Like FB, Twitter does not give users access to an "advertiser profile" and only gives full access to user-created data. | Netflix follows a request-based model of user access. Personal data submitted to the website can be viewed and managed by the Account Settings. But the settings only allow users to review their submitted information and recent streaming activity.<br><br>For a detailed report, users must contact the DPO.<br><br>Note that Netflix's data subject access policies are currently under review after NYOB.eu complained that an access request was delayed with raw data and background information partially missing.[136] | | Users can access their activity and app history through their Profile, but comprehensive data requests are made through Uber's DPO. | Spotify set up a Privacy Center, which deals with all matters related to GDPR.<br><br>Users can access data using the Privacy Center and Settings function on their profile.<br><br>Spotify's data-access policies are also currently debated as NYOB.eu has also filed a complaint against the Controller in Sweden.[137] The complaint alleges that Spotify failed to give background information on data collection and only partially gave raw data, which was only partially intelligible. | The Privacy Policy (and its sections) is helpfully supplemented using video lectures.<br><br>Like FB, Google offers privacy "check-ups" to help users increase security measures on their profile.<br><br>Through the User Settings, the My Activity and Google Dashboard functions help review data processing.<br><br>NYOB.eu also filed an access complaint against YouTube with the Austrian Data Protection authorities for failing to meet GDPR standards of access. The complaint alleges that YouTube failed to give background information on data collection and only partially gave raw data, which was only partially intelligible.[138] |

| | | | | | | | |
|---|---|---|---|---|---|---|---|
| **Data subject rights** | All rights have been provided for in the Settings except the Right to Objection and Explanation to automated processing. | Data subject rights are limited owing to the nature of the service. Users can deactivate or delete their account and edit their information freely. But other GDPR rights can only be enforced by request. | User rights are enforced through Personalization and Data Settings. All GDPR rights are provided for including Objection. Explanation is not provided for. | Data subject rights have not been well delineated and separated in the Profile Settings. Users can manage, delete, and alter data in their profile, but assurances of erasure or an opportunity to object have not been given by the website. | All GDPR rights are carried out through Uber's DPO, who has a specialized page. Users can make erasure, objection, and explanation requests using this web page. | The Privacy Center along with Privacy and Notification Settings help users exercise all GDPR rights on the service. | The user Settings help enforce GDPR rights like erasure, rectification portability, etc. However, GDPR rights are not specifically named and delineated. Objection and explanation are not provided for in the user Settings. |
| **Third-party data-sharing** | The platform lets users restrict and view advertisers who receive data for direct marketing purposes. Additionally, FB Ad Controls explain the process of advertising on the website. However, data sharing by FB overall is highly debated owing to the slew of scandals and legal actions against the company. | Twitter adheres to the Digital Advertising Alliance Self-Regulatory Principles for Online Behavioral Advertising. Processing and analytic service providers along with corporate affiliates are hyperlinked in the Privacy Policy. Advertisers are not listed. | Netflix "supports" the following self-regulatory instruments- ✓ US: Digital Advertising Alliance (DAA) ✓ Europe: European Interactive Digital Advertising Alliance (EDAA) ✓ Canada: Ad Choices: Digital Advertising Alliance of Canada (DAAC) Data sharing on Netflix is primarily focused on enhancing viewing suggestions and features along with advertising. | Unlike other policies, Amazon states that it only shares data with authorized subsidiaries which follow the Privacy Notice or standards that mimic it. The Privacy Statement lists the circumstances of data sharing with the subsidiaries but does not go into further detail. Direct marketing is controlled by a user's Advertising Preferences. | GDPR Section of Uber's Privacy Policy clearly links data collection with a specific legal basis under GDPR. Additionally, Uber lists the circumstances of data sharing with third parties in its policy as well and does not engage in direct marketing services. | Data sharing is clearly linked with a legal basis and purpose for processing in the Spotify Privacy Policy. Marketing and survey data are shared with third parties on grounds of consent and legitimate interest of the Controller. | Though the purposes of data sharing are listed in the Privacy Policy, no link is established with the data collected. Data sharing is primarily internal or with legal authorities, domain administrators, or commercial affiliates. Google gets paid to show advertisers to users but does not sell data for direct marketing purposes. |

*(continued)*

| GDPR requirement | FB policy as on April 19, 2018 | Twitter policy as on May 25, 2018 | Netflix policy as on May 11, 2018 | Amazon policy as on August 29, 2017 | Uber policy as on May 25, 2018 | Spotify policy as on May 25, 2018 | YouTube policy as on January 22, 2019 |
|---|---|---|---|---|---|---|---|
| **Data protection and security** | Data protection standards are unlisted in FB's Data Policy. Website's additional sources mention that messaging services are protected with end-to-end encryption. The website uses "secure browsing" (HTTPS) and also offers users privacy and security "check-ups" through their controls. Users can also implement 2-step authentication for log-ins (optional). For international data transfers, FB utilizes SCCs and Adequacy decisions from the EU. | Though data protection standards are unlisted on Twitter's legal documents, the website maintains a GDPR-Hub that highlighted the addendums made on data transfer agreements between Controller-to-Controller, Processors, and Subprocessors with the company. The contractual changes reflect GDPR mandates. Additionally, data transfers are governed by the Privacy Policy and Master Services Agreement. International transfers of data are governed by the EU-US privacy shield, the Swiss Privacy Shield, along with adequacy decisions and SCC clauses. | The company only states that it implements "reasonable administrative, logical, physical and managerial measures" but does not specify what those are. Additionally, the company expressly states that "Unfortunately, no measures can be guaranteed to provide 100% security.[139] Accordingly, we cannot guarantee the security of your personal information." Netflix also does not list the instruments used in international data transfers, but states that the data will be shared in accordance to the Privacy Statement and "as permitted by the applicable laws on data protection." | Unlike other policies, Amazon expressly states data protection standards. Amazon implements security during transmission by using Secure Sockets Layer (SSL) software, which encrypts information inputted. Credit card digits are anonymized on-screen (barring the last four numbers) but transmitted in full to the payment processor. Amazon follows the EU-US and Swiss-US Privacy Shield for international data transfers. | Data-protection standards are unlisted in the Privacy Policy. The instruments for international data transfers are also unlisted, but the Policy states: "Uber transfers information of users' outside the United States on the basis of mechanisms approved under applicable laws." | Spotify's Privacy Policy expressly lists its data-protection practices by stating that data is anonymized and aggregated for purposes like testing IT systems, research, data analysis, creating marketing and promotion models, improving service, and developing new features and functionality. Additionally, Spotify states that it implements measures like pseudonymization, encryption, access, and retention policies to guard against unauthorized access and unnecessary retention of data. International countries who receive data from Spotify have been listed in the Privacy Policy. Spotify uses SCCs in international data transfers. | Google, like Spotify and Amazon, lists their security measures. These include encrypting data-in-transit, safe browsing, restricting employee access to data and reviewing information collection, storage, and processing practices, including physical security measures. For international transfers of data, Google adheres to the EU-US Privacy Shield along with other instruments of compliance based on the legal regime. The company does not specify the instruments. |

| Accountability | | | | | | |
|---|---|---|---|---|---|---|
| FB does not list a DPO or LSA listed on their ToU or Data Policy. The forum selection clause of the ToU gives jurisdiction to California courts.<br><br>The website maintains a Data Policy Question and Contact page for users who have any data-related questions.<br><br>FB also refers users to the TrustArc Feedback and Resolution System. | DPO has a separate contact page and mailing address found on the Terms of Service and Privacy Policy.<br><br>Twitter lists the Irish Data Protection Commissioner as its LSA for Data Subjects to contact. | DPO's e-mail address has been listed but no mailing address.<br><br>No LSA has been listed by Netflix, but the NYOB. eu complaints indicate its main establishment is in the Netherlands.<br><br>The Netflix Terms of Use contain an arbitration clause with a class action waiver. | The Privacy Statement does not list a DPO or an LSA. The NYOB.eu complaint indicates that the LSA is in Luxembourg.<br><br>The Amazon Conditions of Use contain an arbitration clause with a class action waiver. | DPO has a separate contact page and mailing address for all matters GDPR related.<br><br>The LSA has been listed as the Dutch Data Protection Authority. | The DPO has been listed as the "contact" on Spotify's Privacy Center page.<br><br>LSA has not been listed, but the NYOB. eu complaints indicate the LSA is in Sweden. | DPO and LSA have not been listed.<br><br>The Forum selection clause in the ToU allocates competence to California courts to deal with disputes. As a large conglomerate, Google's policies likely differ based on the location of operation. |

## Notes

1 Scott Galloway, *The Four: The Hidden DNA of Amazon, Apple, Facebook, and Google* (New York: Penguin, 2017), 91.
2 Kate O' Neill, "Facebook's '10 Year Challenge' Is Just a Harmless Meme— Right?" *Wired*, January 15, 2019, https://www.wired.com/story/facebook-10-year-meme-challenge.
3 Mike Isaac and Sheera Frenkel, "Facebook Security Breach Exposes Accounts of 50 Million Users," *New York Times*, September 28, 2018, https://www.nytimes.com/2018/09/28/technology/facebook-hack-data-breach.html.
4 Dustin Volz and David Ingram, "Facebook's Zuckerberg Unscathed by Congressional Grilling, Stock Rises," Reuters, April 11, 2018, https://www.reuters.com/article/us-facebook-privacy-zuckerberg/facebooks-zuckerberg-unscathed-by-congressional-grilling-stock-rises-idUSKBN1HI1CJ.
5 Galloway, *The Four,* 91 onward.
6 Robert McNamee, *Zucked: Waking up to the Facebook Catastrophe* (Penguin Press, 2019).
7 House of Commons Digital, Culture, Media and Sport Committee, *Disinformation and "fake news": Final Report*, HC 1791, published February 18, 2019, ¶76.
8 Gabrial J.X. Dance, Michael LaForgia, and Nicholas Confessore, "As Facebook Raised a Privacy Wall, It Carved an Opening for Tech Giants," *New York Times*, December 18, 2018.
9 For simplicity, these companies will be collectively referred to as *FB* .
10 FB, "What Are the Facebook Products?" https://www.facebook.com/help/1561485474074139?ref=dp.
11 Onavo Inc. and FB Israel Ltd., Privacy Policy, as of December 14, 2018, https://www.onavo.com/privacy_policy.
12 Oculus, Privacy Policy, as of September 4, 2018, https://www.oculus.com/legal/privacy-policy/.
13 WhatsApp, Privacy Policy, as of August 25, 2016, https://www.whatsapp.com/legal/#terms-of-service.
14 Masquerade Technologies, Inc., Privacy Policy, as of June 28, 2016, https://www.facebook.com/msqrd/privacy.
15 CrowdTangle, Privacy Policy, as of May 25, 2018, https://www.crowdtangle.com/privacy.
16 "The Facebook Companies," https://www.facebook.com/help/111814505650678?ref=shareable.
17 Facebook Payments Inc., Privacy Policy, as of December 30, 2013, https://www.facebook.com/payments_terms/privacy.
18 FB, Terms of Use, "5. Other terms and policies that may apply to you," https://www.facebook.com/terms.php.
19 GDPR, Articles 41 and 47.
20 FB, "Data Policy – How do we operate and transfer data as part of our global services?"

21 Note that third-party affiliates of FB are only viewable insofar that it relates to *a particular user's profile*. See FB, Settings, "Your Ad preferences."

22 BBC, "Facebook Ordered by Germany to Gather and Mix Less Data," February 7, 2019, https://www.bbc.com/news/technology-47146431.

23 BBC, "Facebook Ordered by Germany to Gather and Mix Less Data."

24 FB, Terms of Use, "1. Our services."

25 For a detailed discussion on Online Consent, please see Chapter 5 (Section 5.2.1).

26 FB, Data Policy, "How do we use this information?"

27 For example, see CrowdTangle, Privacy Policy, as of May 25, 2018, https://www.crowdtangle.com/privacy, adopted the *very day* of GDPR coming into force.

28 Greg Sterling, "Google Slapped with $56.8 Million Fine for GDPR Consent Violations," *Martech Today*, January 21, 2019, https://martechtoday.com/google-slapped-with-56-8-million-fine-for-gdpr-consent-violations-229813.

29 Sterling, "Google Slapped with $56.8 Million Fine."

30 FB, Data Policy, "How do we use this information?"

31 Such as FB-Instagram-WhatsApp data sharing.

32 FB, Data Policy, "How do we use this information?"

33 Andreas Pawelke and Anoush Rima Tatevossian, "Data Philanthropy: Where Are We Now?" United Nations Global Pulse, May 8, 2013, https://www.unglobalpulse.org/data-philanthropy-where-are-we-now.

34 Adam Satriano, "Facebook Halts Aquila, Its Internet Drone Project," *New York Times*, June 27, 2018, https://www.nytimes.com/2018/06/27/technology/facebook-drone-internet.html.

35 This list was created by viewing features available on FB's homepage and related pages.

36 GDPR, Article 21.

37 Adapted from FB, About Ads, "Why you see a particular ad."

38 FB, About Ads, "Understand what data is used to show you ads."

39 FB, About Ads; Data Policy, "What kinds of information do we collect?"

40 FB, About Ads, Advertising strategy: "Your information."

41 FB, About Ads, "Why you see a particular ad."

42 FB, About Ads, Advertising strategy: "Your interests."

43 It's important to note that FB does not exhaustively list the categories of interests in its own sections.

44 FB, About Ads: "Understand what data is used to show you ads" and related hyperlinks.

45 FB, About Ads: "Understand what data is used to show you ads" and related hyperlinks.

46 FB, Data Policy, "How do we use your data?"

47 Cross reference once pages are finalized.

48 FB, Settings, Notification Settings: "1. On Facebook."

49 FB, "Cookies and Other Storage Technologies."

50 FB, "Terms of Service," §3.3.2.

51 Note, certain jurisdictions *do not* require "commercialization" of the image, and a person can sue for unauthorized use alone.

52  Ari Ezra Waldman, *Privacy as Trust* (Cambridge University Press, 2018), 85–88.

53  Waldman, *Privacy as Trust*, 90–92.

54  House of Commons Digital, Culture, Media and Sport Committee, *Disinformation and "fake news": Final Report,* HC 1791, February 18, 2019, ¶26.

55  House of Commons Digital, Culture, Media and Sport Committee, *Disinformation and "fake news,"* ¶77.

56  James Sanders, "Facebook Data Privacy Scandal: A Cheat Sheet," *Tech Republic*, December 11, 2018, https://www.techrepublic.com/article/facebook-data-privacy-scandal-a-cheat-sheet.

57  House of Commons Digital, Culture, Media and Sport Committee, *Disinformation and "fake news,"* ¶76.

58  House of Commons Digital, Culture, Media and Sport Committee, *Disinformation and "fake news,"* ¶83.

59  Dance, LaForgia, and Confessore, "As Facebook Raised a Privacy Wall."

60  BBC, "Facebook Sues over 'Data-Grabbing' Quizzes," March 11, 2019, https://www.bbc.com/news/technology-47524468.

61  See FB, Terms of Service, §3.2.3: "You may not access or collect data from our Products using automated means (*without our prior permission*) or *attempt to access data you do not have permission to access.*"

62  The *publisher/platform debate* will be discussed later in this chapter (Sections 11.28–11.31).

63  Jasper Hamill, "Facebook Accused of Failing to Remove Shocking Video of Toddler Being Beaten Up," Metro UK, July 17, 2018, https://metro.co.uk/2018/07/17/facebook-accused-failing-remove-shocking-video-toddler-beaten-7724719/.

64  House of Commons Digital, Culture, Media and Sport Committee, *Disinformation and "fake news,"* ¶76.

65  Tony Rom and Drew Harwell, "Facebook suspends tens of thousands of apps following data investigation", *The Washington Post*, September 20, 2019, https://www.washingtonpost.com/technology/2019/09/20/facebook-suspends-tens-thousands-apps-following-data-investigation/.

66  For example, the "Story-Time" feature in Portal, which augments the screen with *face-filtering* technology.

67  Jessica Guynn, "Turkish Man Commits Suicide on Facebook," *USA Today*, October 12, 2016, https://www.usatoday.com/story/tech/news/2016/10/12/turkish-man-commits-suicide-facebook-live/91974112/.

68  See US Communications Decency Act, § 230, the "Good Samaritan Clause."

69  FB, Community Standards, https://www.facebook.com/communitystandards

70  Jason Koebler, "The Impossible Job: Inside Facebook's Struggle to Moderate Two Billion People," Motherboard, August 23, 2018, https://motherboard.vice.com/en_us/article/xwk9zd/how-facebook-content-moderation-works.

71  Hillary Leung, "U.K. Lawmakers Accuse Facebook of 'Intentionally and Knowingly' Violating Data Privacy Laws and Call for Stricter Regulation," *Time*, February 18, 2019, http://time.com/5531618/u-k-disinformation-report-facebook-privacy.

72  Quoted in Jason Koebler, "The Impossible Job: Inside Facebook's Struggle to Moderate Two Billion People," *Motherboard*, August 23, 2018, https://

motherboard.vice.com/en_us/article/xwk9zd/how-facebook-content-moderation-works.

73 Automated accounts that exist to promote accounts, products, services or malicious software. FB fought similar issues with SPAM bots and accounts.

74 Twitter, "The Twitter Rules," https://help.twitter.com/en/rules-and-policies/twitter-rules.

75 This can include the *sale and purchase of illegal goods* or unauthorized dealing in *regulated goods*. See FB, Community Standards, I.5.

76 FB, Bullying Prevention Hub, https://www.facebook.com/safety/bullying, FB, Community Standards, II.9.

77 FB, Community Standards, III.12.

78 FB, Community Standards, V.

79 Note that the numbering in the list directly corresponds to FB's Community Standards. The list is intended to *summarize* the content of the rules. For detail on *definitions, specific examples,* and *unacceptable content,* please see https://www.facebook.com/communitystandards/credible_violence.

80 James Borvard, "Facebook Censored Me: Criticize Your Government and It Might Censor You Too," *USA Today*, October 27, 2017, https://www.usatoday.com/story/opinion/2017/10/27/facebook-censored-cross-your-countrys-government-and-they-might-censor-you-too-james-bovard-column/795271001.

81 Jonathan Vanian "Facebook Gives the Boot to 3D-Printed Gun Blueprints," *Fortune*, August 9, 2018, https://fortune.com/2018/08/09/FB-3d-printed-gun-blueprints/.

82 For example, FB Community Standard II.6 notes that posts raising awareness of self-harm must contain clear, self-injury disclaimers.

83 See "Not without My Consent," https://fbnewsroomus.files.wordpress.com/2017/03/not-without-my-consent.pdf.

84 It's interesting to note that "hacked" materials may only be posted on FB if it's *newsworthy* creating a *journalistic exception* to *data leaks*. See FB, Community Standards, II.11.

85 Samuel Warren and Louis Brandeis, "The Right to Privacy," 4 *Harvard L.R.* 193 (1890), 199.

86 FB, Community Standards, II.8.

87 House of Commons Digital, Culture, Media and Sport Committee, *Disinformation and "fake news."*

88 GDPR, Article 1.1.

89 FB, Community Standards, IV.20: "We do not remove, update, or change anything about the profile or the account because we want to respect the choices someone made while still alive."

90 "Fair Use" under Copyright law allows the public to use copyrighted material in a *limited, transformative, non-commercial* manner for criticism, education, research, etc.

91 FB, Terms of Service, §3.3.3.

92 For a discussion on FB's use of User Publicity Rights for sponsorship and endorsement, please see pages 354 and 355 of this chapter.

93 FB, Terms of Service, §3.3.1.

94 FB, Terms of Service, §3.3.1.

95  FB, Terms of Service, §3.3.4.

96  FB, Brand Resource Center, https://en.facebookbrand.com.

97  Hamill, "FB Accused of Failing to Remove Shocking Video of Toddler Being Beaten Up."

98  Jason Koebler, "The Impossible Job: Inside Facebook's Struggle to Moderate Two Billion People," Motherboard, August 23, 2018, https://motherboard.vice.com/en_us/article/xwk9zd/how-facebook-content-moderation-works.

99  Koebler, *The Impossible Job.*

100  Koebler, *The Impossible Job.*

101  Koebler, *The Impossible Job.*

102  Koebler, *The Impossible Job.*

103  Casey Newton, "Facebook Will Create an Independent Oversight Group to Review Content Moderation Appeals," *The Verge*, November 15, 2018, https://www.theverge.com/2018/11/15/18097219/facebook-independent-oversight-supreme-court-content-moderation.

104  For example, Alexandra Stevenson, "Facebook Admits It Was Used in Myanmar to Incite Violence," *New York Times*, November 6, 2018, https://www.nytimes.com/2018/11/06/technology/myanmar-FB.html.

105  Koebler, *The Impossible Job.*

106  Guynn, "Turkish Man Commits Suicide."

107  *Disinformation and "fake news": Government Response to the Committee's Fifth Report of Session 2017–19*, October 23, 2018, HC 1630 Government response to Interim Report, 2.

108  FB, Community Standards, IV.18.

109  See FB, Community Standards, IV.18: "There is also a *fine line between false news and satire or opinion. For these reasons*, we don't remove false news from Facebook but instead, significantly reduce its distribution by showing it lower in the News Feed."

110  Subsign, "Is Facebook a Platform or Publisher?" *Medium*, May 8, 2018, https://medium.com/@subsign/is-facebook-a-platform-or-a-publisher-f2e2fd04d4eb.

111  Subsign, *Is Facebook a Platform or Publisher?*

112  Sam Levin, "Is Facebook a Publisher? In Public It Says No, But in Court It Says Yes," *The Guardian,* July 3, 2018, https://www.theguardian.com/technology/2018/jul/02/facebook-mark-zuckerberg-platform-publisher-lawsuit.

113  The lawsuit *Manhattan Community Access Corp. v. Halleck,* 587 US _ (2019) Docket No. 17-702 centers on "whether a private operator of a public access television network is considered a state actor which can be sued for First Amendment violations."

114  House of Commons Digital, Culture, Media and Sport Committee, *Disinformation and "fake news,"* ¶14.

115  House of Commons Digital, Culture, Media and Sport Committee, *Disinformation and "fake news,"* ¶¶51 and 52.

116  House of Commons Digital, Culture, Media and Sport Committee, *Disinformation and "fake news,"* ¶¶269 and 270.

117 House of Commons Digital, Culture, Media and Sport Committee, *Disinformation and "fake news,"* ¶210.

118 House of Commons Digital, Culture, Media and Sport Committee, *Disinformation and "fake news,"* ¶212

119 House of Commons Digital, Culture, Media and Sport Committee, *Disinformation and "fake news,"* ¶215.

120 House of Commons Digital, Culture, Media and Sport Committee, *Disinformation and "fake news,"* ¶¶81–83; see also ¶135: "The evidence that we obtained from the Six4Three court documents indicates that Facebook was *willing to override its users' privacy settings in order to transfer data to some app developers, to charge high prices in advertising to some developers*, for the exchange of that data, and to starve some developers—such as Six4Three—of that data, thereby causing them to lose their business. It seems clear that FB was, at the very least, in violation of its Federal Trade Commission settlement."

121 House of Commons Digital, Culture, Media and Sport Committee, *Disinformation and "fake news,"* ¶41.

122 House of Commons Digital, Culture, Media and Sport Committee, *Disinformation and "fake news,"* ¶223.

123 House of Commons Digital, Culture, Media and Sport Committee, *Disinformation and "fake news,"* ¶272.

124 Created by the London School of Economics, the Oxford Internet Institute, and Sheffield University, see: House of Commons Digital, Culture, Media and Sport Committee, *Disinformation and "fake news": Final Report,* HC 1791 Published on February 18, 2019, ¶226.

125 House of Commons Digital, Culture, Media and Sport Committee, *Disinformation and "fake news,"* ¶227.

126 This is analogous to the UK Data Protection Act 2018, Schedule 121–124.

127 House of Commons Digital, Culture, Media and Sport Committee, *Disinformation and "fake news,"* ¶312.

128 House of Commons Digital, Culture, Media and Sport Committee, *Disinformation and "fake news,"* ¶38.

129 House of Commons Digital, Culture, Media and Sport Committee, *Disinformation and "fake news,"* page 34 last line.

130 House of Commons Digital, Culture, Media and Sport Committee, *Disinformation and "fake news,"* ¶129.

131 House of Commons Digital, Culture, Media and Sport Committee, *Oral evidence: Disinformation and "fake news,"* HC 363, November 6, 2018, Questions 3968 and 3969.

132 Vijaya Gadde and Yoel Roth, "Enabling Further Research on Information Operations on Twitter," Twitter, October 17, 2018.

133 House of Commons Digital, Culture, Media and Sport Committee, *Disinformation and "fake news,"* ¶257.

134 House of Commons Digital, Culture, Media and Sport Committee, *Disinformation and "fake news,"* ¶244.

135 "CNIL Fines Google € 50 Mio Based on NOYB Complaint," NYOB, https://noyb. eu/news-update/.

136 "Netflix, Spotify & YouTube: Eight Strategic Complaints Filed on 'Right to Access,' NYOB, https://noyb.eu/access_streaming/.

137 Ibid.

138 https://noyb.eu/access_streaming/.

139 https://gdpr.twitter.com/en/faq.html.

# 12

## Facebook and GDPR

*It is no exaggeration to say that the greatest threat to the global order in my lifetime has been enabled by internet platforms.*
— Roger McNamee, *Zucked*

In Chapter 11 we discussed how Facebook accumulates and uses data within the interface of its website. Facebook as a service creates a self-sustaining ecosystem of personal data exchange for a multitude of economic motivators. In this chapter, we examine how the company operates in the new GDPR regime, how it has complied, and what actions it will likely face in the future.

## 12.1 The Lead Supervisory Authority

Under GDPR, a corporate group which operates across jurisdictions is responsible to one Lead Supervisory Authority (LSA) over its processing.[1] When multiple competencies overlap between Supervisory Authorities, an LSA is designated based on where the Controller has its *main establishment* of business.[2] Currently pending GDPR investigations into FB fall under the authority of the Irish Data Protection Commissioner, who has been assigned as an LSA to investigate the company's behavior-monitoring and data-collection practices.[3]

## 12.2 Facebook nicht spricht Deutsch

Recently, German antitrust regulators ordered the FB Group to reduce and restrict their data sharing activities with third parties. In doing so, the regulator recognized Facebook as a dominant social media company in the market. As a dominant player, the consent policies of the company are subject to greater scrutiny on grounds of adhesion or contractual fairness. In Chapter 5, we studied the recent complaints filed against FB and Google for their consent and information obligation practices under GDPR.[4] Similarly, the German antitrust watchdog suggests that a lack of meaningful choice to deny FB data policies violates the condition for voluntary consent under GDPR.[5]

With 23 million daily active users and 32 million monthly active users with a market share of more than 95% (daily active users) and more than 80% (monthly active users) in Germany alone, there is no denying the company's "goliath" status.[6] FB being "dominant" is relevant for subjecting the company to German Competition Law and antitrust regulation. But an issue arises when we consider a possible overlap of data protection law and antitrust enforcement. As FB's dominance attracted the attention of German antitrust regulators, its abusive practices are linked to their consent policies, which falls under the realm of GDPR. As antitrust overlaps with data protection, consent itself is deeply rooted in traditional contract law making enforcement an issue that runs across regulators.

The FB Group's primary basis for appeal is the regulatory "incompetence" of the German antitrust authority to order GDPR-based measures on the company's personal data processing. Like the multiple orders issued against Google by antitrust regulators globally, the Bundeskartellamt's order reveals an intersection between data privacy and antitrust law. As the world becomes more digitized, it is likely that an overlap between the two regulatory fields will be more common in the future. It is the role of antitrust regulators to protect consumers in the market from abusive practices by those companies "in power." Protection requires regulators to examine the voluntary nature of the "terms" in agreements that consumers are forced to accede to by dominant companies. As contracts also go paperless and companies move services to apps and websites, the question arises as to which regulator will take priority in the future?

## 12.3   Where Is the Beef? Fulfilling the *Information Obligation*

Whether FB has fulfilled its information obligations under GDPR[7] remains under consideration. As discussed above, the traditional social networking company has transformed itself into an all-encompassing conglomerate in the industry. FB on its platform alone provides a diverse range of services relating to human interaction like payments, public polls, "causes" and "live" video feeds. Combined with its products, apps, devices, and subsidiary services, maintaining a coherent and simple "terms of service" is a difficult task in practice. Therefore, the market trend by most large industry-conglomerates is to have bundled privacy policies, which is greatly discouraged by the WP29 (now the EU-Data Protection Board).[8]

In a dominant corporate group like Facebook, being completely transparent about data-sharing practices, specifically for commercial reasons, is clearly not an operation for maintaining public reputation and goodwill. This is evidenced by the steady loss of FB's brand value and repeat users over the past few years as the public consumer base now knows that their data is not safe in the company's hands. A more persuasive reason to justify a lack of "total" transparency is simply because it is impractical to list commercial partners in a data policy. This is because of the following factors:

1. Data sharing happens across many sources.
2. Commercial partners and data recipients change constantly.
3. Explaining the data-sharing ecosystem makes the privacy policy more voluminous.
4. Data subjects are rarely concerned with technical and organizational details of how data is shared.
5. Facebook "Lookalike Audiences" feature only uses inferred data, which takes it outside of GDPR compliance for its ad data sharing.[9]

At present, FB holds all the cards by disclosing only what is commercially sensible for the organization under the confines of GDPR. A change in this culture is likely to be caused by future regulatory action against the corporate group. Perhaps a solution is for the company or a third party to develop a *centralized database* that graphically lays out data sharing on demand to the user based on their individual profile. Providing this data coherently to a user will require a classification of data flows (inward or outward of the company) and then a subclassification of who the recipient is (advertiser or developer). Regulatory action may require the creation of such databases so that Controllers can effectively manage the information obligation.

## 12.4   Data Processing *Purpose Limitation*

On the very day GDPR came into force, Max Schrems, a prominent privacy activist, filed complaints against the FB Group and other giants for their consent policies (leading to Google paying the highest GDPR fine to date).[10] In the complaint, one allegation states that FB fell short of its information obligations by not providing accurate detail of processing purposes in relation to the data collected. The complaint attacks the generic language used in the policies and alleges the company does not state the purpose of data collection with specificity. As examined in Chapter 5 "specificity" has not been qualified by GDPR, and this pending case will likely determine the outcome. For technology conglomerates like FB, personal data is used across platforms, apps, services, and companies for a diverse range of reasons.

It is interesting to note that the website does not allocate a specific GDPR basis for the purposes mentioned above. Rather, it appears that users must link the purposes to the bases under the regulation. From comparing the text of GDPR Article 6 with the purposes mentioned in the Data Policy, FB can arguably claim five out of six legal bases for general processing under GDPR:[11]

1. Consent
2. Necessity for performing or entering into a contract
3. Legitimate interests of Controller
4. Public Interest
5. Compliance with a legal obligation[12]

The excluded basis, namely vital interests, could also be arguably claimed by the FB Group where the website is used for urgent, life-saving purposes such as marking people "safe" during natural disasters or time-sensitive investigations. The diversification of FB's services across apps, websites, devices, and products has led to a point where the company can (arguably) claim a legal basis for all scenarios of social networking.

Facebook has attempted to simplify and condense its data policies, but fulfilling GDPR Articles 12 and 13 is a task that many Controllers across the industry struggle with. Linking personal data usage with specific purposes is difficult when a platform provides more modes of data production than needed for the core purpose. FB at its core is about communication, and logically the data production and collection should be limited to letting users "talk" with one another, avoiding any other superfluous modes of expression, which unnecessarily creates data. However, doing so would reduce the quality of service on the website as users could easily switch to other modes like text-messaging. Part of FB's attraction is its interface and modes of self-expression, which cannot be provided by other competitors. Thus, how can the company be expected to justify the creation of additional emojis into its overall processing purpose? This is how the company uses its dominant position to bring all data collection under the larger umbrella of "social networking," a broader purpose which is defined by the corporation itself.[13]

## 12.5   Legitimate Interests Commercial "Restraint" Needed

FB may legally process data under most purposes listed above, but the most problematic basis, which creates most legal questions, is processing rooted in legitimate corporate interests. These primarily include advertising activities and any other processing that monetizes personal data for the company. The trend of GDPR complaints and penalties seems to target processing carried out under a Controller's "legitimate interests"[14] primarily owing to the ambiguity of the provision.

Under DPD regime, this provision was interpreted liberally by Controllers leading to excessive data collection. GDPR regulators now issue harsh fines to remedy this by having Controllers like FB reduce data sharing for commercial purposes. At a minimum, FB and other companies must adequately inform users of the legitimate interests, educate them on their data use, and eventually receive an informed consent to the processing.[15] But is this requirement economically, legally, and practically feasible?

When considering the scale of the company and services provided, are listing specific purposes and linking them with the legal bases and use of the data practicable. The average person would have to spend 76 working days reading all privacy policies they agree to in the span of a year – reading Amazon's privacy policy takes nine hours.[16] At the same time, consent is only required once and justifies a wide range of processing. After a user gives his/her initial consent, processing is considered legal under GDPR. If a Controller has effectively met the information obligation requirement, all future-related processing is also permissible. Analytics, performance, security, and monetization all require personal data to be fed into the processing algorithm. To explain how personal data is used across the corporate group with precision would require FB to explain the technological aspects of processing, which would sacrifice simplicity. These difficulties exist even after the strong GDPR mandate because of the simple fact that personal data processing contracts are complex.

GDPR remains a consumer-oriented regulation, where most doubts will be resolved in favor of protecting the data subject. Once again, looking into the recent order by the German antitrust watchdog, Facebook has been found to have no legal justification for collecting data from third-party company-owned services by using Facebook Business Tools (such as pixel or FB plug-ins). The order states that:[17]

1. Assigning external data to Facebook user accounts by using business tools is not necessary for fulfilling contractual obligations.
2. Consent was not effective or voluntary as FB's service is conditional on the user agreeing to the data sharing terms.
3. FB's legitimate interests do not outweigh the data subject's privacy rights.

Breaking down the legal bases claimed by FB methodically, the German antitrust regulators conducted a comprehensive GDPR analysis to assess whether the company indulged in *anticompetitive practices,* which is problematic. GDPR assigns enforcement duties to Supervisory Authorities but does not prohibit other agencies from overseeing its compliance. But it remains open for appeal whether the Bundeskartellamt overstepped its authority to pass this order against Facebook. Regardless, the German antitrust authority states that it merely used GDPR as the basis for determining FB's alleged *exploitative abuse* of users. The dominant position held by the company allows it to (attractively) offer its services free of charge, monetizing data through advertisements and amassing information at a scale that other competitors in the market cannot match. Therefore, by using GDPR standards, the Bundeskartellamt determined that contractual terms and conditions can constitute exploitative abuse of FB's consumers, based on case law from the German Federal Court of Justice.[18] Based on this order, one can expect an increased use of GDPR standards in assessing the fairness in online contracts by multiple regulators in the future.

## 12.6   Privacy by Design?

Notwithstanding a debate on FB's data-collection practices and business model, the overall website interface does not support "privacy." While GDPR requires that "privacy" be incorporated into the design of the website and the organization,[19] FB is a platform that encourages sharing information with other users. This is an inherent conflict between the company's business model and GDPR. How can GDPR's privacy culture be incorporated into websites where sharing is assumed remains to be seen and requires clarification from the EU-DPD.

As discussed at length in our previous chapter on FB, the website's interface encourages data production, while the notification practice routinely communicates the activities of other "friend" users.[20] The layout of the service fosters publicity over privacy, which is against the spirit of GDPR, and which conveniently aligns with the commercial goals of the company. For example, FB advertising policies allow for incoming data collection from third parties as a default.[21] Under GDPR, Controllers are responsible to maintain privacy as the default in all data production and collection activities.[22] This preset agreement to such data sharing with third parties is also at the center of the earlier discussed order against FB by the German antitrust regulators. The order specifies that the use of FB plug-ins such as like or share buttons on external sites allowed FB to track each visitor's *IP address, web browser name, version,* and other personally identifiable information.[23] This unrestricted collection and assignment of non-Facebook data to user accounts was allegedly done with insufficient voluntary consent by using preset options and bundled policies.

The fear of German regulators is that the excessive data collection would allow FB to abuse its dominant market position by bringing large amounts of data under the single profile of a user. Therefore, if Facebook wishes to gather personal data from external sources using its products, informed voluntary consent from the user is necessary. The FB group will likely have to change its defaults or get specific consent at the time of creating a profile after this recent order, as many are likely to follow. As long as this inherent tension exists between "social networking" and "privacy," the company can arguably continue its practices to encourage "connectivity" between users.

## 12.7   Public Endorsement of Personalized Shopping

In Chapter 10, we discussed how Facebook's default and irreversible feature of publicizing user shopping habits comes into direct conflict with publicity rights and image interests.[24] Another facet of user "sponsorship" is that it runs contrary to privacy by design under GDPR. Users are contractually required to share their name, profile picture, and information to be disclosed in connection with their advertiser actions without compensation.[25] Though users can customize the audience, these are not the default settings on profiles and cannot be switched off. This website mandate enhances the sharing culture of the service by publicizing personal shopping habits.

**Illustration:** Adnan comes from a traditional, religious family that strongly objects to alcohol and pork, in line with Islamic practices. Adnan himself is not deeply religious and moves to Germany for his master's degree, where he lives a private life and eats pork occasionally, unbeknownst to his family. After ordering online from some grocery apps who partner with FB, Adnan finds a FB page that sells quality pork that is readily cooked. After becoming a regular customer, Adnan's cousin Faisal sees his shopping habits on FB through a suggestion to "Werner's Hog Hauz" which stated that "Adnan & 3 others recently visited this page." Faisal shares this information with Adnan's family, which causes strife.

In the facts above, the damage to Adnan is personal and not economic or reputational in nature, but it can still qualify as damage caused by the intrusion on his privacy. GDPR privacy by design exists for this very purpose of preventing unwarranted disclosure of otherwise private behavior. Therefore, a measure of privacy exists in every aspect of a data subject's activity on Facebook, which *is* the gravamen of why not all endorsements are "public" in daily life.

## 12.8 Customizing Data Protection

Facebook has been heavily criticized for their data-protection practices in the past, both by design and in their security of processing. As a platform premised on sharing, many of the settings are fixed to be public or open for viewing, which may violate of GDPR. Though the website implements encryption in processing, there have been numerous complaints and allegations of data breaches. Data protection serves as one of the pillars of GDPR compliance, and in this section we examine the websites practices under the regulation.

The public-private paradox of FB's services is difficult to reconcile. The FB Group attempts to resolve this issue by employing customizability in profiles and information sharing, but this does not necessarily follow GDPR compliance. FB implements basic security measures but does not publicize it in their Data Policy. These measures include secure browsing (HTTPS), optional enhanced security (like two-step authentication for log-ins), and *end-to-end encryption* in direct messaging. FB does not clarify what security is implemented in the overall platform to combat cyber-attacks.

While GDPR mandates privacy and data minimization at every step of an online service, FB tends to go the other direction and leaves its settings open and public. The job of "privacy" is left to users, who tend to take no action (often due to indifference). GDPR neither prohibits nor allows this as the regulation and only places responsibility for privacy on the Controller and not the users. At the same time, GDPR encourages greater user freedom and control, which is precisely what FB is doing. Thus, here we see a conflict between data subject control over rights and the Controller's duty to maintain privacy.

## 12.9   User Rights versus Facebook's Obligations

As described in Chapter 11, FB adopts a full user control model of enforcing data subjects' rights. In line with GDPR Article 13, FB provides users the modalities to maintain, modify, and enforce their digital rights through profile "settings." The modalities provided help to adjust privacy settings and serve to assist users to enforce GDPR rights. The website does not expressly state that the modalities provided are "rights"[26] but still empowers users to change the nature of their personal data processing based on their preference. Data subject rights are controlled through their FB account settings, which provide the following options to users:

1. **Access:** Data subject access has significantly improved over the years for FB. Rather than "scrolling" down one's profile to review its history, the website provides for a timeline review along with activity logs, which help oversee the social networking activity of users. User activity and information have been categorized and arranged for more specialized searches.[27]

   Personal data published by a user can be accessed freely. Additionally, a user can request a Data Report from FB, which can be downloaded in HTML or JSON format. Access to a profile is limited to a user with two exceptions: legacy contacts (in cases of death or incapacity) and emergency friend contacts (for security breaches). For resolving the issue, the website may temporarily gain access to the FB account. Users are also given an option to manage data, which ultimately is just a help page with a redirection to the settings.

   Note that a user's advertiser profile is not accessible for their review as it only contains inferred data.[28]

2. **Rectification:** This is completely left in user control, with the option of freely editing profile information and deleting/editing older posts.

3. **Erasure:** Initial deletion of profile or content is in user control, but permanent erasure from FB's servers requires a request.[29] The website also provides for removal of data held by third-party apps. This can be done in isolation or along with complete erasure of the account. The data will be permanently erased (irretrievable) within a 30-day period, and the user may change his/her mind within that period.

   In some cases, deletion may take up to 90 days to process data created by the profile. However, the profile will remain inaccessible to others during the process. A user may also download their data before erasure.

4. **Restriction:** FB allows users to deactivate their accounts by restricting any further processing or activity on their Facebook profile, while still using other services (like Messenger). The website also allows users to block users, posts, audiences, messages, invites, apps, and pages. Restriction in cases of disputes with the Controller[30] has not been provided for on the website options. The complaint mechanism of FB services on the website may provide for such an option to users.

5. **Data Portability:** FB has created modalities that allow users to request their data in an interoperable format. As mentioned earlier, users can download their information in HTML or JSON format by selecting types of information and date ranges needed. Downloading personal data is a password-protected process that only the user can access.

In examining the above, we can see that Facebook has covered most GDPR rights in the simplest format possible, except the rights relating to objection and explanation of automated processing.[31] This is because:

1. FB primarily uses AI for direct marketing and advertising purposes, which users can control directly through their settings. We will discuss this further in the next section.

2. FB can argue that their AI does not make "legal or significant" decisions for the users.[32] But as the company increases the breadth its services, it is inevitable that they will implement protections under GDPR Article 22.

## 12.10 A Digital Blueprint and a GDPR Loophole

A collective analysis of all data produced by Facebook and the information it provides likely triggers special data protections under GDPR as a person's profile becomes a digital copy of a person's political and philosophical views. But the steady increase of data-collection capabilities of the service will likely cause more confusion when fulfilling the information obligation under GDPR,[33] which it already has.[34] It is important to note that special data protections on the website are minimal as FB utilizes a clever GDPR loophole that allows it to access such information without specific linkage to a user.

Discussed in the previous chapter, the UK House of Commons' final report on *Disinformation and Fake News* had identified a prominent omission in GDPR that allowed companies to trade personal data with one another.[35] GDPR covers personally identifiable information, which alone or aggregated with other data helps the recipient "identify" an individual. Facebook's current advertising services do not directly identify an individual user but provide "lookalike audiences," which fit the advertiser's targeted demographic.[36] The lookalike audiences tool does not use specific "personal" information but uses inferred data that analyzes the data and matches advertisers to "data profiles."[37] FB itself has admitted that the lookalike audience tool helps advertisers reach users "who are likely to be interested in their business because they are similar to their existing customers."[38]

Consider the following data set: "James Holland, 32 years old, African American, fan of sports, European cinema, lives in X, Texas, ZIP: 1234, mobile #9229, son of Arthur Holland, works at ABC LLC as a sales executive, registered Republican." In the information above, the "identifiable" personal data would be the name, address, mobile number, and father's name. James's place of employment and political affiliation do not directly identify him, but it can become personal data when combined with the first data set. James's race and political affiliation are also protected as special data. The remaining data is supplemental "characteristics," which can become personal data as well when combined with identifiable information. Inferred data involves using AI to find "audiences" with the following "characteristics": male, early 30s, Texas resident, Republican supporter, movie, TV and sports fan. The AI then provides the advertiser with audiences such as James. Using FB hyperlocal targeting services, users can be found within a designated one-mile radius. AIQ, a Canadian firm involved in the Analytica scandal, also used characteristics like race in matching the data profiles.[39]

This GDPR lacuna is slight but has led to commercial and political abuse with visible consequences. By essentially generalizing the process of user identification and utilizing large data sets to conceal direct identification, firms like AIQ, SCL, and Cambridge Analytica were able to use FB to spread targeted disinformation. The final report agreed with the UK Information Commissioner's Office (ICO) and recommended that the government study how privacy protections under GDPR can be expanded to include inferred data.[40] By using GDPR loopholes and ensuring its data ubiquity, FB played an instrumental role in the spread of Russian disinformation, which resulted in electoral influence. As governments and users are becoming more aware of the company's full potential, more rigorous regulation is inevitable.

With GDPR now in force and impending e-communication and content-moderation laws on the horizon, social networking companies in the coming decade are likely to be heavily regulated. Regulation accompanied with deterrent fines has worked well in the past. In Germany, social networking companies were asked to initially self-regulate the removal of hate speech within 24 hours. When self-regulation did not work, the German government passed the Network Enforcement Act (NetzDG), in January 2018. The legislation forced technology and media companies to remove hate speech from their sites within 24 hours and with fines of €20 million if it is not removed.[41] Because of this law, one in six of Facebook's moderators now work in Germany, which is practical evidence that legislation can work.[42]

## 12.11 Investigations Ahead

On June 3, 2018 it was reported that FB maintained data-sharing partnerships with mobile device manufacturers like Apple, Amazon, BlackBerry, Microsoft, and Samsung. Under the terms of this personal information sharing, device manufacturers were able to gather information about users to deliver "the Facebook experience," allowing those parties to obtain data about a user's FB friends, even if those friends configured their privacy settings to deny data sharing with third parties. A month later, FB acknowledged a "bug" that unblocked people that users blocked between May 29 and June 5, 2018. This "bug" allegedly allowed Chinese device manufacturers like Huawei, Lenovo, Oppo, and TCL access to user data under this program leading to potential national security risks. In July 2018, FB discovered and closed a "privacy loophole" in their Chrome plug-in intended for marketing research allowing users to access the list of members for private Facebook groups.[43]

The slew of privacy violations above are outside of the Cambridge Analytica scandal and have occurred since the enactment of GDPR. After the data abuses of the past decade, the coming years will likely see GDPR investigations against the company, which took place after May 2018, with the Irish Data Protection Commissioner's office taking charge as the LSA. The Irish LSA is presently investigating FB's massive data breach in September 2018, which affected over 50 million users when hackers exported access tokens to gain control of user profiles by exploiting a vulnerability in the site's "view as" feature. Additionally, the LSA is investigating the company's monitoring and consent practices following the Analytica scandal and Max Schrem's complaint filed on the day GDPR came into force. The determinations of the Irish Data Protection Commissioner will determine the direction of the company's future data collection and sharing practices in the new data-protection regime.

## 12.12 Future Projects

As seen from FB's diversification of services into the realm of gaming, original IP TV programming, and virtual reality (VR), the company has bold ambitions for the future as a social media and tech giant. The diversification will lead to new regulations applying (such as those relating to internet TV and streaming) but will also help the company to step away from traditional personal data processing. But merely entering the online streaming service industry does not insulate FB from scrutiny. Carriers such as Netflix, Amazon, and Spotify have recently faced their own share of GDPR complaints based on their failures to provide enough user access to personal data.[44] Data subject rights are the driving force for GDPR applicability. As long as FB stays as the anchor of these services, its personal data obligations are unlikely to be diluted.

Moving forward, any new project of FB will likely be subjected to a Data Protection Impact Assessment under the supervision of GDPR regulators. Considering the pending complaints against it, FB should take extreme caution for GDPR compliance, as videochats and voice-based technology create new avenues for abuse. The coming decades will likely see an intersection between FB's obligations across:

1. Personal data protection
2. Online telecommunications and privacy

3. Online streaming services
4. Media and content censorship
5. Antitrust regulations

The overlap of regulations requires that GDPR obligations be kept up to date with a consideration of how these mandates conflict and work together. It becomes important to legally classify which authority should supervise the company and at what point they can do so. A DPIA can help clarify these matters by separating personal data concerns for the SA reviewing the plan.

## Notes

1 GDPR, Articles 55 and 56.
2 GDPR, Article 56.
3 *Investigation into the Use of Data Analytics in Political Campaigns*, ICO, November 2018, p. 9. Note that this investigation relates to the Cambridge Analytica scandal from 2016 to the present.
4 See Chapter 5 (Section 5.2.1); to access the four complaints and its summary please see NYOB, *GDPR: noyb.eu filed four complaints over "forced consent" against Google, Instagram, WhatsApp and Facebook,* May 25, 2018, https://noyb.eu/wp-content/uploads/2018/05/pa_forcedconsent_en.pdf.
5 Press Release, "Bundeskartellamt Prohibits Facebook from Combining User Data from Different Sources," February 7, 2019, https://www.bundeskartellamt.de/SharedDocs/Meldung/EN/Pressemitteilungen/2019/07_02_2019_Facebook.html.
6 Ibid.
7 GDPR, Articles 13–15.
8 EU Data Protection Working Party, *Guidelines on Consent,* April 10, 2018, 6–10.
9 Cross reference to discussion later in this chapter.
10 Greg Sterling, "Google Slapped With $56.8 Million Fine for GDPR Consent Violations," Martech Today, January 21, 2019, https://martechtoday.com/google-slapped-with-56-8-million-fine-for-gdpr-consent-violations-229813; for an in-depth study of this complaint and its ramifications for online contracts, please see Chapter 5 (Section 5.2) of this book.
11 GDPR, Article 6.
12 Facebook, "Data Policy, 'How do we respond to legal requests or prevent harm?'"
13 Chapter 10 (Section 10.8).
14 GDPR, Article 6.1.f.
15 "Bundeskartellamt Prohibits Facebook."
16 The Editorial Board, "How Silicon Valley Puts the 'Con' in 'Consent,'" *New York Times,* February 2, 2019, https://www.nytimes.com/2019/02/02/opinion/internet-facebook-google-consent.html.
17 "Bundeskartellamt Prohibits Facebook."
18 "Bundeskartellamt Prohibits Facebook."

19 GDPR, Article 24.

20 Chapter 10 (Sections 10.15 and 10.21).

21 Facebook, "'About Ads': "Understand What Data Is Used to Show You Ads" and related hyperlinks.

22 GDPR, Article 25.

23 "Bundeskartellamt Prohibits Facebook."

24 Chapter 10 (Section 10.23)

25 Facebook, Terms of Service, §3.3.2.

26 Facebook, Settings, "Your Facebook Information."

27 Facebook, Settings, "Your Facebook Information" – 1. Access your information.

28 For a greater discussion of this subject please see our Section on Content Moderation, "Disinformation and False News" in this chapter.

29 Facebook, Settings, "Your Facebook Information" – 5. Delete your Account and Information.

30 GDPR, Article 18.1.

31 GDPR, Articles 21 and 22.

32 GDPR, Article 22.

33 GDPR, Article 13.

34 "Bundeskartellamt Prohibits Facebook."

35 Note that the United Kingdom presently follows GDPR as their data protection standards along with the domestic Data Protection Act. See House of Commons Digital, Culture, Media and Sport Committee, *Disinformation and "fake news,"* *Final Report,* HC 1791 Published on 18 February 2019, ¶42.

36 For a greater discussion on Facebook's advertising practices and how "lookalike audiences" are created, please see the sections on advertising in Chapter 10 (Sections 10.16–10.20).

37 House of Commons Digital, Culture, Media and Sport Committee, *Disinformation and "fake news,"* ¶42.

38 House of Commons Digital, Culture, Media and Sport Committee, *Disinformation and "fake news,"* ¶42 (specifically the documentary exhibits listed in citation 49).

39 House of Commons Digital, Culture, Media and Sport Committee, *Disinformation and "fake news,"* ¶164.

40 House of Commons Digital, Culture, Media and Sport Committee, *Disinformation and "fake news,"* ¶48.

41 BBC, "Germany Starts Enforcing Hate Speech Law," January 1, 2018, https://www.bbc.com/news/technology-42510868.

42 House of Commons Digital, Culture, Media and Sport Committee, *Disinformation and "fake news,"* ¶24.

43 For an in-depth look at the timeline of events related to the company's data breaches, please see Chapter 10 (Section 10.26).

44 NYOB.eu, "Netflix, Spotify & YouTube: Eight Strategic Complaints Filed on 'Right to Access,'" January 18, 2019, https://noyb.eu/access_streaming.

# 13

# The Future of Data Privacy

*Technology is cool, but you've got to use it as opposed to letting it use you.*

— Prince

## 13.1   Our Second Brain

Your second brain – a digital device without gray matter – is a constant presence in your pocket. It is designed with a single mission: to make your life convenient by assuming your routine and seemingly mindless chores. Its intelligence is called "artificial," but it has an enormous capacity to work across numerous aspects of your life. It is not costly and has a benign purpose: to free your biological mind to focus on what is important. The only side effect of this virtual implant is that it will make your gray-matter brain, well, lazy.

Your digital brain learns constantly. Once it has been programmed, it becomes progressively smarter from your choices and actions. It is not wired to your five, or six, senses. It has a strong pattern recognition ability and can beat your biological brain in chess, unless you are a grandmaster. With experience, it comes close to mimicking aspects of your personality, without the underlying emotions – but for a touch of the real, you can program it to emulate a tense or relaxed voice.

Once the "bare" digital brain is acquired, its training begins with uploads of convenience, with apps carrying out simple daily tasks for you. Don't feel like cooking or talking to a human to order food and provide directions to your house? Tap on Grubhub or Door Dash. You don't have to memorize any phone number – not even your own. Just search your contacts. Need to get out? Speak the destination for an Uber or a Lyft at your doorstep. Want a suit for your cousin's wedding in Japan – what else but Amazon? Your measurements are stored there, and the mall is too far. You can use Expedia, Priceline, Trivago, or numerous other websites to book your flights and hotels. WhatsApp or e-mail your cousin instantly to let them know you are coming; regular/snail mail is a novelty for special occasions.

But how to get around in Japan when you don't speak Japanese? Simple – get Google Translate. Need a travel plan? Just go to TripAdvisor and preset it on your maps. All this is here and now, and getting more sophisticated, intelligent. There is nothing seemingly sinister about all this.

The more your digital brain does for you, the less you have to. There is no need to remember the small details – bank account numbers, addresses, or phone numbers – only passwords. And if your real brain cannot keep track of the passwords, your digital one will recognize your fingerprints, eyes, or tonality – no need for "open sesame."

The learning continues, like a friendly extension of your biological brain. The digital brain knows that you like to wake up at 6:30 a.m. on weekdays and 8 a.m. on the weekends. You love letting your friends and followers on Instagram and Facebook know where you are and what you are doing, so train your digital dragon to do it; it will take a few seconds per day to instruct it and then it will do it on its own. Your "community" of thousands know you're at the Hilton Hotel in Tulsa at this very moment having a drink, because you posted your location on Snapchat. If anyone needs to reach you for a professional interaction or to consider you for a new job, they will find your professionally curated persona on LinkedIn: academic and professional history, areas of expertise, former positions and experience, etc. If someone wants to connect with you at a personal level, they can find you on Facebook, as a dog lover, football fan, etc. Looking for a serious relationship? Numerous applications and tools can assist you, along with millions of other relationship seekers and their own digital brains, to match the personality traits of the "real you" with those of the "real them." The matching algorithm has numerous criteria that you may choose consciously, or you can let your digital brain contrive them through your actions: what type of relationship you are looking for and what you are looking for in a partner; details about yourself accumulated over social media posts, pictures, videos, memes "shared," wines "liked," and text messages help provide a perfect copy of your first brain.

It is now up to you to initiate relationship(s) by sending a message, or you can let your digital brain do the job. You may keep the relationship at the virtual level, and communicate via messages and pictures, or propose in-person meetings. Your digital brain can assist you in maintaining several relationships simultaneously – it can be trained to communicate on your behalf, assist you in composing the content, select pictures or other media, and predict the words coming out of your fingers before you even think of them.

During this journey, providers of the seemingly free bare-bones digital brain are listening and recording your every action. They are voracious for-profit giants that must be fed. They sell your data and persona – in the form of a digital footprint – to providers of what you like to see, communicate with, or seek. This is the point where your digital brain intrudes into your screen. It is designed as a learning organism and starts to think for you.

## 13.2    Utopian or Dystopian?

You adopt a new cat and suddenly advertisements for cat food, litter, and toys come up on your Instagram newsfeed. Facebook declares that you have been in a relationship for seven years now, and projects that it is time for you to propose, and without warning you get prompts for engagement rings on your page. You Google "flights to Paris" and see recommendations for hotels within your budget in Paris when reading a news article online. At a party in Paris, you Shazam a song you like and within days Spotify has a playlist of similar artists for you to explore. Midway through the music you hear an advertisement for the newest political show on Hulu. For a limited time, Spotify also offers *free* Hulu for a month if you upgrade to premium! An offer like that makes you a Hulu member, with all the political shows you could ever want. After binge-watching Sarah Silverman's *I Love You, America*, you log on to Netflix and rewatch *The West Wing* and *House of Cards*. Suddenly YouTube starts to "enhance" your education on left-wing politics, recommending satire and "pertinent" news stories.

Cain Caleb was a liberal college dropout struggling to find his place in the world and was sucked into a vortex of far-right politics through YouTube videos – what he calls a decentralized cult of far-right YouTube personalities who convinced him that Western civilization was under attack. The story is not rare: a young man who is struggling to find his place in the world spends time playing violent video games, visits YouTube looking for tactics, and is directed to a far-right video, and upon viewing he is seduced through other videos created by a community of like-minded people with a mission to grow their organizations. There may be several variants of this story but the common link is YouTube and its algorithm that governs your digital brain.

Recommendations to register as a democratic voter along with articles from liberal news outlets flood your newsfeed as elections approach, which gets you more involved. Political pages and sponsored advertisements demand that you *get up and act!* And so you do.

You engage in political debates across platforms to push the candidate *you think is right* for your country. The journalists you follow are *the most trusted sources* you could rely on, and you share your ideological sermon far and wide in private messages, group chats, Twitter, and Facebook communities, indiscriminately sharing thoughts *you* have been told are true. But frustration mounts when *half* the population you're reaching out to just does not agree with *basic facts*! All the tweets and angry messages aren't forcing the change you want. The boisterous political commentator recommended to you by Spotify a week ago calls for a *PHYSICAL RESPONSE* because it's *time to act!* And so you do.

"Alexa, please order me a baseball bat from Amazon."
"Hey Google! Find me the designs for the Capitol Building."
"Alexa, order a 3-D printer."
"Hey Google! Find me 3-D printer gun designs."

"Hey Portal, message my mother to reschedule our phone call to tomorrow, and tell her I love her."

"Alexa, set my GPS navigator to the Capitol Building please."

With a 3-D printed gun in one hand and a bottle of whiskey in the other, you get into your self-driving car and sit patiently as it drives you to the Capitol Building. It is time. It has been months of protesting and lamenting online – enough digital action, it's time to be *real*. You've planned this attack for months, just you, in your house, along with your blueprints and designs. It is the perfect plan; everything around you has pointed to this act, and you're a cautious, careful person by nature so it's going to go off without a hitch. You sit in your car as it takes you to your destiny, ruminating on the change you'll make in the world by finally acting on what *you're passionate about*. The car stops. You take a moment to breathe, because *this is it*. You grab the gun and dash out of the car ready to shoot, only to find out that your car has driven you straight to the police station, where a pair of handcuffs is waiting for you.

A tragedy prevented, without a doubt, sparing you from serious consequences. But why go through the struggle of denial? Your brain had already programmed your intentions and decided that you will be ready to face the worst.

The principal difference between the first and second brains' effects in our lives is that our second brain sits in a computer server programmed and controlled by a seemingly friendly service provider with deep memory and a mission to exploit your traits and habits, and your individuality, and, if possible, to control your thinking for a small sum paid by someone unknown to you. The brain learns as time goes on and organizes information for us in a simple, accessible fashion so we do not have to expend effort to retain it. But so do the brain's friends – other apps and services providers. Unlike our mind, which processes and filters information before sharing it with the outside world, our devices are *connected* organisms in a larger digital ecosystem. A constant exchange of personal information is happening on or below the surface, letting service providers learn about us, *along with* our second brain.

## 13.3   Digital Empowerment: Leveling the Playing Field

To empower our digital brains and yet keep them sane and under our governance, we must control their access to our personal data. We must also know how they will use it for their learning mechanisms. We cannot let them become too intrusive and passively influence our decisions and lives. We must have conscious control of our data through efficient and effective mechanisms – not through long disclaimers. The information on a can of soup tells us its ingredients and nutritional values for major food groups, with the inherent trust that it will not make us sick or influence our thinking. This information is not provided voluntarily by the manufacturers; they do it because it is mandatory.

A similar framework applies to over-the-counter medications. Prescription medications come with long technical and incomprehensible disclosures in small print. These disclosures are required by law as well, but are directed to medical professionals who have the expertise to understand them and advise us of the medications' curative potential and possible side effects. This type of framework does not yet exist in the realm of private data.

Only users, assisted by laws, can force a change in the personal data ecosystem. The first step in this endeavor is acceptance. We need to consider and appreciate that the free exchange of data and personal information is essential to the "new world order" that it is a *valuable commodity* for service providers. We should be conscious of the fact that free and convenient services come at the cost of using our data for corporate gain – these services make our lives more convenient but by default compromise our privacy.

The next step would be to maintain our *data health*. Our acceptance that our data will eventually be somehow used or sold should not make us cavalier about how and with whom it will be shared. We should start building personal and communal awareness of the abusive data practices and cyber-crimes that exist in today's world.

For example, the first victim of credit card fraud or the notorious "Nigerian prince" phishing scam served as a lesson for *reactive* change, where people learned their mistakes from the consequence itself. Society and law gradually caught up, and now we are generally aware that a suspicious e-mail link is a red flag. Or that anti-virus software is a necessity, along with physically safekeeping computer hardware.

Being mindful of data abuse also requires constant vigilance and trust in on-line service providers and their practices. We should always be aware that our use of and indulgence in services implies, by default, dissemination of our data and vulnerability of our privacy. As tempting as it may be to live-stream our daily ac-tivities, we need to be mindful that each video creates a digital record that can be easily published and shared for anyone to see. If a service provider is found to be blatantly abusing our data-privacy trust, we must reduce our usage of its services even though it is logistically painful. By being selective in the services we use, and by demanding erasure of our information that is not directly applicable to them, we could make a significant impact in the protection of our data privacy.

We should also be cautious not to overshare our private lives online. Our informa-tion is valuable fodder for the data prowlers. For example, Instagram culture dictates that users automatically give a post a "like" if they appreciate what they see. But with each "like," the advertiser profile is boosted through the use of their algorithms. We do not have to necessarily stop "liking" posts altogether, but we should save doing it for when we actually *want* consumers' attention to a product. With cookie collection on websites becoming commonly optional due to GDPR purpose limitation,[1] we should, again, think twice before clicking "accept" on the pop-up consent form.

The children of this generation will be the most recorded people in human history. With Alexa as their home assistant and their parents posting their every "first," they will grow up in a world with profoundly different privacy expectations from the generations preceding them. Old rules of data and personal privacy are becoming redundant, considering the growth of the internet of things, AI, social robots, and sci-fi products like Neuralink, which physically places the technology in one's brain.[2] Crafting new rules of technological privacy will be a struggle for future generations, and the change is already under way. Issues surrounding the dark web, crypto-currency, robotic personhood,[3] and social credit[4] are already surfacing in public discourse.

In summary, we need to act *preemptively* to handle emerging issues rather than being reactive to widespread abuses. If we proactively change our approach towards protecting our data privacy, laws will follow. Toward this goal, we should choose service providers who value and protect the privacy and integrity of our information. We must continually review our active privacy settings on social media. We should be cognizant of our rights as a data supplier to these companies and be mindful of any inappropriate use of our information.

We should also invest in services that protect our passwords and hardware. Once we have addressed our own "data-privacy health," we should push for change and public dialogue on a larger scale. If our rights are violated by a large online conglomerate, we should approach privacy nonprofit organizations and *defend* those rights on public platforms to create broad awareness.

Cultural, societal, and legal transformations are gradual. We expect that legal frameworks will eventually catch up to technologies. But we cannot passively wait in the wings. We should seek a *well-regulated* online environment where concerns regarding our data privacy are at the forefront as a fundamental right. In this framework, websites would be rated by an independent agency based on their "data-privacy hygiene." Technology service providers would be treated like pharmaceutical companies and required to operate with transparency in their services. New technologies or technology-based services would come with *public disclosures* relating to their data use, similar to what the US Federal Drug Administration and similar national bodies around the world require. Naysayers may argue that technology is not a drug and does not require rigorous regulation. However, considering the state of data privacy in the world today, we must pay our digital self the same attention and respect that we have for our physical well-being.

## Notes

1 GDPR, Article 5.
2 Ashlee Vance, "Elon Musk's Neuralink Says It's Ready for Brain Surgery," July 16, 2019, *Bloomberg*, https://www.bloomberg.com/news/articles/2019-07-17/elon-musk-s-neuralink-says-it-s-ready-to-begin-brain-surgery.
3 Janosch Delckler, "Europe Divided Over Robot Personhood," *Politico*, April 11, 2018, https://www.politico.eu/article/europe-divided-over-robot-ai-artificial-intelligence-personhood/.
4 Alexandria Ma, "China Has Started Ranking Citizens with a Creepy 'Social Credit' System – Here's What You Can Do Wrong, and the Embarrassing, Demeaning Ways They Can Punish You," *Business Insider*, October 29, 2018, https://www.businessinsider.com/china-social-credit-system-punishments-and-rewards-explained-2018-4.

# Appendix

## Compendium of Data Breaches

These data breaches are analyzed using the **three pillars** of GDPR data protection:

1. Privacy by design (tokenization, anonymization, etc.)
2. Security in processing (anti-virus and cyber-security)
3. Notification of breach (72 hours)

# 2014

## UPS

- **Breach date:** Between January 20 and August 11, 2014. UPS learned of the threat on July 31, 2014.
- **Notification date:** August 21, 2014.
- **Type:** Malware attack using "memory scraping" software.
- **Targeted data:** Names, addresses, e-mails, phone numbers, and card information.
- **Motive for the breach:** Theft.
- **Damages and data subjects affected:** The hackers affected over 100,000 transactions over the period of breach and attacked 51 stores in 24 states.
- **Preventive measures:** The store's systems were not linked to one another electronically, so the damage was contained to only 1% of the company's systems. UPS investigated the breach after reading a *government notification* on malware attacks.
- **Curative measures and liability:** UPS said that it is providing identity protection and credit monitoring help to affected customers. The company

additionally increased its protection on other stores. UPS also published a list of affected stores, including the breach inception date and duration. The company was lauded by some for its "well-written data breach notification."

- **GDPR compliance:** While it is unclear whether UPS had "privacy-by-design" implemented or whether they maintained security in their processing, at the time they were not under a staunch legal obligation to do so. Their prompt notification of the breach was overdue under GDPR standards, which mandate a 72-hour period to notify the public. Regardless, a three-week period of investigation and notification when there was no duty to do so is still admirable in 2014.

### University of Maryland

- **Breach date:** February 8, 2014.
- **Notification date:** February 19, 2014.
- **Type:** An outside source gained access to a secure records database that holds information dating to 1998.
- **Targeted data:** Names, Social Security numbers, dates of birth, and university identification numbers of people affiliated with the school on two of its campuses. No financial, academic, health, or contact (phone, address) information was accessed.
- **Motive for the breach:** The whistleblower arrestee, David Helkowski, admitted that he mainly did it to *point out the flaws* in the University's systems, and it ended up "going too far" with damage he didn't foresee.[1]
- **Damages and data subjects affected:** 309,079 personal records for faculty, staff, and students who had received identification cards at the University of Maryland were compromised.
- **Preventive measures:** The University maintained the data in a "sophisticated, multi-layered" format; however, someone managed to gain internal access.
- **Curative measures and liability:** The University launched a criminal and internal investigation to investigate the matter further. Additionally, they set up help lines and FAQ pages. On April 9, 2014, a man was arrested by the FBI. The University also offered five years of credit protection to the affected students.
- **GDPR compliance:** The University maintained its database securely but was still vulnerable to physical breach, which is what happened here. Notification taking place the next day shows greater deference to data privacy from the University and is ideal under GDPR. Though not listed in the regulation, provision of *credit monitoring services* seems to be a standard method to abate liability for data breaches in the US and can help *rebuild* goodwill with the customers.

## Trump Hotels I

- **Breach date:** The breach allegedly took place between May 19, 2014 and June 2, 2015.
- **Notification date:** October 2015.
- **Type:** Malware attack.
- **Targeted data:** Payment data such as card number, expiration date, and security code.
- **Motive for the breach:** Unclear at present, but the data stolen suggests theft.
- **Damages and data subjects affected:** Customers who had used their credit/debit cards during the period of breach were possibly affected. The locations hit included the Trump SoHo New York, Trump National Doral, Trump International New York, Trump International Chicago, Trump International Waikiki, Trump International Hotel & Tower Las Vegas, and Trump International Toronto. The hotel collection said transactions on the point-of-sale terminals at the Las Vegas and Waikiki properties may also have been intercepted by card thieves.

## Trump Hotels II

- **Breach date:** The breach allegedly took place between August 10, 2016 and March 9, 2017. The hotel learned of the breach on June 5, 2017.
- **Notification date:** July 11, 2017.
- **Type:** A third party gained access to account credentials that permitted access to the data.
- **Targeted data:** Payment data such as card number, expiration date, and security code. Additionally, they gained reservation information, names, e-mails, phone numbers, and addresses.
- **Motive for the breach:** Unclear at present, but the data stolen suggests theft.
- **Damages and data subjects affected:** The breach had not directly hit Trump hotels, but rather attacked a third party, Sabre SynXis Central Reservations system (CRS), which facilitates the booking of hotel reservations made by consumers. This in turn affected 14 of their properties.
- **Preventive measures (both I and II):** The hotel's then-existing systems clearly did not implicate comprehensive security measures, as *both* breaches were over extended durations of time. Furthermore, the time elapsed among the breaches, discovery, and notice to the public was large.
- **Curative measures and liability (both I and II):** The hotel in its notice suggested acting with the FTC, obtaining a credit report, and placing a fraud alert on the affected account. They stated that a report was filed with the authorities and investigations were under way.
- **GDPR compliance (both I and II):** Minimal if not nonexistent. Prior to these multiple incidents, hotels like the Trump group have been repeatedly been hit

for failing to secure proper means of *encryption* and *tokenization*, which is the standard under GDPR.[2] Furthermore, the extended time of notification would have incurred significant liability under the Regulation.

## Supervalu

- **Breach date:** Two seperate breaches occurred in August and September 2014.
- **Notification date:** August 15, 2014 and September 29, 2014.
- **Type:** The first was a hack and the second was a malware attack.
- **Targeted data:** The hack had resulted in the theft of account numbers and, in some cases, also the expiration date and other details like the cardholder's name. The malware attack focused on the point-of-sale systems, targeting similar data.
- **Motive for the breach:** Unknown, likely theft.
- **Damages and data subjects affected:** The hackers affected the payment systems of more than 200 grocery stores. The malware affected their Shop 'n Save stores, Shoppers Food & Pharmacy, and Cub Foods franchises, along with a few associated liquor stores and certain locations of the Albertsons's grocery chain (for transactions between June 22 and July 17, 2014).
- **Preventive measures:** The store's systems had reportedly prevented the breach from accessing much more sensitive data and prevented the breaches from escalating further. Additionally, the company held cyber-insurance for any such damage.
- **Curative measures and liability:** Investigations showed that the information stolen was subsequently not misused and the damage was contained. They subsequently increased security and filed a report with the authorities. Additionally, the company had set up a call center and provided complimentary identity protection services to assist consumers.
- **GDPR compliance:** While the reporting was timely, it wasn't within the mandated 72-hour period. The existing security measures in place at the time of the breach show that they were mindful of such problems, thereby showing they implemented "security" measures.

## eBay

- **Breach date:** The breach took place over 229 days as hackers got into the company network using the credentials of three corporate employees and had complete inside access to the user database. The breach was discovered on May 23, 2014.
- **Notification date:** It was reported to the public on May 27, 2014.
- **Type:** Hack and internal breach.
- **Targeted data:** Customers' names, passwords, e-mail addresses, dates of birth, and other contact details were exposed.
- **Motive for the breach:** Theft.
- **Damages and data subjects affected:** Approximately *all* 145 million customers were affected.

- **Preventive measures:** Though the then online giant had a fair amount of security measures, this has highly been criticized as their failure to ensure the security over the data for a period that was the greater part of a year. eBay did, however, store their more sensitive payment data on other servers, thereby controlling the damage. Though the passwords were encrypted, they were stolen nonetheless, and the remaining data was not.
- **Curative measures and liability:** Minimal measures were taken. No subsequent arrest was made, and the company refused to provide free credit monitoring (despite requests from the then AG), as they claimed payment data was not taken. They only reset accounts and asked customers to change their passwords.
- **GDPR compliance:** To this day, the eBay hack remains one of the most historic examples of a massive data breach that was handled poorly. In 2014 this served as the *first* wake-up call to the public regarding data protection. Notwithstanding, eBay's notification to the public was timely (though that was likely motivated by the size of the breach).

## JPMorgan Chase

- **Breach date:** The breach took place over the summer of 2014 and was discovered in late July 2014.
- **Notification date:** September 2014.
- **Type:** Hack.
- **Targeted data:** Customers' names, addresses, phone numbers, and e-mail addresses, as well as internal information about the users, pursuant to their filings with the Securities and Exchange Commission. Payment data was not affected but the hackers gained root privileges that would permit them to make account transactions.
- **Motive for the breach:** Targeted attack focusing on several financial institutions.
- **Damages and data subjects affected:** Over 76 million households, 83 million accounts, and 7 million small businesses.
- **Preventive measures:** Though the bank (at the time) annually spent $250 million on cyber-security, the hacker found a way to compromise the system.
- **Curative measures and liability:** In November 2015, federal authorities indicted four men, charging them with the JPMorgan hack plus other financial institutions. The hackers faced 23 counts, including unauthorized access of computers, identity theft, securities and wire fraud, and money laundering that netted them an estimated $100 million. A fourth hacker who helped them breach the networks was not identified.
- **GDPR compliance:** The JPMorgan Chase hack helped demonstrate that comprehensive and expensive security in online processing doesn't mean that an entity is immune from attacks and theft. At the time it could be said that the bank maintained state-of-the-art security, but as the technology evolved, so did the need for a *proportional increase* of the security measures.

## Home Depot

- **Breach date:** The breach took place between April and September 2014 and was discovered on September 2.
- **Notification date:** September 8, 2014.
- **Type:** Malware attack.
- **Targeted data:** Transactions over the four-month period were likely compromised, with relevant contact and payment details taken.
- **Motive for the breach:** Unknown, but likely theft.
- **Damages and data subjects affected:** 56 million credit cards, spread across their brick and mortar stores in the US and Canada.
- **Preventive measures:** Home Depot estimates that the breach has cost approximately $62 million, with more costs likely to come. The company believes it will be reimbursed $27 million thanks to its insurance coverage. This comes on the heels of an **internal breach** in **February 2014** where 20,000 employee names, dates of birth, and SSNs were stolen by three former employees to open fraudulent accounts. The company alleges that the malware was "unique, custom-built" to attack their software.
- **Curative measures and liability:** The company implemented the then prevalent industry practices of *reporting* to the authorities, *investigating* into the matter, *improving* existing security, and of course, providing *free identity protection services*. In March 2016, the company agreed to pay a settlement of at least $19.5 million to compensate US consumers through a $13 million fund to reimburse shoppers for out-of-pocket losses, and to spend at least $6.5 million to fund 1½ years of cardholder identity protection services.
- The settlement covers about 40 million people who had payment card data stolen, and more than 52 million people who had e-mail addresses stolen. The had company estimated $161 million of pre-tax expenses for the breach, including the consumer settlement and expected insurance proceeds.
- **GDPR compliance:** Many of the data breaches at this time, including the Home Depot breach, were for extended durations of time. This clearly indicates that there was a lack of oversight in the security. Furthermore, the company did not come forward themselves; rather, they only *confirmed* a report issued nearly a week prior to making their statements.[3] However, with the lawsuit and the overall expenses, it is clear that Home Depot were made an example of, unlike its counterparts.

## Sony

- **Breach date:** November 24, 2014; the next day, the company shut down its systems to investigate.
- **Notification date:** December 2, 2014.

- **Type:** Phishing scam.
- **Targeted data:** Since the breach, the hackers proceeded to "dump" data over the coming months relating to includes employee criminal background checks, salary negotiations, doctors' letters explaining the medical rationale for leaves of absence, salaries of 6,800 global employees, along with Social Security numbers for 3,500 US staff. There is also extensive documentation of the company's operations, ranging from the scripts for an unreleased pilot, the results of sales meetings with local TV executives, along with several other scripts and movies kept on file.
- **Motive for the breach:** The investigation revealed that the attack was a retaliation from North Korean over Sony releasing the movie *The Interview*, which presented the country in a bad light.
- **Damages and data subjects affected:** Almost 40GB of leaked internal data affected 6,800 global employees and damaged the company's interests, though the hackers did claim that they had 100TB of data to release.
- **Preventive measures:** Though the state of Sony's security was not well reported, the extent of the breach by the phishing scam shows that Sony wasn't expecting an attack of such a nature. As personal data at the time probably wasn't "consumer"-oriented, they were under less scrutiny to maintain it safely.
- **Curative measures and liability:** The company worked closely with the FBI and DHS, as this hack implicated "national security" because it originated from North Korea. Subsequently the US imposed sanctions on North Korea, though they deny the hack. No further action was otherwise taken.
- **GDPR compliance:** At the time, Sony was a business that didn't centrally handle personal data as part of their commercial activities, thereby reducing their burden (at the time) to maintain security for their consumers. However, the hack likely opened Sony's eyes to the fact that the data they hold is an asset worth protecting better, particularly considering the financial loss they subsequently faced.

## NYC Tax Company

- **Breach date:** In March 2014 the data was *voluntarily* released to the public.
- **Type:** Voluntary release of data that suffered from **poor anonymization** of the details.
- **Targeted data:** Home addresses of drivers, their income, and movements across the city. The data also arguably exposes passenger information to the world – which could reveal personal information about their journey points and times.
- **Motive for the breach:** Here there was no specific motive to breach security; Chris Wong, a data activist, had studied the information and pointed out the poor security. He received the data through a *Freedom of Information* request.

- **Damages and data subjects affected:** Taxi trip data of 173 million individuals.
- **Preventive measures:** Nearly nonexistent, considering the data was released without properly ensuring the security of the driver's/customer's privacy.
- **Curative measures and liability:** No action taken subsequently.
- **GDPR compliance:** This is a prime example of an attempt at "privacy by design" but fails to meet the specifications for safety.

### Neiman Marcus

- **Breach date:** Between July 16 and October 20, 2014.
- **Notification Date:** January 11, 2014.
- **Type:** Hack by "scraping" of data.
- **Targeted data:** Payment systems and data of certain brick-and-mortar stores.
- **Motive for the breach:** Likely theft.
- **Damages and data subjects affected:** Neiman Marcus lost 26,829 records for each of its 41 flagship stores, losing approximately 1.1 million records.
- **Preventive measures:** Weak, considering the fact that they later *lost* a class action lawsuit against consumers for the breach of privacy.
- **Curative measures and liability:** On May 22, 2015, in a precedent-setting case, a three-judge bench of the 7th Circuit unanimously ruled against the store in a class action suit, holding Neiman Marcus liable to pay $1.6 million to affected consumers.
- **GDPR Compliance:** The lawsuit and subsequent judgment issued against the store in May 2015 was considered as a historic development in data privacy law, as it created a stronger, positive duty on the part of business entities to protect the data held by them. This demonstrated the beginnings of a new trend in US data privacy law.

### NASDAQ

- **Breach date:** The breach began in October 2010 but was only revealed in July 2014.
- **Notification date:** July 2014.
- **Type:** Malware
- **Targeted data:** Data held by US financial institutions.
- **Motive for the breach:** Speculated to be a "cyber-military" attack from Russia.
- **Damages and data subjects affected:** Remains classified, but the damage was reportedly minimal, as no data taken from the malware was subsequently used.
- **Preventive measures:** When reported, concerns on Wall Street were looming over the security measures implemented, as the malware was found in the central servers.

- **Curative measures and liability:** Investigation and action was launched by the higher levels of government, and while it speculated that Russian spy agencies were involved, no action was subsequently taken.
- **GDPR compliance:** Though this breach does not relate to personal data, it helps demonstrate how *critical infrastructures* need to be protected in the digital age. Often the motives have been theft related, but the power of the data made by these institutions slowly started to join the center stage.

## Mozilla Firefox

- **Breach date:** The breach began on June 23, 2014 and continued for a period of 30 days.
- **Notification date:** August 2014.
- **Type:** Accidental disclosure.
- **Targeted data:** E-mail addresses and encrypted passwords.
- **Motive for the breach:** Error during "data sanitization" process.
- **Damages and data subjects affected:** 76,000 user profiles and 4,000 passwords were accidently disclosed on a public server.
- **Preventive measures:** The company stored the passwords as "salted hashes," encrypting them and rendering them *computationally impossible* to retrieve, thus preventing unauthorized access.
- **Curative measures and liability:** The company immediately removed the "database dump file" from the server to prevent further disclosure.
- **GDPR compliance:** This breach may be a good example of a "harmless," breach as no real damage was caused owing to the encryption of the passwords. Under GDPR the company would be unlikely to face severe liability.

## Michaels

- **Breach date:** The breach began in 2013 and included two *separate* breaches that lasted eight months. The breach was first discovered by an outside source on January 25. 2014.[4]
- **Notification date:** April 17, 2014.
- **Type:** Physical tampering of point-of-sale devices.
- **Targeted data:** Payment data relating to credit/debit cards.
- **Motive for the breach:** Theft.
- **Damages and data subjects affected:** Three million customer credit and debit cards across a varying number of stores.
- **Preventive measures:** As this was a case of physical tampering, the card data stolen was limited to the branches impacted by the breach. As a result the

company says there is no evidence that other customer personal information, such as name, address, or debit card PIN, was taken. They estimate the damage was limited to 7% of their payment cards used at its stores during that period.

- **Curative measures and liability:** An investigation was launched, a complaint was filed, and Michaels provided a full year of identity theft protection.
- **GDPR compliance:** Physical tampering does qualify as a data breach but changes the meaning of "security" in processing, as traditional cyber-security as we know today was hardly implemented into card machines. The delayed notification, however, is well beyond GDPR mandated periods and would likely incur liability.

### MacRumors Forum

- **Breach Date:** November 2014.
- **Notification Date:** November 12, 2014.
- **Type:** Hack using stolen moderator credentials.
- **Targeted data:** Usernames, e-mail addresses, and passwords.
- **Motive for the breach:** Unknown.
- **Damages and data subjects affected:** 860,000 users on the forum were affected.
- **Preventive measures:** The forum kept its passwords in a cryptographically "hashed" format, which makes it hard for outsiders to crack, and subsequent investigations did not reveal the passwords circulating online.
- **Curative measures and liability:** None taken; users were merely directed to change their credentials after the breach.
- **GDPR compliance:** Smaller user forums such as this are unlikely to face harsh scrutiny or large liability when breached because they hold minimal data. Their incentive to achieve "data health" is the loyalty of their consumers rather than governmental oversight.

### LexisNexis and Dunn & Bradstreet

- **Breach date:** The breach is said to have occurred as early as April 2013.
- **Notification date:** LexisNexis and other data-processing houses later admitted to the breach in late September 2013 and began its investigations at that time.
- **Type:** Hack.
- **Targeted data:** Social Security numbers, birthdays, mothers' maiden names, and similar data.
- **Motive for the breach:** A sophisticated group of hackers, the "SSNDOB gang," had stolen the data for resale to data brokerage firms.

- **Damages and data subjects affected:** 860,000 users on the affected forum.
- **Preventive measures:** The company maintained basic security to ensure *compliance* with the then-existing law.
- **Curative measures and liability:** None taken, other than the organization launching its own investigation into the matter. Most of the investigation had been done seven months earlier by *Kerbs on Security*, which shows that external parties were more aware of the lost data than the organization itself.[5]
- **GDPR compliance:** Here the three major firms had *complied* with the then existing law but didn't foresee themselves as a possible victim of an organized attack. This acts as a good example of how criminals such as hackers *forced* the developments in the law by increasing their capabilities for causing damage.

## Korea Credit Bureau

- **Breach date:** The breach is said to have started in December 2013.
- **Notification date:** January 19, 2014.
- **Type:** Employee theft.
- **Targeted data:** Customers' names, Social Security numbers, phone numbers, credit card numbers, and expiration dates.
- **Motive for the breach:** Theft and resale of the data to telephone marketing companies.
- **Damages and data subjects affected:** 20 million users affected.
- **Preventive measures:** The KCB had maintained a fair amount of security, but the employee managed to receive access to the data while working with the company as a temporary consultant to the firm.
- **Curative measures and liability:** The employee, along with several managers of the company who bought the data, was arrested.
- **GDPR compliance:** Maintaining the "physical" integrity of processing has been breached under the regulation, as a "temporary" consultant was given access to such valuable data is a definite contravention.

## European Central Bank

- **Breach date:** The specific date is unknown, but the ECB received the ransom letter on July 21, 2014.
- **Notification date:** July 24, 2014.
- **Type:** Hack.
- **Targeted data:** Customers' names, addresses, and phone numbers.
- **Motive for the breach:** Ransom.

- **Damages and data subjects affected:** 20,000 e-mails and data were taken.
- **Preventive measures:** 95% of the data taken was encrypted and secured.
- **Curative measures and liability:** The bank immediately reset its passwords and the German police immediately launched an investigation into the matter. No critical financial or market data was taken.
- **GDPR compliance:** It is ironic to see the ECB itself hit with a hack, but their response was model to how these matters should be dealt with under GDPR. Immediate action coupled with prompt notification is ideal *regardless* of whether the data stolen is safe or not.

## Dominos

- **Breach date:** Early June 2014.
- **Notification date:** June 16, 2014.
- **Type:** Physical break-in.
- **Targeted data:** Customers' names, addresses, phone numbers, e-mails, passwords, delivery and food preferences.
- **Motive for the breach:** Ransom of €30,000.
- **Damages and data subjects affected:** 592,000 French and 58,000 Belgian customer records.
- **Preventive measures:** The data was encrypted, but not in an unassailable manner. The passwords were in fact stored as plain-text.
- **Curative measures and liability:** The company informed the public of the incident and requested that they change their user credentials. They did not pay the ransom.
- **GDPR compliance:** There appears to be a trend of breach-ransom-refusal-reset that existed in 2014. Most businesses are clear they won't pay an illegal sum to secure personal data privacy, and rather just require that the credentials be reset. This solution may be viable in cases where the breach *only* relates to data that is capable of such a reset but is not a satisfactory conclusion when greater details such as addresses and telephone numbers are stolen.

## Community Health Systems

- **Breach date:** April and June 2014 (two incidents).
- **Notification date:** August 2014. It is important to note that the public was not notified directly; rather, the event became known through the company's SEC filings.
- **Type:** Hack.
- **Targeted data:** Patient names, addresses, birthdates, telephone numbers, and Social Security numbers.

- **Motive for the breach:** Unknown.
- **Damages and data subjects affected:** 4.5 million patients affected.
- **Preventive measures:** CHS was working with cyber-security to help cope with the threat, but the hackers found a way to bypass the security measures. The company additionally had cyber-insurance for such things.
- **Curative measures and liability:** The breach was nonmedical, thanks to the use of cyber-security to fend off the threat, but the company offered free protection to those affected. The company mentioned in its SEC filings that it did not believe that the incident would have a *material adverse effect* on their business or financial interests.
- **GDPR compliance:** Here the failure to notify the public clearly existed, along with a lack of oversight in the storage of the data.

# 2015

### Twitch TV

- **Breach date:** March 3, 2015.
- **Notification date:** March 23, 2015.
- **Type:** Hack.
- **Targeted data:** Username, e-mail address, password (cryptographically protected), the last IP address logged in from, and customers' names, phone numbers, addresses, and dates of birth.
- **Motive for the breach:** Unknown.
- **Damages and data subjects affected:** Unconfirmed, the website merely warned users of the possibility of breach. Twitch TV had 43 million users at the time.
- **Preventive measures:** The passwords were stored in a hashed form, but the hackers may have been able to plant code that was able intercept passwords in the clear as victims logged in.
- **Curative measures and liability:** The website had completely reset user accounts.
- **GDPR compliance:** Twitch TV took an appropriately "safe" response in changing the credentials with immediate effect. In cases where the damage isn't clear, it's better to be cautious than careless. The notification issued, however, lacked a fair amount of detail required under GDPR.

### Starwood Hotels

- **Breach date:** November 2014.
- **Notification date:** November 20, 2015.

- **Type:** Malware on point-of-sale systems.
- **Targeted data:** Cardholder names, credit card numbers, security codes, and expiration dates.
- **Motive for the breach:** Unknown, but likely theft.
- **Damages and data subjects affected:** 54 locations across North America, with transactions during the period being hit.
- **Preventive measures:** As with many other breaches disturbing payment systems, the problem wasn't located until it was too late. Here the breach took place over a year unnoticed, which shows a lack of oversight in the processing.
- **Curative measures and liability:** The company offered a year of credit monitoring and registered a complaint with the appropriate authorities. They also implemented additional security measures.
- **GDPR compliance:** An extended breach of over a year would likely attract heavy penalties under the regulation.

### Slack

- **Breach date:** February 2015 (over a four-day period).
- **Notification date:** March 27, 2015.
- **Type:** Hack.
- **Targeted data:** Usernames, e-mail addresses, hashed passwords, Skype IDs, and phone numbers.
- **Motive for the breach:** Unknown, but likely theft.
- **Damages and data subjects affected:** Undisclosed.
- **Preventive measures:** As the stored passwords were encrypted with a technique known as *salting and hashing*, it's unlikely that the hackers would have been able to crack well-chosen passwords.
- **Curative measures and liability:** The company used the opportunity of the breach to roll out two-factor authentication and password *kill-switches* to revive its security.
- **GDPR compliance:** Though not directly pertaining to the regulation, from a *business perspective* using data breaches as an opportunity to greatly increase one's security is common in the industry. This ensures consumer loyalty and helps assuage any fears.

### Scottrade

- **Breach date:** Late 2013 to early 2014.
- **Notification date:** October 2, 2015.
- **Type:** Hack.

- **Targeted data:** Client information, street addresses, passwords, e-mails, etc.
- **Motive for the breach:** Money laundering and data trade.
- **Damages and data subjects affected:** 4.6 million consumers affected.
- **Preventive measures:** The company had stored its more valuable data such as SSNs and payment data securely, and the data stolen was encrypted.
- **Curative measures and liability:** The company provided identity theft protection services to its consumers as a precaution. Subsequently, four people who were arrested in the **JPMorgan Chase** hack the previous year were implicated in this breach as well and have since been jailed.[6]
- **GDPR compliance:** Once again we can see a disparity in the "urgency" of investigation and notification of the public. This breach also went on for an extended duration of time, which is highly alarming as Scottrade handles very sensitive financial information. The action taken by these institutions reflects how much of a concern cyber-security was only three years ago.

### Natural Grocers

- **Breach date:** Late 2014.
- **Notification date:** March 3, 2015.
- **Type:** Malware in point-of-sale systems.
- **Targeted data:** The company claimed that only credit and debit card numbers were stolen, not names, addresses, PINs, or CVVs.
- **Motive for the breach:** Theft.
- **Damages and data subjects affected:** Undisclosed, but all locations across the country were hit during the period of breach (approximately three months long).
- **Preventive measures:** The company had maintained the then-standard point-of-sale devices that were subject to popular attack in 2014–2015.
- **Curative measures and liability:** The company sped up its plan to revamp their security by providing end-to-end encryption and secure "chip and PIN" devices.
- **GDPR compliance:** After countless attacks on point-of-sale systems, it starts to become evident that the systems need to be replaced with a more secure mechanism, leading to the present-day card payment devices used. Rather than a single isolated incident, it takes multiple events to induce the change needed.

### Medical Informatics Engineering

- **Breach date:** May 7, 2015 and went on for three weeks before discovery.
- **Notification date:** June 2, 2015 (specific clients were notified). Public notice on July 23, 2015.

- **Type:** Hack.
- **Targeted data:** Social Security numbers, lab results, medical conditions, demographic data, children's names, and health insurance policies.
- **Motive for the breach:** Unknown.
- **Damages and data subjects affected:** Approximately 3.9 million individuals had their data compromised. This included patients who received radiology services at 44 locations across Indiana, Michigan, and Ohio, along with providers in Fort Wayne, Indiana, and Ohio, among others.
- **Preventive measures:** The company was HIPAA-compliant in their security measures.
- **Curative measures and liability:** The company has since instituted a "universal password reset," improving password rules and storage mechanisms and boosting active system monitoring. They also provided two years of credit monitoring services.
- **GDPR compliance:** Again, MIE's case acts as a cautionary tale as to why compliance with a law doesn't necessarily mean immunity, as the technological capability of criminals is always growing. MIE's notice to the public is a model one, giving clear details of the breach and affiliates affected, along with time periods of relevant events.[7]

### Hyatt Hotels

- **Breach date:** August 13 to December 8, 2015.
- **Notification date:** Announced in December, but formal notification with the full extent of damage was released on January 14, 2015.
- **Type:** Malware in point-of-sale systems.
- **Targeted data:** The cardholder names, card numbers, expiration dates, and internal verification codes.
- **Motive for the breach:** Theft.
- **Damages and data subjects affected:** Undisclosed, but 250 locations globally hit during the period of breach, and across several affiliate hotels as well.
- **Preventive measures:** The company had maintained the then-standard point-of-sale devices that were subject to popular attack in 2014–2015. The malware was installed in the systems that were *auxiliary* with their services, such as restaurants or gift shops which the company states is a small percentage of their operations.
- **Curative measures and liability:** The hotel subsequently worked with cyber-security experts to revamp their security, along with notifying authorities of the crime. They also provided one year of credit monitoring services.
- **GDPR compliance:** 2015 is the year of hotel breaches, as we'll see, with several locations hit in succession (including the Starwood Hotels). Perhaps the trend grew because it became clear that these entities didn't maintain appropriately safe payment systems in the locations, making them easy targets.

## Hilton Hotels

- **Breach date:** A 17-week period spanning from November 18 to December 5, 2014, and from April 21 to July 27, 2015.
- **Notification date:** November 24, 2015.
- **Type:** Malware in point-of-sale systems.
- **Targeted data:** The cardholder names, card numbers, expiration dates, and internal verification codes.
- **Motive for the breach:** Theft.
- **Damages and data subjects affected:** More than 363,000 accounts were compromised, with the number of locations affected left undisclosed.
- **Preventive measures:** The hotel faced a standard point-of-sale system attack owing to a lack of oversight into the breaches.
- **Curative measures and liability:** The hotel subsequently was fined $700,000 by the UK regulators for the extremely delayed breach notification, notwithstanding media reports that revealed the fact.
- **GDPR compliance:** Among the many hotel breaches of 2015, Hilton as the most prominent faced a big fine from European regulators. The fine was levied as a deterrent to encourage Hilton to be more prompt in their notification measures.

## Experian

- **Breach date:** The breach was discovered on September 15, 2015, and had been under way since September 1, 2013.
- **Notification date:** October 1, 2015.
- **Type:** Hack.
- **Targeted data:** The names, addresses, birth dates, Social Security numbers, driver's license numbers, and passport numbers of customers.
- **Motive for the breach:** Theft.
- **Damages and data subjects affected:** More than 15 million accounts were compromised, with the number of locations affected left undisclosed.
- **Preventive measures:** The data was encrypted but the company claimed that even those measures may have been compromised. "Ongoing" security in the processing, along with privacy by design, was minimal if not nonexistent. As a company that is associated with T-Mobile, a telecom company, regular oversight is assumed by the consumers as a part of the service.
- **Curative measures and liability:** Experian did all the standard measures of investigating and reporting the matter with authorities, and even offered free credit reporting. However, consumers actually *refused* that service as they lost trust in the company's capabilities to check their credit securely. The company's poor notification and investigation of the matter resulted in a class action

lawsuit being filed against them for violating their data protection duties under California law.[8]

- **GDPR compliance:** It's clear that the trend in the US to handle "big" data breaches is to bring a suit against the company on behalf of the consumers. Contrast this with Europe, where the regulators themselves are the ones imposing the fines.

## Excellus

- **Breach date:** The breach was discovered on August 5, 2015, and began in 2013.
- **Notification date:** September 10, 2015.
- **Type:** Hack.
- **Targeted data:** The clients' names, dates of birth, Social Security numbers, mailing addresses, telephone numbers, member identification numbers, financial account information, and claim information.
- **Motive for the breach:** Theft.
- **Damages and data subjects affected:** Approximately 10 million accounts nationwide were affected.
- **Preventive measures:** Minimal, as the breach went on for nearly two years before being detected.
- **Curative measures and liability:** The lawsuits culminated in a larger class action suit where the company agreed in 2017 to a $115 million settlement, which is a large sum but works out to just $1.45 per customer. Additionally, individual plaintiffs will get $50 or two years' additional credit monitoring and can be reimbursed for out-of-pocket expenses incurred dealing with instances of identity theft, such as time lost at work or hiring a lawyer. In January 2018, a district court, following the trends in the *Michaels* and *Neiman Marcus* litigations, had chosen to *expand* the class of claimants against the company.[9]
- **GDPR compliance:** In keeping with the trends of 2015, we can see that hackers have gotten braver and breaches are targeted now to *larger entities* that wouldn't expect the attack. In the absence of regulators to hand down fines, the risk of a data breach is almost exclusively weighed considering the litigation costs that could be incurred. Companies outside GDPR's reach are possibly even at more risk, as their *variable costs* during a breach are likely to be more unpredictable.

## Blue Cross

- **Breach date:** June 2014, two months after the insurance company detected an attack that it believed it had contained. But the hackers had left behind hidden back doors that let them re-enter later, undetected. The breach was rediscovered on April 21, 2015.

- **Notification date:** May 2015.
- **Type:** Hack/phishing attack.
- **Targeted data:** Names, birth dates, e-mail addresses, and insurance identification numbers.
- **Motive for the breach:** Unknown, but likely theft.
- **Damages and data subjects affected:** More than 1.1 million customers of CareFirst BlueCross BlueShield.
- **Preventive measures:** It is clear that some degree of security was implemented as the initial breach was discovered, albeit not effectively disposed of, owing to a creative "back door" implemented by the hackers. However, they failed to encrypt their data, which made it easy to access.
- **Curative measures and liability:** The company provided for two years ID and credit monitoring services in addition to bringing in a cyber-security firm to remedy the issue. However, even though financial losses were not caused (owing to the nature of the data stolen), a lawsuit was still filed against the company for negligently maintaining their data. In 2018 the SCOTUS had remanded the case to Washington Federal Court, where the class action suit is pending.[10]
- **GDPR compliance:** The ruling of the Supreme Court follows the line of cases developing at the time that increases the ambit of liability for data collection entities. The fact that *no sensitive data* (as per GDPR) was even taken but the suit survives shows a shift in judicial tone toward the value of *all* data held by these entities.

## British Airways

- **Breach date:** End of March 2015.
- **Notification date:** March 30, 2015.
- **Type:** Hack by way of an *automated* attack.
- **Targeted data:** Frequent flyer accounts and the personal data contained in those accounts.
- **Motive for the breach:** Unknown, but likely for the purposes of data trade or phishing.
- **Damages and data subjects affected:** Over 10 thousand accounts were taken.
- **Preventive measures:** As an airline that conducts transactions online based in a highly regulated region of the data world, it is safe to say that the company has implemented necessary measures for securing data. The breach was discovered as British Airways (BA) noticed unauthorized activities on the accounts. The problem was then soon disclosed and dealt with.
- **Curative measures and liability:** The BA frequent flyer accounts, along with the website system, were temporarily shut down to fix the problem. It was reopened within a few days thereafter.

- **GDPR compliance:** BA avoided extensive liability in this case; however, the subsequent breaches it faced in 2018 became quite central in light of GDPR being in force. We will discuss this more in the **2018** section.

### Australian Department of Immigration

- **Breach date:** November 2014, with the breach being discovered on November 7.
- **Notification date:** The matter was *reported* on March 30, 2015.
- **Type:** Inadvertent disclosure by employee.
- **Targeted data:** The data released included name, date of birth, title, position nationality, passport number, visa grant number, and visa subclass held.
- **Motive for the breach:** Innocent breach by human error.
- **Damages and data subjects affected:** The employee had disclosed the details (mentioned above) relating to 31 high-level politicians who were to attend the G20 summit in Australia.
- **Preventive measures:** There was no flaw in the security of processing, as the employee mistakenly e-mailed a member of the local organizing committee of the Asian Cup (to be held in Australia) the personal information.
- **Curative measures and liability:** The matter was reported and not disclosed by the Australian government, which was highly criticized by other nations. But such objection led to no liability for the Australian government. This incident closely followed Australia issuing its own staunch and controversial data protection laws for the telecom industry.
- **GDPR compliance:** It is understandable that a State agency is not held liable for such a "high-level" disclosure of personal data, as enforcing punishment would be difficult. This matter raises an interesting point as to whether a country with an incident such as this should be cleared by the EU Data Protection Board for a *third-country transfer*. Of course, this incident is a more innocent example, but can ultimately have a bearing on the commission's decision to allow transfers to another country.

### Anthem

- **Breach date:** The breach began in April 2014 and continued until discovery on January 27, 2015.
- **Notification date:** February 4, 2015.
- **Type:** Hack, which began from a client clicking a phishing e-mail.
- **Targeted data:** The data stolen included names, addresses, Social Security numbers, dates of birth, and employment histories, income data, etc.
- **Motive for the breach:** Its believed that the hack was coordinated by a foreign government.[11]

- **Damages and data subjects affected:** One of the biggest healthcare breaches in history, 80 million records breached.
- **Preventive measures:** The data stolen wasn't encrypted, but that's irrelevant because HIPAA (which Anthem complied with) **does not require encryption** of data on servers. At the time, Anthem was spending more than $260 million on security-related measures.
- **Curative measures and liability:** A class action suit and investigations soon followed the breach, with Anthem agreeing to pay $16 million to the federal government as part of a settlement agreement, with an additional $15 million being set aside for out-of-pocket expenses of the customer.
- **GDPR compliance:** Anthem's predicament perhaps best illustrates the difficulty that Data Controllers will face hereon out. Consider the fact that they complied with the law, paid large sums for security, and subsequently face high risk if the processing is breached. Here the attack was likely done by larger foreign-backed forces, with the resources needed to break the integrity of the system. None of those facts change the reality that *they remain liable* for *any* breach (bearing connotations of the legal concept of **strict liability**). This changes the business of data processing as a sort of high-risk business opportunity.

## Premera

- **Breach date:** May 2014.
- **Notification date:** March 2015.
- **Type:** Coordinated hack by a phishing e-mail.
- **Targeted data:** Social Security numbers, birthdays, e-mails, physical addresses, bank account information, clinical information, and detailed insurance claims held by both past and present customers, dating back to 2002. Bank details provided by individuals who did business with the company were lost as well.
- **Motive for the breach:** It is suspected that the breach was a result of State-sponsored espionage from China.
- **Damages and data subjects affected:** Over 11 million individuals affected.
- **Preventive measures:** Premera has been greatly criticized for the breach, with customers (and subsequent plaintiffs) citing negligence on the company's party. The Office of Personnel Management found many flaws in the company's system weeks prior to the breach.
- **Curative measures and liability:** Soon after the breach, a class action suit followed and is still pending, with allegations that Premera was trying to dispose of evidence in September 2018.[12]
- **GDPR compliance:** Premera's (and other analogous companies') delayed breach notifications could be considered the hardest count to disprove in their class action suit. GDPR allows for *reasonable* delays but only if properly justified with the authorities. Even absent a clear deadline to disclose such a

breach to the public, *disproving* a company's inaction over a period of a year would be incredibly difficult to justify to a regulator.

## The IRS

- **Breach date:** February 2015.
- **Notification date:** May 26, 2015.
- **Type:** Hackers had set up a near identical "Get Transcript" application website (the IRS's filing service) and lured citizens into provide their data.
- **Targeted data:** Social Security numbers, date of birth, tax filing status, and street addresses, in addition to millions in fraudulent tax returns gained. The hackers additionally set up a similar questionnaire that prompted responses to determine *creditworthiness.*
- **Motive for the breach:** Financial gain and theft of data.
- **Damages and data subjects affected:** At first, the IRS said that more than 100,000 people's records had been stolen, later revising the figure up to 334,000 records. The hackers made over $50 million in fraudulent tax returns.
- **Preventive measures:** Despite people coming forward about the breach, the internal bureaucracy within the agency prevented them from effectively dealing with the breach. The IRS had a policy of *not confirming* fraudulent activity, which created difficulty for whistleblowers.[13]
- **Curative measures and liability:** The hackers were based in Nigeria and outside the reach of the US. The IRS followed a creative solution of aggressively prosecuting fraud and identity theft cases in order to collect fines and using that money to refund those affected.[14]
- **GDPR compliance:** A powerful agency such as the IRS being toyed with by criminals thousands of miles away demonstrated that *even government agencies* are not immune from data breaches. In this case, the problem was augmented by the fact that the IRS's internal policies *prevented* effective investigation of the matter. States should be mindful that time is of the essence in data breach cases, and an effective mechanism for dealing with it should be formulated. This is further reinforced when we examine the disparity in the breach dates and when the disclosure was formally made to the public (which was well beyond GDPR standards).

## The Office of Personnel Management

- **Breach date:** Between November 2013 and the discovery on March 20, 2014. A second hacker then struck in May 2014 *right after* the OPM gave their systems a clean bill of health. The second breach was discovered in June 2014.
- **Notification date:** It was first *reported* in July 9, 2014, then confirmed by the OPM on August 6, 2014.

- **Type:** Malware and subsequently hackers gained access through a third-party contractor.
- **Targeted data:** A wide variety of personal data had been stolen, as among those documents included background checks, FBI vetting forms, payments made, etc.
- **Motive for the breach:** Considered to be State-sponsored espionage from China.
- **Damages and data subjects affected:** Approximately 27,000 Department of Homeland Security employees, later rising to more than 31,000, including employees at the National Geospatial-Intelligence Agency, Immigration and Customs Enforcement, and the US Capitol Police. One breach is estimated to affect as many 390,000 current and former DHS employees, contractors, and even job applicants, who may have had their personal information exposed.
- In October 2014 yet another attack is levied on the OPM's interior department shared-services data centers, leading to a loss of more than 4.2 million federal employee files. Unconfirmed reports place the number at 14 million records, though the OPM refused to confirm.
- **Preventive measures:** On June 16, 2015, the OPM testified before Congress that the breach occurred owing to lax security and obsolete technology that left the data unencrypted and unprotected.
- **Curative measures and liability:** A group of hackers in China were arrested on December 2, 2015, by the Chinese government. There were no confirmations regarding their connection to China's government, though it was supported that these were the correct perpetrators.[15]
- **GDPR compliance:** The OPM's handling of the matter was incredibly poor by GDPR standards. The attacks were repeated, the data was not encrypted, and the notification to the public was delayed. The rampant failure of a State to secure its own data accurately reflects what the *general attitude* toward data protection was in 2015; a *non-issue*. This attitude in turn reflects on business practices, breaches, and the laws they must comply with.

## Ashley Madison

- **Breach date:** July 2015.
- **Notification date:** The hack came to the notice of the public on July 15, 2015, when the ransom demand that the site be shut down was released. Ashley Madison confirmed the breach on July 20.
- **Type:** Hack, which acted as a DoS attack preventing the owner from accessing the data.
- **Targeted data:** On August 18 and 20, the hackers leaked more than 60 gigabytes of company data, including user details (account details such as e-mail and profiles).

- **Motive for the breach:** The hackers (aka the "Impact Team") made it clear that the reason for the attack was to send a message and to force the website to shut down its "sinful" operations.
- **Damages and data subjects affected:** The hack affected 32 million of the site's members, releasing delicate information about their extramarital affairs. Toronto police also confirmed two suicides related to the leak.
- **Preventive measures:** Though the site made efforts to encrypt and secure the data, the hackers and many others on the internet were capable of cracking them using password recovery software. Most ironically, it was Ashley Madison's own *data storage policies* that caused the problem to begin with, as they charge users $19 to delete their unsavory data that was provided to the website.
- **Curative measures and liability:** Ashley Madison's parent company offered a *bounty* of Canadian $500,000 to capture the perpetrators.[16] Users whose details were leaked filed a $567 million class action lawsuit against Ashley Madison; the company would eventually settle the lawsuit for $11.2 million.[17]
- **GDPR compliance:** The Ashley Madison hack raised interesting questions about the *ethical* obligations of processing data, *internet vigilantism,* and the processing of *"romantic"* data. Consider the following dilemmas:
  - The Controller of damaging data (Madison) themselves hold the user's personal data "ransom" until a $19 fee is paid.
  - The "hacktivists" primarily wish to deter this policy (albeit by unsavory methods).
  - Did the users *impliedly consent* to the risk of their data being used/stolen/lost at one point when joining the service?

    Under GDPR, all the above doubts will likely be resolved *in favor of the user*, as the regulation recognizes an inherent link between personal data and privacy. Ashley Madison's practice of charging a fee to delete one's data is plainly against the new regulated data market.

## CVS and Walmart (Canada)

- **Breach date:** July 2014.
- **Notification date:** July 17, 2015.
- **Type:** PNI Digital Media, a third-party online photo-processing partner of the companies, had faced a malware attack.
- **Targeted data:** Credit card information, names, phone numbers, e-mail addresses, usernames, and passwords.
- **Motive for the breach:** Unknown, but likely theft.
- **Damages and data subjects affected:** About 2,500 individuals from New Hampshire affected; the total amount affected has been undisclosed.
- **Preventive measures:** Although CVS and Walmart Canada weren't directly hit with the hack, the attack on their vendor, PNI, affected their customers. They subsequently suspended that service. A class action suit alleged that the company failed to encrypt the data properly, maintain proper staff, and otherwise inadequately protect the personal data of its users.[18]

- **Curative measures and liability:** Soon after the breach, a $550 million class action suit followed, with the companies settling the matter by agreeing to pay for credit monitoring, out-of-pocket expenses, administration costs, and legal fees to the plaintiffs.
- **GDPR compliance:** The breach points out well the risk that exists in choosing one's business partners and vendors carefully. The class action suit had a similar result as GDPR would ordinarily have; namely, that Walmart and CVS be held liable regardless of whether the breach was a third-party vendor's fault. Thus, data protection is to be followed as a *chain* rather than in isolation.

## VTech

- **Breach date:** November 14, 2015.
- **Notification date:** November 27, 2015.
- **Type:** Hack of VTech's apps designed for children.
- **Targeted data:** Name, e-mail address, password, IP address, mailing address, and download history (from adults), along with children's name, gender, and birthdays.
- **Motive for the breach:** Unknown, but likely identity theft.
- **Damages and data subjects affected:** About 5 million customer accounts and "related kids profiles" were affected. "Motherboard," which first reported the hack, said that information on more than 200,000 kids was exposed.
- **Preventive measures:** Minimal, as the FTC subsequently filed a suit on behalf of citizens claiming that the company didn't follow its own privacy policy, didn't notify users of its data collection practices, and failed to properly safeguard the data.
- **Curative measures and liability:** VTech ended up paying $650,000 to the FTC as a settlement of the class action suit. The claims were based on the *Child's Online Privacy Protection Act*, which places strict requirements on Data Controllers to maintain integrity in processing.
- **GDPR compliance:** Data relating to children holds a prominent place in most societies with the US having an overarching legislation to protect their interests, which curiously GDPR does not have. GDPR discusses children only in relation to data protection regarding the collection of their data (requiring parental consent) in connection with an *Information Society Services* but not beyond that.[19]

## UCLA Hospitals

- **Breach date:** September 2014 and discovered by UCLA in October 2014.
- **Notification date:** July 17, 2015.
- **Type:** Hack.
- **Targeted data:** Name, Social Security numbers, medical diagnoses, diseases, clinical procedures, test results, addresses, and dates of birth (among others).

- **Motive for the breach:** Unknown, but likely theft.
- **Damages and data subjects affected:** About 4.5 million patients affected.
- **Preventive measures:** Though HIPAA-compliant, UCLA allegedly failed to encrypt the data held by them and didn't notify those affected in a timely manner, leading to a class action suit filed against them.
- **Curative measures and liability:** As HIPAA doesn't mandate encryption, the lawsuit claimed there is a *contractual obligation* to maintain data safely that was violated. The suit has not been resolved as of now.
- **GDPR compliance:** "Sensitive data" such as information provided by a doctor is given the *strongest* level of protection under GDPR. HIPAA serves as the US supplement for healthcare data protection, but doesn't even require the data to be encrypted when stored. Considering that at the end of the day the healthcare industry is a *business*, it is highly unlikely that they will spend additional money on encryption when it is *not even legally mandated*. This is where contractual claims in the US act as the real *teeth* of data protection law supplementing the gaps that exist.

## 2016

### Banner Health

- **Breach date:** June 2016, with the breach being discovered on June 23.
- **Notification date:** August 3, 2016.
- **Type:** Malware installed through point-of-sale systems.
- **Targeted data:** Payment card data, patient information, and health plan member and beneficiary information, as well as information about physicians and healthcare providers. The patient and health plan information included names, birth dates, addresses, physicians' names, dates of service, claims information, and possibly health insurance information, and Social Security numbers.
- **Motive for the breach:** Unknown, but likely theft.
- **Damages and data subjects affected:** About 3.7 million patients affected over 27 locations.
- **Preventive measures:** Though regulated under HIPAA, it is alleged that Banner failed to maintain proper security measures such as multi-factor authentication, firewalls, and encryption.
- **Curative measures and liability:** In March 2018, The US Department of Health and Human Services' Office of Civil Rights (OCR) began an investigation into Banner Health. The OCR has the power to levy fines based on history of noncompliance, patients affected, overall revenue, etc. Additionally, a class action lawsuit is pending against them in Arizona based on the theory of negligence.
- **GDPR compliance:** In absence of a regulation such as GDPR, other US governmental agencies take the role of picking up the duties of investigating

data breaches. The key pitfall of such a system of data breach investigation is that multiple agencies can create problems for one Controller. Imagine a situation in which the FTC, OCR, DOJ, and FBI are involved in tandem with a pending lawsuit. For small and medium-sized Controllers, the legal fees would be astronomical.

## Massachusetts General Hospital

- **Breach date:** The breach was discovered on February 8, 2016.
- **Notification date:** June 29, 2016.
- **Type:** Hack of a third-party vendor.
- **Targeted data:** The hack was limited to MGH's dental practice, with the information stolen being patient names, dates of birth, and Social Security numbers, and may have also included dates and types of dental appointment, dental provider names, and medical record numbers.
- **Motive for the breach:** Unknown, but likely theft.
- **Damages and data subjects affected:** About 4,300 dental records.
- **Preventive measures:** MGH was HIPAA-compliant and contained the damage to their dental wing.
- **Curative measures and liability:** MGH investigated the issue and alerted authorities. No further action or suit has been filed. They have enhanced security features since then.
- **GDPR compliance:** A smaller breach of this size, affecting only thousands, doesn't seem to draw the same amount of "class" attention from the public. A supplementing factor may be the fact that the data stolen relates to merely dental information, which wouldn't be as *sensitive* as other health information.

## Prosthetic & Orthodontic Care (P&O):

- **Breach date:** The breach was discovered on July 10, 2016.
- **Notification date:** July 29, 2016.
- **Type:** Hack exploiting an unknown flaw in the software purchased by P&O.
- **Targeted data:** Patient medical records that included names, contact information, ID numbers, diagnostic codes, appointment dates, and last billing amounts. Some records also contained Social Security numbers, birth dates, medical insurance company, and identification information and photos of procedures.
- **Motive for the breach:** Unknown, but likely theft.
- **Damages and data subjects affected:** Undisclosed.
- **Preventive measures:** Oversight was minimal because the data was found on "pastebin" where it was left in a *plain text* form for anyone to see.

- **Curative measures and liability:** Credit monitoring, new security practices, and greater oversight of security systems. No suits filed against the company.
- **GDPR compliance:** P&O managed to escape liability for this breach, notwithstanding the fact that their notice to the public was delayed and provided minimal detail. Again, here we can see that the smaller *size* of the business tends to be a saving grace for companies that face the occasional breach. As companies become larger and grow deeper pockets, the spotlight and litigation can be difficult to avoid.

### Wendy's

- **Breach date:** Between October 25, 2015 and June 28, 2016.
- **Notification date:** July 7, 2016 (formal disclosure to the public).
- **Type:** Malware attacking the point-of-sale systems, which spread to other databases.
- **Targeted data:** Payment data such as cardholder name, credit or debit card number, expiration date, cardholder verification value, and service code.
- **Motive for the breach:** Unknown, but likely theft.
- **Damages and data subjects affected:** Card payments made at 1,025 Wendy's locations during the breach period.
- **Preventive measures:** Wendy faced the widespread problems on point-of-sales attacks like what was prevalent in the preceding two years. The duration of the breach indicates that ongoing security wasn't maintained.
- **Curative measures and liability:** On August 23, 2018, the US District Court for the Middle District of Florida preliminarily approved a class action settlement in the consumer class action lawsuit *Torres v. Wendy's International, LLC*.
- **GDPR compliance:** After the widespread hack of Wendy's locations, a class action suit is inevitable. Uniquely, Wendy's has openly facilitated the class action process by encouraging affected members to join[20] and providing a search to help any customers to determine if they've been impacted.[21] Facilitating the process seems like an effective method to maintain *goodwill* after a breach of trust with the consumer base.

### Weebly

- **Breach date:** February 2016.
- **Notification date:** October 20, 2016 (first reported by an anonymous source).
- **Type:** Hack.
- **Targeted data:** E-mail addresses, usernames, IP addresses, and encrypted (bcrypt-hashed) passwords.
- **Motive for the breach:** Unknown.

- **Damages and data subjects affected:** 43 million users affected.
- **Preventive measures:** All user passwords were stored in Weebly's database using uniquely salted bcrypt hashing and a cost factor of 8, which ultimately protected them. Weebly since changed each password's cost factor to 10 after discovering the security breach, making future passwords even harder to crack.
- **Curative measures and liability:** Weebly issued password resets, implementing new password requirements and a new dashboard that gave customers an overview of recent login history of their Weebly account to track account activity.
- **GDPR compliance:** Here, no subsequent action was taken against Weebly owing to the security measures placed over the most important data they held: the passwords. A simple investment of good encryption can help protect the gateway which could lead to greater damage, and more importantly, greater costs.

## University of Central Florida

- **Breach date:** January 2016.
- **Notification date:** February 4, 2016.
- **Type:** Hack.
- **Targeted data:** For student-athletes and student staff members supporting those teams, the information involved first and last names, Social Security numbers, student ID numbers, sport, whether they were walk-ons or recruited, and number of credit hours taken and in progress. Meanwhile, for some employees, the information involved first and last names, Social Security numbers, and UCF-issued Employee Identification Numbers.
- **Motive for the breach:** Unknown, but likely theft.
- **Damages and data subjects affected:** Approximately 63,000 current and former UCF students and staff and faculty members were affected by the breach.
- **Preventive measures:** The University did not disclose what measures they put in place, nor has the FBI mentioned the specific cause of the breach.[22]
- **Curative measures and liability:** The University had agreed to spend an additional $1 million annually to protect students' and employees' personal information as part of a legal settlement reached in a class action suit filed by students in January 2018. The University also agreed to add three information security positions, designate a full-time internal senior information security auditor, and tighten access to personal information. Additionally, the University estimated one-time costs of $845,467 related to the changes, which also include using e-mail technology that detects and neutralizes harmful internet links and attachments and adding technology to analyze and report on unusual activity in the network.
- **GDPR compliance:** The settlement arrived at in the present suit is focused more on data protection and online restructuring than on pure money

damages. Perhaps it is because the suit was brought by students, who have a vested interest in a more secure future for their personal data. Regardless, universities, particularly larger ones that immerse themselves in *all aspects* of student life during their education, hold massive amounts of unique data that is highly valuable.

## UC Berkeley

- **Breach date:** December 25, 2016.
- **Notification date:** February 27, 2016.
- **Type:** Hack during software update.
- **Targeted data:** Financial data created though electronic fund transfers, such as financial aid awards and work-related reimbursements. Vendors whose financial information was in the system for payment purposes were also at risk.
- **Motive for the breach:** Unknown, but likely theft.
- **Damages and data subjects affected:** The financial data of 80,000 students, alumni, and current and former employees. Those potentially impacted include about 57,000 current and former students; about 18,800 former and current employees, including student workers, and 10,300 vendors who do business with the campus. The numbers add up to more than 80,000 because individuals may belong to more than one category.
- **Preventive measures:** UCB had security measures in place to protect the data, but the hackers took advantage of a vulnerability in the software that the University was in the process of "patching" up. Though the data was subsequently leaked, it was not misused subsequently.
- **Curative measures and liability:** UCB provided a years' worth of credit monitoring, reported the matter to the police, and removed all potentially impacted servers from their networks to prevent further damage. They also contracted a computer investigation firm to monitor any misuse of the data leaked.
- **GDPR compliance:** The absence of misuse of the data by the hackers once again provided UCB the advantage of avoiding a class action suit (thus far). Though the notification was delayed, quick response and the absence of any quantifiable *damage* is the best way to avoid certain liability for data breaches.

## TaxSlayer

- **Breach date:** The hack took place between October 10 and December 21, 2015. It was discovered by the company on January 13, 2016.
- **Notification date:** January 29, 2016.
- **Type:** The hackers gained access by using false user credentials that were attained by other sources, misrepresenting the identity of users (aka a *validation attack*).

- **Targeted data:** Name, address, Social Security number, Social Security numbers of dependents, and other data contained on the customers' 2014 tax return.
- **Motive for the breach:** Identity theft.
- **Damages and data subjects affected:** The personal and tax information of approximately 8,800 customers.
- **Preventive measures:** Soon after the incident, the FTC filed a complaint on behalf of consumers against TaxSlayer for violations of the Gramm–Leach–Bailey Act in failing to maintain adequate security measures such as having a strong password or failing to inform users of any suspicious activities on their account.[23]
- **Curative measures and liability:** TaxSlayer offered free credit monitoring and $1 million of identity-theft insurance to affected customers. They also recommended that victims change their usernames and passwords not only for their tax forms but also those for other accounts. The subsequent settlement with the FTC had no direct financial penalty, but the company had to bear the costs of the security measures to fix the issues.
- **GDPR compliance:** Tax software businesses are routinely breached because of the host of data they handle to effectively file a return. Businesses such as TaxSlayer face augmented scrutiny from the intimate relationship their service has with the government and ordinary citizens, which assures them liability if their data is lost. Ironically, the IRS themselves did not face similar ramifications when they faced similar issues.

## Taobao

- **Breach date:** Between October 14 and 15, 2015.
- **Notification date:** February 4, 2016.
- **Type:** The hackers used servers hosted on Alibaba's (Taobao's parent company) cloud server platform to try *a brute force attack* on e-mail addresses in Taobao logins.
- **Targeted data:** Usernames, passwords.
- **Motive for the breach:** Promoting products by fraudulently creating consumer reviews to increase its sales.
- **Damages and data subjects affected:** The hackers acquired a database of close to 100 million e-mail addresses and passwords. Additionally, by using existing account information, they managed to log in to nearly 21 million Taobao accounts.
- **Preventive measures:** Taobao's statements to the media maintain that they maintain "world class security" over its cloud computing services and denies any loopholes in Alibaba's platform that could have allowed the breach. Further details have not been disclosed to the public.
- **Curative measures and liability:** As of August 2015, Alibaba had received more than 1,700 complaints from foreign purchasers. In October 2015, police rounded up 25 suspects in Fujian Province for committing the breach.

- **GDPR compliance:** From the Chinese data culture we can see that a "tight" hold over a nation's data sovereignty helps crack down cyber-crime with more ease, with most breaches from China resulting in an arrest. However, Taobao's handling of the situation was far from ideal, with a delayed notification to the public and a failure to intimate the *reasons* for the breach. A lack of transparency would prevent consumers from even being aware of whether the problem has been resolved and whether there was more to the crime and its scope.

## KM.RU and Nival Networks

- **Breach date:** Undisclosed; it is reported to have happened soon after the facts regarding Malaysian Flight MH17 were reported.
- **Notification date:** March 4, 2016 (reported).[24]
- **Type:** Hack.
- **Targeted data:** The hacked databases contained e-mails, encrypted passwords, and secret questions and answers from the TV stations. The database also contained dates of birth, e-mail addresses, genders, and geographic location.
- **Motive for the breach:** The hacker claimed that the attacks were revenge for the MH17 plane crash, which was allegedly caused by Russia. He made it clear on Twitter that he would randomly target Russian companies as revenge.
- **Damages and data subjects affected:** 1.5 million accounts linked to the TV stations.
- **Preventive measures:** Both companies declined to comment, and not much is known of the preexisting security measures; however, it is known that the data was held in plain-text format.
- **Curative measures and liability:** None reported.
- **GDPR compliance:** Russia is well known for its "iron curtain" over the information shared with the public. It would not be surprising to learn that many of the details regarding the breach remain hidden from public knowledge, contrary to the base principles of transparency that center around GDPR.

## Inuvik Hospitals

- **Breach date:** Exact dates not known, but the possibility of breach was cautioned by the Beaufort Delta Health Authority three months earlier.
- **Notification date:** May 9, 2016.
- **Type:** Employee misconduct and inappropriate access.
- **Targeted data:** Personal data such as appointment times, checkout dates, and the reason patients were at the hospital.
- **Motive for the breach:** Unknown.
- **Damages and data subjects affected:** 67 patients were affected by the breach, which was limited to Inuvik's hospital.

- **Preventive measures:** The hospital was subsequently criticized for failing to adequately secure the scheduling system during lunch breaks and didn't implement adequate protections to access it.
- **Curative measures and liability:** The hospital received 46 recommendations from external investigators (many of which call for more staff training) which officials said will be discussed with the territory's health department. Local health authorities soon thereafter investigated how hospitals in the region could maintain privacy better, such as appointing privacy officers and placing more secure barriers in accessing hospital systems.
- **GDPR compliance:** With constant remote attacks being the standard way to breach a computer system, businesses can forget that the damage can come from *within* the organization from their employees. GDPR places a stern chain of command requiring contact between employee-DPO-Controller for accessing data. Additionally, the Controller/DPO are placed with the charge of restricting employee access to data in order to maintain ongoing security of processing.

## Gyft

- **Breach date:** October 3 through December 18, 2015.
- **Notification date:** February 5, 2016.
- **Type:** Hack into cloud servers.
- **Targeted data:** Names, contact information, dates of birth, and gift card numbers. Gift card numbers could have been used to make unauthorized purchases. In addition, Gyft login credentials may have been compromised.
- **Motive for the breach:** Unknown.
- **Damages and data subjects affected:** The damage wasn't extensive but permitted the hackers to access gift card accounts, which potentially allowed them to access accounts or reward points, make unauthorized purchases, or otherwise use the data improperly. The company has not disclosed publicly how many customers it has, but insiders said that the percentage of users affected was in the "high single digits."[25]
- **Preventive measures:** The company immediately logged those affected out of their accounts and refunded any amounts lost on the gift cards.
- **Curative measures and liability:** No evidence of "malfeasance" of the data use was shown, merely the fact that it was stolen. The company did not offer credit protection, as no payment data was taken.
- **GDPR compliance:** Gyft managed to avoid liability since no material damage was caused to its users. Like many of the other breaches in 2016, the details of the breach were not fully disclosed (such as data subjects affected), and the notification was delayed, although not fully concealed. Juxtapose this with earlier data breaches that wouldn't be disclosed but would rather be *reported* as the corporate culture and law at the time did not require them to do so.

## Adult Friend Finder

- **Breach date:** Mid-October 2016.
- **Notification date:** November 13, 2016 (reported); confirmed on November 2ᵗ.
- **Type:** Hack.
- **Targeted data:** Names, e-mail addresses, and passwords. The databases also included site membership data (such as if the user was a VIP member), browser information, the IP address last used to log in, sexual preferences, extramarital preferences, and if the user had paid for items.
- **Motive for the breach:** Unknown, but believed to be an underground Russian hacking site.
- **Damages and data subjects affected:** More than 412.2 million accounts. The hack included 339 million accounts from AdultFriendFinder.com, which includes two decades' worth of data that also includes more than 15 million "deleted" accounts that weren't purged from the databases. Additionally, 62 million accounts from Cams.com and 7 million from Penthouse.com were stolen, as well as a few million from other smaller properties owned by the company.
- **Preventive measures:** Most of the passwords were protected only by the weak SHA-1 hashing algorithm, which meant that 99% of them had been cracked by the time LeakedSource.com published its analysis of the entire data set on November 14. The attack happened at around the same time that one security researcher, known as Revolver, disclosed a local file inclusion flaw on the AdultFriendFinder site, which if successfully exploited could allow an attacker to remotely run malicious code on the web server.[26]
- **Curative measures and liability:** No suit has been filed thus far, only news of an investigation that hasn't produced much information as of now. The website has been gravely criticized for its handling of the incident. They merely assured that they would fix the "vulnerabilities" in the system.
- **GDPR compliance:** The internet and prurient interests such as pornography and online dating go together fluidly, but don't often consider the truly *private* nature of the service provided. GDPR doesn't allude to such matters at all, though much of the "delicate" information does qualify as "special data," as it reveals sexual preferences.

## Eyewire

- **Breach date:** February 11, 2016.
- **Notification date:** February 23, 2016.
- **Type:** Accidental breach by theft of employee laptop.
- **Targeted data:** The laptop contained an Eyewire database dating back to mid-2015 that was intended for statistical analysis. The data included e-mails, IP addresses, and encrypted passwords.

- **Motive for the breach:** The company surmised that the database contents were likely what motivated the theft.
- **Damages and data subjects affected:** Undisclosed.
- **Preventive measures:** The passwords were encrypted, and the laptop was secured from ordinary infiltration attempts but not from more sophisticated attempts.
- **Curative measures and liability:** The website's actions were swift and precautionary: they notified the authorities, updated its security policies (which required employee data to be sanitized), encrypted their hard drives, and deleted their SHA1 legacy passwords from their databases.
- **GDPR compliance:** Theft of electronic hardware that contains personal data of others is an event that is difficult to prevent, but easy to plan for. The response of the company was prompt and cautious. Taking such actions can help reduce the damages and sidestep liability in the long run.

## Department of Homeland Security

- **Breach date:** Unknown, but likely early February, as the breach was discovered a week later.
- **Notification date:** First reported online on February 7, 2016, with confirmation following the next day.
- **Type:** Hack by using a link to a personal computer that took the hacker to an online virtual machine and entered in the credentials of the already hacked e-mail account. After using the link, the hacker had full access to the computer.
- **Targeted data:** DHS employee names, e-mail addresses, locations, telephone numbers, and titles such as "DHS PRISM Support." Additionally, the hacker gained access to the DHS employee directory, which contained data pertaining to all manner of directors, managers, specialists, analysts, intelligence staff members, and more.
- **Motive for the breach:** The hacker left a message that stated, "This is for Palestine, Ramallah, West Bank, Gaza, this is for the child that is searching for an answer."
- **Damages and data subjects affected:** 9,000 records relating to DHS employees, along with those of 20,000 FBI employees, including those who work outside of the US. The hacker claimed to have downloaded an additional 100 GB–1 TB of information from the DHS, with the exact amount unknown.
- **Preventive measures:** It goes without saying that the US government likely had sophisticated firewalls to protect from hacks but failed to fully secure important credentials. The DHS was not aware of the breach until a week afterward and didn't formally notify the public until the matter was reported.
- **Curative measures and liability:** On February 13, 2016, a 16-year-old boy living in England was arrested in connection to the hack.[27] However, the remainder of the "hacking ring" are yet to be arrested.

- **GDPR compliance:** Once again we can see that the US government is failing to lead the charge for data protection in the country. As with the hack of the IRS and OPM, the breach went undiscovered and unreported until after it took place. The government must act as a greater example if it wishes to promote a culture of data privacy on a corporate level.

## The Democratic National Committee

- **Breach date:** The hack began in May 2014, with vulnerabilities identified in the DNC network on March 15, 2016. The Democratic Congressional Campaign Committee and the DNC discovered the hack in May 2016 and only removed the malware in October 2016.
- **Notification date:** Public discovery of the event began on June 8, 2016, when *DNC Leaks* was launched, and Russian involvement was brought to light on June 14, 2016.
- **Type:** A combination of methods including hacking, malware, "spear-phishing" e-mails, and social engineering.
- **Targeted data:** Political candidate and party data, opposition research, and internal communications, along with the accompanying personal data.
- **Motive for the breach:** Believed to be politically motivated attack backed by Russia.
- **Damages and data subjects affected:** The true scope of the damage hasn't been fully assessed to this day, with more than 50,000 records stolen confirmed and with Wikileaks and the hackers claiming there's much more. The true purpose of the hack was to cause *political damage* to the DNC, which it arguably did, as the 2016 election showed.
- **Preventive measures:** Near-minimal measures, considering the widespread and prolonged nature of the hack. The breach spread over several servers, including state election facilities and national DNC and DCCC centers showing the vulnerabilities across the board.
- **Curative measures and liability:** The FBI began its investigation on July 31, 2016, only after Australian authorities reported that they had been offered stolen data. The website DCLeaks was shut down on March 1, 2017, with the 12 Russians affiliated with the hack indicted in July 2017.[28]
- **GDPR compliance:** The 2016 US election is now notorious for the *full power* of the internet and data trade in our modern age. The DNC and DHS hack, accompanied by the Cambridge Analytica scandal, showcased how online information can be used effectively to push forward an agenda of massive proportions. It's amazing to consider that swifter action for data protection hasn't been lobbied for in the government, once again showing how the State can fail to be an example for the people.

## Cox Communications

- **Breach date:** Unknown.
- **Notification date:** March 3, 2016.
- **Type:** Phishing attack.
- **Targeted data:** Names, addresses, and phone numbers. The dump also contained names of employees' managers, the date of their last login, and the last time their password was reset. Some of the logins stretch back to 2007, but some were as recent as December 2015.
- **Motive for the breach:** Sale on the "dark web."
- **Damages and data subjects affected:** 40,000 employees affected.
- **Preventive measures:** The company was just coming off paying a $595,000 settlement to the FTC for failing to inform consumers of a data breach in the preceding year.
- **Curative measures and liability:** No subsequent action taken against the company; the matter was merely investigated. It's likely the matter was internally settled with employees.
- **GDPR compliance:** Cox Communications would be a "repeat offender" under the EU GDPR standards, likely exposing them to a higher measure of damages if they were to be penalized for the violation. However, in this case the data released was not too sensitive, with much of it already being in the public domain prior to the hack. This is where the US shows its more "business-friendly" side of the law by protecting businesses *unless they have been sued by consumers.* The Supervisory Authorities under GDPR, however, have the power to take the matter up *suo moto* (without a complaint).

## Coastal Credit Union

- **Breach date:** February 2016.
- **Notification date:** Reported first on February 25, 2016. Confirmed and notified on February 26.
- **Type:** The hackers retrofitted the credit union's site with a web shell, a backdoor program that provides attackers with remote control of a website and server. Shell components used by hackers can spread malware and promote malicious websites.
- **Targeted data:** Hack and denial of service of website. The company claims no personal data was stolen.
- **Motive for the breach:** Unknown.
- **Damages and data subjects affected:** The credit union said there was no compromise of personal member data but faced harsh criticism from cybersecurity experts regarding the way it handled the event.

- **Preventive measures:** Though a prominent data breach investigator tried to warn CCU of the breach, the compromise of the website prevented such information from being shared quickly. He contacted CCU on February 23, informing them of such a breach, and they did not take him seriously.[29]
- **Curative measures and liability:** Many have criticized CCU as not having any data breach planning in place, as their only measure was temporarily shutting down the site to investigate. No further action was later taken by consumers or the government.
- **GDPR compliance:** Here the damage was caused to the Controller's *own* website, so the CCU is beholden to no one for their own negligence. Though their handling of the incident was widely discredited, it wasn't *horrible* in terms of damage, notification, and liability compared to the hacks that hit the US government itself. If there is no loss of personal data, the only loss that stings is the one that the company and its reputation sustains.

### Apple Health (Medicaid)

- **Breach date:** Unknown.
- **Notification date:** February 9, 2016.
- **Type:** Employee misconduct.
- **Targeted data:** Name, Social Security number, dates of birth, and client ID numbers, among others in the records leaked.
- **Motive for the breach:** Both employees assert that the exchange of information occurred because the HCA employee needed technical assistance with spreadsheets that contained the data. The employees also state that the information was not used for any additional unauthorized purposes or forwarded to any other unauthorized recipients.
- **Damages and data subjects affected:** The personal identification information and private health information of more than 91,000 Apple Health (Medicaid) clients was leaked.
- **Preventive measures:** Undisclosed; however, the misconduct came to light by way of a whistleblower investigation for misuse of State resources.
- **Curative measures and liability:** The hospital arguably handled the matter quickly and as best as they could in such scenarios, thereby avoiding further liability. They also subsequently faced *another hack* of a third-party vendor, resulting in a loss of 382,000 individual data, which didn't gain much news.[30]
- **GDPR compliance:** Isolated acts of employee negligence/misconduct can't always be prevented but they can be *handled* well. Termination of those involved with a frank disclosure to the public and credit monitoring is the best that can be done in cases such as these (depending on the damage, of course). Accepting blame and taking swift action help maintain credibility with one's clients as well.

## 21st Century Oncology

- **Breach date:** The FBI informed the company that they had been hacked in November 2015.
- **Notification date:** March 2016.
- **Type:** The hacker had accessed a database through a remote desktop protocol.
- **Targeted data:** Names, Social Security numbers, physicians, and diagnoses and treatment, as well as patients' insurance data.
- **Motive for the breach:** Unknown, but likely theft.
- **Damages and data subjects affected:** Over 2.2 million data subjects affected.
- **Preventive measures:** The fact that the company had to be informed of their own data breach reveals how little oversight of the data security there was. Though at the time the data had not been "misused" online, the company went on to face heavy penalties.
- **Curative measures and liability:** In December 2017 the company agreed to pay $2.3 million in fines to the OCR as a settlement for the data breach. They also paid $26 million in a class action in Florida for allegations of fraud in their business. Another class action was also filed against them in Florida for the data breach itself, where clients sought to claim the $4.2 million that remained in the company's insurance policy.[31] The proceedings are all overseen and approved by the Bankruptcy Court, with the company going out of business over the fiasco.
- **GDPR compliance:** The consistency in the application of punishments for data breaches in the US are quite inconsistent. Once again, it appears the "size" of the breach seems to be the main motivating factor to attract liability, rather than fault or negligence itself. Many other companies have had breaches much worse than 21st Century Oncology and faced fewer consequences, clearly showing an incongruous system of data privacy.

# 2017

## Uber I

- **Breach date:** May 13, 2014, with discovery of the breach on September 17.
- **Notification date:** February 27, 2015.
- **Type:** The leak was possible because the hacker was able to view driver data on an Amazon Web Services store in plain text using an access key to get that information that had been publicly posted by an Uber engineer to code-sharing website GitHub.
- **Targeted data:** Names, driver's license numbers, 215 unencrypted names, bank account, and domestic routing numbers, and 84 unencrypted names and Social Security numbers. The leak also included physical addresses, e-mail

addresses, cell phone numbers, device IDs, and location information from trips Uber drivers had taken.

- **Motive for the breach:** Unknown, but likely theft.
- **Damages and data subjects affected:** Over 100,000 drivers affected.
- **Preventive measures:** The driver data was unencrypted, and Uber had also failed to properly monitor employee access to consumers' personal data. This includes a "God's View Map" that allowed Uber to monitor all its drivers at once, which was no longer in use but was left unmonitored. These poor protections led to a settlement with the FTC in August 2017.
- **Curative measures and liability:** Uber's loose privacy protections led them to enter a consent decree with the FTC to tighten its practices and subject itself to independent, third-party auditing over the *next 20 years.* This came on the heels of Uber paying the FTC $20 million for exaggerating earnings claims to attract new drivers earlier in 2017. However, the consent decree entered into for this breach did not have much teeth in the following data breach in 2016.

### Uber II

- **Breach date:** The discovery came in November 2016.
- **Notification date:** Uber notoriously did not disclose the breach to the public until a year later on November 21, 2017.
- **Type:** The hackers inappropriately accessed user data stored on a third-party cloud-based service that was used by Uber.
- **Targeted data:** Names, e-mail addresses, and phone numbers. The hackers were also able to access Uber's GitHub account, where they found usernames and password credentials to Uber's AWS account.
- **Motive for the breach:** Unknown, but likely theft.
- **Damages and data subjects affected:** Personal information of 57 million Uber users and 600,000 drivers.
- **Preventive measures:** The CSO of Uber was fired for this event, with most of the blame placed on him for the breach. The breach did not affect the corporate systems or infrastructure, with the company's forensic investigation concluding that no trip location history, credit card numbers, bank account numbers, Social Security numbers, or dates of birth were downloaded. The delayed notification was justified as an error, though that would prove to be an expensive mistake (one that they made *twice* if you include their 2014 breach).
- **Curative measures and liability:** It became public that Uber paid the hackers $100,000 to destroy the data they stole in a way that hid the hack. Additionally, Uber faced a near $20 billion drop in their valuation when the breach became public. On September 26, 2018, Uber reached a settlement with the 50 US states to pay $148 million and to tighten the data security measures that contributed almost *entirely* to their failure to notify the public in a timely manner.

- **GDPR compliance:** The settlement reached with the US requires Uber to comply with state consumer protection laws by safeguarding personal information and immediately provide notifications to authorities in case of a breach. It also included creating strong password-protection policies. In 2017 we can see the full power of FTC consent decrees and lawsuits as a *regulatory instrument* to ensure data protection.
- The settlement from the class action is specific as to how the data should be protected moving forward, acting as a sort of ad hoc control mechanism for the taxi giant. Uber, as a tech giant by its sheer size alone, is a target for being made an example of and the company should begin to take its own consent decrees with the FTC seriously.

### Taringa

- **Breach date:** Unknown, but LeakBase (a data breach notification website) reported the breach on September 4, 2017.
- **Notification date:** September 5, 2017.
- **Type:** Hack, with subsequent passwords decrypted by exploiting vulnerabilities in the previous algorithm.
- **Targeted data:** Usernames, e-mail addresses, and hashed passwords.
- **Motive for the breach:** Unknown.
- **Damages and data subjects affected:** More than 28 million users affected.
- **Preventive measures:** The hashed passwords used an aging algorithm called MD5, which had been considered outdated even before 2012, resulting in 93.79% of them being hacked within a few days.
- **Curative measures and liability:** No subsequent action was brought against the website, which merely reset the passwords and initiated an investigation with no further developments.
- **GDPR compliance:** Taringa is often considered to be the "Latin Facebook," and keeping in line with the Facebook "tradition," a data breach is only appropriate. Here the poor encryption measures were widely criticized as being outdated and affording little control over privileged accounts.[32] GDPR principle of assuring "ongoing security" in processing is precisely meant to impose a duty on Controllers to maintain the most *relevant* practices relative to the danger posed to the personal data. Absent such a directive, businesses would not encourage themselves to keep their security practices up to date.

### Heathrow Airport

- **Breach date:** Unknown.
- **Notification date:** October 28, 2017.
- **Type:** A USB with critical data was discovered in a local library.

- **Targeted data:** The data included high-level security vulnerabilities, such as the Queen's route and security measures, ID disclosure and clearance requirements, and a timetable of officers to protect the airport. The USB also contained detailed maps, CCTV camera locations, minister routes for entry, and the details of ultrasound radar systems to scan speeds.
- **Motive for the breach:** Unknown, but suspected to be terrorism.
- **Damages and data subjects affected: The** lost USB contained 76 folders with maps, videos, and documents. The total drive contained 2.5 GB of data which, if disclosed, would cause irreparable damage to Britain's National Security.
- **Preventive measures:** Undisclosed and unknown, considering *how* the data was breached remains a mystery.
- **Curative measures and liability:** The primary concern of the breach seemed to be *securing* the overall safety of the skies rather than the breach itself. But institutions such as airports are not just for the processing of personal data, but to act as a *wall* between flying and terrorist acts. Here, the *cause is completely unknown*, which investigators themselves are finding alarming. The airport was soon fined £120,000 by the Information Commissioner's Office for the breach.[33]
- **GDPR compliance** The airport admitted that *only 2%* of the (then) 6,500 employees were trained in data protection, which helps to point to how this breach likely happened. It is refreshing to see a deeply intertwined state body being held accountable for a breach, despite the important status it holds for the government. Great examples such as this help to build the culture of "data health" within a nation, rather than letting those agencies go.

### Equifax

- **Breach date:** May to July 29, 2017.
- **Notification date:** September 7, 2017.
- **Type:** Hack by exploiting a weak point in website software.
- **Targeted data:** Names, Social Security numbers, addresses, phone numbers, driver's license numbers, etc. Additionally, credit card numbers for 209,000 consumers were stolen, along with personal information used in disputes for 182,000 people.
- **Motive for the breach:** Unknown, but likely identity theft.
- **Damages and data subjects affected:** More 143 million data subjects were affected, with the data stolen being important to unlock personal information that gives access to medical, banking, and employee accounts online.
- **Preventive measures:** Equifax was criticized for not updating its security practices to protect itself from this breach, particularly because they faced several *other* attacks prior to this where hackers could make off with critical company data through exploiting simple vulnerabilities. Adding to the criticism of

the company, three senior executives sold shares worth almost $1.8 million in the days after the breach was discovered.

- **Curative measures and liability:** Class action lawsuits and action from US government agencies are pending. Equifax received one of the largest fines from the British ICO (£500,000) for the breach as well.
- **GDPR compliance:** The Equifax hack followed several other breaches in 2017 as one of the most notorious in history thus far, particularly because of the lax handling of the event by an entity that holds *massive* amounts of sensitive personal data. With class action suits against the company on the horizon and the events of the 2016 election preceding these breaches, the new culture of "data awareness" had gotten under way in full swing, with the public becoming more informed with each scandal that takes place.

## Deloitte

- **Breach date:** Deloitte discovered the hack in March 2017, but it is believed that the attackers may have had access to its systems since October or November 2016.
- **Notification date:** September 25, 2017.
- **Type:** The hack of Deloitte e-mail servers.
- **Targeted data:** Blue-chip client e-mails, corporate plans for those clients, architectural and security designs, health information, usernames, passwords, and personal details.
- **Motive for the breach:** Unknown, but likely theft.
- **Damages and data subjects affected:** Deloitte claimed the damage was minimal, only affecting a few clients, though some speculate it might have been far larger. *The Guardian* estimated that 5 million e-mails were in the cloud and could have been accessed by the hackers.
- **Preventive measures:** Unknown, but it was reported that password security only required single-step verification.
- **Curative measures and liability:** No further action taken.
- **GDPR compliance:** When a large cyber-security firm such as Deloitte has been hacked, the main damage goes to their *credibility* in the market as a protector of client data and advisor to even bigger giants who hold even more sensitive data. Here, the details of how the breach was handled and notified were all left quite vague, which doesn't create a great example for the rest of the industry to follow.

## Ancestry.com

- **Breach date:** December 20, 2017.
- **Notification date:** December 23, 2017.

- **Type:** The hacker had accessed the company's "RootsWeb Homepage," which is a free community-driven collection of tools that are used by some people to host and share genealogical information.
- **Targeted data:** Names, e-mail addresses, and passwords. Much of the data breached was old and not in use.
- **Motive for the breach:** Unknown.
- **Damages and data subjects affected:** Forensic investigation revealed that the file contained 300,000 e-mail/usernames and passwords, with approximately 55,000 of these being used on both RootsWeb and one of the Ancestry sites; the clear majority of those were from free trial or currently unused accounts. Additionally, about 7,000 of those password and e-mail address combinations matched credentials for active Ancestry customers.
- **Preventive measures:** The fast response time and immediate action that was taken shows ongoing data security in Ancestry's processing operations.
- **Curative measures and liability:** Ancestry immediately reset its passwords for all members and took down the RootsWeb server from any further use.
- **GDPR compliance:** This is one of the few cases where the *breach was notified within GDPR time limits*, which has been rare up until this point. The action taken in this case is what is expected of a company that routinely collects and holds *biological data* of its customers, a "special" type of data under GDPR.

## 2018

### Orbitz

- **Breach date:** The first breach was from January 1 to June 22, 2016, and the second was from January 1, 2016, to December 22, 2017.
- **Notification date:** March 1, 2018.
- **Type:** The hacker had accessed a database through a remote desktop protocol.
- **Targeted data:** Names, dates of birth, phone numbers, e-mail addresses, billing addresses, and genders.
- **Motive for the breach:** Unknown, but likely theft.
- **Damages and data subjects affected:** Thousands of customers affected, including 880,000 payment card records.
- **Preventive measures:** Undisclosed, but the duration of the breach along with the delayed notification suggests that the protections were not comprehensive and the oversight wasn't regular.
- **Curative measures and liability:** Orbitz in its notice mentioned that it would investigate the matter and update its security measures (with a year of credit monitoring), but a class action suit is presently pending against the company for breach of contract, negligence, and violation of unfair competition law.[34]
- **GDPR compliance:** As data breaches enter the "year of GDPR," the tone of data breaches has changed from an unexpected risk to one that *must* be

planned for by businesses. With class action suits becoming the weapon of choice for users to protect their privacy, one can expect multiple judgments and settlements in the coming years, which will likely cement new data culture precedents in the US.

## British Airways

- **Breach date:** The breach took place between August 21 and September 5, 2018.
- **Notification date:** September 6, 2018.
- **Type:** Hack by "skimming" payment transactions.
- **Targeted data:** Names, street and e-mail addresses, credit card numbers, expiration dates, and security codes.
- **Motive for the breach:** Unknown, but likely theft. The hackers are suspected to be Russian.
- **Damages and data subjects affected:** Around 380,000 card payments were compromised over the breach period, with the estimated value of the data as £9.4 million.
- **Preventive measures:** BA noticed the breach when a third party informed them of suspicious activity on their servers. which prompted an immediate investigation.
- **Curative measures and liability:** Britain's government informed the National Cyber Security Centre and the National Crime Agency, along with the Information Commissioner's Office. BA advised customers to contact their bank or credit card provider and took out ads in national newspapers to inform the public. BA also offered financial compensation for any loss. Action against BA under GDPR is pending.[35]
- **GDPR compliance:** BA has faced its fair share of data breaches in the past decade, qualifying it for "repeat offender" status under GDPR for the purposes of assessing fines. This data breach came at a time when GDPR *was in force*, making BA one of the first examples of the regulation. Nothing indicates the looming regulation more than the *immediate notification* to the public about the breach (well within the 72-hour limit). As the hardest violation to *disprove* in a legal action, companies are slowly wising-up to the time-sensitive nature of these breaches.

## Ticketfly

- **Breach date:** May 2018.
- **Notification date:** Ticketfly has been heavily criticized for not informing users formally, by merely sending a tweet in June 2018, which went unnoticed by consumers until September or later.[36]

- **Type:** The hackers usurped the access to the website (a DOS attack) and threatened to post information online.
- **Targeted data:** Names, addresses, e-mails, and phone numbers.
- **Motive for the breach:** Ransom.
- **Damages and data subjects affected:** The hackers defaced the homepage and an estimated 26 million users were affected by the breach.
- **Preventive measures:** Ticketfly allegedly failed to inform users in a timely manner, leaving the stolen data unprotected online for several months following the breach. Aside from the tweet, the company merely created a passive page to inform its customers. Furthermore, the hackers allegedly informed Ticketfly's parent company, Everbrite, of the vulnerabilities in their system, which subsequently led to *no action*.
- **Curative measures and liability:** As of October 2018, a class action suit has been pending against Everbrite and Ticketfly for the breach, particularly for the poor notification and handling of security.
- **GDPR compliance:** An important lesson to take away from the breaches in this list is to *take any warnings or threats regarding system vulnerabilities seriously*. Many companies have been forewarned by the hackers and paid no heed because the internet tends to be full of empty threats. However, the DPO or whichever officer in charge should always *record, investigate*, and *report* the results of the investigation internally. Such a measure may prove invaluable when a subsequent lawsuit is filed.

### Google+

- **Breach date:** The breach is said to have taken place over the three-year (2015–2018) period preceding the *Wall Street Journal* report. It is alleged that Google knew of the breach for *at least* seven months before it became public.
- **Notification date:** It was first reported by the *Wall Street Journal* on October 8, 2018, and subsequently confirmed by Google on the 10th. Google has been criticized for deciding *against* disclosing the glitch publicly to avoid *immediate regulatory interest*.[37]
- **Type:** Public and private data was exposed to third-party developers that knew of a *bug* in the API systems. This allowed many unauthorized parties to access the data.
- **Targeted data:** Names, e-mail addresses, occupations, genders, and ages.
- **Motive for the breach:** Unknown, but likely theft.
- **Damages and data subjects affected:** More than 500,000 user profiles were affected by the bug.
- **Preventive measures:** Google said in a statement that it decided against making the glitch public because it found no sign that third parties exploited the exposed information, but internal memorandums showed that they wished to dodge more regulatory scrutiny. They claimed there was no notification

because their Privacy & Data Protection Office concluded there was no misuse and no action that the developer or user could take regardless. This decision would prove to be expensive in the months to come.

- **Curative measures and liability:** Ironically, by trying to avoid regulatory scrutiny, Google ended up *inviting* it. Following the breach becoming public, EU regulators started investigating the matter, class action suits were filed, and US lawmakers asked for Sundar Pichai's appearance for a hearing after initiating an FTC investigation.[38] On top of all that, Google+'s consumer-facing wing has been shut down.

- **GDPR compliance:** Google felt the noose of regulation and scrutiny tightening and unfortunately followed the *older* practices of handling data breaches, which were proven to be expensive in 2018. The US remains one of the biggest online markets in the world without a comprehensive data protection regulation, and companies are aware of this fact. However, the simple decision to *hide* the breach is a fatal mistake in GDPR age. Google has attracted not only financial loss, but *transcontinental scrutiny* over the breach. Even if the company was within the law in the US, their failure to notify the breach is a different story now in the EU.


## Facebook

- **Breach date:** September 2018.
- **Notification date:** September 25, 2018.
- **Type:** A vulnerability in the site's *"View As"* feature (which lets users see what others do when viewing their profile) allowed hackers take over people's accounts.
- **Targeted data:** Facebook profile details; the information of users who had connected their profile to an Instagram account or any other third-party service were at risk as well.
- **Motive for the breach:** Unknown, but likely theft.
- **Damages and data subjects affected:** More than 50 million users were affected by the bug.
- **Preventive measures:** Hours after the company announced the breach, a class action suit was filed against it alleging that they *negligently* maintained data security when they *remained on notice* of their vulnerabilities coming off the heels of the Cambridge Analytica scandal. The suit also alleges a failure on Facebook's part in adequately informing users of the breach.
- **Curative measures and liability:** The central part of the class action suit against Facebook is that they *ought to have* taken *greater action* after the Cambridge Analytica fiasco, rather than allow such a breach to happen soon after their multiple hearings before lawmakers. Rather than notifying the users of the breach, they merely *logged off* users without further measures. Ultimately, Facebook's representations before lawmakers, coupled with their previous bad

history, required them to take better care moving forward, which they did not do.

- **GDPR compliance:** Placing aside the financial damage the company would face with scandal after scandal, the breach is just a symptom of a larger issue in Facebook's data-processing operations. Constant breaches in their integrity raise issues in the public eye regarding their credibility, which is steadily depleting. As one of the largest companies in the market, they are ripe to be made an example of along with Google, and constant errors will only amplify that problem.

## US Center for Medicaid Services

- **Breach date:** The breach was discovered by CMS on October 13, 2018, with it being verified on October 16.
- **Notification date:** October 19, 2018.
- **Type:** Hack of the *Direct Enrollment System*, which is used by brokers and agents in the healthcare industry.
- **Targeted data:** Agent and broker data for facilitating help for patients. Details were not disclosed, but *no* consumer data from healthcare.gov was stolen.[39]
- **Motive for the breach:** Unknown.
- **Damages and data subjects affected:** 75,000 people in the government health insurance system were affected.
- **Preventive measures:** CMS followed standard and appropriate security and risk protocols for researching and reporting the incident. Unlike other US government breaches, the response and notification were prompt.
- **Curative measures and liability:** No subsequent legal action was taken against the CMS, but on verification of the breach, they took immediate steps to secure the system and consumer information, and subsequently notified federal law enforcement. They also temporarily shut down the enrollment system to investigate.
- **GDPR compliance:** Refreshingly, the CMS handled the breach as appropriately as they could under the circumstances. Unlike the IRS or DHS breach, the matter was resolved cleanly, with minimal damage to their overall operations and credibility.

## Sing Health (Singapore)

- **Breach date:** June 27 through July 4, 2018.
- **Notification date:** July 20, 2018.
- **Type:** The hackers first broke into Sing Health's IT system via a front-end workstation, and later managed to obtain login details to assess the database, according to investigations.

- **Targeted data:** Patient records (between May 1, 2015 and July 4, 2018) that included name, NRIC number, address, gender, race, and date of birth. Most importantly, the hackers stole the Prime Minister's health records and outpatient information.
- **Motive for the breach:** The Prime Minister's records were believed to be the primary target of the breach (for unknown purposes).
- **Damages and data subjects affected:** The largest breach in Singapore's history, with 1.5 million patients and the Prime Minister of Singapore being personally affected.
- **Preventive measures:** The unusual activity was not detected until July 4, after which time investigators immediately halted processing and increased security. But the systems in place prior to the attack, and how they were exposed, were not disclosed. Notwithstanding, the damage was *controlled* and did not spread to other aspects of the Singapore healthcare systems or government systems.
- **Curative measures and liability:** Singapore authorities began working with external experts to conduct a thorough review of Singapore's public healthcare system to better prevent or detect future cyber-attacks. The review will cover areas like cybersecurity policies, threat management processes, and IT system controls, among others. The directive was even ordered in other sectors to ensure overall security in the nation.[40]
- **GDPR compliance:** The Sing Health breach was Singapore's wake-up call to the omniscient nature of digital crime. With more than half the population affected, the hospital did the best it could to handle the situation, but considering the real target was the Prime Minister, the personal data loss of other citizens paled in comparison (owing to national security concerns). The action taken on a *national level* after the breach was ideal, as Singapore realized that such attacks rarely happen in isolation.

## MyHeritage

- **Breach date:** October 27, 2017.
- **Notification date:** June 4, 2018.
- **Type:** It is unclear if the breach was the result of a hacker attack or because of a malicious employee selling the company's data. A security researcher discovered an archive of the data on a third-party server.
- **Targeted data:** The archive contained only e-mails and hashed passwords.
- **Motive for the breach:** Unknown.
- **Damages and data subjects affected:** 92,283,889 MyHeritage users.
- **Preventive measures:** MyHeritage used third-party payment processors for financial operations, meaning payment data was never stored on its systems, while its DNA test results were saved on separate servers from the one that managed user accounts.

The user accounts remained safe, since the passwords were hashed using a per-user unique cryptographic key. The company also had a policy of not storing user passwords, but rather using a one-way hash of each password, with each hash key differing for each customer.

- **Curative measures and liability:** By the time the breach was discovered, the company was under the regulation of GDPR. This prompted them to report the breach the *very day* of discovery, immediately hire a cyber-security firm, and draw up plans to roll out 2FA. In the US, a class action suit was filed in September 2018 against the company, alleging inadequate security in relation to the *value* of the data they held.[41]
- **GDPR compliance:** The strength of GDPR is reflected in how this breach was handled, demonstrating the *deterrent power* of huge fines. Some have raised concerns over whether the protections implemented over the passwords were sufficient under GDPR standards.[42] Genealogy companies such as MyHeritage are attractive targets for hackers because of the nature of the sensitive data they require for their services. But in cases of conflicts between the company's judgment and the public's judgment (with regard to the level of security needed), which should prevail?

## Under Armour

- **Breach date:** The breach was discovered on March 21, 2018.
- **Notification date:** March 25, 2018.
- **Type:** Hack of their recently acquired app MyFitnessPal.
- **Targeted data:** Usernames, e-mail addresses, and encrypted passwords.
- **Motive for the breach:** Unknown.
- **Damages and data subjects affected:** 150 million MyFitnessPal accounts compromised.
- **Preventive measures:** Under Armour states that most of the passwords were encrypted with bcrypt (a relatively strong password hashing mechanism). However, some of the passwords were protected using a significantly weaker 160-bit hashing function, SHA-1. Under Armour's notification to the public was *four days* after discovery, which was criticized for being beyond GDPR deadline.[43]
- **Curative measures and liability:** Despite the aforementioned criticism, Under Armour managed to dodge GDPR liability and was in fact *lauded* for its response and adequate security measures. The SA overseeing found that the password resets and encryption given were appropriate measures.
- On the other hand, in the US a class action suit has been filed against the company for failing to maintain adequate data security, based on theories of negligence. The suit particularly assails the use of SHA-1 legacy passwords when the data was vulnerable to attack.[44] A motion has been made to compel arbitration, which is presently pending.

- **GDPR compliance:** Despite the *technical violation* of informing the public four days after the breach, GDPR showed its gentler side on the UA breach. Harsh deterrence is necessary, but so is *understanding* for breaches. If hackers are dedicated enough, a system could be broken into, and GDPR recognizes this fact in its application. Even though UA didn't follow the minutiae of the formalities, the regulators still concluded that it *did enough.*
- Juxtapose the speedy EU disposition with the more litigious class action method, which will likely tie up UA in court/arbitration for years to come. This is where *regulatory presence* shows its advantage.

## BMO and Simplii (Canada)

- **Breach date:** The breach was discovered on May 27, 2018, when the bank was contacted by the fraudsters for money.
- **Notification date:** May 28, 2018.
- **Type:** Hack.
- **Targeted data:** Banking records that included names, account numbers, dates of birth, and social insurance numbers, among other data.
- **Motive for the breach:** Theft and ransom.
- **Damages and data subjects affected:** 90,000 people customers were affected. Additionally, there was widespread misuse of the data (following the failure to pay the ransom), and the bank had to temporarily shut online service to those accounts affected.
- **Preventive measures:** Inadequate, as alleged in a subsequent class action suit filed against the banks.[45]
- **Curative measures and liability:** Though the bank attempted to control the damage by offering free credit monitoring and reimbursement of any funds misused, a class action suit was filed in Ontario in June 2018 for their failure to secure the data.
- **GDPR compliance:** As much as the bank tried to be prompt in its response, the loss of critical financial data is always a motivator for litigation owing to the valuable nature of the data. Here the loss isn't necessarily the payment card details, but rather the *identity data* that can be used to perpetuate false transactions, which is much worse in the long run. Canada, like the US, is lacking a federal data protection law, which leaves claimants to sue under other Provincial or Common Law theories.

## Pop Sugar Inc.

- **Breach date:** February 2018, with the breach being discovered on April 30, 2018.
- **Notification date:** June 14, 2018.

- **Type:** Hacker gained access to user credentials and accessed the site.
- **Targeted data:** Names, e-mail addresses, and hashed passwords.
- **Motive for the breach:** Unknown.
- **Damages and data subjects affected:** 123,857 users affected.
- **Preventive measures:** The security before the breach was undisclosed, but users and others have criticized Pop Sugar's two-month delayed notification.[46]
- **Curative measures and liability:** The company investigated the matter, addressed their vulnerabilities, and reset their passwords. They also informed local authorities in California.
- **GDPR compliance:** Pop Sugar has managed to avoid liability or news coverage for their data breach thus far, which again demonstrates an inconsistency in the enforcement of US data protection law where the less prominent breaches remain unnoticed.

## Notes

1 https://baltimore.cbslocal.com/2014/04/09/whistleblower-says-he-warned-university-of-maryland-before-data-breach/.
2 https://krebsonsecurity.com/tag/trump-hotel-breach/.
3 https://krebsonsecurity.com/2014/09/banks-credit-card-breach-at-home-depot/.
4 https://krebsonsecurity.com/2014/01/sources-card-breach-at-michaels-stores/.
5 https://krebsonsecurity.com/2013/09/data-broker-giants-hacked-by-id-theft-service/.
6 https://krebsonsecurity.com/2015/11/arrests-in-jp-morgan-etrade-scottrade-hacks/.
7 https://www.mieweb.com/notice/.
8 https://krebsonsecurity.com/2015/07/experian-hit-with-class-action-over-id-theft-service/.
9 https://www.democratandchronicle.com/story/news/2018/01/22/excellus-bluecross-blueshield-hack-lawsuit-ruling-greatly-expands-number-plaintiffs/1053272001/.
10 https://www.healthcareitnews.com/news/supreme-court-rejects-carefirst-bid-review-breach-case.
11 https://www.bankinfosecurity.com/new-in-depth-analysis-anthem-breach-a-9627.
12 https://www.zdnet.com/article/premera-blue-cross-accused-of-destroying-evidence-in-data-breach-lawsuit/.
13 https://qz.com/445233/inside-the-irss-massive-data-breach/.
14 https://www.irs.gov/newsroom/irss-top-10-identity-theft-prosecutions-criminal-investigation-continues-efforts-to-halt-refund-fraud.
15 https://www.washingtonpost.com/world/national-security/chinese-government-has-arrested-hackers-suspected-of-breaching-opm-database/2015/12/02/0295b918-990c-11e5-8917-653b65c809eb_story.html?utm_term=.ae2b84e31610.

16  http://fortune.com/2015/08/26/ashley-madison-hack/.

17  https://www.prnewswire.com/news-releases/ruby-corp-and-plaintiffs-reach-proposed-settlement-of-class-action-lawsuit-regarding-ashley-madison-data-breach-634551783.html.

18  http://www.mondaq.com/canada/x/607024/Security/Settlement+Of+Walmart+Canada+Photo+Centre+Data+Breach+Lawsuits+Lessons+Learned.

19  GDPR, Article 8.

20  https://www.wendys.com/payment-card-incident.

21  https://payment.wendys.com/paymentcardcheck.html.

22  https://www.orlandosentinel.com/features/education/school-zone/os-ucf-hack-suit-20180111-story.html.

23  https://www.cyberscoop.com/taxslayer-ftc-settlement-hacking-identity-theft/.

24  https://motherboard.vice.com/en_us/article/pgkp57/a-teen-hacker-is-targeting-russian-sites-as-revenge-for-the-mh17-crash.

25  https://krebsonsecurity.com/2015/12/password-thieves-target-e-giftcard-firm-gyft/#more-33169.

26  https://www.zdnet.com/article/adultfriendfinder-network-hack-exposes-secrets-of-412-million-users/.

27  https://www.foxnews.com/politics/cops-arrest-teen-for-hack-and-leak-of-dhs-fbi-data.

28  https://www.washingtonpost.com/news/politics/wp/2018/07/13/timeline-how-russian-agents-allegedly-hacked-the-dnc-and-clintons-campaign/?utm_term=.b31a0ce96ce8.

29  https://krebsonsecurity.com/2016/02/breached-credit-union-comes-out-of-its-shell/.

30  https://www.hca.wa.gov/about-hca/apple-health-medicaid/data-breach-apple-health-medicaid-managed-care-plan-what-clients.

31  https://www.fiercehealthcare.com/privacy-security/21st-century-oncology-data-breach-ocr-settlement-class-action-cybersecuirty.

32  https://www.theregister.co.uk/2017/09/05/taringa_data_breach/.

33  https://www.pinterest.co.uk/pin/464785624022658297/?showsignup=1.

34  https://topclassactions.com/lawsuit-settlements/lawsuit-news/839866-orbitz-class-action-lawsuit-filed-data-breach/.

35  https://www.pymnts.com/news/security-and-risk/2018/gdpr-fines-british-airways-lawsuits-compliance/.

36  https://topclassactions.com/lawsuit-settlements/lawsuit-news/860186-ticketfly-data-breach/.

37  https://www.businessinsider.com/google-investigated-lawsuit-over-breach-2018-10.

38  https://www.theverge.com/2018/10/11/17964134/google-plus-congress-privacy-data-vulnerability.

39  https://www.cms.gov/newsroom/press-releases/cms-responding-suspicious-activity-agent-and-broker-exchanges-portal.

40  https://www.zdnet.com/article/singapore-banks-told-to-tighten-data-verification-following-singhealth-breach/.

41 https://topclassactions.com/lawsuit-settlements/lawsuit-news/858174-myheritage-class-action-lawsuit-says-dna-reports-exposed-data-hack/.

42 https://gdpr.report/news/2018/06/06/myheritage-responds-to-data-breach-within-hours-but-was-its-hashed-password-protection-sufficient/.

43 https://www.cm-alliance.com/cybersecurity-blog/under-armour-myfitnesspal-data-breach-cybersecurity-hack.

44 https://www.bankinfosecurity.com/lawsuit-filed-in-wake-under-armour-data-breach-a-11051.

45 https://toronto.ctvnews.ca/proposed-class-action-lawsuits-filed-against-bmo-cibc-s-simplii-after-breach-1.3978967.

46 https://portswigger.net/daily-swig/hack-at-us-website-popsugar-leaks-124k-users-details.

# About the Authors

**Sanjay Sharma** is the founder and chairman of GreenPoint Global (parent of GreenPoint Financial) – a risk advisory, education, and technology services firm headquartered in New York. Founded in 2006, GreenPoint has grown to over 400 employees, with a global footprint and production and management teams located in the US, India, and Israel.

During 2007–2016 Sanjay was the chief risk officer of the Global Arbitrage and Trading Group and the managing director of Fixed Income and Currencies Risk Management at RBC Capital Markets in New York. His career in the financial services industry spans three decades, during which he has held investment banking and risk management positions at Goldman Sachs, Merrill Lynch, Citigroup, Moody's, and Natixis. Sanjay is the author of *Risk Transparency* (Risk Books, 2013) and a coauthor of *The FRTB: Concepts, Implications and Implementation* (Risk Books, 2018) and *Data Privacy and GDPR Handbook* (Wiley, 2019).

Sanjay was the founding director of the RBC/Hass Fellowship Program at the University of California at Berkeley. He is an adjunct professor at Columbia University, New York University, and Fordham University in New York and at EDHEC in London, England and Nice, France. Sanjay has served as an advisor and a member of the board of directors of UPS Capital (a division of UPS) and is a frequent speaker at industry conferences and at universities. He has served on the global board of directors of the Professional Risk International Association (PRMIA). He holds a PhD in finance and international business from New York University and an MBA from the Wharton School of Business and has undergraduate degrees in physics and marine engineering. Sanjay acquired his appreciation for risk first-hand as a merchant marine officer at sea, where he served for seven years and received the Chief Engineer's certificate of competency for ocean-going merchant ships.

**Pranav Menon** completed his BA LLB degree from Symbiosis Law School, Pune, India, in 2016, specializing in intellectual property and media laws in India. While pursuing his undergraduate degree he attained a certificate in Indian cyber laws from the Indian Law Institute, a diploma in media laws from Symbiosis Law School, Pune, and another diploma in intellectual property law and management from Enhelion and Gujarat National Law University through an online program. Pranav completed his LLM focusing on international commercial arbitration and litigation at The Pennsylvania State University and is currently pursuing his doctorate in law. His research is focused on the legal aspects of posthumous existence through the use of technology. Pranav recently passed the New York State bar exam, and his admission to the New York State bar is expected in 2019.

# Index

Page numbers followed by *f* refer to figures.